THE TRANSFER OF POWER IN AFRICA

THE TRANSFER OF POWER IN AFRICA

Decolonization 1940–1960

edited by
PROSSER GIFFORD
and
WM. ROGER LOUIS

Yale University Press, New Haven and London

Set in Caledonia type by
The Composing Room of Michigan, Inc.,
and printed in the United States of America by
The Murray Printing Co., Westford, Massachusetts.

Library of Congress Cataloging in Publication Data

Main entry under title:
The transfer of power in Africa.
Based on a conference held at the Villa Serbelloni,
Bellagio, Italy, Sept.-Oct. 1977, sponsored by the
Rockefeller Foundation.
Bibliography: p.
Includes index.
1. Africa—Politics and government—1945-1960—
Congresses. 2. Decolonization—Africa—History—
Congresses. I. Gifford, Prosser. II. Louis, Wm.
Roger. III. Rockefeller Foundation.
DT30.T73 960′.32 82-1931
ISBN 0-300-02568-8 AACR2

10 9 8 7 6 5 4 3 2 1

CONTENTS

INTRODUCTION

Decolonization is one of the great themes of our age. The passing of the colonial empires, whether by violence or by negotiation, has consumed political energies in much of Asia and Africa since the Second World War. Making sense of the process, from the international or the metropolitan or the colonial vantage point, has led to intense debate about the rise and fall of empires, collaboration and resistance, independence and dependence, and the future of the non-Western world. Does our knowledge of the political and economic history of the era now permit generalization about the worldwide phenomenon of decolonization and independence?

We believe that sufficient time has passed to provide a perspective for reassessment of the years 1940–60 in Africa. Participants in the events of those years could at the time only partially describe and understand the meaning of the two decades. We can now stand back and try to see more clearly the historical developments—the similarities and dissimilarities of chronology and events in different parts of the continent. Although the contributors to this volume deal with many economic, social, and political aspects of the two decades, the emphasis of their interpretative essays is essentially and deliberately historical.

The introductory chapter by Anthony Low provides the background to decolonization in Africa by analyzing the transfer of power in Asia in the 1940s. It argues that nationalist movements in Asia loosened the hold of the imperial powers in Africa. There were Asian precedents for African independence. A complementary theory is introduced by Wm. Roger Louis and Ronald Robinson in the second chapter. The viability of empire in Africa depended upon accommodation at three different levels: in the colony itself, in the metropolitan power, and in the international sphere. Decolonization was by no means inevitable, at least in the eyes of contemporaries. Every step taken by the colonial power was intended to prolong empire, or to sustain control indirectly, rather than to end it.

There is a tension between those two theories. The one holds that independence in Africa followed as a consequence of the success of Asian nationalism, while the other emphasizes the constant interaction of the three levels of African, metropolitan, and international politics which may have had little to do with Asia. This is a crude summation of the two points of view, but such differences of interpretation at the outset characterize other contributions as well, notably those of Jean Suret-Canale and David Fieldhouse, whose chapters offer entirely different economic interpretations of the reasons for the decline of formal empire in Africa. The subject of decolonization invariably provokes controversy.

The chapter by Hollis Lynch deals with popular sentiment (in contrast with the "official mind" of the Louis and Robinson chapter) and discusses influences upon the colonial regimes exerted from the United States. During the Second World War, America proved to be a major training ground for African students, and they returned to Africa to participate in the drive for independence. Black American ideas about African liberation and African activities in America played a distinct part in decolonization.

In chapter 4 Tony Smith assesses the legacy of war in Indochina and Algeria. He compares French and British settler colonies and, as in the case of the introductory chapter, nationalist movements in Asia and Africa. Decolonization was a worldwide process of complex local variation.

John Hargreaves's chapter traces important transformations in British policy in West Africa during the Second World War, focusing on Nigeria and the Gold Coast as the crucial cases. Policymakers initiated programs of social engineering which were seen at that time as a necessary preparation for eventual self-government; but developments both within the colonies and on the international scene changed the nature of this process so that, after the war, power was transferred sooner than intended, and it was transferred to Africans other than those originally envisaged as collaborators. The companion piece by Yves Person argues a different case from the French perspective, though not without similar observations. After examining the contradictions of the French colonial system, he concludes that the French—not least de Gaulle—subordinated African economic and social development to problems of metropolitan France. De Gaulle hoped for decolonization in terms of purely political independence that would be offset by economic, defense, and cultural ties between the metropole and the former colonies. Elikia M'Bokolo's chapter, like Person's, examines not only the evolution of French official policy but also the local and peasant reaction to the colonial regime. He concludes, as does Person, that the French succeeded in controlling the process of decolonization, and that "neocolonialism" exists despite the transfer of political power. Henri Brunschwig's essay pursues the theory of the "three levels" (chap. 2) in the French domain and stresses the part played in decolonization by African elites, establishing similarities between the beginning and the end of the European empires in Africa.

Dennis Austin's chapter raises the question of whether there were decisive "turning points" in decolonization. He argues that the course which seems certain in retrospect was uncertain, and indeed muddled, at the time. The pace quickened, less from increasing conviction about the rightness of the result than from the force of multiplying precedents and growing weariness. Cranford Pratt's essay, in turn, shows the reasons for European disillusionment and the accelerated pace toward independence in Tanganyika. He attacks the view that the transfer of power there (and by implication elsewhere) was "successful." Grace Ibingira, while perhaps more charitable to the British, also argues that in the long run British policies were pursued mainly for British purposes rather than for the economic and social interests of Uganda. British policy perpetuated secessionist or separatist tendencies, at least until it was too late to correct the fatal error.

In the case of the Belgian Congo, Jean Stengers argues that the Belgians genuinely believed they were promoting African welfare through economic development and mass education at the primary level. They paid scant attention to political development and did little to create an African elite. Despite the historical experience of the Dutch (which Anthony Low believes to be important), Stengers argues that the Belgians refused to take account of events in the rest of the world. They believed so fervently in the benevolence of their rule that they suffered from myopic overconfidence. When the troubles came in the late 1950s, the Congo collapsed because the Belgians would not sustain a colonial war. The contrast between this chapter and the following one by Kenneth Maxwell on the Portuguese colonies is striking. To the Portuguese the African colonies were a source of national pride, and they were willing to expend a high proportion of their national income to preserve the empire. As these two chapters demonstrate, studies of decolonization must take into account the psychology of national pride as well as international, metropolitan, and African drives toward independence.

The chapters by Prosser Gifford and Leonard Thompson describe the diverging courses pursued in southern Africa during the years 1945–60. Before the Second World War the outlook for British rule in the Rhodesias did not seem markedly different from the future of the liberal "Cape tradition" in South Africa. But by 1950 the "parting of the ways" toward Afrikaner supremacy had begun in South Africa, and in British Central Africa the federation of the three territories in 1953 accelerated nationalist opposition. Unlike other areas of Africa, including even the Portuguese colonies, "decolonization" in the "white south" appeared until recently to mean the self-declared "independence" of settler-ruled Rhodesia and the successful intrasigence of the Afrikaners.

The chapter by Jean Suret-Canale offers a detailed Marxist analysis of the struggle between the capitalist West and the socialist countries of the world in the arena of French Africa. The author asks the question "What role did economic factors play in the historical process that led the former colonies of French tropical Africa to independence?" He deals with the "myth" of economic aid and the ambiguity of the concept of "decolonization." Like other writers in this volume, he is critical of "Gaullist mythology." Above all, he challenges the reality of the transfers of power in Africa—as does the following chapter by David Fieldhouse, from a vantage point that is not uncritical of Marxist theory. Fieldhouse's chapter is concerned with the economic causes and consequences of decolonization. He asks the question "How should the historian proceed when faced with so many contrasting interpretations?" He surveys the arguments of the "underdevelopment" theorists as well as those of the better-known Marxist writers and liberal economists. This chapter is an exercise in intellectual history as well as an analysis of the economics of decolonization, and its breadth and general interest make it an appropriate conclusion for the volume.

The historiographical essays by Anthony Kirk-Greene and David Gardinier are designed for use primarily as tools of reference in addition to serving as bibliographical supplements. We feel confident that our readers will be grateful for the organization and depth of their references as well as for their historiographical interpretation.

This volume was made possible by the Rockefeller Foundation's sponsorship of a conference held at the Villa Serbelloni, Bellagio, Italy, in September–October 1977, and by Ford Foundation assistance with transportation costs for the participants. We wish to thank the University Research Institute of the University of Texas and Amherst College for additional financial support. We are also greatly indebted to Dr. Robert W. Stookey for the translations of the French chapters and for his assistance in the preparation of the manuscript.

The conference at Bellagio indicated that the subject of decolonization is a matter of intense interest among historians. The participants devoted considerable attention to the nature of archival evidence available on the transfer of power, which in the British and some other cases now extends to the late 1940s. There remains considerable uncertainty about the nature of official motives after that time, and for that reason some of the assessments in this volume should be regarded as provisional. The limited availability of sources applies with even greater force to the African perspectives on decolonization.

If the Bellagio conference is any indication, historians are being increasingly drawn to the subject of the transfer of power in Africa as the archives release their secrets. We hope this volume reflects the intellectual excitement of the conference and, much more important, conveys the present trends of historical analysis.

Prosser Gifford
Wm. Roger Louis

Morocco
(1956)
Rabat
Algiers
Tunis
Tunisia
(1956)
Tripoli
Cairo
Algeria
(1962)
Libya
(1951)
Egypt
(1922)
Spanish Sahara
Mauritania
(1960)
Nouakchott
Mali
(1960)
Niger
(1960)
Chad
(1960)
Sudan
(1956)
Khartoum
Djibouti
(1977)
Djibouti
Ethiopia
Addis Ababa
Somalia
(1960)
Mogadishu
Dakar
Senegal
(1960)
Gambia
Guinea-Bissau
(1974)
Bissau
Bamako
Guinea
(1958)
Conakry
Sierra Leone
(1961)
Freetown
Liberia
(1847)
Monrovia
Ivory
Coast
(1960)
Abijan
Upper
Volta
Ouagadougou
Niamey
Ghana
(1957)
Accra
Togo
Lome
Benin
(1960)
Dahomey
Lagos
Nigeria
(1960)
N'Djamena
Cameroon
(1960)
Yaounde
Central African Republic
(1960)
Bangui

Equatorial Guinea
(1968)
São Tome & Principe
(1975)
Libreville
Gabon
(1960)
Congo (1960)
Brazzaville
Kinshasa
Zaire
(1960)
Uganda
(1962)
Kampala
Kenya
(1963)
Kigali
Rwanda
(1960)
Nairobi
Bujumbura
Burundi
(1960)
Tanzania
(1961)
Zanzibar island
Dar es Salaam
Luanda
Shaba Province
(former Katanga)
Comoros (1975)
Angola
(1975)
Malawi
(1964)
Zambia
(1964)
Lusaka
Salisbury
Mozambique
(1975)
Madagascar
(1960)
Antananarivo
Namibia
not yet achieved
Zimbabwe
(1980)
Botswana
(1966)
Windhoek
Gaborone
Mbabane
Maputo
Pretoria
Swaziland
(1968)
Maseru
Lesotho
(1966)
South Africa
(1910)
Cape Town

1. The Asian Mirror to Tropical Africa's Independence

D. A. LOW

There are two central themes in the history of the attainment of independence by the countries of tropical Africa which warrant closer attention than they have received. In the late 1950s and early 1960s independence came to many of these countries a great deal faster than anyone, most nationalists included, had ever anticipated. And in almost every case it came without a war of independence.

The outlines of this story are well known. Sudan became independent in 1956, Ghana in 1957, Guinea in 1958. Nineteen sixty became "Africa Year," when independence came to three U.N. Trust Territories (Togo, Cameroons, Somalia), to Nigeria, to French West and Equatorial Africa, and to the Belgian Congo. By this time independence was well on the way for Tanganyika and Uganda as well; and at a Lancaster House Conference in February 1960 the crucial corner was turned for Kenya too. By then the Nyasaland riots had occurred. The Devlin Commission had been appointed, to be followed shortly afterward by the Monckton Commission on the future of the Central African Federation. Two years or so later, when the British East African territories actually achieved their independence, the crucial breakthrough had occurred in Northern Rhodesia as well. At that point the winds of change slackened, only to blow hard again in the 1970s in substantially new circumstances.

It is not difficult to trace out the sequitur from the advent of independence for Ghana in 1957 to that for Nigeria, Sierra Leone, and Uganda in the years that followed. The influence of these events upon the ending of the French empire seems clear as well. That, in turn, precipitated the crisis in the Belgian empire. Taken together, these developments placed tremendous pressure on the remaining about-to-be-isolated "British" East Africa colonies. Once their future had begun to clarify too, the pressure spread again to the last British-controlled territories in central and southern Africa; and it was not very long before the final dominoes in that particular array heeled over as well.

All of this had been preceded by the attainment of political independence by the former European-dominated countries in Asia. In seeking to elucidate the characteristics of the tropical African story, a good deal more than has usually been understood is to be gleaned from considering the Asian cases.

Take, in the first place, the American concern in Africa. This would seem to have owed more to the American experience in Southeast Asia than has generally been recognized. It is sometimes forgotten that the United States was a major colonial power—in the Philippines.[1] In the face of Filipino nationalism, the United States was in some respects the most benign imperial power of all. In 1935 it promised independence for the Philippines ten years hence. Despite the intervention of the Second World War, the Philippines did indeed secure its independence as promised, in 1946. At the same time, few colonial powers have shown more solicitude for established colonial elites or more concern to entrench a non-leftist regime where, on the transfer of power, there were doubts that this would occur without its help. Thus, in 1946, the Americans transferred power to the unreformed Filipino oligarchy and then supported it against the leftist Huk revolt. In these same years the Americans also supported, not only the Kuomintang against the Chinese Communists, but the Indonesian nationalists against the Dutch (since Sukarno and his associates looked as if they might well provide a bulwark against the onrush of communism both in Indonesia itself and elsewhere in the region). They soon went on to back the newly independent governments in India and Pakistan. However, where they envisaged the likelihood of the nationalists being led by leftists, as in Vietnam, the Americans took the opposite tack. There they were soon lending their support to the French in their campaign against the Communist-led Vietminh; and despite their refusal to intervene over Dien Bien Phu in 1954, this led on to their support of successive post-Geneva South Vietnamese regimes for another twenty years.

American policy on independence for Africa stood upon similar foundations. The United States regularly lent its weight to independence for Africans. But it persistently concerned itself as well with the relationship between "the reds and the blacks" (as an American ambassador to Kenya was so charmingly to put it). As Kissinger's intervention in Central Africa in 1976 most strikingly confirmed, American policy long persisted in seeking the establishment of right-of-center postindependence regimes.

1. The essentials on the Philippines will be found in: T. Friend, *Between Two Empires: The Ordeal of the Philippines, 1929–1946* (New Haven 1965); Usha Mahajani, *Philippines Nationalism* (St. Lucia, 1971); D. J. Steinberg, *Philippine Collaboration in World War II* (Ann Arbor, 1967). My colleague A. W. McCoy has been very helpful with his comments.

When one turns to consider British attitudes to the transfers of power in Africa, the influence of the British encounter with nationalism in Asia is difficult to gainsay. It is in no way fanciful to assert that many of the critical battles for British colonial Africa were fought, not on the banks of the Volta, the Niger, or the Zambezi, but on the Ganges. Britain, after all, was the most powerful of the Western imperial powers. Had it held onto its empire in Asia, the demise of other Western empires would not have occurred so readily. Thus the epic struggle of the Indian National Congress, particularly during the 1920s and 1930s, is central to the whole story of the transfer of power in the Third World and set the scene for this as did no other anti-imperialist struggle.[2] In particular, it showed what the combination of "tactical action" and "positive action" (to use Kwame Nkrumah's subsequent formulations) could effect. It indicated that widely based nationalist parties were worth creating. It revealed, too, that, however slow British constitutional reforms might seem in coming, they had their own ultimate logic. Above all, it indicated that there could be circumstances where violent colonial rebellion against a reluctant colonial power was not necessarily the only way to move forward.

To attempt to separate the African from the Asian half of the story of the demise of the British Empire—as, indeed, to separate the two of them from the story of the ending of Britain's imperial relationship with its "white" colonies—is to tear at long-continuing historical threads.[3] Four comments here will suffice. In Britain no great debate about the end of empire occurred between the great debate over India in the early 1930s and the great debate over Central Africa in the late 1950s. There was an all-but-smooth progression in the public realm in Britain from independence for South

2. There is a large, relevant literature on India. See, for a start: David Arnold, *The Congress in Tamilnad. Nationalist Politics in South India, 1919–1937* (New Delhi, 1977); J. H. Broomfield, *Elite Conflict in a Plural Society. Twentieth-Century Bengal* (Berkeley, 1968); Judith M. Brown, *Gandhi's Rise to Power, Indian Politics, 1915–1922* (Cambridge, 1972); Judith M. Brown, *Gandhi and Civil Disobedience. The Mahatma in Indian Politics, 1928–1934* (Cambridge, 1977); J. Gallagher, G. Johnson, and A. Seal, eds., *Locality, Province and Nation, Essays on Indian Politics, 1870–1940* (Cambridge, 1973); S. Gopal, *Jawaharlal Nehru, A Biography, I, 1889–1947* (London, 1975); R. Kumar, ed., *Essays on Gandhian Politics. The Rowlatt Satyagraha of 1919* (Oxford, 1971); D. A. Low, ed., *Soundings in Modern South Asian History* (London, 1968); D. A. Low, ed., *Congress and the Raj. Facets of the Indian Struggle, 1917–1947* (London, 1977); R. J. Moore, *The Crisis of Indian Unity* (Oxford, 1974); C. H. Philips and M. D. Wainwright, *The Partition of India, Policies and Perspectives, 1935–1947* (London, 1970); Francis Robinson, *Separatism among Indian Muslims. The Politics of the United Provinces' Muslims, 1860–1923* (Cambridge, 1974).

3. D. A. Low, *Lion Rampant. Essays in the Study of British Imperialism* (London, 1973), Chap. 5.

Asia in the late 1940s and the beginning at that time, by those who read the signs, of preparations for Britain's later withdrawal from Africa. The significance of their previous experiences in Southeast and South Asia for, respectively, Sir Charles Arden-Clarke and his chief secretary, Reginald Saloway, in the Gold Coast in the years before independence provides a footnote to the larger point. It should always be remembered, too, that the prime minister who presided over Britain's transfer of power in South Asia, and over the Cabinet in which Arthur Creech Jones, the reforming British colonial secretary, sat, was one and the same man, Clement Attlee—a member of the much abused Simon Commission in India in the late 1920s, but also the man who secured reconsideration of Britain's policy there when it took its final conservative turn in the middle of the Second World War.

The French revision of the end of empire in Asia was much more traumatic for them than for the British, and as a consequence its impact upon their African policy turned out to be much more sharply delineated. In the late 1940s the French strove more mightily than any other colonial power to maintain their Asian empire. Their bitter denouement came with the defeat of French arms at Dien Bien Phu in 1954.[4] In the years that followed, France's reaction in Africa to its Asian experience trifurcated. In *Afrique Noire* those inclined to disown their French connections, as in Guinea, were quickly isolated. But where "Bao Daist" regimes (Senghor, Houphouët-Biogny) could be created, there was little argument about an early transfer of power. Where, however, there seemed to be no case for a transfer of power—as in Algeria—then the honor both of French arms and of French colonialism was to be upheld at well nigh any cost. The shadows—and they were sharply varying shadows—of Dien Bien Phu seem, from an Asian perspective, to lie right across the last decade of France's empire in Africa.

The Belgian experience was rather different. They had no empire in Asia as they did in Central Africa. But in Europe they were neighbors to the Dutch, and the Dutch had had their fill of disappointment, abandonment, defeat, and protracted recriminations over the ending of their empire in Asia. It may perhaps be suggested, therefore, that the Belgians' precipitate

4. On Indochina see: W. J. Duiker, *The Rise of Nationalism in Vietnam, 1900–1941* (Ithaca, 1976); D. G. Marr, *Vietnamese Anticolonialism, 1885–1925* (Berkeley, 1971); Jean Lacouture, *Ho Chi Minh: A Political Biography* (New York, 1968); Ellen J. Hammer, *The Struggle for Indochina, 1940–1955. Vietnam and the French Experience* (Stanford, 1954); John T. McAlister, *Vietnam, the Origins of Revolution* (New York, 1970); A. B. Woodside, *Community and Revolution in Modern Vietnam* (Boston, 1976). I have been much helped by my colleague David Marr.

actions in the Congo in 1959–60 owed more than has been generally appreciated to their conclusion that once their antinationalist stance—which was as strong in the Congo as it had been among the Dutch in Indonesia—had cracked, there was no point in any way prolonging the agony, as their Netherlands neighbors had, at so much commercial and diplomatic cost to themselves.[5] Belgium's proximity to France in Europe reinforced this thought, particularly following the Algerian crisis.

Amid all the now innumerable stories of the transfer of power across the world—we in Australia watched at close hand in the 1970s yet another example in Papua New Guinea—one can discern a great range of variations on a number of quite regular themes.

Some of these (to make an arbitrary beginning) relate to the economic interests of the colonial powers and to the economic viability of the newly independent countries. In the 1940s the Dutch believed that their Asian empire was crucial to their economic well-being; they were, of course, wrong. The British by that time had seen their Lancashire preferences in India go altogether and India's sterling balances in London transformed into Britain's rupee debt to India. So they already knew that more was to be gained for British interests by maintaining the postindependence economy in India than by continuing to try to rule India. The Americans in the Philippines were never in any doubt that this was the path of wisdom. The British picked up the point a decade later and provided considerable financial support, with just this end in view, toward maintaining the otherwise wavering Kenyan economy. The French variation on this particular theme in Africa was perhaps the most explicit of all.

On the other side, it would be no less possible to trace out extensively the form of nationalist movements in different colonial contexts: their provenance in various elites; their linkages with what, in truth, were highly localized discontents; their painful mobilization against—again to be

5. On Indonesia, here and elsewhere, see: Susan Abeyasekere, *One Hand Clapping: Indonesian Nationalists and the Dutch, 1939–1942*, Monash Papers on Southeast Asia, 5 (1976); Benedict R. O'G. Anderson, *Java in a Time of Revolution: Occupation and Resistance, 1944–1946* (Ithaca, 1972); Harry J. Benda, *The Crescent and the Rising Sun: Indonesian Islam under the Japanese Occupation, 1942–1945* (Bandung, 1958); Bernard Dahm, *Sukarno and the Struggle for Indonesian Independence* (Ithaca, 1969); John Ingleson, *Road to Exile, The Indonesian Nationalist Movement, 1927–1934* (Canberra and Singapore, 1979); G. McT. Kahin, *Nationalism and Revolution in Indonesia* (Ithaca, 1952); J. D. Legge, *Sukarno: A Political Biography* (London, 1972); R. T. McVey, *The Rise of Indonesian Communism* (Ithaca, 1965); A. J. S. Reid, *The Indonesian National Revolution, 1945–1950* (Hawthorn, Australia, 1974); J. R. W. Smail, *Bandung in the Early Revolution, 1945–1946: A Study in the Social History of the Indonesian Revolution* (Ithaca, 1964). I am indebted to my colleague A. J. S. Reid for his guidance here.

precise—an equally fragile colonial power; and so on. At the interface between colonial power and nationalist movement there is a host of issues for comparative investigation. One can take some further examples from the final stages of terminal colonialism: the balance of control over political forces between colonial power and nationalist leadership, about which, in the final run up to independence, both became concerned; the ultimate common interest of the two sides in effecting a smooth transfer of power (thus, in the Philippines, MacArthur-Roxas; in Burma, Rance–Aung San; in India, Mountbatten-Nehru; in the Gold Coast, Arden-Clarke-Nkrumah; in Tanganyika, Turnbull-Nyerere, and so on); the perennial question in the end (in the Philippines, Vietnam, Indonesia, India, Ghana, Nigeria, Uganda, Angola, Zimbabwe, and so on), not of whether independence was coming, but of who was to have power or how it was to be shared upon its actual attainment; not to mention the often neglected question of the actual bases of political authority for the successor regimes once independence had been achieved. Some of these are well-worn themes, and, as has been hinted above, the Asian stories are as replete with them as the African.

It used to be tempting to say that the chief contrast between the history of the transfer of power in Asia and that in Africa was that the former was so much more protracted than the latter. Certainly the Indian struggle took several decades longer than the Ghanian. But with independence in south central Africa not achieved until three and a half decades had passed since the end of the Second World War, this contrast warrants qualification. It should be made in this way: the struggle in tropical Africa was indeed conflated; it was the struggle elsewhere in Africa, especially in the south, which became so prolonged.

So far as *tropical* Africa is concerned, there remains a major contrast with the Asian story that is at once striking and intriguing. Across tropical Africa as a whole the sequence of events was remarkably cumulative. There were fairly direct cross-flows from developments in one part of the region to those in another. This was very largely not the case in Asia. There events occurred more by fits and starts, and with next to no direct reference to events in neighboring countries. Because of this, the various Asian stories have tended to be considered in isolation from one another. It can, nevertheless, be argued that, with obvious qualifications as to different particularities, the sequences in the Asian stories over the first half of the twentieth century were, if not cumulative as in the African case, nevertheless much more strikingly parallel to each other than has been generally appreciated, and this would seem worth exploring.

The argument would run as follows. As the twentieth century opened (with, for example, the American annexation of the Philippines at the expense of both Spain and the Filipino revolution), nationalism and independence were already both well-developed conceptions, at all events among the Asian elites: in the Philippines of Aguinaldo; in the India of Tilak, Gokhale, Banerji, Aurobindo, and Naoroji; in the Vietnam of Phan Boi Chau and his contemporaries; in the Java of Kartini and Wahidin Sudironusodo; and even to some extent in Malaysia.[6]

A great fillip to these developments was then given in so many quarters in Asia by the dramatic Japanese defeat of the European power, Russia, in the Russo-Japanese war of 1904–05; and in the ensuing ten years there were a variety of violent nationalist upheavals that had many characteristics in common. They were organized by elitist groups, usually on a small scale, and designed essentially to scare the imperialists. They occurred most strikingly in India and in Vietnam—and were all uniformly disastrous for their participants. That made it essential for far-sighted nationalists to consider other possibilities.

As it happened, these possibilities seemed to be forthcoming along the lines adumbrated by the Chinese revolution of 1911, and then more especially as hammered out by the greater Russian revolution of 1917. Following upon these events, the similarities between the major movements for change in the major countries of Asia surfaced quite plainly—and for the time being, as we shall see, China should be included in our consideration here.[7] For against this background there emerged from the First World War a quite new temper in almost all the larger countries of Asia. This change was exemplified in the May Fourth movement in China, in Gandhi's first national satyagrahas in India, in the student eruptions in Rangoon, in certain important new developments within Sarekat Islam in Indonesia, and so on.

Sarekat Islam was particularly significant; for, while most other movements still tended to have an elitist flavor, in the first quarter of the twentieth century it spread well beyond the small westernized elite. It represented, in fact, the Indonesian version of the wider religiopolitical upheavals which, in the first twenty-five years of the twentieth century,

6. W. R. Roff, *The Origins of Malay Nationalism* (New Haven, 1967).

7. The literature on China is, of course, voluminous. See, for a start: Lucien Bianco, *Origins of the Chinese Revolution, 1915–1959* (Stanford, 1971); Jerome Ch'en, *Mao and the Chinese Revolution* (London, 1965); Jean Chesnaux, *Peasant Revolts in China, 1840–1949* (London, 1973); Chalmers A. Johnson, *Peasant Nationalism and Communist Power: The Emergence of Revolutionary China, 1937–1945* (Stanford, 1962); B. I. Schwartz, *Chinese Communism and the Rise of Mao* (Cambridge, Mass., 1951); S. R. Schram, *Mao Tse-Tung* (Harmondsworth, 1966); C. P. Fitzgerald, *The Birth of Communist China* (Harmondsworth, 1964). I am indebted to my colleagues Wang Gungwu and Lo Hui-min for introducing me to this literature.

were widely characteristic of the Islamic world. These reached their climax with the defeat and final destruction of the centuries-old Ottoman Empire at the end of the First World War. That event very directly powered the Khilafat movement in India; and, as recent scholarship suggests, it was these Muslim movements rather than embryonic Asian nationalisms as such which, in a crucial way, first generated extensive support in Asia for anticolonialism.[8] The significant fact is that although both the Indian and the Indonesian nationalist movements soon loosened their connections with this Muslim tide (which in any case itself soon ebbed), they were from this time onward inspired by the belief that they could be *mass* movements. In other words, they lived in the confidence that it was well within the bounds of possibility to draw country-wide support for their campaigns. Such confidence only came to their contemporaries in other Asian countries later. Because the Muslim movements in India and Indonesia indeed had no counterpart in the Philippines, China, or Vietnam, the course followed in those countries differed substantially. It is striking, for example, that while by the 1920s the days of almost unalloyed elitist nationalism in India and Indonesia were already past, in Vietnam, where there was no Muslim movement because there were no Muslims, elitist nationalism persisted and soon reached its climax with the unsuccessful, violent uprising in 1930 of the recently formed elitist Vietnam Nationalist Party, the VNQDD.

The change that did then come in Vietnam stemmed largely from the Russian Revolution, which through the Third International elicited support for the Communist movement from among the more ardent opponents of the existing regimes—indeed, in several cases for the Communist International itself, particularly perhaps among the French-speaking Indochinese elite. Some of the most important individuals who were caught up in this movement in due course became key figures in their countries: Mao Tsetung, Ho Chi-minh, Tan Malaka, Musso, M. N. Roy. They were not, of course, confined to Vietnam.

One striking fact, however, about the 1920s in Asia was that these various Communist initiatives soon suffered severe setbacks. The Communist revolts in Java and Sumatra in 1926–27 were easily crushed. In 1927 Chiang Kai-shek wheeled upon the Chinese Communists and destroyed four-fifths of them. In 1929 the British, via the long-winded Meerut Conspiracy Case, swept the Indian Communist leadership into jail; while over the following two years the French in Vietnam ruthlessly crushed a Communist-led

8. Robinson, *Separatism among Indian Muslims;* Kahin, *Nationalism and Revolution in Indonesia.*

peasant revolt (and its accompanying Soviets) in the provinces of Ha Tinh and Nghe An. Nevertheless, in the late 1920s the Indonesian Dutch-educated elite joined with the young engineer Sukarno to form the Partai Nasional Indonesia. In India, meanwhile, Gandhi and the new Congress peasant-oriented leadership of such men as Rajendra Prasad, Vallabhbhai Patel, and Abdul Ghaffar Khan, along with younger leaders like Jawaharlal Nehru and Subhas Bose, were soon mounting a major new campaign against British dominion in India, knowing that they had done this once already in the Khilafat-Noncooperation Movement of 1920–22.

In the early 1930s, however, it soon became clear that almost all of the regimes that were still paramount in Asia had set their minds upon suppressing, not merely the first Communist enterprises there, but any and all of the movements which challenged their dominion. Thus the French White Terror of 1930–31 was directed as much against the VNQDD as against the Indochinese Communists. The Meerut Conspiracy Case against the Communists in India was soon overshadowed by Britain's eventually unremitting repression of Gandhi's two civil disobedience movements (1930–31, 1932–34). During these very same years Chiang Kai-shek's Five Encirclements pressed hard upon the Chinese Communists, and Mao was eventually squeezed out upon his Long March. Then, first in 1929 and more particularly in 1933, Sukarno was arraigned by the Dutch, who the second time around all but destroyed the Indonesian nationalist movement. Indeed, when one looks around in the mid-1930s for the major figures of a decade or so later, one finds Mao cooped up in Yenan, Ho in exile in Moscow, Nehru in Dehra Dun prison, and Sukarno in isolation in Endeh.

Yet in a quite remarkable way the mid-1930s saw some very important recoveries. During the preceding years the American regime in the Philippines had always been much more liberal toward its local nationalists than the other imperialist powers. Under the Republican Coolidge, Harding, and Hoover, and their successive nominees, Wood, Stimson, and Welles, the prospects throughout the 1920s for Philippine independence had never, however, been dimmer. But with Roosevelt's presidential victory in 1932 the outlook improved; and out of the to-ing and fro-ing of the Hoare-Haws-Cutting Act of 1933, its rejection by the Filipino oligarchy and legislature, followed by Quezon's support for the Tydings-McDuffie Act, came the establishment of the Commonwealth of the Philippines under Quezon's presidency in 1936, with the promise of full independence a decade later. In that same year, 1936, the advent of the Popular Front Government in France led to the momentary revival in Vietnam of a few political freedoms which the lately formed Indochinese Communist party used in a highly skilful way to build up popular support. In December 1936 the Sian Incident gave Mao and the Chinese Communist party a quite new position in China, of which over the following decade they were to make spectacular use. In the early part of 1937, the Indian National Congress capped its recent series of electoral victories by securing control of seven of the eleven provincial governments of India; while that same year "Responsible Government," as the British called it, came to Burma as well, with Ba Maw as its first prime minister. In Indonesia alone was there still no movement, with only the collaborating parties enjoying the freedom to operate.

Taken together, these various developments in the 1930s were to be of great importance for the future. While they entrenched the Filipino oligarchy (the only nationalist leadership which had secured a clear promise that it would shortly take over from its existing rulers), they everywhere else undermined the existing regimes' local supporters: the supporters of the Kuomintang in China, the anti-Congress Liberals and so on in India, Gerindo and Parindra in Indonesia, and the Constitutionalist party in Vietnam. At the same time, on the other side Mao had now established himself as the prime Chinese Communist leader. The Indochinese Communist party had replaced the VNQDD as the leading Vietnamese nationalist party. The Indian National Congress, despite patent British opposition, had succeeded in winning a massive electoral victory, while in Indonesia Sukarno's preeminence as a nationalist leader had become firmly established. The casts for the dramas of the 1940s were largely chosen.

It was now that the Second World War supervened, and late in 1941 extended to all of Southeast Asia. This very directly cut across these older confrontations and raised some quite new possibilities for their resolution. The Vichyite French stayed on in Vietnam—but at the mercy of the Japanese. The British were driven from Malaya and Burma, the Dutch from Indonesia, the Americans from the Philippines, and at one stage it looked as if the Japanese would soon be marching into India. The previous apparent inviolability of the Western imperial regimes was gravely shaken, where it was not altogether destroyed.

In these circumstances the future for the nationalist and radical movements was nevertheless very often quite unclear. Given the stark intensity of the moral-political issues which the Japanese onslaughts posed, it is remarkable that Mao did not break at this time with Chiang; that Osmena stuck with Quezon and went into exile with him from the Philippines to America; and that Nehru in India, Sjahrir in Indonesia, and many others besides, stood up unrelentingly against the Japanese.

Yet there were others who took a different course—perhaps from expediency, perhaps in an effort to hold their existing gains intact, perhaps because they saw no end to the Japanese occupation. Thus, in 1940, the former revolutionary and Kuomintang leftist leader Wang Ching-wei became premier of a Japanese puppet government in Nanking. A few months later, Subhas Bose, Nehru's rival for the plaudits of the younger Indian nationalists, fled to join the Axis Powers and later formed the Indian National Army to support the Japanese. In the Philippines, Quezon's secretary, Vargas, remained behind in Manila to head the Philippines Executive Commission, which cooperated with the Japanese. Shortly afterward, Ba Maw, prime minister of Burma under the British, agreed to serve as his country's head of state under the Japanese; while, following his release by the Japanese from detention in July 1942, Sukarno and his later vice-president, Hatta, both took prominent positions under the Japanese. (In March 1943, Sukarno, for example, formed Putera, an association organized to mobilize the Javanese urban elite to support the Japanese war effort.)

As the war turned against them, the Japanese sought to push these processes further. In October 1943 they established the Republic of the Philippines under the presidency of a typical Filipino oligarch, José Laurel. Aung San became prime minister of a more independent Burma. In March 1945 the Japanese eventually turned on the Vichyite French and elevated the former Emperor Bao Dai to become head of an independent Vietnamese state; while in September 1945 some of Japan's now defeated military leaders gave active encouragement to the Indonesian nationalists under Sukarno as they moved toward proclaiming the independent Indonesian republic.

The ambiguities which suffused such situations could be traced out in some detail. It is fascinating to note, for example, the skill with which some of those who walked the knife-edge managed to survive the Japanese defeat—Sukarno for a start, who was chairman of Putera under the Japanese but president of the Indonesian republic after their defeat. Likewise, the first president of the postwar American-supported independent Republic of the Philippines was none other than Manuel Roxas, a collaborator with the Japanese but General MacArthur's protégé following their defeat. Similarly, Aung San, who originally actively collaborated with the Japanese, nevertheless linked up in good time with the British commander-in-chief, Lord Mountbatten, and placed himself securely in a position to lead Burma to independence.

As the Asian world teetered on several brinks at once in late 1945, there continued to be parallels in its countries' affairs. It is noteworthy, for example, that the leaders of the radical forces opposing the older, and in a number of cases now once again dominant, regimes not only moved very cautiously but actually entered into negotiations with them. They all began by feeling, that is, that more was to be gained by *diplomasi,* as the Indonesians called it, than by *perdjuangan* (the Indonesian term for "struggle"). Thus Chou En-lai and Mao parleyed with Chiang. The Indian leaders met Wavell in Simla in 1945 and negotiated with the British Cabinet Mission in the following year. Ho Chi-minh signed the March 6 Agreement with Sainteny and attended the Fontainbleau Conference in Paris in 1946. The Indonesian leaders signed the Linggajati Agreement with the Dutch in March 1947, and the Renville Agreement in January 1948. The most important parallel was the most striking of all. It was in the aftermath of the Second World War, between 1946 and 1950, that the final triumph of the new forces in all these countries occurred—except in Indochina where substantial independence was delayed in part until 1954, and then again until 1975.

Thus, while the direct interactions between the imperialist and nationalist struggles in the various countries of Asia seems to have been very limited, over forty years and more these nevertheless seem to have oscillated almost in parallel between periods of confrontation and periods of accommodation. In the combination of euphoria and anxiety produced by the First World War, the nationalist and radical forces in Asia flexed their muscles. As, during the 1920s, the war years receded and western Europe once more regained a degree of self-assurance, very strict curbs came to be placed upon these nationalist endeavors. Indeed, during the depression years of the early 1930s they were often harshly repressed. Yet as the Western world moved back to a further time of troubles, there was some let-up during which the new generation of nationalist leaders firmly staked out their claims on the future. That future was thrown into considerable confusion by the victories of the Japanese in the middle years of the Second World War. But with the Japanese defeat in 1945, the by now entrenched Asian nationalists finally moved in to claim their inheritance. At first this involved all of them in negotiations with their corresponding colonial power. And the outcome then turned, as we shall see, not on the ability of the nationalists to expel their Western rulers—which was soon no longer in doubt—nor even on whether their particular colonial power had decided to forego its Asian empire or not, but rather on the much narrower issue of the terms on which residual connections acceptable to the imperial power could be established. Where, accordingly, as in Asia, there would seem at first sight to have been so many differences between the experiences of the nationalist movements, it turns out on closer scrutiny that there was a much greater commonality than has generally been supposed. We should not be surprised, therefore, that where such common experiences were even more prevalent, as in tropical Africa, the course which events took there should have been even more similar.

For all the similarities in the Asian stories up to the 1940s, there were nevertheless differences. It was during the last years of empire there that the contrasts became particularly striking, and this raises another set of issues for consideration. These contrasts had already begun to emerge at the very moment of the Japanese defeat, more especially in respect of the position which the imperial powers held, or did not hold, in their ex-colonial territories. The British were still just barely in control of their empire in India. But they did not immediately control Burma. In the months before the war ended, the Americans effectively reestablished their control of the Philippines. But even several months after the Second World War was over, the Dutch, to their fury, were still not back in control of Indonesia, nor the French of Vietnam. Thus, while the British in India and the Americans in the Philippines could still largely, in the short run at least, determine the course of events in the territories they claimed as theirs—as the nationalists in both cases generally understood—in September 1945 the French in Vietnam found themselves confronted by Ho Chi-minh's declaration of the independent Democratic Republic of Viet Nam, and the Dutch by Sukarno's proclamation, in the same month, of the independent Republic of Indonesia. What was more, both Ho and Sukarno controlled some of their countries' major cities.

These contrasts were soon compounded. In 1946, contemporanious with the Philippines' peaceful movement toward independence, a full-scale war broke out between the Communists and the Kuomintang in China. Two years later this culminated in Lin Piao's great victory in the Huai-hai campaign, which was soon followed by Mao's declaration of the People's Republic of China in Peking in October 1949. These massive events provided the ever-present backdrop to contemporary developments elswhere, particularly in Southeast Asia. They were not, however, readily repeated elsewhere. For none of the colonial territories had suffered the extensive collapse of an ordered society to the extent that China had; none of them saw the decisive military overthrow of the previous dominant regime that China did; and thus, not only was the Chinese revolution unique in its time, but its concerns became separated for a decade and more from those which predominated in most other Asian countries.

This was not for lack of activity on the part of Communist, or at all events markedly leftist, movements elsewhere. In the late 1940s there were considerable leftist revolts in India (in Telengana, Kerala, and Bengal); in the Philippines (the Hukbalahap); and in Indonesia (under the Moscow returnees Tan Malaka and Musso). Nehru's India repressed all of the first. American support for the Filipino oligarchs just held the Huks at bay in the Philippines; while the incautious precipitancy of the Madiun affair in September–October 1948 thwarted the hopes of the Partai Kommunist Indonesia, for the time being at least. Only Ho Chi-minh, with his Yenan in Cao Bang, managed to survive the postwar onslaughts against the Communists and their like in the ex-colonial territories, and even there Giap's great victory at Dien Bien Phu did not come until five years after Lin Piao's in northern China, and even then only secured control of North Vietnam.

In each case the imperial powers sought to establish at this time regimes with which they could subsequently live. But here again contrast abounded. In China General Marshall and others sought to bolster the Kuomintang, or at all events to ensure that it become the dominant partner in a coalition with the Communists. They failed, of course; the situation was not amenable to their control. But in the Philippines where the Americans did have control, MacArthur's choice, Roxas, became the first president of the independent postwar Republic of the Philippines in 1946. In India in 1947, Mountbatten made his settlements with Nehru and Gandhi and Patel and Jinnah. Thereafter in Burma, Rance cut Britain's losses and transferred power to Aung San.

The course taken by D'Argenlieu in Vietnam was, however, significantly different. Hostile to the Vietminh, and to its Communist core in particular, he strove to elbow Ho Chi-minh aside and reinstate the former emperor, Bao Dai, with whom he hoped France might perhaps live—and for some years so it turned out. Van Mook in Indonesia followed a similar line. The Indonesian nationalists, despite Musso and Tan Malaka, were never led by their Communists; but they were led by a man whom the Dutch (still seared by their experience of a German occupation) considered a Quisling. Thus the Dutch, too, wanted to elbow their colonial nationalists to one side: and to this end van Mook sought to mobilize the non-Javanese in a federation under the Dutch crown in a way that would confine the Indonesian republic to its Javanese heartland.

It was in these connections that the most striking contrasts in Asia appeared. For while the Americans and the British had by the Second World War clearly decided to depart, the French and the Dutch were evidently determined to remain. This meant that, for the Indonesian and Vietnamese leaders, there were strict limits to the efficacy of diplomasi. Armed conflict with their controlling power accordingly occurred in both countries, as it did not elsewhere.

The remarkable fact here was that, while those movements which did not need to take military action against the formerly dominant regimes were those which had not had an opportunity during the war to develop their own military forces, those that *did* need to take military action against the older regimes happened, in one way or another, to have had an opportunity during the war to build up an effective nucleus of their own military forces. Thus Mao had built up the Red Army to an impregnable position in north China. In Indonesia, the Japanese had encouraged the creation of PETA, which became the starting point for the Indonesian republican army against the Dutch; while in Vietnam, Ho and Giap had been able to develop a key military base for their revolutionary army in northern Tonkin. Paradoxically, were it not for this contrast, the divergencies in the histories of the transfers of power in Asia would have been still greater. Here one can see at the same time the importance of the Japanese defeat. In each of the countries they had overrun (Malaya included) a significant, and sometimes strong, armed uprising sooner or later occurred in the vortex thereby created.

Of the four main histories outlined above the most straightforward occurred in the Philippines. Here, from the days of their takeover from the Spaniards the Americans had maintained the Filipino oligarchy in power. This elite managed to hold onto its position throughout the Japanese occupation; and after the war authority was transferred to it by the Americans with remarkable smoothness. For this the Americans reaped their reward in the special commercial and military privileges which they continued to enjoy in the Philippines for decades thereafter. As a consequence, the Philippines has one of the most unreconstructed social orders in Asia. There has been a modicum of land reform; but power is still held by those who have owned large estates, and so far all attempts to break their position have proved abortive.

A transfer of power was similarly effected in India and Pakistan in the immediate postwar years without armed conflict between Britain and the Indian nationalist movement. But by contrast with the Philippines, the transfer, particularly in India, did not see the entrenchment of a landholding oligarchy but the coming to power at national level of those who had long held power at village level.

India's attainment of independence was in every respect the outcome of a much more strenuous struggle than that in the Philippines. It greatly depended on the extraordinarily magnetic leadership of Gandhi. His prime achievement had been to bring into the nationalist movement tens of thousands of activists from the towns and villages of India, who eventually secured hundreds of thousands of supporters. During the period from 1917 to 1937, the tactic the British primarily employed against the Indian nationalist movement was to stretch the franchise for the provincial legislatures in British India beyond the bounds of those groups from which the Indian National Congress had up to then recruited support. By enfranchising something like 4 to 5 percent of the population the British were not unsuccessful, in the years between 1920 and 1935, in maintaining their position; the elected provincial legislatures of British India, and the executives partially linked with them in the "Dyarchy" period, generally withstood the Congress onslaught. At the same time, the British deflected the thrust of Congress-led peasant agitations, first by making concessions and then, when concessions proved ineffectual, by displaying a determination to confiscate lands. But their extensive use of police repression against Congress's two major civil disobedience campaigns of 1930–34 alienated many people of influence. As a result, when in the mid-1930s the British sought once again to undercut the nationalist movement by extending the franchise to nearly 12 percent of the population, they found that Congress had now undercut *them.* In consequence, at the provincial elections of 1937 Congress not only achieved a dramatic electoral victory, but because of the provisions of the new Government of India Act of 1935, went on to secure control of seven of the eleven provincial governments in India.

It is true that during the Second World War there was a marked conservative reaction in British Indian policy. But as Churchill's appointee in 1943 to the viceroyalty, Field Marshal Lord Wavell, immediately appreciated, Britain's interest in maintaining its empire in India had now distinctly declined. British preferences and British trade with India had dropped. India, indeed, was now becoming costly for the British. The Indian army, moreover, was not the inexpensive asset it had been in the past. Accordingly, Mountbatten, Wavell's successor, took energetic steps to transfer power to those who, at the further elections of 1946, had amply demonstrated the very considerable political support they possessed in various parts of India. Since the preceding decade had seen in the movement for Pakistan the most striking case of the classic end-of-empire dispute about how power should be disposed upon the attainment of independence, the eventual transfer ultimately entailed the appalling trauma of the partition between the two successor states, India and Pakistan. But as between Britain herself and the leaders of these states the transfer itself was scarcely less smooth than in the Philippines.

By contrast, the transfer of power in Indonesia involved considerable armed conflict. Though the Dutch had created a small Volksraad (assembly), they had not made any significant constitutional concessions to the Indonesian nationalists. Ultimately, this precipitated Sukarno's unilateral declaration of Indonesia's independence in September 1945. In Java the defense thereafter of the embryonic Indonesian republic regularly involved armed conflict—often of heroic dimensions, as, for example, against the British-led forces assisting the Dutch at the Battle of Surabaya in November 1945. That, and various other events which followed, brought about the Linggajati Agreement of 1946, by which the Dutch agreed not, it is true, to Sukarno's independent Indonesia, but to the establishment in due course of a federal Indonesia of which Sukarno's Java would be one part. But since there were soon differing interpretations of what all this meant, the Dutch in July 1947 eventually sought to settle the issue by mounting their first military action against the Indonesian forces. However, this only precipitated intervention by the United Nations through a Good Offices Committee, which in January 1948 patched up the precarious Renville Agreement. Later that year, in the course of the ill-fated Madiun affair, Sukarno's nationalists outwitted the Indonesian Communists. But, still dissatisfied, the Dutch then mounted their fatal Second Military Action. Since this aroused such strong United Nations, and particularly American, support for the Indonesian nationalists—who had just emerged on top of their Communist associates—international pressure forced the Dutch to transfer sovereignty to the United States of Indonesia before the end of 1949.

Vietnam in some significant respects followed a similar course. Back in 1941 Ho Chi-minh, building upon the Communist experience in Vietnam in the late 1930s, formed a united front nationalist organization, the Vietminh. Under Giap's remarkable military leadership this formed a military base in northern Tonkin during the Japanese occupation. Following the Japanese defeat in 1945, Ho dramatically proclaimed the independence of Vietnam. But the French nevertheless reestablished themselves in south and central Vietnam, and in March 1946 forced Ho to accept Vietnam's participation in the newly formed French Union in exchange for French recognition of his Vietminh government. But such compromises, as in Indonesia, soon collapsed, and before 1946 was out, full-scale war—the first Indochina War (1946–54)—had broken out between France and the Vietminh.

In the years that followed, the Vietminh forces steadily increased their hold on the northern countryside. But, unlike the Indonesian nationalists, they won little support in the West, particularly when, following the victory of the Chinese Communists in 1949, they more openly proclaimed their Communist attachments. French arms, moreover, were more substantial than Dutch ones. The French were able to play on Communist control of the Vietminh to hold at least some Vietnamese nationalists to their side; and in 1949 they once more made the former emperor Bao Dai head of a Vietnamese puppet state. But in the end the Vietminh forces wore down the French and at Dien Bien Phu in 1954 delivered their brilliant coup de grace. By then the Geneva Conference had been called and this granted full control over northern Vietnam to Ho and his Vietminh.

The contrasts are thus plain. In the Philippines the Americans transferred power to the Filipino oligarchy, which readily provided them with a continuing commercial and military presence. In South Asia the British accepted the legitimacy of the Indian, Pakistani, and Ceylonese nationalist leaderships and thankfully clutched at their readiness to remain members of the British Commonwealth of Nations. In both these major instances, transfers of power were accordingly effected without armed conflict. But it was different elsewhere. The Dutch did not accept the right of what they saw as the Javanese Quisling, Sukarno, to rule Indonesia, and they had no confidence that he and his regime would uphold the Dutch notion of an Indonesian federal state within the "Realm" of the Queen of the Netherlands. Armed warfare accordingly followed. Likewise, many Frenchmen abhorred the Vietminh leadership in Vietnam because of its Communist commitments; and still more they questioned its readiness to accept Vietnam's place in the French Union. So war followed there too.

Thus far the Asian mirror to independence in tropical Africa can therefore be said to have contained the following reflections. Even though the circumstances in various Asian countries differed considerably, there were enough broad similarities in their varying colonial experiences to suggest that where the general circumstances did not differ so greatly, as over so much of tropical Africa, even closer similarities were likely. The Asian experience indicated, too, that armed conflict in the ending of empire was a distinct possibility. Wherever such conflict occurred, the effect was traumatic—and it could be quite appallingly prolonged. But it was now also evident that there could be an alternative to violence. If certain terms were accepted by both sides (which in the last analysis turned on the acceptance by the departing imperialists of the assurances of their likely successors), a transfer of power without armed conflict could be achieved. In view of the clear tendency for there to be a concurrence in the patterning of events, it is perhaps especially significant here that peaceful transfers had occurred in Asia where America—now the greatest of the world's powers—and Britain—still the largest of the imperial ones—had held sway. The potentialities for peaceful transfers were thus rising.

In every case where an active nationalist movement had existed, however, independence had eventually come. And perhaps the most significant point here for subsequent African history is quite simply that the main imperial powers in tropical Africa happened to be the same as those which had experienced the ending of empire in Asia (or, as has been suggested above, in the case of the Belgians, had witnessed the experience of their immediate neighbors there), whereas those groups which held power elsewhere in Africa—Spain, Portugal, and the whites in Rhodesia and South Africa—had had no such experience.

If one then picks up some other threads of the Asian story, particularly in relation to the nature of nationalist upheavals, some further characteristics of the tropical African story soon become apparent.

In the Philippines, as we have seen, the Americans granted independence to a preexistent westernized elite that already possessed both urban and rural power. In Indochina, first the French, and up until 1975 the Americans, sought a similar result. Late in 1957 the British did likewise in Malaya, with success. About the only similar case of a successful transfer of power to a preexisting elite in tropical Africa occurred in northern Nigeria, where in the 1950s and early 1960s the British transferred power to the ruling emirate elite. Elsewhere some kind of struggle was invariably the order of the day, and it is to the range of variations here that some attention may be directed.

Because of the example of the Russian revolution of 1917, it was expected by many of those involved that independence in the colonial world would most probably come by way of a leftist urban revolt. Here the case of the Communist party of India (CPI) is particularly suggestive. In the two decades preceding the Second World War, it was probably the most substantial urban Communist party in Asia. In the 1920s it secured a remarkably strong base in Bombay. By the early 1940s it was influential in other cities as well, such as Calcutta. In 1929, as we have seen, its leaders were imprisoned by the British as a consequence of the long-drawn-out Meerut Conspiracy Case. But by contrast with what occurred elsewhere—in China, Indochina, and Indonesia—the leaders of the Communist party of India were not largely exterminated. During their imprisonment they relied on the Comintern to maintain their position, and on their release in 1933 most of them returned to their old party bailiwicks in the cities.[9]

Paradoxically, this constituted their first serious setback. Unlike their counterparts in Indonesia, Indochina, and China, the Indian Communists had had no involvement with a leftist rural revolt: indeed, the collapse of these revolts elsewhere may well have reinforced their proneness to concentrate on the cities. But to confine themselves to the cities, as they very largely did, was to limit their access to less than 15 percent of India's popu-

9. Roger Stuart, "The Formation of the Communist Party of India, 1927–1937: The Dilemma of the Indian Left" (Ph.D. diss., Australian National University, 1978).

lation. Even in the cities, moreover, they at no time held a monopoly of the existing radical impulses; they always had to share these with the ideologically very different Indian National Congress.

From the mid-1930s onward the CPI was caught in two further difficulties which climaxed in a major disaster. The doctrine of their mentors in the Comintern called at this time for "United Fronts." In India that meant muting its ideological conflict with the Congress governments in power in the provinces of British India. Then, in 1941, there followed the enormously damaging period of "People's War," when just as the Indian National Congress was mounting its major "Quit India" movement of August 1942 against the British, the CPI in effect aligned itself with the British. It never fully recovered from this mistake, and by the time the Zhdanov line was being propounded in the late 1940s, the revolutionary moment had passed. With the coming of independence to India all the levers of power had passed into the hands of the Congress.

The key failure of the CPI seems, in retrospect and by comparison, to have been its failure to "go rural." It should be emphasized that this occurred, not simply because for nearly two decades it had had some remarkably strong urban bases, but more particularly because the situation in the rural areas made it hard for it to do so. For, in general, the patterns of political authority at rural and village level in so many parts of India were at this time still remarkably intact, so that leftist movements encountered great difficulties, as they continue to do, in securing an entry there. The importance of this consideration is most illuminatingly exemplified by the case in the 1930s when the Communist party in India did in fact "go rural." In north Malabar in southwestern India, following the switch of the previously dominant Nayar caste from matrilineal to patrilineal succession, a breakdown of the structure of authority in the rural areas occurred, and as a consequence significant numbers of younger, Western-educated Nayars became seriously alienated from their society and moved into the leadership of a rural Communist movement.[10] Such developments were most unusual elsewhere in India, as they were to be later in tropical Africa.

Against this particular background the characteristics of the Communist movements in Indonesia, Indochina, and China become more readily apparent. By the early 1930s all three had experienced a largely rural Communist revolt, which stuck in their memories. All three, moreover, had suffered the virtual elimination of their urban parties; all that was open to the survivors was long-term exile. For the Indonesian Communists there

10. Robin Jeffrey, "Matriliny, Marxism and the Birth of the Communist Party in Kerala, 1930–40," *Journal of Asian Studies*, vol. 38, no. 1, pp. 17–20.

was never to be much respite from their expulsion, until Sukarno magically established the Republic of Indonesia in 1945 and made it possible for them to return. Although the Partai Kommunist Indonesia (PKI) had some successes in the rural areas in the two decades that followed, its ability to "go rural" was, as a consequence of its tardy reappearance on the scene, very much hampered.

In the early 1930s the possibility of "going rural" for the Communist party of China (CCP) and the Indochinese Communist party (ICP) was severely restricted as well. Since, however, unlike the CPI, they had been destroyed in the cities, their only hope if they were to operate at all was in fact to "go rural," and as it transpired the opportunities for them to do so were marginally more favorable than for their counterparts in Indonesia. As is well known, the inability of the Kuomintang government to control effectively the whole of China allowed the CCP to establish a rural base in Yenan. The corresponding opportunity in Indochina came first with the advent of the Popular Front government in France in 1936 and then with the Japanese invasion in 1941, which allowed the ICP to develop its rural cadres and its rural base sooner than might otherwise have occurred. In both these cases, moreover—in contrast with the Indian and the Indonesian ones—the Communist movement came to enjoy a substantial hold over the radical tendencies in their countries: in China, as the Kuomintang moved politically to the right; in Vietnam, following the French extermination of the VNQDD in the early 1930s.

But more to the present point, in both China and Vietnam, in contrast to so much of India, and for that matter Indonesia, the chances of the CCP and the ICP "going rural" seem to have been substantially assisted because, in both countries during the crucial period there were serious breakdowns in the structures of authority at rural level. The circumstances were different from those in Malabar. China suffered the ravages of warlordism on the one side and social banditry on the other, while Vietnam had to endure the serious dislocation of patterns of authority in the rural areas caused by sustained French assaults upon the rural scholar-gentry.[11] In both instances the way was open for Communist intrusion.

In both instances, what is more, there was no question of being caught at a critical moment on "the wrong side" of the preeminent local issue, as the CPI had been in August 1942. Mao (however half-heartedly, as has been suggested) joined Chiang in fighting the Japanese; Ho and Giap fought likewise. Both parties, moreover, were able to hold on to their redoubts (in Yenan and in northern Tonkin); while the CCP in particular seems to have

11. Woodside, *Community and Revolution in Modern Vietnam.*

benefited greatly from the succor it provided to those devastated by the rural rampages of the Japanese armies. In the event, an armed Communist-led revolution was eventually effected in both these countries—though it required a major war in China and a grotesquely protracted one in Vietnam to achieve this.

One can find some parallels to these events in Africa in the classic period of the attainment of independence there, more particularly, in Algeria. But it is difficult to think of others, until the further developments in the Portuguese territories and elsewhere in south central Africa in the 1970s.

When one turns to consider Indonesia a further possibility suggests itself. It is important to note that there were many indications that the structures of power at the rural level in Indonesia were kept largely intact during the Dutch period. Indeed, the "agricultural involution" of which Geertz wrote may well have served to reinforce the position of the *pamong desa* (village officials) at the head of the grievously hard-pressed but closely interlocked village society, particularly in Java. Certainly the opportunities for the PKI to "go rural" were always very restricted. It would also seem that in the 1920s and 1930s the Indonesian nationalists of Sukarno's ilk did not "go rural" either—not even to the extent that Sarekat Islam had done before them. Herein, no doubt, lay one of the major weaknesses of Indonesian nationalism, which would seem to explain why it was so much more easily crushed by the Dutch than Indian nationalism was by the British.

Accordingly, it would seem highly significant in the present context that when in the 1940s the opportunity for Sukarno and his associates did eventually come, it was powered by a ferment *in the cities*, particularly among the younger men.[12] Sukarno and his associates had to be careful not to be outmarched on the Left; in this, however, they were not unsuccessful. Moreover, rural support was of some importance to them in their armed conflicts with the Dutch, and that of many small towns even more so. But all signs point to the fact that the eventually successful Javanese Indonesian nationalist movement owed its critically important initial thrust to a series of well-coordinated nonleftist urban revolts in the Javanese cities of Jakarta, Bandung, Jogjakarta, Surabaya, and so on, and to some corresponding upheavals in Sumatra and even Makassar.

It is difficult to think of any comparable example of such events in Africa. The closest parallel might perhaps be in the Congo (now Zaire) on the collapse of the Belgian position there in 1960. But the dissimilarities are substantial.

The Indian case was different again. In terms of the argument outlined above, the central facts here would seem to be that, while the CPI for the

12. Anderson, *Java in a Time of Revolution*.

most part did not "go rural," the Indian National Congress in the 1920s and 1930s under Gandhi's leadership *did* "go rural." But when it did, it did not do so in a situation where the structure of power at rural and village level had broken down, but rather, and very precisely, through association with those whose power at village level remained intact. The British successfully repressed both rural and urban revolt in India. The Indian National Congress nevertheless successfully edged its way to power by securing the support of leading rural as well as urban elements, and then (as these were enfranchised) by winning the elections which the British instituted at local, provincial, and eventually national levels. In marked contrast to the Indonesian case, the Indian nationalists themselves took steps in the 1940s to damp down urban revolt. Despite events in Kerala, Telengana, and elsewhere, they had little to fear from the forces of the Left. It was therefore essentially a Congress increasingly linked to established village powerholders which won political independence for India.[13]

What all this implies for events in tropical Africa, and in particular for the great changes that occurred there with such rapidity between 1957 and 1964, may now be suggested. It is clear from a comparison with the Asian cases that, with perhaps one exception (northern Nigeria), the crucial advances toward independence in tropical Africa did not come through transfers of power to long-established elites. But they did not come by means of leftist-led urban revolutions either; nor through leftist-led rural revolutions; nor by nonleftist, urban-based revolutions. Since there were successful nationalist parties in most of tropical Africa whose political victories were registered in ballot boxes, it might appear that independence came to the main British and French colonies there by the same means as in India. But the distinctions from India remain striking. When mirrored in the experiences of Asia, the main tropical African stories appear indeed to have had important characteristics that were distinctly their own.

The essential difference from India was that in tropical Africa linkages were not created by westernized nationalist leaders with established village powerholders at the rural level to anything like the same extent, largely because the structures of power at the rural level in tropical Africa were, in general, nowhere nearly as firmly entrenched as they were in India.

Coupled with this is the fact that, although tropical Africa's nationalists never succeeded in effecting a successful rural revolution, they nevertheless periodically moved into situations where some of the rural power structures that did exist had broken down, or at all events were breaking down, as in Vietnam and China. In this connection it is important to notice one very important sea-change that took place in colonial Africa from the

13. Low, *Congress and the Raj*.

1940s onward. Previously (particularly in British colonial Africa under the influence of Lord Lugard's doctrine of indirect rule, the impact of which spread well beyond its prime seed bed in northern Nigeria), great emphasis had been placed by the imperial rulers upon "the chiefs." Although there were great variations in what this term implied, a common ethos prevailed. In some places chiefs belonging to previously existing hierarchies were confirmed in their positions of power; elsewhere direct appointees of the colonial territorial governments were given chiefly authority. But by the 1940s, various colonial bureaucracies had become increasingly irritated by the unreliability and lack of Western education, particularly of minor chiefs, and by their deep involvement in local power struggles. Furthermore, with the swing at this time by several colonial bureaucracies to a greater emphasis upon policies of "development and welfare," they developed an increasing anxiety that these chiefs would not provide the commitment and capacity that such reforms would require.

As a consequence, there was the particularly important switch in British colonial Africa in the late 1940s toward the creation of locally elected councils, which it was hoped would be better placed to take local responsibility for the local implementation of the new development policies. This had some very serious implications for the chiefs. Not only was their near-monopoly of local power undermined; they were often made subject to the newly elected councils' authority. Worse still, these councils were frequently captured by those who had hitherto been the chiefs' prime critics and rivals. There is, in fact, now increasing evidence that the democratic changes introduced by the colonial powers in tropical Africa in the late 1940s and 1950s weakened the one element of authority in rural areas—and often a tenuous authority at that—upon which colonial authority had hitherto depended.[14]

There was, perhaps, one especially significant miscalculation here. Among British policymakers there appears to have been some expectation that by instituting democratic elections at the local level a disjunction could be effected between local leaders and those who claimed to lead the (still embryonic) nationalist movements. The reasons why this disjunction was not in fact brought about lie at the heart of the differences between the Asian events we have considered and the tropical African ones.[15]

14. See Louis and Robinson, in this volume.

15. It is almost invidious in a volume of this kind to list relevant studies. The following may, however, be specifically mentioned: David E. Apter, *The Gold Coast in Transition* (Princeton, 1955); David E. Apter, *The Political Kingdom in Uganda* (Princeton, 1961); Dennis Austin, *Politics in Ghana 1946–60* (Oxford, 1964); James S. Coleman, *Nigeria, Background to Nationalism* (Berkeley, 1965); Thomas Hodgkin, *Nationalism in Colonial Africa* (London,

In China and Vietnam the new mobilizing forces had found it necessary to develop dedicated cadres that would go to the rural areas and, often with the backing of important military forces, correct the negativism of a world out of joint and win support for a new revolutionary doctrine for the improved ordering of society.

It would not be difficult to point to fissures and fractures in the social orders of Africa. But the dominant impression in the innumerable studies we now have of events in tropical Africa in the period following the Second World War is not, as for China and Vietname, one of breakdown and disintegration but rather of burgeoning local activists—and not least in rural areas—busily engaged in bursting forth into new enterprises and then periodically erupting when their initiatives were misconstrued or frustrated.

The reasons for this growth still need a great deal of elucidation. A bold suggestion might be that those societies having contact with Western technology which had already lived through the great experience of an agricultural revolution but had not been encapsulated in a high culture—the commonest situation in tropical Africa—have been among those best placed to respond with speed and vigor to the new opportunities such contact offered them. One thinks in particular here of such peoples as the Ibo of Nigeria or the Kikuyu of Kenya, but of many others besides. More specifically, one can trace the substantial development in tropical Africa by the mid-twentieth century, and not least in rural areas, of means of communications undreamt of before, of literacy in so many quarters where it had not hitherto been available, of the very extensive spread of cash crops bringing access to wealth that transformed social existence, and of the building of innumerable local retail stores selling a range of industrial goods that were frequently novel in the extreme. It is plain that the management of all these new areas of activity provided opportunities for—indeed demanded—enterprising individuals in unprecedented numbers. Many such became clergymen and school teachers, cash-crop farmers, storekeepers, officials of farmers' cooperatives, and elected members of local

---

1957); Martin Kilson, *Political Change in a West African State* (Cambridge, Mass., 1966); René Lemarchand, *Political Awakening in the Belgian Congo. The Politics of Fragmentation* (Berkeley, 1964); G. Andrew Maguire, *Toward 'Uhuru' in Tanzania* (Cambridge, 1969); David C. Mulford, *Zambia: The Politics of Independence 1957–64* (London, 1967); Cranford Pratt, *The Critical Phase in Tanzania 1945–1968* (Cambridge, 1976); Carl G. Rosberg and T. Nottingham, *The Myth of Mau Mau, Nationalism in Kenya* (New York, 1966); R. L. Sklar, *Nigerian Political Parties* (Princeton, 1963); Herbert Weiss, *Political Protest in the Congo* (Princeton, 1963); Crawford Young, *Politics in the Congo. Decolonization and Independence* (Princeton, 1965); A. R. Zolberg, *One Party Government in the Gold Coast* (Chicago, 1964).

councils. A new world of existence for these people, and at one remove for so many of those which whom they interacted, quite suddenly opened up.

Inevitably things did not always go smoothly. There could be serious local rivalries, distortions in particular developments, deep-seated disjunctions, and, it seems clear, grievous misconceptions by the colonial powers as to how to handle some of the more uncertain issues which appeared amid this torrent of events. Two specific examples will here suffice. Just as so many Africans were excitedly moving into a host of new political and economic roles, the numbers of local "export" representatives of the colonial powers often escalated dramatically; at some of the most important levels the new world was thus found to be dominated by foreigners to an even greater degree than the old. More specifically, the succession of the Korean war boom and the subsequent economic decline in the 1950s caused great disturbances to the whole situation which entailed all manner of small upsets.

In this pullulating situation there were consequently a good many disruptive episodes at the local level. These varied enormously, from short-lived and locally confined riots, to widespread patterns of disorder, and even to some major outbreaks, of which perhaps the Mau Mau revolt in Kenya was the greatest. Against this troops were used on a large scale, as they were from time to time elsewhere. But because of the previous loosening of the imperial bolts in Asia, the imperial reaction tended to be muted, except where the colonial power was substantially aroused by such a revolt. The responsibility for containing local eruptions was placed upon the very many territorial colonial bureaucracies, who were often in no fit state to bear it successfully. In many places they could no longer look effectively to their African chiefs, while the police available to them were generally far too thin on the ground as well. As a consequence, by the 1950s, the territorial colonial bureaucracies in many parts of tropical Africa found themselves increasingly hard-pressed to maintain their control (and it is clear that they were generally far less successful in doing so than their counterparts, had been, for example in India, a few decades earlier).

The most salient phenomenon in so many parts of colonial tropical Africa as the end of empire drew nigh was thus that of innumerable ebullient individuals, especially in the rural areas where most Africans lived, who were carving out a new society for themselves.[16] When, for reasons beyond their comprehension, brakes were applied to their pulsating ambitions, they became very easily enraged. The often tiny numbers of those in this

16. For example, D. A. Low and Alison Smith, eds., *History of East Africa*, vol. 3 (Oxford, 1976), passim.

situation who developed particular nationalist objectives did not often have to stir the general populace into activity. Rather, their prime task was somehow to aggregate discrete local, generally rural, energies into some larger political enterprise, and (to use Lonsdale's useful language)[17] to shift popular political concerns from a "local focus" to a more "central focus." Once they began to do this—and by contrast, say, with India or Vietnam it is notable how relatively little organization it required—then political forces were set loose in tropical Africa which its colonial powers, remembering their Asian pasts, were usually very hesitant, if not actually unable, to resist.

A further consideration warrants particular attention here. Since territorial boundaries in tropical Africa were so much newer than in Asia, and so much less coterminous with distinct cultural and historical borders, the singularity of developments in one territory in tropical Africa (which, as we have seen, was a great deal less even in Asia than has sometimes been imagined) was exceedingly hard to contain. There were clearly innumerable variations in the character of the burgeoning and of the outbreaks that occurred in different parts of tropical Africa. Nevertheless, the striking fact is that these differences did not correlate to anything like the degree the colonialists believed they should have done in terms of whether they occurred in British or French or Belgian colonial Africa, or in British West, East, or Central Africa. The upsurge characteristic of tropical Africa in the post–Second World War period occurred right across the continent, and the propensity toward vigorous protest when those affected found their energies being unwarrantedly curbed, proved to be no respecter of the carefully contrived regional and territorial demarcations which the imperial powers had imposed.

The fond belief, therefore, of the imperial powers that they could somehow control the course of events in tropical Africa turned out to be a sorry delusion. They were regularly caught off balance—and thus they had to relinquish power between 1957 and 1964 at a speed that no one had foreseen. They miscalculated the political effect of giving elected councils their head in place of their previous reliance upon chiefs. (These new councils usually quite failed to devote their minds simply to "modernizing" local government; and, ironically, their memberships often had less Western education than did the new generation of chiefs.) Moreover, many of tropical Africa's admittedly very varied populations displayed an effervescence not found anywhere near so widely in the former colonial empires in Asia.

17. J. M. Lonsdale, "Some Origins of Nationalism in East Africa," *Journal of African History* 9, no. 1 (1968):119–46.

For this reason the arbitrary distinctions which the colonialists sought to maintain between different parts of tropical Africa proved to bear so little relation to political realities, that they quite failed to hold back the overall torrent of events.

It was not, therefore, primarily the mobilizing of existing local powerholders, nor the negative aspects of social change in the countryside, nor messianic ferment in the cities, which provided the key to the nationalist forces in tropical Africa, as they had in Asia, but rather the widespread upsurge there, particularly among rural folk grasping the new opportunities within their reach, who then eagerly displayed their readiness to be mobilized by those who argued, "Seek ye first the political kingdom and all the rest shall be added unto you." Political primacy in Africa came to those nationalist leaders who most successfully rode this tide. And in the event, it moved very much faster than any of them had bargained for.

We may say therefore—as the other chapters in this book variously exemplify—that by contrast with events in Asia, independence came to tropical Africa after the Second World War with remarkable rapidity. Quite obviously the imperial grips in tropical Africa were loosened by the immediately preceding upheavals in Asia. It may seem at first sight that in their day the various Asian histories ran independently of each other. But upon closer inspection this does not seem to have been quite the case. Despite significant differences in the outlooks of the various imperial powers, and substantial differences in national cultures, parallel developments abounded in Asia. Where there was a greater congruence of outlook among the colonial powers (not least as a consequence of their experiences in Asia), as in tropical Africa; where (as in tropical Africa) there was a lesser degree of cultural diversity between different countries; and where, in the post–Second World War era, boom and recession propelled and then frustrated a great continent-wide burgeoning. There the parallelism in the steps toward independence turned out to be even greater than in Asia. There was as a consequence little holding the immediacy of the repercussions of events occurring in one part of Africa upon those in another. The ebullience which characterized tropical Africa in the two decades after the Second World War (of which there had been no real counterpart in Asia) soon broke the tenuous authoritarian and territorial barriers which the imperial powers had imposed upon her. For this reason there was little need in Africa for nationalist forces to develop the degree of dedication and organization that leftist forces in particular had established in Asia. (Socially radical movements were thus rarely in vogue in Africa.) In short, nationalist movements in Africa were less dependent upon systematic political organization, and to a greater extent were the political embodiment of continent-wide social impulses than they were in Asia; being more diffuse, they were, moreover, more difficult for the imperial powers to curb, but easier for them to accommodate, than they had been in Asia. Herein lay the central elements, it may be suggested, which made for the relatively non-violent precipitancy which in retrospect still seems to characterize the story of tropical Africa's attainment of political independence.

2. *The United States and the Liquidation of British Empire in Tropical Africa, 1941–1951*

WM. ROGER LOUIS AND RONALD ROBINSON

The fall of Europe's colonial empires in Africa has usually been attributed to a magpie's choice of African nationalism, shifts in national ideology, and changes in the international balance of power. Clearly a catalogue of such forces is not enough. The difficulty in assessing the collapse of the European regimes lies in relating the international, metropolitan, and colonial factors in a comprehensive framework that reveals both the chronology and the interacting forces. This chapter attempts to move the subject forward toward such an explanation by examining the problem through one particular but cardinally important aspect. It begins with the emergence of the United States as a global power—a global power that during the Second World War suddenly developed an intense interest in the British Empire, including its African components. When the center of world power shifted from London to Washington (and eventually to Moscow as well), the British felt the blow to their economy and their colonial position throughout the world. Did this shock trigger the changes of mind on the part of the British that eventually accelerated the transfer of power and the nationalization, or Africanization, of colonial administration?[1]

A brief historical comment may help to explain the background of these remarks. After the partition of Africa at the turn of the century, the colonial

1. Parts of this essay are drawn (but with important modifications and reflections) from Wm. Roger Louis, *Imperialism at Bay: The United States and the Decolonization of the British Empire, 1941–1945* (Oxford, 1976), and from various seminar papers and publications by Ronald Robinson, for example: "Andrew Cohen and the Transfer of Power in Africa," in W. H. Morris-Jones and George Fischer, eds., *Decolonisation and After: The British and French Experiences* (London, 1979); "Sir Andrew Cohen: Proconsul of African Nationalism," in L. H. Gann and Peter Duignan," *African Proconsuls* (New York, 1978). For the background to theoretical aspects of this chapter, see Ronald Robinson, "European Imperialism and Indigenous Reactions in British West Africa," in H. L. Wesseling, ed., *Expansion and Reaction* (Leiden, 1978); and, by the same author, "Non-European Foundations of European Imperialism," in W. R. Louis, ed., *Imperialism: The Robinson and Gallagher Controversy* (New York, 1976).

powers of Europe supported each other against Africans. They only rarely interfered in each other's affairs. There was, in fact, what could be called an international colonial system (interrupted, of course, by the First World War). Through international treaties the African powers of Europe accepted each other's colonies as exclusive spheres of influence—spheres recognized in international law. Though there were important protests against this sytem, notably on the part of Woodrow Wilson in 1919, the European powers administered their territories without fear of external intervention. So long as Europeans dominated the balance of power, colonial administrators could enjoy freedom of action without fear of international subversion. One way of looking at the beginning of the end of the "colonial system" is to analyze the impact which the emergence of the United States from isolation had on colonial affairs.

The momentous shifts in the bedrock of world politics during the Second World War raised one set of problems in Washington and another set in London. Should the Americans collaborate with British "imperialism" for purposes of winning the war and securing the peace? Or would their anticolonial tradition and expansive economic strategy bring them to insist on the liquidation of the empire? On the other side of the Atlantic, how could the British adjust to their unaccustomed dependence without giving up the empire? This chapter probes these questions from both sides, and more particularly, it assesses the relation between American expansion and the future of the British Empire in tropical Africa in the 1940s. Though it deals primarily with the international aspect of decolonization, it also attempts, in conclusion, to set that dimension in broad perspective.

The American Scare, 1941–44

From the time of the Atlantic Charter in August 1941, the United States officially espoused the principle of self-determination. Self-determination for whom? Churchill thought that the pledge referred exclusively to the conquered peoples of Europe under the Nazi yoke. Roosevelt believed that it should apply to colonial peoples as well. With that mixture of disarming idealism and intuitive realism that characterized him, the president held that the European colonial empires should be placed under some sort of international administration. The colonies would eventually become independent on the model of the Philippines. But to the British this was a dubious example. Would the Philippines be truly "independent" politically or economically? And was not the scheme for international administration perhaps camouflage for the beginning of a gigantic, even if informal, American empire?

Like most Americans, Roosevelt usually made no distinction between India and the Colonial Empire. The emergency in India in 1942 colored his view of the British Empire as a whole. Nevertheless, he and many of his fellow countrymen were realistic enough to admit that some peoples would acquire independence sooner than others. India certainly would acquire it sooner than the peoples of tropical Africa. Roosevelt was typical of his generation in believing that the headhunters of New Guinea might take several hundred years to be educated and trained for independence. In this sense the Americans, like the Europeans, were gradualists with a common outlook; but there were also real differences. Throughout the war the State Department requested *timetables* for independence. The war created a sense of urgency to set colonial peoples free. According to the editors of *Life* magazine in "An Open Letter . . . to the People of England" in October 1942, the American people might disagree among themselves about war aims, but they were unanimous on one point: "one thing we are sure we are not fighting for is to hold the British Empire together. . . . If your strategists are planning a war to hold the British Empire together they will sooner or later find themselves strategizing all alone."[2]

Grand strategy and the great events of the war of course also had a bearing on the colonial problem. Churchill's famous remark, made in November 1942, that he had not become the king's first minister in order to preside over the liquidation of the British Empire was made little more than a week after the victory at El Alamein. Roosevelt instructed the joint chiefs of staff to formulate plans for an "international police force" shortly after the turn of the tide in the Pacific.[3] For both sides the victories of late 1942 stimulated postwar planning for the colonial world.

In Washington sharp lines of controversy developed over the extent to which American influence should be exerted through an international trusteeship system, and the extent to which the solution to the problem of military security might be found through annexation pure and simple. Enthusiasts in the State Department might wax eloquent about the replacement of "imperialism" by "international trusteeship," but in the eyes of the Navy there was one overriding concern: security in the Atlantic and Pacific. Roosevelt held the delicate balance, and he did not lose sight of the main goal at hand: winning the war against the Axis powers. Though the president, like many Americans, distrusted British imperialism, the British and Americans were comrades-in-arms. Perhaps he assumed, un-

2. *Life*, October 12, 1942.

3. Memorandum for Admiral Leahy by Captain John L. McCrea, naval aide to the president, December 28, 1942, Roosevelt Papers (Hyde Park, N.Y.), map room box 167.

consciously if not consciously, that American economic power would eventually reduce the European colonial regimes to the status of American satellites. In any case, Roosevelt took definite steps toward decolonization, though he moved slowly because of the circumstances of the wartime alliances; and like almost all others, he did not foresee how rapidly the colonial empires would collapse.

Roosevelt agreed with his advisers in the State Department that there should be eventual independence for the colonies. As early as November 1942 the State Department proposed, in a document entitled "Declaration on National Independence for Colonies":

> [T]hat the *independence* of those nations which now possess *independence* shall be maintained; that the *independence* of those nations which have been forcibly deprived of *independence* shall be restored; that opportunity to achieve *independence* for those peoples who aspire to *independence* shall be preserved, respected, and made more effective. . . .

To aid those people aspiring to independence, definite dates would be established for decolonization:

> It is, accordingly, the duty and the purpose of each nation having political ties with colonial peoples . . . *to fix at the earliest practicable moment, dates* upon which the colonial peoples shall be accorded the status of full independence within a system of general security. . . .[4]

With timetables to mark the pace, colonial peoples progressively would be granted self-government, which would lead to independence. Thus, within the State Department in 1942 can be found the grand design of the United States in the postwar era of decolonization—a design, as later became apparent, that was not always in harmony with the requirements of national security, especially against the threat of communism.

In London the head of the General Department of the Colonial Office, Christopher Eastwood, examined the declaration in detail and observed that the word *independence* occurred in the document nineteen times altogether. He concluded that the Americans were attempting to establish a sort of informal empire:

4. "The Atlantic Charter and National Independence," November 13, 1942, Papers of Stanley Hornbeck (Hoover Institution), box 48, italics added. Hornbeck, the Adviser on Far Eastern Affairs, was a moving force behind the Declaration. See also U(nited) S(tates) S(tate) D(epartment) "Notter Files" (hereafter USSD NF), i.e., postwar planning files, boxes 63–66 and 117–18.

> Independence is a political catchword which has no real meaning apart from economics. The Americans are quite ready to make their dependencies politically 'independent' while economically bound hand and foot to them and see no inconsistency in this.[5]

Though he did not pursue this line of reasoning, Eastwood clearly expressed what he believed would be the result of American enthusiasm for independence: "this emphasis throughout on independence implies that the hope for the future lies in a great multiplication of small national sovereignties."[6] Furthermore, it would probably mean the end of the British Empire.

The Colonial Office officials took a skeptical view of the American proposals for colonial independence. But they now fully recognized that not only the empire but Britain herself depended militarily and economically on the support—and perhaps even the whim—of America. While it seemed vital to the British to obtain agreement from the Americans "that would include defence of the colonial areas without impairing our right to administer them," it appeared equally important not to jeopardize British administration.[7] Thus the Colonial Office attempted to counter the American proposals with a set of regional consultative commissions designed "to bring in America in defence and in economic matters," and also to satisfy "Clem Attlee and the Left in Britain [by providing] an element of internationalism."[8]

The State Department still insisted on international control over the colonial powers in order to coordinate development programs in education, welfare, and health. There would have to be an international "executive authority" in the West Indies, Africa, and Southeast Asia to enforce timetables to advance colonies to independence. And there would be "international accountability." The British, however, would not accept these schemes for intervention in their colonial affairs. According to one report, the colonial secretary "would see us [the Americans] in Hades" before he would agree to an external executive authority.[9] In the schemes for re-

5. Minute by Eastwood, April 21, 1943, C(olonial) O(ffice) 323/1858/9057B; all F(oreign) O(ffice), D(ominions) O(ffice), CAB(inet Office), and PREM(ier) Papers on which this chapter is based are at the Public Record Office, London.

6. Minute by Eastwood, April 21, 1943, CO 323/1858/9057B.

7. Draft Cabinet Paper enclosed in Eden to Attlee, October 25, 1942, CO 323/1858/9057B.

8. Cranborne to Emrys-Evans, October 9, 1942, CO 323/1858/9057B.

9. Isaiah Bowman's comment to the key American State Department committee discussing colonial problems at this time, the Committee on "International Organization," May 12, 1944, USSD NF box 142.

gional commissions, as in the proposals for the national declaration of independence, the British and Americans were at loggerheads.

These issues were discussed intensely at all levels of the American government during 1944. The president's military advisers complained about the lack of realism in the State Department: internationalism might sound all right in theory, but in practice it had many implications for military strategy. Roosevelt himself intervened spasmodically; early in 1944 he solidly backed the State Department's proposals. After his return from the conferences in Cairo and Teheran, his proposals for international trusteeship became more and more emphatic. On January 12, 1944 he gave a breathtaking sketch of his ideas to the Pacific War Council. Japan would be stripped of her empire and the islands "would be taken over by the United Nations." The western Pacific would be policed by powers capable of exercising effective military control. Korea would be placed under international trusteeship for a forty-year term. Dairen would become a free port. The United States would act as a "police agent" in the Marianas, Carolines, and Marshalls. One important strand in his thought was the provision of military bases for the proposed international police force at such places as Truk, the Bonins, Tuamotus, Rabaul, Dakar, and Ascension Island. Another was the use of trust territories and free ports to achieve equal access and free trade for all nations in colonial areas; for example, he wanted to bring Hong Kong, Dairen, and a port at the northern end of the Persian Gulf under international trusteeship in order to guarantee free trade—or, as British observers put it, freedom of American trade. In all these proposals the president seemed to regard international trusteeship as a kind of universal panacea. His basic solution was international control in which the American voice would be influential, if not predominant. Roosevelt's enthusiasm for international trusteeship reached its peak in the winter of 1943–44.

In April 1944, Isaiah Bowman, Roosevelt's trouble-shooter on colonial issues, went to London with the Stettinius mission to put American plans for international trusteeship to the British colonial secretary and his officials. Bowman returned to Washington a disenchanted man to report that the British had rejected the proposals outright. They objected in principle to international supervision and accountability for colonial administration. "Such a procedure would be like trying to get the Ten Commandments to fit all dependent areas," Bowman reported about British opinion. He went on to say to his colleagues in the State Department, "It simply could not be done, and even if it could be done it would be merely an incitement to riot for agitators all over the world."[10] More than that, he reported, the British

10. "International Organization" minutes 52, May 10, 1944, USSD NF box 142.

bitterly resented the Americans sticking their fingers into colonial pies. Stanley Hornbeck, adviser on Far Eastern affairs, expressed the State Department's reaction to the British attitude:

> He [Hornbeck] felt like replying to the British that it happened to be their pie which was under our nose and which did not smell too good to us . . . what becomes of these dependent peoples was everybody's business.[11]

Joseph C. Green (assistant secretary of state), however, presented a less ambitious approach to international trusteeship. He proposed to limit the system to former mandates and ex-enemy colonial territories. He hoped that trusteeship there would set an example which would raise the standards of colonial administration throughout the world. He reasoned:

> [M]oral aspiration . . . applicable only to trust territories would be reflected throughout the world—in Puerto Rico, in Mississippi, in Malaya, in Burma, and elsewhere. . . . it would then be possible for us to insist upon the application of these principles without being accused of sticking our fingers into other peoples' pies.[12]

The moral principles applied in specific trust territories would, he hoped, "create a standard of conduct for the whole world and would influence such areas as Mississippi and the Navajo territory as well as British and Dutch dependencies."[13] So great was the State Department's enthusiasm for the ethics of trusteeship that the moral influence would extend from colonial areas into the backwater sections of the United States itself. At least up to the summer of 1944 it seemed probable that the State Department's proposals for an international authority to preside over the liquidation of the European colonial empires had the backing of the president and might inspire American policy after the war.

The British Response to American Pressure, 1943–44

During the latter part of the war the British turned to the sharpening of their trusteeship standards, not least in order to appease American anticolonialism, which as early as 1942 had given them their first intimation of colonial mortality in Africa. Sir Arthur Dawe (assistant under-secretary) wrote, for example: "Nineteenth century conceptions of empire are dead.

11. Ibid.
12. Ibid.
13. Ibid.

Forces released by the war are gathering great velocity . . . after the war this Island will be exhausted. . . . To surmount this danger will require statesmanship, or we shall lose the African continent as we did the American in the 18th century."[14] Dependence on the United States strengthened the demands of British liberals, humanitarians, and socialists that colonialism be given a new and more attractive image.

In 1943–44, now that the Americans as well as the British radical Left, not to mention the Indian nationalists, were denouncing the empire, the Foreign Office came to the aid of the Colonial Office in demanding a better deal for the colonies. And so, like most empires, the British Empire improved its morality as its power declined. From 1943 it began to live up to the moral pretentions which had been raised in statements of policy since the native paramountcy declaration of 1923. According to this often reiterated pronouncement, the British promised to administer their African territories as "trustees before the world for the African population." They had also pledged themselves to give the economic and social development of the African population priority over the interests of the European and Indian settlers in the east and central African territories; but for twenty years they had done little to fulfill these promises. They feared that, if they did so, the British settlers would rebel, as the Rhodesians eventually did in 1965.

At the same time as the danger from Washington reached its peak in 1943–44, the Colonial Office succeeded in persuading the British Treasury to contribute on a large scale to African welfare for the first time. For example, in 1943 Harold Macmillan, then a junior minister, proposed that the Treasury should buy out the Kenya settlers and repatriate them. Also in that year the colonial secretary, Oliver Stanley, asked the Treasury to purchase the mineral rights of British companies in Northern Rhodesia and Nigeria on behalf of their African inhabitants. The thin lips of the treasury lords did not smile on the idea of paying for all past imperial sins in Africa; if they began to do so, they felt, there would be no end to it. Nevertheless, 1944 was to be an annus mirabilis: for in that year, to gild the old image of empire and make it more acceptable in the eyes of British and American public opinion, £120 million was squeezed out of the Treasury for colonial development and welfare.

The negotiations for the new Colonial Development and Welfare Act had begun in 1943. A year later a treasury official observed, in language unusual for one of his breed, "As regards the money we are conscious that we must

14. Memorandum by Dawe, "A Federal Solution for East Africa," dated July 1942, CO 822/111/46709.

justify ourselves before the world as a great Colonial Power."[15] There followed, more characteristically, a bitter dispute between the Colonial Office and the Treasury over the amount and control of the expenditure. Finally, in September 1944, the colonial secretary wrote privately to the chancellor of the exchequer:

> The end of the fighting in Europe will, I am convinced, be the psychological moment at which to announce our intention to make fully adequate provision for the assistance from His Majesty's Government which will be necessary for a dynamic programme of Colonial development. It is the moment at which to demonstrate our faith and our ability to make proper use of our wide Colonial possessions. It is also the moment when the minds of administrators in the Colonies will be turning . . . towards planning for the future permanence and adequacy of our policy. . . .[16]

It is notable that the need to demonstrate sincerity and to raise the standards of British colonial trusteeship was uppermost in the colonial secretary's mind, rather than the material benefits that might accrue to Britain. He mentioned in passing that the investment would increase colonial production, which in turn would strengthen Britain's general financial position; but ultimately he did not rest his case on economic returns:

> I make no pretence . . . that this is going to be a profitable transaction on a purely financial calculation. The over-riding reason why I feel that these proposals are essential is the necessity to justify our position as a Colonial power.[17]

He rested his case implicitly on justification in the eyes of America.

A major conclusion can be drawn from this exchange between the Colonial Office and the Treasury in late 1944. It seems likely from the timing of the Colonial Development and Welfare Act of 1945 that one of the strongest incentives for investing the money was to appease American opinion. But the act was more than an exercise in public relations; fear of American anticolonialism had strengthened the arm of British politicians and officials who had previously lacked the financial sinew to carry out imperial good intentions. In this sense the new resolution to develop the colonies economically and socially was inspired by changing conviction.

15. Sir Bernard Gilbert (Treasury) to Sydney Caine, September 13, 1944, CO 852/588/19275.

16. Stanley to Sir John Anderson, September 21, 1944, CO 852/588/19275.

17. Ibid.

Thus American influence helped to bring about a moral regeneration of British purpose in the colonial world. It also helped to bring to power a new generation of officials who were resolved to reform the old colonial regime.

The American Bogey and British Plans for the Transfer of Power in Africa, 1945–49

While the Colonial Office was moving forward with the Colonial Development and Welfare Act and with its postwar planning for the colonies, the joint chiefs of staff in Washington continued to attack the State Department's proposals for international trusteeship. A controversy of the first magnitude arose over the Japanese mandated islands. The State Department insisted that unless those islands became trust territories, they would have no ground for arguing with the British that the Italian colonies should be placed under international supervision. To the officers of the navy, however, it seemed preposterous that the State Department wanted to make these islands into a sort of international property. Their population was negligible. They served no purpose other than as strategic outposts. They were being won at the high cost of American blood and treasure. In short, the navy insisted on annexation pure and simple.

In this clash between the military and the State Department, the president's position, though central, was not altogether clear. On the one hand, he encouraged the State Department to proceed with plans for trusteeship, while on the other he instructed the military to plan for permanent bases throughout the Pacific and other parts of the world. Roosevelt refused to concur in the joint chiefs' plea for annexation of the Japanese islands. "I am working on the idea," he wrote to them on July 4, 1944, "that the United Nations will ask the United States to act as Trustee for the Japanese Mandate Islands. With this will go . . . the military authority to protect them (the inhabitants), i.e., fortifications, etc."[18]

These words did not placate the joint chiefs. Frustrated by the president, the Joint Chiefs Strategic Survey Committee now turned to the State Department and insisted that further discussion of trusteeship arrangements would prejudice the conducting of the war. Russia might refuse to help defeat Japan if the Japanese Empire were prematurely divided. The State Department had to admit that the joint chiefs' case was unanswerable. If controversies over trusteeship were likely to prolong the war, then these issues must be put into cold storage. Moreover, the State Depart-

18. Memorandum for the Joint Chiefs of Staff, July 4, 1944, Papers of the Joint Chiefs of Staff, CCS360 (12-9-42), National Archives; Roosevelt Papers, map room box 167.

ment officials were beginning to see that if they pressed for universal trusteeship, it would be difficult to justify excluding such territories as Puerto Rico and the Virgin Islands from international supervision. It also seemed unlikely that Congress would ever agree to such a proposal, still less the navy and the Department of the Interior.

The schemes for placing *all* colonial territories under international trusteeship were never realized, in part because of the opposition by American military officers. They held strong opinions about the future of the colonial world. The decline of the British Empire was obvious to them. According to the Joint Chiefs Strategic Survey Committee:

> As a military power, the British Empire in the post-war era will be in a distinctly lower category than the United States and Russia. The primacy of the British Empire in the century before World War I, and her second-to-none position until World War II, have built up a traditional concept of British military power which the British will strive to profit by and maintain in the post-war era.[19]

The joint chiefs emphasized the need to regard the British less sentimentally and more realistically: "Both in an absolute sense and relative to the United States and Russia, the British will emerge from the war having lost ground both economically and militarily."[20]

To Roosevelt and his advisers, who were conscious that the *Pax Britannica* was being replaced with a sort of *Pax Americana,* it was perhaps tempting at first sight to try to take over Britain's imperial bases under the guise of internationalization; but in view of British opposition to internationalization, it seemed better in the long run to shore up the British ally and her empire and achieve security for as long as possible at second hand. The British Empire, though in decline, would still serve as an instrument of American security.

At Yalta in early 1945, Roosevelt and the State Department obtained a trusteeship formula that was limited to the former mandated territories and to parts of the Italian colonial empire. Colonial powers were invited to place their colonies under the same authority, but in the event none of them did so. The general policy of the United States government had shifted gradually from one of dismantling the British Empire to one of giving it tacit support. The watchword "security" had begun to eclipse that of "independence." At the San Francisco conference in the spring and

19. Memorandum entitled "Fundamental Military Factors in Relation to Discussions concerning Territorial Trusteeships and Settlements," JCS 973, July 28, 1944, CCS092 (7-27-44).
20. Ibid.

summer of 1945, the British had little reason to be dissatisfied with the limited American proposals for trusteeship that were incorporated into the United Nations Charter. The British could congratulate themselves that, as far as the United States government was concerned, pressure for the liquidation of the British Empire had ceased, at least temporarily.

Nevertheless, the psychological effects of possible American intervention continued to be felt in London. The British still feared that anticolonial public sentiment might force the American government to renew its insistence on decolonization if the British did not advance the colonies toward self-government. When Attlee's Labour government came to power in 1945, the transformation of policy which had begun in the economic and social field carried over into political plans for the transfer of power in Africa. The men of the new course had come into office. In 1946 the Labour colonial secretary, Arthur Creech Jones, set up a committee of officials under Sydney Caine and Andrew Cohen to chart "a new approach" to Africa, not only by way of economic and social advance, but also of political progress. The report submitted in May 1947 implied a revolution in African policy. It was assumed that "within a generation . . . the principal African territories will have attained . . . full responsible government," which in effect meant independence within the Commonwealth.[21] According to this plan, power was to be transferred in stages, according to circumstances in each colony. The transfer was to begin with the democratization of African local government and end in African ministries responsible to democratically elected assemblies.

On what grounds had the Cohen-Caine committee given colonial rule in British Africa a life expectancy of a mere twenty years when up until then it had been given a century or more? The committee in effect contended that the chiefs who had been the mainstay of colonial rule were useless as agents of economic development. If the African empire were to be developed, colonial rule would have to be nationalized to bring the hitherto excluded African educated elites into collaboration; but they would not cooperate except on the conditions of a progressively swift transfer of power. If this were true, it seemed better to concede too much power too early than too little too late, for magnanimity was expected to put the brake on demands for the transfer of power and end in a moderate rather than a revolutionary succession. In effect, this was a plan to convert (or reconvert) formal into informal empire as the need arose.

The Cohen-Caine report indicated a radical shift not only in the perspective of the planners but also in their social and political values. They

21. Cohen-Caine Committee Report, May 1947, Cohen Papers (in the possession of Ronald Robinson); CO 847/46.

seemed to be losing interest in governing Africa from London precisely because they had become interested in developing and modernizing it. As they did so, they changed the aim of policy from one of jealously conserving imperial power in alliance with African kings and chiefs to one of nation-building hand in hand with modern African elites.

In the years 1948 to 1951, the Cohen-Caine plan was implemented in British West Africa much faster and with different consequences from those intended by the planners. When Creech Jones issued his celebrated local government dispatch, which in 1947 ordered the democratization of colonial authority from below, the new course encountered bitter resistance from senior colonial officials. But the riots in Accra of 1948 and subsequent events in the Gold Coast confirmed the wisdom of the Cohen-Caine plan. The disturbances persuaded the Colonial Office to introduce direct elections and a quasi-ministerial system into the Gold Coast, so that the time scale of Colonial Office plans were foreshortened by fifteen years. The British then miscalculated the electoral odds in the new Gold Coast constitution of 1951. As a result, the more extreme African party won at the polls and its leader, Nkrumah, had to be let out of jail and made leader of government business. The victory gave his party a popular following on a national scale.

The British soon realized that the advanced constitution which had been given to the Gold Coast could not be denied to Nigeria and other west coast territories; and so the involuntary transfer of power spread with a domino effect throughout West Africa. The ballot box and directly elected assemblies, which had been planned in 1947 as bargains with leaders of nationalism, were conceded prematurely, at least according to previous Colonial Office calculations. British constitution-making thus contributed much to the development of nationalism as a popular movement. In this sense, the Cohen-Caine committee helped to determine the shape of things to come. Wittingly and unwittingly, the British had sown the wind of colonial concessions and reaped the whirlwind of African nationalism.

The plan of 1947 therefore had momentous effects; but what had inspired its tenets? How had the empire's rulers been brought to see the futility of continued colonial administration unless it served as scaffolding for building self-governing nations? The reasons given followed a three-pronged formula which had become customary since early in the war: this was "the internal situation in the territories themselves, the state of international opinion, [and] the public relations of the Labour Party."[22] There is in fact no specific evidence that any of these pressures had become more acute. In 1947 African nationalism was still in its infancy. Its leaders had not yet

22. Minute by Ivor Thomas dated November 1946, Cohen Papers.

organized the elite and the people into a popular party, nor would they be able to do so until the British introduced the ballot box and democratized colonial government. Naturally the Labour government wished to show that the shibboleths for colonial reform, which had been applied in opposition, were being respected in office; but on the whole Labour's anti-imperialism, never strong, weakened further with experience. As Labour ministers grappled with the dollar crisis and learned the economic value of the African colonies to Britain, they became prouder of the feats of progress which they proposed to bring about under the Union Jack. Like earlier generations of British anti-imperialists, as they raised the standard of colonial trusteeship toward their ideals, most Labour leaders became more and more reluctant to give up the empire and the means to achieve their aspirations. Only by retaining the empire could they demonstrate the progressiveness of their colonial rule.

If neither the strength of nationalism in Africa nor the force of anti-imperialism in Britain seems fully to account for the new course of the postwar period, how far was the international or American factor responsible for it? It is generally true that after 1945 the fire of anticolonialism burned much less brightly within the United States government. By the time of the San Francisco conference, the American military had prevailed over those who sought to liquidate colonial empires by placing them under international supervision. In 1945 the United States had acquiesced in the return to their former rulers of many colonies which had been occupied by the common enemy. During the period of the Loan and Marshall aid the United States pledged its economic resources to the recovery of its European allies with no conditions attached to colonies except that they should be more accessible to American trade and investment. During the early years of the Cold War there was very little question of American pressure to decolonize, though the dilemmas of orderly imperial liquidation persisted.

In the immediate postwar era, American involvement in European colonial affairs can be summed up in the names Cyrenaica, Indochina, and Indonesia. Each of these carried a chilling message to the British. In the dispute over the future of the Italian colonies, Ernest Bevin, the foreign secretary in the Attlee government, hoped that Britain would be able to acquire trusteeship status over Cyrenaica and create a strategic base there in order to lessen British dependence on Egypt. When the negotiations for the renewal of an Anglo-Egyptian alliance broke down in 1946–47, and when it became clear that the Palestine problem could not be resolved to British advantage, the question of Britain's security in the Middle East became acute. To Bevin's dismay the Americans could not be counted on to back British trusteeship claims to Cyrenaica. American policy fluctuated in reaction to possible Russian expansion into the eastern Mediterranean and in relation to the strength of the Communist movement in Italy (for European reasons, the Americans were willing to consider an Italian trusteeship if it would strengthen an anti-Communist government in Italy). In 1945–48 the British were forced to turn to Iraq as the linchpin of British defense in the Middle East. What the British learned from the episode of the Italian colonies was that American policy toward colonial areas in North Africa and the Middle East would change according to the fortunes of the Cold War and would not necessarily accommodate the strategic requirements of the British Empire.

The specter of communism similarly checked the American aversion to French colonialism in Southeast Asia. From the time of the earliest days of the Cold War American officials regarded Indochina as the key area in preventing the spread of communism to the Philippines, Indonesia, and Malaya. Sympathy in Burma and India for Ho Chi Minh led the State Department to believe that the call for liberation in Vietnam might become a rallying-cry for all anti-Western forces in Southeast Asia. Roosevelt's enmity toward French colonialism continued to flavor American postwar attitudes; but this deep-seated animus was offset by an even stronger emotional reaction to Ho Chi Minh and the belief that he was a Russian puppet. "We do not lose sight of [the] fact that Ho Chi Minh has direct Communist connections," Secretary of State George C. Marshall wrote in February 1947, "and it should be obvious that we are not interested in seeing colonial empire administration supplanted by [the] philosophy and political organization emanating from and controlled by [the] Kremlin."[23] To British observers, who were less alarmist and certainly much less inclined to ideological interpretation, nothing less than an American crusade against communism had the countervailing power to hold American anticolonialism in check.

Nowhere did the contradictory aims of the American government become more sharply apparent to the British than in Indonesia. On the one hand, the United States hoped for the political and economic stability of the Netherlands and, in turn, the unity of western Europe against communism. On the other hand, the American anticolonial tradition encouraged Indonesian nationalists to look toward the United States for encouragement in their struggle against the Dutch. Within the State Department attitudes differed between the Division of Northern European Affairs and the Division of Southeast Asian Affairs. The former held that, economically, the Netherlands East Indies were indispensable to Dutch re-

23. Marshall to Caffery, February 7, 1947, *Foreign Relations 1947*, 6:68.

covery in Europe and therefore that the Dutch should be supported in the colonial issue. The latter warned that the Dutch were moving toward a prolonged colonial war by resisting reasonable nationalist demands. The response within the British Foreign Office was similar. With British initiative the Dutch and the nationalists reached a fragile truce (the Linggadjati agreement of January 1948) whose purpose, from the American point of view, was (1) the rehabilitation of Dutch authority and economic development of the Netherlands East Indies; and (2) accommodation of the nationalist movement, including the conferral on nationalist or Republican leaders of governmental responsibilities that would eventually facilitate a smooth transfer of power.

Both British and American observers agreed that the Dutch were much too slow in responding to nationalist demands. For example, in May 1947, on the eve of Indian independence, Attlee warned the Dutch ambassador that if concessions were not made to the moderate nationalists then the initiative would pass to the extremists. For Americans the crux of the issue was that moderate and pro-Western nationalists might be superseded by Communists. When the Dutch undertook a large-scale "police action" in December 1948, the State Department feared that it would plunge Indonesia into a colonial war in which communism would emerge as the victor.

Postwar American policy favored the European colonial regimes rather than the nationalist movements. The French and the Dutch would not have been able to combat colonial nationalism as effectively as they did had it not been for the economic and military resources provided by the United States through the use of lend-lease and indirect economic assistance. Publicly the Truman administration disassociated itself from French and Dutch counterrevolutionary activities, but privately American officials were quite aware that considerable amounts of financial aid under the Marshall Plan were being siphoned off into Southeast Asia. In the case of Indonesia, however, the American government feared that the Dutch flouting of the United Nations good-offices committee would weaken the United Nations organization itself, and that Dutch intransigence with the moderate or Republican nationalists would lead to a Communist revolution. In December 1948 the American government suspended an unexpended balance of Marshall Plan aid of about five million dollars designated for the Netherlands East Indies. The United States made it clear that economic assistance to the Netherlands itself might be in jeopardy. The Dutch capitulated. No move by the Americans could have been more dramatic to the British: it became apparent that the United States was prepared to cut off economic aid to a European ally in order to promote colonial independence.

Dependence on the United States since 1941 and the witnessing of the American response to such crises as the one in Indonesia profoundly influenced the official mind of British imperialism. The course of American anticolonialism in the 1940s helped to undermine the confidence and shatter the traditional perspectives of British colonial rulers. It also armed British liberal reformers with compelling arguments that reform was vital in order to preserve the American alliance. There were powerful reasons for the belief that the anticolonial sentiment of the American public might yet provoke the United States government to interfere if the British did not continue with a progressive colonial policy. Above all, dependence on the United States was probably the one experience humiliating enough to convince the British psychologically that the age of empire was ending. The change of perspective resulting from this reversal of international roles encouraged a new spirit and direction in British policy that favored the eventual transfer of power in Africa.

As far as officials in Washington were concerned, the dismantling of the British Empire led to balkanization and local instability. They were confronted with a lengthening series of local crises similar to those faced by the British in the nineteenth century. In one way or another these crises compelled the Americans to extend their "responsibilities" in order to fill the vacuum left by the contraction of the British Empire. In Africa the rapid fragmentation was a phenomenon the United States neither planned nor welcomed, but to some extent it was the logical outcome of the goal of the American government to save as much as possible of the non-Western world from communism and to do so in the historic American tradition of anticolonialism.

The Interaction of International, Metropolitan, and Colonial Politics

The considerations at international, metropolitan, and colonial levels that led the British by 1947 to plan for, and in 1951 actually to begin, the transfer of power in Africa may now be analyzed.

It was the American "scare" in 1941–44 at the international level that first jolted the imperial complacency of officials in London. Proposals from Washington for liquidating the colonial empires might have seemed somewhat academic under German bombing; they might be rejected; nevertheless, they signified to the British that the shifting of the center of world power from Europe to America had ended the insulation of African colonial affairs from international rivalry and pressures which, since 1919 at least, had made the governing of colonies a relatively easy task. After 1941, American anticolonialism and American expansion had to be accommodated if the empire was to be preserved.

Colonial Office officials also worried about the possible impact of these changing international relations upon the colonies. The demands of war complicated the tasks of colonial rule.

In Africa, British governors were exerting pressure on their indigenous collaborators for the purpose of mobilizing colonial resources for the war effort, with requital mainly in promissory notes of repayment after victory. Colonial loyalty came under increasing strain as rulers took more from their subjects in return for less than ever before.

To appease American and domestic anticolonial feeling, and to reward the patient loyalty of their African allies, the chiefs and kings, Colonial Office planners until about 1946 concentrated mainly on schemes of economic and social development. There was as yet no question of transferring substantial power, though some token advances in representation were conceded to chiefs and settlers. The Colonial Office assured itself that, for all practical purposes, modern nationalism did not exist in tropical Africa. The empire there would continue to be upheld through the well-tried alliances with chiefs and kings based on the political strategy of indirect rule. As long as the war lasted, the wind of African political change was merely a portentous breeze from the quarter of Britain's international requirements.

The international situation that necessitated the planning and actual beginning of the transfer of power from 1947 to 1951 looked very different from that of the wartime era. It was no longer simply a question of Anglo-American relations, of keeping the colonies without risking loss of the American alliance. With the beginning of the Cold War, colonies and ex-colonies became potential or actual pawns of great power rivalry on a scale not seen since the comprehensive partitions of the late nineteenth century. Now once again there were competing centers of expansion in world politics. A major domestic crisis in a colony might attract the intervention of one of the great powers. Immediately after the war, the Cold War mainly affected the colonial area of Southeast Asia; but the possibility of Africa becoming involved could not be ignored. The international factor was impinging upon colonial affairs more and more intensely.

The onset of the Cold War helped the British in their colonial problem with the Americans in one way but made it more difficult in another. While the United States gave priority under the Marshall Plan to the reconstruction of Europe and the containment of communism, it tended to act more often than not as a guarantor of Europe's remaining colonies. But there were two implicit conditions. Colonial policies had to be adopted that would provide internal tranquility and future political stability; and the colonies had to serve American strategic requirements as buffers against Russian expansion. The difference that these two conditions could make in a colonial emergency was shown when the Americans gave their blessing to the French in Indochina and withdrew it from the Dutch in Indonesia. The difficulty the British found in fulfilling the American conditions was twofold. First, the United States continued to identify colonial stability with liberal advances toward independence. Though the Americans were not as outspoken on this issue as during the wartime era, the British could not rely on the relaxation of American pressure. Second, the British found it difficult to forecast where the State Department or the Pentagon would discover a strategic interest. It often proved to be far from where the British Foreign or Colonial Offices thought it should be. London regarded American support of the British Empire as too sporadic and unpredictable to be relied upon. British anxiety not to provoke American anticolonalism continued. In the shadow of their powerful American ally, the British followed certain golden rules more warily than ever: handle the colonies with kid gloves; concede to subjects rather than risk confrontations with them; and above all avoid all dangers of possible uprisings, armed repression, and colonial wars. Only thus could the possibility of American intervention in the African empire be averted. Colonial imbroglios that might drag the area into the international arena could be forestalled.

Dependence on the United States together with the experience of nationalism in India, Burma, Palestine, and elsewhere altered British perspectives on the African empire. The Colonial Office, it is true, rarely considered the implications of the fall of the empire in South and Southeast Asia. Africa, it was assumed, was different. To compare Africa with India seemed as foolish as thinking of the Taj Mahal in terms of a grass hut. As far as the Colonial Office was concerned, there was no immediate prospect of nationalism of the populist Indian kind emerging in Africa, nor of the spread of communism. The impact of Asian nationalism nevertheless could be read between the lines of such documents as the Cohen-Caine report of 1947. Colonial Office officials perceived rising risks in Africa and diminishing prospects of international support. They began to assume that the nineteenth-century empire was dying, if not already dead. Their estimate of the African empire's life expectancy dwindled from a century to a generation. The Colonial Office assumed that the spread of nationalism to Africa sooner or later was inevitable. Once it began, it would spread like wildfire over the kindling of economic discontent in British inflation-ridden colonies. Looking into the future, with India and Palestine in mind, the British contemplated in a theoretical sort of way the real possibility of losing control of the African colonies—of the colonies slipping into anarchy. They believed that extremist nationalism could be headed off only by a progressive transfer of power.

Such were the forebodings behind colonial reform in Africa. By 1947 they were perhaps no more than that; but such apprehensions were taken seriously enough to bring about a "palace revolution" in the administration of the African empire. For the first time the Colonial Office took the formulation of policy out of the hands of local governors and laid down a new course to be followed uniformly throughout the different dependencies. Colonial politics had become too important in the international and metropolitan context to be left to colonial officials. The spirit of the new course between 1947 and 1951 nevertheless was supremely confident. Forebodings of colonial collapse and anarchy were allayed by hope of economic development and political stability through constitutional safeguards. If the African planners in retrospect seem to resemble men building a house of cards while American cousins and turbulent subjects jogged their elbows, the British did not feel it after the war. As far as Africa was concerned, there was no loss of imperial nerve. The resolute and perhaps self-righteous content of the new African policy probably derived from metropolitan idealism as well as international and local colonial realpolitik.

The British, after all, had won the war. The Labour government believed, rightly or wrongly, that it had been elected to carry out the ideals of social democracy—abroad as well as at home. In the period of postwar euphoria it was essential that Labour's African policy be different. The unacceptable face of "capitalist exploitation" and "laissez-faire stagnation," which the Labour party had criticized in opposition, would be exchanged for benevolent state control and social welfare. Colonial autocracy and its reactionary indirect-rule alliances would give way to progressive collaboration with educated Africans in order to nurture democracies and build nations. All this would take time. As the British began to export to Africa the welfare state designed for home consumption and took up the tasks of "nation-building" rather than "empire-building," they persuaded themselves that they were prolonging the empire's life, not liquidating it. So firmly did the Colonial Office believe in these goals that it opposed independent India's reception into the Commonwealth in 1946–47 because Indian admission might hasten the development of nationalism in Africa.

By 1947 British plans therefore represented such a mixture of international realism, domestic utopianism, and imperial traditionalism as to seem paradoxical in two respects: one paradox is that of transferring power in order to keep it; the other is that of dismantling colonial rule in order to develop the colonies precisely at the time when their economic value to the ruling power was greatest.

In 1947 the British abandoned indirect rule, began democratizing African colonial administration from below, and planned a controlled transfer of power to seduce the African intelligentsia into cooperation. They foresaw that these measures would bring the colonies to self-government within a generation; and yet they also believed that such colonial reform would extend the life of colonial control.

The paradox of transferring power in order to keep it is resolved if it is understood that the British had never regarded the colonial empire as part of Great Britain or believed in ruling it from Downing Street as an end in itself. Financially and constitutionally the colonies had always been treated as autonomous and potentially self-governing entities. When they became able to sustain a politically self-sufficient order and, not least, when they were able to look after British commercial and strategic interests, it had been customary to grant self-government and eventually Dominion status. In this sense the "new course" for Africa derived from imperial tradition. The planners had inhaled the dust of precedent on Colonial Office files. They intended to preempt the emergence of nationalism in the colonies by setting up democratic local institutions in order to delay the political impact of the nationalist movements. Nationalism would be diverted into moderate and constructive channels. It had all been done before successfully in Canada, Australia, and, for a time, even in Ireland and India. The African version of this strategy was unique only in its application at such an early stage of colonial development to such disparate and divided groups of peoples. Most senior officials in the African colonial governments felt that this strategy was premature. But London insisted on it, which suggests that international and metropolitan pressures more than fear of African insurgency brought about colonial reform.

A resolution of the paradox of transferring power in order to keep it helps to resolve the other paradox, which is that power was to be transferred when the economic stakes were highest. The latter is not so remarkable as it might seem. Traditional colonial rule for the British, with the exception of India, had never been regarded as the ideal means of promoting British trade. The motto for national expansion on the cheap had long been "trade without dominion if possible, dominion for trade only if absolutely necessary." In other words, the British much preferred informal to formal empire. When it is understood that the British in their African plans of 1947 intended an eventual transition from formal rule to informal economic leadership and political influence within the Commonwealth (a transition to be achieved in partnership with the United States), then the second paradox disappears.

The British in 1947, in short, planned in the long term to apply the formulas for dealing with colonial nationalism that had been put forward a century earlier by Lord Durham for Canada, though in Africa they believed that nationalism scarcely existed. The place was unlikely and the timing unexpected. The outcome was the result of the narrowing of British options in the international field and in domestic politics. In the late 1940s the transfer of power in Africa was merely a design on a drawing board. Nevertheless, the planners evidently had prepared themselves only too well intellectually and psychologically to make substantial concessions should a serious crisis arise in an African colony.

If great movements in history seem to begin almost at random, it is perhaps because they have been first invented in the minds of statesmen groping for the reality of the moment among their fears for the future. So it may have been, at least, with the beginning of the end of the British African empire. For it was an event in a single colony that confirmed the Colonial Office's worst forebodings and brought British plans for the transfer of power into accelerated operation. The plan that had been predicated on a hastily revised estimate of colonial nationalism and the imperial future in the new age of American and Russian expansion was triggered into action from the local level. When Accra rioted in 1948 and the Gold Coast government momentarily feared that it was losing control of the situation, Arthur Creech Jones, the colonial secretary, and his chief adviser, Andrew Cohen, took it as the warning signal that they had expected. In former times they would have sent in a battalion to show the flag, and the landing of British troops would have ended the riot; but after withdrawing from India and Palestine, which were of the greatest strategic importance, what was the sense of repression in western Africa? In any event, the Labour government, the British people, and doubtless also the Americans wanted no more colonial troubles. To tranquilize with a modicum of constitutional concessions seemed not merely expedient but conscientious; to concede earlier rather than later, according to Whiggish lessons from British and Indian history, would avert national or democratic upheavals. By 1951, with the introduction of the ballot box and other constitutional devices into indigenous Gold Coast politics, the British had set up a framework in which a popular nationalist movement was quickly manufactured. It is a tribute to the cogency of their original design that they went on throughout the 1950s transferring power on the same principle and with the same result with a minimum of civil disturbances. It is also a tribute to the steadfastness of the

British belief that nationalism would accomplish the purposes of colonialism by other, and, in the light of international circumstances, safer and far more effective means.

In 1947 the Colonial Office thought it foresaw the probable fate of the African empire. The confidence of British officials in that vision lured them into doing what they could to make it come true. Between 1947 and 1960 the African empire toppled into decline and fall. In this sense it was lost as it had been acquired, with illusions about the nature of man and the destiny of nations.

A Framework for Studying the Fall of Colonial Empires in the Twentieth Century

How can the appeasement of American anticolonialism be assessed in relation to the decline of the British Empire as a world power, the rise of the Labour party in domestic politics, and the advent of the nationalist movements in Asia and Africa? In answering that question (which has a bearing on the French, Dutch, Belgian, and Portuguese colonial empires as well), it may help to advance certain propositions concerning the transfer of power. The viability of empire depended upon a substantial accommodation at three different levels: in the colony itself, in the metropolitan power, and in the international sphere. More explicitly, the maritime colonial empires of western Europe could continue to exist only so long as three requirements were fulfilled: (1) that their colonial subjects acquiesced in their authority; (2) that the politicians and electorates of the metropolitan countries accepted colonial commitments as not entirely unethical and on the whole worthwhile; and (3) that these empires received international recognition. The colonial regimes could not survive the breach of these conditions.

In international politics—with which this chapter has been especially concerned—conditions became more exacting as the imperial nations lost their domination of the world balance of power; at the metropolitan and colonial levels, attitudes hardened as ideologies changed and political movements and parties became more assertive. In these circumstances the terms for the acceptance of colonial rule could still be found on some levels, but it became increasingly difficult to achieve compatible terms on all three levels at once. Indeed, readjustment or renegotiation of the terms for the acceptance of empire on one level or another tended to disrupt the agreements already concluded on other levels by making them unattractive or impracticable. In other words, the practical politics of retaining a colonial empire consisted not only in finding viable "bargains" in colonial, metropolitan, and international politics, but also in keeping them compatible with each other.

The interdependence of terms for the toleration of colonial empires became sharply apparent in the mid-twentieth century. For example, the decline of the European powers in world politics tempted not only the Soviet Union but also the United States to stiffen the conditions for acquiescing in the continued existence of the overseas colonial regimes; the international balance of power, in turn, encouraged nationalists in the colonies to organize support and demand more concessions. Increasing international pressure together with growing resistance from colonial subjects thus tended to test the willingness of the metropolitan peoples to tolerate the burden of colonial empires. The extent of that toleration varied with the financial and military cost of colonial upkeep, the supposed economic benefit, and the prevailing ethic or ideology. In the British case (and perhaps in that of some of the other European powers also), so few politicians knew enough about colonial economics that most were forced to rely on ethical yardsticks of trusteeship to measure the value of empire and hence their own willingness to tolerate the burden. As the humane values of democracy, pacifism, and social welfare increasingly pervaded a war-weary Europe, the limits of metropolitan toleration tended to shrink from coercion to concession; in other words, where once the colonial power coerced its subjects, it now made concessions to them. The increased reluctance of the metropole to pay the cost of retaining colonies in turn diminished the imperial administrators' power to bargain for the acquiescence of their colonial subjects.

Just as international and metropolitan conditions reflected in part the tensions in the colonies, so the circumstances in the colonies themselves were profoundly affected by the changing balance of forces at the international and metropolitan levels. Colonial governments have always stood or fallen as the rulers and the ruled have accommodated or resisted each other's major interests. The rulers usually came to the negotiating table with the idea of retaining imperial authority up to the brink of a crisis in which they would have to "shoot or get out"; subjects, on the other hand, came with the intention of enlarging their share of governing power up to the point of "getting shot or backing down." For the proconsul the colonial problem was how much power to share with subjects in exchange for their cooperation; for the subject the question was how much noncooperation would elicit the maximum share of power. Between the two extremes the terms for obtaining acquiescence in colonial rule depended on several variables: for example, the expenditure of finance and use of force which the peoples of the metropolitan country would tolerate for purposes of keeping a colony; the extent of a colonial government's demands on its subjects for land, labor, and produce and of the resistance thus provoked; the volume of metropolitan investment offering partnerships to subjects in the profits of the international economy; and the extent of power-sharing with indigenous elites.

In short, the existence of the Western overseas empires depended on conditions which made them acceptable to the politics of the metropolitan countries, and these terms also had to be practicable both in international relations and in the local politics of colonial or quasi-colonial societies. Empires eventually fall when the conditions necessary for their survival at one of these levels become impossible to translate acceptably at the other two levels. If this thesis holds good, it would be futile to debate the question whether the main cause of the fall of empires is to be found either in shifts in the international balance, or in the vicissitudes of metropolitan politics, or in the rise of colonial nationalism. No simple, single-cause explanation can be found. Change at any one level caused changes in the others. In the British case, Colonial Office planners ultimately concluded that there could be no resolution of the tensions—international, metropolitan, and colonial—other than by swift transfers of power. The "transfers of power" were intended to sustain British influence through African agents.

3. *Pan-African Responses in the United States to British Colonial Rule in Africa in the 1940s*

HOLLIS R. LYNCH

The establishment of European colonial rule in Africa at the end of the nineteenth century, legitimized by the belief in social Darwinism and the Eurocentric view of the history and culture of black peoples, had called forth an immediate pan-African response on the part of westernized blacks in Africa and also those in the Americas, who themselves suffered a subordinate status.[1] Before the Second World War, this response took organizational form in four pan-African conferences held between 1920 and 1927: Marcus Garvey's Universal Negro Improvement Association (UNIA)[2] and the National Congress of British West Africa of the 1920s;[3] the West African Students' Union founded in London in 1925;[4] and the Ethiopian World Federation founded in New York in 1937 to mobilize black Americans in order to help restore freedom to Ethiopia after its recent conquest by Italy.[5]

All these organizations had as their political goals the end of European colonial rule and the promotion of unity in Africa. All but one was small, moderate, and elitist, hoping to achieve its goals with the cooperation of the European colonial powers. Only one—Garvey's UNIA—was mass-based, international, and prepared, at least in theory, to use violence to end European colonial rule in Africa. But this potential threat to European colonialism was removed with the collapse of the Garvey movement by 1927 as a result of external pressures and internal conflicts. Thus, up to the

1. See Immanuel Geiss, *The Pan-African Movement: A History of Pan-Africanism in American, Europe and Africa* (New York, 1974).

2. There are several scholarly studies of Garvey. The latest is Tony Martin, *Race First: The Ideological and Organizational Struggles of Marcus Garvey and the Universal Negro Improvement Association* (Westport, Conn., 1976).

3. Eee Ayo Langley, *Pan-Africanism and Nationalism in West Africa, 1900–1945* (Oxford, 1973), chaps. 3 and 4.

4. Geiss, *The Pan-African Movement*, chap. 14; P. Garique, "The West African Students' Union," *Africa* (January 1953), pp. 55–69.

5. William Scott, "A Study of Afro-American and Ethiopian Relations, 1896–1941" (Ph.D. diss., Princeton University, 1971), chap. 5.

outbreak of World War II, the European colonial powers did not have to respond seriously to pressure from the black world to end their rule.

But after 1940 black opponents of European colonial rule in Africa found themselves in an increasingly favorable position. During the war the major colonial powers, Britain and France, were substantially dependent on colonial Africa for manpower and strategic resources. In addition, the Allied powers, in their struggle against the fascist Axis, were forced to engage in the propaganda of adherence to democracy and self-government. The anticolonial stand of the Soviet Union and the United States—at least during the war itself—was particularly strong and forthright. All these factors helped to give a strong impetus to the international black movement to end European colonial rule in Africa. The strength and determination of this movement, already evident by 1947, were a major contributing factor to the end of European colonial rule in most of black Africa by the early 1960s. It is the purpose of this chapter to examine the efforts of three major pan-African organizations in the United States—the Council on African Affairs, the African Students Association of the United States and Canada, and the African Academy of Arts and Research—to accelerate the process of decolonization in Africa in the 1940s.

The Council on African Affairs and Radical Pan-Africanism

The Council on African Affairs (CAA), which formally came into being in October 1941, was an outgrowth of the International Committee on African Affairs.[6] The idea for the committee was that of Max Yergan, an Afro-American YMCA official who had returned to the United States in 1936 after working for fifteen years among black students and teachers in South Africa. Founded in 1937, with Yergan as executive director, the committee was only modestly active because of lack of adequate support. However, under the stimulus of events during the war (and with Africa's increasing importance because of its strategic location as well as its manpower and natural resources), the committee was renamed the Council on African Affairs in October 1941, and was reorganized.

By the summer of 1943, the council's reorganization had been completed. By then it had twenty-seven formal members, a five-member Executive, and had started a regular monthly publication, *New Africa*. The council's main leadership consisted of Yergan as executive director, Paul

6. For a fuller analysis of the council, see Hollis R. Lynch, *Black Americans and the Liberation of Africa: The Council on African Affairs, 1937–1955*, Cornell University Africana Research Center Publication, no. 6 (Ithaca, N.Y., 1978).

Robeson, the world-famous actor and concert singer as chairman, and William Alphaeus Hunton, a former Howard University professor of English as educational director. Two of the five white members of the council, all of whom were wealthy and progressive, held the positions of vice-chairman and treasurer. All three black leaders adhered to Marxism, admired the Soviet Union—both Robeson and Yergan had visited there—and were on close terms with the leadership of the American Communist party. Together, they gave the council a stamp of ideological radicalism. The membership consisted of highly educated black Americans who were professionally affiliated with the church, labor, higher education, and journalism. Most of them were from New York, but there was some representation from each major region of the country.

Despite its small membership, the council did succeed in attracting significant national and international attention. This was because of its able, energetic, and skillful leadership, and its success in utilizing an urban network of influential and sympathetic labor, civic, and church leaders who were not formal members.

Council funds came through concert benefits performed by Robeson and other black entertainers, from the contributions of members and supporters, and as a result of Yergan's access to wealthy whites. Its budget grew from about $11,000 in 1942 to a peak of almost $40,000 in 1946.[7] Through *New Africa*, press releases, radio programs, pamphlets, lecture series, conferences, and mass meetings, the council sought in a systematic way to enlighten the public about developments in Africa and to enlist support for its goals of political liberation and material and social progress for Africans. To advocate its pro-Africa policy, the council, its members, and sympathizers sent letters, petitions, and telegrams to the United States and European colonial governments, as well as to international agencies. And it gave material aid and encouragement to labor and nationalist groups in Africa.

The influence of the council derived, to a very considerable extent, from *New Africa*, which was edited by Hunton. Although a minitabloid of generally only four pages, it was professionally produced. It carried news of major developments in Africa; of the actions, policies, pronouncements of the European colonial powers, the United States, and Russia, which would or could affect developments in Africa; of the activities of the council on behalf of Africa; and of the burgeoning interest in the United States in that continent. It recommended to its readers significant new books on Africa and reviewed some of them. It occasionally carried an up-to-date profile on an African country or leader. In the United States it was certainly the single

7. Minutes of CAA meetings for January 29, 1942, and January 9, 1947, *Frazier Papers*.

most important source of information and enlightened opinion on Africa. Its circulation peaked at more than three thousand in 1946.[8] But *New Africa's* influence was considerably larger than its circulation suggests, as it was subscribed to by church, labor, educational, and political organizations, and was also read by U.S. government officials. It also circulated in Europe, particularly among British leftist and government circles, and in Africa among nationalist and labor groups. Indeed, by 1950 there was a government ban on it in three African countries—Kenya, South Africa, and the Belgian Congo.[9]

During the war the council held two mass rallies and one major conference. On April 8, 1942, at a rally featuring Pearl Buck, the novelist and internationalist, and attended by some three thousand people, speakers called for an end to colonialism and racial discrimination.[10] On September 2, 1942, the council held a "Free India Rally" attended by some four thousand at the Manhattan Center, New York. The meeting called for the freeing of jailed Indian nationalists, including Nehru, the formation of an Indian national government, and the opening of a second front in Europe to relieve the pressure on Russia. The council believed that freedom for India "would speed a free Africa."[11]

Undoubtedly the single most important public meeting organized by the council during the war was the conference on "Africa—New Perspective" which met on April 14, 1944, at the council's headquarters. One hundred and twenty-seven black and white delegates representing fifty-nine labor, civic, church, and women's organizations attended; among them were a few representatives from British West Africa, the Caribbean, and India. The conference was concerned to increase the extent and effectiveness of Africa's contribution to the Allied victory, and to achieve this it recommended immediate reforms to boost African morale: an end to forced labor, to racial discrimination, and to monopolistic and other unfair trading practices of Europeans. More fundamentally, the conference discussed means to promote rapidly the political independence and social and economic progress of Africa. It recommended that the United States take the lead in establishing international agencies and in promoting international action that would secure the council's goals for Africa. Although aware of the reactionary forces in American society, the Council still felt that the solidar-

8. Minutes of CAA meeting, January 6, 1946, in ibid. Hunton gave the circulation for 1945 as 3,000 and it is reasonable to assume that it increased in 1946, the council's most active year.

9. *New Africa*, May–June 1950.

10. *New York Times*, April 9, 1942; *California Eagle*, May 7, 1942.

11. *People's Voice*, September 12, 1942; *News of Africa*, October 1, 1942.

ity of black people in alliance with liberal and radical forces would succeed in persuading the United States government to adopt its Africa program. The conference also sent "to the leaders of the African people and their organizations our pledge of wholehearted cooperation in working with them towards the achievement of the goals of freedom and progress. . . ." The council published the proceedings of the conference and circulated it in labor, church, and government circles.[12]

In addition to its general propaganda, the council sought directly to influence United States policy through correspondence and meetings with State Department and White House officials. The council foresaw that World War II might result in the emergence of the United States as the world's undisputed leading military and economic power, with a substantial and growing stake in the natural resources and strategic importance of Africa; it thus thought it vital to ensure that the United States have a progressive policy toward that continent. The council was greatly encouraged by the action and pronouncements of President Roosevelt. He was the main architect of the Atlantic Charter, which held out the possibility of freedom for oppressed and colonial peoples—a principle that was regularly reaffirmed by the Allied powers during the war. He had been markedly friendly to Liberia and Ethiopia, which had regained its sovereignty in 1941 after a short-lived Italian rule. On his way from the Casablanca Conference, Roosevelt made a stopover in Liberia in January 1943—the first American president to visit black Africa. This was followed by an official visit of President Barclay, who was given a reception and dinner at the White House and appeared before Congress.[13] In December 1943, Roosevelt received the first Ethiopian minister to the United States, His Excellency Blatta Ephrem Tewelde Medhen, and in February 1945, on his way home from the Crimean conference, met with the Ethiopian emperor, Haile Selassie. By the early fall the Roosevelt administration had evolved an African policy which the council characterized as "progressive but not completely adequate."[14] On January 15, 1944, a separate division of African Affairs was created in the State Department under Henry S. Villard, former assistant chief of the Near Eastern Division, under which Africa had hitherto been subsumed. In mid-March three members of the executive board of the council—Yergan, Hunton, and Field—met cordially with officials of the new Africa Division and urged a more progressive pro-

12. *For a New Africa: Proceedings, Conference on Africa, New York, April 14, 1944*, Council on African Affairs (New York, 1944).

13. See *Amsterdam News* and *Pittsburgh Courier*, May 29, June 5, 12, 19, 1943.

14. *New Africa*, January 1944.

Africa policy.[15] The council executives had invited State Department officials to attend its major conference on Africa, but they had pleaded being too busy. The new Africa Division showed itself responsive to some black American wishes: by the end of 1944 the State Department had for the first time made use of black American experts in Africa, primarily Liberia and Ethiopia, and also sponsored the visit of a group of black American newspapermen to West Africa.

Fully aware though it was of the reactionary forces in the United States and abroad, the council sought to keep up the pressure on the United States to play a progressive role in international politics. In the early summer of 1944, the council, together with other major black national organizations, submitted a manifesto to both Republican and Democratic conventions urging them to support "political and economic democracy for Africa."[16] And in a letter of December 15, 1944, on "African and Post-War Security Plans" addressed to President Roosevelt and Secretary of State Edward R. Stettinius, Jr., the council enjoined the United States to ensure that "the promotion of the welfare of the millions of Africans and other dependent peoples of the world must be an integral part of the projected international organization's program and functions."[17] The letter was signed by 170 educators, journalists, and churchmen. Stettinius replied on January 5, 1945, thanking the council for its "constructive efforts" and assuring it that serious attention was being paid to the problems it cited. On February 28, 1945, Hunton, as well as delegates from other progressive national organizations, were assured by state and treasury officials that the Bretton Wood proposals would form the "cornerstone for international economic cooperation" and that the International Monetary Fund would also be used for the benefit of colonial peoples. In anticipation of the United Nations meeting, Yergan and Hunton met with Assistant Secretary of State Archibald Macleish on March 23 at the State Department and briefed him on the council's anticolonial pro-Africa views.[18] These were embodied in a nine-page pamphlet entitled "The San Francisco Conference and The Colonial Issue," copies of which were sent to all official delegates to the conference.

15. Ibid., April 1944; cf. Robeson to Villard, June 26, 1944, State Department Archives, 111.75316-2644, in which the latter was asked for help in raising the council budget of $25,000.

16. *New Africa,* July–August 1944.

17. Ibid., December 1944.

18. Mr. Yergan to A. Macleish, March 20, 1945, State Department Archives, 500.cc 3/-2045 cs/LE.

THE MILITANT PHASE

On the eve of the San Francisco Conference, the council remained acutely aware that the attitude of the United States would be a crucial factor in determining whether the new United Nations would serve the interest of colonial peoples. Thus, on May 15, Chairman Robeson sent Stettinius a telegram requesting "a forthright affirmation of the traditional American principle of freedom for colonial peoples such as our Government has guaranteed the Filipinos."[19] For the council saw the European powers as giving every indication that they would not easily relinquish their African colonies nor allow international inspection or supervision of them under an effective trusteeship system. In the United States, the death on April 12—less than two weeks before the San Francisco Conference—of President Franklin D. Roosevelt, widely regarded by blacks as a champion of the oppressed, seemed ominous for the cause of colonial peoples. It was becoming clear that powerful racist, military, and business interests would not permit the United States to take the unequivocal anticolonial stand that the council and other progressive American organizations desired.

The San Francisco Conference, which met from April 25 to June 26, attracted considerable black attention, so the council was only one of several black organizations unofficially represented. The only black U.S. official was Dr. Ralph Bunche, associate chief, Division of Dependent Affairs, Department of State; and among black official observers were four major figures: Mordecai Johnson, president of Howard University, and a representative of the United Negro Church; W. E. B. DuBois and Walter White of the NAACP; and Mary McLeod Bethune, president of the National Council of Negro Women. Of the fifty nations represented, three were black: Ethiopia, Liberia, and Haiti. The council was represented by Max Yergan and Eslanda Robeson, both of whom were vigorous publicists of the council's point of view.[20]

The council was disappointed in what it saw as the easy willingness of the United States at the San Francisco Conference to accommodate the reactionary position of the European colonial powers. In a July 1945 editorial, *New Africa* commented: "The inadequacies of the U.N. trusteeship

19, *Pittsburgh Courier*, May 19, 1945.

20. Ibid.; also M. Yergan to Macleish, May 17, 1945, State Department Archives, 500.cc/5-2245 CS/LE. See also Eslanda Robeson, *What Do the People of Africa Want?*, CAA Pamphlet (New York, 1945).

plan . . . must be attributed as much to the pressure of forces right here in America as to the influence of imperialist interests abroad."

Evidence of the government's contempt for the council's opinion, and indeed that of all major black organizations, came with the appointment in July 1945 of James F. Byrnes, a Democrat from South Carolina as secretary of state. Black leaders regarded him as racist. In the face of such lack of sympathy, the council became more harshly critical of United States policy toward Africa. This is well exemplified in an editorial in the *New Africa* for January 1946:

> The pursuance of the practice of intervention on the side of imperialism and feudal reaction and against colonial and semi-colonial peoples struggling to achieve freedom and democracy has made or is making America an object of hate and fear in the minds of hundreds of millions of people in the dependent areas of the world.

However, the council continued to act on the assumption that it could influence United States policy. In September it recommended for adoption by the United States and the United Nations a six-point program that included the placing of the African colonies of Italy (with the exception of Eritrea, which should go to Ethiopia), Spain, and Portugal, as well as the mandated territories, under effective UN trusteeship, and the promotion of the economic and social welfare of Africans, as well as their democratic rights, leading to early independence.[21] And on October 26, 1946, Yergan sent a letter to the secretary of state expressing strong opposition to South Africa as a member of the interim, trusteeship council—a letter endorsed by about a hundred labor, church, education, civic, and government leaders.[22]

By 1946 the postwar militancy of the council was manifesting itself not only in sharp anti-American editorials but also in mass meetings, demonstrations, and picketings, and in more direct and regular communications with African labor and nationalist groups, particularly in South Africa. From the start of its career, the council showed a special concern about South Africa—partly because Africans there suffered from the most extreme form of white colonial expolitation and degradation on the continent, partly because, through Yergan, it had extensive contacts with progressive South Africans and particularly with the African National Congress, the oldest and largest African nationalist organization in all of black Africa.

The increasing postwar repression of nonwhites, plus extensive famine

21. *New Africa*, October 1945.
22. Ibid., November 1945.

stemming from drought, led to the council spending much of its time and effort in 1946 in exposing the inhumane conditions under which nonwhites lived in South Africa and raising funds and foodstuffs in a major relief campaign. In response to appeals from the African National Congress for aid for the famine victims, the council set up a twenty-eight-member National Sponsors Committee for South African Famine Relief. The relief campaign started off on January 7 with an overflow crowd of some five thousand at the Abyssinian Baptist Church in Harlem.[23] During February and March the council and its supporters organized South African relief meetings in about forty major cities throughout the United States. These climaxed on Sunday, March 31, designated by the council as "Help Africa Day," when money and gifts were collected in dozens of churches and civic centers in the nation. The drive resulted in more than $5,000 and 22,000 cans of food being sent to South Africa.[24]

The Harlem mass meeting of January 7 had also approved resolutions condemning South Africa's increasing apartheid rule and its "parody of trusteeship in South West Africa." The resolutions were sent to UN delegates and Prime Minister Smuts of South Africa. Continuing concern about retrogressive developments in South Africa led the council to organize another mass meeting at Madison Square Garden on June 6 specifically to "cast a searing spotlight on the vicious discrimination in the Union of South Africa and on the plight of the African millions resident there," and more generally to "rally American support for the African demand for freedom and full democratic rights."[25] This was the council's most successful mass public meeting. An interracial audience of about 15,000 attended. The meeting urged President Truman to direct the State Department and the U.S. representative at the UN to "translate into immediate and concrete action the pledges of democratic rights and self-determination for all peoples made by the UN and by the heads of our Government" and also adopted a "Charter for African Freedom." Proceeds from the meeting were also sent to the famine victims of South Africa.

The council took advantage of the presence in New York of a distinguished unofficial three-man South African delegation, representing nonwhites, to arrange two meetings which focused on the union. The delegation was comprised of Senator H. M. Basner, a leading South African left-wing politician and the representative in parliament of Africans from

23. *New York Times*, January 8, 1946; *New Africa*, January 1946.

24. *New Africa*, March and April 1946; *New York Times*, February 12, March 5, and May 15, 1946.

25. *New York Times*, June 7, 1946; *New Africa*, September 1946.

the Transvaal; H. A. Naidoo of Natal, a major figure in the Indian National Congress; and Dr. A. B. Xuma, president-general of the African National Congress. On November 8 the South Africans addressed a meeting held at the council headquarters and attended by two hundred leaders of progressive organizations and members of delegations to the UN. On Sunday afternoon, November 17, the visitors talked to a much larger crowd at the Abyssinian Baptist Church in Harlem. The meeting expressed solidarity with the African mine workers, nine of whom had been killed and more than a thousand injured between August 12 and 16, 1946, during what was then the largest strike in South Africa's history, involving 50,000 workers in eight mines.[26] The Harlem mass memorial meeting was planned to coincide with similar meetings held in several South African cities on the same day. Four days later, on November 21, under council auspices, some two hundred representatives of trade unions, civic, and church organizations picketed in front of the South African consulate at Fifth Avenue and Forty-second Street.

To bolster its campaign against the oppression of nonwhites in South Africa, and to prevent South Africa's annexation of South West Africa, the council within a year during 1946–47 published and distributed three major pamphlets.[27]

The unprecedented militant drive of the council in 1946 seemed to have carried over into the new year. At a membership meeting on January 9, the council decided to increase its membership and "broaden its work."[28] During the ensuing months membership was augmented to a maximum of seventy-two. The new members belonged to the same social and political network as the old; many of them had prior informal association with the council. They comprised black university professors—four new members were from Howard University—clergymen and bishops, doctors, lawyers, social workers, and entertainers. Whites, very largely radical Jewish in-

26. *New Africa*, December 1946; Edward Roux, *Time Longer Than Rope: A History of the Black Man's Struggle for Freedom in South Africa*, 2d ed. (Madison, Wis., 1964), pp. 338–41; and Mary Benson, *The African Patriots: The Story of the National Congress of South Africa* (New York, 1963), chap. 12.

27. The first was *8 Million People Demand Freedom! What About It, General Smuts?* (1946). This was a reprint with introduction and notes of a 23-page pamphlet written by I. B. Tabata, a Bantu South African, and first published in the Union by the African National Congress in December 1945. The second, *Stop South Africa's Crimes, No Annexation of South West Africa* (1946), was 24 pages long and written by Hunton. The third was a graphic pictorial essay of 25 pages, compiled and written by Hunton and entitled *Seeing Is Believing—Here Is the Truth about the Color Bar, Land Hunger, Poverty and Degradation, the Pass System, Racial Oppression in South Africa* (1947).

28. Minutes of CAA meeting, January 9, 1946, *Frazier Papers*.

tellectuals, formed 20 percent of the enlarged membership. It continued to have a primarily northeastern base, with New York and Washington, D.C., accounting for about two-thirds of the total.

In its role as lobbyist, the council was the only nongovernmental organization with a regular accredited observer at the United Nations. It was represented by Hunton, with Mrs. Robeson substituting occasionally. Hunton attended the sessions of the Ad Hoc Committee on Non-Self-Governing Territories, the Trusteeship Council, and the General Assembly. He prepared and distributed special memoranda and council pamphlets to delegates. Thus, to thwart the attempt of General Smuts in late 1946 to win UN approval for South Africa's annexation of South West Africa, Hunton had widely circulated the council's pamphlet, *Seeing Is Believing—The Truth about South Africa*. And with evidence supplied by the Reverend Michael Scott, the white liberal South African leader, he compiled a detailed report of the oppressive condition of Africans in South West Africa. In addition, he personally lobbied with representatives on the Trusteeship Council. In this instance the council's view prevailed: to Smuts's chagrin, South Africa failed to win UN approval for the annexation of South West Africa. Several delegates, among them Sir Majaraj Lingh of India, were highly appreciative of Hunton's efforts in providing pertinent information on African questions. Hunton also sent weekly reports of relevant proceedings at the UN to African nationalist organizations in Britain and Africa and to sympathetic organizations within the United States.[29] Finally, Hunton on several occasions published the vote of each country in the United Nations with regard to Africa and colonial questions;[30] and this showed the United States voting regularly on the side of the European colonial powers.

The Rift

The inauguration by 1947 of the Cold War, with its atmosphere of growing "anti-Communist" hysteria, led to an irreparable rift in the council, which resulted, after a protracted struggle, in the expulsion of Yergan, who had suddenly and sharply swung ideologically to the right, and in the resignation of several "moderates." However, the council did gain new adherents,

29. "Report of the Educational Director, W. A. Hunton, to the Meeting of the Council on African Affairs, February 2, 1948," *Hunton Papers*.

30. For a letter of appreciation for this, see Leslie S. Perry, Administrative Assistant in NAACP's Washington Bureau, to Hunton, February 28, 1947, *Hunton Papers*. See also *New Africa*, February and December 1947: *Spotlight on Africa*, January 8 and December 17, 1953; *Freedom*, February 1953.

the most significant of whom was W. E. B. DuBois, who was named vice-chairman in 1945. As activist and writer, he had worked all his adult life toward the liberation of African peoples. As director of special research at the NAACP, he had recently published two books, *Color and Democracy* (1945) and *The World and Africa* (1947), both intended as contributions to the psychological and political liberation of Africa.

The council continued to use the conventional democratic methods—rallies, demonstrations, picketing, petitions, and letters—in seeking to win support and exert influence. The rallies were relatively few, were held in Harlem, and were almost exclusively black. Thus, on June 19, 1949, five thousand people attended a "Welcome Home Rally" at Rockland Palace, Harlem, for Paul Robeson, who had been on a concert tour abroad. In a passionate, defiant speech, Robeson rededicated himself to the struggle for the freedom of blacks everywhere.[31] On April 5, 1952, the council held another major rally in Harlem in support of the civil disobedience campaign being waged by nonwhites in South Africa.[32] On April 24, 1954, it conducted "a working conference in support of African liberation" at the Friendship Baptist Church, Harlem.[33] And in the early summer of 1954 it held a series of public meetings on Harlem streetcorners where "Africa Must Be Free" buttons were sold. Acting alone or occasionally in conjunction with other organizations, the council directed a regular flow of letters, petitions, and memoranda to U.S. and UN authorities. Both the South African consulate and the White House were among targets of occasional picketing by the council leadership.

Nonetheless, in the 1950s the council, like other radical and liberal organizations, found formidable obstacles in the way of its functioning. Its leaders and members were harassed and intimidated by the FBI and the Department of Justice. It finally yielded to intense pressure and dissolved in June 1955.

But before that, despite its difficulties, the council did manage to continue fulfilling its essential roles. Its news publications (though irregular in

31. See Paul Robeson, *For Freedom and Peace* (New York: Council on African Affairs, 1949).

32. *Spotlight on Africa*, April 14, 1952.

33. See *Pittsburgh Courier*, May 8, 1954. In the same issue, a reader, Mrs. L. A. Jiggetts, commended the council as "one of the few organizations . . . in the country which has concerned itself with African life. . . ." She believed that "for most of us [Afro-Americans] our admiration and sympathies are with our African brothers" and she wished to see these given concrete expression in more widespread support for the council: "Are we . . . Americans to be less courageous than the brave African peoples in actively voicing our support to the just grievances of our African brothers?"

some periods) and pamphlets continued to be the most up-to-date, accurate, and important sources of information on Africa in the United States. It published *News of Africa* until 1951, after which it was renamed *Spotlight on Africa*.

Also, the post-Yergan period found the council in more regular communication with, and offering greater aid and encouragement to, a larger number of African nationalist and labor groups than ever before. The accelerating movement toward independence had brought Africans in direct confrontation with their European colonial oppressors, creating tension, strife, and even violent conflict, particularly in territories like South Africa and Kenya where white interests were well entrenched. The council also maintained regular contact with Nigerian nationalist and labor leaders. A careful scholar has attested to the impact the council had on Nigerian nationalism: "Azikiwe's [West African] *Pilot*, which frequently quoted inflammatory articles from *New Africa* on the front page, gave literate Nigerians the impression that 15 million American Negroes were closely following the nationalist movement with strong moral support."[34]

The Impact of African Students

African students abroad articulately and actively pressed for the liberation of Africa. This section will examine their nationalist and pan-African activities in the United States during and immediately after World War II. It is estimated that there were "over sixty" African students in the United States during the war,[35] the vast majority of whom were from English-speaking West Africa. The British colonial authorities had generally discouraged, and in the case of East Africa had banned, Africans from studying in the United States, partly out of the fear that, under the influence of black Americans, they might become troublesome nationalists.[36] But by the late 1930s the United States and its institutions of higher learning had found an influential champion in the youthful and dynamic Nigerian, Nnamdi Azikiwe, already the leading journalist and nationalist in West Africa.[37]

Azikiwe had studied and worked in the United States for nine years

34. James S. Coleman, *Nigeria: Background to Nationalism* (Berkeley, 1963), p. 235.

35. K. O. Mbadiwe, "Africa's Hope of Democracy," *Survey Graphic* (November 1942), pp. 519–21, 550–52.

36. Kenneth James King, *Pan-Africanism and Education: A Study of Race Philanthropy and Education in the Southern States of America and East Africa* (Oxford, 1971), p. 71.

37. See K. A. B. Jones-Quartey, *A Life of Azikiwe* (Baltimore, 1965); and Nnamdi Azikiwe, *My Odyssey* (New York, 1970).

between 1925 and 1934. An indigent student, Azikiwe completely identified with black Americans, like them suffered discrimination and hardship, particularly during the Depression, and involved himself in their struggles for freedom and dignity. This was a particularly vigorous period for black American assertiveness and creativity, exemplified by a militant press, the mass-based Garvey movement and the "Harlem Renaissance," and all this served greatly to stimulate in Azikiwe a strong racial consciousness and pride.

As a result of his own experience, Azikiwe believed that the United States was a much better training ground than Britain for future African leaders. Between 1935 and 1938 he persuaded fourteen young Africans to study in the United States, securing admission for all of them at his own alma mater, Lincoln University, the oldest and one of the best black American institutions of higher learning.[38] The first three students sent to the United States between 1935 and 1937 were from the Gold Coast and came under Azikiwe's influence while he was a controversial editor in that colony during that time. They were Kwame Nkrumah, a young Achimota-trained teacher; Ako Adjei, a recent graduate from Accra Academy; and J. A. B. Jones-Quartey, a former teacher who had been Zik's assistant sports editor on the *African Morning Post.* In 1938, eight Ibo and three Ibibio protégés of Zik left for the United States.

These fourteen students were a remarkable group. All were privately supported, all were academically able and well-prepared, all were already fiercely nationalistic. From among them came the founders and leaders of two major African nationalist organizations in the United States—the African Student Association of the United States and Canada and the African Academy of Arts and Research. On their return home, they were in the vanguard of West African nationalism and held highly influential positions after independence.[39] Thus, Kwame Nkrumah became prime minister and later president of Ghana; Adjei, foreign minister; and Jones-Quartey, a distinguished professor at the University of Ghana. Among the Ibo students, three who worked very closely together in the United States stand out: K. O. Mbadiwe, future holder of several cabinet positions in Nigeria; Prince A. A. Nwafor Orizu, future president of the Senate of Nigeria; and Mbonu Ojike, future author, journalist, and major Nigerian nationalist figure.

38. Horace Mann Bond, *Education for Freedom: A History of Lincoln University, Pennsylvania* (Oxford, Pa.: Lincoln University, 1976).

39. Ibid., pp. 530–50; also Leonard L. Bethel, "The Role of Lincoln University (Pennsylvania) in the Education of African Leadership" (Ph.D. diss., Rutgers University, 1975), appendix 5.

When the eleven Zik-sponsored Nigerian students started at Lincoln University in February 1939, they increased the African student population to sixteen, including the three from the Gold Coast. The African student population at Lincoln accounted for about a quarter of the entire African student population in the United States. It was within the context of their regular informal discussions at Lincoln that the idea of an all-embracing African student organization first emerged. Although several of the students went on the following academic year to study at major Northern public and private universities, they maintained a network of communication and generally reconvened in Harlem during the summers.

Indeed, African students received much of their political education in the United States in major black urban centers—particularly in Harlem, which was widely regarded as the political, cultural, and intellectual capital of black America. Here African students gathered in the summer in search of jobs and excitement. Here their informal headquarters was the apartment of Mrs. Jessie Douglass, an intelligent, kind, and generous West Indian woman.[40] In Harlem black nationalist organizations proliferated, and African students became involved with several of them, including the Africa-oriented Ethiopian World Federation and Marcus Garvey's remnant Universal Negro Improvement Association.[41]

The African Student Association of the United States and Canada

The initiatives which led to the founding of the African Student Association (ASA) were taken by John Karefa Smart of Sierra Leone together with the Nigerians Orizu, Ojike, and, above all, Mbadiwe.[42] On August 18 and 19, 1940, an important preliminary conference was held at the Harlem YMCA. On New Year's Day, 1941, Mbadiwe, then a student at New York University, journeyed to Columbus, Ohio, and along with Ojike and Orizu, students at Ohio State University, spent four days drafting the constitution of

40. Mbonu Ojike, *I Have Two Countries* (New York, 1946), p. 38. Kwame Nkrumah, *Ghana: Autobiography* (New York), p. 46. Interview with Dr. K. O. Mbadiwe in Lagos, Nigeria, January 12, 1977.

41. Roi Ottley, *New World A-Coming: Inside Black America* (1943; rpt. New York, 1968), pp. 41–61.

42. *African Interpreter*, February 1943, pp. 5–6; Ojike, *I Have Two Countries*, pp. 37, 71. Nkrumah's claim that "at the first conference, I was elected president, a position I held until the day I left for England" in his autobiography, *Ghana* (Sunbury on Thames, Middlesex: Thomas Nelson and Sons, 1957, p. 44), is not borne out by the evidence. However, as shown below, during 1942/43 he did play a major role in the Association.

the ASA. At a meeting, again held at the Harlem YMCA on September 2–5, 1941, the ASA was formally begun. The executive committee was dominated by Nigerians: Ojike was president; Mbadiwe, executive secretary; Orizu, director of information; and Ibangu Akpabio, a graduate student at Columbia University, treasurer. Jones-Quartey of the Gold Coast was recording secretary.

Also on the executive committee were two remarkable Ugandans, Ernest B. Kalibala and Akiki K. Nyabongo, vice-president and director of education, respectively. They had first come to the United States in the early 1920s, just managing to avoid a ban by colonial authorities on Ugandans studying in the United States. Both had since established distinguished careers as students and nationalists. Kalibala studied at Tuskegee Institute, received his B.A. from New York University, and his M.A. in education from Columbia University in 1934. He returned to Uganda and in 1935 opened the independent, nonsectarian Aggrey Memorial School.[43] He came back to the United States in 1939, and taught at Lincoln University in Jefferson City, Missouri, and later at Morris Brown College, Atlanta. In 1946, he obtained his Ph.D. in anthropology from Harvard University, published a book of Ugandan folktales,[44] and became one of the first United Nations area specialists. Prince Akiki Nyabongo was a nephew of the Omukama of Toro. He, too, first studied at Tuskegee Institute, but received his B.A. from Howard University, where in the academic year 1927–28 he shared a dormitory room with Azikiwe. He obtained his M.A. from Yale and his Ph.D. in anthropology from Oxford University, where he was a Rhodes Scholar. Between 1935 and 1937 he became celebrated as the author of a Ugandan folk novel and three volumes of children's folktales that were well received in England and America, and translated into several foreign languages.[45] On returning to the United States in the late 1930s, he taught for several years at the State Teachers' College, Montgomery, Alabama. Interestingly, both Ugandans had been members (and Nyabongo the president in 1929) of an earlier organization, the African Student Union

43. King, *Pan-Africanism and Education.* The school was named after James Kwegyir Aggrey, the saintlike and influential educator from the Gold Coast who studied and worked at Afro-American College, Livingston (Jefferson City, Mo.) for most of his adult years, and who was directly responsible for Azikiwe and other Africans coming to the U.S. to study in the 1920s: see Edwin Smith, *Aggrey of Africa: A Study in Black and White* (London: Student Christian Movement, 1929).

44. Ernest B. Kalibala, *"Wakaima and the Clayman" and Other African Tales* (New York, 1946).

45. King, *Pan-Africanism and Education,* pp. 215–25; also A. K. Nyabongo, "African Life and Ideals," *Journal of Negro History* (July 1945), p. 179.

of America, which functioned throughout the 1920s.[46] Both men were married to Afro-American women.

In the first three years of the association about forty-one students were active members.[47] The association used as its headquarters International House, a well-known, private student hostel near Columbia University, where two members of the executive of the association—Mbadiwe and Akpabio—resided. It is evidence of the extensive contacts that African students had already made with Afro-Americans and liberal white Americans that the ASA was able to assemble a prominent, interracial but largely black advisory board of about sixty members. Among the stated goals of the association was "to interpret Africa to America" and to work toward that continent's "complete economic and political freedom."[48]

The association did not have the resources to engage in much organized activity during its first year. But as interest in Africa was rapidly growing, association members, as lecturers, panelists and authors, had increased opportunities to correct distortions and misrepresentations about Africa and to argue the case for early political independence from European colonial rule. An example of this kind of activity was a symposium on "Africa and the War" conducted by six African students at a large public meeting at City College, New York City, on May 8, 1942. This was reportedly the first time in New York City that a group of African students had been given a public forum for their political views.[49]

Under the dynamic leadership of Mbadiwe, who transferred from New York University to Columbia's Business School in the fall of 1941, the association was quite active in New York City. A major event for Mbadiwe and the association took place with the publication in March 1942 of his book, *British and Axis Aims in Africa*, which had originated as a series of lectures.[50] An impressive and passionate nationalist document, the book argued that Africans "have left significant traces of their existence in the progressive march of human history," called on Africans to help defeat Nazi

46. See Akiki K. Nyabongo, *The Story of an African Chief* (New York, 1935; this volume was published by G. Routledge in London in 1936, under the title *Africa Answers Back*); *The "Bisoro" Stories*, 2 vols. (Oxford, 1937); and *Winds and Lights: African Fairy Tales* (New York: The Voice of Ethiopia, 1939).

47. This figure is derived from names listed or mentioned in the four extant issues of the *African Interpreter*, the publication of the Association, as well as from two signed, undated attendance lists in the Archives of the African Academy of Arts and Research, Africa House, New York City.

48. *African Interpreter*, February 1943, p. 3.

49. *People's Voice*, May 16, 1942; L. D. Reddick "Africa Speaks," *Opportunity* (July 1942), pp. 205–06.

50. Kingsley Ozuomba Mbadiwe, *British and Axis Aims in Africa* (New York, 1942).

Germany, as otherwise "Africa will be plunged into the gloomiest period in all its life," expressed support and admiration for Britain (though critical of her colonial rule), and demanded independence for the African colonies within the British Commonwealth of Nations. But Mbadiwe and the association were soon to repudiate the goal of commonwealth status for independent African countries. Nonetheless, Mbadiwe's book served to attract considerable attention to himself and the association.

Mbadiwe and other African students had assumed that the Atlantic Charter would apply to Africa. The joint declaration of President Franklin D. Roosevelt of the United States and Prime Minister Winston Churchill of Britain, issued on August 14, 1941, had affirmed "the right of all peoples to choose their form of government" and supported the restoration of "sovereign rights and self-government to those who have been forcibly deprived of them." African students were therefore chagrined when Churchill stated in the House of Commons on September 9, 1941, that the Atlantic Charter was intended to apply to "the states and nations of Europe . . . under the Nazi yoke" and not to British colonies.[51] Mbadiwe expressed his keen disappointment in a two-part article published in *Opportunity*, the monthly organ of the National Urban League and a major black political and literary journal.[52] "When I wrote my book," he complained, "I took for granted that the age when democracy was for England and totalitarianism was for the colonies was ended and would never return." He characterized Churchill's statement as "shocking" and criticized the United States government for not denouncing it.

This militant and urgent tone was again expressed by Mbadiwe in his next article, which appeared in the November 1942 issue of *Survey Graphic*, a quarterly journal.[53] This was a special issue, guest-edited by Alain Locke, a distinguished black philosopher at Howard University. It was entitled "Color: Unfinished Business of Democracy" and dealt mainly with the Americas, but also with Asia and Africa. Of the twenty-two major contributors, Mbadiwe was the only African. In his article, he pointed to Africa's "no small . . . contribution of men and resources for the defense of democracy," and warned that "Africans see no really successful and satisfactory outcome of this world struggle which does not offer us a change in

51. The American Committee on Africa, "The War and Peace Aims," *The Atlantic Charter and Africa from an American Standpoint* (New York, 1942), pp. 31, 35.

52. K. O. Mbadiwe, "Africa in the War of Destiny," *Opportunity* September 1942, pp. 260–64, and October 1942, pp. 298–301, 317.

53. K. O. Mbadiwe, "Africa's Hope for Democracy," *Survey Graphic*, (November 1942), pp. 519–21, and 550–52.

political status and in economic relationship to the rest of the world." He expressed impatience with liberal European and American opinion which "sticks too closely to the familiar tune of gradualism and stays too much within the restricted orbit of paternalism." He recommended that the United Nations draw up and put into practice after the war "a full democratic program for Africa."

Further recognition of African students in the United States as spokesmen for their continent came when several of them were consulted in early 1942 by the newly formed Committee on Africa, the "War and Peace Aims." The committee was formed in August 1941 as a result of the initiative of the officers of the Phelps-Stokes Fund, a foundation with a long interest in African education. It came into being in response to the Atlantic Charter and the fast-growing, war-stimulated American interest in and involvement with Africa. The committee was comprised of forty Americans, all wih substantial interest in and knowledge of Africa. Ten members of the committee were Afro-Americans—itself a recognition of their special interest in Africa.[54] There was an executive committee of ten, three of whom—Ralph Johnson Bunche, Charles S. Johnson and Channing H. Tobias—were Afro-Americans. The committee was concerned to "develop an intelligent public opinion . . . regarding conditions in that vast continent . . . and how they might be improved." At a meeting on February 21, 1942, of the executive committee, five Africans, four of whom were students, presented their views on Africa's future: Walter F. Walker, Liberia's consul-general in New York; Ross Lohr of Sierra Leone; and Adjei, Nkrumah, and Akpabio.[55] Other African students submitted memoranda. Although the committee's recommendations in its final report were moderate and gradualist, it had taken into account the militant and urgent views of African students. The committee itself seems to have become defunct with the publication of its report.

In contrast, African students continued their active propaganda. Indeed, their association was most successful during its second year, 1942–43. This was a result of the imaginative leadership of Kwame Nkrumah, who was elected president at its first annual convention held in New York City between September 6 and 10, 1942. In his presidential address he echoed the familiar call for pan-African unity in order to build a strong, free Africa:

> the cause of Africans everywhere is one with the cause of all people of African descent throughout the world. . . . Unity, Freedom, Indepen-

54. *The Atlantic Charter and Africa*, pp. 151–53.
55. Ibid., p. ix.

dence, Democracy—these should be our watchwords, our ideals. . . . This is the time to remember Mother Africa and build for her a glorious and independent future.[56]

Nkrumah demonstrated skills as a publicist by taking the initiative in founding a journal, *The African Interpreter*, edited by his countryman, J. A. B. Jones-Quartey. Altogether five issues of between fourteen and twenty pages were published. The first three issues, which were mimeographed, appeared in February, March, and April of 1943. The next two issues were printed; one, a special number and the most ambitious, appeared in the summer of 1943, and the final one appeared in the spring of 1944. Although relatively short-lived, the *African Interpreter* had served to project the image of the association as a militant African nationalist organization. It reported and commented on major African initiatives for political independence and economic and social progress. Thus it carried the entire text of a memorandum submitted in London in August 1943 by eight visiting West African journalists, led by Azikiwe, to the secretary of state for the colonies, demanding an immediate crash-training program for Africans, representative government in ten years, to be followed by full independence within the British Commonwealth of Nations in another five years. Editorially, the *Interpreter* considered the demands of this "quite remarkable" memorandum "to say the least, reasonable." But the ultimate goal of membership in the Commonwealth was objectionable on the grounds that it would diminish African independence. The memorandum commented thus: "We hereby affirm that such a political destiny is not that to which we look forward as befitting a proud and numerous race of men. On the contrary, we look forward to the day of complete independence. . . ."[57]

The association did have limited contact and communication with British officialdom. When in early February 1943, Arthur Creech Jones, influential Labor M.P. who was later to be colonial secretary, visited New York, the association, represented by Mbadiwe, made its views known to the British official.[58] That same month the association sent cables to Prime Minister Churchill and President Roosevelt protesting the jailing of Gandhi and demanding his release.[59] The African students, too, had clearly seen their struggle for freedom as linked with that of other colonial peoples.

Helping to project the association into public consciousness was Robert Kweku Attah Gardiner, a brilliant Gold Coast student and an influential

56. *African Interpreter*, Summer 1943, p. 5.
57. Ibid., Spring 1944.
58. *People's Voice*, February 13, 1943.
59. *African Interpreter*, February 1943, p. 10.

member of the West African Student Union (WASU) in London. He spent most of the academic year 1942–43 in the United States, during which time he traveled and lectured extensively. From its inception the association had been influenced by WASU, which had long functioned as a nationalist organization, and the former had been in regular contact with the latter through correspondence as well as by an exchange of publications. During the war, WASU had submitted several nationalist memoranda to the secretary of state for the colonies, one of which, dated April 6, 1942, demanded "Internal self-government now with a definite guarantee of complete self-government within five years after the war."[60] WASU had also organized a parliamentary committee which met twice a month with British members of Parliament interested in Africa. In an article entitled "African Opinion and World Peace," published while he was in the United States, Gardiner sought to dispel the widely held notion that Africans were not ready for self-government. He wrote:

> The history of West Africa is replete with evidence which vindicates the leadership and statesmanship of African public men. It is not to be forgotten that even the African illiterate can weigh evidence and make decisions. He does this every day in his household and native courts. On what political grounds do we or can we condemn his political wisdom?[61]

While there is evidence that the association continued to function throughout the war,[62] the discontinuation of its publication and the establishment in November 1943 of a new broad-based pro-African organization in which African students played a central role seriously blurred its identity and function. From late 1943 on, African student nationalism in the United States can best be seen through examining the history of the African Academy of Arts and Research.

The African Academy of Arts and Research

The African Academy of Arts and Research was founded by the energetic and persuasive Mbadiwe, who had been among the most active and best known of the African student nationalists.[63] Already there existed two

60. Coleman, *Nigeria*, p. 240.

61. Kweku Attah Gardiner, "African Opinion and World Peace," *The Negro Quarterly* (Winter 1943), pp. 345–359.

62. For example, Ojike attended the U.N. San Francisco Conference in May 1945, both as president of the association and as vice-president of the academy.

63. The papers of the academy are in an uncatalogued state at Africa House in New York City. This section, unless otherwise indicated, is based on research in those papers.

major Afro-American-led organizations concerned with Africa's welfare—the Ethiopian World Federation and the Council on African Affairs—but Mbadiwe, despite discouragement from both black and white friends who foresaw insuperable difficulties in founding a new organization, thought the time propitious for a broad-based organization in which Africans themselves would take the lead in speaking on behalf of Africa. And he did succeed in mobilizing support among Afro-American professionals and influential white liberals. Mbadiwe had graduated in February 1943 with a B.S. in business and finance from Columbia University, and was enrolled as a part-time student in political science at New York University. But overwhelmingly, until he left to return to Nigeria in December 1947, his time and attention were focused on the academy. This was possible because he received regular financial support from his elder brother Green, an early Nigerian entrepreneur and millionaire.[64]

The academy opened its office on Saturday, November 13, 1943, at 55 West Forty-Second Street, but was formally incorporated in New York State as a nonprofit organization on December 30. The first officers of the academy were as follows: Lawrence Reddick, curator of the Schomburg Collection in Harlem, chairman of the Board of Directors; Mbadiwe, president; Ojike, vice-president; D. Buyabuye Mdodana, a South African clergyman, secretary; A. A. Austin, a wealthy West Indian-born businessman, treasurer; and Alain Locke, chairman of educational research. The academy was listed as having two representatives in West Africa: George I. Mbadiwe, Kingsley's brother, who was an editor of the *West African Pilot* in Lagos, Nigeria; and W. J. Kwesi Mould, a businessman of Accra, Gold Coast. President Mbadiwe was the main administrator and was assisted by a small regular staff as well as by volunteers.

By April 1945, the academy had an impressive all-black twenty-five-member Board of Directors comprised of eight Africans—Azikiwe, Jones-Quartey, Kalibala, Mbadiwe, Mdodana, Nyabongo, Ojike, and Orizu—and seventeen Afro-American professionals, among them educators, clergymen, businessmen, union leaders, and medical doctors. By September 1945, there were some changes among the officers: the Reverend James H. Robinson, a Lincoln-educated, Harlem-based, Presbyterian clergyman who was later to become well known as founder and administrator of the successful Crossroads Africa Program, became chairman of the Board of Directors; Dr. A. George Daly, Jamaican-born director of Mt. Morris Park Hospital, New York City, vice-president; and Nyabongo, educational director. By this time, too, the academy claimed a

64. Mbadiwe, *British and Axis Aims in Africa*, p. 33.

national membership of a thousand. Early in 1946, in keeping with the expanding ambitions of the academy, three whites were added to the board: the academy's long-time patron, Eleanor Roosevelt; Roger N. Baldwin, director of the American Civil Liberties Union; and Maurice F. Davidson, a lawyer and industrialist. Before this, whites had been extensively used on ad hoc advisory and fund-raising committees.

To help raise funds for its operations, and at the same time educate the American public about Africa, Mbadiwe hit upon the idea of the academy organizing spirited presentations of authentic African culture—music, drama and dance. Such talent existed in the form of two already quite well-known dance troupes led by Asdata Dafora of Sierra Leone and Effiom M. Odok of Nigeria. These were to be supported by talented Afro-American and Caribbean artists. With the help of distinguished patrons like Eleanor Roosevelt, Mary McLeod Bethune, president of the National Council of Negro Women, Governor Raymond Baldwin of Connecticut, and of a large and influential African Dance Festival Committee, the idea succeeded magnificently. The festivals were held at Carnegie Hall on five occasions in three years: December 13, 1943; April 4 and 6, 1945; and April 25 and 26, 1946. They were artistic successes and played to capacity crowds, a total of almost 15,000 people watching the performances. Each year Mrs. Roosevelt and other American dignitaries attended, and the performances attracted wide and favorable press comments.

The academy's skill in attracting attention was again in evidence in its establishment and annual presentation of a Wendell Willkie Award. Willkie, an apostle of internationalism, humanism, and equality, was one of the major liberal American figures to whom Mbadiwe had been attracted. In a seven-week round-the-world trip in August through September 1942, Willkie had made stops in Ghana and Nigeria, and on his return had made an unequivocal call for an end to European colonial rule. Encouraged by this, Mbadiwe had met with Willkie and had persuaded him to play an honorary role in the academy; but Willkie died of a heart attack in October 1944. In February 1945 the academy established a Willkie Memorial Award "to promote, encourage and recognize leadership in the field of international goodwill." The first recipient was Henry A. Wallace, former vice-president, then secretary of commerce, and a leading liberal American political figure. The presentation of the award was made on November 1, 1945, at a unique colorful and well-publicized ceremony in the Department of State. The following year the award went to Haile Selassie, emperor of Ethiopia, and the presentation, attended by a large number of American and United Nations dignitaries, was made on November 22, 1946, at the Capital Hotel in New York City.

The three Nigerian leaders of the academy performed an outstanding feat of propaganda through their lectures and writings. With their paid lectures organized by lecture bureaus, they propagandized in all parts of the country. Their articles—very often rebuttals of a proimperialist perspective—appeared in such liberal American journals as the *New Republic* and *Harper's Magazine*.[65] A book by Orizu was published in 1944, and two by Ojike in 1946 and 1947.[66] All three, like Mbadiwe's, were nationalist in perspective, condemning European colonial rule and demanding early independence for former colonies; all were widely reviewed and attracted considerable attention. In addition, between 1945 and 1947 both Orizu and Mbadiwe had regular columns on Africa, respectively, in the *Pittsburgh Courier* and the Oklahoma City *Black Dispatch*, two of black America's leading weekly newspapers.[67] The academy issued regular press releases that were carried in black American newspapers and also supplied Azikiwe's newspapers with relevant American stories.

The academy itself had plans to publish a monthly journal. In October 1945 the first issue of the *African Eagle*, "symbolizing the freedom of African man," appeared. It was a modest four-page tabloid. Apparently a second issue did not appear: the academy did not have the resources and skills to publish a regular journal.

But before this, in April 1945, the academy had succeeded in putting out a book entitled *Africa: Today and Tomorrow*, edited by Jones-Quartey. There were eighteen major contributors, African and American, to the

65. See, for instance, Mbonu Ojike, "Nigeria and the Colonial Problem," *New Republic*, March 20, 1944, p. 182 (written in response to an article, "Colonies and Freedom" by Sir Julian Huxley in the January 24 issue, in which the British biologist argued against early political independence for African colonies); and idem? "Modern Africa," *Harper's Magazine*, January 1945, p. 59.

66. A. A. Nwafor Orizu, *Without Bitterness* (New York, 1944). Mbonu Ojike, *My Africa* (New York, 1946), and *I Have Two Countries* (New York, 1947).

67. That Afro-American interest in Africa was substantially stimulated by World War II is well reflected in the leading contemporary Afro-American newspapers and journals. An illustration of this is the editorial comment of the *Chicago Defender* of January 6, 1945:

> One of the really gratifying developments of the war has been the increasing interest of Americans in African affairs. . . .
>
> The new approach to an understanding of the African problem comes at the same time that the thirteen million Negroes of this country are becoming increasingly aware of the color problem on a world-wide scale and are coming more and more to regard Africa as "their old country." American Negroes today are talking more about imperialism and colonial rule . . . because they have learned that what happens in distant . . . colonies has a great deal to do with what happens to them here at home.

However, space limitation does not permit me to elaborate on this theme here.

book. The articles dealt with aspects of the economic, social, and cultural life of Africa and envisaged political freedom and economic progress in the postwar African world. Reportedly six thousand copies of this book were sold.

The academy also organized a successful public lecture series on Africa. Between November 1945 and April 1946, it sponsored six free lectures—one per month—at the American Museum of Natural History. These were intended to be a basic introduction to African culture and history. Lecturers and discussants consisted of African students, knowledgeable Afro-American supporters such as Reddick and W. E. B. Du Bois,, and white scholars such as Melville J. Herskovits, the renowned anthropologist. The lectures were well attended, and after discussion the audience was introduced to the African art works in the "African Hall" of the museum. The academy conducted a similar lecture series during 1946–47.

In New York City on October 4–6, 1946, the academy held its only major conference. The theme of the conference was "Africa Looks Ahead" and there were panels and discussions on such subjects as "Education and Culture," "African Resources," and "Colonialism and World Peace." Several hundred members and observers attended the conference, including representatives from the Council on African Affairs, the NAACP, and the mayor's office. The conference endorsed a memorandum, which was later submitted to the United Nations General Assembly, containing "an appeal for justice on behalf of nongoverning peoples of Africa who fought and died for freedom, but were denied the most elemental of human rights." It asserted that "the continuation of colonialism and imperialism endangers the efforts of peace-loving peoples of the world."

A notable achievement of the academy was the establishment of Africa House, strategically located near City College, Columbia University, and Harlem in Upper Manhattan. In the summer of 1947, after a long, strenuous campaign waged primarily by Afro-American clergymen in the metropolitan New York area, the academy succeeded in purchasing a four-story townhouse for twenty-five thousand dollars. Africa House, as it was named, became the headquarters of the academy and a major social center for African students and visitors. The establishment of Africa House was partly to facilitate the fast-growing numbers of Africans who were coming to the United States to study in the postwar years. Indeed, the propaganda and aid of the academy, as well as that of an allied organization headed by Orizu, the American Council on African Education, were, in large part, responsible for the new influx.

The academy remained alert to all major developments in the struggle for African independence. Thus it took a strong interest in the Pan-African

Conference held in Manchester, England, between October 13 and 21, 1945.[68] This was the sixth in a sporadic series of Pan-African conferences which had started in 1900. The academy was formally invited to participate but could not afford to do so. In any case, West Africa was well represented at the Manchester conference. Indeed, two former members of the African Students Association of the United States and Canada who had left for England in early 1945, Adjei and Nkrumah, played important roles there. The conference was attended by some two hundred delegates. It was the largest, most representative, and the most militant of the Pan-African conferences. It set as its goal "complete and absolute independence" and a unified Africa with a socialist economy. As a result of the conference a West African secretariat was set up, with Nkrumah as secretary-general, to work toward one united, independent West Africa. But this organization failed, and Nkrumah returned to the Gold Coast in late 1947 to spearhead the nationalist drive there.

The academy leaders from Nigeria had kept in especially close touch with developments in their country, where, during the war, union and nationalist activities were organized on a country-wide basis for the first time. Country-wide nationalism was expressed first through the Nigerian Youth and, from 1944, through the National Council of Nigeria and the Cameroons (NCNC), an organization that Azikiwe had been instrumental in founding and in which he held the key position of general secretary.[69]

The Nigerian academy leaders were in regular communication with Azikiwe himself. Thus, when the NCNC failed to persuade the Nigerian legislature to send two observers to the UN San Francisco Conference, the academy thought it imperative to send an observer. Ojike was selected and charged with "casting the impression . . . that the sleeping giant of Africa had finally awakened." His own memorandum, dated May 14, 1945, demanded "an international charter based on the principle of justice and equality for all peoples" and recommended that the United Nations enjoin colonial powers to set freedom dates not exceeding fifteen years for all their colonies. Furthermore, the academy had sent a telegram to the leaders of the American delegation which read: "Any compromise of the colonials falsifies the whole purpose for which the war was fought. Our choice is either total freedom or a Third World War."

Ojike carried out his assignment vigorously. He conferred with delegates from Arabia, Egypt, Ethiopia, Haiti, and Liberia, as well as with the large number of Afro-American observers, and tried to get as much public-

68. Geiss, *The Pan-African Movement*, chaps. 20 and 21.
69. Coleman, *Nigeria*, pp. 264–65.

ity as possible for the cause of colonials. He tenaciously but unsuccessfully tried to meet with British and American officials. The end of the conference left the academy greatly disappointed with the British and Americans for failing to show signs of accommodating the aspirations of Africans for political independence within a reasonable time. On the other hand, the academy praised Russia and China for "triumphantly championing the cause of weaker nations."

The aftermath of the UN San Francisco Conference was a stiffened resolve on the part of academy leaders and all Nigerian nationalists to struggle on for independence. Coincidentally, in late June 1945, just as the conference was ending, there occurred in Nigeria its first general strike involving thirty thousand technical workers of the fast-growing but still fledgling Nigerian Trades Union Congress.[70] The strike, which lasted six weeks, was easily the most dramatic manifestation of the potential power of organized labor in an African colony. It was supported by Azikiwe's newspapers and by the NCNC. The academy also expressed strong sympathy for the Nigerian workers and feared that the colonial authorities would make reprisals against the union leaders and Azikiwe. Through an exchange of cables and letters with the Nigerian union leaders, the academy was kept informed about the labor crisis. It aggressively publicized the strike in the United States and succeeded in winning some American sympathy and support for it. Mbadiwe retrospectively commented: "The reaction in America was spontaneous. Cables were going to Nigeria and London and even white ministers' groups broke all precedents by sending letters of protest to the London Government." He credited this publicity with preventing the Nigerian colonial authorities from carrying out stern reprisals against the labor leaders and Azikiwe.

The academy joined Nigerian nationalists at home in fiercely attacking the new Richards Constitution of 1945 on the grounds that it was brought into existence without consulting the Nigerian people, that it represented no advance whatsoever in the training of Nigerians for responsible self-government, that it failed to increase the number of Africans elected to the Legislative Council, and that it did not give Nigerians a real majority within that body.[71] It joined, too, in the protests against four "obnoxious ordinances" enacted in 1945. The Nigerian nationalists interpreted three of these—the Minerals Ordinance, the Public Lands Acquisition Ordinance, and the Crown Lands Ordinance—as arrogating to the British crown the title to Nigerian minerals and lands. The fourth ordinance, the Appoint-

70. See Wogu Ananaba, *The Trade Union Movement in Nigeria* (New York, 1970), chap. 5.
71. Coleman, *Nigeria*, pp. 276–78.

ment and Deposition of Chiefs Ordinance, they objected to on the grounds that it made puppets of traditional rulers.

And when *Time* magazine for December 16, 1946, reported that the besieged British governor of Nigeria, Sir Arthur Richards, had called Azikiwe "a bloody bastard" in an interview, the incident was used to further fan the flames of Nigerian nationalism. An academy cablegram of January 31, 1947, to the British colonial secretary called Sir Arthur's remark "not only greatly offensive to millions of Africans but to Americans of both African and non-African descent as well;" the telegram went on to demand that the governor be reprimanded and removed from office. Similarly, the alertness and sensitivity of the academy to racial discrimination in Nigeria is evidenced in the Ivor Cummings case. Cummings, a black official of the Colonial Welfare Department, was refused accommodation in Feburary 1947 at the Greek-owned British Hotel in Lagos, even though the Nigerian government had reserved a room for him. The academy cabled the Nigerian government, press, and nationalist organizations, urging that the licenses of the owner be revoked and the owner repatriated. "Nigeria cannot tolerate discrimination and ingratitude," the cablegram added. The incident evoked a strong unified nationalist protest, which resulted in the governor banning all forms of discrimination in public places.

In order to air its grievances and to raise funds for a protest delegation to London, the NCNC undertook an unprecedented eight-month Nigeria-wide tour from April to December 1946. The tour started out under the leadership of Herbert Macaulay, president of the NCNC and the oldest and most venerable of Nigerian nationalists, together with Azikiwe and Michael Imoudu, Nigeria's most outstanding labor leader. On May 7, Macaulay died in Kano at the age of eighty-two. Millions of West Africans mourned his death, and his funeral in Lagos on May 11 was the largest in Nigerian history, with more than a hundred thousand people attending. Academy leaders, too, paid warm tribute to Macaulay, vowing that "His death is a gage of battle flung at our feet." An academy press release announcing Macaulay's death and funeral and providing a biographical sketch of this "greatest of African nationalists" was carried by most black American newspapers. Of course, the NCNC had continued its tour. It was a great success, raising £13,000 and creating a firm sense of Nigeria-wide nationalism.

A national seven-man NCNC delegation was due in London in the summer of 1947. Azikiwe, its leader, left ahead of the others in late May in order to spend a month in the United States. It was his first return visit since completing his studies in 1934, and it was a triumphant one. Thanks partly to the efforts of the academy, Azikiwe was given considerable publicity in both the black and white presses. He was officially welcomed to New York by Mayor O'Dwyer. He was awarded honorary degrees from two black colleges he had attended, Storer and Lincoln. He was received by UN and U.S. officials, as well as by Mrs. Roosevelt at Hyde Park. On June 27, the academy gave him a splendid banquet at the Pennsylvania Hotel attended by four hundred prominent guests. On leaving Azikiwe had every reason to believe that there was substantial support in the United States for his goal of early independence for Nigeria.

In London the Nigerian delegation, after holding discussions with WASU and other supportive groups, met with A. Creech Jones, secretary of state for the Colonies, on August 13, 1947. But the secretary insisted that the Richards constitution be tried. On their return to Lagos in October 1947, the delegation was met by the tumultuous and supportive welcome of a crowd of about a hundred thousand. Nigerian nationalism was now full-blown and could only be satisfied by full independence.

Two months after the NCNC delegation had returned home, Mbadiwe left the United States to return via Britain to Nigeria. He had been preceded by Ojike, Orizu, and others. The United States during the war had proved a major training ground for African students, and they had returned home to participate in the final drive for the political independence of their respective countries. Their confidence and determination in pursuing their goals rested, in part, on the knowledge of the strong moral support of Afro-Americans and liberal white Americans. In the United States the African Academy of Arts and Research became largely a paper organization: its energies had been transferred to Nigeria and other parts of Africa.

During World War II the United States emerged as an important arena from which to stage a battle for decolonization in Africa. Several factors were responsible for this: The United States had the largest concentration of people of African descent—some thirteen million in 1945—outside of Africa itself; during the war the United States quickly emerged as the leading world power, with a rapidly growing interest and involvement in Africa; and, with the considerable leverage it exerted over the weakened European colonial powers, the United States could, if it so chose, profoundly affect developments in Africa in the postwar world.

As we have seen, the two most vocal and organized groups seeking to persuade the American government and public to play a leading role in accelerating decolonization in postwar Africa were radical blacks and African students together with their Afro-American and liberal white supporters. Radical pan-Africanism, as exemplified by the Council on African Affairs, was a new phenomenon in the United States. While having its beginnings in the late 1930s, its effective functioning was made possible by the wartime alliance between the United States and the Soviet Union and the consequent temporary rapprochement between the U.S. Communist party, a friend and ally of the council, and capitalist America. The inauguration in 1947 of the Cold War between the United States and the Soviet Union brought the council, as well as other radical organizations, under attack—leading to its demise in 1955. Nonetheless, the council had played a significant role in educating the American public about Africa, and in winning some support among them for a constructive and progressive American role on that continent, though far from enough to shape American policy. Also, the council played a central role in propagating and maintaining the vision of a united socialist Africa, to which many African leaders were to pay lip service, and which such influential ones as Kwame Nkrumah, Sekou Touré, and Julius Nyerere were to adopt.

The war years also saw the emergence for the first time of African students as an organized, articulate, and influential group. Although generally supportive of pro-African, Afro-American organizations, they felt that the time had come to take the lead in speaking out on behalf of Africa. Yet they realized that the support of Afro-Americans, West Indian immigrants, and liberal whites was indispensable to achieving their goals. Their role as educators of the American public about Africa was major, and the close ties they forged with Americans, particularly blacks, was to lead to a highly substantial increase in Africans who came to the United States to study,[72] thereby creating even more and stronger bonds. These were the developments which facilitated the functioning of such black-created, pan-African, or goodwill organizations as the American Society of African Culture, Crossroads Africa, and the American Negro Leadership Conference on Africa.

World War II had served to universalize the struggle of oppressed peoples against colonial domination, and because of this the pan-African nationalist activities of Afro-Americans and Africans abroad must be taken into account in any full evaluation of the process of decolonization in Africa.

72. The sixty students who were in the United States during the war increased to more than 300 in 1949, and despite the development of universities in Africa, now stands at about 26,000. See *A Survey of African Students Studying in the United States* (New York: Phelps Stokes Fund, 1949), and *The Chronicle of Higher Education*, April 17, 1978, p. 12.

4. Patterns in the Transfer of Power: A Comparative Study of French and British Decolonization

TONY SMITH

Although definite political options were open to Britain and France in imperial policy after 1945, the historically conditioned realm of the possible precluded the adoption of certain courses of action. The material hardships following the havoc of World War II combined with the clear ascendance of the two "anti-imperial" powers, the United States and the Soviet Union, and with the increased maturity of nationalist elites throughout Africa and Asia, to force a decided retrenchment of Europe overseas. In retrospect, we can see that the truly important political decisions that had to be made by Paris and London after 1945 concerned, not whether the colonies would be free, but, rather, which local nationalist factions they would favor with their support and over what piece of territory these new political elites would be permitted to rule. What would be federated, what partitioned, who should govern and according to what procedures constituted decisive issues where the Europeans continued to exercise a significant degree of control. When the Europeans did not respect the historically imposed limits of their power, however, their policies were destined to meet with defeat. Thus, although the Suez invasion of October–November 1956 constituted a political crisis of the first order in Britain, it was the only occasion when colonial matters occupied such a prominent position. In France, by contrast, the interminable wars in Indochina and Algeria cost not only the lives of hundreds of thousands of Asians and Africans but eventually brought about the collapse of the Fourth Republic as well.

A comparative analysis of British and French abilities to withdraw from their empires after 1945 suggests four respects in which the British were favored. First, there was the legacy of the past in terms of ideas and procedures on imperial matters, precedents built up over the decades before the Second World War which served to orient European leaders and organize their responses to the pressures for decolonization. On this score, the British proved to be temperamentally, and especially institutionally, more fit than the French to cope with overseas challenges to their rule. Second, there was the international "place" of Britain and France and especially the different relations with the United States maintained by the two countries. Third, there was the question of the domestic political institutions of France and Britain, with their very unequal capacities to deal with a problem of the magnitude of decolonization. The French multiparty system with its weak governing consensus clearly was not the equivalent of the two-party system in Britain. Even had the French system been stronger, however, it is not evident it would have dealt more effectively with decolonization; for national opinion, and especially the "collective conscience" of the political elite in France, was significantly different from that in Britain. The fourth variable to be analyzed directs attention from Paris and London to the character of the nationalist elites with whom the Europeans had to deal. Here, it will be argued that the situations in Indochina and Algeria presented France with serious problems that Britain was simply fortunate enough to escape (at least until Suez).

So the comparative study of European decolonization depends in important measure on the comparative study of colonial nationalism. These four factors correspond to the three analytical "levels" proposed by Wm. Roger Louis and Ronald Robinson in their chapter in this volume, with the category of "imperial traditions" warranting special attention, in my view, as a bridge between the colonial and the metropolitan spheres of action.

With respect to prewar preparations for the transfer of power, the Government of India Act of 1935 must appear as the first major step in the decolonization process which began in earnest after 1945. For although the act itself fell far short indeed of according independence to India, it was not undeniable that the "white" Dominions would eventually be joined in their informal alliance by peoples of other racial stock. To the Indians, of course, this was scant satisfaction, because not only the time of their independence but, more importantly, the politically most crucial features of their emerging state seemed to be outside their ability to control. But in London the act was in many ways decisive. It reconciled the majority of popular and elite opinion to the eventual independence of this "crowning jewel" of empire, considered along with the British Isles themselves to be the other "twin pillar" of Britain's international rank.

Of course, there is the mistake, encountered in the works of British writers especially, of seeing in retrospect a grand design for decolonization which in fact did not exist. Closer inspection commonly reveals the British to have been following Burke's sage counsel to reform in order to preserve: London made concessions more usually to subvert opposition to British rule than to prepare for its demise. So, for example, to see Indian independence in 1947 as necessarily following from the Government of India Act of 1935, which in turn unerringly confirmed the intentions of the Government of India Act of 1919 (itself the natural product of the Morley-Minto reforms of 1909), assumes belief in a British gift for foresight which a detailed examination of the historical record makes it difficult to sustain. What is lacking in these accounts is a sense of the conflicts, hesitations, and uncertainties of the past and of the attempts to reinterpret or renege on the promise of eventual independence for India.

Nonetheless, the British *did* establish a tradition of meeting colonial discontent by reforms which associated the subject peoples more closely with their own governing. The prior evolution of the Dominion system *did* exert an important influence on the style of British policy toward India. And the ultimate decision to grant India independence and to to permit her to withdraw from the Commonwealth if she wished *did* constitute a momentous precedent for British policy toward the rest of the colonies. The chapters in this volume by John Hargreaves and Cranford Pratt offer additional documentation that, however shortsighted London may have been about the eventual speed of decolonization, British foresight was remarkable indeed relative to that of the French (not to speak of the Belgians or Portuguese).

How limited, by contrast, was the French experience in handling political change within their empire. When, in January–February 1944, a group of colonial civil servants met in Brazzaville, capital of French Equatorial Africa, to draw up proposals for imperial reorganization in the aftermath of the war, the many worthwhile recommendations they made—the end of forced labor and special native legal codes, the creation of territorial assemblies and their coordination in a "French Federation," the representation of colonial peoples at the future French Constituent Assembly—failed to deal with the truly central problem, the possibility of a colonial evolution toward independence.[1] That is, the French are not to be criticized for failing to provide complete and immediate independence to their colonies, but rather for their steadfast refusal to consider even eventual separation as a viable political option. As the conference report preamble put it:

> The ends of the civilizing work accomplished by France in the colonies exclude any idea of autonomy, all possibility of evolution outside the French bloc of the Empire: the eventual constitution, even in the future, of self-government in the colonies is denied.[2]

Nor were matters to improve with time. Despite the rapid enactment of a host of unprecedented reforms proposed by the conference over the next

1. For a discussion of the conference, see D. Bruce Marshall, *The French Colonial Myth and Constitution-Making in the Fourth Republic* (New Haven, 1973), pp. 102–15.

2. *Brazzaville: 30 janvier–8 février 1944*, published by the Ministère des Colonies, 1944, p. 32.

two years, there was no thought of conceding political advantages to colonial nationalists which might lead to independence. By the summer of 1947, this had been made clear on successive occasions to the Indochinese, to the Tunisians and Moroccans, to the Malagasies, to the blacks of West and Equatorial Africa, and to the Algerians. Indeed, the matter had become fixed by the Fourth Republic's Constitution in the terms providing for the "French Union" in its Title 8.[3]

Experts in jurisprudence have convincingly pointed out the ambiguity and contradictions with which the final text establishing the French Union abounds. Its one central feature stands out clearly enough, however: the authority of France over the Union was beyond dispute. Neither in the immediate nor in the distant future would there be a partnership among equals within this "federation." The only significant power whatsoever conferred on the Union was that of pooling members' resources for the common defense (article 62). But it was "the Government of the [French] Republic [which] shall undertake the coordination of these resources and the direction of the policy appropriate to prepare and ensure this defense." In legislative matters, the Union was totally subordinate to the National Assembly (articles 71–72). Nor could foreign nationalists convert the Union into a platform from which to dislodge France from her overseas possessions, for its key institutions (the Presidency, the High Council, and the Assembly) were safely under metropolitan control (articles 62–66 and article 77). What the Union assured, in essence, was that the peoples of the empire would be neither French nor free.

Compared with the British case, the French position is especially striking. For what Paris seemed intent on doing was to form an equivalent to an imperial federation which the British, working with people similar to them racially, economically, and culturally, had abandoned some twenty years earlier. How, then, are we to understand this historically outdated institution, the French Union?

Perhaps the most frequently advanced explanation has to do with ideology: the French goal of "assimilating" their colonial peoples was never as realistic as the British expectation of eventual self-rule for their dependencies. On closer inspection, however, this explanation presents difficulties, for not only was the British pledge capable of indefinite postponement, but there is good reason to think that the French were not so naive about the feasibility of their doctrine as many seem to think. A better approach is to understand the respective French and British outlooks in terms of past experiences and established institutional procedures. In the former re-

3. Tony Smith, "The French Colonial Consensus and People's War, 1945–1958," *The Journal of Contemporary History*, October 1974.

spect, the British were practitioners of "informal empire"—that is, of supporting a dependable local elite in order to assure a stable environment for trade and investment free of the inconveniences of direct political control.[4] For the French, on the contrary, direct rule alone permitted domination, since their economic strength was too feeble to ensure their presence otherwise. To be imperialists the French were perforce protectionists. But perhaps the best way to understand the difference between the French and the British handling of their colonies lies in their respective methods of colonial government. Since the Durham Report of 1839 relative to Canada, the British had been experimenting with a system of institutionalizing the transfer of powers from London to the various colonial governments. No similar tried means of dealing with colonial nationalism existed for the French to draw upon after 1945.

Yet, whatever the differences between them, the French and British colonial systems in Africa shared similarities that made them unlike their Belgian and Portuguese counterparts. In the latter cases, not only were educational and economic advancement denied the Africans more completely than was the case in the British and French territories, but metropolitan trade unions and parties were dormant there—again in contrast with the African experience under British and French rule, as Jean Stengers's chapter in this book clearly indicates in the case of the Belgian Congo.

Prewar theory and practice alone did not decide postwar imperial policy, however. That the United States emerged after 1945 as the world's dominant power clearly helped the British to accept their declining role in international affairs more than it did the French. Thus, wartime cooperation in the development of the atom bomb had extended into an important place for Britain within NATO, where the British held five of the thirteen principal command posts, with seven reserved for the Americans and one for the French. But the most salient aspect of the difference in Washington's relations with Paris and London emerges, perhaps, from an analysis of the quality of the bonds linking Franklin Roosevelt to Winston Churchill and to Charles de Gaulle. Whereas Roosevelt held Churchill in high esteem, "he hates de Gaulle with such fierce feeling that he rambles almost into incoherence whenever we talk about him," Cordell Hull reported in the summer of 1944.[5] With the North African landing of November 1942 and the assassination of Darlan a month later, the Ameri-

4. John Gallagher and Ronald Robinson, "The Imperialism of Free Trade," *Economic History Review*, 2d ser. 6, no. 1 (1953).

5. Cited in Gabriel Kolko, *The Politics of War: The World and United States Foreign Policy, 1943–1945* (New York, 1968), p. 83.

cans moved to make General Henri Giraud, not de Gaulle, head of civilian administration there and commander-in-chief of the surrendered French army of several hundred thousand men. Despite de Gaulle's ability in 1943 to rally behind him the National Liberation Committee (CFLN) and the support of certain resistance groups operating inside France, the Americans continued to oppose his leadership. Even at the moment of the liberation of France, Roosevelt refused to recognize the general's authority, insisting instead that a military administration run the country until the wishes of the population were made known by elections. It was the end of October 1944 before the United States finally recognized de Gaulle's Provisional Government.[6]

Certainly more than personality factors were in play; for the features of de Gaulle's personality that the Americans, and sometimes the British, found so antipathetic had to do with his determination not to let France be absorbed by her allies during the war and relegated to a satellite role deprived of all initiative thereafter. So, early in the struggle, he had protested the manner in which the British occupied Diego Suarez on Madagascar and conducted operations against the Vichy troops in Syria. Similarly, the general had intimations of Roosevelt's plans for the French Empire; that Indochina or Morocco might be made trusteeships of other powers; that British or American bases might be permanently established on New Caledonia or at Bizerte and Dakar; even that a new buffer state might be created between France and Germany, to be called Wallonia and to extend from Switzerland to the Channel. De Gaulle's sharp reaction to such considerations was in perfect accord with his amibition to regenerate France as a nation. As he told Roosevelt:

> I know that you are preparing to aid France materially, and that aid will be invaluable to her. But it is in the political realm that she must recover her vigor, her self-reliance and, consequently, her role. How can she do this if she is excluded from the organization of the great world powers and their decisions, if she loses her African and Asian territories—in short, if the settlement of the War definitely imposes upon her the psychology of the vanquished?[7]

This wartime experience was to have a permanent mark on French attitudes toward the United States whenever colonial questions arose. All

6. A. W. DePorte, *De Gaulle's Foreign Policy, 1944–1946* (Cambridge, Mass., 1968), chaps. 2 and 3. Also Ibid., chap. 4.

7. Charles de Gaulle, *The Complete War Memoirs of Charles de Gaulle* (New York, 1967), p. 574.

shades of French political opinion were suspicious of Americn moves in North Africa after the Allied landing there in November 1942, believing that Washington wished to expel the French in order to move in itself. British efforts to pry the French out of the Levant at the end of the war were similarly believed to be dependent on American support. And the possessiveness with which the French tried to protect their monopoly over affairs in Indochina after 1946, despite their reliance on ever-increasing American aid, serves as yet another instance of their suspicion of American designs.[8] One need only reflect on the welcome London gave to American involvement in British spheres of influence in Greece and Turkey in 1947, and in Iran in 1953, to appreciate the importance of the impact which relations with Washington made in the overall process of European decolonization.

Thus, if the actors at center stage in the decolonization process were Europeans, Asians, and Africans, their deliberations were informed throughout by the altered postwar international context in which they occurred, especially by the predominance of the United States in the affairs of Western Europe. The essay by Louis and Robinson in this book points to the changes going on in American thinking in regard to the colonial empires of their European allies during the war and in the postwar period. Thereafter, American thinking was to develop still more in response to the intensification of the Cold War. Whatever the different phases in American policy, however, there was all the while a common denominator to it: an effort to establish independent local governments as immune as possible to communism and as open as possible to trade and security arrangements deemed important by Washington. To be consistent, such a policy necessarily had to be varied in application. It was not inconsistent, therefore, that the United States *withdrew* from the Philippines after the successful political institutionalization of what D. A. Low, in his chapter in this volume, appropriately calls "the most unreconstructed social order in Asia" shortly before Washington greatly *increased* its presence in Greece in order to insure there a political structure resistant to communism.

Again, with respect to the Netherlands East Indies, the United States initially supported its Dutch ally (though with some reservations) only to increase the pressures for the transfer of power to local nationalists once it became evident by late 1948 that these forces were strong indeed, and that

8. Anti-Americanism flared up in France each time the dependent role became evident: over the Marshall Plan, the EDC, the "nuclear shield," and American funds for the Indochinese war. See, among others, Georgett Elgey, *La République des illusions* (Pris, 1965), pp. 101, 133, 139–41, 248; and Alfred Grosser, *La Politique extérieure de la Vè République* (Paris, 1965), pp. 17, 47 ff.

Indonesian Communists might be in a better position to take control of the nationalist movement if the struggle there should turn out to be prolonged and intensified.[9] By contrast, in Indochina the American opposition to the transfer of power to local nationalists increased after 1947 as the Communist character of the struggle for independence emerged more unequivocally. In short, American anticolonialism presupposed the establishment, in Asia as elsewhere, of stable regimes capable of being dependable allies. According to circumstance, this might mean a policy of withdrawal (the Philippines in 1946, Indonesia in 1948) or one of intervention (Greece in 1947, Indochina in 1950). Of course, Washington's European allies did not necessarily share this perspective. But the British proved far more amenable to it than the Dutch or, more especially, the French.

The third major difference in the respective abilities of the British and the French to decolonize takes us from international considerations to an analysis of the domestic political institutions of these two countries. Britain had a "loyal opposition," a stable two-party system, and a strong executive. France, on the contrary, was plagued by disloyal opposition from both the Right and the Left, by a multiparty system, and by a notoriously weak executive. Hence the French were not so able as the British to deal with a problem of the magnitude of decolonization.

To an observer with a background in French domestic politics, surely the most striking thing about the British political system during this period is the manner in which its institutions seemed to function more effectively during crisis. Faced with a challenge to its authority from abroad, the system organized its responses by closing ranks and asserting the hierarchies of command. This resilience of British institutions was highlighted especially at the time of the invasion of the Suez Canal Zone, the single occasion when matters related to empire focused the concerned attention of the British public and its leaders. The question here is not whether the policy was a colossal blunder or whether the fault for its failure lay with Eisenhower and Dulles. the point is simply, as Leon Epstein demonstrates in his careful study of British politics at the time, that the system performed remarkably well in the sense of responding to the crisis (which to some extent it was responsible for creating in the first place).[10]

Not that there was always unanimity. As the most thorough study of party politics during decolonization suggests, imperial issues were perhaps as much a matter of serious bipartisan dispute during the 1950s as at any

9. George McTurnan Kahin, *Nationalism and Revolution in Indonesia* (Ithaca, N.Y., 1952), pp. 417–18.

10. Leon D. Epstein, *British Politics in the Suez Crisis* (Urbana, Ill., 1964).

time in modern British history.[11] But the discipline of the parties, the institutional strength of government leadership, and the way partisan conflict tended to increase party solidarity (rather than create centrifugal struggles as was so often the case in France), meant that from the mid-1940s until the mid-1960s, British imperial policy was characterized by coherence, consistency, and strength.

The most delicate balance point in British politics at this time was the effort by the Conservatives not to let these issues tear them apart after they came to power in 1951.[12] As David Goldsworthy documents, the Conservatives were the party of empire, tied to it emotionally in perhaps their most vital collective myth, the pride in empire, and connected to it concretely through settlers, business interests, and the Colonial Service, all of whom sought their place in its ranks.[13] The single serious misstep under their leadership was Suez. A part of the reason for their success was surely that Labour had shown the way by granting independence to the several territories of south Asia and by preparing the road for the future independence of the Gold Coast. In addition, there was luck: Churchill was out of office after the spring of 1955 and so was not able to maintain the mistaken policies he had supported, paramount of which was the creation of the Central African Federation in 1953.[14] Harold Macmillan (from 1957) and Iain Macleod (from 1959) proved themselves more realistic leaders. They were substantially aided in the pursuit of their policies by the logic of the British political system, which made it quite difficult for the recalcitrant reactionaries in the party—probably no more than 10 to 15 percent of its strength, though on specific issues they could rally greater support—to create enough instability in the system for concessions to be made to them. Try as they might, first over Egypt, then over Cyprus, and finally over Central Africa and Katanga, they remained isolated and impotent.[15]

In contrast, if there is one point on which French Socialist politicians, academic observers, and right-wing military officers are in agreement, it is that they all hold the manifold structural shortcomings of the governmental system under the Fourth Republic (pejoratively referred to as "le système") responsible for the terrible trials of French decolonization. Charles

11. David Goldsworthy, *Colonial Issues in British Politics, 1945–1961* (Oxford, 1971).

12. On party politics during decolonization, see especially Miles Edwin Kahler, "External Sources of Domestic Politics: Decolonization in Britain and France" (Ph.D. diss., Harvard University, 1977).

13. Goldworthy, *Colonial Issues*, pp. 166 ff.

14. Patrick Keatley, *The Politics of Partnership* (Harmondsworth, 1963), pp. 393 ff.

15. Ibid., pt. 5; Goldsworthy, *Colonial Issues*, chap. 8 and pp. 352 ff; Rudolph von Albertini, *Decolonization* (New York, 1971), pp. 245–47.

de Gaulle expressed with characteristic bluntness the sentiments of many when he replied in 1948 to an interviewer who inquired how he would "significantly modify the foreigh policy of France" should he return to power:

> I will not have to change the foreign policy of France since at present France has no foreign policy. Her regime does not permit it any more than it permits her to have an economic policy worthy of the name, a social policy, or a financial policy, etc. The truth is there is nothing. Thus I will not change this policy which does not exist, but I will make the policy of France.[16]

A general theory of the Republic's weakness could readily amalgamate the various criticisms of "le système" into a unified explanation of its difficulties.[17] Under both the Third and Fourth republics, the root cause of political weakness was to be found in political division which, although not so serious as to prevent a governing center coalition for France, nonetheless habitually precluded the unity indispensable for effective government. We are told[18] that this political division was the product of the simultaneous playing out of several historical conflicts wracking French society at large (Williams, Hoffman), of the difficulty of governing in the face of the cynical opposition of those who denied the entire system legitimacy (Aron), of French attitudes toward power which hindered the growth of effective authority relations (Crozier)—all aggravated by a form of constitutional government which, with its multiple parties and weak executive, exacerbated these conflicts in the very seat of power (Wahl, MacRae, Barale), and thus encouraged the irresponsibility of elected officials (Leites). Inability fed upon inability until the default of government authority reached such proportions that, at the first serious threat of military insubordination, the regime totally collapsed.

At first reading this seems to make good sense of the French experience and to contrast meaningfully with the case of British domestic institutions.

16. Charles de Gaulle, *La France sera la France* (Paris, 1951), p. 193.

17. The following comments are drawn from Smith, "The French Colonial Consensus."

18. Philip Williams, *Crisis and Compromise: Politics in the Fourth Republic* (New York, 1966); Stanley Hoffman, ed., *In Search of France* (New York, 1965); Raymond Aron, *Immuable et changeante: de la IVè à la Vè République* (Paris, 1959); Michel Crozier, *The Bureaucratic Phenomenon* (Chicago, 1964); D. MacRae, *Parliament, Parties and Society in France, 1946–1958* (New York, 1967): Jean Barale, *La Constitution de la IVè République à l'épreuve de la guerre* (Paris, 1963); Nicholas Wahl, "The French Political System," in Samuel Beer and Adam Ulam, eds., *Patterns of Government* (New York, 1962); Nathan Leites, *On the Game of Politics in France* (Stanford, 1959).

But on closer analysis this account reveals serious problems, as it neglects to point up the stubborn colonial consensus which held from the Socialists to the Right and which contributed as much to the ineffectiveness of the political system as this, in turn, made a sound policy impossible to agree upon or implement. For, as a review of the Indochinese policy of the Blum and Ramadier governments in 1946–47 and the Algerian policy of the Mollet Government of 1956–57 demonstrate, it was unity, resolution, and action which at these critical junctures of Socialist national leadership emerge as the hallmarks of the regime. What typified these truly decisive periods of Socialist leadership was not so much the shortcomings of the political system through which it had to govern, as its own unrealistic, tenaciously held positions on colonial matters. Admittedly, the French political system was a weak one whose divisions clearly complicated the reaction to colonial nationalism. But it is all too tempting to use the system as a scapegoat and so to forget the dedication of the Fourth Republic to an image of France which found its highest expression through de Gaulle: that to be internally stable, France required international greatness, and that to obtain this rank she must count on her empire since in this enterprise she had no certain friends.

Time and again throughout the history of the Fourth Republic, beneath the invective of political division one finds a shared anguish at the passing of national greatness, a shared humiliation at three generations of defeat, a shared nationalistic determination that France retain her independence in a hostile world—all brought to rest on the conviction that in the empire they would *maintenir.* Thus the Socialists shared with most of their fellow-countrymen an image of France, a kind of collective conscience, born of the political paralysis of the 1930s, the shame of the Occupation, the stern prophecies of General de Gaulle, the fear of domestic communism, and the initial expectations and ensuing disappointments of the Resistance. With most of their fellow-countrymen, they, too, experienced the loss of Indochina as the failure, not of a historically absurd colonial policy first launched by de Gaulle, but as the failure of a regime. They feared, then, that the decline of France to second-power status marked not so much an inevitable phase of world history as the inner failing of a people. The charges of being a *bradeur d'empire* raised much more profound self-doubt in the National Assembly than did charges of "scuttle" at Westminster.

Therefore, not only the political institutions of France and Great Britain were dissimilar but, perhaps more importantly, there were great contrasts between the national moods or psychologies of the political elites in these two countries. Where, for example, does one find in the annals of French leaders anything equivalent to the entry in the journal of Hugh Dalton, who closely followed Lord Mountbatten's handling of the independence of India, dated February 24, 1947?

> If you are in a place where you are not wanted and where you have not got the force, or perhaps the will, to squash those who don't want you, the only thing to do is to come out. This very simple truth will have to be applied to other places too, e.g., Palestine.[19]

One may object that this analysis fails to disaggregate sufficiently the constituent forces in each country. How important was it, for example, that Labour was in power immediately after the war and so could set an example in Britain of how to deal with colonial nationalism? Doubtless the influence of the Fabian colonial bureau and the work of Arthur Creech Jones as colonial secretary from late 1946 until 1950 had their positive impact. But it should be recalled that Socialists led the government in France as well in the crucial years 1946–47, when the decision to fight nationalism in Southeast Asia was made. Thus, at the very time when the British Socialists were deciding to hasten the withdrawal from India, the French Socialists were staging emotional appeals in the National Assembly in favor of supporting military action in Indochina.[20] The leaders of both parties wore socialist labels, but they were more clearly to be recognized by their national than by their party memberships.

In France there was one place where a realistic colonial policy was held. Despite the usually prejudiced attacks on the French Communist party's colonial stand, it was the PCF alone of the major parties in France which respected the historical limits of the moment and recognized very early the kind of flexibility a successful postwar imperial policy must possess. Thus, while the Party did tend to discourage independence movements in the empire, it preferred to work with them rather than repress them, seeking to ensure that, should separation become inevitable, it would occur under the auspices of a nationalist elite best able to represent the interests of the local population and preserve the area from the encroachments of foreign powers other than France. In these respects, the PCF compares well with the Labourites.[21]

19. Hugh Dalton, *High Tide and After: Memoirs 1945–1960* (London, 1962), p. 211.

20. For the very different attitudes of Prime Ministers Attlee and Ramadier, see the excerpts of parliamentary debates of 1946–47 reprinted in Tony Smith, *The End of European Empire: Decolonization after World War II* (Boston, 1975).

21. For a fuller discussion of Communist policy, see Tony Smith, *The French Stake in Algeria, 1945–1962* (Ithaca, N.Y., 1978); and Irwin M. Wall, "The French Communists and the Algerian War," *The Journal of Contemporary History*, vol. 12 (July 1977).

It is similarly difficult to argue that economic interests offer more than a partial explanation of the different patterns of decolonization, although Miles Kahler has shown that French interests were more basically concerned and that they found ways to vent their fears.[22] Kahler's evidence suggests that, in several respects, the relatively more mature British economic interests found the transfer of power easier to accommodate than the French: from the beginning British business and finance had been relatively more exposed to the strains of free trade and so were less likely to need a protectionist harbor guaranteed by direct colonial control; the large, diversified international firms and banks headquartered in Europe understood that they could cooperate with moderate nationalists better than with smaller European economic interests, the latter of which were more likely to be British; and the more advanced colonial economies under British rule threatened to compete with home industries, so that their independence was actually welcomed by an important part of the economic community. Of course, it is possible to find the hand of business wherever one wishes, in theoretically if not historically logical terms. So economic interests are damned if there is federation (in Nigeria, it is sometimes alleged, this allowed for more rational exploitation by outside groups) and equally damned if there is decentralization (in French West Africa, so one hears, these same interests would balkanize in order to divide and rule). But so long as nationalists were not avowed Communists, or, unlike Mossadegh in Iran and Nasser in Egypt, did not appear to represent threats to basic European overseas interests, leaders in Paris and London could realistically hope to count on the pressures of economic development to create a strong working arrangement with European business. Indeed, in some instances a strong leftist nationalist was to be preferred to a compliant but incompetent collaborator.

In short, disaggregation of the "nation" into its constituent political forces offers insights into specific periods or cases but does not appear to have conditioned the overall pattern of European decolonization. Just as military insubordination in France was far more a reflection of the national crisis than it was the cause, so other political forces at work are better understood in terms of their national context than with respect to their own power of initiative. None of these considerations is complete, however, unless we turn our attention from ideas and institutions of the European capitals to a study of the character of insurgent nationalism in the overseas empires.

22. Miles Kahler, "Decolonization," chap. 6.

However thorough a comparison might be made between the policies of Paris and London, such an approach focuses the study of decolonization too narrowly on the imperial capitals, neglecting the decisive role played by the peoples of Asia and Africa in their own liberation. For it is possible to trace the history of decolonization not in terms of European, but of Asian and African developments. The victory of Japan over Russia in 1904; Lenin's rise to power in 1917 and his subsequent aid to national elites striving to reduce European influence in their countries; the triumph of Mustafa Kemal in Turkey after World War I; the rise of Gandhi to leadership of the National Congress Party of India in 1920; the increasing importance of Cairo in Arab affairs following the defeat of efforts at Arab unity in World War I and the emergence of modern Egyptian nationalism under Saad Zaghlul Pasha; the rapid growth of colonial economies during the interwar period, with corresponding shifts in local social and political structures; the Japanese conquest of European colonies east of India and the hardships suffered by colonial peoples in all other parts of the globe during World War II; Kwame Nkrumah's return to the Gold Coast in December 1947; Mao Tse-tung's entry into Peking in January 1949—all these developments offer an alternative way of charting the course of history and analyzing its decisive movements.

From this perspective, concentration on the formal boundaries of empire or on events deemed significant in European capitals at the time risks obstructing our vision of those determining processes of history which occurred silently within colonial territories giving a local pedigree to nationalism, or which took place regionally without respect for imperial frontiers on the basis of communication among Asians or Africans. Looked at from this angle, history ran by other clocks, whose timing mechanisms synchronized only occasionally with the pacing of events in Europe. In order to form a just appreciation of the colonial problems facing Paris and London, our attention must turn from these capitals to Hanoi and Delhi, to Cairo and Algiers, to Accra and Abidjan.

Whatever their political values, what Bourguiba, Ataturk, Sukarno, Nkrumah, Nyerere, Ho Chi Minh, Bandhi, and Houphouët-Boigny all shared, was their leadership at the moment of national independence over groupings, both traditional and modern in values and structure, with a scope so broad that the split between the countryside and the city was overcome. Obviously such nationalist alliances varied enormously among themselves, depending on the interests represented, the solidity of the party apparatus aggregating anticolonial forces, the relative power of local groups outside the nationalist fold, and the international dangers which a young independence movement had to face. But it is, I believe, through an analysis of these forces that we can best elaborate a typology of colonial nationalism and so understand the contribution of the peoples of Asia and Africa to the character of the decolonization process. In a word, *who mobilized, or could claim to mobilize, the peasantry?* (In his essay in this volume, Jean Suret-Canale seems to be making somewhat the same point with respect to French sub-Saharan Africa.)

A comparison of reactions in black Africa and Madagascar to postwar French colonial policy with those of nationalists in Algeria and Indochina offers a good illustration of the importance of local conditions in determining this historical movement. For it is important to emphasize that *French policy was essentially the same throughout the empire:* political reforms were granted only so long as they could be seen tending to preserve French rule. Demands for change which might ultimately destroy the French presence were immediately to be squelched. De Gaulle was the chief architect of this plan, and he made its terms clear to the Vietnamese by his Declaration of March 25, 1945, which his successors in power reaffirmed in their negotiations with Ho Chi Minh at Fontainebleau in the summer of 1946. The Second Constituent Assembly adopted the same stand with the Algerians, and the first legislature of the Fourth Republic confirmed it in the terms of the Statute of Algeria voted in the summer of 1947. General Juin took the message to Morocco after having delivered it in Tunis. Marius Moutet, the Socialist colonial minister, was relying on the same view when he called for a boycott of the extraordinary conference called at Bamako, Soudan, by the black Africans under French rule in October 1946.

The French subsequently demonstrated the seriousness of their resolve. In November 1946 they shelled the port of Haiphong, taking the lives of several thousand Vietnamese in their determination to rid the city of the Vietminh. In March–April 1947, they responded to a nationalist raid on an army base on Madagascar with a repression which by official estimates killed 86,000. Since the Sétif repression of May 1945 had momentarily cowed the Algerians, rigged elections commencing in the spring of 1948 kept the peace in North Africa. But shortly thereafter, the French felt obliged to launch a concerted repression south of the Sahara against the Africans of the Rassemblement Démocratique Africain (RDA).

If the policy was the same, the results were not. Within a month of the French attack on Haiphong, the Vietminh had responded with a coup attempt in Hanoi. While the Sétif repression effectively fragmented the Algerian political elite for a time, a revolution willing to give no quarter finally broke out in 1954. But in black Africa the policy succeeded. A closer analysis of the situation there may suggest why by reviewing the variables mentioned earlier: the ability of a nationalist party to harness the forces it represents; the relative strength (actual or potential) of the party's local opponents; the degree of need of such a party for aid from the international system in order to maintain its local predominance. Thus, to understand the process of European decolonization means to perceive some particulars of the variety of colonial situations, as a French policy that was anachronistic in certain areas proved well suited to master the events in others. For instance, why did French policy succeed so well in Africa when it so totally failed elsewhere?

Immediately after World War II, African nationalism in the French territories found its most advanced expression in Senegal and the Ivory Coast. But as we shall see, it was the Ivory Coast which was quickly to emerge as the key territory in French policy south of the Sahara. Here the leading political formation was Félix Houphouët-Boigny's Parti Démocratique de Côte d'Ivoire (PDCI) which was founded on the base of the coffee and cocoa planters' voluntary association, the Syndicat Agricole Africaine (SAA). As president of the SAA, Houphouët had been elected to the French Constituent National Assembly, and there, in the spring of 1946, had proved instrumental in passing the legislation which ended the bitterly hated forced-labor regulations that were in effect throughout French Africa under the Third Republic and were intensified under Vichy. By this legislation, Houphouët was able, in one stroke, to secure a decisive advantage for his own class against the European planters in coffee and cocoa (who could not compete with the African without the help of cheap, requisitioned labor) and to enlist the support of the great mass of the territory's inhabitants who were subject to these terrible regulations. So Houphouët-Boigny, the largest planter in the Ivory Coast, became, in the words of Ruth Morgenthau, "a hero and liberator. This achievement was the beginning of a myth around Houphouët, the first truly national Ivory Coast tradition."[23] By October 1946, the PDCI had 65,000 members and was the largest party in French tropical Africa.

At the very time when the Ivory Coast was in the process of securing an initial measure of national unity behind Houphouët, the country found itself in increasing turmoil with the French administration. The economic aspects of the problem were familiar throughout the postwar world: shortages and inflation. But these were aggravated in the Ivory Coast by the sharp decline in world-market prices for coffee and cocoa, which together constituted 75 to 92 percent of the country's exports between 1947 and

23. Ruth S. Morgenthau, *Political Parties in French-Speaking West Africa* (Oxford, 1964), p. 181.

1957.[24] In the Territorial Assembly, at the same time, a number of political issues served gravely to divide the PDCI from the settler delegates and the colonial administration. What made these local issues a matter of intense concern to Paris, however, was the alliance which had grown up between the PDCI and the French Communist party, and the increasingly dominant role the PDCI was playing throughout the Federation of French West Africa (AOF).

In the first French Constituent Assembly (October 1945–May 1946), the African deputies had recognized both the Socialist and Communist parties as their allies in the effort to secure liberal reforms in colonial rule. Although the leaders of the Provisional Government assured the Africans that these reforms would not be modified whatever the fate of the first draft of the constitution, this promise was not kept. The combined pressures of settler lobbying, de Gaulle's warning that firmness must be displayed, and the need to come to some unequivocal stand in the negotiations with the Vietminh during the summer of 1946 worked together to produce a text in which the second Constituent Assembly (June–October 1946) defined the French Union in terms distinctly less liberal than those earlier proposed.[25] In response, therefore, some eight hundred delegates from French Africa assembled at Bamako in October 1946 to coordinate their efforts to secure liberal reforms. In an effort to sabotage the congress, Colonial Minister Moutet used his influence inside the Socialist party to convince affiliated Africans, most notably the Senegalese, to boycott the meeting. In the absence of the well-organized Senegalese, the PDCI with Houphouët at its head emerged as the unrivaled leader of both French West and Equatorial Africa through the creation of the interterritorial party, the Rassemblement Démocratique Africain (RDA). Several years later this was to prove critically important, when the issue of attaining independence as a federation arose and the unionists within the RDA found themselves cut off from their Senegalese allies outside and so less able to thwart what came to be Houphouët's goal of breaking the federation up into sovereign states. At the time, a boycott on the part of the French parties which had also been invited to the conference as observers meant that the Africans responded favorably to the one metropolitan party in attendance, the PCF. It was hardly surprising, then, that the newly formed RDA would affiliate itself (*apparentement*) with the Communists in the first legislature of the Fourth Republic elected in November 1946.

24. Aristide Zolberg, *One Party Rule in the Ivory Coast* (Princeton, 1969), p. 163.
25. Marshall, *Colonial Myth*, chaps. 5, 7, 8; Morgenthau, *Parties*, chaps. 2, 3.

With the exclusion of the Communists from the French government the following May, and especially with the railway strikes in West Africa in the fall of 1947, Paris began to anticipate the need to apply the same firm hand in West Africa that it had already shown in Indochina, Algeria, and Madagascar. In January 1948, Socialist deputy Paul Béchard was appointed governor-general of AOF and Orselli was named governor of the Ivory Coast. Initially these men pursued a somewhat conciliatory policy, trying to woo the RDA and the PDCI away from the Communists. But when this method showed no signs of progress, Orselli was replaced by Laurent Péchoux, and the administration cracked down to rid the territory of the RDA by the time of the elections to the second legislature in 1951. Naturally this repression (as it was frankly called) fell most heavily in the Ivory Coast. PDCI officials were imprisoned en masse, villages favorable to the Party found their taxes raised, and even pilgrims to Mecca were prohibited to leave if they were members of the Party. In a move familiar in all the French territories after the war, administrators reorganized electoral districts and rigged election results to favor their hand-picked candidates. The repression did not go unanswered. Between February 1949 and January 1950, the Party responded to these measures in kind. Hunger strikes, mass demonstrations, acts of civil disobedience, and actual street fighting took the lives of several score of Africans, while hundreds were injured and thousands arrested.[26]

For our concerns, the most striking thing about these developments is that ultimately the policy achieved its aims. Unlike the situations in Algeria or Indochina, but like the case of Madagascar, force worked. From the spring of 1950, when Houphouët-Boigny met with François Mitterrand in Paris and determined to break with the Communists, until the present day, France has had no better friend in Africa than Houphouët. Here, then, is the signal success of French decolonization, the exemplar of the policy of reform within order designed to guarantee a continued French presence in the overseas territories. It raises the obvious question of what factors were present in the case of the Ivory Coast that were lacking in Indochina and Algeria.

The most serious problem immediately facing Houphouët-Boigny in the period from February 1949 to January 1950 was the inadequacy of his party organization. Relative to other political formations in French Africa, the PDCI may have seemed a potent force, but it simply could not tolerate the pressures put upon it by the French administration. It should be recalled that the PDCI only came into existence in 1946, and that it built on the

26. Zolberg, *Ivory Coast*, pp. 131 ff.; Morgenthau, *Parties*, pp. 188 ff.

foundation of the SAA, created just two years earlier. While it is true that the SAA associated tribal chiefs with commoners and that Houphouët had important credentials both as a planter and as the scion of a leading chiefly family, this fact simply did not bear enough weight to oppose the French. The root weakness of the party seems to have been the tribal structure of the country (indeed, wherever we turn in colonial situations these "primordial divisions"—to use Clifford Geertz's term—constitute the basic obstacle to party formation, regardless of whether the society is "tribal" or "peasant").

The PDCI was, in fact, an "indirect party" in the sense that its structure depended more on the loyalty of elites who had their bases independent of party control than on authority the party could muster on its own account. Beneath its upper levels, party structure mirrored rather than bridged the cleavages within society at large. Once the top split, the party, devoid of horizontal linkages at lower levels, simply fragmented into its constituent parts. As Aristide Zolberg puts it, "the structures created in 1947 helped maintain ethnic ties even when economic and social change might have diminished their importance . . . basic party units coincided with ethnic wards, and party life also reinforced ethnicity. . . . Those who were particularly responsible for party organization knew that its machinery was adequate only for electoral purposes."[27] What occurred under French pressure was, quite simply, the disaggregation of this elite, as some succumbed to hopes for personal gain while others responded to fears of personal loss.

This alone, however, cannot explain Houphouët's capitulation to the French. Other parties at other times have been fractured by repression only to arise more powerful thereafter. Is it not conceivable that Houphouët could have gone over the heads of his fellow party leaders to the people, retired to the bush, and begun a war of national liberation against the French? If a West African specialist might balk at the idea, certainly a student of Asian politics would not. Houphouët was, after all, widely agreed to have charismatic personal qualities, and the election results after his reconciliation with France suggest that, in the eyes of the people, his previous opposition had served to heighten his prestige. But this is not the course of action Houphouët chose, and while the reasons may seem apparent to the Africanist, they may be illuminating for a comparative study of decolonization which attempts to encompass the Middle East and Asia. In a word, as the largest planter in the Ivory Coast, Houphouët-Boigny realized the obvious: that the future of his class, and thereby of his people, lay with

27. Zolberg, *Ivory Coast*, pp. 143, 237; Morgenthau, *Parties*, pp. 188 ff.

France. Mobilize the peasantry? Conduct guerrilla warfare? Nothing seemed less probable. As this Catholic, this traditional chief, this leading spokesman of the African bourgeoisie put it to his compatriots at the opening of a fair in 1953: "If you don't want to vegetate in bamboo huts, concentrate your efforts on growing good cocoa and good coffee. They will fetch a good price and you will become rich."[28]

In order to promote these export crops, the Ivory Coast of the early 1950s needed the cooperation of France, for the former country produced only 3 percent of the world's coffee output, and this of an inferior quality, which made it especially vulnerable to price fluctuations on the international market. Under a 1954 agreement with France, however, Ivory Coast coffee (accounting in those days for some 57 percent of its total exports) received both a quota guarantee and a price floor in metropolitan markets.[29] The growing middle class of African planters, along with their upper-class colleagues on the great estates, depended for their livelihood on the stability of these contracts.

Houphouët-Boigny and the interests he represented faced another challenge as well: the threat of incorporation into a federal West Africa. Since 1904, French practice had been to finance the entire federation from indirect taxes levied throughout the area. Wealthier territories perennially complained about this practice in the Grand Council in Dakar, but to no avail. After 1945, the Ivory Coast confirmed a trend begun earlier, so that by the mid-1950s it was the undisputed economic leader of the AOF, accounting for 45 percent of the region's exports. As a result of the federation's taxing system, the Ivory Coast received an average of only 19 percent of the money it remitted to Dakar. These taxes paid to the federal authority amounted, in turn, to two or three times the amount collected and retained locally, so that of the total governmental revenue levies in the Ivory Coast, well over half left never to return. In addition, the area has traditionally been a heavy importer of labor from other territories, so that by the 1950s some one-fourth of the work force came from outside the Ivory Coast and the percentage was growing.[30]

In order to make good its separation from French West Africa, the Ivory

28. Cited in Zolberg, *Ivory Coast*, p. 151. Tribal cultivators are, of course, very different from peasants, so that for reasons of social structure they may be more difficult to mobilize in revolution.

29. Elliot J. Berg, "The Economic Basis of Political Choice in French West Africa," *American Political Science Review* 54 (1960):290; Zolberg, *Ivory Coast*, p. 165.

30. On taxes and migrant labor, see Zolberg, *Ivory Coast*, pp. 159 ff., 41; and for more recent figures on migrant labor, U.S. Department of State, *Handbook for the Ivory Coast*, 1973, p. xvii.

Coast needed the support of France, for throughout the federation in the early 1950s the mood was for union. Houphouët's preference for decentralization met with opposition from Léopold Senghor from outside the RDA, while from within the party, Sékou Touré of Guinea began to challenge the Ivory Coast leadership. As a result of French support, however, Houphouët could disregard the opinions of his fellow West Africans. The French National Assembly's framework law of March–April 1957 severely weakened the federal authority of the AOF by transferring certain of its powers to Paris and devolving others onto the reinforced territorial assemblies. Senghor complained of the "balkanization" of West Africa, and most observers have agreed with him that this was the conscious intention of France.[31] At the Bamako RDA Conference held in September 1957, Touré was much more popular than Houphouët (who found his only backing from wealthy Gabon), but the Ivory Coast's Paris connections made it quite invulnerable to African objections.

Before the territorial assemblies had fully assumed their new prerogatives, however, the Fourth Republic fell. The French scheme of things for Africa was now expressed in de Gaulle's idea of the "French Community." By the terms of the Fifth Republic's Constitution, Africans had two choices: either "federation" in subordination to France, or independence. In other words, the policy of the Fifth Republic was essentially the same as that of the Fourth so far as African federations were concerned. They could expect no comfort from Paris, for France would not support a gradual evolution toward a federal structure for the AOF which reduced metropolitan control. (The contrast with the British in Nigeria during the same period is striking. Here the pressures for decentralization—at least after the Richards' Constitution of 1946—came from the Africans themselves, and especially from the Northern Region.)

A comparison of the Ivory Coast with other colonial situations suggests that the key variable to analyze in order to understand the colonial response to metropolitan policy is the local power position of the predominant nationalist elite. For every war of colonial liberation carries within it a civil conflict, so that in fact the nationalist elite is fighting on two fronts: against the imperial power and against other local groups striving to replace it. Dominant elites are therefore prudent to avoid armed confrontation with the imperial authority. This is not only because it is sensible to recognize that, given the great disproportion of military resources, it is mostly their fellow citizens who will be killed. The elites understand as well that the first

31. This judgment is shared by Morgenthau, Zolberg, Michael Crowder, and Pierre Gonidec, among others.

military setbacks they can expect to suffer may well release the centrifugal forces of class and ethnic division which so profoundly mark most colonial societies. Since warfare in the colonial context will almost inevitably be a protracted, decentralized affair, the initially dominant nationalist elite may find their position subsequently assumed by rival leaders. It is, after all, a theme of nationalist fairy tales that nationalism feeds on its own reversals, rising from the earth each time more powerful than before, until the entire "people" is united on that great day of liberation. In fact, as closer inspection of virtually any colonial situation will warrant, there are a variety of nationalist movements behind what, to the casual observer, may seem like a single wave of nationalism, and these diverse groups frequently are seriously at odds.

Thus civil war lurks in the heart of every movement for national liberation. Thus, shortly after the signing of the Anglo-Irish Treaty of 1921, serious strife broke out within Ireland and lasted for two years before the Provisional Government was able to bring it under control. The terms of the dispute continued to mar Irish life for decades thereafter. Again, in the very midst of fighting the Dutch effort to regain the Netherlands East Indies, the Communists attempted a coup against the Hatta-Sukarno government (the Madiun Rebellion of 1948) which the Indonesian army never forgot. In the case of Tunisia, Bourguiba found his agreement to "internal autonomy" as a prelude to eventual independence hotly contested by Salah ben Youssef, secretary-general of the Neo-Destour party, who secured important backing within the country as well as from the Algerians and the Egyptians. Only because his leadership of the nationalist movement was so undisputed could Kwame Nkrumah accept the 1950 constitution for the Gold Coast, which offered him a good deal less than independence. What he must certainly have feared was that his continued recalcitrance would prompt the British to support the separatist movement in Ashanti and the Northern Territories (as they might easily have done). "We have no program but independence," declared the Moroccan Istiqlal party in the early 1950s. This made good sense indeed for a party that represented landed interests in a country where 60 percent of the rural population was landless and the nationalist movement was divided into three autonomous forces. It was the same slogan adopted by the Wafd party in Egypt on the occasion, in 1951, of their unilateral abrogation of the Anglo-Egyptian Treaty of 1936. But the Wafd quickly saw things pass out of its hands with the mobilization of the Muslim Brotherhood and the Free Officers, and the coup against the monarchy in 1952. More wisely than the Wafd, Ho Chi Minh avoided confrontation with the French until it was literally forced upon him, realizing that whatever the apparent strength of the Vietminh, Indochina was far from securely in its grasp in 1946. In the case of the Ivory Coast, there is a slight variation in this pattern. For what Houphouët-Boigny had to fear was not so much local as federal interference with his position. That is, other forces in the AOF constituted the functional equivalent of an internal threat to his leadership. (G. S. K. Ibingira's chapter in this volume points to the similar importance of ethnic cleavages in Uganda.)

Yet however reluctant virtually any nationalist elite may be to enter into war against the imperial authority, such confrontations do occur, and we must investigate further to see the possibility of establishing categories of nationalist leadership, determining in each case its likelihood of heading a militant insurrection. Dominant groups *least likely* to mount a sustained challenge to the colonial order are those which recognize the fragility of their local control and the interest they may well have in a European connection. In his contribution to this volume, Elikia M'Bokolo points to an instance of this form of collaboration in French Equatorial Africa around 1960. Politically and economically more complex and dynamic systems may want to collaborate as well, however. A particularly clear case of this, as we have seen, is the Ivory Coast. Here local factors (the threat of the AOF to incorporate the territory) combined with international considerations (the preferential treatment given in French markets to coffee and cocoa production, the economic basis of the ruling class) to dictate a policy of prudence toward Paris. Not that an elite based on export revenues is necessarily a willing collaborator with European interests—Colonel Qadhafi of Libya is evidence enough of this. But even in the case of Qadhafi, it should be recalled that petroleum products have demonstrated a special immunity to international pressures, and that even this is true only of the present period, as the experience of Prime Minister Mossadegh testifies.

The royal court of Cambodia provides another instance of elite collaboration with the Europeans. The Cambodian king welcomed the French return since this promised to destroy the antimonarchical forces the Japanese had fielded before their defeat and to return to his rule the territory seized by Thailand during the Second World War. Royal courts do not make the best collaborators, of course, since economic development tends to advance classes whose attitudes undermine their legitimacy. European interests are most effectively represented, rather, by what may be called an import-export elite whose capacity to develop economically—even if only within certain limits—allows it to cooperate usefully with the international system while at the same time assuring domestic stability.

In light of the foregoing analysis, what sorts of nationalist elites may be expected to enter into violent conflict with an imperial regime? Three situations tend to produce such leaders: where a native elite dependent on foreign power has never been created; where such an elite, once created, is destroyed; where such an elite has been displaced by the rise of a rival political formation. Each of these ideal types has its historical example.

The case of Algeria is one where a strong Muslim elite which depended for its position on the good favor of the French was simply never created. The role of a local native elite was preempted by the settlers. As a result, the rise of an important Gallicized Muslim class failed to occur, and it became increasingly likely as the twentieth century progressed that the terrible grievances of the Muslim peasantry would be directly expressed against the French instead of being mediated by a native bourgeoisie. To be sure, there were the various bourgeois movements associated with Ferhat Abbas and Dr. Bendjelloul which had a certain activity from the mid-1920s until the mid-1940s; but these never created any ties with the masses. In retrospect, they must be seen as highly visible but politically insignificant compared to the efforts of Messali Hadj and the Reformist Muslim Ulama who gave a popular base to opposition to the French. Once the revolution began in November 1954, the French sought desperately for some group with authority with whom they could negotiate a settlement on better terms than those held out by the National Liberation Front (FLN). None was found, partly because the history of rigged elections served to stigmatize any Algerian who worked with the French as their puppet, but more importantly because the class of people who might have seen their future interests tied to France and who might have feared a radical peasant uprising just did not exist in any important number.[32]

In the case of Indochina, a nationalist elite that might have had an interest in cooperating with the French after 1945 was destroyed. Here the decisive factor was the Japanese Occupation. As George M. Kahin and John W. Lewis write:

> Japan's role in Indochina was radically different from her occupation of any other Southeast Asian country. In the rest of the colonies there, the Japanese realized the advantage of working through the native elites, whom they regarded as more satisfactory instruments of administration than Western colonial civil servants. In order to secure the support of the educated indigenous groups in these other areas, the Japanese were obliged to grant them concessions. . . . The one great exception was Indochina. There the pro-Vichy French administration was willing to come to terms with the Japanese. . . . Thus, during the war the major channel open to those Vietnamese who wished to free their country from

32. Smith, *The French Stake*, chaps. 4–6.

> Japanese, and ultimately French, control was an underground movement where Vietnamese communists already had a strong and entrenched position.[33]

Other developments contributed to making it difficult to find a local counterweight to the Communists after 1945. Economically, the French presence in the 1930s had rested on the investments of a number of large capitalist firms like Michelin, the activities of a Chinese merchant class (with their families totaling perhaps 4 percent of the country's population), and the influence of a few thousand wealthy landowners whose property for the most part was located in the Mekong Delta.[34] In addition, between 1929 and 1932, the French had liquidated the most important non-Communist opposition to their rule when a combination of the Tan Viet and the Viet Nam Quoc Dan Dang had risen against them. Despite the simultaneous suppression of Communist insurgents in Nghe-Tinh Province in 1930–31, the Indochinese Communist party (ICP) proved far more resilient than their fellow Vietnamese nationalists. Thus the economic base on which a collaborating nationalist elite might stand was exceedingly narrow, while politically the French repressions of the thirties and the occupation of the early forties worked to the advantage of the Communists.

While these considerations suggest that the French presence in Southeast Asia would have to be drastically modified after 1945, one is not justified in concluding immediately that a Communist-sponsored peasant revolution would necessarily triumph there in the end; for the congeries of political forces existing in Vietnam that the Communists did not control—the Catholics, the Cao Dai, the Hoa Hao, and perhaps even the Buddhists—might have been welded together with other potentially anti-Communist forces to split the union of communism with nationalism. Thus, had the French seriously backed Bao Dai in 1947 and granted his demands for the unity and independence of Vietnam as they apparently debated doing, Cochin China might effectively have been denied to Ho Chi Minh, and in the process the Cambodian monarchy preserved. Paris could have counted on the threat from the north to persuade Bao Dai to limit his claims to sovereignty in favor of a veiled French presence. However much one may admire the Communist-led Vietnamese Liberation Movement, it does not do justice to its achievement to assume that its

33. George M. Kahin and John W. Lewis, *The United States in Vietnam* (New York, 1967), pp. 14–15.

34. John T. McAlister, Jr., *Viet Nam: The Origins of Revolution* (New York, 1969), chap. 6; and Joseph Buttinger, *Vietnam: A Political History* (New York, 1968), chap. 9.

victory was somehow inevitable. In Malaya, where admittedly the Communists were in a more difficult situation for a variety of reasons than their counterparts in Vietnam, a crucial part of the final British success was their willingness to respect the independent power base of Tengku Abdul Rahman, head of the Alliance party associating Malays with Chinese, in order to crush the insurgents. Perhaps the "Bao Dai formula" would have failed whatever the French position, for as the preceding analysis shows, the social structure there was not favorable to the French return. But one must be cautious not to confuse the political predispositions of a particular structure with a necessary historical outcome.

There is a third type of situation in which a nationalist elite may be expected to oppose the colonial order on the basis of its local power position. This is the case of a national manufacturing bourgeoisie whose rise displaces the previously dominant elite in the name of tariffs to protect their young industries and, for the sake of more rational agricultural production, to feed the urban proletariat and increase rural demand for manufactured goods. Such a situation is illustrated by India. Here the alliance of the peasantry and the rising urban bourgeoisie brought about by Gandhi after 1920 through the vehicle of the National Congress party created the force which eventually would evict the British.[35] The roots of this manufacturing bourgeoisie lay in the 1850s in the textile mills of Bombay and the jute industry of Calcutta. The *Swadeshi* movement, which began in 1905 over the British decision to partition Bengal, involved a boycott of British goods in favor of domestic products, so demonstrating to this bourgeoisie in tangible terms the utility of nationalism. But the period of greatest expansion for this group began after World War I when the British permitted the first important protective tariffs for India, since it was increasingly the Japanese who were profiting from the subcontinent's low custom duties.[36]

At the same time the Indian manufacturing bourgeoisie was gaining strength, Gandhi was effectively extending the nationalist creed to the Indian peasantry. His first great success was his 1920 program of "full noncooperation" with the Constitution of 1919, but he gained still wider support in the early 1930s with his world-famous campaigns of civil disobedience. However much Gandhi may have inveighed against the evils of the modern world, preached the rights of Untouchables, and promoted the interests of factory workers, it also seems correct to stress that his respect

35. The importance of this alliance for the political development of India is given central importance by Barrington Moore, Jr., *Social Origins of Dictatorship: Lord and Peasant in the Making of the Modern World* (Boston, 1966), pp. 370 ff.

36. Angus Maddison, *Class Structure and Economic Growth: India and Pakistan since the Moghuls* (London, 1971), chap. 3.

for property rights and insistence on nonviolence gave the Indian industrialists no serious cause for alarm. Simultaneously, Gandhi provided the ideological vehicle whereby the peasantry and the manufacturing elite could join forces.[37]

Indian specialists seem agreed that had the British not granted independence to the subcontinent within the first few years after the end of World War II, there would have been a revolution.[38] The Congress party declared its militancy clearly in its 1942 "Quit India" resolution, and the incidents of the interwar years combined with scattered disturbances in the military immediately after the surrender of Japan to make British minds turn once again to memories of the Great Mutiny of 1857. India would be done with the British.

Nevertheless, it is not clear that the organization of interests which ultimately brought India to independence would have maintained its hold on the country had an intense revolution of long duration been necessary. For not only was there the serious problem of minorities, and especially the Muslims, but there was a destitute class of peasants as well, whom revolution would doubtlessly rouse to political activity. An official study of landholding in India (exclusive of Pakistan) in 1953–54, found that 23 percent of the rural households were landless, another 24 percent owned less than one acre, while 14 percent owned between one and two and a half acres.[39] One may legitimately speculate in these circumstances on the fate of the 3.5 percent of the population who were reported (in what was certainly an underestimate of their property since the census was part of an effort to reduce large holdings) to own 36 percent of the land. As it was:

> India has been governed since independence by a coalition consisting of the bureaucratic-military establishment, which implements policy, the big business groups, which have backed Congress financially, the rank and file politicians who mainly represent the rural squirearchy and richer peasants, and the intellectuals who articulate policy. . . . [Nehru] was a leftist flanked by conservatives who know from experience that it was not worth opposing progressive resolutions or legislation which were not likely to be implemented.[40]

The case of India presents us, then, with a nationalist elite which would surely have hesitated long before launching into revolution, but which gave

37. Moore, *Social Origins*, pp. 373 ff.

38. See, among others, Francis Hutchins, *India's Revolution: Gandhi and the Quit India Movement* (Cambridge, Mass., 1973).

39. Maddison, *Class Structure*, p. 106; Moore, *Social Origins*, pp. 368 ff.

40. Maddison, *Class Structure*, p. 89; Moore, *Social Origins*, pp. 385 ff.

every indication of pursuing such a course should the British prove obstinate and refuse to grant independence. It is to the credit of British statesmanship that they could view the changed status of such an important possession so realistically and attempt as best they could to harmonize their interests with the future of a country which, for over a century, had been the base of their foreign policy from the Mediterranean to China.

The foregoing case studies offer examples of a spectrum of colonial responses to the maintenance of European rule after 1945, ranging from militant revolutionary opposition to the call for independence within the framework of a continuing European presence. They are not intended to establish rigid, predictive models for the likelihood of colonial uprisings, but to establish instead a heuristic typology. The factor which this study suggests should be most closely analyzed is the place the momentarily predominant elite occupies in respect to the double challenge it faces: that from the international system and that from local rivals. Import–export elites and traditional rulers are threatened in both respects and are well-advised to moderate their nationalist demands in order to assure continued foreign support for their regimes. On the other hand, a national manufacturing elite allied with rural forces representing more than a handful of great landlords is clearly more able to press its autonomous claims. But it must avoid if possible the radical suggestion to push for an all-out war of national liberation, as it should recognize that the radicals intend to take advantage of popular mobilization, not only to oust the foreigners, but to create a revolution from below and be done with them as well. By this same token, the most militant elite will be one which fears no local rivals—since none exists to any politically significant degree—and at the same time sees the outsiders with whom it must deal as the inveterate enemy of its most essential demands.

In these respects, Algeria and Indochina were idiosyncratic in the challenge they posed to France. These two colonies simply had no genuine parallels in the British experience. Kenya might be thought comparable to Algeria, but in essential respects this was not the case. For how could this relatively insignificant East African land be the equivalent to the British of what Algeria meant to France: the home of more than 2 percent of the national population; the location of badly needed petroleum resources; and a strategic outpost of France whose capital, Algiers, was only 500 miles southwest of Marseille? It was largely because Kenya was so unimportant that the British could arrange for the sale of the European farms to the Africans at full value and so create, virtually overnight, an export elite on whom they could base their postindependence relations.[41] In Algeria, to the contrary, the incomparably more powerful settler presence negated any attempt to create a politically important Muslim bourgeoisie. Nor could the French copy the example of the Republic of South Africa and cut themselves off from their North African territory. This was not because of "centralizing traditions," but because, unlike South Africa, Algeria was far too poor for a small minority of the population to maintain its rule without constant aid from the outside. For these reasons—which had to do with Algeria and not with France—withdrawal was especially difficult. Had the French had the experiences and institutions of the British it is not evident that they would have responded more ably to the crisis.

This chapter has reviewed a range of factors determining the character of the process of European decolonization, with special emphasis on Africa. I have attempted to stress the distinctive contribution to this great historical movement of the colonial peoples themselves: the character of their economic, social, and political organization. At the same time, I should emphasize that I am not at all persuaded that the history of the expansion and contraction of European empire is best understood by giving primary emphasis to the study of the "periphery" or colonial areas, in the manner of John Gallagher, Ronald Robinson, and D. K. Fieldhouse,[42] or of Henri Brunschwig in his chapter in this volume. In my opinion, the decisive events in world history continue to be determined by the actions of the industrial powers. Thus the study of decolonization must reflect centrally the impact of the Second World War, the relations of the European countries with the United States, and the formative impact of France and Britain (as well as Portugal and Belgium) on their colonial possessions. Africans have nonetheless had an important hand in the making of their history, and one can hope that this will increasingly be the case, without at the same time supposing that the power of industrial Europe was, or is today, without critical importance to the character of modern Africa.

41. Colin Leys, *Underdevelopment in Kenya: The Political Economy of Neo-Colonialism, 1964–1971* (Berkeley, 1974).

42. See William Roger Louis, *Imperialism: The Robinson and Gallagher Controversy* (New York, 1976), and D. K. Fieldhouse, *Economics and Empire, 1830–1914* (Ithaca, N.Y., 1973).

5. *Toward the Transfer of Power in British West Africa*

JOHN D. HARGREAVES

After 1865, the year of an often quoted and often misunderstood parliamentary committee, the transfer of power in British West Africa was a subject to which far less thought was given in Great Britain than among Africans. For supporters of empire, the question was removed from the agenda when vast new imperial commitments were undertaken during the partition. Among the critics, anti-imperialists who aimed at the destruction of colonial empire were always fewer and less effective than those who aimed to transform colonial dominance into more just (and so potentially more durable) forms of relationship. Under economic and political pressures during the interwar years, the ideas and programs of colonial reformers began increasingly to penetrate the "policy-making elite." The Colonial Development and Welfare Act of 1940 crowned the first phase of a major reappraisal. But despite political rhetoric concerning gradual progress toward self-government, ambiguity persisted about the political goals toward which the new "planned colonial policy" would lead West Africa; economic and social development could equally well culminate with their closer incorporation into the empire-commonwealth system as in a transfer of political power. At the outbreak of the Second World War, constitutional changes in central government remained very low on the working agenda of West African administrations.

The opening of official British archives allows us to study that agenda, and the gradual transformation of its priorities, with greater precision than before. Snap judgments on this subject may be dangerous; the Colonial Office, like all the machinery of British government, was growing increasingly complex in its internal organization, and in its capacity to intervene in the colonies,[1] and essays like this, which are based on evidence relating to a portion of the field, are liable to grotesque distortions of perspective. The first and longest section of this chapter will nevertheless attempt to show

1. On this, see J. M. Lee, "'Forward Thinking' and War: The Colonial Office in the 1940s," *Journal of Imperial and Commonwealth History* 6 (1977): 64–79.

how, under the intensive and complex pressures generated by the war, new constitutional policies were evolved through dialogues between the Colonial Office and the West African periphery. Within the colonies, it seems that governors still largely held the initiative, anticipating rather than responding to powerful African pressure for political change. Later sections of the chapter, which more briefly review relatively well-known evidence about the postwar period of political transfer, naturally place greater emphasis on effective initiatives taken by Africans, though I do not attempt here to analyze these in depth. But it appears that much of the thrust of the wartime policies was maintained, even though the greatly accelerated timetable which it was necessary to adopt produced fundamental changes in the expected effects.

The new thinking generated by the Depression of the 1930s had largely been focused on "development policy" and the extension of social welfare, rather than on political change as a policy in itself. As far as West Africa is concerned, political thought centered on methods of applying Lugardian principles of Indirect Rule to "native administration," their general suitability being taken for granted. In theory, indirect rule provided a framework within which the conflicting claims of "progress and security" could be reconciled in various ways; in practice, "security" usually won. At their best, Native Authorities were like vintage cars—elaborate and dignified structures with little capacity for acceleration and strong tendencies to steer to the right. The great extensions now envisaged in the responsibilities of colonial government made it urgent to improve the capacity of such bodies to discharge them, and in the longer term raised the question of their role in an ultimate political future tacitly assumed to involve "self-government based on representative institutions."[2]

The problem may be rephrased with reference to the view that the character of colonial rule depended on "the indigenous collaborative systems connecting its European and Afro-Asian components."[3] British rule in West Africa rested on the active participation in local administration of supposedly "traditional" rulers, operating under various degrees of direction from above; and on the acquiescence of a small Western-educated "national bourgeoisie," who were permitted access to a narrow range of professional and business opportunities, to the junior levels of public office, and to a narrowly circumscribed "sphere of civic usefulness" in a few ports

2. Hailey, *An African Survey* (1938), pp. 529, 537–42, 1639.

3. Ronald Robinson, "Non-European Foundations of European Imperialism: Sketch for a Theory of Collaboration," in R. Owen and Bob Sutcliffe, eds., *Studies in the Theory of Imperialism* (London, 1972), p. 138.

and capitals. The many frustrations of this latter group had so far been contained within a framework of empire loyalism by the distant prospect that they would one day inherit control of the colonial state. Hitherto this day had seemed too distant to be relevant to the daily concerns of colonial administrations; but if Africans were to collaborate in the new roles required by the development policy, they might reasonably expect some clearer statement of political prospects.

The outbreak of war, which placed new demands on Africans for servicing of ports and airfields, increased production of raw materials, and service in the armed forces, made it still more urgent to redefine the political basis of collaboration. Early perception of this fact lay behind the extended tour of British African colonies which Lord Hailey was asked to undertake in December 1939. His ostensible mission was to follow up his magisterial *African Survey* by more detailed study of Native Administration in the several colonies; but, as West African governors were told, he was to do this in a wider political context:

> It may be that one of the results of the war will be to stimulate the political consciousness of Africans and to give emphasis to the demand for a quickened pace of development towards more representative and liberal institutions of government. In any case it seems very desirable from the standpoint of high policy that H.M.G. should attempt now to clarify in their own minds the important problem of the future development of unofficial African representation in Legislative Councils in relation to the evolution of indirect rule and the future development of native administration. Important decisions may have to be taken to prevent Native Administrations on the one hand and Legislative Councils on the other from developing upon diverging lines.[4]

This did not imply any drastic shift of priorities from economic toward constitutional reform. Indeed, the immediate effect of the war was to sharpen the British government's commitment to initiate and carry through long-term programs of colonial development and reconstruction. In April 1941, Hailey, while still drafting his report, was asked to chair a Colonial Office committee consisting of four assistant under-secretaries with the wide remit of "post-war reconstruction in the colonies." The agenda[5] of

4. Macdonald to West African Governors, December 18, 1939, quoted in C.O. 847/21/47100/1/1941. The wording to East African governors was slightly different, and that to Central Africa referred to conversations with Huggins "as to the possibility of coordinating native policy in Southern Rhodesia, Northern Rhodesia and Nyasaland."

5. The agenda (revised in April 1942) and records of four early meetings are in C.O. 967/13.

over fifty headings which it produced had the effect of stimulating enquiry and formulation of views throughout the Office. Priority was given to economic problems likely to arise in the direct aftermath of war and to improving the capacity of colonial governments to handle the technical problems of longer-term development. Constitutional and political matters were less prominent; and the general conclusions which Hailey drew from his mission did not provide unambiguous guidance.

In many ways, *Native Administration and Political Development in British Tropical Africa* is a far-sighted document. Hailey foresaw a continuing growth of "African racial consciousness" and of the influence of the African middle class; his Indian experience added extra weight to his perception of "rapid change, and of greater changes impending," and to his rhetorical questions, "Can we be sure of the continuance of that degree of acquiescence in our rule which is a necessary condition of administrative progress?" But Hailey doubted whether acquiescence could be secured by what he disparagingly called "constitution-mongering"; his approach was, rather, to identify potential political and administrative elites who could gradually be trained to assume the enlarged responsibilities of the colonial state. As required by his brief, he concentrated upon the diverse problems of "native administration"; while decisively rejecting the idea that, even in Northern Nigeria, Native Authorities were embryonic states with "inherent rights" which might become the direct heirs of colonial sovereignty, Hailey did regard them as the key, not only to efficient local government, but to constitutional advance.[6] When eventually it became necessary to reconstitute the central legislatures, regional councils, based upon reformed authorities, would become channels for indirect election which could be trusted to return hardheaded men of the people.[7] Even the conservative Lord Moyne found this emphasis on "local tribal institutions" as the major channel of political advance and education over-cautious and "hardly democratic."[8]

The political philosophy implicit in Hailey's approach was still dominant in Colonial Office and colonial service a year later, when his reports were

6. Quotations are from chapter 1 of this report [NAPD], which was confidentially printed in 1942 but submitted in cyclostyled form in March 1941 (C.O. 847/21/47100/1).

7. Cf. this sentence, deleted at Burns's suggestion before the printing of Hailey's Report on the Gold Coast: ". . . when dealing with such questions as the extent to which electoral systems should be introduced into the townships, due weight should be given to the consideration that a broad policy of concessions in local government may make it easier for the Government to feel its way with some caution in planning constitutional changes." C.O. 847/22/47100/9.

8. Note of Hailey's discussion with Moyne and others, March 18, 1941, C.O. 847/21/47100/1/1941.

printed for wide circulation among officials and suitable outside persons.[9] But now the case for some clearer declaration of political intent had become much strengthened by disputes over the interpretation of the Atlantic Charter, by America's entry into the war, and by the traumatic shock of the fall of Singapore. Despite Churchill's well-known addiction to imperial ideas, it was essential to convince allies and potential allies that victory would bring positive benefits to Britain's colonial subjects; it was equally urgent to convince West African collaborators of this, as the demands of the war effort upon them were intensified. Statements of long-term policy would hardly do; nor would municipal reform, which few West Africans accepted as a sufficient "sphere of civic usefulness." The need to supplement indirect rule by more imaginative gestures was understood by Sir Alan Burns, who, having served on Hailey's reconstruction committee during secondment to the Colonial Office, went to the Gold Coast as governor in October 1941.

Born in 1887 in Saint Kitts into a third generation of colonial civil servants, Burns had divided a distinguished career between the Caribbean (he governed British Honduras from 1934 to 40) and Nigeria (of which country in 1929 he published a history that is still frequently cited). Though paternalistic and even authoritarian in many of his attitudes (as might befit Lugard's former A.D.C.),[10] Burns had acquired a reputation among his Colonial Office colleagues for an "ardent temperament" that was liable to express itself particularly strongly on matters of color prejudice (on which subject he published a book in 1948).[11] A devout Catholic, Burns prided himself on his ability to cooperate with Africans according to their character and abilities—he later collaborated with an eminent Ghanaian in writing a pamphlet designed to reduce racial misunderstanding;[12] but by the same token he could react strongly against African politicians who failed to measure up to his own strict ethical standards. Though capable of expressing remarkably libertarian views for a governor,[13] he found it difficult to main-

9. On the question of publication and circulation, see the interesting discussion in C.O. 847/21/47100/1/1942, 1943.

10. His interesting autobiography, *Colonial Civil Servant* (London, 1949) does not seem to do full justice to his readiness to innovate within the limits of current assumptions.

11. Minute by Gater on Williams draft of January 20, 1943; C.O. 96/774/31336; minute by Dawe, June 5, 1943, C.O. 96/770/31013/5/1943.

12. Alan Burns and Robert Gardiner, *Other People, Other Ways: Some Suggestions to Africans and Europeans Visiting One Another's Countries* (London, 1950).

13. For example, Burns to Parkinson, January 24, 1942, C.O. 96/770/31032, refusing to allow the director of education power to close African schools—"to my mind the liberty of subject (even the African subject) is of more importance even than education"; Burns to Williams, June 29, 1943, C.O. 96/776/31486.

tain them when faced with a challenge to colonial authority or colonial values. Nevertheless, his abundant energy and good will, and his recognition that the times called for active imperial initiatives, were to prove valuable assets during difficult years. Before leaving London he discussed with Moyne a range of desirable reforms: increased Africanization of senior posts (including some in district administration), ending of residential segregation, municipal reform, extended African representation in Legislative Council, the appointment of African members to the Executive Council. Although warned that the latter points would require further consideration after discussion by the Governors' Conference, Burns was encouraged to "experiment" with proposals along these lines, and the important point was conceded that reforms for which the Gold Coast seemed ready should not be delayed solely on grounds that time was unripe elsewhere in West Africa.[14]

On arriving in Africa, Burns soon had to deal with serious strikes over the cost of living, in Nigeria as well as the Gold Coast, and this confirmed his resolve to press ahead with reforms.[15] His Africanization proposals were hailed by the Colonial Office as "sensible and moderate" (hence they proved less than adequate for the postwar expansion of the colonial state);[16] on residential segregation he fought a drawn battle against the contention of medical authorities in London and Africa that "the preservation of the health of the Europeans . . . is of such paramount importance that the political effect of racial segregation must be accepted as inevitable."[17] His first political initiative was to press a reluctant Colonial Office to agree to the appointment of African members of the Executive Council. "I believe," Burns argued, "that the rising tide of anti-British resentment, and the disturbances which in recent years have been symptoms of this resentment, are due to the policy of deferring constitutional concessions until it is too late for them to be appreciated by the people. The Negro peoples, both in the West Indies and in West Africa, are learning that the colonial administrations take no notice of popular feeling until this feeling is manifested in disturbances."

Perceiving "a growing feeling of antipathy to Europeans and an under-

14. Minutes by Burns, September 22, by Williams September 24; record of discussion with Moyne, September 30, 1944, C.O. 96/775/31444.

15. C.O. 96/774/31312; *Colonial Civil Servant*, pp. 186–88.

16. Burns to Stanley, December 17, 1942 (confidential), and minutes, C.O. 96/776/31466.

17. Burns to Cranborne, 219 and July 28, 1942 (confidential), C.O. 96/774/31336. It is interesting to compare Burns's strong stand against residential segregation in this extremely interesting file with his readiness to defend segregated clubs in print in 1949 (*Colonial Civil Servant*, pp. 58–59).

current of discontent which affords a fertile field for the subversive activities of enemy agents," Burns, backed by Bourdillon from Nigeria, persisted against objections raised by Hailey and other Colonial Office pundits. In September, Lord Cranborne, as secretary of state, was persuaded to authorize such appointments, in Nigeria as well as the Gold Coast.[18] But these were grace and favor appointments; the crucial point for African opinion would be Burns's recommendations for constitutional reform.

In his interview with Moyne, Burns had specifically suggested unofficial majorities only in municipalities, proposing an unspecified increase in African representation on the Legislative Council. By December 1942 his mind was clearly moving toward accepting an unofficial majority there also;[19] this was no doubt connected with his desire to turn aside African opposition to the introduction of income tax, which the Colonial Office had just decided to impose against his advice.[20] It did not, however, indicate any intention to move toward an early transfer of power; even in 1949 Burns did not believe the Gold Coast was "yet fit for self-government."[21] In the first place, unofficial majorities were to be linked with a reaffirmation and definition of the governor's reserve powers; Burns's Caribbean experience had led him to believe such a system could work well, and that there should be little need to put these powers into practice. But besides this, Burns now saw more clearly the link between the future composition of the legislature and the distribution of power in the localities.

Hailey's report had emphasized the weak control which the Gold Coast government exercised over traditional states of the colony; chiefs and councillors, claiming to exercise "inherent rights" of government, effectively controlled the substantial revenues produced by the concession of stool lands for cocoa-farming and gold-mining, and by the consequent litigation. (African lawyers also benefited.)[22] One of Burns's priorities was to establish stronger central control by applying the principles of Indirect Rule; working with Sir Ofori Atta, most important of the traditional rulers, he sought to make this acceptable by associating the changes with increased representation at the center, and by promises of central government grants to reformed authorities. Experience during these negotiations made Burns

18. The episode is documented in C.O. 554/131/33701/42; quotations from Burns to Cranborne June 30, 1942 (secret). Cf. *Colonial Civil Servant*, pp. 194–96.

19. Burns to Stanley, December 14, 1942 (telegram), and minutes, C.O. 96/770/31013/5.

20. Swinton to Cranborne, October 13, 1942 (private), C.O. 554/131/33696/1942. Cranborne to Burns and Stevenson, December 6, 1942 (telegram).

21. *Colonial Civil Servant*, p. 69.

22. Jarle Simensen, "Commoners, Chiefs and Colonial Government: British Policy and Local Politics in Akim Abuakwa" (Ph.D. diss., University of Trondheim, 1976), 2:300–06.

contemptuous of many of the "intelligentsia" and "demagogues" with whom he had to deal, especially Afori Atta's learned kinsman, J. B. Danquah; in planning municipal reforms, which were to provide "training for the further political advance of the Gold Coast," he was anxious to minimize their influence. Whereas his proposal to establish a municipality in Kumasi envisaged half the members directly elected on an occupier franchise, by December 1942 Burns was temporarily flirting with a suggestion that the franchise in Accra should be abolished in favor of indirect elections through the Ga traditional authorities.[23] Though he resisted that dangerous temptation, Burns had no intention of promoting a legislature dominated by such men.

One immediately crucial factor was that the existing Legislative Council represented only the Colony; Asante and the Northern Territories (as well as the Togoland mandate) lay outside its competence. Hailey had recommended "as our ultimate objective the establishment of a Central Legislature, with three territorial councils"; and in February 1943, Burns took a step in this direction with proposals to establish an Advisory Council for Asante.[24] But at this stage the Asantehene and his fellow chiefs did not wish to be brought under the central legislature nor to seek representation there; constitutional reform thus remained a matter of balancing different interests within the Colony. Burns, having been warned not to expect approval for an unofficial majority,[25] deferred any proposal pending the planned visit to West Africa of Oliver Stanley, the new secretary of state.

After Burns left London, Colonial Office thinking continued to concentrate on long-term plans for economic, social, and educational development rather than on constitutional reform. Some impetus was given in this direction by the appointment in May 1942 of Lord Swinton as Resident Minister in West Africa. This arose from the desire of the armed services for more direct means of influencing policy (they would have preferred a military governor-general); but besides coordinating operational priorities and external relations, Swinton presided over governors' conferences, reconstituted as the Civil Members Committee, and began to build up a policy-making capacity of his own, with distinguished specialist Advisers serving all four colonies—Noel Hall on development, Maxwell Fry on town planning. This side of "Resmin" was beginning to resemble the office of

23. Burns to Cranborne, July 29, 1942 (confidential), C.O. 96/773/31229/6; Burns to Williams, December 29, 1942 (private).

24. NAPD, p. 138; Burns to Stanley, February 14, 1943 (secret), C.O. 96/772/31096/6.

25. Williams to Burns, January 20, 1943, C.O. 96/770/31013/5.

comptroller set up in the West Indies after the Moyne report of 1939; but in Swinton it had a shrewd and active political head who had been secretary of state in 1931–35. On February 24, 1943, Swinton presented to the Civil Members Committee a comprehensive paper on economic policy, envisaging colonial governments pursuing very actively interventionist policies for an indefinite period after the war.[26] Swinton was strongly skeptical about the "Westminster model;" his prescription was: "pressing on with the things that matter to the common man, agricultural and industrial development, cooperative farming and marketing, health, education; staffing the services concerned with Africans as quickly as they can be trained; assigning to African local administrators more and more responsibility for these services. The more Africans are playing their part in the things that really matter, the less they will bother about constitutional forms. . . ."[27]

Curiously enough, the Colonial Office was quicker than Swinton to understand that the increased social pressures of wartime would raise constitutional claims which "will then demand attention as being themselves factors in the immediate wartime situation."[28] Some shift in emphasis was marked by their decision to activate plans for a Commission on Higher Education in West Africa, which had been under leisurely discussion since the governors' conference in August 1939 had identified a West African University as "an ideal at which they should aim." During 1942 the Colonial Office, while still assuming that the commission could not conduct its main enquiries in wartime, decided to appoint a nucleus to begin work, under a chairman who would recognize that (as Stanley put it when approaching Lord Harlech) "the most important aspects of the question are political."[29] But during 1943 the full commission (including three West African members) was in fact appointed with Walter Elliot as chairman, and its active enquiries began later that year. The development of a high-class university was thus recognized, not only as a concession highly valued by the West African elite, but as an essential preliminary to an eventual transfer of power. The Elliot Commission worked on the assumption that "somewhere in West Africa within a century, within half a century, a new African state will be born," and that it was urgent to begin the political and technical formation of its future rulers.[30] But political transfer would follow

26. Economic Policy in West African Colonies: Memorandum by Swinton, February 24, 1943, C.O. 96/776/31475.

27. Copy of Minute by Swinton, July 14, 1943, C.O. 554/132/33727.

28. Cranborne to Stevenson, August 18, 1942 (confidential), C.O. 847/22/47100/8/1942.

29. Minute by Dawe, May 15, 1942; Stanley to Harlech, December 1942, C.O. 847/21/47029/1942.

30. P.P. 1944–45, V, Cmd. 6655, p. 18.

the maturing of the university and of other development programs; the time-scale was shortening but would still allow plenty of opportunities to guide the course of decolonization.

During the summer of 1943, while Stanley prepared for the first tour of the West African colonies ever undertaken by a secretary of state, the Colonial Office attempted to sketch out this course. On July 20, Stanley presided over a discussion of a paper by O. G. R. Williams, an experienced assistant secretary. While agreeing that political advance ought to remain dependent upon social progress, Williams argued that West Africans needed assurances that their progress would not be retarded to keep step with East Africa. Williams's "tentative plan for constitutional development" was based on Hailey's proposals to reform local and regional government on foundations of Indirect Rule, but suggested five stages which might lead to political change at the center. The emphasis of the first stage would be largely on local government, the "gradual modernization" of Native Authorities being accompanied by increased African representation on Municipal Councils, and by the formation of advisory Regional Councils based on the Native Authorities; but there would also be increased representation of African interests, by elected and nominated members, on Legislative Councils. Unexpectedly, Hailey himself proposed to extend this phase by appointing Africans as heads of departments with seats in the Executive Council, though without full ministerial powers; he justified this as "education in responsibility," and a means of preventing educated Africans from adopting the role of "chartered opposition." Williams's second and third stages would consist largely of extending the functions of Regional Councils, together with measures to make both municipalities and Legislative Councils more directly representative. The fourth stage might see African unofficial majorities in Legislative Councils; but the Colonial Office was still unhappy about unofficial majorities without responsibility for government and also feared that Europeans in eastern Africa might demand similar status. Williams therefore thought it might be desirable to move directly to Stage Five, somewhat tentatively entitled "towards self-government."[31]

Beyond the first stage, this was not really a "plan" at all, even a tentative one, but a well-guarded declaration of intent. Williams's paper was wholly imprecise about Stage Five, suggesting only that it would have to be preceded by a lot of consultation with African interests, and it seems to have

31. Note by Williams on "Constitutional Development in West Africa"; note of meeting in secretary of state's room, July 20, 1943, C.O. 554/132/33727. For earlier discussions on unofficial majorities, see C.O. 96/770/31013/5, minutes on Burns telegram, December 14, 1943.

been generally accepted that it would require "a good many generations for its evolution."[32] The purpose of the discussion was not to produce immediate proposals but to permit Stanley to give the African deputations he was about to receive general political reassurances (if hardly the unequivocal commitment which Hailey, on the basis of his Indian experience, was now suggesting). But before Stanley reached the Gold Coast, Williams's program was called into question by an African initiative.

Among the papers prepared for presentation to Stanley was an impressive petition signed by African members of the Asante Confederacy Council as well as of the Legislative Council and the Joint Provincial Council of Gold Coast Colony. Without questioning the ultimate authority of the governor, this called for an elected majority on the Legislative Council, with formal provision for members of that majority to be appointed to the Executive Council, and to a new "Ministry of Home Affairs."[33] Such a petition might have been politely pigeon-holed but for what Burns called an "astonishing change" in the attitude of the Asantehene and his councillors, who now requested early representation for their country on the Legislative Council. To resist this request might jeopardize the basis of collaborative rule in Asante; but if it was accepted, the existing official majority of one could be maintained only by reducing the representation of other elements or by adding more officials—both courses certain to arouse African hostility. Burns therefore urged Stanley to agree to the unofficial majority—"the one demand that will really satisfy the politically-minded people in this country"—so that he could resist more dangerous claims for a footing in the executive.[34] Burns's political strategy had been shaken by the death on August 20 of Ofori Atta, whose collaboration was the key to reform of the Native Authorities, and by the rising influence of J. B. Danquah; this unforced gesture of political intent seemed the best way to regain the initiative.

This suggestion of course ran counter to the strategy of Williams's five stages, and the first reaction of the Office was that it would be a "lesser evil" to match Asante representation by appointing additional official members.[35] But Stanley's discussion with Burns in Accra, and his discovery that

32. Minute by Williams, September 4, 1943, C.O. 96/770/31013/5; cf. Grantham to Stanley, October 11, 1943.

33. Burns to Stanley, October 4, 1943 (secret), enclosing petition, C.O. 96/782/31499/1.

34. Burns telegram, August 31, 1943, C.O. 96/770/31013/5; Burns to Stanley, October 5, 7, and 8, 1943 (secret), C.O. 96/776/31499. Cf. *Colonial Civil Servant*, pp. 282–84.

35. Minutes by Williams September 1 and 6, 1943, Stanley to Burns, telegram, September 6, 1943, C.O. 96/770/31013/5.

Bourdillon in Nigeria and Blood in the Gambia also favored unofficial majorities subject to reserve powers, removed his opposition. The argument that African unofficial majorities in the West might set precedents for Europeans on the other side of the continent was discounted, and Burns was authorized to elaborate constitutional proposals which he had already drafted as an alternative to those in the Danquah petition.[36] While African appointments to the Executive Council were still to be at the governor's discretion, the Legislative Council would be reconstituted with a substantial African majority: this would consist primarily of members indirectly elected through advisory councils for Asante and the Colony, reconstituted on the basis of the new Native Authority legislation which was simultaneously being prepared. (The Northern Territories would temporarily be represented only by the chief commissioner.) In May 1944, Burns visited London and secured Stanley's agreement to negotiations on this basis with African representatives, "but on the distinct understanding that apart from the four municipal members [it had been agreed to accept direct elections in Kumasi] . . . the form of election would be substantially that at present in force in the case of the six Provincial members. . . ."[37] Unofficial majorities, in other words, were acceptable only on safe foundations of Indirect Rule.

The basis of a new pattern of collaboration now seemed to have been laid. At two meetings in July and August with African members of existing councils, Burns made a number of detailed concessions and in return secured their cordial consent, not only to the new constitution which was to bear his name, but to the Native Authorities legislation. Stanley himself had now grasped the symbolic importance of the unofficial majority and was anxious not to jeopardize the good atmosphere its acceptance had created by delay in preparing new constitutional instruments.[38] The change was not expected to involve any significant shift of power; a contemporary regarded Burns's handling of public opinion as "not so much consultation as education" and did not expect the new council to "assert its independence in obstructive or uncooperative ways."[39] But Burns had fundamentally

36. Ibid.; minute by Williams, October 22; note of discussions with Stanley October 27–28, 1943. Minutes by Cohen, November 29, Seel, November 30, Gater, December 1, 1943, C.O. 96/776/31499.

37. Burns's original proposals are evident in Burns to Stanley, October 7, 1943 (secret), C.O. 96/776/31499. The discussions with Stanley in May 1944 are documented in C.O. 96/782/31499/1944.

38. Minutes by Creasy, September 16, Stanley, September 20, 1944, C.O. 96/782/31499/ 1944.

39. M. Wight, *The Gold Coast Legislative Council* (London, 1947), pp. 202–06. Wight also provides a convenient contemporary study of the emergence of the new constitution.

changed the stages of Colonial Office planning, and it was necessary to consider implications for the other West African colonies.

Nigeria was, of course, the critical case. The political activists in the south of the country were no less active and articulate, though no more effectively united, than their Gold Coast contemporaries; but the country was vastly larger and more complex, and Indirect Rule had already created powerful interests opposed to ideas on the political future in the south. These were most strongly voiced by British officials in the north, led by Chief Commissioner Sir Theodore Adams, an ex-Malayan official who aimed to promote the autonomous development of the emirates as "Protected States," and believed "the policy of a central African Government incompatible with the Emirate system."[40] Such a view was rejected by Sir Bernard Bourdillon, governor from 1935 to 1943, though less categorically than by Hailey. Bourdillon, who considered the basis of Nigerian opposition to colonial rule to be "99% economic," had been an early advocate of a vigorous development policy, for which Nigerian unity provided the appropriate administrative framework. Instead of trying to exclude southerners from the north, the emirs should be encouraged to demand their own "finger in the Nigerian pie," taking their place along with the "Progressives" in the central legislature.[41] But if immediate steps were to be taken to constitute political unity, it could only be on the basis of the diverse regional structures which Indirect Rule had fortified. That this would ensure the dominant influence of conservative British advice during the gradual process of political advance was a welcome corollary.

Since 1939 Bourdillon had favored the creation of advisory councils with legislative and financial powers within the three existing regions, and had regarded these as the basis for gradual constitutional change at Lagos. As Hailey pointed out, there was nothing "natural" about these regions; developing them as political authorities might create future conflicts, and Bourdillon himself thought the structure should be thoroughly reexamined.[42] But any serious administrative reconstruction would have tended to delay constitutional change, and events in the Gold Coast during 1943 made this undesirable. At a meeting in the Colonial Office in November

40. Memo by Adams, August 29, 1942, C.O. 847/22/47160/10/1942.

41. Printed comments by Bourdillon on Hailey's general report, C.O. 847/21/47100/1/1943.

42. NAPD, p. 175: Bourdillon, "A Further Memorandum on the Future Political Development of Nigeria" (confidential print; Lagos, October 1942). Memo by Bourdillon, August 30, 1943, C.O. 847/22/47100/10/1943.

1943, Bourdillon's designated successor, Sir Arthur Richards, accepted his general approach (although, having been briefed by Adams, he emphasized the need for cautious handling of the emirs, who retained the key to British authority in the north). But Stanley, fresh from his African tour, pointed out that the confidence of the "Lagos politicians" was also relevant; he pressed Richards toward granting an unofficial majority in the new Legislative Council and to keep in step with developments in the Gold Coast.[43] The basic foundations of the famous "Richards Constitution," including its transformation of administrative regions into embryonic states, were thus laid before the new governor arrived in Nigeria.

The implications for constitutional change in the smaller West African colonies seemed less urgent, and less clear. "It would be obviously absurd to think of all the existing Colonial units as being equally fit for self-government," Williams had written in his paper of 1943. No doubt the slender territorial, economic, and demographic resources of the Gambia were uppermost in his mind, but Sierra Leone seemed hardly better able to meet vague Colonial Office criteria of "viability," and the social foundations on which political progress would have to rest were seriously defective. Reform of the 216 small chiefdoms which were to form the grass roots of political progress was proceeding slowly and unimpressively; and the Creoles, no longer regarded as suitable collaborators and heirs of empire, were commonly despised and rejected. Stanley, who had been depressed by his visit to Freetown, accepted advice of Governor Hubert Stevenson that cautious reconstitution of the Freetown City Council was "the most expedient step in the direction of self-government";[44] here at least it seemed possible to control the application of Williams's "tentative plan." But Stevenson's conservatism encountered more resolute opposition than expected; Freetonians refused to register to elect what they feared would be another subordinate municipality, and consequently any consideration of reconstituting the legislature was delayed. This delay was possibly more welcome than otherwise to officials with urgent priorities elsewhere, but the result was that the program of political education envisaged for Phase One proved largely abortive.[45]

The transfer of power in West Africa thus ranked low among the priorities of Colonial Office "forward thinking," even at the end of the war.

43. Note of meeting, November 19, 1943, C.O. 554/132/33727.

44. Notes of talks with Sir H. Stevenson, July 16, August 12, 1943, C.O. 267/683/32375.

45. John D. Hargreaves, "Assumptions, Expectations and Plans: Approaches to Decolonisation in Sierra Leone," in W. H. Morris-Jones and George Fischer, eds., *Decolonisation and After: The British and French Experience* (London, 1980), pp. 73–103.

Constitutional reform was largely an addition to a "planned policy" centered on the theme of development and had been brought forward by governors more sensitive than Whitehall to the changing tone of African opinion. It was hoped that reformed institutions would provide a framework for cooperation with a wider spectrum of African leadership, embracing trade unionists and other spokesmen for the commoners as well as the traditional intermediary elites, and that this might secure not merely the "acquiescence" of Africans but their active acceptance of the new goals of colonial policy. The new catchphrase of "partnership" (another word for collaboration) was intended to apply in West Africa as well as in the colonies with settler minorities; even in the municipal government of Freetown, one official at least regarded "harmony of the black and white keys" as a long-term necessity.[46] (Even such harmony involved a shift in attitudes which not all officials found it easy to make; the new Nigerian constitution would have had a better start had Richards shown the same readiness to consult as Burns.)

But it became increasingly clear that only on new political foundations could the resources of the colonial empire be used to restore Britain's battered strategic and economic interests in the postwar world. It is arguable that the importance of the West African colonies to the United Kingdom had become greater than ever before. West Africa was a prolific source of raw materials and foodstuffs, with dollar-earning cocoa as one of the sterling area's few immediate assets; and new routes of international communications developed during the war had enhanced the strategic importance of its harbors and airfields. But Britain's diminished resources, and her appreciation of the colonial contribution to victory, meant that these imperial purposes would have to be served within new collaborative frameworks where the power of initiative would be more evenly shared between metropolis and periphery.

In eastern Africa (which always played a more important role than the West in imperial strategy) such a framework seemed in the 1940s to depend upon interracial power-sharing with built-in European leadership, and upon intercolonial cooperation to ensure stronger blocks of power.[47] Traces of both ideas can be found in the West African files also, for example, in the Colonial Office desire to perpetuate the interterritorial organization of the Resident Minister in a West African council, where a British Minister with a strong and independent secretariat would preside over the periodic

46. Minute by Varwill, November 22, 1945, C.O. 267/688/32348, Part 2.

47. See the introductory chapter by D. A. Low and J. M. Lonsdale in *The Oxford History of East Africa*, ed. D. A. Low and A. Smith, vol. 3 (1976), esp. pp. 2–3.

governors' meetings.[48] As noted above, there were also occasional flirtations with ideas of multiracialism. But the Colonial Office, if not all the politicians, understood that: "East Africa differs so much from West Africa, both as regards the state of political advancement of Africans and as regards the admixture of immigrant communities, that only on the very broadest of principles is anything done in West Africa likely to affect East Africa."[49] Whereas in the east it was feasible to regard Europeans as the long-term collaborators of empire, hoping for some future Capricornian Smuts, in West Africa, as in Asia, there would eventually be only the indigenous peoples. Hence the political changes somewhat timidly accepted during the war, together with the programs for African advancement, economic development, and social improvement, became crucial means of ensuring West African collaboration in Britain's last attempts to maintain an imperial role in the world of superpowers.

Recent studies of British political history tend to diminish the historical significance of the Labor electoral victory of 1945 (which the writer, like many of his contemporaries, hailed as the start of a new political era). Paul Addison's masterly study presents the Attlee government as heir to "a broad agenda of safe and constructive progress,"[50] adumbrated during the miseries of the 1930s but given practical form under urgent wartime pressures. Though he regards the essential political framework as provided by the Coalition, Addison perceives the solid content of this new reforming consensus as originating in the new commitment to planning of civil servants, increasingly allied with academics and the emergent technocrats of the policy-making elite.

Addison's book appears to contain only one passing reference to colonial policy: in 1943, Attlee, Bevin, and Morrison included it in a list of subjects suitable for consensual decision.[51] But his general thesis seems eminently applicable; Hailey could well have appeared in his book as the Beveridge of the colonial empire. While the 1945 election certainly gave office to men whose professions of faith (unlike those of some of their opponents) firmly committed them to new approaches, the general course had already been mapped out in a bipartisan or nonpartisan atmosphere around Whitehall, under the political and economic impulses of depression and war. George

48. Study of this interesting topic might begin in C.O. 554/139/33768 and in C.O. 554/140/33829/1.

49. Minute by Seel, November 30, 1943, C.O. 96/776/31499.

50. Paul Addison, *The Road to 1945: British Politics and the Second World War* (London, 1975), p. 43.

51. Ibid., pp. 233–34.

Hall, Attlee's first secretary of state, had served his colonial apprenticeship under Moyne, Cranborne, and Stanley; since he seems to have preferred to do business orally rather than on paper, his personal influence is hard to trace, but it does not seem to have been profound. Arthur Creech Jones, who succeeded him late in 1946, is a more significant figure, not least because his long-standing concern to investigate African grievances and his role in the Fabian Colonial Bureau since 1940 had earned him good expectations among African leaders. Rather than a political innovator, Creech Jones was a sincere colonial reformer coopted into the policy-making elite (as a member of the Advisory Committee on Education in the colonies since 1936, and as vice-chairman of the Elliot Committee); his absorption in the details of worthy projects may sometimes have blinded him to wider issues.[52] In December 1946 he addressed to a meeting of the Fabian Colonial Bureau an extensive "profession of faith" under the title "Labour's Colonial Policy"; virtually every innovation there mentioned could be shown to have originated in the Colonial Office under the wartime coalition.[53] This does not mean that the radical and socialist writers from whom the Fabians claimed descent had counted for nothing—rather, that the reforming conscience had been coopted to support a new colonial consensus.

Revisionism need not go so far as to suggest that the Labor victory had no importance for Africa. Apart from reinforcing such specific reforms as those designed to encourage a "responsible" trade-union leadership, it ensured that the new Development and Welfare Act would be applied under a Parliament more sensitive to African needs and aspirations than its Conservative-dominated predecessor might have been. But as Low and Lonsdale point out,[54] the indirect institutional effects of that act were arguably more important than its direct financial contribution. While the technical capacity of the Colonial Office itself to intervene was being vastly enlarged, colonial governments too were encouraged to draw up long-term plans (or shopping lists); when funds available from London proved disap-

52. As under-secretary in 1945–46, Creech Jones devoted much effort to trying to force through the Minority Report of the Elliot Committee, which he had signed. This document was strongly favored by the educational technocrats; it was the logical conclusion of their working assumptions about the supply of staff, students, and finance, all of which subsequently proved erroneous. Its acceptance would have involved ignoring the deep attachment of Africans in the Gold Coast and Sierra Leone to existing institutions which, whatever their deficiencies, were living concerns with real assets. Creech Jones was far slower than many officials to recognize the force of these political considerations. See his minutes and comments in C.O. 554/134/33599 and C.O. 554/135/33599/1.

53. *Labour's Colonial Policy: A Survey by Mr. Arthur Creech Jones M.P., Secretary of State for the Colonies* (Fabian Colonial Bureau, 1947).

54. *Oxford History of East Africa*, pp. 12–16, 43, 54.

pointing but revenue from export crops and the new income tax proved buoyant, they could choose to finance development locally. But the execution of such plans (however financed) produced a "second colonial occupation" in the form of a large-scale infusion of technical experts, whose activities not only increased the "intensity" of colonial government but seemed to imply its continuance in some form until the new policies had an opportunity to mature. Ardent socialists were among the warmest supporters of this technocratic approach: Ian Mikardo, in a Fabian pamphlet of 1948 entitled *The Second Five Years*, gave pride of place to "joint British–French–Belgian–South African–Egyptian planning and development of the greater part of Africa." The imperatives of domestic reconstruction could lead colonial reformers to press colonial development schemes (as for Tanganyikan groundnuts) without carefully calculating those benefits to Africans which their rhetoric assumed to be the real justification for development.

There is a related aspect of this "second occupation" which Low and Lonsdale hardly mention. Some of the specialists who carried out the second occupation were themselves convinced radicals or socialists, who believed that the transfer of their own particular expertise or knowledge to African successors was an essential part of that wider transfer of power to which they saw themselves committed. Elsewhere I have discussed the way in which Edgar Parry, commissioner of labor in Sierra Leone, "discovered" Siaka Stevens as a man capable not only of guiding the embryonic trade-union movement along soundly constitutional lines, but of leading a wider social democratic movement "with its hooks well into both sides of Transport House."[55] But it was perhaps the educationalists, moving out to teach in the Elliot University colleges and elsewhere, who best exemplify this urge to form successors in their own image. Thomas Hodgkin, persuading the Colonial Office in 1946 to sponsor an extension to West Africa of the political education offered by the Oxford Extra-Mural Delegacy, provides an example of radical neocolonialism which even the strongest anti-imperialist must applaud.[56] It would be interesting to estimate the effects of the classes which grew out of this visit on the developing ideas and objectives of African political leaders.

But even the radical decolonizers still expected the preparatory period of partnership to be lengthy; nobody knew better than a specialist how long the economic and social foundations of nationhood would take to lay. Plans

55. Fabian Colonial Bureau Papers, Rhodes House, Oxford (MSS British Empire S.365), box 86, fols. 125–27, Parry to Hinden, Nov. 24, 1946; cf. my paper, "Approaches to Decolonisation in Sierra Leone," cited above, n. 45.

56. C.O. 554/135/33599/4/1946.

were being initiated which would take decades to mature fully; it seemed desirable to most experts, and feasible to the officials, to govern the timing of political transfer accordingly. As another chapter in this volume argues, the Cohen-Caine memorandum prepared for the African Governors' Conference of November 1947 did give a new priority to political and constitutional change. It prescribed a greatly shortened time-scale for Williams's "tentative plan" of 1943, breathed urgency into the policy of reconstructing the foundations of local government, and sought to relate political change to programs of social and economic development.[57] As officials became aware of rising African expectations, they grasped the need to anticipate them in order to retain the political initiative. Yet any further acceleration of the timetable was bound to upset newly calculated relationships between social and economic advance and "the slow work of nation-building"; only within limits could one accelerate the capacity of new universities to train highly sophisticated cadres or the implementation of carefully balanced proposals for improved patterns of land use. At *some* stage changes in the timing of constitutional development would involve qualitative change in the whole concept of planned preparation for the transfer of power.

The need to accelerate came much sooner than Cohen could have expected. From late 1947, after Burns's departure, unrest in the Gold Coast intensified; inflationary pressures produced a well-organized boycott of high-priced European manufactures, and in the countryside cocoa farmers protested against government measures to enforce the "cutting-out" of diseased trees. The United Gold Coast Convention, led by its new general secretary, Kwame Nkrumah, used these and other grievances to organize support. On February 28, 1948, a demonstration by ex-servicemen in Accra was fired on by police, who killed two men and wounded four or five others; three days of rioting followed, extending from Accra to other towns, including Kumasi. Governor Creasey declared a state of emergency, and Nkrumah appealed for international support by sending telegrams to assorted recipients in New York, London, and Moscow. But by March 4 the country seems to have been relatively calm. Total casualties (including three killed and four injured during renewed outbreaks in Kumasi on March 15–18) were officially estimated at 29 dead and 237 injured.[58] In the context of imperial history this hardly seems a major crisis; one may specu-

57. Cf. Louis and Robinson, above, pp. 42–43; and for Williams, above, p. 126. At the time of writing I had not seen the Cohen-Caine memorandum, still unavailable in the P.R.O.

58. *Report of the Committee of Enquiry into Disturbances in the Gold Coast*, Colonial no. 231 (London, 1948), p. 85.

late whether a more experienced and resolute governor, confident of the support of police and officials, might not have contained the situation locally. But the magnitude of the consequences far exceeded that of the events themselves; these riots led directly to Ghanian independence nine years later.

Part of the explanation may be found in the international background. Nineteen forty-eight, which would prove to be a year of destiny for the Commonwealth in Africa, was also a crucial year in the Cold War. The Communist seizure of power in Prague earlier in February had converted many liberals and Social Democrats to the thesis that the Communists were driving toward world mastery; in June such fears were reinforced by the Berlin blockade. Mao Tse-Tung's decisive offensive was about to begin; during this same month of February Asian Communist Youth movements were conferring in Calcutta, and by June the grumbling disorders in Malaya were to reach the status of "emergency."[59] Maladroit British responses to the inconclusive evidence of Nkrumah's communism must be understood in this alarming context.[60] We still have little direct evidence about military influence on colonial policy, but the general climate nourished broad concepts of world strategy, worked out upon small maps. In November 1948 the chief of Imperial General Staff could solemnly harangue African legislative councillors about the need for a "Master Plan" to contain communism by a union of African territories under "the great dominion in the south";[61] more sober appraisals must have suggested that a more realistic policy would be closer collaboration with an authentic West African leadership capable of resisting Communist blandishments.

In 1948, that seemed to exclude Nkrumah. Even those who discounted his Communist affiliations must have seen danger to established economic interests and social relationships in a leader who was appealing so effectively not only to new portions of the urban population but also to discontented rural commoners. How far British policymakers drew direct analogies with India, recognizing a class of "dominant peasants" in the militant cocoa-farmers, we do not yet know.[62] But the riots did provide a

59. Anthony Short, *The Communist Insurrection in Malaya, 1948–1960* (London, 1975), pp. 27, 44–47, 80 ff.

60. Colonial no. 231, pp. 17–20, 91–94; Hansard, 5th ser., vol. 448, Commons, March 1, 1948, pp. 37–38.

61. Speech by Montgomery to conference of African legislative councillors, October 4, 1948; J. B. Danquah's circular letter, November 8, 1948, in H. K. Akyeampong, ed., *Journey to Independence and After* (Accra, 1970), 1:87–89.

62. Indian analogies were certainly drawn by the chief secretary, newly arrived from the ICS. Reginald Saloway, "The New Gold Coast," *International Affairs* 31 (1955):469–76.

clear warning that, unless the British broadened the basis of their rule in West Africa, sooner or later they would be faced with something worse. The Lagos strike of 1945 may have suggested that such a crisis could well develop in Nigeria (it might have been provoked by the Enugu shooting of November 1949, had Sir Hugh Foot not by then begun to recover the all-important "initiative");[63] and in that vast and complex country it would have been harder to improvise a technique of controlled transfer of power. Although the Gold Coast was no straightforward case, it did seem to provide enough of the supposed preconditions for self-government to make acceleration of the constitutional timetable an acceptable gamble.[64]

So, during 1948 and 1949, the Watson and Coussey committees sought to reconstruct the system of collaboration within a traditional Gold Coast framework of "chiefs and intellectuals," and so to invalidate Nkrumah's claim to speak for those African masses whose interests never lacked self-appointed defenders. The British Cabinet, now convinced "that in the present state of political development in the Gold Coast no system would be workable which did not provide for a very considerable degree of African participation in the control of policy,"[65] approved the apparently far-reaching Coussey proposals, but with one major qualification. By rejecting as premature the idea of an embryonic prime minister who would nominate Africans for appointment to the Executive Council, the Cabinet in effect denied that any African political party could yet bridge the gap between the aspirations of rural Africans and the political rituals of Accra: they had learned the lesson which Namier was teaching from British history, that until the advent of "strongly organized, disciplined parliamentary parties," the sovereign retained the initiative in appointing ministers.[66] But Nkrumah, too, must have included some history in his spasmodic studies at the London School of Economics; success in the colony elections of February 1951 marked a temporary capture of the initiative by his Convention Peoples' party. Sir Charles Arden-Clarke could recover it in part only by

63. *Report of the Commission of Enquiry into the Disorders in the Eastern Provinces of Nigeria*, November 1949. Colonial no. 256 of 1950. Hugh Foot, *A Start in Freedom* (London, 1964), pp. 103–06. Cf. below, p. 138.

64. The indispensable account of events in the Gold Coast remains Dennis Austin, *Politics in Ghana, 1946–1960* (London, 1964).

65. Creech Jones Papers, Rhodes House, Oxford. (MSS British Empire S.332), box 18, file 4, fols. 32–34. C.O. note on constitutional proposals, October 15, 1949. The guide to the official papers in box 55, still closed, shows that the Cabinet discussed the Gold Coast on October 13, 1949.

66. Colonial no. 250. Statement by H. M. Government. Creech Jones to Arden-Clarke October 14, 1949, p. 9. L. B. Namier, *Monarchy and the Party System* (Oxford, Romanes Lecture, 1952).

recognizing the necessity of accepting those collaborators whom the electorate had designated and hoping that the six-year transitional period would permit the transfer of objectives and values, as well as of power, to African successors. Efforts, as Creech Jones put it, had to be made "to direct these new forces into constructive channels."[67] By 1957 there was some guarded official optimism that the Ghanaian regime to which power was being transferred would maintain at least some of its predecessor's constructive policies, domestically and within the Commonwealth.

Though the social and ethnic diversity of Nigeria made the transfer of power in Lagos a more complex operation, that very complexity also gave the colonial government certain opportunities of initiative. Although the Colonial Office had rejected the separatism favored by some northern administrators, it still seemed possible—even necessary—to use the weight of the conservative north to restrain the ambitions of southern politicians. But Richards's maladroit handling of his constitutional proposals, together with the social pressures revealed by the Lagos strike of 1945, showed that there were deep sources of discontent in the south and that it was important to regain the confidence of the leaders. Here the manifest sincerity of Hugh Foot, chief secretary from 1947 to 1951, was an undoubted asset. By sponsoring widely based committees to examine the sensitive questions of constitutional revision and Africanization of the public service, the Government of Nigeria avoided such losses of initiative as had occurred in the Gold Coast in 1948 and 1951. The improvement in prices for primary products after the Korean War, accentuating the general improvement in barter terms of trade between 1945 and 1960, also helped to blunt the political radicalism which had begun to seem menacing during the later 1940s.[68]

Once the process of constitutional revision had been reopened, the pressure of events in the Gold Coast alone was sufficient to ensure an accelerating momentum in Nigeria. The southern leaders would not be satisfied with less than their Ghanaian brothers; northern conservatives increasingly saw the necessity, and the tangible advantages, of joining in. But the tempo of political transfer at the center left no opportunity to reconsider the unwieldy triregional structure on which successive constitutions rested. The decolonizers could only work through those specific groups of

67. A. Creech Jones, "British Colonial Policy with Particular Reference to Africa," *International Affairs* 27 (April 1951):177.

68. The interaction between economics and politics during the period clearly requires fuller discussion than it receives here; for a beginning, see A. G. Hopkins, *An Economic History of West Africa* (London, 1973), pp. 267–92.

leaders who had emerged within the old administrative regions; and in varying degrees the NCNC, the Action Group, and the Northern Peoples' Congress came to be regarded as controlled by Ibos, Yorubas, and conservative Muslim aristocrats, respectively. Not only Hailey and Bourdillon but Azikiwe and Awolowo had suggested that the regional pattern required reconstruction; but, quite apart from the Northern Peoples' Congress's interest in maintaining a monolithic north, there simply was not time for this. The Willink Commission of 1958 was instructed to assume the existence of "Minorities," and to seek means of allaying their fears; though authorized to recommend the creation of new states "as a last resort," they were in no doubt that the consequent delay in the transfer of power would be as unwelcome to the Macmillan government as to Nigerian leaders. Their elegant application to the Nigerian federation of western liberal-democratic doctrines, reread in light of the Nigerian civil war, seems essentially a justification of the politically unavoidable.[69]

Although during the Second World War the Colonial Office repeatedly asserted that the four West African territories would have to be treated individually in light of such criteria as "viability" or "readiness for self-government," it soon became clear that there would be no attempt to retain Sierra Leone and the Gambia once Ghana and Nigeria were independent. Despite the Committee on Smaller Territories which the Colonial Office established during the later 1940s, events in Sierra Leone at least were now shaped by reactions on the periphery rather than by debates at the center of empire. In 1951 the political deadlock created in Freetown by the intransigent particularism of the Creole National Council was broken by Governor Beresford-Stooke, who after the election took the first decisive steps toward a transfer of executive responsibility to the elected leaders of the Sierra Leone People's Party. Though their political influence rested largely on very imperfectly modernized chieftaincies, they now were the only credible "collaborators" in sight. The incipient diamond boom, besides increasing the political stakes, provided some short-term answers to questions about "viability"; (only today, as Sierra Leone's mineral resources are threatening to run out, is the full significance of that concept about to be tested). The Gambia's minute size seemed to raise graver problems, and for a time there was even some discussion of integration with Britain; but since metropolitan wisdom could devise no politically acceptable alternative, independence came here, too, in 1964, and the Gambia has so far proved more "viable" than many larger and richer states.

69. P.P. 1957–58, IX, Cmnd. 505. Nigeria: Report of the Commission Appointed to Enquire into the Fears of Minorities and the Means of Allaying Them, July 1958.

The argument of this chapter may now be summarized. During the Second World War the transfer of political power to West African hands, formerly a vague aspiration for an indefinite future, was specifically envisaged as the culmination of comprehensive programs of social engineering designed to reconstruct African societies to accord with the ideals and interests of a changing British Commonwealth. But pressures from within Africa, and from the changing balance of international power, radically modified these intentions; although the Colonial Office had much success in retaining the tactical initiative, this meant reversing the priorities of their strategy. They moved from a policy of subordinating controlled constitutional experiment to programs of social and economic development, through a phase of "nation-building" and accelerated preparation for self-government, into conditions where the speedy transfer of power to acceptable African collaborators became an end in itself. The British government, genuinely converted during the 1930s by the colonial reformers, ended by discovering that the political objective of the anti-imperialists was more in accordance with the economic and strategic realities of their diminished position in the world.

Tactical flexibility enabled the British largely to determine the institutional framework within which radical African leaders like Nkrumah and Azikiwe agreed to collaborate in the transfer of power. In the process of collaboration the radicalism of some of these leaders, perhaps never very deeply grounded, became attenuated or corrupted—sometimes by material temptations, sometimes by the prospects of influence within the political contexts of Commonwealth or United Nations, sometimes perhaps by simple despair at discovering discrepancies (already well known to colonial governments) between constitutional responsibility and effective power. Few historians would dare to predict the fortunes of any African state over the next quarter-century; but those fortunes are likely to differ almost as much from the visions of Pan-African ideologues as from officially sponsored plans for the postcolonial order.

6. *French West Africa and Decolonization*

YVES PERSON

The fifteen years from the end of World War II to the political liberation of French West Africa have already been the subject of numerous studies, varying in quality from country to country; some, like Senegal or Ivory Coast, have been more fortunate than others in the scope of such scholarly analysis. As there can be no question, here, of reviewing events in detail, but only of recalling their dynamics, the more important studies of major developments will be cited in the footnotes.

Beneath the apparent political uniformity of the colonial order, the various separate territories composing French West Africa in 1945 had great cultural, economic, and social diversity.[1] Extending from the heart of the desert to the forests along the Gulf of Guinea, this immense country was divided among seven colonies grouped under the authority of Dakar: Mauritania, Senegal, Guinea, Soudan (Mali), Ivory Coast, Niger, and Dahomey. To these must be added Togo, which was separate by reason of its mandate, and then its trusteeship, status. Upper Volta, partitioned in 1932 among Ivory Coast, Soudan, and Niger, was to be reestablished in 1948.

The coastal colonies may, in general, be contrasted with the countries of the interior. The latter were distinguished by their drier climate and their isolation from the sea; economic development did not occur, except for a few agricultural export crops, such as peanuts and cotton, the cultivation of which was enforced by the colonial government, and urban growth remained quite limited (to Bamako, Ouagadougou, Niamey). These countries were already exporting laborers to the coastal areas, both French (Senegal, Ivory Coast) and British (Gold Coast). Here the educated group possessing the knowledge that linked it to the modern organization of power was confined to a narrow stratum of civil servants and commercial

1. For a good description of the country at the end of the war, see J. Richard-Molard, *Afrique Occidentale Française* (Paris, 1949); and Eugène Guernier, ed., *Afrique Occidentale Française* (Paris, 1949). The latter is quite detailed but rather diffuse.

representatives. Among the coastal colonies we may leave aside Mauritania, which was simply a desert inhabited by nomads ruled from the Senegalese city of Saint-Louis.

Senegal was set apart from the other coastal territories by its relatively dry Sudanese climate, by the early date of its colonization, and also by a political acculturation symbolized in its four communes, its "native" French citizens, and its deputy, as well as by the role of Dakar, the federal capital, a crossroads of the Atlantic and an industrial center already of long standing. The agricultural base provided by the cultivation of peanuts lent its economy a certain dynamism, and a small bourgeoisie of businessmen existed alongside a very large administrative bourgeoisie with ties to a sizable nucleus of intellectuals.[2] The laboring class was still quite small, working chiefly for the administration or for such public services as the railroads. The railway workers played an avant-garde role, as they had already done between 1936 and 1938. Except for the planters in Ivory Coast, Senegal was the only country with an appreciable white minority (20,000), which included many poor laborers. Thus was created a racial problem which, however, remained a marginal one. To it must be added the problems of the native "mulatto" ethnic group in Saint-Louis.

The other coastal colonies—Guinea, Ivory Coast, Togo, and Dahomey—were characterized by a relatively rich agriculture (timber, coffee, cocoa, bananas, coconuts), which in Guinea and Ivory Coast had permitted the growth of a rather large plantation sector. Already before the war a small bourgeoisie of African planters had appeared in Ivory Coast, which outnumbered the civil servants paid by the colonial power: a unique phenomenon.

Some urban growth had taken place at Conakry and particularly at Abidjan, with railway terminals penetrating deeply into the interior; but it also occurred to a lesser extent at Lomé and Cotonou. Moreover, Dahomey, a country of ancient cities, had produced a large number of civil servants and commercial agents who emigrated, as the Senegalese had done in the past, to all the French-speaking countries.[3]

The period under consideration can clearly be divided into two segments. From 1945 to 1956 there was a quest by the colonial system, disrupted by the war but encouraged by French ideology in its will to survive,

2. Samir Amin, *Le Monde des affaires sénégalaises* (Paris, 1969).

3. Maurice A. Glélé, *Naissance d'un etat noir: L'Évolution politique et constitutionnelle du Dahomey de la colonisation à nos jours* (Paris, 1968). An excellent study, really the only one, of the complex ramifications of Dahomeyan politics just before and after independence.

for a new equilibrium. On the level of political history alone, this period itself could be divided into two phases: before and after 1950, the date of the break between the Rassemblement Démocratique Africain (RDA) and the French Communist party. From 1956 to 1960, in a fluid international context, the Loi-Cadre regime led to political independence at a much more rapid pace than had been anticipated.

Although this discussion centers upon political and cultural data, it will obviously be necessary to examine the economic and social evolution along the way.

The New Colonial System 1945–1956

After the turn of the twentieth century, colonized black Africa no longer had a separate political history aside from the Senegalese elections; but the upheavals of the Second World War put an end to this period of silence.

Brazzaville and the New Colonialism

After the liberalization—albeit brief and narrowly restricted—of the Popular Front, the cities where it had made itself felt, like Dakar and Abidjan, found Vichy's authoritarianism, accompanied by an increasingly racist ideology, very hard to bear. The war effort, which was stepped up especially after 1942, had alienated the peasant masses—all the more so as the colonial system had prevented any industrialization worthy of the name.[4]

Having joined Free France very late, French West Africa responded all the more enthusiastically to the ideal of the liberation of peoples the Allies had propagated in their struggle against Nazi Germany.

As the end of hostilities drew near, it was obvious that the population, and particularly the educated stratum of *évolués*, would not accept a maintaining of the status quo. Moreover, the reconstruction of a France ruined by the Occupation made better organization of production desirable. Furthermore one could foresee strong international pressures toward decolonization, for example, those already discernible in the attitude of the Americans toward North Africa and Indochina. The United States and the USSR were, in fact, soon to outbid each other on colonial issues in the United Nations.

The Free French authorities were sensitive to this situation, which explains the holding of the Brazzaville Conference in January and February

4. The Vichy period and the war have not been thoroughly studied. However, see Jean Suret-Canale, *Afrique noire occidentale et centrale*, vol. 2: *L'ère coloniale* (Paris, 1964), pp. 567–94.

1944.[5] In retrospect, it has been erroneously viewed as the beginning of decolonization. Whether some of the orientations adopted there objectively provided impetus in that direction is another question. In the minds of de Gaulle, Pleven, and most of the participants, the great majority of whom were high-ranking colonial officials, the aim of the conference was, on the contrary, to consolidate the colonial system definitively by renovating it. To this end, the termination of forced labor and of the native code (*indigénat*), a limited participation in elections, and extension of the voice of the Africans in public affairs were recommended. Similarly, the Brazzaville Conference endorsed the expansion of education which lagged far behind that of English-speaking Africa—but to the exclusion of African cultures and with the view of broadening the role of the collaborationist elite. Finally, the major act was the rejection of the old principle whereby each colony must pay its own way. The metropole decided to make capital investments in the social and cultural public sectors, but this was obviously in order to foster an economic development by which it would profit, which would link the territories more closely to itself, and which would permit it to refute the accusation of bad colonial rule. In any case, this change was to receive practical expression only in 1947, with the creation of the Fonds d'Investissement pour le Développement Economique et Social (FIDES). But the essential principle was also clearly stated: any idea of independence or self-government, even in the long term, was solemnly thrust aside. "The African peoples want no other liberty than that of France," Pleven stated. The Brazzaville Conference thus serves admirably to illustrate the beginning of a period: that of renovating the colonial system from top to bottom so as to ensure its permanence.

The development of public and private investment, and of industrialization, is beyond the scope of this chapter, but a few aspects should be mentioned. Investment was especially substantial from 1947 to 1956. Some

5. Ibid., pp. 595–600. See also Franz Ansprenger, *Politik im schwarzen Afrika* (Cologne, 1961), pp. 59–64. This is a work of exceptional quality, based on detailed, on-the-spot investigation at the time of independence. Social and economic evolution is studied, although, as the title indicates, the emphasis is on political life. Also, Edward Mortimer, *France and the Africans, 1941–1960: A Political History* (London, 1969), pp. 49–52. Written by a former *Times* correspondent at Paris, this book is concerned exclusively with the history of events and politics; but it is the most detailed work available on the African policy of the parties as seen from Paris. Its territory-by-territory account of local politics, however, is cursory and at times incorrect (R. Schachter-Morgenthau, *Political Parties in French-Speaking West Africa* (Oxford, 1964), pp. 37–40). An essential work, particularly for Senegal, Guinea, and Ivory Coast. A useful complement to Ansprenger on many points. A great effort is made to study local dynamics, territory by territory.

countries, such as Guinea which enjoyed a strong mining base, were transformed by it. Industrialization produced substantially increased social differentiation in Senegal. With the opening of its deep-water port in 1951, Ivory Coast saw the dawn of a period of growth lasting more than twenty years. Integration into the world market was thus greatly accelerated.

The Birth of Politics[6]

The essential political phenomenon is the sudden appearance of active political and social life after 1945. After seven years of silence, Senegal in effect took up where the effervescence of the Popular Front had left off. Demobilized infantrymen still experienced repression in 1945 (as, for example, in the Tiaroye massacre), but this was the swan song of the old order.

At the end of 1945, and again in 1946, one election followed another and small numbers of Africans participated in them for the first time elsewhere than in Senegal. Although they sent only a few legislators to France, they were in a position to participate in the jockeying for power; they found themselves led to identify politically with one or another of the French parties; and they organized their political machines and constituencies on the spot. Thus new power structures appeared.

These structures were, however, able to operate only within a quite restricted framework. Exploiting the general intellectual confusion that resulted from the war and from the leftward drift of the French electorate, the first-draft constitution, written early in 1946, provided for considerable autonomy in the territories, and in fact assumed an evolutionary complexion.

But this constitution was rejected in May, and partisans of the old order took the opportunity to recover their balance. At Douala in September 1945, some planters and merchants, with the support of certain large business firms, organized the Etats Généraux de la Colonisation, in which Ivory Coast, Cameroun, and Madagascar were particularly well represented. They expressed their opinions over a period of about fifteen years through the weekly periodical *Climats*. They protested against any sort of political evolution and, in the social sphere, against the abolition of forced labor.

6. Suret-Canale, *Afrique noire*, vols. 2 and 3, pt. 1 (Paris, 1964 and 1972). Volume 3, part 1, *La décolonisation*, comprises a study of the political awakening between 1944 and 1946 and an analysis of economic evolution until 1960. The latter is remarkably rich and exact. Two additional volumes are anticipated, dealing with social and political life; they should supersede earlier works in part, if and when they are published.

The pressure group they comprised was to be quite active and effective, notably in Ivory Coast.[7]

French national ideology, furthermore, clung so tightly to the myths of unity and assimilation that the trends reflected in the constitution appeared disquieting even to men fairly far to the political Left. This was the case, notably, with Marius Moutet, Minister of France Overseas. This quite moderate socialist had, it is true, been the moving spirit behind the African Popular Front of 1936, but he shuddered at the idea of secession or autonomy. To justify himself, he invoked the ideal of assimilation.

In the summer of 1946, therefore, Moutet induced the Section Française de l'Internationale Ouvrière (SFIO) to make common cause with the Mouvement Républicain Populaire (MRP), and particularly with Prime Minister Georges Bidault, who was now stricken by a frantic nationalism, during the drafting of the second constitution, which was to be approved on October 13. In August the Etats Généraux de la Colonisation had convened with great fanfare in Paris to make its pressure felt. The clauses respecting what was henceforth called the French Union now became much more restrictive. Basically, the system of two electoral colleges was instituted to ensure a disproportionate influence for the French minorities, and the franchise remained quite exclusive. As for the second college, the small number of Overseas parliamentary seats made a mockery of the assimilationist myths of the Republic "One and Indivisible." More seriously, powers of the administration, and consequently of the ministry, remained almost intact, each governor being assisted by a territorial assembly with scarcely more power than a General Council in France. The same was true of the Grand Councils assisting the governors-general of French West Africa and French Equatorial Africa. Nothing was done to expand the system of municipal government, except in the mixed communes, which were supervised by the administration. The evolutionary article remained such only in theory; in practice, it prevented any evolution. In Madagascar, where the nationalist movement was strong, an effort was made to split up the territory; the administration's maneuvers were to precipitate the desperate insurrection of 1947, repression of which blocked the situation well beyond the date of independence.[8] Dull-witted and overdetailed, this conventional constitution was simply verbiage intended to impede political progress.

7. Ansprenger, *Politik*, p. 193; *Marchés coloniaux du monde* (Paris), Dec. 8, 1945.

8. Ansprenger, *Politik*, pp. 65–80; Schachter-Morgenthau, *Political Parties*, pp. 48–83; Mortimer, *France and the Africans*, pp. 71–104; Suret-Canale, *Décolonisation*, pp. 28–53.

In French West Africa the nationalist movement was much less advanced, and the fixation on French ideology was so strong that demands focused upon social emancipation and civil equality failed to lead to the idea of political liberation. A few brilliant minds, like Senghor, dreamed of it, but were prudent enough not to express themselves unequivocally.

Adoption of such a constitution was nevertheless a great disappointment. The structure it created was to last until the Loi-Cadre of 1956. No significant autonomy being granted, it was on the level of the French Parliament that action had to be taken; the African deputies were too few to be sure of making themselves heard. In any event, it was in that autumn of 1946, when the rules of the game were laid down for the next ten years, that African political forces were organized and chose their orientation, and that lasting oppositions were established.

At the outset, in 1945, this political life was improvised at the base, in each territory. Associations and unions of civil servants and planters, the Catholic missions, the traditional chiefs, and of course the administration, had brought forward candidates in line with their desires. The first elections served as a sorting-out process in the teeming mass of ambitions.

But no clear political principle emerged from this chaos of desires and aspirations, except perhaps in Senegal. The very logic of French centralism, however, was soon to make a clarification necessary. At the level of each territory, groups quickly reorganized, often according to personal or ethnic sentiment rather than political ideas. But the parliamentarians, finding in Paris the only arena for effective action, were inevitably drawn to regroup themselves along the lines of the French parties, upon which they were forced to rely in order to gain anything at all. This necessarily forced them to create broad, Federation-wide alliances in the search for ideological cohesiveness.

The Socialists[9]

At first all the odds appeared to be on the side of the Socialists, who benefited from the prestige of the lawyer, Lamine Gueye, whose sway in Senegal seemed unchallenged after 1945. Well used to handling the urban voters, he was led by the extension of the franchise to many rural people to entrust the rural sector to the brilliant poet Léopold Sédar Senghor, the

9. Lamine Gueye, *Etapes et perspectives de l'Union française* (Paris, 1962), and *Itinéraire africain* (Paris, 1966); Schlachter-Morgenthau, *Political Parties*, p. 145; Bakary Traoré, *L'Evolution des partis politiques du Sénégal depuis 1946* (Paris, 1966); François Zuccarelli, *Un Parti politique africain: L'Union progressiste sénégalaise*, mimeograph (Paris, 1970).

first Senegalese *agrégé* and well known in Paris literary circles. But Lamine Gueye had been totally deranged by French national ideology and was to reject to the end, even to the point of political suicide, the evolution of Africa toward independence which all the English-speaking public figures were already demanding. By contrast, the African socialism that Senghor (who, moreover, knew Marx's writings well) was formulating eventually led in that direction, although cautiously and although in 1946 the problems were as yet very timidly defined. Outside of Senegal, the socialists had enlisted some rather influential men in Mali and Guinea (Fily-Dabo Sissoko and Yaçine Diallo), and minorities of some significance in western Ivory Coast. At the beginning of the year they had reason to think that the majority of African parliamentarians would join them.

Some Catholics, notably in Dahomey, were already looking toward the Mouvement Républicain Démocratique (MRD), even though its imperialist ideology was already discernible except for among brilliant individualists such as Robert Buron or Dr. Louis-Paul Aujoulat. The latter, working with missions in Cameroun, was beginning a remarkable political career, utilizing moderate Africans against the colonists.

The Rassemblement Démocratique Africain (RDA)[10]

But the nucleus of what was to become the Socialists' greatest rival already existed in the form of the Parti Démocratique de Côte d'Ivoire (PDCI), founded at Abidjan in April 1946. As is well known, this country had been harshly colonized and was dominated by a large community of white planters who impeded the growth of the small African farming bourgeoisie. The latter, who were bullied by the administrative services, denied labor, and sometimes even saw their property confiscated, founded their agricultural union in 1944 on the initiative of one of their number, the physician Félix Houphouët-Boigny, a descendant of the Akwe (Baulé) tribal chiefs. Supported by Governor Latrille, Houphouët succeeded in organizing his political machine by attracting African civil servants, the Dioula merchants (an excellent propaganda instrument), and some tribal chiefs, such as Gbon Kulibali of Korhogo. For socioethnic reasons, the Bété and some Malinke notables refused to join and allied themselves instead with the Socialists. We now see clearly that this party was neither socialist nor even nationalist, but it could be revolutionary in defending its class interests and in opposing a certain kind of corruption of African dignity. Like many Ivorians,

10. Ansprenger, *Politik*, pp. 123–52; Schachter Morgenthau, *Political Parties*, pp. 181–83; Mortimer, *France and the Africans*, pp. 105–10; Suret-Canale, *Décolonisation*, pp. 60–72; Aristide Zolberg, *One-Party Government in Ivory Coast* (Princeton, 1964), pp. 81–105.

Houphouët distrusted the Senegalese and was already accusing Dakar and the Federation of devouring the Ivorians' resources.

From 1945–46 on, this distrust excluded the possibility of his collaborating with the SFIO, but Houphouët needed allies against a more than ordinarily reactionary colonist community, and one that was to procure Governor Latrille's recall. Now he was welcomed and supported in this struggle by the Communist party of France, whose Abidjan study group had succeeded in developing contacts. As the Communist party was at the time a major component of the French government, it is understandable that Houphouët agreed to associate himself with it, or more correctly, with the fellow-traveling Mouvement Unifié de la Resistance (MUR). He was soon to bring into this alliance the great RDA, of which he would be head.

Early in 1946, in view of the constitutional debates and of powerful pressure by the colonialist faction, it was a matter of urgency for the African legislators to group themselves in an interterritorial alliance if they wished to preserve a modicum of political effectiveness. The ideal was to rise above personal rivalries and ideological differences so that all might join in defending African interests. This is, in fact, the way things were going in the early summer of 1946, when it was decided to hold a large congress at Bamako as a riposte to the Etats Généraux de la Colonisation and to the return to the Right in the second Constituent Assembly. Despite Houphouët's important role, well advised by the Communist party, all the African members of Parliament were to attend, and one could foresee that the Socialists' influence would be great.

It was then that Moutet, appalled at the birth of a policy that threatened French sovereignty, threw his full weight against the Socialists' participation at the very time when he was supporting centralist formulas for the constitution. Lamine Gueye submitted without qualms. Senghor did so in a spirit of discipline but reluctantly, and it was then that he decided to break with the SFIO, whose ideology clearly closed the door to restoration of the African's identity and political liberation. But the harm had been done: the cleavage between the Ivorian and the Senegalese poles of African demands was irremediable and was long to survive independence. Personal animosities that could have been overcome took on a permanent character.

At Bamako itself, Fily Dabo Sissoko, who was to preside over the congress, was uneasy at the rise of Mamadou Konate, supported by the Muslims, and was subjected to pressure by Moutet. He was at first inclined to withdraw in spectacular fashion. He finally agreed to play out his role, but this did not prevent the rupture from occurring.

Thus the Bamako Congress, as it took place in October 1946, did not culminate in a great regrouping of Africans but in the organization of an activist movement provisionally linked to the Communist party and agreed on a certain number of aims but otherwise quite heterogeneous. The RDA, carefully taking its cue from the Communist party's methods of organization, was to become the largest mass movement in French-speaking Africa. It often succeeded in mobilizing not only the urban workers but also the peasant masses, and in bringing them to political consciousness and hope. But it was a federation of parties quite diverse in the social composition of their leaderships, in ideology, and also in their objectives, beyond a certain minimum.

The Parti Démocratique de Côte d'Ivoire (PDCI)[11]

The PDCI, dominated by African planters, sought to create favorable conditions for an African bourgeoisie. Houphouët soon concluded that such conditions could not be brought about without the support of France, and that close ties with her were necessary to forestall any reckless adventure on the part of the masses, whose actions were beyond control. He had, furthermore, embraced the myths of France's civilizing values; this led him to reject African identity and to take advantage of Ivory Coast's wealth by disassociating it from the other states while continuing to rely on the metropole.

His subsequent development was therefore predictable. The alliance with the Communist party was merely a matter of expediency and became less and less desirable after 1947, when that party withdrew from the French government and the developing Cold War made it a compromising tie. It remained necessary that the white colonists and the French authorities allot some social and political sphere to the PDCI. Nevertheless, the administration, exploiting the current witch-hunt, worked to crush it by encouraging defections from its ranks and by instigating the formation of pro-French parties such as the Progressives or the Socialists—at times, it is true, based on genuine ethnic foundations such as Bété particularism. Repression reached its peak between 1948 and 1950 under the cynical administration of Governor Péchoux, a socialist of nationalist leanings; with the assassination of Senator Biaka Boda; and with the bloody incidents at Treichville in 1949 and at Dimbokro and Seguela in 1950.

The PDCI apparatus was disrupted, activists were persecuted, and the

11. Mortimer, *France and the Africans*, pp. 105–10; Schachter-Morgenthau, *Political Parties*, pp. 176–87; Zolberg, *One-Party Government*, pp. 81–105; P. H. Siriex, *Felix Houphouët-Boigny* (Abidjan, 1976), the only biography of the Ivorian leader; useful, although hero-worshiping.

results of the 1951 elections were obviously going to be falsified; the situation was unpromising despite the loyalty of the masses. It was then that, thanks to François Mitterand, then Minister of Overseas France, Houphouët decided in July 1950 to sever his tie with the Communist party of France, to the great indignation of the colonists.[12] At first, the administration was not in the least grateful, and the parliamentary elections of 1951 were falsified, as were the Territorial Assembly elections in 1952 (with the exception of Ivory Coast). The repression was, however, suspended. The PDCI rebuilt its organization, concluded a compromise with the colonists, and triumphed in the 1956 parliamentary elections. While Houphouët began a ministerial career in France, his friends were consolidating their power in Ivory Coast in anticipation of imminent political changes.[13]

Expansion of the RDA

The 1950 break with the Communist party was accepted in Ivory Coast without much regret; but elsewhere, where territorial parties, often quite powerful, had other social bases and ideological orientations, the break was more difficult. Nevertheless, Gabriel d'Arboussier, who had resigned in July 1950 from the RDA's secretariat-general, unsuccessfully led the campaign against disaffiliation until 1952. Except for the Union des Populations du Cameroun, (UPC) only a majority of the Union Démocratique Sénégalaise (UDS) and a minority of the Parti Populaire du Niger (PPN) refused to follow Houphouët. Expelled, Djibo Bakari founded the Union Democratique du Niger (UDN) at Niamey in 1954.

Upper Volta followed without difficulty. The profound nationalism of the Mossi, and their desire for reunification and for better control over the emigration of workers to the coast, had contributed to the reestablishment in March 1948 of the autonomy of this territory, which had been partitioned in 1932 so as to facilitate the supply of labor to the plantations. But it is certain that France sought above all to ensure that this region should not

12. Ansprenger, *Politik*, pp. 137–43; Mortimer, *France and the Africans*, pp. 148–60. In April, Houphouët had still attended the Communist party (PCF) Congress, but on June 23 he had the new orientation approved by the parliamentary group over the objection of Félix d'Arboussier, who resigned from the General Secretariat on July 7. The negotiations received a new impetus from Mitterand, who became Minister of Overseas France in the Pleven government in July. The SFIO and Indépendents d'Outre-Mer endeavored to win over the RDA, and a secret understanding was concluded with them on August 9. Disaffiliation was finally announced on October 17, 1950 (the communiqué was dated October 19), but the group actually joined the Union Démocratique of Socialiste de la Résistance (UDSR) out of loyalty to the RDA and under Mitterand's influence.

13. Zolberg, *One-Party Government*, pp. 106–46; Schachter-Morgenthau, *Political Parties*, pp. 188-202.

fall under the influence of the RDA, which was preponderant in Ivory Coast. The operation succeeded at first, Joseph Conombo's Union Voltaïque reducing the RDA to insignificance. After 1948 a prestigious RDA figure, Ouezzin Coulibaly, who was closely linked with Houphouët and, having been William Ponty's inspector general at Dakar, enjoyed great influence with his generation of intellectuals, led the struggle in the western part of the country against Nazi Boni's Progressives, the Mouvement Populaire d'Evolution Africaine (MPEA) and, in the central area, against the friends of the Morho-Naba (Union Voltaïque, Parti Social d'Education des Masses Africaines). The latter eventually confessed defeat, and the RDA-Parti Democratique Voltaïque triumphed in the 1956 elections. However, after the death of Ouezzin in 1958, the latter party was to fall into the unsure hands of Maurice Yaméogo, a recent defector from the Union Voltaïque.

In Soudan (Mali) the Union Soudanaise (US) was a large party intimately associated with the civil servants' unions influenced by the Confédération Générale du Travail. Under the distinguished leadership of Mamadou Konate, it gradually reduced the influence of F. D. Sissoko's "Socialists," who were supported by the administration. The US permanently remained a civil servants' party of bureaucratic and authoritarian leanings, a tendency further reinforced after the death of Konate before independence, under the presidency of Modibo Keita.[14]

In Guinea, on the other hand, the Parti Démocratique de Guinée (PDG)[15] was extremely weak in 1946, while self-styled Socialists supported by the administration and the chiefs seemed all-powerful (Yaçine Diallo, Mamba Sano, formerly of the RDA). A revised socialism appeared after 1952 in the person of Ibrahima Barry, known as Barry III. But it was too late. Guinea had in fact become the stage for a remarkable adventure in which the trade unionist and PDG leader, Sékou Touré, seized uncontested power. Long regarded as a fellow-traveler, he was in reality an African nationalist for whom power was prerequisite to all else and justified all means. He followed Houphouët unenthusiastically in his break with the Communist party. Deeply influenced by Nkrumah's pan-African ideas, Touré was above all concerned with asserting his own unrivaled supremacy within the framework of his own state. He was to succeed in this, thanks to

14. Schachter-Morgenthau, *Political Parties*, pp. 255–98.

15. Bernard Charles, "Un Parti politique africain: Le Parti démocratique de Guinée," *Revue Française de Science Politique* (June 1962), pp. 312–59; Gray Cowan, in G. M. Carter, ed., *African One-Party States: Tunisia, Senegal, Guinea, Ivory Coast, Liberia, Tanganyika* (New York, 1962); Schachter-Morgenthau, *Political Parties*, pp. 220–53.

the remarkably effective action of the civil servants, railway workers, and miners unions. The great Federal strike in support of the Labor Code, and the Conakry strike of September–October 1953 for a 20 percent increase in wages, placed him in a position of strength, and he won the 1956 elections. By then he had eliminated all opposition and held undisputed power at all levels when the 1958 crisis occurred. It will be recalled that Touré broke with Houphouët on the structure of the Federal executive and, alone among French tropical African leaders, had the audacity to demand immediate independence and the strength to assert it, which he did in September 1958. This earned him, within the black world, an extraordinary prestige that his catastrophic domestic policy destroyed only gradually.

In Niger, by contrast, the RDA of Hamani Diori and Boubou Hamma, also composed of civil servants, was quite moderate and had difficulty in asserting its influence. Revolutionary virulence was confined to the UDN and later the Sawaba, led by Djibo Bakari, who left the RDA at the time of the disaffiliation crisis. He formed a government in 1957 under the Loi-Cadre, but fell from power in 1958, having made the miscalculation of voting "no" in the referendum without possessing the means to enforce his will.[16] The RDA was introduced into Togo under Martin Aku, but only ephemerally, since the rules of the political game were distorted by the Ewe nationalist problem. Its first representative in Dahomey was S. M. Apithy, an expert accountant and converted Catholic who enjoyed a strong personal position at Porto-Novo. He left the RDA in September 1948, however, under MRP influence, and founded the Indépendents d'Outre-Mer (IOM) in cooperation with Aujoulat. The RDA was later reconstituted by dentist Justin Ahomadegbe, who represented only one of three regional factions, that of Abomey. It is impossible to give any clear ideological definition of these leagues, whose rivalries, as shortsighted as they were sterile, were to lead the country into catastrophe after independence.[17]

In Senegal, finally, the RDA was represented by the Union Démocratique Sénégalaise (UDS), promoted by Dr. Doudou Gueye, a courageous and honorable man and a personal friend of Houphouët. The political stage, however, was occupied, and aside from some hold it exerted over the labor unions, the UDS was never more than a small, marginal group reinforced from time to time by intellectuals returning from France. At the instigation of trade unionist Abdoulaye Gueye, however, the UDS refused

16. Schachter-Morgenthau, *Political Parties*, pp. 102, 317.

17. Glélé, *Naissance d'un etat noir*.

to break with the Communist party after 1950 and was expelled from the RDA, of which the Senegalese branch was reconstituted by Doudou Gueye under the name of Mouvement Populaire Sénégalais(MPS). These two groups led a shadowy existence until they were absorbed into Senghor's party: the UDS in 1956, the MPS in 1958.[18]

This cursory review indicates the profound heterogeneity of the RDA within French West Africa. Even before it broke apart in 1958, this great edifice, which had done so much to awaken the masses, had an illusory quality. Nonetheless, nothing comparable existed among its adversaries.

Senghor and the Bloc Démocratique Sénégalais (BDS)[19]

It is a striking fact that in Senegal the Socialists (SFIO), who appeared so strong in 1946, sustained a total defeat and paid dearly for their unconditional adherence to the pro-French faction's nationalism. As we have seen, Senghor resigned because he was forbidden to attend the Bamako Congress. Aware of Gueye's weaknesses, particularly his inability to organize outside the cities, Senghor exploited them to his own advantage. In September 1948, seizing the occasion of events in Madagascar, he rejected the SFIO as hostile to the liberation of Africa and founded the Bloc Démocratique Senegalais. Thanks to the remarkable energy of the Senghorand schoolteacher Mamadou Dia, the BDS entirely supplanted the SFIO outside the urban centers: it won the elections of 1951 and 1956; it absorbed the UDS in 1956, and the remnants of the SFIO in 1958, to form the Union Populaire Sénégalaise (UPS), which became the Parti Socialiste Sénégalais (PSS) in 1977. Mamadou Dia, who became a notable economist under the guidance of François Perroux, was for Senghor its principal organizer, and it was he who formed the Loi-Cadre government in 1957.

The BDS was a mass party, like the RDA branches, which explains why it left no room for the latter. Except for a few urban centers remaining loyal to the SFIO, a few trade unionists associated with Abdoulaye Gueye (UDS), and the adherents of Doudou Gueye (MPS), it brought together the great majority of civil servants and intellectuals, who were numerous in Senegal, and also drew strength from the peasant masses and the quasi-traditional structure of the marabout brotherhoods. This heterogeneity made it a genuinely national party, and its ideology was indeed far more nationalistic

18. Schachter-Morgenthau, *Political Parties*, pp. 138, 158–60.

19. Ansprenger, *Politik*, pp. 160–77; Schachter-Morgenthau, *Political Parties*, pp. 139–64; L. V. Thomas, *Le Socialisme et l'Afrique* (Paris, 1962); Traoré, *Evolution des partis;* Zuccarelli, *Formation de l'unité*, pp. 44–54.

than that of the PDCI. However, when its progressive faction, at Dia's initiative, endeavored to introduce Socialist processes, the party fell apart and the attempt failed (1958–62).

With the loss of Senegal and the progressive collapse of its constituencies in Guinea and Soudan, the SFIO had finally lost out in Africa, having failed to rise above its French nationalism. It remained barely alive for ten years before resigning itself to extinction.

In Paris, meanwhile, Senghor, master of Senegal, found himself isolated, face to face with the RDA, and in search of alliances which might provide him the means of exerting pressure upon French officialdom. It is understandable that he, too, attempted to play the game of shifting affiliations and interterritorial regroupings. It must be acknowledged that he did so much less successfully than Houphouët. Left out of the RDA by his refusal, at SFIO demand, to go to the Bamako Congress, and how having broken with the SFIO, Senghor and his Senegalese friends joined with elected representatives from Dahomey (Apithy), Togo (Aku), and Upper Volta, who had combined in September 1948 with Aujoulat, deputy from Cameroun, to found the IOM. Several were former RDA members. They affiliated with the MRP, of which Aujoulat had been a member. This regrouping lacked balance, however, since only the Senegalese had a mass party comparable to the RDA, their partners being either notables supported by the administration or local leaders heading personal factions, as in Dahomey or Upper Volta. This parliamentary bloc became a genuine movement only in February 1953, at the Bobo-Dioulasso Congress.[20]

It nevertheless remains true that the political scene did not appreciably change until the turn of the year 1957, when the march toward independence began. On the other hand, French West Africa was profoundly transformed during these ten or twelve years.

The Reforms[21]

In 1944–45 the Provisional Government, sometimes even without awaiting the end of hostilities, had granted certain reforms, such as abolition of the *indigénat* (December 22, 1945) and a first step toward electoral franchise. On April 11, 1946, Houphouët succeeded in having his renowned law abolishing forced labor adopted by the first Constituent Assembly. On May

20. Ansprenger, *Politik*, pp. 160–77; Schachter-Morgenthau, *Political Parties*, pp. 93–105; Mortimer, *France and the Africans*, pp. 188–96.

21. Ansprenger, *Politik*, pp. 235–52; Schachter-Morgenthau, *Political Parties*, pp. 59–73; Mortimer, *France and the Africans*, pp. 179–87.

7, Lamine Gueye saw passed his law theoretically extending French citizenship to all the inhabitants of the overseas territories.

At the end of the year, the Constitution having finally been adopted, a parliamentary battle was joined to place the law in conformity with the principles announced for the French Union. The debate was unusually protracted, bitter, and obstructed by delaying tactics on the part of the administration and of rightist politicians, prominent among whom were Coste-Floret of the MRP, the Radical-Socialist Caillavet, and the majority of the Gaullists Rassemblement du Peuple Français (RPF). Until his 1951 defeat, Gueye devoted himself to questions of terms of public service; in harmony with his assimilationist ideology, he endeavored to place the African corps of civil servants on the same basis as that of their metropolitan colleagues; in this he succeeded, with the second Lamine-Gueye Law of June 1950, which was seriously to burden the budgets of the future African states.

The greatest struggle, however, was over the Labor Code, which aroused fierce opposition in economic circles. Signed by Moutet in October 1947, at the end of the decree period it was rescinded by an act of questionable legality by the new minister, Coste-Floret; despite Aujoulat's efforts, it remained suspended till 1952. The great strike of November 4 promoted by Sékou Touré unblocked it in that year, and it was finally passed, notwithstanding last-minute intrigues by Caillavet, then secretary of state.

These reforms were not made for the benefit of the indifferent masses. The RDA and UDS were meanwhile thoroughly politicizing the people into the farthest corners of the bush.

The Trade Unions[22]

After 1945 it was the trade unions that established effective hold over the body of civil servants and the small laboring class. One of the latter's most active elements was the railway workers guild. At the outset, most of the unions, and the most active ones, were organized by the French Confédération Générale du Travail (CGT). During the period of the RDA's affiliation, Communist influence among them was often strong. The Confédération Française des Travailleurs Chrétiens also endeavored to establish a

22. Ansprenger, *Politik*, pp. 217–25; Jean Meynaud and Anisse Saleh-Bey, *Trade Unions in Africa* (London, 1967); Ioan Davies, *African Trade Unions* (Harmondsworth, 1966); Schachter-Morgenthau, *Political Parties*, pp. 111–12, 159, 252–53. Ansprenger writes incorrectly that the railway workers' strike brought about their break with the CGT; the exact opposite actually occurred, at least for the Senegalese.

foothold, adopting the name Confédération des Travailleurs Croyants (CTC) in addressing the Muslims. The administration, dismayed by what it considered a "communist danger," often eased its way; but the administration soon perceived that the social combativity of the "believers" was frequently as lively as that of the "communists." After the disruption of the WFTU as a result of the Cold War, the Force Ouvrière also tried to enter the field but was able to attract only a smattering of civil servants.

In the circumstances, social and political effervescence was intense, and the period was marked by historic strikes. The first was that of the French West African railway workers, which took place from October 1947 to May 1948 and was led by Ibrahima Sar, one of Dia's future ministers, who died in 1959 after a harsh imprisonment. The strike was especially intense at Thiès, in Senegal, where it recalled the events of 1938. It inspired the famous novel by Sembène Ousmane, *Les Bouts de bois de Dieu.* It was a failure, but it stimulated militancy among the workers, and definitively broke the affiliation of the union, which had recognized that it was within the CGT. We should also mention the Conakry strike for implementation of the Code du Travail, which lasted from September to November 1953 and was a decisive stage in the rise of Sékou Touré and the PDCI.

The close association between the unions and the parties is a notable feature of this period. The workers sought direct participation in the political struggle, and that is why the accusations of communism were unfounded, despite certain organizational ties. Sékou Touré was a revolutionary nationalist, and was determined to rely upon himself alone. Now the French CGT maneuvered very clumsily, opposing any direct affiliation by the Africans with the Prague Centrale. The result was the rupture of 1955, when Sékou Touré organized his own Union Générale des Travailleurs d'Afrique Noire (UGTAN). It lasted only five years, however, for the political fragmentation following the 1958 watershed encouraged each state to exercise control over its own unions and to prevent any contact between them and Conakry. The unions were thenceforth considered an instrument to be used by the state.

As noted above, economic development, due in part to FIDES credits, was uneven but often remarkable during the period from 1947 to 1960. Guinea and Ivory Coast were the principal beneficiaries, but this is not the place to discuss the subject in detail. It resulted in a strong impetus for urbanization of the uneducated rural people, bringing into being an unqualified and unemployed mass but at the same time producing a rapid growth in the number of qualified workers. Dependence upon the world capitalist system accelerated, and the breath of the outside world touched even the most isolated peasants.

Education and Culture[23]

Economic development was accompanied in many places by rapid development of "education," always conceived of by the French as being exclusively aimed at the radical destruction of the African cultures, and at the selection of individual members of an elite while leaving the bulk of the students to fend for themselves.

It was only natural that the reaction in favor of African identity occurred first, not in Africa but in Europe, among the students. The new phenomenon, an important one at the cultural level, was that African students, who had been extremely few before 1939, flocked to the French universities after 1945. There was, in fact, no higher education in French-speaking Africa. The University of Dakar opened timidly in 1951 and became autonomous only in 1957; Abidjan's followed after 1960. The students in France were obviously highly politicized, and their association, Fédération des Etudiants d'Afrique Noire (in France) (FEANF), became a center of virulent radicalism, engaging in unbridled criticism of the politicians in power. Furthermore, they followed with enthusiasm the evolution of the English-speaking Africans, and it was here (and quite soon—as early as 1948) that the demand first appeared for total independence and cultural separation, which the elected representatives, paralyzed by French ideology, were incapable of formulating—except perhaps for Senghor, who masked it with extreme prudence.

Beginning in the years 1953–55, these students began to complete their studies and to return to their countries in large numbers. There they revealed themselves as far less radical than they had been at Paris; some reversed their positions in the most spectacular fashion (one thinks of Konan Bedié, a revolutionary socialist while an economics student at Poitiers and an apostle of the crudest kind of capitalism as minister of economy at Abidjan). Many, nevertheless, retained some of their youthful ideals, so that their integration into African politics profoundly altered its climate around 1955, on the eve of the great change that was to take place. In Senegal some of the newcomers followed the old UDS/RDA only momentarily in its association with Senghor, and in 1956 established the Parti Africain de l'Indépendence (PAI), which invoked a narrow, dogmatic

23. Ansprenger, *Politik*, pp. 226–38; Léopold Sédar Senghor, *Liberté 1: Négritude et humanisme* (Paris, 1964), and *Liberté 2: Nation et voie africaine du socialisme*, 2d ed. (Paris, 1970). Senghor's works may be consulted with great profit, particularly these two first volumes of *Liberté:* the transition from Négritude to politics is revealed in striking fashion, in writings of high literary value. See also Jabez Ayodele Langley, *Pan-Africanism and Nationalism in Western Africa* (Oxford, 1973); Imanuel Geiss, *The Pan-African Movement* (London, 1974).

form of Marxism; its influence did not extend, however, beyond a nucleus of trade unionists and intellectuals. (Banned in 1960, one of its factions was legalized in 1976.)[24]

More important was the influence the intellectuals exerted within the large parties themselves, particularly in the UDS-UPS, with which some periodically broke only to rejoin later, and in the PDCI-RDA. In Guinea, Sékou Touré's autocracy left them no freedom of action.

Decolonization on the Way[25]

The final factor which contributed to preparing the way for the 1956 turning-point was the change in evolution of the global equilibrium. In the context of the Cold War, advanced decolonization everywhere, even though peoples of the Latin tradition, such as France, resigned themselves to it reluctantly because of their dream of eternal empire. The USSR pressed for the dismantling of empires in order to weaken the rival camp. But the United States, while hesitant through fear of placing "reds" in power, pushed in the same direction insofar as solidarity with its allies permitted. In the view of the political Left, at least, for America, the ideal was a political independence that would open up the new states to the capitalism of the multinational companies and put an end to tariff barriers.

France clung to Indochina, where many blacks fought until 1954, when the Mendès-France government began the process of decolonizing that country as well as Tunisia. Morocco's turn soon followed in 1956. After November 1954, however, it was the Algerian war that captured the attention of France and profoundly upset its political life. Partisans of colonialism concentrated their effort upon this crucial case, which engaged all the passion of the nationalist tradition. The other colonies, including black Africa, became minor cases well outside the limelight. This was fortunate for them, for clear-sighted, benevolent men were able to exploit this propitious penumbra to set in motion irreversible processes of separation.

The political liberation of French-speaking black Africa, however, was not only a matter of the world context and of France's fixation upon the most inflammatory cases. The demand for it was late in developing by reason of the French ideology, which impeded the rise of consciousness among Africa's politicians. But the evolution of the region, pressure by radical intellectuals trained in Paris, and especially the rapid rejection of the colonial

24. Ansprenger, *Politik*, pp. 376–82; Schachter-Morgenthau, *Political Parties*, pp. 155–60.

25. Ansprenger, *Politik*, pp. 241–60; Mortimer, *France and the Africans*, pp. 201–26.

framework by its English-speaking neighbors and the trusteeship territories all led in the opposite direction.

For French West Africa the decisive role was played by the Gold Coast, soon to be metamorphosed into Ghana.[26] Many leaders imbued with French ideology, like Houphouët, mistrusted the English language and pan-Africanism, but Senghor had encountered them on the banks of the Seine, and others, like Sékou Touré, found in them the reaffirmation of their revolutionary nationalism. In any event, Kwame Nkrumah, who had for many years been in contact with the Sherif of Kankan in Guinea, placed his colingual colleague, Houphouët (the Nzima and Baule languages are mutually intelligible), somewhat in the shade; but the rapid pace at which he led Ghana toward independence was destined to produce a decisive collision. It will be recalled that after his imprisonment Nkrumah headed an autonomous government in 1951, expanded its powers after the 1956 elections, and proclaimed independence in March 1957. One month later, on April 6, during a visit to Abidjan, Houphouët issued his famous challenge to Nkrumah opposing the venture toward independence.

This development first swept Togo along and, more slowly, Cameroun, which is beyond the purview of the present study. The former's trusteeship status had prevented France, to her disgust, from assimilating this former German colony. But the ethnic nationalism of the Ewe, who demanded unification with those in Ghana while maladroitly ignoring the rest of Togo, made it possible for the French administration to play its hand cleverly while Nkrumah, belying his pan-Africanism, hoped to exploit the situation by annexing Togo. In order to ease international pressure after the decolonization of Indochina and Tunisia, and after the onset of the Algerian war, France, having disbanded the Comité d'Unité Togolaise (CUT) of Sylvanus Olympio and its youth group Juvento, led by the lawyer Santos, decided in 1955 to proclaim an autonomous state governed by her own creature, Grunitsky. But dusting off the myths of assimilation was not enough. Olympio was the victor in the 1957 elections, and it was the CUT that led Togo to independence.[27]

Thus we see that a French-speaking state had been torn away from the myths of imperial unity and launched on the road to political sovereignty and reconstruction of its identity. In spite of the stubborn blindness prevalent in Ivory Coast or Gabon, the course that events would take in the near

26. Dennis Austin, *Politics in Ghana 1946–1960* (London, 1970).

27. Claude E. Welch, *Dream of Unity: Pan-Africanism and Political Unification in West Africa* (Ithaca, N.Y., 1966). The best available study of Togo and Ewe nationalism, this study, deals also, though less satisfactorily, with Cameroun and the Ghana-Guinea-Mali Union.

future appeared clearly as early as 1955. A procedure remained to be found by which the ideological and juridical impasses created by the French constitution could be discreetly circumvented.

From the Loi-Cadre to Independence, 1956–1960

From 1956 on, the political history of French-speaking Africa accelerated. While the Algerian crisis, which was to bring about the fall of the Fourth Republic, was intensifying, a center of pan-African agitation had been formed in Ghana, and the British, to the consternation of the French colonists, were doing their best to push their other territories toward independence even when they were hesitant, like Nigeria or Sierra Leone.

Invigorated by the intellectuals returning from Paris, the French West African parties were effervescent; everywhere the masses, increasingly politicized, were stirring. In Guinea incidents occurred daily. Were we to witness a war of liberation like the one that seemed to be adumbrated in Cameroun with the armed action of the Union des Population du Cameroun (UPC)? This was hard to conceive at a time when all French forces were earmarked for Algeria.

The Loi-Cadre[28]

The most clear-sighted among French political officials thought, on the contrary, that the time was ripe to break the yoke of French ideology and the French constitution without calling attention to what they were doing, and to bring about an evolutionary situation in black Africa that would make it possible to avert an explosion. The idea doubtless originated with Buron, Mendès-France's Minister of Overseas France, who placed it under study during the 1954 decolonization wave; in 1955, Minister of State Senghor was unable to move it forward. Despite the nationalism of the old SFIO, it was a member of that party, Gaston Defferre, Minister of Overseas France in the Mollet cabinet, who directed the operation by having the 1956 Loi-Cadre drafted and passed, with Houphouët as minister of health.

This action does honor Defferre, although it won him symmetrical insults, both from those who accused him of scrapping the empire and from those who blamed him for the "Balkanization," or fragmentation, of Africa into ministates incapable of genuine independence. As early as 1955–56, some senior officials of the ministry undoubtedly entertained the idea that, since it was necessary to set Africa free, it was preferable to split it up into

28. Ansprenger, *Politik*, pp. 241–52; Schachter-Morgenthau, *Political Parties*, pp. 65–73, 110–15; Mortimer, *France and the Africans*, pp. 233–40.

mini-stages, each of which would be forced to remain attached to the metropole. Defferre did not embrace this idea, but neither did he fight vigorously against it, as the British did by enforcing unity in Nigeria and the Sudan against the wishes of minorities who did not want it. But it is too easy to lay everything at the door of the French. The Africans were deeply divided over the choice between autonomy—or, later, independence—within a French West African framework or within the narrower one of each colony by itself; the rich colonies, such as Gabon or Ivory Coast, were fiercely opposed to the former alternative. We have seen that the RDA was to break up over this problem in 1958; Houphouët was the leader of the opposition to federalism, not only out of Ivorian selfishness, but also because he feared he would be left in the minority and be drawn into a dangerous venture through the victory of irresponsible revolutionaries at the head of the other territories.

Now, after the 1956 elections, which represented a total victory for the PDCI, Houphouët, a minister of the French government, became its most influential councillor on African politics. He remained so for many years, even after independence, and particularly after de Gaulle's return in 1958. In such circumstances it was unthinkable that federal principles, which were already incompatible with the administration's profound desire for fragmentation, could win out. One cannot, therefore, lay the blame on Gaston Defferre. Rather, one must emphasize the fact that the game's outcome was not decided in advance, no matter what one may believe retrospectively. French nationalism was still on the lookout for any threat to the empire, and but for the Algerian war, which diverted attention, nothing—probably—would have been possible. Furthermore, the French constitution was so unwieldy that only by violating it—knowingly but discreetly, as he himself has said—did Defferre succeed in effecting passage of his draft law.[29]

This unprecedented document was not revolutionary in tone, but it was profoundly and totally contrary to the French tradition of centralization. Georges Bidault, a devout Christian in his ultranationalism, was not deceived. "Soon," he said, "there will be governments everywhere except in Paris." Above all, the Loi-Cadre was a cunningly evolutionary document. The processes it set in motion led straight to independence, thanks to a favorable combination of circumstances.

The fact which was unprecedented in French tradition was that, while leaving the question of federations such as French West Africa open, it permitted the creation in each territory of a governing council chosen by an

29. Author's conversations with Gaston Defferre.

assembly elected, at last, by universal suffrage. This council was to administer all public services except those affecting "sovereignty," which were reserved to the governor, who was also the council's president. In the event, this latter arrangement was called into question in 1958, and the governor was replaced by an elected president (previously the vice-president). The institutions of the French community contemplated by the 1958 constitution, which were to be the capstone of the entire edifice, remained a dead letter. Thus, the only step left to take was to transfer the sovereign functions (defense, foreign affairs, and so on), and this was accomplished by the independence agreements of 1960.

Formation of the Governments

From this time on, political life in French West Africa became feverish. Everyone felt, indeed, that evolution would now be rapid, although no one dared to utter the word *independence*. Moreover, by virtue of the authoritarian colonial heritage and the shunting aside of African traditions, one could anticipate that the teams in office when the French departed would have every chance of staying there indefinitely. It was thus urgent to occupy positions of power at any cost during the decisive years that were beginning. The period after 1956 witnessed a general realignment of political forces.

Elections to the assemblies having proceeded without incident on March 31, the governing councils were formed in the spring of 1957.[30] In Senegal, Senghor left the vice-presidency to Mamadou Dia, who undertook an experiment based on peasant communities, with the help of Father Lebret's technicians. This quest for a program of self-governing socialism began with a thorough reorganization of the marketing of peanuts, which mobilized all the conservative forces against him and brought about his fall in 1962. But the first struggles were both practical and symbolic. They consisted in the transfer of the capital from Saint Louis to Dakar, which was accomplished early in 1958 amid intrigues and violent protests.

Constituent parties of the RDA took power as expected in Guinea, Ivory Coast, Upper Volta, and Mali. In Guinea, Sékou Touré immediately abolished the office of customary chief and instituted autocratic power, often by terrorist methods, down to the village level. Master of the trade unions and supported by the great majority of the people, he had the means to place, and win, the bet of voting no in the September 1958 referendum.

In Ivory Coast, Houphouët set great store by his office as minister in

30. Ansprenger, *Politik*, pp. 248–50; Mortimer, *France and the Africans*, pp. 262–69; Schachter-Morgenthau, *Political Parties*, pp. 107–23.

Paris, conscious of the effective pressure he exerted upon France's African policy.[31] He therefore left the vice-presidency to schoolteacher Auguste Denise, a self-effacing and completely loyal aide. Houphouët's positions were by now well defined. He absolutely rejected a federal government as well as independence. In his view, the Ivorian bourgeoisie was to establish itself under the direct protection of France against any foreign threat or domestic trouble. Development excluded any idea of African identity, being conceived purely as material growth, and it is in this sense that one should interpret the famous challenge to Nkrumah in 1957.

A rigid, authoritarian party, on the model of the PDG but less ramified in the country, assumed power at Bamako under Modibo Keita, Konate having died in May 1956.[32]

In Niger, on the other hand, the RDA was eclipsed by Djibo Bakari's Sawaba, an offshoot of the UDN; Bakari obviously tried to follow Sékou Touré's example but lacked the latter's control over his country. The irresponsible choice of no in September 1958 made it possible for Hamani Diori's RDA, combining with the customary chiefs, to supplant him very quickly.[33]

Finally, in Dahomey, still sharply divided among three regional clans, power was placed in the hands of Sourou Migan Apithy, who had been elected deputy in the 1946 elections; his authority, however, was largely confined to the Porto-Novo area.[34]

The Failure of Federalism

While the local authorities were getting settled in their positions, a lively polemic began over the problem of the federal executive, of which the formation at Dakar had changed the rules of the game. At the same time, regroupings and ruptures appeared at the interterritorial level in view of the deepening crisis.

The scattered remnants of SFIO, led by Lamine Gueye, founded the Mouvement Socialiste Africain (MSA)[35] at Conakry in January 1957. It was stillborn. Except for Gueye's Senegalese, who were to rejoin Senghor the following year, it included chiefly partisans of the Guinean, Barry III, genuine Socialists though confined to members of Futa Djallon, who were

31. Schachter-Morgenthau, *Political Parties*, pp. 212–16; Zolberg, *One-Party Government*, pp. 149–216.

32. Schachter-Morgenthau, *Political Parties*, pp. 294–300.

33. Ibid., pp. 317–18.

34. Glélé, *Naissance d'un etat noir*.

35. Ansprenger, *Politik*, pp. 143–59; Schachter-Morgenthau, *Political Parties*, pp. 302–11; Mortimer, *France and the Africans*, p. 255.

to join Sékou Touré in voting no in the referendum the following year. Of more importance was the effort of the Parti du Regroupement Africain (PRA), since it was formed around the well-organized UPS; the latter had recently found itself isolated, because at the Dakar Congress of February 1957 the IOM had dissolved to make way for Senghor's Convention Africaine (CA), which included a strong left wing.[36] The Sawaba of Niger added its strength to this revolutionary vigor. But the other territorial parties merely represented groups of notables or regional factions (Apithy, the Bété in Ivory Coast) who had in common only the impassioned struggle against the RDA's branches. There was nevertheless one problem which, although setting them against Houphouët, should have brought them together with some of his friends. In a spirit of revolutionary pan-Africanism, and by the clear intellectual decision of Senghor, the PRA declared itself strongly against "Balkanization," and thus in favor of a West African federal state. In fact, a general regrouping of the African parties was begun at a conference held in Paris on February 2, 1958. But the Congrès du Regroupement which followed at Dakar (March 26–April 5) witnessed the withdrawal of the RDA, while the others decided to create the PRA. The latter held its organizing congress at Cotonou July 25–27, after the May events and just before the constitutional studies announced by de Gaulle; to general surprise, the congress opted in favor of immediate independence. In September, however, Senghor coldly ordered a yes vote, and this brought about the defection of his left wing (Ly, Seck, Mbow), which founded a local party with little influence, the PRA Sénégal. They returned to the fold in 1964.[37] After the referendum and the fall of Sawaba, the PRA, having lost its raison d'être, disappeared. After independence, there was no longer any question of interterritorial alliances. The failure of the PRA as a regrouping attempt was accompanied by the decline of the RDA, which appeared to have succeeded in the same operation more than ten years before.

The increasingly revolutionary and autocratic tendencies of Sékou Touré were in sharp contrast, particularly after 1956, with the policy of Houphouët, the French minister, but it was over the question of a federal government that the break was finally made. A fervent pan-Africanist, and seeking a broader field than Guinea for his revolutionary action, Sékou Touré was an ardent proponent of a federal state centered at Dakar. Nevertheless, he was not prepared to make common cause with the friends of

36. Ansprenger, *Politik*, pp. 160–77; Mortimer, *France and the Africans*, p. 256.

37. Mortimer, *France and the Africans*, pp. 281–94; Gil Dugué, *Vers les Etats-Unis d'Afrique* (Dakar, 1960); Schachter-Morgenthau, *Political Parties*, pp. 302–11.

Senghor, whose influence he feared. He therefore intrigued to carry along the RDA apparatus; but given the unshakable opposition of Houphouët, this was a hopeless ploy. The explosion in fact occurred at the time of the RDA interterritorial congress at Bamako in September 1957.[38] It was papered over, however, and the moral authority of Ouzzin Coulibaly was counted upon to avoid the worst. But he died in September 1958 and, by a very African contradiction, Guinea's negative vote sealed the breakup of the unity to which Sékou Touré had claimed to be so fervently attached. That was the end of the RDA as an interterritorial coalition. The member parties thenceforth followed increasingly divergent paths, each within the framework of its nation-state. A few branches, especially those composing the Conseil de l'Entente, remained grouped around Houphouët and endeavored to keep the tradition alive.

The 1958 Crisis and the Community[39]

The process leading to independence with fragmentation was thus well advanced when the French crisis of 1958 acted as a catalyst and substantially accelerated the course of events.

De Gaulle's reputation as a decolonizer is strangely undeserved. We have observed this with respect to the 1944 Brazzaville Conference, but the same can be said of the address he delivered in the same city in 1958.

When returning to power in June 1958 as a result of the Algerian affair, de Gaulle certainly did not place black Africa in the forefront of his preoccupations, but he was too imbued with French grandeur really to neglect the old Empire. The role that the clandestine services of M. Jacques Foccart played in this field is well known. The influence now enjoyed by Houphouët, who revealed himself a fervent Gaullist, has perhaps not been sufficiently emphasized. Deeply steeped in French ideology, he was prepared to forgive past insults and render the best and most loyal of services, on the sole condition that the local bourgeoisie be assisted in strengthening itself and increasing its wealth. Convinced that no African country, and particularly the wealthy Ivory Coast, would be safe in a dangerous world except with a direct and intimate link with France, Houphouët was, with the approval of Michel Debré, the architect of the chapters of the 1958 constitution in respect to what would be called no longer the French Union, but the Community. Now, by rejecting any access to national sov-

38. Ansprenger, *Politik*, pp. 148–52; Schachter-Morgenthau, *Political Parties*, p. 310; Mortimer, *France and the Africans*, pp. 270–80.

39. Ansprenger, *Politik*, pp. 261–84; Mortimer, *France and the Africans*, pp. 303–26.

ereignty, by imposing an unwieldy and uneven federal structure with broad reserved powers, while rendering any inter-African federation impossible or at least difficult, this constitution amounted virtually to a challenge to those who had now become radical nationalists, whether in the RDA or the PRA. The first draft, made public in July, explains the PRA's position at the Cotonou Congress. The final version, written in August, did permit rapid evolution in another direction, as de Gaulle was to declare in Brazzaville. But ambiguities and mental reservations persisted, which explains the negative decisions of Sékou Touré and Djibo Bakari, as well as the unenthusiastic "yes" votes of Senegal or Mali.

De Gaulle thus hoped that by expanding the powers of the loyal local bourgeoisies France would keep a firm grasp of Africa generally, and that this would enhance her weight in the world at large while gaining for her, at small cost, a decolonizing reputation. He doubtless contemplated a purely political independence, but fairly distant in the future; he anticipated that it would be compensated for by cultural and economic ties, which could only grow stronger. The military presence, strongly maintained, would in any case be there to guarantee the future.[40]

Houphouët's responsibility for this web of illusions appears great, but the Ivorian leader fervently believed in it.

The challenge furthermore appeared to have succeeded since, on September 29, everyone voted "yes" except Guinea, which received exemplary punishment; cast into the outer darkness, it was denied credit and other facilities, and avoided collapse only by a headlong flight into increasing autocracy. Without minimizing Sékou Touré's responsibility, one must nevertheless remember that France had a hand in the catastrophic evolution that plunged this unhappy country into economic disaster and a paranoid dictatorship. Houphouët himself was to strive jealously for years to make sure that nothing should be done to breach the boycott of these delinquents, whose immediate rapprochement with Nkrumah was taken as a further insult.[41]

Elsewhere, the Community seemed to be establishing itself without too many problems. Houphouët devoted his full talents to ensuring that the framework he had given it not be distorted. Thus he fought vigorously against any effort toward inter-African federation, although Senghor and most leftist intellectuals remained obsessed by this idea. Although entirely refuted by the facts, the idea of unity was still Africa's pattern of thought as

40. Mortimer, *France and the Africans*, pp. 309–28.

41. Ansprenger, *Politik*, pp. 285–318; Mortimer, *France and the Africans*, pp. 329–33.

it moved toward liberation. It was to culminate in 1963 in the formation of the OAU, which personifies quite well the homage that hypocrisy pays to virtue.

As early as November 1958, Senegal, Soudan, Upper Volta, and Dahomey decided to organize the Mali Federation.[42] Using all the economic power of Ivory Coast, and manipulating friendships and prestige, Houphouët succeeded in effecting the secession of Upper Volta and Dahomey early in 1959. Along with his friends in Niger, as yet hardly consolidated in power, he grouped them in a loose not even confederal, structure—the Conseil de l'Entente. Watching jealously over their moderate orientation, which he was in a position to reward financially, after independence he was to make them one of the pillars of moderate Africa: the Monrovia group, opposed to the Casablanca group.

By this act, however, Houphouët had set off a chain reaction which led to the very independence he desired to avoid at any price. This evolution was doubtless inevitable, but he hastened its pace.

The March to Independence[43]

Many think that Guinea's example was decisive, and that without its "no" the Community might have survived awhile. Certainly, the audacity of Sékou Touré's gesture won him extraordinary prestige and strengthened the will of radical nationalists everywhere, notably those in Soudan (Mali), who were particularly close to the Guineans.

But another factor, which to this writer seems more important, is usually neglected: by reducing the Mali Federation to Senegal and Soudan, Houphouët had deprived it of balance. No arbitration is possible within a federation of only two members. The Senegalese, who were democrats in search of a delicate equilibrium between moderates and self-management socialists, found themselves a minority confronting a Soudan with a larger population, vast, authoritarian, and less advanced. Proud of their progress, the Senegalese, except for an extremist minority, were determined to face up to the Soudanese. In the long run this contradiction brought about the collapse of the Federation after independence, in August 1960. But in the

42. Ansprenger, *Politik*, pp. 330–56; William J. Foltz, *From French West Africa to the Mali Federation* (New Haven, 1965). This book is a thorough and well-organized study of the breakup of French West Africa, essentially as seen from Dakar; Mortimer, *France and the Africans*, pp. 349–54, 362–66.

43. Ansprenger, *Politik*, pp. 319–28; Zolberg, *One-Party Government*, pp. 319–49; Mortimer, *France and the Africans*, pp. 360–70; Schachter-Morgenthau, *Political Parties*, pp. 313–25.

near term, it created a situation where national liberation and reconstruction of the African identity were objects up for auction. Senghor's "yes" in 1958 moreover carried the clear implication of eventual independence, without violent upheavals.

Meanwhile, it had been hoped that de Gaulle would quickly put an end to the Algerian war; but the conflict dragged on and on, and this made association with France increasingly unbearable for the African nationalists. Passions rose while the rest of Africa was marching at an impressive pace toward liberation. Several English-speaking states, including great Nigeria nearby, acceded to it in 1960, as well as the Belgian Congo, of which the ultra-rapid evolution upset all expectations. French-speaking Cameroun would soon follow.

Throughout 1959 and early 1960, to Houphouët's disgust, Mali's leaders made repeated approaches to obtain from France by amicable means the transfer of functions which would lead to sovereignty. Disappointed and disillusioned by the Algerian affair, and believing it possible to preserve powerful economic and cultural links, de Gaulle allowed himself to be persuaded. After careful negotiation, and in the best possible conditions, the agreements acknowledging Mali's sovereignty were concluded in April, and independence was proclaimed in June 1960. Senegalese separate independence followed two months later, but that is another story. Madagascar had followed in Mali's footsteps and at the same pace, within a few days.[44]

This retreat by France embittered Houphouët, who regarded it as a virtual betrayal. His pride led him, though not without anguish, to demonstrate his strength. Where Mali had negotiated, he decided to declare Ivory Coast's independence unilaterally, leaving cooperation agreements to be negotiated later. Given the ideological, economic, and political links that united Houphouët with France, de Gaulle seems to have taken this setback philosophically. The Community was an empty framework that could be discarded and replaced with a series of less formal, but more concrete, ties.

Ivory Coast having proclaimed its independence on August 7, its friends and the other moderate States could do no less. Between July and November all the French-speaking states of Africa, except for the Empire's "confetti"—Djibouti, the Comoros, and Réunion, which lacked statehood status—proclaimed their independence and, as the supreme accolade, entered the UN under the sponsorship of France. Thereafter, they negotiated

44. Mortimer, *France and the Africans*, pp. 352, 362, 369.

with good humor the cooperation agreements that tied them more or less closely with France in all fields, including the military, revision of which was not seriously considered for fifteen years or so.[45]

Conclusion: The People Excluded

We need not examine here the history of the first decades of independence; we shall simply sum up, and draw a few conclusions for the future.

Independence was the aspiration of the African masses, who wished to end a situation in which they were humiliated, exploited, and relegated to the margin of public affairs. For a time they were strongly politicized, but disillusion came quickly, as notably demonstrated by their total apathy in the face of the many coups d'Etat that have shaken the continent since the assassination of Sylvanus Olympio in Togo in 1963. The liberation of French West Africa, in fact, was accomplished without armed struggle, and the masses in whose name the leaders claimed to speak had no need to involve themselves directly.

How is this to be explained? Colonial society was an amalgam of phenomena of social oppression and of national oppression. One cannot, as in Gramsci's classical model, set political society, represented by the state apparatus, apart from civil society, embodied in the mass of the people. The colonial state absolutely excluded those who had not been acculturated to its system, reducing them to the level of marginal, exploited objects. The system thus united political and civil society in a single bloc dominating the inchoate nonentity, without culture or recognized personality, represented by the mass of the people.

Political independence in no way changed this. On the contrary, it reinforced it, justifying itself by empty talk of so-called nation-building.

The extension of power over the people at the time of colonization had constituted a profound rupture, in cosmology as well as in the relations among men. Decolonization, on the other hand, was achieved by subtle degrees, without brusque rupture.

The dominant white group was indeed replaced, particularly in the political field. But it was replaced by a new political stratum composed of elected officials and civil servants, even planters and merchants, recruited exclusively from the acculturated minority which had mastered the European knowledge that provides access to modern techniques of organiza-

45. Zolberg, *One-Party Government*, pp. 233–49; Mortimer, *France and the Africans*, p. 367; Guy de Lusignan, *l'Afrique noire depuis l'indépendance* (Paris, 1969), pp. 22–87; Schachter-Morgenthau, *Political Parties*, pp. 326–27.

tion. They are thus more or less broken off from the national culture, which they generally despise, their acculturation justifying, in their eyes, their social advancement. This is especially serious in French-speaking Africa, where an exceptional effort was made to break completely with the indigenous languages and cultures, and entirely to negate their value. While a few planters and businessmen remain within the traditional culture, this does not affect the overall phenomenon. Similarly, the demand for distinct cultural identity came late, and from the most acculturated element, the students returning from Europe. This reconstructed identity is necessary in order to avoid corruption and to escape from cultural domination, but its symbolic implications prevent the people from even dreaming of it. Indeed, by the present system's logic, it is by rejecting as completely as possible his collective being that any individual is able to climb the social ladder. The destruction of African communities in favor of the increased production made possible by competition among individuals is in fact the watchword of those states that have chosen the liberal path, such as Ivory Coast, Cameroun, or Gabon.

The dream of this petite bourgeoisie, which has assumed power with the people's support, is to transfer itself into a high bourgeoisie: that is, in the absence of the means to nourish a national capitalism, to secure by negotiation a larger share in the profits of the global system, for which they are only too ready to serve as go-betweens.

The values of the market—"le système des objets," to use Jean Baudrillard's term—being fully internalized, one need not hesitate to speak of social classes, whether or not one believes they existed in the old society.

This new class, however, is not homogeneous, and its behavior is unpredictable and variable. It sought emancipation from Europe in order to restore its derided dignity, and so as not to leave to the whites the offices it could occupy itself. Having attained this position, however, it saw focused upon itself the gaze of its own people, from whom it was separated by an ever-widening social and cultural gulf. It then usually did its best to maintain relations with the former metropole, renewing the themes of alienation and scorn for the local cultures, so as to justify its newly-won exclusive power and to contain the threat represented by the indigenous "savages." To close the gulf, it furthermore needed another sort of intermediary, of the sort already manipulated by the colonial system: either the customary chiefs, or pseudo-traditional structures that had permitted the masses to escape the colonial grasp, such as the marabout system in Senegal.

After 1945 the massive penetration by world capitalism, increasingly in the form of multinational corporations, into the somnolent domain previously reserved to the marginal commercial capitalism of the colonists, created a need for many new middlemen. The new bourgeoisie came forward to play this role.

Renewal of the African economy has thus simply increased its dependence upon the global system, and political independence has facilitated this trend more often than it has resisted it.

The nation-state thus became a fertile field for this phenomenon, for it had lost the market-constructing function it possessed according to the eighteenth-century ideology of Adam Smith. But this ideology of the absolute sovereignty of the state, and the contract among abstract citizens, has been faithfully reproduced, since it justifies the marginalization of the masses, the carriers of the national culture, exploitation of whom supports the whole system. Physical violence no longer sufficing, ideology and education inflict symbolic violence upon them, and bury them under disdain. Domination requires that the dominated live in a culture of the dominated.

It is thus easy to understand the disappointments that have followed political independence. Refusing to accept the organic nature of their peoples and to set free the powerful latent forces of the communities at the base for the sake of genuine development, the African states have remained in a condition of social and cultural schizophrenia. The results are the impossibility of restoring collective identity, the socialization of the state's apparatus, immovable obstacles to any development beyond the purely quantitative, and the total halt of the movement toward African unity.

Such is the present situation, and it offers no ground for optimism. These contradictions, however, cannot be left to grow indefinitely. There is some sober thought in progress, and many experiments are being undertaken—in the context, for example, of the Internationale founded in 1975 by Mamadou Dia upon his release from detention.

But hope will be limited until Africa calls Europe to account by demanding that it choose another type of development and until Africa rids itself of that poisonous heritage of colonialism: the logic of the nation-state.

7. *French Colonial Policy in Equatorial Africa in the 1940s and 1950s*

ELIKIA M'BOKOLO

French Equatorial Africa felt more keenly than any other colony of France the changes that took place in French colonial policies during the 1940s and 1950s. Formed in 1910 by the uniting of Gabon, Middle Congo, Ubangi-Shari, and Chad on the model of French West Africa, French Equatorial Africa remained in all respects less advanced than its sister. It was said, with some justice, that it was the "Cinderella of the French Empire."[1] No one has underlined better than Félix Eboué the misdeeds of the regime that dominated French Equatorial Africa between the end of the nineteenth century and 1940. In 1941, speaking frankly of the "errors of the past," the governor-general analyzed it thus:

> The Colony is threatened, threatened from within like a granary that is being depleted. Whether one finds the cause in the protracted system of large concessions, in chaotic economic exploitation, in a sometimes clumsy proselytization, in a slumbering education, or finally and above all in neglect of, one might even say contempt for, the native political and social structures, the result is there, and we can put our finger on it: this is a population which in some places is not increasing, and in others is diminishing; this is a country incapable of providing commerce, public works, and administration with the managerial and auxiliary personnel that are quite indispensable; this is a mass of people that is disintegrating and dispersing; voluntary abortion and syphilis are spreading within a nascent proletariat; these evils of an absurd individualism are inflicted all together on the colony.[2]

Except for the liberal interim period under Governor-General Reste (1935–39), who attempted unsuccessfully to introduce some reforms, French Equatorial Africa remained the domain of brutal economic exploitation and uncompromising political domination. No territory in the

1. M. Devèze, *La France d'Outre-Mer* (Paris, 1948), p. 181.
2. Félix Eboué, *La Nouvelle Politique indigène en A.E.F.* (Brazzaville, 1941), p. 2.

Federation was spared: in Gabon and Ubangi-Shari, where there was a large nucleus of white colonials, the system weighed as heavily as in Chad and the Middle Congo, where little settlement had developed. During the 1920s and 1930s the natives' reaction assumed singularly diverse forms, permitting one to distinguish among the levels of political consciousness in the respective colonies. In Gabon, the small group of mulattoes composing the Libreville petite bourgeoisie, soon followed by the cultured elite of Mpongwe and Fang, formed study circles and pressure groups. The Middle Congo was agitated by politicoreligious messianisms aroused by Simon Kimbangu and André Mastoua. Resistance in Ubangi-Shari was still in the "primitive" stages—the flight of the people into the neighboring Sudan or the Belgian Congo, and large-scale spontaneous revolts such as the Kongo-Wara War (1928–31). Agitation was absent only from Chad, which for a long time remained a military territory.[3] Faced with these various forms of resistance, the French colonial system remained curiously frozen. The lower levels of the administration were static; there were barely a thousand officials in 1939. The concessionary system continued: massive uprooting of populations, for example, at the time of the construction of the Congo-Océan railway (1921–34). Abuses were perpetrated by civil servants sent to French Equatorial Africa against their will or who came without enthusiasm: the outraged testimony of Maran, Gide, Londres, and Homet hardly differed from that published at the time of the 1904–05 scandals.[4]

French colonial policy was thus falling behind and was in contradiction to the evolution of the black society, mentality, and consciousness. This contradiction, inherent in the colonial system, was the more pronounced as the authorities continued to preserve the features peculiar to French Equatorial Africa: delay and immobilism.

This is the reason why, although the general lines of French decolonization were the same in French Equatorial Africa and French West Africa, the chronology and pace of events appear rather different. In French West

3. See particularly M. Sinda, *Le Messianisme congolaise* (Paris, 1972); Nzabakomoda-Yacoma, "La Guerre de Kongo-Wara, un chapître de la résistance anticoloniale en Afrique équatoriale 1928–1931" (thesis, University of Paris, 1975); Thompson and Adloff, *The Emerging States of French Equatorial Africa* (Stanford, 1960), p. 350; P. Kalck, *Histoire centrafricaine* (thesis, University of Paris, 1970), vol. 3.

4. C. Coquery-Vidrovitch, *Le Congo au temps des grandes compagnies concessionnaires 1898–1930* (Paris, 1972); G. Sautter, "Le Chemin de fer du Congo-Ocean," *Cahiers d'Etudes Africaines* (1967):219–99; R. Maran, *Batouala* (Paris, 1921); André Gide, *Voyage au Congo* (Paris, 1927) and *Retour du Tchad* (Paris, 1928); A. Londres, *Terre d'Ebène* (Paris, 1929); M. Homet, *Congo, terre de souffrances* (Paris, 1934).

Africa two periods are easily distinguished, both determined by initiatives from the metropole: from 1945 to 1956 France sought to transform its colonial regime the better to perpetuate it; between 1956 and 1960, she resigned herself to granting independence. This overall policy was also applied to French Equatorial Africa; but there other factors came into play. First were the absence of continuity in the government-general's policy and instability in its personnel. Second, French colonial policy was decided here, as elsewhere, on at least two levels: that of the government-general at Brazzaville and that of the French metropolitan authorities. Third, the immobilism of the territorial governors and the hostility of French economic interests exerted a braking effect on implementation of the measures selected. A final factor was the degree of availability of the local populations.

French Equatorial Africa was thus distinctive in two respects. On the one hand, the initiatives that changed the course of French colonial policy date, not from the Brazzaville Conference of 1944, but from the assumption of power by Governor Félix Eboué in 1940. On the other hand, there was a give-and-take in the making of the decisions that determined the course of events between the level of metropolitan authority and that of the local authorities.

One may thus suggest the following phases.

1. Between 1940 and 1944, a period of change was decided upon through the sole initiative of the government-general; this change, aimed chiefly at correcting the backwardness of French policy with respect to conditions in French Equatorial Africa, was only partially achieved and appears more doctrinal than real.

2. Between 1944 and 1952, approximately, the policy of change continued. Initiative passed into the hands of the metropolitan authorities who, pursuing more or less the policy worked out in the preceding period, mapped out a global policy for the French Empire. This new policy seriously aggravated the tensions peculiar to French Equatorial Africa.

3. From 1952 to 1956–57, the government-general, faced with an accelerating course of events, particularly following reforms decided upon by the metropole, redoubled its efforts to meet the most urgent situations while at the same time endeavoring to make up for past delays and to appease opposition.

4. The last phase consisted in the march to independence, during which the initiatives reverted once again to the metropole.

Emphasis here will be placed more heavily upon the two periods 1940–44 and 1952–57, during which the policy adopted flowed more from local considerations and from interforce relationships peculiar to French Equatorial Africa than from calculations by the metropole, where factors external to French Equatorial Africa entered into the balance.

I

It is worth noting that the new "native policy" put forth by its author, Félix Eboué, as a revolutionary innovation was conceived, perfected, and to some extent put into effect in wartime, when priorities were of another order and energies were polarized by the requirements of national defense.

General de Gaulle's nomination of Félix Eboué to the post of governor-general of French Equatorial Africa on November 12, 1940, was the final episode in a cascade of events and dramatic surprises that had kept public opinion in colonial circles and the urban African elite in turmoil since the armistice.[5] These consisted of the spectacular about-face by Governor-General Pierre Boisson who, having asserted on June 18 his determination to pursue to the end the fight to save France, on July 13 suddenly announced that the Vichy regime had appointed him High Commissioner, and that he would soon leave for Dakar; the no less astonishing shift by General Husson, commander-in-chief of French Equatorial African forces and Boisson's successor-designate, who in June favored withdrawal to British territory to continue the struggle, but in August was the sworn enemy of all the Resistance groups among the colonials and officials; the total absence of information or instructions from Vichy; the atmosphere of patriotic conspiracy kept alive by Eboué's early adherence to Free France on July 3; the goings and comings of Gaullists—Leclerc, René Pleven, and Colonna d'Ornano, among others—in French Equatorial Africa and the Belgian Congo; and finally, the threat of civil war with Husson's arrest on August 28 and the adherence of Masson, governor of Gabon, to the Vichy regime and the Dakar authorities (a military campaign lasting three months—September-November 1940—was required to align Gabon with the position of the Federation's other territories). Recognition of these exceptional circumstances places Eboué's policy in its proper perspective.

Having been an administrator in Ubangi-Shari for twenty-three years (1909–32), secretary-general of French Soudan from 1934 to 1936, and governor of Chad beginning in 1939, Félix Eboué had a solid knowledge of African affairs.[6] His instructions, however, set certain priorities for him.

5. E. Guernier, ed., *Afrique Equatoriale Française* (Paris, 1950), pp. 68–72.

6. Brian Weinstein, *Eboué* (New York, 1972); idem, "Félix Eboué and the Chiefs: Perception of Power in Early Oubangui-Chari," *Journal of African History* 11 (1970):107–26.

During his visit to Brazzaville (October 24–November 17, 1940), General de Gaulle confined himself to reorganization and to creating administrative structures to give Free France a juridical basis; thus the Empire Defense Council and the High Commission for Free French Africa came into being. On November 9, 1940, de Gaulle wrote a personal letter to Eboué that reflected the same preoccupations:[7] the African domain must fully engage itself in the struggle and work in concert with the British, while maintaining its independence. Not one word was said about "native policy," relations among the peoples of French Equatorial Africa, or their administration.

It was nevertheless precisely in this area that Eboué would seek to innovate. Convinced that thoroughgoing reforms were necessary, as much for the immediate success of the Resistance as for the mid- and long-term future of the Federation, he strove equally, from the first, for the war effort and for the flexibility of administrative and political methods. His first great "General Circular," dated January 19, 1941, reflected this dual preoccupation.[8] Having exalted the "duty" to dedicate "all efforts and all thought" to the war, he insisted, "ending the war must not prevent us from accomplishing things in the administrative field; on the contrary, it would be bad procedure to defer the necessary reforms until the day of victory." The government, first, must be decentralized by giving the governors of the Federation's four territories in "full exercise of their natural prerogatives" and the power to ensure, "personally and in freedom," the carrying out of the orders issued by the governor-general. This principle was placed in effect on January 20.[9] One may wonder how suitable this decision was, since the governor-general's powers, already counterbalanced by those of the High Commissioner for Free French Africa,[10] might conflict with initiatives of the territorial governors, especially in the area of "native policy."

7. Letter quoted in Weinstein, *Eboué*, pp. 257–58. Eboué was well aware of the spirit in which his appointment was made: see his general circular of January 19, 1941, in which he wrote: "The meaning of this promotion is no secret to anyone: the determination to continue the war, the steadfast refusal to accept defeat, the clear realization of the impasse into which compromises were inevitably leading France and the Empire. . . . After the holidays we must set aside frivolous details and address ourselves solely to the serious matter of war." *Journal Officiel de l'Afrique Equatorial Française* (hereafter *JOAEF*), Feb. 1, 1941, p. 86. Eboué's second general circular, of May 20, 1941 (ibid., June 1, 1941, pp. 345–50), was almost exclusively dedicated to war problems.

8. General circular of Jan. 19, 1941, *JOAEF*, Feb. 1, 1941, pp. 86–90.

9. Governor-General's "Order (No. 205) defining the authority of territorial governors and delegating certain powers to them," Jan. 20, 1941 (*JOAEF*, Feb. 1, 1941, pp. 96–98).

10. The post of High Commissioner, instituted in 1940 and occupied successively by de Larminat and Sicé, was abolished in July 1942, following protests by Eboué.

The latter, in fact, constituted Eboué's other major preoccupation. His ideas in this field, expressed as soon as he took charge, were not to be spelled out in systematic fashion until the too-famous but ill-understood "Circular of November 8, 1941."[11] This text, praised by all for its lucidity and humane spirit, and quoted several times as a model at the Brazzaville Conference, deserves detailed analysis that permits an appraisal of the nature and real scope of the changes it introduced.

For the sake of convenience, the following will be successively examined: the spirit of the new native policy; comments and propositions relating to traditional society and urban society; and finally, the role assigned to various agencies of colonization.

The Spirit of the New Policy

The spirit of the new policy is highly contradictory and characteristic of what one might call, for lack of a better term, "liberal colonialism," partaking both of "imperial ideology" and a certain humanitarianism.[12] On one hand, there is clearly no critical questioning of French colonization, not the least shadow of a "guilty conscience," nor of doubt concerning France's "civilizing mission." It is true that triumphal declamation is absent, but the basic convictions remain those of all colonialist circles. This is true, for example, of the statement in which "Equatorial Africa, instead of being served by France, as has been too often seen, [must] tomorrow be in a position to serve France" (p. 1); of the faith in the educational and beneficent role of the various agents of colonization; and also of the conviction that, despite the "errors of the past" and the survival of certain abuses, the French presence remains necessary and could tolerate no sort of criticism, reserve, or, even less, resistance on the part of the natives. It is thus understandable that the "new" policy intended to improve the condition of French Equatorial Africa's blacks[13] was conceived and drawn up without any participation in it by them. In the governor's eyes, all that counted was "the necessity for associating representatives of *all the Colony's creative elements* [emphasis mine] in a policy toward the indigenous population,

11. According to statements in private conversation by Laurentie, who was the government's secretary-general under Eboué, he played a role at least as important as the governor-general's in writing this document; the question remains to be cleared up. Except where otherwise indicated, references are to *Nouvelle Politique Indigène pour A.E.F.* (Paris, 1945).

12. Ideas borrowed from R. Girardet, *L'Idée coloniale en France* (Paris, 1972).

13. The agenda of the Consultative Commission for November 6, 7, and 8, 1941, lists: "Receive information concerning the native population, the ills threatening it and, with it, all productive work in the country, and, finally, the remedies proposed." *Nouvelle Politique*, p. i.

and to establish in this field a doctrine and statute which not only would reflect the administration's concepts but would be the overall program of all the colonizing values in French Equatorial Africa."[14]

On October 6, 1941, the governor extended an invitation to a number of prominent personalities; the consultative commission they composed became virtually the only forum in which the governor's proposals were discussed. The twenty-seven members, under the chairmanship of Eboué and Henri Laurentie, the governor's secretary-general, were eight administrators, including the territorial governors, six prelates, five presidents or vice-presidents of chambers of commerce, and eight private individuals representing forestry, mining, and commercial interests. The proposals were indeed presented before the commission, but along with other measures of a budgetary and administrative nature for the purpose of referring them to the French Equatorial Africa Administrative Council which, among its seventeen members had, in addition to officials and representatives of French economic interests, four native personalities chosen by a quite restricted electorate.[15]

Notwithstanding its content and these colonialist features, the new policy did make innovations. In the first place, the previous policy and the "Jacobin" leanings of French colonization were condemned. Having stigmatized the errors and abuses of the concessionary period, Eboué made a direct attack upon the principles of assimilation and direct administration.

> To attempt to make, or re-make, a society in our own image or even according to our habits of thinking, would court certain failure. The native has a way of behaving, laws, and a homeland which are not ours. We cannot make him happy by applying the principles of the French Revolution, which is our revolution, nor the Napoleonic Code, which is our code, nor by replacing his chiefs with our officials, because our officials will think through him, not within him. [p. 3]

He advised the officials to "move, in all fields, from direct action to supervision" (p. 12). This utopian and generous colonialist mystique, which firmly believed it was possible to make the blacks of French Equatorial Africa "happy," was accompanied by a radical assertion of which no one, not even Eboué, perceived the explosive potential content. On January 19, 1941, Eboué stated that "the natives, too, had a homeland"; he was to revert

14. Governor-general's Order no. 2.089 of Oct. 6, 1941. *JOAEF*, Nov. 15, 1941, p. 667.

15. The composition and powers of the council were defined by a decree of Feb. 27, 1941. Eboué's address to the council on Nov. 10, 1941; *JOAEF*, March 15, 1941, pp. 167–70, and Dec. 1, 1941, Annex.

constantly to this theme, demonstrating that the native, "if kept within the framework of his traditional institutions . . . will be happier, capable of more progress, and better disposed to perpetuate his race than in any other way."[16]

In short, the spirit of this policy was innovative as compared with policies previously applied in French Equatorial Africa, but not as compared with other colonial traditions; it borrowed wholesale from Hubert Lyautey's actions in Morocco, which were cited as an example and model (pp. 4, 38), but also from British and Belgian practices in Nigeria and the Congo.[17]

Native Society and Traditional Institutions

On this subject, Eboué delivered a downright apology, at once disinterested ("to deprive the natives of these two motivations in human life, their homeland's traditions and the love of country, would be tantamount to despoiling them without recompense") and self-seeking, out of concern for effective administration ("if we do not bolster the foundations of native political institutions, these foundations will give way to unbridled individualism, and how could we act upon an unorganized mass of individuals?" (p. 4). From this he derived a glorification of the legitimate chieftaincy, inspired in part by Jean-Marie Lanessan and Louis Lyautey: "The institution of the chief is the most important, and he should be the object of our greatest concern. . . . There is no better chief: there is only one chief, and we have no choice" (p. 5). The situation had certainly changed since the time when Eboué had served in Ubangi-Shari. Traditional society had begun to disintegrate, sweeping the institution of chieftaincy along in its decline. A new class, the petite bourgeoisie of public employees and traders in the cities, had come into being and was advancing its claims. Between these two elites Eboué chose that of the past: "It must be kept in mind that there is no common measure as between even the most senior native civil servant and the chief. The two persons are placed on different footings and, though they *both* deserve esteem and solicitude, it cannot be the *same* esteem nor the *same* solicitude" (p. 9). He added that even when besotted with strong drink and women, or when he employs poison in order to govern arbitrarily, the "legitimate chief" commits fewer abuses than a native civil servant, and his coercion of the citizens is no more onerous than that of the modern state.

16. Governor-general's circular of Jan. 19, 1941; *JOAEF*, Feb. 1, 1941, p. 89.

17. It appears that Eboué was not informed in detail concerning British policy in Nigeria, and particularly concerning Lord Lugard's activity. His information probably came from conversations with Lord Hailey, among others. See Weinstein, *Eboué*, pp. 262–63.

On the basis of these principles the governor proposed a series of urgent reforms. First, the administration's methods and traditional attitude toward the chiefs had to be done away with; he had especially in mind the "deplorable" and "absurd" practice of removing and replacing chiefs, and the correlative treatment of them as government officials. Since power belonged by right to the legitimate chiefs, the "upstarts, scullions, and opportunists" who had been hastily invested with the trappings, if not the dignity, of chiefs, should be evicted; "the chief . . . is an aristocrat: for that reason he enjoys broad freedom of conduct, and is not subject to the rules imposed on the administrative staffs" (p. 9). Misled by its prerogatives and omnipotence, the colonial administration did not realize that its frequent inopportune interference created two sets of powers in native society:[18] the official power, ostensible but inoperative, entrusted to the chief who had been installed by the administration, and the genuine power, the only effective one, "the occult power [which] persists because it is the traditional power" (p. 7).

The great reform thus consisted in sharing power, in accepting at least a partial "transfer of power" from the administration to the traditional chiefs.[19] A de facto partition in fact already existed:

> the Colony is composed of two stable elements: French sovereignty and native authority rising from the land. Administrators are the *representatives* of French sovereignty, while the chiefs are the *repositories* of local authority. Respect and obedience are due the former because of their functions, and to the latter because of their birth. This is an essential distinction, and I cannot too strongly advise all administrators to reflect upon it. [pp. 7–8].

In this desire to share power with the chiefs there was also a political calculation, a mid- or long-term strategy: in Eboué's mind, it was preferable to give up a portion of power rather than to have it wrested entirely from one's hands:

> instead of allowing a mob of proletarians, more or less badly dressed, speaking more or less French, to grow up through contact with us, we would do better to create an elite, beginning with the chiefs and notables

18. "If we replace the chief arbitrarily, we split command into two parts, the official one and the true one; no one is deceived except ourselves, and if we flatter ourselves by believing we shall obtain better service from *our* chief, we are usually unaware that he himself obeys the true chief, and we have thus made a fool's bargain." *Nouvelle Politique*, p. 6.

19. "We [should] restore to the country its own cadres and . . . give them the share in deciding affairs which is properly theirs." Ibid., p. 6.

> who, having been made by us personally responsible for power, will progress by their experience in dealing with the difficulties they encounter and, as they become attached to their work, will win their spurs on behalf of the country and within it. Is this not better than a crowd of soured individuals bringing in unsuitable slogans from who knows where?" [p. 7]

In practice, this boiled down to seeking out and rehabilitating the legitimate chiefs, and then conferring on them a status different from that of the masses: thus, unless for an "exceptionally serious reason," they ought not to be summoned before the courts; similarly, they should be subjected to the *indigénat* only with "the most extreme prudence."

Native Urban Society

Regarded by the governor simply as the result of corruption and the alteration of traditional society by reason of the French presence, urban society was far from being his favorite. Probably with excessive subtlety, Eboué distinguished three types of urban society. In one group he placed urban centers like Abéché and Fort Lamy, which possessed a strongly Muslim structure, which were organized on the model of the traditional society, and which he felt should receive the same treatment. The second group included the real cities such as Libreville and Bakongo, a native suburb of Brazzaville, characterized in the governor's view by a "homogeneous population close to the land" and by the existence of a "true native bourgeoisie, quite well developed," although it had taken on only the superficial appearances, "the bloom, of Europeanism: fancy clothes, refined language, liberated manners." Eboué nevertheless proposed reforms that were heatedly debated in the consultative commission: the granting of a privileged status to *notables évolués;* the right for them to combine in circles or associations of a social and political nature; the establishment of native communes in which the "municipal corps" constituted by the *évolués* would have decision-making power in the areas of town planning, sports, and quasi-academic education. Here, there is no discernible disposition to share power, as in the case of the chiefs: what is involved is a sort of experiment under the direct supervision (the phrase is repeated several times) of the colonial administration.

Finally, in the third group Eboué lumped centers like Bangui, Port-Gentil, Pointe-Noire, and Poto-Poto, Brazzaville's other black surburb. In his eyes, none of these agglomerations exhibited the features of a city. "There one generally finds," he emphasized,

> one socially stable element composed of public servants, veterans, artisans, and employees of commercial firms, and an unstable element

> (domestic servants, unskilled laborers, soldiers' families, etc.) properly described as a floating population. Neither of these elements has roots in the country, and neither comprises a community: wards haphazardly adjoining each other, none constituting a distinct village, and therefore lacking the identity of orientation and attitudes from which civic spirit would develop. [pp. 17–18]

In these towns the governor saw only a danger, and found no solution to it except rigor: "discipline will be the best remedy for this scar on the social body; repressive discipline, employing all the sanctions of the indigénat and the Vagrancy Decree; special prisons should be built, and an incorruptible sanitation service formed; discipline should furthermore address itself to improvement, drawing on the help of sports and educational organizations to retrieve those capable of improving themselves."

A special problem in these cities had to do with the mulattoes, a particularly acute problem in Gabon, where they had joined in the early 1930s in an "Amicale" (friendship society) comprising between 10 and 15 percent of the population; they were in open conflict with the black petite bourgeoisie, who were Myènè or Fang.[20] The same rivalry, although in less explosive form, was found in the other French Equatorial African cities. Eboué took a firm stand against any discriminatory treatment between the blacks and those of mixed race: "anything that sets the mulattoes apart from the native society, since they cannot become a part of European society, has the disadvantage of creating a pernicious rivalry between blacks and mulattoes, without any benefit to the mulattoes" (p. 16). The two elements should therefore be combined in a single class, the urban elite of notables évolués.

The Agents of Colonialism

The question of the agents of colonialism is somewhat marginal to the present discussion. It may, however, be noted that Eboué, in a spirit of some utopianism, called upon the various forces present—the administration, the missionaries, and the colonists—to cooperate closely.[21] Missionary activity could be integrated into the governor-general's new policy

20. Thompson and Adloff, *The Emerging States*, pp. 350–51; Brian Weinstein, *Gabon: Nation Building on the Ogooué* (Cambridge, 1966), pp. 169 ff.

21. "Our colony can function only through the overall effort of all the European corporate bodies. The colonist is the administrator's associate, as is the missionary or the miner. The time has passed when the administration sought to do everything by itself while the colony's other essential elements lazily trusted in this presumption or looked upon it with resentment. Common effort is indispensable in all fields." *Nouvelle Politique*, pp. 31–32.

without changes, at least where urban society was concerned. In view of the religious component of traditional authority, however, it may be questioned whether the task he set the missionaries was possible to accomplish: "you will accept things as they are, and above all the country's political organization; evangelization must not contribute to undermining the chief's power: it will buttress it, on the contrary, by lending it an additional justification" (p. 24). As for "transforming the colonist's role," here the governor departed from the realm of the possible. Forgetting the weight of habits inherited from the concessionary system and ignoring the omnipotence of the cotton and lumber companies and the abuses of trade-based commerce, the governor lost himself among purely theoretical ideas. Observing that "the more the Colony produced the poorer it became" (p. 32) because of abusive exploitation of resources and men, he proposed that the colonist become a sort of educator: "he will manage the villagers' first undertakings, advise them in all circumstances, furnish them the necessary seeds, plants, and tools and, in a word, guide and encourage their endeavors; in return, he will promise to buy their harvest at a fair price. Building on his own concession, a vital center of the area, the colonist will enliven an entire region, and will share with the natives the rewards of success" (p. 30).

Thus formulated, the new doctrine had an extraordinary destiny: the circular was printed as a separate pamphlet by order of the French National Committee in London, and thousands of copies were distributed—to the British and Americans, above all, who had just signed the Atlantic Charter, in order to show them that French colonial doctrine and practice were in accord with, or even an advance over, the charter's provisions.[22] It was sent, furthermore, to imperial officials to serve as a model.

To move from doctrinal formulations to practical accomplishments was a much more difficult task. The contradiction is indeed striking between the relative boldness of the theory and the slowness with which it was applied, between the genuine effort behind the reforms and the no less obvious hardihood of the habits and attitudes of the past. But that was not all: priorities were reversed. In the circular, traditional society and institutions were the principal focus of concern; in practice, preoccupations centered upon urban society and its "elites." Never, finally, was misunderstanding so clearcut between the Federation's local officials and the metropolitan authorities in London; where Eboué spoke of "revolution," de Gaulle saw only the will to pursue "despite the war . . . the progressive development of France's subjects and protégés and their status, *in conformity with*

22. Weinstein, *Eboué*, p. 274.

France's traditional policy."[23] Practice, thus, was chiefly marked by innovations, cross-purposes, and survivals from the past.

Innovations

By the end of 1941 Eboué had drawn up three reform projects concerning the problem of labor, the status of the notables évolués, and the creation of native communes. Questioned by René Pleven, the national commissioner for economy, finance and the colonies, Adolphe Sicé, the high commissioner for Free French Africa, expressed an unfavorable view: the preparatory studies, according to him, had been insufficient. In May 1942 the Legislation Commission objected to labor reform on the pretext that it would lead to forced labor (which still existed), and to the proposed status of the notables évolués, which, it alleged would likely create a "native aristocracy." Eboué had to threaten to travel personally to London in order to remove these obstacles and secure de Gaulle's agreement.[24] The labor reform established an Office of Labor and Native Manpower responsible for protecting the freedom of labor and ensuring, if recruitment proved necessary, that workers' villages would be kept ethnically homogeneous.[25]

The change most widely debated, in Brazzaville as in London, concerned the notables évolués.[26] The latter's personal status, it is true, did not change, as they remained subject to customary jurisdiction and judiciable in the native courts. At the same time, they did acquire a large number of rights. Thus, they were exempt from administrative police sanctions (the indigénat); they were permitted to purchase immunity from requisitions of personal service (namely, were exempt from forced labor); and were entered on special rosters for the capitation tax. Set apart from the masses, they furthermore achieved participation in public affairs: ex officio members of the electorates in all local elections, they were eligible to participate in the "municipal corps" of native communes. (It will be noted that these "privileges" did not extend so far as to grant the notables évolués full French citizenship.)[27] The entrance requirements did not appear to be

23. Telegram from de Gaulle to Eboué, Aug. 1, 1942. *JOAEF*, Nov. 1, 1942, p. 572.

24. Weinstein, *Eboué*, pp. 274–75. The Aug. 1, 1941, telegram: "I have just signed with great satisfaction your three decrees . . . I wish to take this occasion to tell you how much I appreciate and approve the principles of the native policy you are pursuing in F.E.A." *JOAEF*, Nov. 1, 1942, p. 572.

25. Decree no. 376, July 20, 1942. *JOAEF*, 1942, pp. 572–73.

26. Decree no. 377, July 29, 1942. *JOAEF*, 1942, pp. 573–74. Its provisions were a step backward from the decree of July 23, 1937, which provided for accession to French citizenship by right or by option.

27. In 1938 there were about 5,000 black or mulatto French citizens of local origin in French Equatorial Africa. See Le Cornec, *Histoire politique du Tchad*, p. 81, n. 3.

demanding: aside from the usual administrative provisions, it was enough to have education equivalent to a primary-school certificate (except for members of the order of the Legion of Honor and the Liberation Order, who were exempt from this qualification) and to be either "fully competent" in a trade or a representative of "interests important to the local economy." This apparent generosity nevertheless affected very few people. On the eve of the war there were only about 10,500 students in French Equatorial Africa,[28] and holders of a primary certificate practicing a stable trade—whether natives of French Equatorial Africa or of other French colonies—did not exceed three hundred out of a population of three and a half million inhabitants. This was, therefore, an elite policy par excellence, closely controlled by the administration; the new status was precarious, as any évolué could be deprived of it by reason of "unworthiness." In the event, two hundred persons were granted évolué status.[29] Other, less spectacular, measures followed. In February 1943 Eboué appointed four Africans, including Jean Aubame, a Gabonese, to positions in the local secretariats previously reserved for Europeans.[30] Also to be included in this field was an impressive series of measures designed to regularize the status of the administration's local employees and to improve their standard of living,[31] as well as the reorganization of education[32] and financial aid to institutions—private or public, Catholic or Protestant, French or foreign—engaged in education.

The status of native commune[33] was reserved for "towns where the feeling of unity and the sense of civic life were sufficiently well marked."

28. G. Bruel, *La France Equatoriale Africaine*, p. 449.

29. Weinstein, *Eboué*, p. 277. In a sample of 93 grantees (Order dated Aug 27, 1943, *JOAEF*, 1943, pp. 562–63), analysis of the distribution by professional categories gave the following results: 29 clerks, 25 accountants, 23 secretaries and secretary-interpreters, 4 nurses, 4 chiefs, including the Sultan of Ouadaï, 3 monitors, 3 police officers, and 2 merchants. For purposes of comparison, in French West Africa (see n. 25) French citizenship was granted over a period of six years to only 73 persons, including 43 by the optional procedure, which most nearly resembled the procedure for registration as évolué. *Archives nationales, section Outre-Mer* (hereafter ANSOM), Affaires politiques 2201/6 ("Dossier politique indigène").

30. Weinstein, *Eboué*, pp. 275–77. In addition to Aubame, these were Jean-René Many, Jean-Baptiste Viérin, and Jean-Rémy Ayouné, all appointed third-class clerks in the French Equatorial African secretariats-general. Orders of Feb. 23 and 27, 1943. *JOAEF*, 1943, p. 183.

31. See especially the twenty orders, no. 649 through 668, dated March 26, 1943. *JOAEF*, 1943, pp. 246–79.

32. Note particularly the organization of agricultural education (Order no. 244 of Feb. 9, 1942, *JOAEF*, 1942, p. 137), reorganization of the Ecole Edouard-Renard on the model of William Ponty, and the creation of a secondary education program at Brazzaville (*JOAEF*, 1942, pp. 293–382, 671).

33. Decree no. 378, July 29, 1942, *JOAEF*, 1942, pp. 574–75.

Although all the resident blacks, regardless of their status (French citizen, French subject, or foreigner) were its citizens, its administration was restricted to "a municipal corps of from six to twelve members, appointed by the Territorial Governor from among *notables évolués* or French citizens born in French Equatorial Africa or in other French colonies." The government, though not transferring any of its own functions to the municipal corps, undertook the obligation to consult it concerning questions of finance, town planning, general public interest, the organization of native associations, and advances granted to the natives, and to enlist its participation in the assessment and collection of taxes, the census of the population, and the recruitment of labor quotas.

Cross-Purposes

That doctrine and practice were at cross-purposes was particularly typical of policy toward the chiefs. After his great circular, Eboué no longer concerned himself with the legitimate chiefs. He went no further than to create, in 1943, a Centre des Recherches Ethnologiques for French Equatorial Africa, which, in addition to its purely scientific tasks, was to set up a documentation center for public officials and colonists, to give ethnological instruction to students at the Ecole Edouard Renard, and to maintain a "liaison with the Direction des Affaires Politiques, to which it [would] transmit information of possible assistance to the local administration." The center began operating in December 1943.[34]

In this field, initiative was in the hands of the territorial governors, and this gave rise to another kind of cross-purpose. According to the precolonial sociopolitical structures of the various ethnic groups, the evolution of the territory since the institution of the colonial regime, and its particular situation with respect to the war, the territorial governors themselves decided whether or not to act on Eboué's ideas. Chad, where the institution of the chieftaincy was still solidly rooted, was too preoccupied by the war effort because of its geographical situation; the fact that the chiefs at Baguirmi and Dar el Kouti, former slave-traders, professed and practiced an anti-French Islam was a further deterrent to raising the question of promoting or modifying chiefdoms. In Ubangi-Shari, the opposition of the cotton companies and the subordinate officials, both black and white; rivalries among the leading families; and the dispersal of the Zande and Nzakara ethnic groups, especially into the Belgian Congo, all contributed to obstructing any innovating policy in the sultanates.[35] Gabon was also a

34. Governor-General's Order no. 2,070, Oct. 9, 1943, *JOAEF*, 1943, p. 729.
35. Kalck, *Histoire centrafricaine*, 3:446–63.

special case, where prudence had been made desirable by recent events—namely, the pro-Vichy leanings of Governor Masson and a majority of the officials and the untimely death of the new governor, Colonel Parant, who shared Eboué's ideas. The latter himself acknowledged that the new governor's task would not be an easy one: "Gabon," he stated, "suffers from the fact that it has never been the subject of a clear, consistent policy. The imperious needs felt by a declining population, the wage-scale and all its consequences, the disruption of the native leadership structure, and the presence of a mulatto community, all present a difficult problem. To face it we need, not a theory, but a guiding principle taking account of mutually contradictory facts."[36]

There remained only the Middle Congo, whose governor, G. Fortuné, having built an "Artisan's House" at Brazzaville for the display and sale of the best artisans' work, devoted most of his energy to a "virtual restoration" of the chieftaincy; the traditional chiefs saw their powers increased, especially in the judicial and agricultural fields, through savings, relief, and credit-union institutions.[37]

Survivals from the Past

Despite Eboué's cautionary remarks on the subject of the mulattoes, the discriminatory policy instituted by the decree of September 15, 1936, remained in effect. On May 14, 1941, the High Commissioner for Free French Africa, Larminat, decided to reaffirm this decree by extending its provisions to mulattoes throughout French Africa.[38] Eboué himself confirmed this group's privileges in the field of education. The institutions specialized in teaching them received increased subsidies; the best living conditions were reserved for them, as well as priority of admission to the schools in places where there were no schools especially for the mulattoes.[39]

For the masses of the people, the "new native policy" period did not represent a break with the past. Forced labor remained in effect, with an obligation of twelve days' duty and optional purchases of exemption at the rate of one to four francs per day, according to the place of residence.[40] But the economic and financial effort imposed by the war left them even less cash resources than in the past. In practice, recruitment was intensified so

36. Governor-General, General Circular of May 20, 1941, *JOAEF*, 1941, p. 346.

37. G. Fortuné, "Circulaire sur la politique indigène au Moyen-Congo," Feb. 11, 1942, *JOAEF*, 1942, pp. 150–54.

38. Decree no. 152, May 14, 1941, *JOAEF*, 1941, pp. 335–36.

39. Governor-general's order of July 20, 1943, *JOAEF*, 1943, pp. 560–61.

40. Governor-general's order of Nov. 10, 1941, *JOAEF*, 1941, pp. 701–02.

as to stimulate production of gold, lumber, and particularly rubber, which was required for the war industry. A new Labor Office, composed exclusively of the administration's representatives and delegates from the chambers of commerce, placed the former under the latter's thumb, as in the heyday of the concessionary regime. The indigénat system remained in effect; in November 1941 the governor-general issued a list of fourteen infractions for which "administrative police sanctions" might be imposed, scarcely differing from previous lists.[41] Not until 1943 and 1944 were penalties somewhat eased, although the list of infractions remained unchanged: "both fine and prison sentence could be assessed only in the case of a repeat offense."[42] Tax pressures weighed heavier. The poll tax was increased. Additional taxes were levied (on livestock, for example). "Voluntary" contributions were called for: at the end of 1941, half of the Voluntary War Contributions Fund had been provided by French Equatorial Africa (4,570,000 francs out of 9,420,000). Epidemics and endemic disease spread; in some regions as much as 44 percent of the population suffered from trypanosomiasis. The years 1940–44 were lived through and preserved in popular memory as "le temps de la chicotte."[43]

Eboué, furthermore, inherited from previous governments a repressive policy toward certain communities and individuals that he dared not disavow. Léon M'Ba discovered this through sad experience: at a time when Eboué was advancing the évolués' status, this most representative Fang notable, who generally shared the governor-general's ideas, saw the latter confirm the sentences imposed upon him in 1931 and 1932.[44] More serious was the problem of the Amicaliste movement, founded by André Matsoua in the Lari country. After the policy of relaxation inaugurated by governors Georges Renard and François-Joseph Reste, Boisson had reverted to systematic repression.[45] Eboué and Henri Laurentie considered this policy "idiotic."[46] They nevertheless rejected appeals for pardon by Amicalists condemned to death and let justice pursue its course. After the execution in December of three Amicalists, Eboué declared his solidarity with his predecessors and his subordinates: "Just measures have been taken since October [1941] to prepare the way for the natives' submission, or rather their liberation [*sic*]. To achieve this without reservation, it was sufficient for the

41. Governor-general's order no. 2,249, Nov. 10, 1941, *JOAEF*, 1941, pp. 701–02.

42. Governor-general's order of Dec. 20, 1942, *JOAEF*, 1943, p. 44.

43. Kalck, *Histoire centrafricaine*, 3:463.

44. Brian Weinstein, "Léon M'Ba: The Ideology of Dependence," *Genève-Afrique* 6, no. 1 (1967):49–62. Order of Oct. 20, 1942, *JOAEF*, 1942, p. 589.

45. Sinda, *Le Messianisme congolais*, pp. 151–231.

46. Weinstein, *Eboué*, p. 269.

Governor-General to demonstrate publicly, while on tour, that the policy of a department head was also his own, and that there was but a single authority, informed and responsible. This example will be remembered. It proves that, once a proposed measure has been studied, discussed, and decided upon, the administrative mechanism can be effective only if it operates as a whole and without self-contradiction."[47] Matsoua's death in prison in 1942 only exacerbated Lari nationalism and helped to give it an exclusively political and anticolonialist content.[48]

II

Between 1944, the date of the conference at Brazzaville, and 1952, the beginning of an intense politicization of life in French Equatorial Africa, the initiative in the conception and formulation of colonial policy passed almost exclusively into the hands of the metropolitan authorities. This policy, truly new in French colonial history, was at the time represented as "emancipatory," "democratic," and even revolutionary.[49] The more or less direct part played by French Equatorial Africa in the formation of this policy, and its repercussions on the Federation's life, will be examined here.

The issue first arises in connection with the French Africa Conference at Brazzaville (January 30–February 8, 1944). There can be no doubt that the conference was convened partly in reaction to the anticolonialist ideas that were being increasingly disseminated by the United States after the signing of the Atlantic Charter.[50] But independent desire for change certainly existed too, doubtless imposed by circumstances. In this respect French Equatorial Africa was not only, in Governor Cornut-Gentille's expression, the conference's "godmother"; Eboué's ideas also served as guidelines:[51]

47. Governor-general's general circular of May 20, 1941, *JOAEF*, 1941, p. 346.

48. Wagret, *Histoire et sociologie politiques de la Republique du Congo* (Paris, 1963), pp. 62–63. See also Sinda's judgment: "[Eboué] made himself the accomplice of all those who had decided upon repression. . . . Thus, at the time when he was prosecuting militant Amicalists he was creating a leadership composed of *notables évolués;* he sought thereby to surround himself with subordinate employees dazzled by the position offered them, and entirely devoted to the colonial authorities." *Le Messianisme congolais*, p. 231.

49. Suret-Canale, *Afrique Noire* (Paris, 1972), vol. 3, pt. 1, p. 9.

50. Ibid. 2:596–600; 3:10. Also the conference program: "Finally, the foreigner is watching us. We must respond to his searching observation not only by setting forth our past successes but also by a program relying upon the confidence we have inspired to demonstrate that France is an active and methodical nation worthy of carrying forward the Empire it has succeeded in attaching to herself." *Programme général*, Jan. 1944, ANSOM, Affaires politiques, 2201.

51. *JOAEF*, 1948, p. 496.

"Governor-General Eboué's Circular on native policy was conceived and written for French Equatorial Africa. It would be absurd to attempt to apply it in all our colonies. Certain principles can be drawn from it, however, which may be regarded as universal, and will serve as the starting point for the discussion."[52] French Equatorial Africa's new policy thus served as a model, the more so as the conference's secretary-general, Henri Laurentie, recently promoted director of political affairs in the Commission for the Colonies, had been Eboué's secretary-general and in this capacity was closely associated with the governor's innovations. Furthermore, French Equatorial African representatives proposed a number of the reforms adopted in the conference's concluding recommendations.[53]

The conference also had to take into account the aspirations of one native group which, although excluded from the discussions, attentively followed their echo over the radio. On January 23, 1944, the Brazzaville Cercle des Evolués sent Governor Eboué a petition summarizing its aspirations and the hopes it reposed in the conference's resolutions.[54] It stated that it believed in the coming of a "truly humanitarian ideal of colonialism," emphasizing in particular that "the men of old France seem to have given priority to matter over man; those of the new France appear to have a clear tendency to give man priority over matter. One might say that, purified by hardship, humanity is getting ready for a giant step forward." On the central question of the future and the place of Africans in French colonialism, the evolués showed themselves very moderate. Choosing "free integration of the colonized people with the colonizing people" in preference to "complete emancipation through self-government," these men who claimed to be "French Equatorial Africa's elite" proposed that an "Empire citizenship" be created; this status would give its beneficiaries the same civil and political rights as French citizens, although they would be effective only within the colonies. However, and this was an important restriction, this status would be granted only to those "individuals" meeting the conditions provided for in the decree of July 29, 1942, establishing the status of *notable évolué* in French Equatorial Africa." The same ideas were

52. Brazzaville Conference, *Programme général.*

53. Notably, Mgr. Biéchy, Apostolic Vicar of Brazzaville and spokesman for the "desiderata of the ecclesiastical leaders" concerning customs, society, and the missions; and especially Delmas, Chief Administrator and spokesman for French Equatorial Africa, a dominant personality of the conference, for which he wrote a "contribution to imperial political doctrine" (ANSOM, Affaires politiques 2201/6).

54. "A propos de la colonisation: vues de quelques intellectuels de l'Afrique centrale." ANSOM, Affaires politiques 2291/1. Extracts published in *La Conférence africaine française* (Algiers, 1944), pp. 87–105 and passim.

encountered in a long petition by the Brazzaville évolué, Jean-Rémy Ayouné.[55]

Thus, there existed a desire for participation in power—but an elitist and antirevolutionary one—which might have made it possible to ease certain tensions in the colonial society at this time when the Amicaliste movement was demanding, in Brazzaville itself, "self-government" for the Lari.[56] Read by Eboué at the February 3 session, these manifestos made a strong impression on the delegates; they encouraged them in their conviction that autonomy and independence should be rejected, whereas a free concession of rights, though under the control of the colonial authority, was desired by the natives themselves.

The conference made its decisions along this line. As is well known, "eliminating any idea of autonomy or any possibility of evolution outside the block of the French Empire, or of self-government in the colonies, even in the distant future,"[57] it adopted, to the great joy of the évolués, the principle of representation of the colonies in the French Legislative Assembly and proposed a series of measures inspired by Eboué's recent policy. The recommendations relating to "social questions" presented the dispositions concerning traditional chiefs and the notables évolués, among others, as a "safe and tested method," and a "model" [applicable] to all the black colonies in Africa.[58]

The Cercle des Evolués at Brazzaville greeted the resolutions of the conference favorably. One of the personalities most pampered by Eboué, the Gabonese Jean Aubame, a future deputy from Gabon, wrote five years after the event that "the Brazzaville Conference may be regarded as a veritable Declaration of the Rights of African Man: a declaration as yet timid, incomplete, and reticent, perhaps, but rich in possibilities."[59] He nevertheless criticized the delegates for their refusal to allow the African elites to participate in the discussions, their tendency to generalize from isolated facts, and above all their hesitation to decide "between federal principles and an assimilation which some desired, although they knew it to be impossible in practice, which would, under Governor-General's Eboué's influence, safeguard native institutions but would subject them to a rigorous control distorting their operation; on the other hand, the dele-

55. Ibid., pp. 88–94.

56. Wagret, *Histoire et sociologie*, p. 35.

57. *La Conférence africaine*, p. 35.

58. Reservations concerning the évolués expressed by Cournarie, Governor-General of French West Africa, were rejected. Ibid., pp. 41–82.

59. J. Aubame, "La Conference de Brazzaville" in E. Guernier, ed., *Afrique Equatoriale Française* (Paris, 1950), p. 186.

gates dared not state questions forthrightly and propose effective solutions, as in the case of matters of marriage, dowry, and divorce, or else ignored very thorny questions completely, such as the ownership of real property."

A more resolute and stable policy line came from the metropole, without participation of the Africans, with the adoption of the "great liberating laws"[60] by the Provisional Government, and more particularly by the 1946 Constituent Assembly. Like the empire's other colonies, French Equatorial Africa experienced a total disruption of the legislative, administrative, political, and economic system that had characterized the colonial regime before 1940. It is difficult to say which of these measures was the most important. The Africans' social condition was juridically transformed by the law of February 11, 1946, which abolished forced labor and instituted labor freedom, and by the decrees of August 7 and 17, 1944, which introduced trade unions and a labor inspectorate. Relations between the administration and the people were fundamentally altered by the elimination of the indigénat (February 20, 1946), unification of the judiciary, and application in principle of the metropolitan penal code (April 30, 1946) and extension of French citizenship to all nationals of the overseas territories, but without change in their civil status (the "Lamine-Gueye Law" of May 7, 1946). The institution of local assemblies in the territories (October 7, 1946), representation of the overseas territories in the French National Assembly, and the creation of the Assembly of the French Union at a time when the governors-general were becoming mere "ministers resident" responsible to the National Assembly all implied effective rights and increased participation in the exercise of political power. Finally, the creation of FIDES (Fonds d'Investissement et de Développement Economique et Social des Territories d'Outre-Mer) on April 30, 1946, seemed to usher in a period of harmonious economic development centered upon improvement of the natives' living conditions.[61]

The contradictions inherent in these measures as a whole, and their juridical and political ambiguities, have been emphasized at length and are indeed subject to various interpretations.[62] But there was no doubt that

60. Aujoulat, *Aujourd'hui l'Afrique* (Paris, 1958), p. 263.

61. See, for example, Governor Cornut-Gentille's addresses to the Grand Council of French Equatorial Africa: "Our firmest hope for development in all respects is the Plan, which for us is synonymous with vast accomplishments through generous credits" (2d sess., 1948); and "everything in French Equatorial Africa, including political equilibrium and material and human well-being, depends upon the breadth and depth of the economic advance it is practical for us to achieve" (1st sess., 1949).

62. Le Cornec, *Histoire politique du Tchad.* Suret-Canale, *Afrique Noire*, vol. 3, pt. 1, pp. 9–60. Kalck, *Histoire centrafricaine*, p. 466.

"Brazzaville had been overtaken by events."[63] The question then arose whether, as seen from French Equatorial Africa, the reforms did not amount to a stampede. At one and the same time, they quite likely stunned French colonial interests in French Equatorial Africa, which were accustomed to enjoying exclusive and abusive privileges, and surprised the local évolués who, as previously mentioned, with rare and extreme exceptions[64] were not asking for this much. As for the masses, one would judge that, even taking due account of the slogans propagated during the Kongo-Wara revolt (1928–31) and of the pervasiveness and intransigence of Kongo messianism, these measures went beyond their aspirations.[65]

The politicization of local life in 1945—both theoretical and potential—became actual between 1946 and 1952, punctuated by two legislative elections in 1946 and 1951 and two territorial elections in 1947 and 1952. Political representation of French Equatorial Africa, organized along the same lines as in the other French colonies, is shown in the following table.[66]

	Representative Councils			*Grand Council*	*National Assembly*			*Council of the Republic*			*Assembly of the French Union*
I	I	II	Total		I	II	Total	I	II	Total	
Gabon	12	18	30	5	1	1	6	1	1	2	1
Middle Congo	12	18	30	5		1		1	1	2	1
Ubangi-Shari	10	15	25	5	1	1		1	1	2	2
Chad	10	20	30	5		1		1	1	2	3
Total F.E.A.				20	2	4	6	4	4	8	7

Notes: I: Elected by First College (citizens of both sexes having French civil status) II: Elected by Second College (certain categories of citizens of both sexes retaining their personal status)

The local administration asserted that these new institutions were operating well. This, for example, was the view of Cornut-Gentille, governor of French Equatorial Africa:

> on the political level the effort put forth has produced equally good results. Except in a few very restricted localities, and for subjective

63. Pierre Cot, quoted by Suret-Canale, in ibid., p. 43; and Aubame in Guernier, *Afrique Equatoriale Française,* p. 186.

64. Kalck reports radical demands formulated "within small groups" of government employees. *Histoire centrafricaine,* p. 466.

65. See Nzabakomoda-Yacoma, ("La Guerre de Kongo-Wara" Cabore, n. 3); the very fine testimony of René Maran in *Batouala,* p. 77; and G. Balandier, *Sociologie actuelle de l'Afrique Noire* (Paris, 1955), pp. 397–486.

66. According to Guernier, *Afrique Equatoriale Française,* pp. 177–78.

reasons, no tension exists within our populations, and if *implanting the new institutions was a very risky venture*, reasonable minds cannot but be astonished that the *upheaval* that took place so recently in the underpinnings of *such a backward community* has been, all in all, substantially made up for. . . . The fact that the desire for union and understanding prevails among the majority in our local assemblies, thanks to concentration of attention by the elected representatives on *economic and social problems not of a specifically political nature*, must be marked as a real success for the French Union's institutions. [Address before the Grand Council of French Equatorial Africa, April 20, 1949, first session. Emphasis added.]

Here it was the spirit of harmony that was praised; elsewhere, it was the importance of participation: the results are reflected in a more intense political life, a more well-defined awareness among the *évolués*, and the growing influence of the elected representatives. The needs and desires of the people are now making themselves heard more effectively, and a *close and trustful* cooperation is beginning between the Representative Councils and the administration. . . . The peoples concerned are *today participating directly* in the management of their own affairs, and have the capability, which they are in fact using, of making their voice heard in the councils of the French Union.[67]

With the new institutions, economic development was the second major axis of French policy after 1945.[68] Within the framework of FIDES, a ten-year plan was drawn up for the period 1947–56 to which was allocated some 51.344 million CFA francs, or considerably less than for French West Africa (133.890 millions). These credits were apportioned as follows:[69]

	Millions	*Percent*
I. Infrastructure	31.513	61.4
—Communications	26.858	
—Telecommunications	2.028	
—Electricity, materials, mapping	2.627	
II. Production	7.345	14.3
—Agriculture	3.953	
—Forests	782	
—Livestock	1,820	
—Mining	790	

67. M. Riedinger, "Colonial Servant," in ibid., p. 181.

68. For the general context, see Suret-Canale, *Afrique Noire*, vol. 3, pt. 1, pp. 92–132.

69. *Afrique Equatoriale Française: Plan décennal d'équipement et de développement 1947–1956* (Brazzaville, 1948), fols. 5–31.

	Millions	*Percent*
III. Social Services	12.486	24.3
—Public Health	5.131	
—Education	4.148	
—Town Planning	.573	
—Urban sanitation	2.634	

Aside from the smaller amount of credits allocated, the differences from the French West African plan bore principally upon (1) the large share for social services (24.3 percent as against 18.3 percent), explained by the enormous backwardness of French Equatorial Africa, notably in the fields of education and sanitation, and by the recrudescence of endemic diseases and epidemics as a result of the war effort;[70] (2) the favored role of communications: more than half of the credits. But in both cases the plan accelerated the process of integration with the metropolitan economy and accentuated the outward orientation of the local economy (development of cotton, lumber, and gold production, and petroleum prospecting). In the sociocultural field the credits permitted a building construction policy that was eventually recommended by the Minister for Overseas France as a model for the other colonies; included were the extension of credit to the évolués so as to meet their "legitimate aspiration to own property," the opening of cultural circles for these same évolués "devoid of any political purpose, and without a questionable paternalism," and the completion of the lycée and general hospital at Brazzaville.[71] Successive governors made the economy, in Cornut-Gentille's words, the "essential activity" of their government and sought to impose this point of view upon the local assemblies: that is, to depoliticize them to the extent possible.

Here one encounters what appears to be the salient characteristic of this period. The dominant feature was not constructive accomplishment in the "spirit of Brazzaville," but resistance by the local colonial authorities to the full application of the new measures, and their disinclination to play by the new rules of the game.

This disinclination is explained first of all by the attitude of French economic interests and by their weight in local life. The chambers of commerce in the four territories had no intention of submitting passively. They were the better able to press their demands as the postwar governors, going beyond the provisions of the April 5, 1935, decree establishing the

70. Kalck, *Histoire centrafricaine*, p. 466.

71. Address to the Grand Council, April 20, 1949, pp. 11–12. Ziéglé, *Afrique Equatoriale Française* (Paris, 1952), pp. 181–87.

chambers, accorded them increased powers.[72] On August 16, 1945, a local ordinance authorized the formation of "exporters consortiums" enjoying a monopoly of the export of certain groups of products; seven were created immediately and others followed later. On December 22, 1948, another ordinance made it obligatory for the governors to consult the chambers of commerce on subjects as varied and important as the fixing of prices, customs duties and "all other taxes," the creation of new business establishments, "any basic reform of the economic system," and "all questions affecting the Colony's economic activity." There was, of course, a conflict of jurisdiction between the chambers of commerce and the new representative assemblies, whose functions were of a specifically economic nature; the conflict was settled by a lame compromise between the economic interests and the representatives of the local peoples.[73] The most extreme attitude was that of the Bangui Chamber of Commerce; in a petition addressed to the Governor-General in May 1946, it took a position in open opposition to the reforms, adducing the danger of economic chaos: "the measures just adopted can be suitable only for less backward peoples than those of French Equatorial Africa; it is obvious that the termination of forced labor is interpreted here as the legal confirmation of the right to do nothing. . . . No one who knows these countries can believe that a piece of prose can suddenly modify the black man's mentality."[74] A very obvious racism, characteristic of the "poor white" (*petits blancs*) community which was particularly numerous in Ubangi-Shari, was revealed in these views; the very same opinions were defended by René Malbrant, the First College deputy, in the Chamber of Deputies, and also at the meeting of the Etats Généraux de la Colonisation convened upon his initiative at Paris in July and August 1946.[75]

72. Cf. Genty (President of the Brazzaville Chamber of Commerce), "Les Chambres de commerce," in Guernier, *Afrique Equatoriale Française*, pp. 415–18. The chambers similarly denied entry of competitors to French Equatorial Africa, whence a long dispute between the traditional companies in Ubangi-Shari and the Boussac firm (Kalck, *Histoire centrafricaine*, p. 485). In 1945, also, an "Association des colons de L'A. E. F." was formed, with corporate status (*JOAEF*, 1945, p. 619.)

73. "Since . . . 1946 and 1947 some confusion has arisen in the respective jurisdictions of the representative assemblies and the commercial associations. The administration believed that the powers given to the representative assemblies could abrogate those of the commercial associations, and a finding by the finance section of the Council of State was required in order to place things in order and restore each agency to its legitimate jurisdiction." Genty, "Les Chambres de commerce," in Guernier, p. 418.

74. Kalck, *Histoire centrafricaine*, p. 474.

75. Ibid., pp. 460–61; Suret-Canale, *Afrique Noire*, vol. 3, pt. 1, p. 49. A typical assessment of the "poor white" in Ubangi is in R. Monmarson, *L'Afrique franco-africaine* (Paris, 1956).

As for the colonial administration, it was neither quantitatively nor qualitatively able to cope with the situation created by the reforms. Quantitatively, because it suffered from particularly serious problems: its chronic illness of underadministration and a new one, instability. At the end of the 1940s French Equatorial Africa appeared to be truly threatened by paralysis; there were only seven public-works engineers, 100 public school teachers, 78 doctors, 23 magistrates, and less than a thousand administrators for a population of five million.[76] Although improved between 1948 and 1951, staffing remained manifestly insufficient, thus lending additional immediacy to Eboué's warnings.[77] The newer illness of administrative instability was no less grave; between February 1944 and March 1948, when Cornut-Gentille was appointed (March 1948–September 1951), French Equatorial Africa saw eight governors-general succeed one another, of whom five were only interim appointees. Not only was implementation of the new measures therefore hasty and pro forma, and local policy lacking in continuity, but above all decisions by the transient governors lacked force, especially in the face of powerful economic interests. Eboué's successor, André Bayardelle, found this out to his cost. In December 1945 he drew up a sweeping plan for administrative and territorial boundary reform. The governor's powers were to be "strengthened"; French Equatorial Africa was to be governed from a single capital (that is, Brazzaville, not Paris) and administered from a limited number of departmental towns. Gabon and Middle Congo were to be united, Chad diminished so as to embrace only the Muslim districts, and Ubangi-Shari extended to include the Sara country. Submitted to the chambers of commerce, the plan was rejected.[78] From that time on, the federal principle lost ground, and fragmentation of French Equatorial Africa appeared to be the only possible outcome.[79]

Qualitatively, at the level of mentality and political conviction the administration was unwilling to put the "new deal" of power into practice. This was, of course, inevitable inasmuch as an effort was being made to accomplish new things through men of the past. But this is not the full explanation. During his tenure, Cornut-Gentille (1948–51) in fact brought in young career colonial servants and contract employees from the metropole.

76. Cornut-Gentille, Address to the Grand Council on Sept. 29, 1948, p. 17.

77. Ziéglé, *Afrique Equatoriale Française*, pp. 181–86.

78. Bayardelle's comment: "I did not take into account the creation of certain interests which probably find in the mediocrity of the present institutions sources of satisfaction commensurate with themselves." Quoted by Kalck, *Histoire centrafricaine*, p. 479.

79. Cf. Cornut-Gentille: "The four territories must be given a maximum of autonomy." Address to the Grand Council on April 20, 1949, p. 15.

The men changed, but the spirit remained the same. The administration thus found itself in disagreement with the laws it was entrusted to apply. Two examples will illustrate this disagreement.

For the masses, the most noticeable change was the abolition of forced labor. But practice did not confirm the principle. In Gabon and Middle Congo, freedom of labor was seriously compromised by the "work card" system. This card, introduced in Middle Congo in 1942 and extended to Gabon when that territory was liberated, was required of all blacks employed by European enterprises. Those who happened to become unemployed lost the advantages pertaining to the card and became liable to penalties under the vagrancy law unless they placed themselves at the administration's disposition and accepted whatever job was assigned them. In Ubangi-Shari and Chad, labor recruitment proceeded for a very long time. Thus, the French Equatorial African Chambre Syndicale des Mines requested additional workers in Novembet 1947. The governor of Ubangi, on the pretext of preventing depopulation of the cotton-growing areas, took the initiative of designating by decree the regions where recruitment was *authorized* and the *maximum* number of workers by subdivision. The officials in charge of the subdivisions interpreted the *authorization* as an *order*. The situation in the cotton fields remained unchanged. The Inspectorate of Labor was nowhere in evidence.[80]

For the elite, the problem was above all political. It has been shown above that in Eboué's time the administration was already aware of the conflict between the two elites, the chiefs and the évolués, and favored the chiefs in its doctrine while in practice promoting the évolués. Representatives in the new assemblies were recruited principally from among the évolués. The administration saw no harm in this so long as they were "moderates." In Chad, for example, it provided all sorts of assistance to Issembé, candidate for Deputy in 1946, whose platform stated that "the natives of Chad and Ubangi were not demanding their independence" and were preoccupied solely by "improvement of social conditions and the economic situation."[81] But the voters were turning increasingly toward "radical," or reputedly radical, candidates: d'Arboussier in Gabon, Jean-Félix Tchicaya in Middle Congo, Gabriel Lisette in Chad, and Bartélémy Boganda in Ubangi-Shari.

To face up to this drift, the administration devised a subtle strategy extending from repression of the "radicals" to the search for a substitute

80. Kalck, *Histoire centrafricaine*, pp. 485–88. Other evidence in Dampierre, *Un Ancien Royaume du Haut-Oubangui* (Paris, 1967).

81. Le Cornec, *Histoire politique du Tchad*, p. 102.

elite with moderate positions. Strong-arm tactics were well illustrated by the difficulties encountered by Boganda in Ubangi-Shari, the den of the "poor whites" and the large cotton companies. Elected and reelected Deputy beginning in November 1946, the founder of Mouvement d'Emancipation Sociale de l'Afrique Noire (MESAN, September 1949), a movement staffed by *évolués*, Boganda saw himself sentenced for "incitement to riot" in November 1951 and threatened with loss of his office. But this maneuver was not found profitable,[82] and attempts were made to nurture a more reassuring elite.

In Chad the administration colluded with the chamber of commerce to promote the popularity of the commercial branch of the new black "bourgeoisie"—Ibrahim Babikir and Béchir Sow, Fort-Lamy merchants—against the "bush peddlars."[83] In all the territories it looked to the chiefs, endeavoring to revive the "traditional" institutions. This is how the genesis of the Pahouin de Mitzic Congress (February 26–28, 1947), and the administration's attitude toward it, must be interpreted.[84] Convened "under the auspices of the Governor of Gabon," the congress nevertheless had an ambiguous outcome. The Fang notables expressed the desire to give themselves a paramount chief, an idea the governor heartily approved; nevertheless, the congress appeared above all like a plebiscite in favor of Léon M'Ba, an évolué recently condemned to prison and exile.

Faced with these repeated setbacks, the local administration reconciled itself to the obvious: henceforth it had truly to accept the new institutions as a fact, and furthermore to come to terms somehow with the évolués.

III

After 1951–52 several circumstances reinforced this desire for accommodation. Decisions taken on the metropole's initiative accentuated the autonomy of the territories and expanded opportunity for participation in public affairs. The Municipalities Law of 1955 and, more particularly, the Loi-Cadre of 1956 and the introduction of the single electoral college, had as their consequence an intensive politicization of the popular masses. As the locus of decision on territorial affairs passed from the faraway Ministry for Overseas France to locally elected officials, the level of participation in elections rose abruptly at a time when the size of the electorate doubled, or even quadrupled, according to the territory. In Chad, for example, the

82. Kalck, *Histoire centrafricaine*, pp. 273–81.

83. Ibid., p. 103.

84. G. Balandier, *Sociologie des Brazzavilles noires* (Paris, 1955), pp. 198–201.

number of voters rose from 308,000 to 1,200,000 between 1952 and 1957; in Middle Congo it rose from 230,000 to 400,000 between the 1956 and the 1957 elections, while the rate of participation, which had been a mere 45 percent in 1951 (7.5 percent of the total population) increased to an average of 80 percent in 1956 (99 percent in certain subdivisions) and remained at that level until independence.[85] The "legal" country was thus corresponding more and more closely to the "actual" country.

This politicization, which might have been expected to disturb the colonial authorities, seemed to them the more reassuring, as it was accompanied by growing moderation in the African political parties, whether because of the appearance of new parties supplanting the "radical" tendencies of the immediate postwar period or because some of the first nationalist leaders embraced conciliatory positions. In Gabon the situation had clarified as early as 1951.[86] The withdrawal of d'Arboussier left the Union Démocratique et Sociale Gabonaise (UDSG) of Jean Aubame, who was a member of the Indépendants d'Outre-Mer, in confrontation with Léon Mba's Bloc Démocratique Gabonais (formerly the Comité Mixte Gabonais), the local section of the Rassemblement Démocratique Africain (RDA). The rivalry between the two men was indeed intense, Aubame being elected Deputy in 1951 and 1956, M'Ba mayor of Libreville in 1956 and vice-president of the Government Council in 1957.

Both, however, maintained excellent relations with the administration, a rare phenomenon in French Equatorial Africa. They spoke with one voice in praise of Gabon as an "example of Franco-African unity," carrying the desire for interchange so far as to give responsible posts in their respective parties, and even places on party slates, to colonials. Furthermore, the fact that both belonged to the dominant Fang ethnic group, and Léon M'Ba's leadership of the Mpongwé and other non-Fang groups, served to de-fuse many potential conflicts. The Parti d'Union Nationale Gabonaise (PUNGA) was handicapped by its late formation (1958) and by its aspect as a heterogeneous coalition, uniting men as diverse as former members of the UDSG, trade unionists, "radical" students, and non-Fang natives of southern Gabon.

Although moving in a similar direction, evolution was more uneven in the Federation's three other territories. Thus, in Middle Congo Jean-Félix Tchicaya was regularly elected Deputy until 1956; a former vice-president of the RDA, he and his party, the PPC (Parti Progressiste Côngolais),

85. Wagret, *Histoire politique du Congo*, pp. 56–73; Le Cornec, *Histoire politique du Tchad*, p. 102.

86. Thompson and Adloff, *The Emerging States*, pp. 348–57; Weinstein, *Gabon*, p. 171.

followed the Rassemblement's general evolution. After the break with the Communist party of France, however, the Deputy's moderation appeared to many as "collaboration" with the administration. Ethnic particularism further clouded the political picture. The PPC was looked upon as the "southerners'" party (Vili and Lari), while Jacques Opangault's MSA (Mouvement Socialiste Africaine) was regarded as that of the "northerners" (particularly the Mbochi). Both parties nevertheless continued to alarm French interests and some administrators—the PPC because of Tchicaya's past record, and the MSA because of Opangault's socialist Section Française de l'Internationale Ouvrière (SFIO) convictions of very long standing. In 1951, therefore, a local section of the Rassemblement du Peuple Français (RPF) appeared under the leadership of an African physician, Samba Dehlot; but the experiment failed, its candidate receiving barely 18 percent of the vote in the Lari district. The true turning point was reached in 1956, when Abbé Fulbert Youlou founded the Union pour la Défense des Intérets Africains (UDDIA). This party, of regionalist leanings, affiliated with a group of French colonists, l'Union du Moyen-Congo, in the "Intergroupe Libéral du Moyen-Congo." Its success in the municipal elections of 1956 and "Monsieur l'Abbé's" maneuvering skill made the UDDIA the territory's leading party between 1956 and 1958.[87]

In Ubangi-Shari at the end of 1954, Deputy Boganda renounced "purely negative demands" and "sterile letters" and embarked upon "a new path, one of positive, constructive work, which presages a better future." His warm endorsements of High Commissioner Chauvet for his "understanding," and of Sanmarco, the territorial governor, for his "humane spirit," amounted to an appeal for solidarity with the French.[88]

Within this general evolution only Chad might have been an exception. Until the territorial elections of 1952, and except for the election of Gabriel Lisette by the Second College in 1946, the majority adhered systematically to the most reactionary of the Europeans (René Malbrant) and a few conservative notables, sultans, or large merchants, such as Béchir Sow, Sou Quatre, or Arabi el-Goni, grouped together in the Union Démocratique Tchadienne, later renamed Action Sociale Tchadienne. Their very intransigence, and the barely concealed support lent them by Governor Colombani (1951–56), were at the core of serious disturbances in 1952 and permanent tension in the territory between 1952 and 1956. In 1956 the appointment of a liberal governor, Troadec, coincided with an election victory by the Parti Progressiste Tchadien, led by Gabriel Lisette. The latter, like

87. Wagret, *Histoire politique du Congo*, pp. 60–73.
88. Kalck, *Histoire centrafricaine*, p. 287.

Tchicaya in Middle Congo and Houphouët-Boigny in Ivory Coast, had aligned himself since 1950 with the moderate RDA line.[89]

During the 1950s, then, the new African elite clearly demonstrated its desire to share responsibility and power, in an amicable and progressive spirit, with the tutelary authority.

It was precisely during this period that High Commissioner Paul Chauvet (1951–58) introduced a series of measures and arrangements to ensure that the colonial authority would be replaced by this elite calmly and without disorder. The new official, formerly Résident at Lang Son and Secretary-General of French West Africa, assumed power at a particularly difficult juncture. The Federation's financial situation, and that of certain territories, was disastrous. Debts accumulated since 1945, adjustment of officials' salaries, interest and amortization on loans contracted to carry out infrastructural works in the ten-year plan and the first four-year plan—all combined to produce a substantial budget deficit. According to the governor himself, "a suspension of payments was barely avoided, thanks to the sympathy of the metropolitan treasury."[90] The political situation appeared chaotic. While the legislative elections of 1951 and the 1952 local elections aroused only verbal effervescence, tension remained acute between the local population and the French, both private individuals and officials, in Chad and Ubangi-Shari. Incidents at Logone in 1952 and at Berbérati in 1954[91] served as reminders of this tension. Paul Chauvet's policy was at once a mid- and long-range one, intended to prepare the way for transfer of the colonial authority's powers, as had been decided upon by the metropole, and an ad hoc policy seeking to do away with the survivals of the old colonial system revealed by these incidents.

In the latter category one may place Chauvet's efforts to improve relations between whites and blacks and his relations with the "traditional" chiefs. Following the Berbérati riots, which had been provoked by a French official's brutality and in which three persons (two Africans and a Frenchman) were killed, Chauvet warned Europeans against "white racism . . . as deplorable as ever, and as dangerous to public order," ordered officials to maintain strict neutrality in dealings between whites and blacks,[92] and took a series of procedural measures, including banning the

89. Le Cornec, *Histoire politique du Tchad*, pp. 125–42.

90. Address to the Grand Council on Sept. 30, 1952, p. 20.

91. Ibid., p. 5; Kalck, *Histoire centrafricaine*, pp. 528–31.

92. "This must be made understood by the Europeans, first, who are too inclined to believe that the soldiers, gendarmes, and police are there only to watch over their personal security; by the Africans, whom excessive abuses have convinced that the gendarmes and territorial guards are there only to force them to work; and finally by all the personnel of the Army, the

use of the familiar "tu" in addressing Africans and participation of Africans in public and private ceremonies designed to "reform the Europeans' mentality." Many of the latter did not hesitate to charge the administration with "weakness" and "demagogy," or to accuse it of pursuing an "anti-European and anti-colonist" policy. Their resistance led the High Commissioner to return to the charge in 1956; he had a pamphlet written addressed to new officials and colonists, threatened officials who were "incapable of improvement . . . or incompetent" with dismissal, and attempted by various means to encourage heads of business firms to "train African elites and facilitate in all appropriate ways their employment in responsible positions."[93]

Circumstances also dictated measures relating to the chiefs. Chauvet's first circular in this field, dated July 1, 1952, was prompted by the Logone riots, and that of April 4, 1955, by the acute crisis the chiefs were then passing through, especially in Chad and the sultanates of eastern Ubangi.[94] In Chad, for example, the people had exhibited increasing impatience with economic and financial exactions by the chiefs. The latter, in order to round out their income, had become accustomed to require the cultivation of lands that the villagers christened "chiefs' fields"; thus, chiefs' fields sown to cotton, millet, and rice were common sights.[95] During a tour in 1955, Chauvet observed that "demands which were perhaps excessive, but which no one would have dreamed of eluding until quite recently, were looked upon as intolerable abuses. Even obligations established by custom . . . were difficult to accept, even when they were based on firmly rooted practice or religious duties." This dissidence had certainly been accelerated by the reforms, which since 1946 had been introducing among the people a new concept of power and legitimacy, thus directly threatening the institution of the chieftancy.

Chauvet accurately perceived the contradiction between the new laws

---

Gendarmerie, the Guards, and the police, who must be convinced that they are not there to protect one category of citizens against another, but to protect them all and to ensure peace and tranquility for all. This implies rigorous impartiality on the part of all officials, of whatever kind and whatever rank." Letter to the governor of Ubangi-Shari dated May 29, 1954, and to the governors of Gabon, Middle Congo, and Chad dated June 3, 1954, in *Circulaires de base*, pp. 53–74.

93. Circular of May 12, 1956, *Circulaires de base*, p. 63.

94. Circulars of July 1, 1952, and April 4, 1955 (*Circulaires de base*, pp. 11–15 and 19–34). It should be emphasized that the former breathes not a word on the measures taken by Eboué, while the latter concludes, "It must be admitted that Governor-General Eboué's instructions have been lost sight of, and that since then no general line of conduct has been identifiable." One indication, among others, of a remarkable discontinuity in the local authorities' policy.

95. Le Cornec, *Histoire politique du Tchad*, pp. 92–93.

and the chieftaincy regime.[96] But how was the contradiction to be overcome? Should the chieftaincy simply be abolished or should one try to adapt it? He chose the latter solution; but, faithful to the reforms introduced since 1946, Chauvet decided to retain the viable chieftaincies while democratizing them. From then on, "customery" chiefs were to be treated with consideration at the expense of "administrative" chiefs, an attitude which came in a straight line from Eboué's thought. In order to reinforce the chiefs' authority, villages were regrouped in territories where political authority was the most fragmented (Gabon, Middle Congo, western Ubangi-Shari); thereby, several landed chiefs, mostly administrative appointees, disappeared. In order to democratize the institution, the "Councils of Notables," which had been created as early as 1936 but had never been able to function, were replaced after 1955 by elected district or division councils with budgetary responsibility. Training was provided to all chiefs down to the level of *canton* chief.[97] The transformation instituted by Chauvet thus consisted, in principle, in aligning the old chiefly elite with the new elite of évolués, by demanding that the former be properly qualified and imposing on them obligations that represented exactly the values and aspirations of the latter.

In the mid-term, the policy inaugurated by Chauvet bore upon two preoccupations: to satisfy certain demands on the part of the mass of the people and, especially, to associate the modern elite as closely as possible with public responsibilities. In his first statement before the Grand Council of French Equatorial Africa on June 9, 1952, he showed that the colonial authority "could build nothing solidly based without the support and participation of the people." To this end, several decisions were made, but their actual effect was uneven. Officials were urged to "resume contact—human contact—with the people." After 1952, in fact, tours were made more frequently, and were no longer simply "inspection and police sorties." In regions where European enterprises depended upon African labor to obtain products for export (lumber in Gabon, cotton in Chad and Ubangi-Shari), care was taken to ensure that "production was not unneces-

96. "It was precisely the reform of 1946 that accelerated evolution, by orienting it toward democratization. . . . The creation of representative assemblies has brought new elites into being, and the tie of dependence that bound the subject to his chief is tending more and more to be transferred to the person of the elected representative." Circular of April 4, 1955, in *Circulaires de base*, p. 21.

97. The program provided instruction in the organization of the French Union; the organization of the Federation, the territory, and the region; organization of the judiciary; the Gendarmerie, the Police, and the Territorial Guard; basic notions on financial legislation, public accounting; and some "technical" courses (stock-raising and agriculture, public health, etc.). Ibid., p. 28.

sarily regimented." Elsewhere in the countryside[98] the administration strove to promote small-scale, independent production. In 1952 three officers of the Agricultural Services went to the Belgian Congo to take advantage of its *paysannats* experiments; but the related measures and appropriations were not decided upon until 1956 and produced no practical results between 1956 and 1960.

The truth is that the authorities' principal preoccupation was with the évolués. The problem had been well formulated in 1952 by Chauvet himself. "It will be these *évolués,*" he told the Grand Council, "*whether we like it or not,* who will gradually take over from the old elites and the customary authorities. If this take-over is not accomplished in collaboration with us and under our supervision, it will inevitably be done beyond and against us."[99] The problem was the more urgent as the development, however relative, of education was continually enlarging the évolué class. In 1957–58 there were twelve lycées in French Equatorial Africa with 4,500 students, whereas in 1950–51 the Federation had only 1,700 students in secondary schools. Between 1950 and 1958 nearly 300 students passed the first part of the baccalaureate, and 160 the second part. The number of scholarship students sent to France for higher education rose from 23 in 1949–50 to 150 in 1957–58.[100] While there, many of these students embraced the radically anticolonialist ideas of the Fédération des Etudiants d'Afrique Noire en France (FEANF). To these must be added the youths who went in increasing numbers to study in French West Africa (at the Bamako School of Public Works, Dakar Nursing School, and Rufisque School of Posts, Telegraph, and Telecommunications).

Although the first évolué generation—that of Léon M'Ba, Jean Aubame, and Jean-Félix Tchicaya—had become quite satisfied materially (with the rise in salaries under the Lamine Gueye Law) and morally (with access to responsible positions, and the systematic use of "vous" in contacts between whites and blacks), it was imperative to find some way to calm the youths' impatience. The new policy consisted in opening wide the administration's doors, according to two principles Chauvet laid down in 1955: "Any position that can be filled correctly by an African must be entrusted to him rather than to a European. . . . Between two equally qualified candidates, the African must always receive preference" (circular letter of July 26, 1955). Faced with reservations on the part of some European officials, he

98. See "Production agricole," in ibid., pp. 106–74.

99. Ibid., p. 14.

100. Gardinier, "Schooling in the States of Equatorial Africa," *Revue Canadienne des Etudes Africaines* 8, no. 3 (1974):521.

replied, "I now order that the recruitment file of every approved candidate from the metropole include *proof* that the necessary search and advertising to recruit an African candidate have been carried out" (circular letter of December 8, 1955).[101] The French Equatorial African administration thus renounced the practice, instituted by Cornut-Gentille, of hiring European contract employees, as a "facile solution." As a consequence, more room was made for graduates of higher and secondary schools (baccalaureate and Brevet d'Etudes de Premier Cycle), and even for those with only primary education (there were 20,000, for example, in 1957–58). The new recruits were incorporated, with or without competitive examination, in the local staffs of the French Equatorial African financial and administrative services.

This policy, it would seem, had lasting consequences for the political history of French Equatorial Africa. One consequence was rapidly to make bourgeois the second generation of the modernist elite at a time when the first generation was embracing moderate political views. On the material level, these young officials received remuneration comparable with that of their European colleagues. A holder of the baccalaureate, for example, began at the index level 150 on the pay scale, which in 1952 carried a monthly salary of 21,000 CFA francs.[102] At that time, the average monthly expenses of a European family were between 11,500 and 12,400 CFA francs, while an African laborer's wages were about 3,000 francs per month. On the political level, meanwhile, the openings generously made available by Chauvet required of applicants a solemn pledge that the colonial authorities need fear no "subversive activity" on their part.[103] The black political elite on the eve of independence was thus isolated from the African masses socially and politically conditioned to come to terms with the tutelary authority.

This situation explains the fact that, in French Equatorial Africa generally, independence was freely granted by the colonial power to the African elite at the close of friendly negotiations.[104] Indeed, in 1958 total independence appeared to be desired only by the trade unionists, in particular those of the CGAT in Middle Congo, French Equatorial Africa's most powerful union, and by a few intellectuals. On the contrary, all the political parties signed a joint manifesto in August 1958, on the occasion of de

101. In *Circulaires de base*, pp. 68 and 73, respectively.

102. *Notice sur les cadres supérieurs de L'A.E.F.* (Brazzaville, 1954); *Conditions de vie et formalités de départ en A.E.F.* (Paris, 1952); Balandier, Sociologie des Brazzavilles noires, p. 85.

103. Circular of July 26, 1955, in *Circulaires de base*, p. 70.

104. The expression used, notably by Kalck, *Histoire centrafricaine*, p. 363.

Gaulle's proposal for a referendum. Although in appealing for a yes vote they requested independence in a more or less distant fugure,[105] this request was expressed on the basis of very strange considerations, among which the following may be noted:

> —Considering the threat of strangulation by the former British colonies hanging over the French African territories, and especially French Equatorial Africa which is nearly surrounded, on the north by Libya, adjacent to Algeria, on the east by the Republic of the Sudan, and on the west by Nigeria and Cameroun, all of which are independent states;
> —Considering that, confronting the African states associated with the Commonwealth, we have the imperative duty to defend and preserve the invaluable patrimony that France is bequeathing us, so as to pass it on to future generations. . . .
> —Considering that there is no respect except among equals, and that today we are suffering from an inferiority complex vis-à-vis the former British colonies which are now independent states. . . ."[106]

The demand for independence was thus based less upon a feeling of antagonism toward France than upon a feeling of inferiority and claustrophobia with respect to the neighboring territories.[107] At the same time, the plan for a federation among the four future states proposed by Opangault and Boganda was rejected by all the other parties and by the High Commissioner.[108] The Federation's territories thus became independent in 1960 each on its own.

In these conditions, the "neocolonial" nature of the cooperation agreements concluded between France and the states of the former Feder-

105. "The Conference requests the Government of the French Republic to insert the provision in the constitutional document that France recognizes the independence of the Overseas Territories; that they can take advantage of it when they please; and that, consequently, the simple unilateral decision by the local Assemblies and Councils of Government would be sufficient for such independence to become effective." Manifesto quoted *in extenso* in Wagret, *Histoire politique du Congo*, p. 76.

106. Ibid., p. 75.

107. One may thus accept Gardinier's statement, "The States of Equatorial Africa were not prepared for independence when it arrived" ("Schooling in the States of Equatorial Africa," p. 522), but in a sense very different from that author's; for him, the lack of preparation resulted from the incompetence of the leadership personnel and from weaknesses in economic development (but what colony has ever been ready for independence according to this criterion?); in the present writer's view, the lack of preparation consisted of the African elite's ideological and political disposition.

108. Wagret, *Histoire politique du Congo*, pp. 79–80; Kalck, *Histoire centrafricaine*, pp. 299–300; Thompson and Adloff, *The Emerging States*, p. 356.

ation stemmed both from the determination of the former colonial power to preserve its interests and from the desire of the new governing teams to maintain privileged relations with it.[109] There is not sufficient space here to give a detailed analysis of these agreements. It should nevertheless be noted that the "quadripartite agreements" signed among France, Chad, Congo, and the Central African Republic included very restrictive articles. In the military field, a mutual defense system was established that was responsible for ensuring the security (external or internal?) of each of the three states and was designed to organize common facilities of a military sort; hegemony within this system clearly rested with France. In the economic field, the agreements specified certain "strategic materials" (petroleum, uranium, thorium, lithium, beryllium, helium), concerning which the signatories undertook to consult regularly; while the former colonies agreed to give France preferential rights and priority of purchase, as well as to inform France of any measures they might take respecting these materials. The bilateral agreements signed between France and the three states covered substantially the same fields (except for the Centre d'Enseignement Supérieur de Brazzaville); the basic agreements, and those relating to foreign relations and military assistance, were written in identical terms and followed the same lines as the quadripartite agreements.

In conclusion, one may raise the question of the role played by the three levels—international, metropolitan, and local—of which Wm. Roger Louis and Ronald Robinson have pointed out the interaction in the evolution of the colonial empires.

The significance of international pressure is difficult to determine. It was certainly operating in 1944, at the time of the Brazzaville Conference; but this pressure was less in the direction of a transfer of power than of bringing about a new, less explosive, equilibrium. The pressure was stronger in the mid-1950s; it was doubtless the disillusionment of French colonialism in Indochina and Algeria that led the metropolitan authorities to contemplate, after 1956, a more flexible response to the aspirations of the local peoples.

At the local level, the pressure of the black social forces changed profoundly during this period. Before the 1950s, challenge to the colonial order in the form of mass rebellion and political-religious messianism appeared among the peasants and exhibited genuine vigor. During the 1950s,

109. *Journal Officiel de la République Française, Accords quadripartites franco-centrafricains, franco-congolais et franco-tchadiens* (Paris, 1960). The above analysis is even more viable for Gabon, which left France in possession of very important privileges.

on the other hand, it was the new elite that took the center of the stage, but without opposing the colonial regime in any fundamental way. The process of decolonization, therefore, was controlled from start to finish by the French metropolitan authorities.

Which leads to the question of the nature and reality of the transfer of power in Equatorial Africa. In this respect, one is struck by the conservatism of the colonial authorities. Those in the metropole who accepted decolonization, even if they did not wish it, may seem to have been more progressive than those in the colonies who, at best, long contemplated a very gradual sharing of power within the framework of the imperial regime. Both, however, sought above all to preserve the basic core of French interests. French policy, which consisted in granting power without jeopardizing fundamental interests, succeeded the more easily because the African elites in French Equatorial Africa—surprised by the swift pace of events, cut off from the mass of the people, and won over to the idea of collaboration—conceived of independence as merely obtaining powerful positions, without there being any change in the structure of society or in the nature of their relations with the former tutelary power. This is why, in French Equatorial Africa, colonialism was replaced by neocolonialism.

8. *The Decolonization of French Black Africa*

HENRI BRUNSCHWIG

I

The chapter in this volume by Louis and Robinson on the United States and the liquidation of the British Empire in tropical Africa proposes a methodological framework for all similar studies. In accepting this framework I have found it useful to elaborate it as a general schema for consideration of the problems of colonization and decolonization.

It is obvious that in order fully to understand events one must place them in a worldwide context, and the three levels—international, metropolitan, and colonial—chosen by the above authors, are certainly valid for everything that concerns colonization as well as decolonization. This broadening of the geographical horizon is as indispensable as that of the chronological horizon proposed in 1958 by Fernand Braudel in his well-known article on "la longue durée."[1] One must determine the location of an event occurring in the "short term" (ranging from a day to a few years) in its mid-term, the combination of circumstances of a few decades of which it is a part, and which in turn enters into the long term of several centuries whose permanent characteristics persist despite changes in circumstances.

But the timing and location of an event of interest to the historian thus lead to certain questions. If its occurrence reacts upon the three levels that evolve parallel one to another and constantly interact, are there not places and times where the event seems particularly important and from which it radiates upon the other levels? If examination of the various levels does not lead to definition of their differences, to discussion of the event's significance, its origin, its consequences, and its specific weight, of what use are levels? One might raise many questions concerning the event located in time and space. Three will be singled out here:

1. Fernand Braudel, "La Longue Durée," *Annales E.S.C.* (October, 1958), pp. 725–53; *Ecrits sur l'histoire* (Paris, 1969), pp. 41–83.

1. At what level, when, and by whom was the decision taken? When and where did the necessity for decolonization, namely, the relinquishment of the metropole's sovereignty, become apparent?

2. Was this relinquishment foreseen and prepared for over an extended period, or was it decided upon suddenly?

3. Who benefited by it?

Confronted with the complexity of interactions, these authors refuse to give preference to one or another of the levels. But does not the remainder of their chapter demonstrate that the Anglo-American negotiations at the international level, even if there was no direct pressure, weighed more heavily than local circumstances—and perhaps even the weakening of the will of the metropole—in the government's decision? To take another example, is it not true to say that, whereas decolonization of British West Africa was in gestation in the mid-term—at least since the 1864 Commission of Inquiry in the Gold Coast—in the Belgian Congo the decision was made suddenly, at the local level, and in the short term, in the wake of quite unforeseen disturbances?[2]

One may add that decolonization follows upon colonization, and that it may be useful to recall briefly its basic characteristics and to analyze not only the peoples concerned, with their mutual rivalries, but also the social structures of the colonial era. This leads to a concept that seems essential: that of the *evolutionary tempo* typical of each population. It would appear indeed that peoples, like individuals, have their distinctive temperaments. They evolve according to a more or less rapid tempo which may be speeded up or slowed down. A violent acceleration imposed from without may result in a spectacular adaptation or in the disappearance of a group recalcitrant to innovators. Well before colonization one may identify in Africa populations with rapid tempo, such as those which accepted colonization, cooperated with the whites, assimilated foreign cultural elements, followed the tempo of global evolution (which itself had accelerated), and adopted liberal or socialist programs; whereas others maintained a slow tempo, whether because the colonial power did not force them to progress or because their temperament did not allow them to bear the shock of an excessively drastic modification of their way of life and thought. Thus, side by side, the Bateke were recalcitrant whereas the Bakongo adapted. The colonizer was clearly the essential agent of acceleration but, long before the partition of Africa, the coastal peoples of western Africa had adopted a quicker tempo than those of the interior. There were nuclei of African

2. Jean Stengers, "La Belgique et le Congo," in *Histoire de la Belgique contemporaine* (Brussels: Renaissance du Livre, n.d.), pp. 415–36.

Colonization and Decolonization in Black Africa: Dahomey

Levels		COLONIZATION			DECOLONIZATION		
		Long-term	*Mid-term*	*Short-term*	*Long-term*	*Mid-term*	*Short-term*
	Governments		A				A
International	Public opinion						A
	Economic interests		A				B
	Governments (political)		D (Porto Novo)	D (Abomey)			A
Metropole	Public opinion		A	A			A
	Pressure groups (economic or religious)		D	B			A
Local: Coast	Advanced		D B				D B
(Porto-Novo, Cotonou)	Slow-tempo		A				A
Kingdom of Abomey	Advanced			R			D B
	Slow-tempo			A			A
North Dahomey	Advanced						
	Slow-tempo			A			A

Key:
A = Acceptance
B = Beneficiary
D = Decision
R = Refusal

bourgeoisie who cooperated in colonization, and their numbers were swelled by a broad fringe of gendarmes, junior civil servants, domestics, and so on, more or less urbanized and detribalized. Accepting the white or resigned to his presence, they felt themselves capable, in the end, of carrying on his work for their own benefit, at the expense of slow-tempo peoples whom the colonists had not, or had less fully, "civilized."

There are many sociological studies of cooperation (or collaboration), but acceptance of foreign colonization, (or resignation or resistance to it), whether active or passive, may constitute a deciding factor in the decolonization process. It explains subsequent evolution—and neocolonialism, which is the quest for acceleration in tempo toward that of liberal or socialist types of societies and economies. This does not mean that others, on the metropole or the international levels, may not also have profited from decolonization. On this point the present writer's views appear to coincide with those of Louis and Robinson.

The existing case studies—for example, on French West Africa, British West Africa, and the Belgian Congo—reveal so much diversity that it seems necessary to use the model proposed below for each territory. An attempt has been made to apply it to Dahomey. On this chessboard are placed the pawns Decision (D), Acceptance (A), Refusal (R), and Beneficiary (B). Thus we see that the international level had scarcely any influence; that between colonization and decolonization attitudes were reversed, the metropole moving from D to A and the colonized people from R or A to D; and that ethnic reactions vary within a single colony, the acculturated populations being placed in D, the slow-tempo ones in R or A.

II

In endeavoring to characterize the decolonization of French Tropical Africa, of which M'Bokolo, Person, and Suret-Canale study particular aspects, we shall place special emphasis on features that distinguish it from the emancipation of the Belgian or the British colonies. French decolonization, like the colonization that preceded it, appears to be unique and specific. The impact of international relations or economic interests upon it is less important than elsewhere; metropolitan public opinion is less well informed and, finally, less persuaded to break with the past. The colonization and decolonization of black Africa are marginal phenomena, secondary aspects of France's foreign policy and of its colonial policy, which was oriented much more toward Indochina or the Maghreb. Also, the role of the colonized peoples was a greater one, more decisive than elsewhere.

Jean Suret-Canale, in his critique of the thesis I advance in *Mythes et*

Réalités, objects that "one cannot attribute to a fact peculiar to French history (the defeat of 1871) a phenomenon that is not specifically French: the partitioning of the globe's territory." But, on the one hand, I did not say that the loss of Alsace-Lorraine was the cause of the world's partitioning. I was looking for the reasons why France participated in it; they are above all political, just as Leopold II's reasons were above all economic. On the other hand, the nationalism of the years 1871–1914 was not specifically French; to me it appears common to most of the powers, and certainly entered into the colonizing motivations of Germany, Portugal, and Italy. Finally, I do not think it a vice for scholarship to search for distinguishing features; on the contrary, it is one of the historian's basic virtues, and it is precisely French specificity that I would like to elucidate, rather than drowning French decolonization beneath waves of general and abstract theories.

The nationalist expansionism of the years 1880–1900 encountered no serious obstacles at the international level, thanks to the willingness of the powers to negotiate among themselves, within an atmosphere of a common faith in the superiority of western civilization and in the mission of the white nations with respect to "backward" peoples.

Nor is it some international pressure, comparable to that of the United States obliging the Netherlands to decolonize Indonesia, which explains the relinquishing of French sovereignty over black Africa. Memory of the errors committed in Indochina at the moment when the British were decolonizing India may have moved de Gaulle, attentive to international opinion, to put an end to the Algerian war. In black Africa, however, the decolonizing process had already been set in motion by the Loi Cadre of 1956. The General's genius consisted in reaping an increment of prestige from decolonization, which would normally have appeared as a defeat in the eyes of a metropolitan opinion long accustomed to consider as defeat any abandonment of sovereignty on the part of the "Republic, One and Indivisible."[3]

There was, furthermore, no interaction between British policy and that of France in black Africa. Decolonization was always foreign to French ideology. It was, however, already inherent in British doctrines of tutelage, which presupposed emancipation; as a result, the Africans had no need to engage in British domestic politics, and their presence in the Parliament of Westminster would have seemed incongruous. In French Tropical Africa

3. Cakpo Vodouhé, "La Création de l'Afrique Occidentale Française 1895–1904" (thesis, Sorbonne, 1974); Joseph-Roger de Benoist, *La Balkanisation de l'Afrique Occidentale Française* (Dakar, 1979); Joseph-Roger de Benoist, "L'Afrique Occidentale Française de la conférence de Brazzaville (1944) à l'indépendance (1960)" (thesis, Ecole de hautes etudes en sciences sociales, Paris, 1978).

there were no organized white minorities as there were in East and South Africa. Finally, mutual influences at the local level between French and British governors of neighboring colonies were always virtually nonexistent.

Some writers have stressed the fact that explorers, merchants, or soldiers sometimes confronted governments with accomplished facts, as Brazza did in signing the Makoko treaties, as Goldie-Taubman did in Nigeria, the French troops in the Soudan, and so on. It has been noted that the behavior of administrators in the bush, acting as local circumstances demanded, was often identical. But beyond these coincidences the fundamental fact that governs the entire history of French black Africa from 1871 to 1960 is that the action of the French colonizers was always dictated by the attitude of the colonized Africans.

The decision to colonize was doubtless made at the metropolitan level, in the short term, under influence of the chauvinism born of the 1871 defeat and reinforced by the traditional rivalry between the French and British navies.[4] French governments, little aware of the profound indifference of public opinion which was oriented more toward the Rhine than the Niger, dared not strike the flag and renounce the ways of a great power proud of its 1789 ideology and of its civilizing mission. But though they were able to acquire immense territories at modest cost, they lacked the means to organize them, administer them, and make them productive.

In 1914 there were, according to the *Annuaires,*[5] 2,175 administrators and officials of various public agencies in French West Africa and 533 in French Equatorial Africa. In French Equatorial Africa, French colonists were enumerated at 532 at the time of the mobilization. The figure is less precise for French West Africa, where the black citizens were not distinguished from the white. The statistics mention 2,932 reservists, from which figure the 2,175 civil servants must, moreover, be deducted. Even with a generous estimate of those ineligible for conscription, one finds hardly more than a thousand or so private citizens residing in the various colonies composing this group. This handful of some 4,200 white Frenchmen, dispersed over a territory fourteen times the size of the metropole and inhabited by between 15 and 16 million, could not have maintained themselves without the assistance of the blacks cooperating voluntarily with coloniza-

4. Henri Brunschwig, "Anglophobia and French African Policy," in Prosser Gifford and Wm. Roger Louis, eds., *France and Britain in Africa* (Yale University Press, 1971), pp. 3–34.

5. *Annuaires de l'A.O.F.*, 1913–1914; *Annuaires de l'A.E.F.*, 1912–1913; ANSOM: AEF 20.

tion, which was more widely accepted by the colonized peoples than is generally believed.

The local disturbances, the resistance to colonization, and the scandalous abuses on the part of the colonizers have been much insisted upon—with good reason, and with reference to the echo of the abuses in Parliament and the press. But these local disturbances, which were ephemeral and harshly repressed, did not give birth to general hostility, to a feeling common among all blacks, or to an early form of pan-Africanism. Perhaps this was because the excesses of the conqueror, and the rebellions, were nothing new in Africa, and because the precolonial African states and societies had always known ones just as serious.

In any event, during the organizing phase that preceded the First World War and afterward, and indeed until about 1945, the colonies' governors always found black collaborators without whose assistance government would have been paralyzed. At first, each governor recruited them from among those who applied. Sometimes they came from the acculturated, rapid-tempo populations along the coast, who provided excellent interpreters and clerks; sometimes they were military veterans, accustomed to discipline and speaking broken French, who became policemen (or rather, guards) or customs officers; sometimes they were *dyoulas*, peddlers who spoke several dialects and were acquainted with the trails; and sometimes even "boys" trained by their employers, like Boubou Penda, whom the administrator Ernest Noirot, after educating him, placed in the civil service as an interpreter. The governor paid such collaborators wages, and regulated them according to his means and needs; but little by little he made them into public servants, assimilating them at first with the white local staffs, then later grouping them separately in the "local native cadres" which became more and more numerous after 1906. At Paris and Dakar awareness of this necessity for the natives' assistance developed later on, and the governors' initiatives were formally ratified. On May 24, 1911, in a circular addressed to the governors-general of French West Africa and Madagascar regarding personnel expenditures in the local budgets, Minister of Colonies Adolphe Messimi declared:

> that substantial economies could be accomplished, while carrying forward an endeavor to which, like my predecessors, I attach particular importance, if greater advantage were taken of the natives' collaboration. . . . At the present time a very great number of junior posts which require of their incumbents no particular qualifications and involve no heavy responsibility are entrusted to officials from the metropole. This

practice must cease. . . . A large number of secretarial or accounting-clerk jobs, to mention only administrative posts properly speaking, could be entrusted to natives.[6]

The governor-general of French West Africa, William Ponty, in a circular distributed from Dakar on June 26, 1911, remarked that the employment of natives was of long standing in French West Africa and encouraged the formation of native local cadres to the extent that this would not excessively burden future budgets.[7] In the event, such cadres proliferated in all the public agencies: administrative clerks, draftsmen-interpreters, post and telegraph employees, nurses, native doctor's aides, customs officers, orderlies, chauffeurs, and so on each received civil service classification.

This is not the place to undertake a detailed study, but some statistics should be mentioned, not as absolute figures (for the sources are suspect) but to give an idea of the order of magnitude. As early as 1914 the proportion of Europeans was, according to the French West Africa yearbook, 1.04 percent in the French West African police services; in Posts and Telegraphs it was 8.30 in Senegal, 6.25 in Guinea, 7.69 in Ivory Coast, and 5.95 in Dahomey. In short, virtually all the working-level colonial servants were natives. Subsequently, the number of Africans continued to rise; above all, their competence improved, thanks to the development of education, and many of them, after 1945, considered themselves qualified to replace the white bureau chiefs.

The acceptance of colonization can also be explained by the absence of widespread frustrations. Much has been said about the large concessionary companies in the Congo, but it has not been sufficiently noted that they represented an anomaly in French black Africa. Comprehensive study of the permanent concessions of "vacant" and ownerless lands" granted in the various colonies between 1890 and 1914 reveals that natives obtained 37 percent of the concessions in Guinea, 54 percent in Dahomey, and between 12 and 15 percent in Ivory Coast. Land was not scarce. The large capitalist enterprises were in no hurry to invest. Individual applicants were few. Most of the concessions were for small areas, intended for commercial agencies or warehouses in the new cities, for modest craft enterprises, or for small-scale farms.

All these people, often of quite modest station, constituted the flesh and blood of the colonial system. They owed to it a sort of upward social mobility which did not conflict with their customary beliefs or with their

6. *Bulletin officiel du Ministère des Colonies*, June 1, 1911, pp. 624–26.
7. *Journal officiel du Dahomey*, Aug. 1, 1911, p. 265.

membership in different ethnic groups. They were everywhere, more or less active, more or less useful; but without their help colonization could not have survived. Little by little an elite of advanced Africans emerged from among them. What were the thoughts and aspirations of its members? It is difficult to say, because they themselves did not always know very clearly, they were not always agreed among themselves, and they rarely expressed themselves. On the one hand, a survey of the Dahomean press, to which M. Lokossou has devoted a good thesis,[8] and statements by certain Senegalese, on the other, seem to establish the fact that until about 1920 the collaborators believed more firmly in assimilation than did the theoreticians in Paris. This was because they had not undergone the influence of Anglo-Saxon pan-African schools of thought, and because in French literature they found abundant equalitarian and humanitarian declarations that assuaged their wounded dignity. They knew, moreover, that in Franch a black man could become a Deputy, a professor, or a physician on the same conditions as a white without encountering racist reactions on the part of the whites subordinate to him. Many of them aspired to French citizenship and believed that colonization led to it. As one example, we may mention the Congolese Jean-Rémy Ayoumé, an évolué of Poto-Poto at the time of the Brazzaville Conference. In an article on "Westernism and Africanism" filled with references to works by French evolutionists, he noted that "within the general trend toward universality of civilizations and toward uniformity of all men there are stages in evolution toward progress," and "the need for leveling and equalization . . . has led certain groups, those we assume to be advanced, to concern themselves with other groups called 'primitive' or 'backward' in order to hasten their development. We call this need 'colonization.' From the human point of view, thus, colonization is the act by which man seeks to establish a vital equilibrium among all the groups comprising mankind." He concludes, "To sum up: we favor the extension into Africa of Western civilization in its entirety. One may, if need be, momentarily restrict this extension for practical, transitory reasons stemming, for example, from needs that must be satisfied immediately. But in our view the extension, without any discrimination, gives rise to no irrefutable or decisive objection."[9]

By 1944 this radicalism had become anachronistic, if only because France herself no longer believed in assimilation and scarcely applied the

8. Clément Koudessa Lokossou, "La Presse du Dahomey 1894–1960: Evolution et réaction face à l'administration coloniale," (thesis, Sorbonne, Paris, 1976).

9. Jean-Rémy Ayoumé, "Occidentalisme et africanisme," *Renaissances*, nos. 3–4 (1944), pp. 258–63.

principle. In 1938 there were, in French Equatorial Africa, only 5,000 native French citizens out of 3,400,000 blacks, and 90,000 out of 14,900,000 in French West Africa; at the first Constituent Assembly of 1946 there were only nine black Africans among the 63 overseas deputies.[10]

Advanced Africans had meanwhile become conscious of their cultural identity, and their opinions were doubtless closer to those of the Soudanese canton chief, Fily Dabo Sissoko. In 1944, in the same periodical, *Renaissances*, the latter also invoked evolutionism while condemning total integration, which he saw as a "chimera," a "mortal danger" for the colonizer, and a form of "sterilization" for the colonized: "A totally assimilated man, or one who thinks he is, is a derelict." Sissoko preferred association or, preferably, "cooperation." He wished "to find in race itself elements capable of assisting its own evolution." Evolution, he thought, "does not consist in aping the white man, nor in renouncing our blood and our past." And the white man ought to endeavor "by all appropriate means to ensure that the black man evolves according to his black path of evolution." This was echoed in the slogan of the young Senghor, *agrégé* in grammar: "Assimilate, don't be assimilated." And this attitude aroused the enthusiasm of liberal French intellectuals, centered around M. Pleven, Robert Delavignette, and others, who were discovering "black" cultures.

No one dreamed of independence; the great word was "cooperation." A new France, Free France, associating the blacks in a new policy that would turn over to them the responsibility for their own evolution in Africa; cooperation in an amicable, peaceful atmosphere; a striving toward mutual understanding, not opposition, violence, or revolt—this seems to be where the blacks' collaboration with colonization had led between about 1890 and the end of World War II.

What about the others, the illiterate masses living in the bush at the slow tempo of their ancestral traditions? Seen from outside, they are easy to describe. They emerge as exploited, the victims of French capitalism or that of the advanced Africans, wretched and subject to limitless forced labor and taxation. But were they aware of this? Had they not always been exploited in the course of the precolonial intra-African wars, the Muslim raids, and the whims of transitory potentates? They certainly did not expatiate on the laws of evolution. They persisted at the slow tempo of days and seasons, enduring the contingencies of good and bad harvests, good

10. Fily Dabo Sissoko, "L'Evolution et la colonisation française en A.O.F.," *Renaissances*, nos. 3–4 (1947), pp. 247–57.

11. Michel Devèze, *La France d'Outre-Mer de l'Empire colonial à l'Union Française 1938–48* (Paris, 1948), p. 16.

and bad administrators, in a world alien to all others despite incursions by the great religions and by techniques which eroded their traditions without attacking them in any brutal way.

Did these people reap no benefit whatever from colonization between 1890 and 1945? How can we tell? Demographic statistics, relatively reliable only after 1921, are meaningless. Depopulation may accompany a rise in the standard of living; demographic growth may intensify poverty. Objectively, they were beyond doubt oppressed, reacting locally against the most flagrant abuses by initiating revolts that were quickly crushed. Resignation, passive resistance, inability to rise above day-to-day concerns? Who knows? Neither whites nor advanced blacks were much concerned with understanding this segment of the population. This was not the pastoral euphoria of the Belgian Congo, but even if the compartments which set apart slow- and rapid-tempo populations were not that watertight, they were nevertheless real.

III

The harmony between French governments and their African collaborators was shattered between the years 1945 and 1960. Why, precisely? At which level did the events that imposed this change burst forth? When? To whose benefit?

In the first place, both sides sought to avoid violence and war. Second, during this period those responsible vacillated, were subjected to various sorts of pressure, and competed among themselves. But the most important thing appears to be that the behavior of the French governments was dictated by that of the advanced blacks rather than by international circumstances or by the interests of metropolitan economic circles. The dominant fact is that the colonization undertaken by the metropole functioned for thee-quarters of a century, thanks to the collaboration of Africans who were advanced or in the process of rapid advancement. Once they ceased to accept it, French sovereignty was bound to crumble.

The origin of the rejection would have to be determined and documented colony by colony. The tactics adopted by the African leaders were flexible and skillful. At first they did not mention the word *independence* nor—except perhaps in Guinea—seek conflict. Decolonization, which arose from the 1956 Loi Cadre, was the deed of Senghor and Houphouët-Boigny as much as of Defferre. The first-named was a French Deputy, the second a French minister. These collaborators, who had first accepted, then rejected, the metropole's sovereignty, nevertheless did not wish to alter the direction of the evolution on which Africa had embarked.

The French governments did not bow to injunctions from the United States, as the Netherlands did, nor did they undergo the influence of international events to the extent the British did. Did they really even believe that they were decolonizing by relinquishing their juridical sovereignty? What they were bringing about amounted, after all, simply to the *transfer of power* to groups with which they had long collaborated. Whether their compatriots Houphouët or Senghor were ministers in Paris or presidents in Dakar or Abidjan, the difference, substantial in appearance, was perhaps less so in reality. In any event, the two men differed on the question of preserving the Federation of West Africa. It is by no means clear that, in opting for "Balkanization," the government followed the "divide and rule" principle. One would, moreover, think that it would have been easier to exert its influence on the federal capital than to allow negotiations and expenditures to proliferate. When one recalls the slowness and the difficulties with which the governors-general laboriously imposed their authority, when one thinks of the disturbances that centralization might have engendered through incitement by thwarted elites in various colonies, when one remembers that Houphouët's influence would have predominated because he was a member of the government and that, after all, black Africa was not the central preoccupation of the government, one will suspend judgment until the day when access to the archives will permit a supportable conclusion.

The French did not surrender to victorious enemies such as Nkrumah or Kenyatta; they stood aside before friends of long standing and with whom, in their turn, they were to collaborate. Furthermore, public opinion remained indifferent and ill-informed. "Decolonization" of black Africa, to its way of thinking, certainly seemed preferable to a new Indochina or Algerian war. And economic circles, while perhaps regretting the loss of their monopoly positions, were not badly situated vis-à-vis foreign competition for the business they would conduct with their former partners.

So who benefited from this new regime? First, the new states, to the extent that they received from abroad greater means for their economic development than before; and second, the foreign powers, whether capitalist or socialist, which furnished these means and expanded their own political influence. Who suffered from it? That is hard to say exactly, without the perspective only time can bring. The masses, perhaps, who were subjected more harshly to an accelerated tempo? Their protests, intensified by the resurgence of ethnic rivalries that colonization had appeased, are creating constant troubles. Their integration into the new states is a slow process, and the emergence among them of new elites jealous of the collaborators who seized power may presage new, inter-African transfers, possibly less amicable than the previous ones.

Decolonization has engendered a neocolonialism under the aegis of the former collaborators. This neocolonialism is haphazardly endeavoring to achieve a new equilibrium, to develop an African civilization distinct from foreign models; it is torn between the influence of capitalists and of socialists whose assistance is, furthermore, indispensable. In the face of difficulties constantly arising from demographic pressure, climatic vagaries, penury of natural resources, slow intellectual advancement, and rivalries among external powers, it is striving to bring into being national cultures appropriately rooted in the past. David Fieldhouse in chapter 17 of this volume, has competently analyzed these problems, which neither optimists nor pessimists have, in the short term, been able to resolve. His conclusion appears correct when he asserts that the future of decolonized Africa depends above all upon the Africans.

Can one, as Dennis Austin has done for British decolonization, divide the decolonization of French black Africa into phases and point out the crucial turning-points? This is difficult without fuller knowledge of the course of development in internal relations among the African groups concerned; these are as important as relations between metropoles and colonies, and they dominate the politics of the decolonized states.

In French black Africa there were no spectacular climaxes, as there were in India, but only changes in pace following the two world wars. After World War I, France did not fundamentally alter her conduct, notwithstanding the programs set forth in the Sarraut Plan, or at the time of the Vincennes Colonial Exposition of 1931. But, on the one hand, some 150,000 black veterans who had lived in France were added to the sparse ranks of the advanced group, while on the other hand, the image of the "black" as a big, smiling, trusting child took the place, in metropolitan public opnion, of the somewhat racist image of the "black" as a savage. In 1946, after World War II, the vehicle of politicization in the French manner, with growing numbers of voters in Africa and of African parliamentarians in France, started down the road toward decolonization.

Contrary to experience elsewhere, even that of France in other colonial theaters such as Indochina and the Maghreb, colonization and decolonization took place within a watertight compartment. The metropole had extended its sovereignty over Africa; it had organized administrations and ensured peace, thanks to the help of Africans. So long as they played its game, it was able to control them. They remained in the game and assimilated the metropole's culture. Whereas the leaders of British West

Africa—Nkrumah, Azikiwe, and others—pursued their political studies in the United States, the French African political chiefs pursued theirs in Paris. They took active part in French political parties and movements, and remained outside the general current of English-speaking African nationalism. They were the ones who, by and large, inspired the metropole's African policy. From Blaise Diagne, the Senegalese assimilationist, to Houphouët-Boigny, the Ivorian nationalist, it was, broadly speaking, the colonized people themselves who colonized and decolonized French black Africa.

9. *The British Point of No Return?*

DENNIS AUSTIN

Exponents of imperialism who catalogue its crimes have had little to say, except in the most apocalyptic fashion, about its end. It has been left to Polybius, Ibn Khaldun, Gibbon, Ostrogorsky, Lewis—historians sifting the remains of former empires—to describe its downfall. Many have noted the diseases rooted in a governing class, or in the general populace, for which the Roman or Arab or Byzantine or Chinese or Turkish empires had no remedy. The most general, if the most expressive, chronicler is Gibbon, who observed that the rise of a city that grew into an empire was "a singular prodigy . . . but the decline of Rome was the natural and inevitable effect of immoderate greatness. Prosperity ripened the principle of decay; the causes of destruction multiplied with the extent of conquest and . . . the stupendous fabric yielded to the pressure of its own weight." Eisenstadt has singled out specific dangers in particular empires: high taxation, a swollen bureaucracy, foreign conquests, infertile lands, a declining population, class conflict, the tug and pull of tradition against modernity or of priest against warrior.[1] Writing of the Han dynasty, Pan Piao added that the failures and successes of history could be explained by omens and signs, or by strange markings on the face and body of the ruler.

All these observations are helpful. But when we reach the former British Empire and the colonial possessions of the European states, I confess to being puzzled. Of course, one can say that they collapsed under their own weight, becoming too complicated and onerous to sustain, and loose generalizations can be framed about the contradictions of capitalism or the assertion of nationalist demands. But Britain, France, Holland, and Belgium still stand in the sense that Rome did not—or Byzantium or the Pharoahs or the Han dynasty did not. There was the protection of distance between the European metropolitan powers and their overseas dependencies. Some shadow of Rome, it is true, lingered over France and Portugal.

1. S. N. Eisenstadt, ed., *The Decline of Empires* (Englewood Cliffs, N.J.: Prentice-Hall, 1967).

The latter tried to retain the notion of provinces in Africa. The French sustained a belief in integration through representation in Paris and the legality of *territoires et departements d'outre-mer*, distinct from Protectorates in Morocco and Tunis and the Associated States of Indochina. The British had no such illusions. Imperial federation was rarely a serious proposition; integration with Malta was only a momentary aberration. The empire kept its distance from London. There were times, indeed, when quarrels between London and Delhi, or the Colonial Office and Nairobi, or the Dominions Office and Salisbury, put on some of the characteristics of international disputes, as in earlier arguments with the American colonies and Canada. But there was no breakdown of authority at the metropolitan center. The notion of "decolonization" suggests a process of dissolution: but it has been only the formal links of subordination which have been dissolved, not—or not yet, we should perhaps add—the structures of power in London or Lagos or Delhi or Suva.

What was the solvent? In an amused aside, Gibbon dismissed as mere superstitition an ancient belief that the rise and fall of Rome should be ascribed to Fortune.[2] And very few today see history as chance, unless it is over millennia. Nor is it comfortable to believe in destiny except in relation to class or race. Yet belief in the validity of *fortuna* was less difficult to accept when reflected in the faded splendor of an Italian villa, and it was at Bellagio, in the Villa Serbelloni, that I first began to wonder whether it was possible to find any "point of no return" in the history of British decolonization. Such a point would have to carry the notion of irreversibility, almost of fate—a fate determined perhaps by chance or accident, or by a sequence of events which carried with them a mark of inevitability, so that one had to recognize that the end was contained in the beginning, or at least was unavoidable once a point had been reached from which there could be no turning back. (One might add, more prosaically, that "a point of no return" might also be interpreted rather differently: not that a path of action once begun had to be followed to the end, but simply that no other end was worth the candle, was, in a word, profitless, because there was "no return" to be had politically, economically, or nationally.) Fortune had carried the British overseas across huge tracts of the world, but there were elements of

2. "The Greeks, after their country had been reduced into a province, imputed the triumphs of Rone, not to the merit, but to the *fortune*, of the republic. The inconstant goddess, who so blindly distributes and resumes her favors, had *now* consented (such was the language of envious flattery) to resign her wings, to descend from her globe, and to fix her firm and immutable throne on the banks of the Tiber."

mortality within the very process of expansion and consolidation, of a kind that brought colony after colony—*suo proprio motu*—to an inevitable end once a "point of no return" had been reached?

It is true that British rule abroad exists still. Circumstances almost defeated policy over Rhodesia and have produced a puzzled state of no policy at all in Belize, Gibraltar, Hong Kong, and the Falkland Islands, along with various atolls of such diminutive size as to be below even the present tolerant notion of sovereignty. Pitcairn has yet to enter the United Nations. But the 1960s saw the Colonial Office put up its shutters, and the 1970s brought the reduction of the Commonwealth to a subtitle of the Foreign Office: a tattered cloak upon a stick. The dissolution has been swift, and we are still close to the main events which marked its progress. Hence the belief among historians that, if the dependent world of the colonial empires cannot be rejuvenated, at least it can be understood. The time was ripe for a study. And it was in the falling dusk of a lovely autumn evening that those who met together at the Rockefeller villa drew from their memories a portrait of that awkward age of empire when the final transfers of power were taking place under British or French or Belgian rule. The historians spread their wings and looked back through the twilight of those years. No longer dazzled by the light of empire, they tried to find the decisive events which determined the end of European rule.

In more modern guise, historians are like the aerial photographers of my Air Force days; they bring back their distant views, neatly framed for approval, as evidence of this or that conjunction of events, or unwind the film of their observations for scrutiny. So it was in Bellagio, in the shade of the dark tall cypresses that mark out the terraced steps down to the sunshine of the lake. And in the pictures drawn for such scrutiny a number of critical events began to seem conspicuous. Within the British Empire there were half a dozen apparent turning points: the independence of India, the 1948 riots in the Gold Coast, the attack on Suez in 1956—that last spring of the once rampant lion, the period of "Emergency" in Kenya, Malta 1964, and the breakdown of the Caribbean Federation. Others no doubt might choose different aspects of the story, but each was certainly significant over the range of colonial rule considered as a whole.

India 1947—to which we must add Pakistan and Ceylon. So much has been written on the theme that there seems little else to say. Not all the murders and enforced migrations of dispossessed communities could quite blot out the peaceful symbol of that first transfer of power under a title of independence. The cordial exchange of flags amidst mutual protestations of affection in colony after colony—dependence at midnight, sovereignty in the morning—turned the original act into a ritual. Where was the point of no return in India and in what sense was the 1947 Act of Independence a turning point in the empire as a whole?

"To the end," writes D. A. Low, "the apparatus of the Raj maintained by the British remained intact and was never physically destroyed."[3] Success through the ballot box by Congress leaders and by "the dominant peasant communities" had ensured that "the game, in the terms the British had determined it, was up. Despite grievous last-minute alarms and excursions the transfer of power inexorably ensued."[4] There it is once more: "inexorable." What does it mean? That nothing could stop the transfer taking place? It was beyond entreaty or prayer or will: a point of no return had been reached where the momentum of events, if not always of policy, had become irresistible and irreversible? But were earlier decisions and events of a different order, less consequential because alternatives were present? In retrospect, a path of reform can be traced back *ad originem* by which India had moved toward independence: 1947, 1942, 1935–37, 1931, 1929, 1919, 1917.[5] Were such steps critical at each stage? Or did they become *accumulatively* critical, in the sense that the options open to Britain, and the ends pursued by nationalist leaders, narrowed until all sides to the argument were brought inexorably to August 15, 1947?

The readiest answer is, I suppose, yes. For was it not less easy for the British to change course after the 1937 elections than after 1921, and more difficult after 1942 than in 1937? Such is the effect of hindsight. It offers a progressive view of events, programmatic in nature. The picture it presents of India is that of a widening political consciousness, accumulative concessions, and successive turning points of increasing significance. Yet there is a familiar paradox here. Teleological arguments always present the view that developments are due to the purpose and design served by them: thus the goal of self-government may be said to contain each critical event from which there was no turning back. But when a term of years is looked at in detail, there is always an awful lot of movement backward and forward. There is often a groping about for remedies to meet a particular crisis, reform alternating with suppression. At one level, it can be argued that Congress and viceroy struggled to adjust competing claims and did so—

3. D. A. Low, ed., *Congress and the Raj* (London, 1977), p. 47.

4. Ibid.

5. 1947—Independence; 1942—Quit India campaign; 1935–37—Government of India Act and Elections; 1931—Gandhi-Irwin Pact; 1929—Irwin's declaration of the offer of Dominion Status; 1919—Montagu-Chelmsford reforms; 1917—Montagu's declaration of policy for "the progressive realization of responsible government."

despite periods of conflict—by reaching out for agreements which fell within an "old Dominion pattern": ballot boxes, legislatures, ministerial government, a widening franchise, and Commonwealth membership.

At another level of action, however, alternatives to that model were always visible. There were, even teleologically considered, grim alternatives for which the end and the means would match, not Canada or Australia or New Zealand, but Ireland, Palestine, Burma, Aden, and Rhodesia. Then the point of no return might have been very different from that described by Low. It might have been a "finale with chaos," to use the title applied to Palestine, or a story of force against force, one "resting on the will of the people and the other on an alien Government depending for its existence upon military power—the one gathering more and more authority, the other steadily losing ground. . . ."[6] Moreover, even within the pattern of conflict that actually took shape, it is hardly possible to say when the point of no return was truly reached. Was it as late as the arrival of Lord Mountbatten, or the onset of war, or a middle point in the 1930s, or the drawing together of a Muslim League or of Congress, or the return to India of Gandhi? Everything depends on the view of the observer, and on the length of view taken. Low uses familiar phrases, of the British being "hoist with their own petard," blown up by engines of their own device, by the use of the ballot and the acceptance of tbe legitimacy of Dominion status. But the origins of that particular trail of gunpowder would lead very far back—beyond South Asia—along a continuous line of sappers!

It would certainly include Ceylon, though in a very mild setting, where the movement toward self-government, writes Kingsley de Silva, was "so bland as to be virtually imperceptible to those not directly involved."[7] The island took independence almost by stealth. Was there any point of no return? De Silva has traced with meticulous skill, through Colonial Office files, the negotiations which enabled Ceylon, by Order-in-Council, to achieve "fully responsible status within the British Commonwealth." I once read all the Command Papers, dispatches, petitions, and memorials between Colombo and London from 1921 to 1945. There is hardly any demand for self-government, and certainly none for "independence" as an immediate goal. That was not the kind of language of reform used. Yet running through all the documents is an assumption, whether in petitions from the Sinhalese community or dispatches from the secretary of state,

6. Michael Collins, *The Path to Freedom* (Cork, Ireland, 1968), p. 65.

7. K. M. de Silva, *Sri Lanka: D. S. Senanayake and the Passage to Dominion Status, 1942–1947* (London: Institute of Commonwealth Studies, 1976).

that Ceylon ought to move toward a "more popular control of government."[8] De Silva shows how indeterminate the whole progress was even at a quite late stage.

It is true that a novel form of home rule was introduced in 1931—it was much disliked not only by many party leaders but by the governor—and I am sure that Kingsley de Silva is right when he observes that the outbreak of war in 1939 did not accelerate reform as it is often assumed to have done in respect of the colonial empire; it probably delayed the granting of self-government. Even so, as late as 1944, at the time of the Soulbury proposals, there was still indecision in London over how long the final period of colonial rule should be—whether, indeed, it should have a predetermined end. There was vague talk in cabinet of a further six years at least. That independence came in 1948 was not primarily because of events in the Indian subcontinent or Burma but through Senanayake's adroit, steady, confident handling of Whitehall and Westminster at one end and of his own legislature in Colombo at the other. There were no sudden changes, no abrupt change of course, nor any direct line of advance. The image is one of meander. Relations between individuals—Senanayake, Caldicott, Oliver Stanley, Monck-Mason-Moore, A. S. Ranasinha, Creech Jones, Goonetileke—were always more important than any dramatic turn of events.

If we had surveyed the colonial world of 1947–48 what kind of landscape would we have seen? I am thinking mainly, though not exclusively, of the once familiar universe of British rule. We would have looked out over a wide field of dependent territories and sovereign "commonwealth governments." An intelligent observer of a mathematical turn of mind, by the application of a simple Markov chain of probability, might have predicted the increase in the number of independent states over future years. But politicians are not mathematicians. To predict is easy: to face the immediacy of events is quite another matter. Secretaries of state, or colonial governors, or nationalist leaders, have to decide what to do in all the uncertainties of the present, and statistical determination has only a secondary place in any vocabulary of action. Nor do politicians easily accept as inevitable what they may later be obliged to endorse. Arguments which purported to show that the independence of South Asia must have a sharp effect on Africa or the Caribbean or Southeast Asia would have encountered familiar beliefs that "India was different" or "that Ceylon was unusual."

From the vantage point of today, looking back to 1947, the case is clear. The hunt was up and colonialism its prey, from India in 1947 to Saint Lucia in 1979. But that was not as it appeared at the time. In 1947 the French

8. Secretary of State to Governor of Ceylon, June 18, 1923, *Cmd. 1906*.

were successfully quelling an armed uprising in Madagascar. European settlers were moving out once again to Kenya, Rhodesia, and the Congo. Over the British in particular there still hung a bright sword of expectation forged in war. There was great pride in achievement as a nation which alone had fought the war from beginning to end to emerge victorious as one of a triumvirate. Hugh Tinker might write: "August 1947 demonstrated that British governments of whatever political complexion could dispose of the remaining imperial possessions as soon as they wished. The politicians were not slow to dismantle the 'imperial museum.'"[9] But that was too indulgent. South Asia might be free, but colonial territories in Africa, Southeast Asia, the Caribbean, and the Pacific and Indian oceans were still in the business of empire. Historians can indeed lay bare what was not seen at the time. They are, after all, grander than mere pilots. They are like gods who ride above the chronology of events. But they falsify their trade if they translate the consequences of a particular set of events back into the intentions of those who acted at the time.

In brief, it was very far from clear that colonialism was soon to be over. Between 1947 and 1957 recruitment into the colonial service increased by more than 50 percent. At the end of the Second World War not a single nationalist party existed in any of the African colonies under direct British control.[10] Colonial rule was actually being reimposed in Southeast Asia, and although academics were beginning to map the future retreat of British rule, the prospect of independence for each and every territory was quite remote. Britain was still a global power. There was civil war in Greece, the Russians were advancing, the Americans beginning to look for bases overseas in safe hands under the Truman Doctrine. It was a cold new world of no peace at all, in which the vulnerable or poor or small were thought to be greatly at risk. It is true that there was a large measure of reform in many colonies. But that was seen as enabling colonial rule to be more effective, not as hastening its demise. Indeed, the overriding preoccupation in the Colonial Office at the end of the 1940s was reform of local government and encouragement of colonial production. The empire had been harnessed for war and was now needed to establish peace.

Lord Swinton was quite sure about what was needed. "Before I left for West Africa, Lord Woolton told me that all his nutrition experts had told him that the one cut above all others he should try to avoid was a cut in our fat ration."[11] Swinton had been appointed Resident Minister in Africa in

9. Hugh Tinker, *Experiment with Freedom* (London, 1967), p. 164.

10. Unless one includes local parties in Nigeria.

11. Lord Swinton, *I Remember* (London, 1950), p. 192.

May 1942 to coordinate economic and military policies, and four chapters in his memoirs describe his success in "winning the battle of the fat ration." Similar preoccupations marked the postwar years from Tanganyika to the Gambia: margarine and eggs on the largest scale to improve the British breakfast table. So, too, in Southeast Asia. It was the need for tin and rubber, in addition to global strategy, that determined the British to suppress the Communist insurrection in Malaya. Constitutional changes were introduced to soften discontent or to meet new demands: but the intention was still reform, not dissolution. The Moyne Report on the West Indies had driven home the danger of economic stagnation and political reaction, but the policies worked out in the Colonial Office by Andrew Cohen and Sydney Caine—eloquently defended by Ronald Robinson—were largely concerned with reform of local government and the encouragement of economic planning. Of course, it was proposed to move in the direction of "more and not less participation by the people in the work of government [as] a real necessity for lasting social advancement."[12] But moves toward greater "participation" simply reflected the way in which the British controlled their colonial dependants, preferring acquiescence to coercion. The core of such a policy might be described very simply as: "the power structure in [the colonies] is changing. Authority is no longer obeyed for its own sake. There are severe limits on what governments can do."[13] Under Cohen's energetic direction, responding to Hailey's questioning of the obedience now capable of being exacted by Native Authorities in many African territories, efforts were made in many colonies to extend "the limits on what government can do" by encouraging reform at district level in favor of the educated young in place of the old and traditional. But in Africa, as elsewhere, it was still to be collaboration between colonial rulers and a local elite. It was very far from abdication.

Such views were put to severe test in the Gold Coast in 1948. So much so that the abrupt and forward rush of events, leading to independence in 1957, is frequently singled out as a major turning point not only in the Gold Coast itself but throughout the colonial empire. The riots of 1948, it is said, forced a path to independence; independence for Ghana forced the pace of reform throughout Africa and the empire. Both assumptions seem to me valid in a very general sense of affecting the tempo—and possibly the temper—of change. But (at least in respect to British policy) the reser-

12. The phrase used by the (Moyne) *West Indian Royal Commission 1938–1939, Cmd. 6174.*

13. A familiar *cri de coeur* which might have come from any colonial governor in the 1950s. It is actually James Callaghan in 1974, in his address to the Labour party conference.

vations that need to be entered against too sweeping a conclusion are also substantial. It seems most probable that the Gold Coast would have moved toward independence even had the 1948 riots not occurred. On a wider front, self-government in Accra sent a thrilling note of alarm and expectation through many other colonial capitals; but the contagious effect was surely very marginal.

I can write with some feeling in the matter since I was once guilty of extravagance in the writing up of the events of 1948 to 1957. I gave them dramatic form and made the beginning of the change coincident with my arrival as a young man in Accra. Now, if I could, I would question the degree of novelty and stress the element of continuity. I notice that Ghanaian scholars have come to a similar revision—namely, that the 1948 riots, the Watson Commission and its recommendations, the subsequent Coussey Report, and the bringing together by Nkrumah of a People's party, reflected a mood of discontent and a quickening of reform already apparent in the 1930s and 1940s. That the speed of change quickened once the franchise had been extended (on an indirect basis of election) in 1950 is certainly true, and the success of Nkrumah's party owed more, perhaps, to that than to any other single factor. But chance or Fortune, too, played a part in the favorable conjunction of events and of able individuals—the reformist lawyer Henly Coussey, Governor Arden-Clarke, the Watson commissioners, and temperate politicians, among whom Nkrumah, Botsio, and Gbedemah were very representative. After its initial dismay over the disturbances, the Colonial Office was prepared (by its own deliberations) to accept substantial reforms at a local level. The Commission of Inquiry thought it proper to cover national and local problems.[14] The Coussey Committee then enlarged the scope of the recommendations; and Nkrumah, seizing the opportunity that the Coussey Report presented, gave the whole movement for reform a further radical shove along the road to "responsible government."

Thus, what began as "disturbances" and as proposals for reform along lines fully approved in the Colonial Office slipped into a nationalist movement for self-government. There were ancillary causes—the initial unpreparedness of the colonial administration in the Gold Coast and then the competence of the new governor who patrolled the road to independence, armed or compliant as occasion demanded, with great force and surety. It was also the case that West Africa was not very important in any assessment

14. "The Watson Commission, appointed by the Colonial Office . . . stretched and, some said, went outside its terms of reference in recommending radical reform." Sir Andrew Cohen, *British Policy in Changing Africa* (London, 1959), p. 43.

of global strategy. The Anglo-Nigerian Defence Agreement in 1960 was a halfhearted affair, and Accra was rated well below Lagos. Nigeria is interesting by comparison in other respects too, since without rioting, without a nationalist party, without more than the peaceful pressure of local politicians on the colonial government, the country moved by negotiations into independence. It is true that Sir Hugh Foot noted the effect on Nigeria of the 1948 riots in Accra:

> Not long after [Sir John Macpherson's] arrival we had a vital conference in Government House. The Richards constitution had then been in full effect for little more than a year and it had been stipulated that it must remain in force unchanged for nine years. We reviewed the whole political situation; we took into account the disorders and changes which had recently taken place in what was then the Gold Coast. We came to the conclusion that we must at once take a new initiative.[15]

But such decisions simply gave the movement for reform and its nationalist response a push forward along a line of advance already begun.

Still, it is clear that the level of agitation in the Gold Coast and Nigeria was far below that needed in India to bring about a British withdrawal. There was no General Dyer, no civil disobedience, no prolonged period of nationalist struggle. Ceylon offers a closer parallel, although the stages of British retreat, of the kind marked out by Martin Wight (who preferred the notion of "stages of advance"), were less widely spaced in West Africa than in South Asia.[16] *The curve of reform was shortening.* Was it because of the influence of India and Ceylon? Among those with whom I once worked and lived in West Africa in the 1950s I can remember some interest in Asia, but not very much. Self-government had an appeal which seemed self-evident once it was heard, and I am sure that the assertion of what were seen as national interests had only to be made to be endorsed. At a simple level of explanation the movement against colonial rule reflected no more than the growth in number of educated leaders, particularly in the small towns that linked the countryside.

More complicatedly, the rise of an anticolonial sentiment surely represents the transfer to Asia and Africa of nationalist beliefs, carried as part of that immense outward movement of Europe which the rest of the world at first embraced and then resisted. From a narrowly *British* stance, however, the effect of Commonwealth independence in South Asia was almost

15. Sir Hugh Foot, *A Start in Freedom* (London, 1964), pp. 103–64.
16. See Martin Wight, *British Colonial Constitutions 1947* (Oxford, 1952).

certainly to persuade successive governments in the United Kingdom, Labour and Conservative alike, that the goal of self-government was a manageable proposition. In the history of British decolonization the resolution of a particular crisis by constitutional rearrangements, portioned out in instalments, invariably encouraged further demands for further reform. But they also established useful precedents. Very likely the principles grew out of the precedents. Success bred a belief in success, and to know how to decolonize helped to justify the need to do so. Practice began to shape decisions by precedent and was thus brought into consciousness as policy.

There was a good deal of uncertainty in the 1950s about where and when to move forward. Policy had still to wait upon events. More than ten years after the Accra riots, an interesting comment was made in the House of Commons by the secretary of state, Alan Lennox Boyd. He expressed uncertainty about the momentum of reform and its relevance to the whole of the empire, and added: "If we had a hundred years of steady progress in which to bring all our colonial territories to maturity, their independence would cause no misgiving, but we are now working in terms of a decade or so."[17] Yet he could also declare in respect to East Africa that he was "unable to envisage a time when it will be possible for any British Government to surrender their ultimate responsibilities for the destinies and well-being of Kenya."[18] It was a view noted by the Monckton Commission on Central Africa the following year: "Conditions in West Africa were thought to have little relevance for the multi-racial countries of the Eastern and Central portions of the Continent."[19] The Minister of State for the Colonies, Henry Hopkinson, had said much the same for Cyprus: that the island would "never" become a sovereign state.[20]

Year by year, however, the reservations were overcome, borne down by the pressure of events. The transformation of colonies into Commonwealth members, of dependencies into sovereign states, became a yearly occurrence in the early 1960s. There was an extraordinary array of conferences to settle the affairs of Kenya, Cyprus, Uganda, Malta, Jamaica. It took three secretaries of state—Macleod, Maudling, Duncan Sandys—to negotiate Kenya into independence. It required three Offices of State to dissolve the Central African Federation: the Colonial Office, the Commonwealth Relations Office, and R. A. Butler's Central African Office. But both tasks were completed by the end of 1963, although there was unfinished business still

17. *Parliamentary Debates*, November 13, 1958.
18. *Parliamentary Debates*, April 11, 1959.
19. *Cmnd. 1148*, 1960, paragraph 31.
20. *Parliamentary Debates*, July 10, 1954.

in Rhodesia. Commonwealth membership doubled during these few years, as colony, protectorate, and trust territory alike underwent their conversion, each fully equipped for self-government with parties, parliament, a Speaker, adult suffrage, a governor-general (or local king), a prime minister, cabinet, a chief justice and—still holding his sword ceremoniously—a commander-in-chief. One by one the barriers to full sovereignty were set aside. Too divided racially or communally? Kenya proved otherwise. Too vulnerable or strategically important? Malta regained a freedom the Maltese had not known for a millennium. Too small? There now seemed no limits on size of territory or paucity of population.

Here then, surely, in the 1960s was the last and decisive turning point. Although there were detailed shifts of power, they became in essence one decision: to put an end to empire, by free negotiation where possible, but by exerting pressure if needed on reluctant nationalists who might not want to be "free." Was that not the case in Kenya after Mau Mau?

There were early signs of impatience to be gone. Macleod prefaced the January 1960 conference on Kenya with the words, "We intend to lead Kenya to full self-government or, if I may use a plainer word, to independence."[21] Michael Blundell believed that Macmillan and Macleod had decided some time in 1960 to move toward an East African Federation under independent African control.[22] Turnbull, as governor in Dar-es-Salaam, was said to be in agreement. Macmillan was warning his own party and trying to teach even the Afrikaner about the need to run with the tide and sail with the wind, picking up an earlier phrase—the winds of change—used by Baldwin about India.[23] Later in the decade, Macleod was to claim personal credit for the change:

> It has been said that after I became Colonial Secretary there was a deliberate speeding up of the movement towards independence. I agree, there was. And in my view any other policy would have led to terrible bloodshed in Africa. This is the heart of the argument.[24]

That was in 1964–65, and I suspect that hindsight had once again translated, with too great a precision, consequences back into intentions. Still, it is true that Kenya was critically placed.

The old debate over "White Man's Country" versus the "Paramountcy of Native Interests" still hovered over the colony during the Mau Mau Emer-

21. *Cmd. 960,* 1960.
22. Michael Blundell, *So Rough a Wind* (London, 1964), pp. 220 and 261.
23. See K. Middlemas and J. Barnes, *Baldwin* (London, 1969), p. 713.
24. *Spectator,* March 20, 1964, and April 23, 1965.

gency. The 1950s were pivotal in that 50,000 British soldiers had been needed to put down the revolt. So many troops were used under direct British control and so much money spent to mend the destruction that settler rule was now out of the question. There then began a familiar search for acceptable African successors. Nor were they lacking. Who brought Kenya into independence? Kenyatta of course, and Mboya. KANU, too—but also that small, well-educated nationalist elite to whom the loyalist Kikuyu looked for leadership and whom the British saw as capable of governing.

> The modern Kenya elite would appear to have emerged as a group . . . some time in the mid-1950s. The Legislative Council elections of 1956–57 at which, for the first time, Kenya Africans were asked to choose by secret ballot their eight representatives, probably marked the open emergence of that elite. It seems clear now the colonial authorities had by 1954 realized that given the vote, Africans would elect the elite.[25]

That may be to credit the "colonial authorities" with rather too great a prescience; but the search for a way forward was, after all, a resumption of what had been interrupted under the Lyttleton Constitution of 1954, which, in turn, looked back to those far-off times when Dr. Eliud Mathu was nominated to the Legislative Council (1944–57) and to the appointment of five Asian members in 1925. It may well be that by 1960 the British had sufficient confidence in those who had stood out against (or who were now prepared to disown) the "Mau Mau freedom fighters" to move forward once again. For, as B. A. Ogot has observed in his admirable study: "Unlike the loyalists in the American Revolution who lost their argument, their war and their place in American society, the Kenya loyalists won the military war, lost their argument but still dominate Kenya society in several significant respects."[26] In brief, the more one looks at Kenya, the more familiar is the picture. The colonial administration in Nairobi, like its master in London, constantly sought partners in collaboration, and was forced to change them from time to time, until at last those with whom it worked and negotiated insisted on being left to govern by themselves. It was a search for allies, the price of cooperation being the introduction of reforms which drew the administration further and further along the road to self-rule. That is the mildest description of the "winds of change" or the force of nationalism, and the story in Kenya is only a more dramatic version of the

25. B. A. Ogot, ed., *Politics and Nationalism in Colonial Kenya* (Nairobi, 1972), p. 251.
26. Ibid., p. 135.

change in partners—from chiefs and elders to an educated elite, and then to a more numerous, less educated leadership—in Ghana and Nigeria. Even on so vital an issue as land-ownership in Kenya, the conclusion is much the same. What happened in 1960–63 between European and African farmers, it is argued, needed to be seen as "the politics of adaptation."

> To view African independence as a victory of a nationalist movement over a colonial system is to narrow and presume a question which deserves detailed study. Independence can also be seen as 'a deal': a bargain struck between contending parties over the terms and conditions of independence.[27]

It is the absence of any major turning point of a radical kind between the end of colonial rule and the continuation of African politics under Kenyatta and Arap Moi which provokes criticism today. But that is quite another matter.

Nevertheless, if one watches the rapidity with which independence was bestowed in the mid-1960s (a rapidity so great that earlier notions of preparation or trusteeship became a mockery), it is difficult not to conclude that a major change had taken place. Would any British government in 1947 have agreed to self-government for Ceylon had the island been as singularly ill-equipped to maintain its independence as, say, Zambia in 1964? Were there truly forces at work (either in London or Lusaka) of such strength as to compel the Labour government to grant independence? The question is not quite as easy to answer as the rhetoric suggests. Something had happened to make it very difficult for Sir Evelyn Hone to remain as governor in Lusaka—the force of events if not the strength of local nationalism, or the circumstances of the time which made independence a ceremony of courtesy, whereas the effort to prolong colonial rule would surely have led to the need for coercion. Not only was there no going back, as in British Guiana in 1953 or Malta in 1933 and 1958 or Newfoundland in 1933; it was far easier to go forward than to stay still. But before we reach any conclusion there is a prior question: is it really the case that some colonies had independence thrust upon them?

I turn to Malta, that "fortress and harbour" colony which "came voluntarily under the British Crown 150 years ago and continued to accept . . . the difficulties of an island Fortress economy."[28] Because of its strategic importance, "the road to self-government" was held to be blocked," in that

27. G. Wasserman, "The Politics of Adaptation" (1970), quoted in Ogot, *Politics and Nationalism*, p. 147.

28. Malta Round Table Conference 1955 Report, *Cmd. 9657* (London, 1955), p. 23.

Parliament at Westminster must, in order to maintain the defence of Malta and the facilities necessary to enable it to fulfil its role as one of the principal Commonwealth and NATO bases in the Mediterranean, exercise overriding powers in the fields of defence and foreign affairs."[29] The Nationalist party under Borg Olivier agreed that Malta was unique in its capacity for self-government and its inability to achieve it: "Imperial interests have so far been involved to deny the Maltese people the full measure of self-government to which, by their history and traditions . . . they are justly entitled."[30] The Labour party under Dom Mintoff tried in 1955 to meet the problem by proposing "full integration" with Britain and, after a good deal of hesitation, the Conservative government agreed. A bill was presented to the Westminster Parliament; a referendum was conducted in Malta to gauge local opinion. When opposition from the Nationalists and the church produced a low poll (though one in favor of integration), Mintoff began to back away from the idea, and the House of Commons had second thoughts. There was a flurry of uncomplimentary letters between Lennox Boyd in London and Mintoff in Valletta, until by April 1958 the Malta Labour party was demanding separation from Britain, the Nationalist party was refusing to cooperate, and—as in 1903 and 1933—the Malta constitution was suspended.[31]

Here was an unexpected check to the rush to decolonize. The resumption of "Governor's rule" under a Crown Colony form of administration was a very unusual sight—quite antiquated. Yet what one must note is the speed with which the islands began, very soon, to move forward again to full independence. By 1961 new proposals had been formulated for a "State of Malta" under a reshaped diarchy. There was also a change of roles. The Nationalists now cooperated with the administration and pressed for a second referendum, not on integration with but independence from Britain. In 1962 a general election brought Borg Olivier to office as prime minister. In July the following year, Duncan Sandys convened a conference of Maltese delegations from which all but the Nationalists withdrew before the end of its deliberations. "We in Britain have no desire," the delegates were told, "to hustle Malta into independence or to lay down our responsibilities so long as you need us."[32] That may have been so. But there was no attempt now, in 1963, to repeat the warning given by Lennox Boyd

29. Ibid.

30. *Times of Malta,* December 3, 1953.

31. For details of the referendum, see D. Austin, *Malta and the End of Empire* (London, 1971), p. 125.

32. Ibid., p. 96.

in 1958: that "the unrealities of full independence would cause mass unemployment and untold suffering to the people of Malta."[33] On the contrary. At the end of the conference, H. M. government appointed a day—May 31, 1964—by which the islands should be independent and agreed to a referendum to elicit local opinion.

Once again the outcome was unsatisfactory: indeed, it was a repetition of that of 1956. There was a marginal yes majority for independence, but not if those who abstained were added to those who voted no.[34] A period of uncertainty followed, as the target date came and went. Amendments, which modified the rights of the Catholic church, were made to Borg Olivier's draft constitution, and two Agreements on Finance and Defence were prepared. The debate in the House of Commons on the outcome of the referendum was full of uneasy questioning. Mintoff and his colleagues were still in London, lobbying the government and the opposition, and members on both sides of the House pointed out that it was the first time—or almost the first time—that a colony had been given independence without a formal agreement on the constitution between local political leaders: Zanzibar was an exception, but that had led to revolution and murder. Where was the need for hurry? Why not wait and seek a further measure of agreement between the Maltese parties? The opposition, said Mr. Bottomley, would put down an amendment to provide "for elections to take place in Malta before independence," and he wanted to "make it clear that we on this side of the House say that the Government themselves have the full responsibility for the content of the constitution." Mr. Griffiths added his own warning: "This constitution is not an agreed constitution, agreed between the Government of Britain and people representing the majority of those in Malta. . . . If the House of Commons agreed with the Bill we shall be adopting a constitution which has not been approved by the majority of the people of Malta."

But Mr. Sandys would have none of this kind of argument. The necessity was to get the deed done. Catholics and the Catholic church had a special position in Malta just as Muslims and Islam had a special place in the constitution for Malaya. And "if we fail to pass the Bill now, it would be difficult to get independence much before the beginning of next year." Malta was not like Zanzibar or Guinea said Mr. Sandys, the difference being that "while these people [in Malta] say rather beastly things about each other they do not kill or burn one another every night." Later in the day, Mr. Bottomley's amendment was moved in the committee stage, when fresh arguments broke out again; it was defeated, and there was a

33. *Parliamentary Debates*, October 7, 1958.
34. Austin, *Malta and the End of Empire*, p. 127.

final grudging acceptance by the whole House of the closing statement by the secretary of state: "I really think that we have got to the point where we have got to take it that we have decided that Malta is to be independent." The bill then went through its third reading among a dwindling number of members from both sides of the Commons, was passed by the Lords on July 29, and received the Royal Assent two days later.[35]

Malta became independent at midnight on September 20–21, 1964, to the delight of the Nationalists and the dismay of the Labour party whose supporters still, today, refuse to celebrate the anniversary. Why was it done? Part of the explanation may lie in the parallel with Zanzibar (a disaster) and Kenya (a success)—namely, that the British wanted to transfer power to acceptable successors. It is not easy to see the Nationalist party in that guise, although it is true that the Malta Labour party under Mintoff proved recalcitrant allies during the 1970s. More likely—and it is very relevant to the problem of "turning points"—was that sense of finality about the end of colonial rule which had begun to haunt Labour and Conservative governments in Britain. But before drawing such conclusions I would like to look briefly at the last of our examples.

Within the broad sweep of the empire, the West Indies were interestingly placed. They were "settled islands"—settled by immigrants; but many were also conquered territories. Crown Colony rule had its origins in the Caribbean. Yet Barbados had, and still has, an unbroken parliamentary history, though of course the basis of the Assembly has been enlarged.[36] Once rich, then very poor, the islands have been categorized almost endlessly in respect of slavery, class, race, and the plantation economy which linked them to the New World. In the universe of British rule, the perennial question—can the structures and ways of government be advanced politically toward self-government?—was hardly capable at first of being answered. The islands were like Malta, although lacking the overriding strategic importance of that Mediterranean base: that is to say, by the middle of the twentieth century, West Indians were thought to be capable of governing themselves as an educated, middle-class elite, but the islands themselves were still seen as too small and too poor for independence.[37]

35. Ibid., p. 102.

36. See R. L. Cheltenham, *Constitutional and Political Development in Barbados 1946–1966* (Manchester, 1970); George A. V. Belle, *The Politics of Development: A Study in the Political Economy of Barbados* (Manchester, 1977); and A. J. Payne, *The Politics of the Caribbean Community* (Manchester, 1978).

37. It is "clearly impossible in the modern world for the present separate communities, small and isolated as most of them are, to achieve and maintain full self-government on their own." *Memorandum on the Closer Association of the British West Indian Colonies, Cmd. 7126* (London, 1947), pt. 2, par. 11.

The answer seemed to be federation. Yet not only geography but history pulled them apart. There was so much they had in common, and so little to hold them together. By the 1940s, a double phenomenon, already noted by Lord Halifax in the early 1920s,[38] began to have effect. The islands' leaders were meeting together to discuss closer union while pressing for constitutional reforms within their own political structures of control. What should have brought them together—the prospect of federal independence—was put at risk by the pursuit of reform at the territorial level. As Sir John Mordecai observed: "the desire for self-government now began to work against federation instead of in its favour."[39] It would be as vulgar to believe that the United Kingdom was seeking to "divide and rule" as it would be naive to suppose that it was striving to "unite and quit." There was nothing so plain or direct as that. The story is one of muddle.

The idea of closer unions was in the air from a very early date, but the first detailed plans for federation were made at the Montego Bay Conference in 1948. They were pushed forward in 1953 and 1956 and brought into being at the beginning of 1958 as the Federation of the West Indies.[40] Meanwhile, constitutional reforms were also being introduced in the individual islands and in British Guiana: universal suffrage as early as 1944 in Jamaica, 1946 in Trinidad, 1949 in Barbados, 1951 in the Leeward and Windward Islands; ministerial government in Jamaica in 1952, then in Trinidad and Barbados and the Leewards and Windwards in 1956. (Guiana moved toward ministerial government only to have its constitution suspended in 1953.) In theory, no doubt, island self-government might have become a stepping stone to federal independence. But local pressures on each of the colonial governments, and the ambivalence with which the richer and poorer islands viewed each other, eroded what little popular sentiment existed for federation. Within three years it had fallen apart, enthusiastically torn down in Jamaica by popular vote in the referendum of September 1961. And one by one the islands moved toward independence, either directly or by way of an association agreement under continued British protection.

The Malta story had no simple progression because of the constitutional game of snakes and ladders to which the islands were subjected. The West Indies were less vulnerable to such changes: but the uneasy movement

38. *Report by the Hon. E. F. L. Wood, M.P., on His Visit to the West Indies and British Guiana, December 1921–February 1922, Cmd. 1679* (London, 1922).

39. Quoted in Payne, *Caribbean Community*, p. 25.

40. D. Lowenthal, ed., *The West Indies Federation* (New York, 1961), and Hugh Springer, *Reflections on the Failure of the First West Indian Federation* (Cambridge, 1962).

between fusion and fission also made progress toward "the fuller association" of their local populations with their own affairs very uncertain.[41] Here again is the paradox noted earlier in respect to India. For what was true of the very large became true of the very small. Early in the twentieth century, independence for the Caribbean was unthinkable. By the end of the 1970s it was inescapable. Where was the turning point? The 1960s, it may be said, when independence began to be bestowed on island after island from the quite large (in Caribbean terms) to the very small—Jamaica to Trinidad to Dominica and Saint Lucia. The change in attitude had to be made on both sides, since (as Dr. Payne has observed) the West Indian leaders, along with the secretaries of state in London, had to adjust to the mini-scale of sovereignty that the world had begun to accept.[42] Yet the *basis* of independence was certainly older than the 1960s. It was laid during the 1940s, during and after the Second World War, in the number of liberal measures of a representative kind. Yet they, too, can be traced back through the miseries of the 1930s to the limited changes introduced in the 1920s. The move to independence, therefore, has to be seen less as a reversal of policy than as an unexpected twist in a constantly rearranged pattern of change and movement, increasing in tempo but within a familiar framework of reform.

Between the loss by Britain of the American colonies and the independence of the Caribbean lie huge tracts of time during which British rule overseas grew enormously and then declined. Is there any single connecting theme of withdrawal? Was there always the promise of emancipation: the bestowal of liberty? Or simply the fact of revolt: a failure of empire? Historians who charted the fortunes of the Dominions used to argue that the Commonwealth had solved the problem of *imperium* and *libertas*. It had done so (it was said) by putting aside theory and concentrating on practice: reconciliation not legality. They quoted Burke: "I am not deter-

41. *Report by the Conference on British Caribbean Federation, February 1956, Cmnd. 9733*, par. 8. See, too, *Cmnd. 8575, British Dependencies in the Caribbean and North Atlantic 1939–52*, 1952; *Cmnd. 8837, Report by the Conference on West Indian Federation*, 1953; and *Cmnd. 9618, Plan for British Caribbean Federation, Report of the Fiscal Commissioner; Cmnd. 9619, Report of the Civil Service Commissioner;* and *Cmnd. 9620, Report of the Federal Commissioner.*

42. "Manley, for example, at Montego Bay argued in very similar terms to the British Government that it was 'impossible to suppose that every single one of these territories, or perhaps even the largest of us, can achieve alone the basic services which it is the whole aim of politics to create and make possible for the common man.'" Payne, *Caribbean Community*, p. 22.

mining a point of law. I am restoring tranquility." From such a standpoint, the slow evolution of the Dominions by adaptation within a political culture drawn from Britain was not essentially different from the less peaceful progress of India. "From 1917 onwards India was accepted in the conference circle as 'the juniormost traveller on the highroad of self-government'—the same road which the Dominions had already travelled."[43] Where the Dominions led and South Asia followed, the rest of the colonial empire also moved—in the same direction along the same road. That is why it has been very difficult to locate any decisive turning point either in the history of particular colonies or in that of the dissolution of the colonial empire as a whole. There was often indecision and a fumbling about for solutions to particular crises; but the changes introduced invariably took the same forward course toward self-government. Setting aside the failures, the British Commonwealth appeared as having fulfilled the end of the British Empire: "it is nothing else than the 'nature' of the British Empire defined, in Aristotelian fashion, by its end."[44] It was the distinct *fortuna* of the British Empire, therefore, to have experienced the rise and fall of empire without suffering its eclipse, a *fortuna* which expressed not simply the operation of chance but the inner nature of British society.

How splendid such phrases were, and how comforting! The enlargement of Commonwealth membership became an enlargement of liberty and a story of reconciliation between former master and former colony. But, if the end was truly implicit both in the beginning and in the history of each colony-turned-sovereign-state, it is a little surprising to find, in many of the examples examined, so large a number of obstacles to their journey—obstacles defined at the British end. Many were said to be too poor, or too divided, or too small, or too vulnerable, to be able to surmount the difficulties which lay athwart the road to self-government. Was it really the case, then, that the only shift of policy between, say, 1900 and 1979, or even between 1950 and 1979, was one of tempo, not a qualitative change in judgment or policy? The transmutation of many of the colonial territories was tortuous rather than tranquil, and the present Commonwealth of forty or more members would certainly have surprised the older Dominions: it would have astonished and, no doubt, dismayed the signatories to the 1926 Declaration with its confident assertion of "free institutions" as being the "life-blood" of the association. Was it not also the case that much larger forces were at work—more powerful than those generated from British

43. W. K. Hancock, *Survey of British Commonwealth Affairs* (London, 1937), 1:61. The words quoted are from *Cmd.* 2769 of 1926, p. 31.

44. Hancock, *Survey*, p. 61.

experience? Should we not look to the changes of *fortuna* not simply of Britain but of Europe as a whole? After all, by 1960 the British had ceased to be unique. The French and Belgians, and later the Portuguese and Spanish, had been decolonizing, as indeed the Dutch had been obliged to do in the 1940s. They had reached a turning point of an abrupt kind, requiring an abrupt change in policy, and the cause was fundamental—the resurgence of non-European identities and longings:

> The relative weakening of England and France, the defeat of Italy and the subordination of Holland and Belgium to the designs of the United States; the effect produced on the Asians and Africans by the battles fought on their soil for which the colonizers had needed their support; the dissemination of doctrines which, whether liberal or socialist, equally demanded the emancipation of races and of individuals; and the wave of envious longing aroused among these deprived masses by the spectacle of the modern economy—as a result of all these factors the world was faced with an upheaval as profound, though in the opposite direction, as that which had unleashed the discoveries and conquests of the power of old Europe.[45]

The argument is extreme and might not be thought to fit the British case. It was certainly very late in the day before the British were brought to see how little they were able to do beyond their own islands. Of course, no government liked the costs of coercion. The Liberal party gave way to force in Ireland in 1921, the Labour party in Palestine in 1948 and Aden in 1968. But these were seen as exceptional cases and did not change the insistence, by Labour and Conservative governments alike, on the need for Britain to remain "a global power." Pretensions of that sort died very hard, surviving well into the 1960s.[46] The attack and enforced withdrawal at Suez in 1956 is often said to have marked a turning point of powerlessness but that, too, is very much a matter of hindsight. As late as 1964, long after the suppression of a Communist uprising in Malaya and of the Mau Mau in Kenya, the United Kingdom was willing to deploy over 30,000 troops in Malaysia against Indonesia. There were some 54,000 on active service in Southeast Asia.

The imperial lion was still prepared to fight. And yet, despite such

45. Charles de Gaulle, *Memoirs of Hope* (New York, 1970), pp. 11–12.

46. For example, "I want to make it quite clear that whatever we do in the field of cost effectiveness, value for money and a stringent view of expenditure, we cannot afford to relinquish our world role." Harold Wilson, *Parliamentary Debates*, December 16, 1964. Similar phrases appeared in the *Statement on Defence Estimates 1965, Cmnd. 2592*, p. 6.

endeavors, it is possible to detect the growth of a certain *weariness* in the 1960s. The accession to full Commonwealth membership of India had been a grand occasion, Ghana and Malaya were both received with satisfaction, Nigeria with considerable élan; but the swift transition to independence in the late 1960s and 1970s of Swaziland and Mauritius and the Seychelles—many others too—began to have the appearance not simply of haste but indifference. It was not so much the possible costs of maintaining a residual empire as the disproportionate effort that might be required to "restore tranquility," as in the imperialism of the absurd in Anguilla. Too much, perhaps, had happened to weary the United Kingdom: wrangling at Commonwealth conferences, abuse from Nkrumah or Kapwepwe, military takeovers, arguments over immigration, pan-African assertions, wars between Commonwealth members, new opportunities in Europe. No wonder that what had been ceremonies of welcome now began to seem like rituals of retreat.[47]

If, therefore, among the examples looked at, one strong theme to single out is that of continuity, it is not difficult to discern its antithesis: shifts in policy which were unforeseen, enforced by circumstance, and accepted without demur by London once the transformation of empire into Commonwealth had settled the more important areas of conflict. But is it also possible, by way of conclusion, to lift each argument to a level that encompasses both views? It might at least be a tribute to Hegel to attempt to do so; and perhaps such a synthesis, very briefly, might run as follows.

The unique aspect of the British Empire—quite without parallel—lay in that peculiar combination of colonial rule and self-government which characterized the late nineteenth- and early twentieth-century world of Britain and the old Dominions. Its evolution by the 1920s enabled the transfer to South Asia in 1947–48 of an adapted "Westminster model of government" at a time when the Commonwealth was still an attractive force. Thereafter a rough pattern of reform was available, known and able to be applied as a remedy wherever a crisis arose in a particular colony that required a rearrangement of power. Precedents created principles of reform. Events enforced their use through practice, at a quickening pace, to such a degree that earlier notions of a desired set of prerequisites for independence simply disappeared.

The most general impetus behind such a movement was, I suspect, twofold: the use of the ballot box—an instrument of popular demand; and whatever is meant by nationalism—a sentiment of popular assertion. The

47. The best account of changes in mood within the British Labour party is by Michael O'Neill, *The Changing Concept of the Commonwealth 1964–70* (Manchester, 1977).

ballot box rid the colonies of British rule since it obliged the colonial elite to seek local mass support. It prevented the possibility of a cooptive imperialism, although very likely such a system would have required a much greater degree of wealth and power at the center than twentieth-century Britain could exert. It was also the case that the assertion of nationalist sentiments across the colonized world gave overriding force to territorial interests of a kind that may yet put an end to Commonwealth ties. The slackening of many of the former bonds of advantage contrasts very sharply with nineteenth-century confidence: the present Commonwealth lacks the cohesive force that gave the Victorian empire its immense attraction. Indeed, the strongest impression conveyed by the association today is that of a constant moving away from, rather than toward, any positive endeavor. Hence, one must suppose, the turning to new centers of power by many of its member governments—to Europe (east and west), to South Asia, to the Americas. Whether, however, as I suspect, the Commonwealth has begun to reach a point of no return on the road to its own dissolution cannot be decided yet. It must await proper inquiry.

10. *Colonial Governments and the Transfer of Power in East Africa*

CRANFORD PRATT

"The British are too inclined towards the extremities of apology or confession." This is George Woodcock's recent judgment of British historical writing on India.[1] Concerning the British in Africa there have been few confessions. This is particularly true in regard to the role of the colonial governments during the last decade of colonial rule. A great deal of highly sympathetic scholarly and semischolarly writing has praised the planning and foresight of the Colonial Office and the activities of the colonial governments during the period in which power was transferred.[2]

This chapter seeks to establish a more critical perspective, at least in regard to East Africa. I will try to do this with reference to the two major areas of policy, constitutional and administrative, in which the highest claims are often made on behalf of the Colonial Office and the colonial governments, and with particular reference to a British African territory which still tends to be seen as one of the real successes of British statecraft in the transfer of power in Africa—namely, Tanganyika. Crawford Young, for example, lists Tanganyika, along with Tunisia and Zambia, as his examples of countries where the transfer was a success.[3] Margery Perham takes a similar view,[4] and almost all the writers of more extended studies of the Tanganyikan experience treat the British colonial regime very respectfully

1. In a review of Stanley Wolpert, "A New History of India," in the *Manchester Guardian Weekly*, July 17, 1977.

2. See, for example, J. M. Lee, *Colonial Development and Good Government* (Oxford, 1967); D. A. Low, *Lion Rampant* (London, 1973); K. E. Robinson, *The Dilemmas of Trusteeship* (London, 1965); Margery Perham, *Colonial Sequences*, vol. 2: *1949-69* (London, 1976) and *The Colonial Reckoning* (London, 1963); W. P. Kirkman, *Unscrambling an Empire* (London, 1966); C. E. Carrington, *The Liquidation of the British Empire* (London, 1961).

3. Crawford Young, "The Coming Independence," in Gann and Guignan, eds., *Colonialism in Africa*, vol. 2 (Los Angeles, 1974).

4. Margery Perham, *The Colonial Reckoning*, p. 73.

and each writes far more fully and with far more knowledge of the British side of the colonial equation than of the African.[5]

The Colonial Office Strategy for the Transfer of Power in Africa

The most detailed of the sympathetic scholarly treatments of official British attitudes toward colonial development in the period between 1945 and 1960 is provided by J. M. Lee in his *Colonial Development and Good Government*.[6] He identifies what he calls a commitment to good government among Colonial Office officials. This is the application to the colonies of that "idea of good government [which] was a discernable philosophy in upper-middle class circles."[7] He even compares the official classes engaged in these activities with the antislavery movement, seeing the two groups as comparable in their efforts to "improve the social and economic conditions of the colonial peoples."[8]

Lee traces the immediate origins of this concern for "good government" to Lord Hailey's important report, *Native Administration and Political Development in British Tropical Africa*,[9] which, though confidential, was widely circulated within the Colonial Office and the African colonial governments. Hailey brought to the consideration of the political policies which Britain ought to follow in Africa a sensitivity toward the dynamics of colonial politics and a clear perception of how these dynamics could be contained. In regard to each of these aspects he was far ahead of most officials. Very few at that time were yet contemplating the possibility of a vigorous upsurge of African nationalism, and fewer still had given any thought to the policy responses that would be necessary. There was at the heart of Hailey's perspective what can fairly be called its Indian dimension. This "Indian dimension" was the recognition that in Africa, as in India, nationalism was bound to become a powerful force and that major concessions to it would need to be made. Hailey expressed the point in these terms:

5. See, for example, Claggart Taylor, *The Political Development of Tanganyika* (1963); Lady Listowell, *The Making of Tanganyika* (1965); and Margaret Bates, "Social Engineering, Multi-Racialism and the Rise of TANU: The Trust Territory of Tanganyika 1945–61," in D. A. Low and Alison Smith, eds., *History of East Africa*, vol. 3 (1976).

6. New York: Oxford University Press, 1967.

7. Lee, *Colonial Development*, p. 31.

8. Ibid., p. 32.

9. Lord Hailey, *Native Administration and Political Development in Tropical Africa* (London, 1942).

> There are forces both at home and in the dependencies which will exert increasing pressure for the extension of political institutions making for self-government, and the fuller association of Africans in them. The strength of this pressure is likely to be largely enhanced as the result of the war. Unless we have a clear view of the constitutional form in which self-government is to be expressed, the answer to this pressure will be ill-coordinated, and may lead to the adoption of measures which we may afterwards wish to recall.[10]

The "clear view" which Hailey advocated had three basic components. First, the highest priority should be given to the social and economic advancement of the people. Development was to be the primary concern of each colonial government. Britain, he argued, was committed to the eventual self-government of the African colonies. These intentions "will lack realism unless we can build up a social foundation adequate to bear the structure of the political institutions in which they will eventually find expression."[11] Second, there should be a rapid introduction of Africans into the administrative and other important cadres of the public service of the colonial governments. This was not, at the time, a popular idea within the Colonial Service. In East and West Africa, the colonial governments had long taken the position that educated Africans with political ambitions ought to engage themselves in the affairs of their Native Authorities. Sir Edward Grigg, then governor of Kenya, had affirmed in 1931: "I think that it would be a great mistake to offer any alternative whatever to the able and young African at the present time."[12] This was also the official view of the Nigerian government as late as 1938.[13] Hailey was particularly critical of this attitude:

> Whatever form the institutions of self-government may eventually take, the executive government must have officers who will not merely supervise the working of the Native Authority, but will deal with the considerable range of activities which will be outside the field of their work. Self government would not be a reality if the cadre of these officers were confined to Europeans.[14]

He went on to observe:

10. Ibid., p. 50.
11. Ibid., p. 5.
12. *Joint Select Committee on Closer Union in East Africa*, vol. 2: Minutes of Evidence, H. C. 156. H.M.S.O. (London, 1931), p. 60.
13. Hailey, *Native Administration and Political Development*, p. 47.
14. Ibid.

in our Eastern dependencies, the first ambition of the political-minded elements was the substitution of a native for the European official establishment. . . . There can be no doubt that African ambition will also center in the first instance, on gaining a share in the official organization. . . . It is in our readiness to admit Africans to such posts that they will see the test of the sincerity of our policy of opening to them the road to self-government.[15]

However, Hailey did not wish to bring urban, educated Africans into the Legislative Council in any significant numbers. He recognized that they were likely to want this; nevertheless, Hailey's intention in their regard was to involve them directly in the promotion of development policies, in the work of the native administrators, in town councils, and in the public service of the central government. He urged that no political concessions should be made which would suggest that the African colonies were going to be developed into parliamentary regimes on the Westminister model. He wanted to keep open the question of the future political institutions of the African colonies. He noted that as political consciousness grew there would be an increasing demand for directly elected representatives. Nevertheless, for an intervening and apparently quite lengthy period, Hailey wanted the colonial regimes to concentrate on the devolution of activities to the Native Authorities and to have African representation on the legislative councils very largely selected indirectly by these Native Authorities.

After 1945, a group within the Colonial Office led by Sir Sidney Caine and Andrew Cohen, then head of the Africa Division, carried Hailey's analysis forward, though with important modifications. In this they were strongly supported by Creech Jones when he became secretary of state. With his assistance, they conducted a sustained campaign over a period of several years to secure a recognition of the force of their analysis within the Colonial Service in Africa.

The famous secretary of state's dispatch of February 25, 1947, marked the beginning of this "campaign." It continued with a summer school on African administration, the first of an annual series of such conferences, held in Cambridge in August 1947 and attended by senior members of the administrative services of the British African territories. The African colonial governors themselves were gathered in London for a conference in September 1947, and in the following year there was a conference of members of the legislative councils of the British African territories. The African

15. Ibid.

Studies Branch of the Colonial Office then launched the *Journal of African Administration* in 1949 in an important effort to overcome the isolation of the members of the Colonial Service and to generate within that service an awareness of the importance of the policy objectives of the secretary of state's dispatch.

This whole "campaign" certainly had as one of its starting points the recognition that it was probable nationalism would quickly become a powerful force. Concessions to it, therefore, should be made sooner rather than later. Creech Jones, in the February 25 dispatch of 1947, made the point in these terms: "The rate of political progress cannot be regulated according to a pre-arranged plan; the pace over the next generation will be rapid, under the stimulus of our own development programs, of internal pressure from the people themselves, and a world opinion expressed through the growing international interest in the progress of colonial peoples."[16] He expressed the point again a year later when, with blunt irritation, he "intervened to remind the governors that the demand for responsible government was there and though it is said to come from a few, it will spread. . . . We had to satisfy the demand whether we liked it or not; we could not afford to wait."[17] It is interesting that Ian MacLeod, the secretary of state who perhaps did more than any other to win British acceptance of this truth, referred back to the Indian experience to explain the need for a rapid advance to independence:

> Any other policy would have led to terrible bloodshed in Africa. . . . Were the countries fully ready for independence? Of course not. Nor was India, and the bloodshed that followed the grant of independence there was incomparably worse than anything that has happened since to any country. Yet the decision of the Attlee Government was the only realistic one. Equally we could not have held by force to our territories in Africa.[18]

The final feature in the strategy being recommended by the Colonial Office related to constitutional reform. It was in this area that the post-1945 policy was a distinct advance over the Hailey proposals. Hailey had hoped still to build the central institutions of the African colonies on the foundation of the native administrations. Both the Burns Constitution in Ghana in

16. Secretary of State for the Colonies Dispatch of 25 February 1947, para. 4.

17. *Papers Presented to the Africa Conference*, vol. 2. African Studies Branch, Colonial Office, A. C. (48) (2). Mimeograph, 1947, p. 22.

18. Quoted in David Goldsworthy, *Colonial Issues in British Politics 1945–61* (Oxford, 1971), p. 263.

1945 and the Richards Constitution in Nigeria reflect this conception. By 1947 Caine and Cohen—and with them Creech Jones—had come to a much more critical view of the native administrations. They doubted their efficiency as agencies of development and they felt that they would provide but a weak and inadequate foundation for national political institutions.

The political cooperation of the African urban intelligentsia required more than recruitment to the administrative service and greater participation by educated commoners in the native administration. Educated Africans had also to be given a predominant role among the unofficials in the legislative councils: they alone in the African community would be effective allies of the government's development policies; they alone could provide the political foundations for future self-governing African states.

The British colonial governments were therefore urged by the Colonial Office to make immediate and major political concessions to African nationalism so that the politically ambitious would have adequate scope for their talents within the political system. In September 1947, Cohen proposed that the colonial governments (or at least the West African governments) should:

1. move swiftly to concede unofficial majorities on their legislative councils;
2. disperse the responsibilities then concentrated in the office of the Chief Secretary and group these responsibilities into government departments;
3. group these departments into shadow ministries;
4. appoint some elected unofficial members of the legislative council to the executive council, initially with a responsibility to oversee one of these groups of departments. Soon thereafter these members should be appointed ministers within an executive council on which, however, there would continue to be an official majority.[19]

Cohen argued that constitutional arrangements such as these would reassure the educated and politically active African and would therefore make possible an extended period under these arrangements before full, internal self-government would have to be conceded. Cohen predicted that internal self-government would be achieved in West Africa in not much less than a generation's time. In East and Central Africa he felt that constitutional progress would be much slower.

There is much in all this that is ideological. As Britain could not long

19. These four points are a summary of Cohen's presentation to the Conference of African Governors in 1947 as it appears in the *Papers Presented to the African Conference*.

retain its rule in Africa without having to pay too high a cost in repression and in international opprobrium, it was clearly in her interest to arrange a transfer of power to an elite that would look to Britain for assistance and would not challenge the British dominance in the economies and trade of British Africa. All that Hailey, Cohen, and their colleagues advocated can be interpreted as shrewdly designed to protect and advance British economic and political interests in these changing circumstances. Yet there is little evidence to suggest either cynicism or deceit in their concern for African development. Neither is there any suggestion that there was elsewhere in the British power structure a hidden set of decision makers who were using and manipulating the idealism of these reformers for more selfish and more narrowly British ends.

One must, therefore, either use the language of structural Marxism and speak of the state acting through its public servants to ensure that it fulfills its central function of maintaining and advancing the interests of capitalism, which surely is a mystifying reification, or one must accept the position that these public servants were motivated by the considerations that predominated in their advocacy and argument at the time. If one does the latter, then one is able to do justice to their integrity and concern for African welfare and to the historically progressive role they played in moving public and official opinion in Britain to an acceptance of African independence. One is also able, however, to recognize the degree to which their background, training, and imperial presumptions blocked them from an adequate sense of the dynamics and power of political nationalism and an awareness of the deep contradictions which persisted between the reality and the requirements of colonial rule and African development.

The Colonial Office analysis of the immediate postwar years which is discussed above, and the strategy deduced from it, involved a major and important change in one of the basic assumptions of Colonial Office thinking about Africa. Colonial Office officials accepted the fact that independence would mean that government power would be transferred very largely to educated Africans rather than to the traditional Native Authorities. This was a revolutionary change in official thinking. Before the war there had been some speculation in the literature on indirect rule about the long-run pattern of political development in the African territories.[20] Margery Perham, for example, envisaged an eventual self-government in terms of a loose federation of independent Native Authorities which would themselves, by then, have evolved into full-fledged native

20. These speculations are briefly discussed in my "The Politics of Indirect Rule," in A. D. Low and R. C. Pratt, *Buganda and British Over-rule* (London, 1960), chaps. 10 and 11.

states.[21] A variation on that theme, more appropriate to countries in which Native Authorities were too small and too numerous to become native states, was the expectation that regional councils of Native Authorities would eventually be created to which the central government would delegate important powers. A third view, particularly with reference to the East African territories, envisaged the development of an assembly of Native Authority delegates that would stand alongside of the legislative council with powers and a status equal to those of the legislative council. The fourth approach, which was recommended in 1942 by Hailey and was actually followed in the constitutions introduced in Nigeria and the Gold Coast immediately after the war, would develop the central legislature by drawing its African members primarily from the Native Authorities, with the only directly elected members being a tiny number coming from the urban areas.

In contrast to these approaches, the Colonial Office in 1947–48 was urging the colonial governments to anticipate and accept that the chiefs would be of declining importance in the politics of the African territories and that adequate scope must be provided in the legislatures for the educated and politically active commoner. Cohen gave particular attention to the question of how this new political class could be kept close and responsive to the great mass of rural Africans. He did not foresee the rise of strong nationalist parties uniting masses of men and women behind national political leaders. He accepted the view that direct elections were fundamentally inappropriate in tropical Africa: "Direct elections can only succeed when the majority of the electors are in a position to take an intelligent interest in the proceedings of the body for which the election takes place."[22] Because Cohen and his colleagues assumed that the interest of Africans in rural areas could not be raised above local and tribal matters, as planners they sought a network of intermediary institutions to link the parochially minded peasant with the national politician. They settled upon representative local governments as the solution to the problem which they had thus set for themselves. They argued that local governments were needed as the crucial tier in a system of indirect elections for the central legislature.[23] This led, then, to the further conclusion that if local governments were to

21. Margery Perham, *Native Administration in Nigeria* (London, 1937).

22. *Report of the Proceedings of the Conference of African Governors*, Nov. 8 to Nov. 21, 1947. African Studies Branch, Colonial Office, p. 151 (mimeograph).

23. The local government councils would not, in fact, be the first tier, as this strategy recommended that these councils should themselves be indirectly elected by lower councils. Only at the lowest tier, the village level or its rural equivalent, were elections to be direct.

play this important role in national political institutions they must themselves be elected, representative bodies. The point was put to the Colonial Office Summer School on African Administration in these terms:

> Besides being suited to the present conditions in the African territories, the system of indirect election is genuinely democratic at all stages, provided that, at the local government level, adequate provision is made for the representation of all classes of the population. To make this system completely representative, the method of appointment of members to the lowest council must be democratic.[24]

There was a wide variety of additional arguments which also favored the early development of representative local governments. These overlapped and reinforced each other, each augmenting the importance attached to the establishment of a representative local government system, making the need for such a system finally as much of a dogma for the more enlightened members of the British Colonial Service in the late 1940s as indirect rule had been in the 1930s.[25]

In many ways the Colonial Office strategy for the development of democratic institutions was given its most complete trial when Cohen was made governor of Uganda in 1952. His arrival brought a sudden escalation in the pace of reform, each initiative reflecting a different component of the strategy. The local governments were democratized and their powers enlarged; the effort was made to secure direct election of African members to the Legislative Council; the cooperation of the African urban intelligentsia was cultivated in a wide variety of ways. This was social engineering with a vengeance.

Cohen quickly realized, however, that it was not working. Ethnic loyalties proved far more resilient than he had anticipated, even among educated Africans; local governments were far less able than he had hoped to take up new and modern responsibilities.

24. African no. 1173, p. 32.

25. The reform of local government in the British African territories in the fifteen-year period 1945–60 has been the subject of a number of able studies. See, for example, Hailey's monumental five-volume *Native Administration in the British African Territories* (London: H.M.S.O., 1950–52), and the following two succinct analyses: Bryan Keith Lucas, "The Dilemma of Local Government in Africa," in F. Madden and K. Robinson, eds., *Essays in Imperial Government* (Oxford, 1963), and Lucy Mair, "Representative Local Government as a Problem of Social Change," *Journal of African Administration*, vol. 10, pp. 11–24. There is also a series of important reports published in the period from 1947 to 1956 on the reform of local government in the individual African territories. The most important of these are listed by Keith Lucas.

In retrospect, this strategy for the transition to independence can be seen to have been deficient in at least four important ways. First, it seriously overestimated the feasibility of an African colonial government being able to delegate significant responsibilities to autonomous representative local governments. In almost all territories the administrative competence of these local governments was just too low for such delegations to be seriously considered. Moreover, many of the governmental activities which might seem appropriate for administrative control by local governments (activities such as agricultural and veterinary field services or middle and junior secondary education) are of such importance to national development that no central government, colonial or independent, would happily transfer them to local governments.

This observation leads to the second criticism of the strategy. The strategy, where it was followed, did not in fact assure a lengthy period of continued British rule, which certainly was its expected consequence. African political leaders were not willing to accept a set of reforms which directed their energies into local governments for a considerable period of time, and which gave them only minority participation in the executive council. The period immediately prior to the achievement of responsible government was, therefore, much more likely to be marked by political turbulence than by a cordial cooperation between African nationalists and colonial administrators. This strategy assumed that rapid concessions would lead to several more decades in which Africans would exercise important political and administrative responsibilities while still remaining under British rule. This proved to be a fundamental misjudgment. In territory after territory, the choice which the British had to face in fact was between a very rapid advance to full self-government or the use of force to try to assure an adherence to a more gradual constitutional timetable.

Third, the strategy made inadequate provision for the maintenance of the authority of the central government. Under colonial rule, the source of the authority of the central government was external to the society being ruled. It rested upon the overwhelming power which the colonial government was able to mobilize if faced with any significant opposition within that society. With independence, the authority of the national government had to be founded in the society itself. The Colonial Office strategy underestimated the importance of this problem. Cohen and his colleagues did not realize how fragile were the societies that were soon to be independent. They did not envisage the contribution to national integration which can be made by national political parties. They sought instead to achieve the involvement of rural peoples in the national institutions of government by building these institutions upon the basis of representative local governments. It is hard to imagine that any state other than a very fragile one would emerge on this basis. At the most it would have produced a government which would be dependent upon the bargaining of locally based and locally oriented politicians; at worst it would have failed to provide an adequate base for a stable national government.

There is a further aspect to the failure of this strategy to recognize the political requirements of a national government. In countries where there are no solidly established national institutions, a representative local government council easily becomes a structure through which the local community expresses its separate identity in contradistinction to that of the wider national community. Even colonial governments which had the power of an imperial Britain to underwrite their authority tended to see any district council which refused the advice of its district commissioner as a challenge to the authority of the colonial government. It is small wonder that independent African states, whose power base was much less secure, proved equally anxious to exercise close political supervision over local governments. The strategy for decolonization in Africa, which the Colonial Office was urging upon colonial governments in the late 1940s, paid far too little heed to the political fragility that would be so prominent a feature of the independent states of Africa.

The Colonial Office Strategy for Central and East Africa

The Colonial Office's recommendation that there should be major constitutional concessions was intended primarily for the West African colonies. Cohen and his colleagues, in these initiatives in 1947 and 1948, paid only passing attention to the application of their strategy to Northern Rhodesia, Nyasaland, Tanganyika, Kenya, and Uganda, the five territories in East and Central Africa in which there were permanently settled European and Asian minorities. In these territories, in contrast to West Africa, the demand for greater local participation in the legislature and for a lessening of Colonial Office control did not come primarily from African nationalists. It came from the leaders of the European minorities. These minorities had already secured for themselves significant representation in each of the five legislatures. The white minorities, particularly in Northern Rhodesia and in Kenya, were pressing for further constitutional concessions that would give them an increasing control of the legislatures and greater representation in the executive councils.

In so far as Cohen and his colleagues had a strategy at all in the late 1940s in regard to East and Central Africa, it was, in effect, a repetition of the liberal position of the 1920s and 1930s. They argued that the official majority must be maintained until "the Africans are in a position to play their full part in the system of representative government."[26] They entirely avoided any discussion of the racial distribution of power they wished to see once Africans were able to play this full part in the institutions of the central governments.

Nevertheless, it was the East African governors who reacted with particular vehemence to the ideas being promoted by the Colonial Office. Sir Philip Mitchell, governor of Kenya, replied bombastically to the secretary of state's dispatch of February 25, 1947. That dispatch, in most moderate terms, had presented the case for the development of efficient and democratic local governments in Africa and the introduction of more elected members to the legislature. Mitchell's response was rude and racist. He declared himself "bound to resist processes which might be called political progress by the misinformed or opinionated." He continued, "how primitive the state of these people is and how deplorable the spiritual, moral and social chaos in which they are adrift are things which can perhaps only be fully realized by those who are in close personal touch with the realities of the situation."[27]

The vulgarity of such rhetoric was avoided by the other East African governors, but they nevertheless expressed their general agreement with Mitchell. They had no sense that they were, or would soon be, under any nationalist pressure. They were certain that British rule was in the best interests of the Africans of their colonies. They had no confidence whatsoever in the educated African whom London was pressing upon them. The acting governor of Tanganyika concluded his reply to the February 25, 1947, dispatch with this sad evidence of languid hauteur: "It is a melancholy fact . . . that we have failed to advance to any appreciable degree the moral and ethical standards of a great number of those Africans who have had the longest benefits of our schools and the training centres." The governors were determined to persevere with the activities and programs which their governments were reviving and initiating after the war and which they were confident were in the best interests of their colonies. Lee has underlined how frequently this was taken to mean the eventual creation of a society that would be attached to British social and political values. Mitchell made the point with typical bluntness: "We are not here to create

26. *Papers Prepared for the African Conference* (1947), p. 34.

27. Cranford Pratt, *The Critical Phase in Tanzania* (Cambridge, 1976), pp. 15–17. The several quotations in the subsequent paragraph each appear in more extended versions in this book.

a succession of Bulgarias but to develop and civilize this continent as part of what I may call Western European civilization and economics."

Creech Jones and Cohen at first sought to avoid the question of whether the East African colonies should also move toward African majority rule on the West African pattern. But they could not avoid it for long. With the buildup of settler pressure for a Central African federation and for greater unofficial European participation in the legislatures and executive councils of Northern Rhodesia and Kenya, the pattern of constitutional development for East Africa had to be decided. The decision was taken that there should be balanced representation of the major racial communities in the legislative and executive councils of each of these territories. The actual balance that was sought in each case reflected the political influence of these communities as experienced by the British at that time. In Kenya, the British determined upon a ratio of 2:1:1 as the ratio of European to Asian to African unofficial members. In Uganda, it was to be 1:1:2. In Tanganyika, it was initially to have been 1:1:2, but in 1951 under strong European pressure, it became 1:1:1.

For ten crucial years, 1949 through 1959, the British sought to win African acceptance in East Africa of the idea that the minority communities were sufficiently important that they should receive equal representation in the legislature, despite the fact that the minority races were only tiny communities in contrast to the numbers of Africans. (For example, the numerical ratio of European to Asian to African in Tanganyika was approximately 1:4:430.) The British intention was not necessarily to place the African permanently in a minority position in the legislature. It was, rather, to entrench the disproportionate representation of the minorities in the near- and middle-term, thereby placing them, at some quite distant future date, in a strong position to bargain for the long-term protection of their special community rights and privileges.[28]

The immediate importance of this strategy was that it brought British policy into very sharp conflict with African nationalists in every one of the territories of East and Central Africa, for Africans quickly recognized that "multiracialism" and "racial partnership," the slogans under which the power-sharing proposals traveled, involved a denial of the primarily African character of their societies. Nevertheless, in Kenya, Uganda, and Tanganyika, as in Central Africa, the Colonial Office persisted in its efforts to fix upon these African territories constitutional arrangements that gave the local white minority a measure of political power vastly disproportionate to

28. See the secretary of state's authoritative statement of the British position, which he made to the House of Commons on June 25, 1952. It is quoted in ibid., pp. 28–29.

its population. This whole effort finally collapsed, at the time of the acceptance of an African majority among the elected members in Uganda in 1957. The acceptance of the principle of majority rule was then extended to Tanganyika in October 1958, to Kenya at the Lancaster House Conference in 1960, and to Central Africa with the constitutional proposals for Northern Rhodesia and Nyasaland in 1962.

There are one primary and two supporting reasons for this collapse of British resolve to entrench minority rights. The primary reason was African resistance. Throughout East and Central Africa, Africans finally made it clear that Britain could persist in this effort only if she was ready to send troops to suppress African opposition. The earliest and most dramatic demonstration of this fact was, of course, the Mau-Mau uprising in Kenya, not a straightforward African liberation movement but nevertheless an example of deep African antipathy to European rule which the local settler community was unable to contain without direct British military intervention. In Northern Rhodesia and in Nyasaland, African discontent over the imposition of the Central African Federation also became more and more intense, culminating in the Nyasaland riots of 1959.

In theory Britain could have responded to these challenges by further political repression. That option was unattractive because of the strength of anticolonialism in the international community and the widespread sentiment in Britain that, indeed, the sun should now set upon the empire. In that climate of opinion, the government in Britain became vulnerable to charges of abuses of power—abuses that were nearly inevitable when colonial governments sought to contain African hostility. Incidents such as the murder of African prisoners in the Hola detention camp in Kenya and the identification of Nyasaland as a "police state" by the Devlin Commission in 1961 quickly led to political costs which no British government could bear. The full force of African nationalism finally made itself felt. The "Indian dimension" was recognized. Rapid concessions leading to majority rule had to be made.

Assisting that final volte-face in East and Central Africa was an important division that emerged within the white minority in Kenya and in Northern Rhodesia. In each of these colonies the settler-farmers who had tended to dominate European politics held out against any advance toward majority rule. Plantation and commercial interests, on the other hand, came to realize that they could probably continue to pursue their activities under African rule. That prospect, however, would be threatened if Britain sought to delay the transfer of power, thereby embittering and radicalizing political leaders. These commercial groups therefore favored a more rapid transfer of power to African nationalists than the main body of European settlers. In Kenya this inclination received direct political expression through the New Kenya Group, a new party formed by Michael Blundell and others to win Kenyan European support for a fuller integration of Africans into the country's social and political life.[29]

The abandonment of the effort to entrench European political dominance in Central Africa and to maintain highly disproportionate European representation in East Africa came very late in the day. The constitutional policies promoted by the Colonial Office for these substantial portions of Africa can hardly be counted as a positive contribution to an effective and peaceful transfer of power.

Can it also be argued that colonial government contributed far less to the success of the transfer of power to Africans in Tanganyika than is often claimed?

THE TANGANYIKAN GOVERNMENT AND THE TRANSFER OF POWER, 1945–58

Some Basic Presuppositions of British Rule

Before 1949 there was, in fact, nothing that could legitimately be referred to in Tanganyika as a national political policy. There had been, on rare occasions, speculation about the institutional arrangements which might be appropriate for an independent Tanganyika. Sir Donald Cameron, for example, had spoken in 1931 before the Joint Select Committee of the House of Commons of the possibility of a two-house legislature, one house representing non-Africans while the other house would include chiefs, who would represent the large mass of rural Africans, and educated Africans representing those who had achieved a level of educational and economic advancement.[30] Speculations of this sort were about arrangements for a very far-distant future. They had little or no impact upon constitutional policies before the end of the Second World War, or indeed even immediately thereafter.

A legislature was established in 1926 with an official majority and without any African participation. The appointment of three African chiefs to this Legislative Council in 1945 was little more than a polite acknowledgment that some constitutional advancement was needed in Tanganyika to parallel the much greater rate of political progress which was being achieved in the

29. This view of the pattern of Kenyan European politics in the 1959–62 period is brilliantly developed in Gary Wasserman, *Politics of Decolonization: Kenya Europeans and the Land Issue, 1960–65* (Cambridge, 1976).

30. *Joint Committee on Closer Union*, 2:175–226.

West African colonies. Little thought was given, and certainly no public announcements were made, about the longer-term pattern of constitutional advancement which the British would seek to introduce in Tanganyika.

The Tanganyikan government, however, did have a well-articulated policy of local administration to which its serving officers were deeply committed. This policy, well known as "indirect rule," involved the administration of rural areas through traditional authorities rather than through appointed nontraditional authorities. The policy made use of these traditional authorities as agents of social change and permitted the traditional societies under their own leadership to adapt to the demands and circumstances of colonial rule.

In its detailed implementation, indirect rule often involved a most transparent undermining of the political institutions of African tribes. Traditional councils were often ignored; government officers intervened in the selection of chiefs; and the chiefs were required to exercise authority over a wide range of matters which bore little relationship to their traditional functions. Nevertheless, indirect rule constituted a coherent, comparatively humane, and, for a period, workable political strategy. Where it operated well, it provided an effective and locally accepted channel through which the central government could secure the cooperation, or at least the acquiescence, of the countryside.

The effectiveness of indirect rule depended upon the continuing validity of these three propositions: (1) that the chiefs who were appointed as Native Authorities[31] were competent to perform the governmental functions assigned to them; (2) that they were acceptable to their peoples and able to win their cooperation within government policies; and (3) that colonial rule itself was not significantly challenged. As long as these propositions remained true, the Tanganyikan government was able to direct and control governmental welfare and development activities in the rural areas while also working through structures which helped to make that direction and control acceptable to the rural masses.

The first and second of these assumptions began to lose their validity before the third did. The whole process of social change that followed colonial rule slowly undermined the earlier natural acceptance of chiefly rule. Simultaneously, the colonial government was increasingly able to finance a widening range of local services in rural areas. Many chiefs proved incompetent to deal with these new functions. The Provincial Administration then began to assert its authority more openly, and in particular it

31. The title of the office which they held within the government system.

interfered more frequently in the appointment of the Native Authorities, in an effort to secure the appointment of men who would be able to deal with the increasingly complex range of activities with which they were involved. The government also began to press forward more vigorously with the amalgamation of Native Authorities so that they would form more reasonable units of local administration, and to introduce small local bureaucracies at the district level to manage the finances and to strengthen the administration of the Native Authorities.

These administrative reforms were accompanied by an effort to convince the chiefs to consult with and indeed share power with native authority councils which would include educated commoners. Once the Tanganyikan government was able to expand the services which it could provide in rural areas, members of its administrative service grew increasingly critical of an overreliance upon the Native Authorities. A reading of district commissioners' annual reports for the years 1945–48 shows that a surprising number of district commissioners were tending to regard their Native Authorities, not as the natural and accepted leaders of their people but rather as reactionary and authoritarian barriers to progress and development.[32]

The Tanganyikan government exercised a good deal of ingenuity in its careful efforts to expand the representative nature of the Native Authorities. These reforms began rather tentatively and cautiously in 1945. By 1951, sixteen of the fifty-seven districts had councils which included elected commoners, though in every case the chiefs and subchiefs continued to be an important and often a majority component. In ten more districts, mainly in the Lake Province, a different pattern had emerged, with councils of commoners being established alongside the chiefs and advisory to them. In the remaining districts in 1951, there was still no popular participation on these councils at all.

A third development relating to the Native Authorities was the increasing importance of the local services financed through their treasuries. By 1947 native treasury estimates included expenditures on primary education, rural medical services, agricultural, veterinary, and forestry services, and rural water supplies. This pattern continued and became more impor-

32. The District Commissioner, Geita District, for example, wrote of the few nonofficials on the council: "They act as an ever present brake on abuse of power by the constituted authorities and are, as it were, the watch dogs of the common man . . . the traditional authorities realize that these councils sound the—however faint at present—death knell of the era of authoritarian rule in Africa." *1955 Progress Report on African Local Government*, Geita District (mimeograph). This and other unpublished materials are located in the Dar es Salaam archives.

tant. However, these increases in the expenditures of the local treasuries did not involve any significant relaxation of central governmental control over these funds or over the activities financed by them. The native treasury estimates were prepared by the district commissioner. The most senior African staff member was in almost every case a treasury clerk who was in no position to act as an autonomous finance officer for the native treasury. The committees of the district councils, to the extent that they existed at all, were not yet sufficiently competent or self-assured to challenge a district commissioner. The district commissioners therefore had little trouble in winning the approval of the Native Authorities for the native treasury estimates which the commissioners had prepared them.

There is every evidence that the Provincial Administration in Tanganyika never for a moment doubted that it was very much in charge of these matters. In 1952, for example, the provincial commissioners in conference decided that the Native authorities should pay for school materials supplied by the government to the native administration schools and should, as well, contribute to the salaries of teachers in both the native administration and the voluntary agencies' primary and middle schools. After this had been approved by the Minister, the provincial commissioners were then instructed to arrange for all 1953 native treasury estimates to make provision for the payment of 1953 Native Authority contributions under the new formula.[33]

These several reforms affecting the functions and staffing of the native authorities and increasing the participation of elected commoners within them amounted to the beginning of a gradual transformation of the Native Authority system into a local government system. It was, however, only the beginning. In some British territories by 1950 these reforms had led to the creation of local structures which had achieved a competence and an autonomy which made them genuine local governments rather than subordinate structures within a central government administrative system. This was, however, not the case in Tanganyika. The reasons are several: the absence of any senior bureaucracy in the local authorities which could be responsible for the administration of local services; the newness of the councils and the consequent initial timidity of most elected councillors; the major role, within the councils, of chiefs who were government appointees and therefore particularly sensitive to government advice. The continuing dominant role of the district commissioner, together with these reasons,

33. From the memorandum "Contribution by Native Authorities toward Teachers' Salaries." The Member for Local Government to all Provincial Commissioners. (mimeographed 25 November 1952).

meant that, whatever might have been the longer-term purposes of these reforms, their more immediate purpose was an improvement in the ability of the central government to reach the masses and to win their cooperation. The governor, Sir Edward Twining, in a communication to the Legislative Council in 1953, wrote:

> There can be no doubt that the steps that have been taken, particularly with regard to the establishment of councils have been for the general good and have gone some way to ensure that the people can be consulted so that the district commissioners and their team of specialists can carry the people with them in the framing and execution of their programs for economic and social development.[34]

These reforms in local administration in Tanganyika were introduced to increase efficiency and political control. They are evidence of the continued faith of the colonial government that it knew best what was in Tanganyika's interest.

Further evidence of this self-confidence is provided by the government's decision to continue after the war to use Native Authority orders and rules to secure peasant compliance with a wide range of practices which it felt would promote rural development. Native Authorities Ordinance no. 18 of 1926, had permitted the Native Authorities to issue orders on a wide range of subjects. The majority of these were matters that clearly required regulation if rural life was to be orderly and peaceful. However, the list also included a number of subjects which reflected the preoccupations of the Provincial Administration at the time the law was first passed. Thus, for example, the authorities could require adult males to work on essential public works for up to sixty days a year. Gradually the government added to the list of matters that could be covered by Native Authority orders. In 1937, for example, the Native Authorities were given the power to issue orders relating to soil erosion, the cultivation of cotton, and the use of grazing land. In 1942, by a special government notice issued under the Emergency Powers (Defence) Act, the Native Authorities were empowered to issue orders "requiring any native to cultivate land to such extent and with such crops and to take such other measures as will secure an adequate supply of any product which is essential to the well-being of the community."[35]

34. *Legislative Council, Council Debates 28th session (1953–54).* (Dar es Salaam: Government Printer, 1954), pp. 7–8.

35. Government Notice no. 177 of 1942, as amended by no. 37 of 1946. *Laws of Tanganyika, 1947. Vol. VI* (Dar es Salaam: Government Printer, 1947), p. 2133.

Although the form and wording of Native Authority orders might suggest otherwise, in fact when issuing these orders the Native Authorities almost invariably acted on the advice of the district commissioner. They were not autonomous local rulers. They were quite clearly subordinate to the district commissioner, and they used their power to issue orders only when advised to do so.[36]

For a crucial decade beginning in 1946, the government greatly increased its use of compulsion, exercised through Native Authority orders, to enforce improved practices relating to agriculture, livestock care, terracing, and land usage. As I have argued elsewhere: "It was not a case of a few Africans being compelled by law to comply with new agricultural practices after a process of public education had won widespread popular acceptance of the rules being enforced. The practice in these matters after 1946 came much nearer to an effort to educate through compulsion."[37] The arrogant self-confidence of the colonial service in Tanganyika after the war as it did what it felt it should do (or, to use Lee's language, as it followed the dictates of its own commitment to good government), was well expressed by one officer who wrote in 1945 of the need for "an understanding by those who govern that in place of the stress which forces Europeans to do things, the African must be compelled—and forcibly—to improve the condition under which he lives with his own hands."[38] It is not surprising that a colonial service in the grip of such self-confidence should give little thought to any real delegation of power to elected Africans.

One further component of the attitudes and values that dominated the Tanganyikan government must now be noted. This relates to the position of Europeans within Tanganyika. Chidzero has noted that even in the 1920s and 1930s, when the doctrine of the paramountcy of African interests was accepted as the cornerstone of British policy in Tanganyika, the British also favored the development of a modern non-African sector of the economy, parallel to the African sector. It is Chidzero's judgment that, nevertheless, the commitment of the Government of Tanganyika to the protection of African rights was sufficiently strong (and the attractiveness of Tanganyika to European settlers sufficiently slight) that "there can be no doubt that British land policy in Tanganyika remained deliberately protective, and only cautiously permissive of alienation."[39]

36. This is also the judgment of Lord Hailey in his *Native Administration in the British African Territories*, pt. 1, chap. 3, p. 276 and passim.

37. Pratt, *The Critical Phase*, p. 25. This issue is discussed more fully in that book, pp. 24–28.

38. Quoted in ibid., p. 25.

39. Bernard Chidzero, *Tanganyika under International Trusteeship* (Oxford, 1961), p. 228.

Gradually Tanganyika's commitment to the protection of African rights shifted. In 1938 the government appointed a Central Development Committee which, in 1940, reported its view that "the economic structure of the territory must be made to rest on a broader foundation than African agriculture" and that "the objective of increasing the non-native population should be accepted."[40] Sir Wilfred Woods, who conducted a fiscal inquiry for the three East African governments in 1945, came to the same view.[41] He foresaw that there would be strong pressures from London and from within East Africa for increased government expenditures, particularly on education and health. He felt that these could not be financed without greater non-African participation in the economy. A widespread reaction against the purely protective approach toward the rural areas (which had typified British policy toward land tenure and land alienation in those colonies in which there was no significant white settlement) reinforced this ill-founded, but generally accepted, fiscal concern.

The older trusteeship approach to British responsibilities in Tanganyika was challenged by those who wished to make land usage, rather than traditional claims and African paramountcy, the basis of land policy. By 1950 their view had become the new conventional wisdom of the Government of Tanganyika. In that year it set up a Land Utilization Board to facilitate the alienation of land to non-Africans and more particularly, to European farmers. In the five years from 1949 to 1953, a total of just under 920,000 additional acres were alienated to private individuals or bodies, and a further 520,000 acres to public and semipublic bodies.[42] By 1953 about 5 million acres of land were in non-African hands. This constituted 0.49 percent of the total land area of Tanganyika.[43] Thus the alienation of land to non-Africans never, in fact, became extensive. However, it was a persistent objective of policy throughout this period; it marked a major shift in government thinking.

An official statement issued in 1953, explained the shift in these terms:

> The old theory that Africans should be protected by declaring . . . large areas in which alienation would or would not be permitted and by endeavouring to keep the non-African farming areas segregated from mainly African zones has been abandoned and the general notices on this

40. Quoted by Sir Wilfred Woods in his report on a *Fiscal Survey of Kenya, Uganda and Tanganyika* (Nairobi: Government Printer, 1946), pp. 129–30.

41. Ibid.

42. *United Nations Visiting Mission to Trust Territories in East Africa, 1957. Report on Tanganyika*, T/1401. (New York: United Nations Organization, 1958), p. 26.

43. *Report of the Commission on Land and Population, Cmd. 9475* (London: HMSO, 1955), p. 22.

> subject have been cancelled. It is now accepted that the health, wealth and general interests of the Africans are not best served by leaving him in isolation, surrounded by great tracts of undeveloped land which may be needed for this anticipated progeny. On the contrary, the development of the territory is now believed to depend on the combined effects of all communities working and thriving in mutual interest and assistance for a common goal of territorial prosperity.[44]

The circular recorded the government's view that the minority communities were to be regarded as belonging fully to the territory and that:

> The Secretary of State has made it clear that non-African Settlement by suitably selected persons of the right type and under conditions of proper government control is likely to be conducive to the economic development of the territory and in this connection, he has stressed the vital necessity of pressing on with development by all suitable means.[45]

This concern to increase European immigration led to the disappearance of "the paramountcy of African interests" from the various British affirmations of their objectives in Tanganyika. The Minutes of the *Constitutional Development Committee* in 1951 record with surprise that certain missionaries and chiefs appeared still to be "under the impression that the doctrine of the paramountcy of African interests was still operative."[46] The government's concern to maintain and augment the non-African contribution to the economy led it to the view that equal individual rights for all inhabitants regardless of race would not be appropriate to the conditions of Tanganyika. The Tanganyikan government assumed that the protection of individual rights would hardly satisfy the European or Asian immigrant communities. It assumed, not critically or regretfully but as a statement of natural fact, that these communities would need to have their position *as communities* carefully safeguarded if they were to remain in Tanganyika.

One reflection of this protection of immigrant communities was the concern of the Government of Tanganyika to build a European residential secondary school in Tanganyika. Governor Twining saw this as an important symbol of the fact that Europeans should not be regarded as transients in Tanganyika. If Europeans were to be an integral part of Tanganyikan

44. *Land Utilization and the Allocation of Individual Rights over Land.* Government Circular no. 4, 23 April 1953 (mimeograph, Dar es Salaam, 1953).

45. Ibid.

46. Committee on Constitutional Development. *Evidence and Memoranda Submitted to the Fact Finding Sub-Committee*, file 1146-1, fol. 12 (Dar es Salaam Secretariat Library, 1959).

society, he felt that they should not have to send their children outside Tanganyika for their secondary school education. Neither he nor his colleagues seriously considered integrating European children into African secondary schools; they assumed that there needed to be a secondary school for European children. In 1956 Tanganyika secured a windfall of some £2.4 million, the proceeds from the sale of enemy property seized in Tanganyika during the war. Twining divided it into four equal portions. One quarter was held in the Tanganyika Higher Education Trust and £600,000 each was earmarked respectively to African, Asian, and European education. The European portion was used to build Saint Michael's and Saint George's School in Iringa, a well-appointed and totally European secondary school. Without hesitation and with a natural sympathy, the Government of Tanganyika acted on the assumption that the protection of the rights of the minorities in Tanganyika required that the state promote and facilitate their separate existences as socially autonomous racial communities.

Mr. Paul Bomani, who was a nominated member of the Legislative Council at the time, questioned the decision to put such a substantial sum into a racially exclusive school. The financial secretary replied: "I would suggest in the present case that the honourable member might possibly consider the source from which these funds came and I think if he gives full consideration to that point he will see nothing unfair in the proposed distribution."[47] It was an audacious reply, revealing the degree to which the financial secretary thought in racial categories. In his view, because the properties in question had been expropriated from Germans (who were European) it was only fair that a significant proportion of the proceeds from their sale should be used for the benefit of the European (though non-German) community.

The government's concern to promote the interests of the non-African communities, and more particularly the European community, as separate racial communities was also a feature in the famous Meru land case. In 1951 the Government of Tanganyika forcibly moved to other lands some three thousand Africans of the Meru tribe from a plateau which separated two areas of European alienated land. The Meru land was well watered and was thought to be of good quality for ranching and dairy purposes. What is significant for the purposes of the present discussion is that the government included in its defense of this action the argument that the alienation would improve the homogeneity of both the alienated and the tribal lands. The government had not previously been responsive to the desire of Europeans

47. *Tanganyika Legislative Council Official Report*, 30th session, 1955–56, vol. 1, col. 369.

to live in large, racially homogeneous blocks. That it was willing, in 1951, to take land from Africans for this purpose, in the face of strong African resistance and a good deal of international criticism, indicates the degree to which the government had accepted the view that the European community had rights as an autonomous racial community which could properly be promoted.[48]

There was, it is fair to say, more to all this than mere acceptance of the logical corollaries of the economic role which the government wished Europeans to play. There was also a growing racism within government circles. Despite the efforts of some younger administrative officers, the European clubs remained closed to the middle-class Africans, and the private nursery schools continued to be all-white. The Colonial Service in Tanganyika in the 1920s and 1930s had strongly supported the principle of African paramountcy. At the time, what that in fact meant was a continuation of effective colonial rule rather than an expanding role for the leaders of the local European community. However, once the rise of African nationalism was expected, the Colonial Service in Tanganyika became far more protective of the minority communities. In 1951 some twelve senior officers individually submitted memoranda to a committee of the legislature that was to make proposals concerning constitutional development. None of these officers talked the language of trusteeship and none sought an assurance of eventual majority rule. Instead their main preoccupation was to find a way to entrench the political position of the minority communities.[49]

Tanganyikan Responses to the Colonial Office Proposals of 1947–1948

The Tanganyikan government that received Colonial Office exhortations in 1947–48 to respond to African nationalism was thus a government full of self-confidence in its own wisdom, very suspicious of educated Africans, and increasingly sympathetic toward the European and, often, the Asian minority communities. It is no surprise, therefore, that its response was unenthusiastic; in fact, it failed entirely to respond to the demand that it devise a special entry for Africans into the Provincial Administration. Not until 1957 was an African appointed a district officer. Not until 1961, the very year of independence, was there a serious effort to recruit more than a

48. The Meru land case was discussed at several sessions of the United Nations Trusteeship Council and was commented upon critically by the 1951 UN Visiting Mission. The case is discussed in some detail in Chidzero, *Tanganyika*, pp. 236–45, and in John Iliffe, *A Modern History of Tanganyika* (Cambridge, 1979), pp. 499–503.

49. For a fuller discussion of this point, see Pratt, *The Critical Phase*, pp. 28–31.

tiny number of Africans to the Provincial Administration. This tardiness was a major fault, caused, essentially, by a failure to heed the advice given in 1942 by Hailey and vigorously repeated in 1947 by Creech Jones and Cohen, that they must begin immediately to prepare for decolonization. As a result, in June 1961 every senior civil servant in Dar es Salaam at the principal assistant secretary level and higher, every provincial commissioner, and fifty-five of the fifty-seven district commissioners were still British expatriates.[50]

The government was equally reluctant to take the force of the recommendation that it attach a high priority to the development of a democratic local government system. Tanganyika presented its own cautious local government reforms as if they showed that the Tanganyikan government and the Colonial Office shared a common set of objectives and a common analysis. They did not. The fact that each talked about local government reform did not demonstrate an underlying harmony. The key point to be made is the following:

> The assumption behind the Secretary of State's proposals was that independence was likely to come more swiftly than expected and that representative local governments should therefore be introduced rapidly. . . . In contrast the Tanganyika Government's self assurance as a colonial regime was unshaken. Its local government reforms were intended to improve the efficiency of colonial rule not to prepare it for dismantlement.[51]

Indeed, Twining, who became governor in 1950, argued in September of that year that constitutional advance at the center should wait upon the successful establishment of the local government system.[52] Thus local government reform, though viewed in London as necessary because of the inevitability of swift political advancement, was used by Twining as a further reason to delay political concessions at the level of the central government.

Multiracialism

The point has already been made that the Creech Jones proposals in 1947 for rapid constitutional advancement were intended primarily for West Africa, and that by 1949 the Colonial Office was promoting an alternative

50. For a further discussion of the argument of this paragraph, see my *The Critical Phase*, esp. pp. 17–19 and 91–95.

51. Ibid., p. 18.

52. Twining's dispatch of September 20, 1950, is reproduced in *Development of African Local Government in Tanganyika*, col. no. 277 (London, 1951).

pattern of multiracialism for East and Central Africa. This was not the first time this issue had been raised in Tanganyika.

In the 1930s, when there was strong pressure to bring Tanganyika into a closer union with Kenya and Uganda, the Tanganyikan government opposed it strongly, seeing the idea as an effort to extend the power of white settlers over Tanganyikans. This was not the reaction in 1949. It is one thing for a colonial regime to oppose European encroachment when the alternative is a continuation of rule by that regime; it is another matter when the alternative to an entrenchment of disproportionate political power for the minority communities is a rapid advance to African majority rule. By 1949, as was discussed in the previous section, the Tanganyikan government was much more sympathetic to the minority communities—and much more convinced of their importance to the economy. The government, therefore, in 1949 took up the cause of multiracialism and championed it. In contrast to its position at the time of the governorship of Sir Donald Cameron, Tanganyikan government was now ready to abandon its older trusteeship values.

A great deal of ingenuity, time, and energy went into the planning of how "multiracialism" should be achieved in Tanganyika. Sir Edward Twining and Andrew Cohen discussed the whole question before Twining became governor. Twining, several months after arriving in Tanganyika, decided what he wished the policy to be. He cleared his ideas with the Colonial Office, assured himself that they were acceptable to the nonofficial members of the Legislative Council, and then appointed, from among these members, a Constitutional Development Committee whose purpose was to recommend to Twining what ought to be done. Not surprisingly, the recommendations that finally came forward included the proposal that the official majority be continued in the legislature, with the unofficial side to be divided between the races in a ratio of 1:1:1. Multiracialism, though decided upon by London, was thus launched in Tanganyika, as if on the initiative of this Constitutional Development Committee.

It was, however, no mean task to devise an electoral system that could produce this balanced representation in a country in which, in fact, Africans outnumbered Europeans by more than 400:1, and Asians by 100:1. Academic expertise was recruited and, following a report by W. J. M. MacKenzie[53] and much additional discussion within the government, the decision was taken that there should be a common electoral roll with very high qualifications, which would reduce, though not eliminate, the African majority among the potential voters. It was also decided to divide Tan-

53. *Report of the Special Commissioner Appointed to Examine Matters Arising Out of the Report of the Committee on Constitutional Development*, (Dar es Salaam, 1953).

ganyika into ten constituencies, each to return three members to the legislature: an African, an Asian, and a European. However, there was not to be communal voting. Instead, each voter was to vote for one candidate for each of the three racially identified seats.

MacKenzie had recognized that even with high educational and income standards, there would be a substantial African majority on the rolls in almost all the constituencies. He therefore felt that in most constituencies, there would have to be communal voting. He recommended that common roll elections could be held only in the one or two towns where there would be a significant number of Asian and European voters.

It is an extraordinary indication of the self-confidence of the Colonial Service that it ignored MacKenzie on this point. Perhaps this requires amplification. The risk was that, where Africans predominated on the common roll, common roll elections (in which each voter voted for a European, an Asian, and an African candidate) could easily produce successful Asian and European candidates who would not be acceptable to their racial community. Twining ignored this risk. He was confident that a new party, the United Tanganyika party, which he engineered into existence and which supported multiracialism, would be able to win substantial African support.[54]

There was another, equally important, component to the Tanganyikan government's commitment to multiracialism. Twining felt that if multiracialism was to win full acceptance it should also be a feature of governmental institutions below the national level.[55] This involved a sudden, blunt, and total reversal of a basic attitude toward local rule in British Tanganyika that had been universally accepted within the Colonial Service not only during the decades of indirect rule but also in the more recent years in which the effort was made to promote the development of efficient and democratic African local government. In each of these earlier phases there had been total acceptance that the local institutions of rural Tanganyika were African. Twining himself in 1949 had quoted with approval Cameron's view that "the indigenous system had its foundations in the hearts and minds of the people" and could be made modern only by "enlisting the real force of the spirit of the people," and he had stressed the necessity "of encouraging development by evolutionary means."[56]

54. The constitutional innovations of the 1950s are discussed in Claggart Taylor, *The Political Development of Tanganyika* (Stanford, 1963), chaps. 5 and 6. The argument of the previous several paragraphs is developed at greater length in Pratt, *The Critical Phase*, chaps. 2 and 3.

55. See his memorandum to the Constitutional Development Committee, quoted in Pratt, *The Critical Phase*, p. 31.

56. Ibid., p. 32.

This old and seemingly deep-rooted attitude toward local institutions was swept aside in a major effort at social engineering. What was suddenly felt to be essential was that the participation of the minority communities, as communities, must be acknowledged and made visible and explicit throughout the country. This became a major preoccupation of the Provincial Administration from 1953 to 1958.[57] The effort was made, at first, to establish multiracial county councils, the county being a totally new level of government created between the district and the central government. When that innovation proved totally artificial and unworkable, the government then used the full influence of its administrative officers to try to replace the old all-African Native Authority councils by new district councils in which there would be minority representation. Until 1958 the government would not approve the establishment of any district council under the 1953 Local Government Ordinance unless it included representatives of the minorities. Africans of all classes, including the chiefs, were vigorously hostile to this effort to achieve multiracialism at the district level. There was very little support for the idea among the non-Africans in the rural districts, who very often consisted of a few score Asian traders and a handful of European missionaries. Moreover, the policy was entirely the idea of the local Colonial Service. Indeed, in 1955, a Colonial Office adviser, Claude Wallis, urged the abandonment of specially reserved racial representation on district councils. Yet the effort continued until it collapsed in 1958 in the face of mounting African opposition.

There can be few clearer examples of the overweening arrogance of the senior officers of the Tanganyikan government than is provided by their persistent efforts in the decade 1949 to 1958 to achieve "multiracialism" in the political institutions of Tanganyika. Certainly they were men of integrity; certainly they were pursuing their conception of what was required by "good government." But this was little comfort to Tanganyikans.

The Reaction to the Rise of the Tanganyikan African National Union

African nationalism became a national political force in 1954 with the creation of the Tanganyikan African National Union (TANU).[58] Its rapid rise, no

57. I have written at length on the theme of the next few paragraphs in my "Multiracialism and Local Government in Tanganyika," *Race* (London), November 1960, pp. 33–49, and more recently in *The Critical Phase*, pp. 28–35.

58. There is much good material available on TANU. See, in particular: Lionel Cliffe, "Nationalism and the Reaction of Enforced Agricultural Change in Tanganyika during the Colonial Period," paper presented to the East African Social Science Research Conference, 1964; John Iliffe, "The Role of the African Association in the Formation of Territorial Consciousness in Tanzania," a paper presented to the University of East Africa Social Science

doubt, owed a good deal to the political culture of the British who ruled in Tanganyika. Although ill disposed to this challenge, the British were but hesitant repressors. TANU was able to spread its influence widely and rapidly without its leaders being imprisoned or its followers cowed.

It is also true that the Tanganyikan government unintentionally aided TANU by two of its most important general policies in the 1950s. The persistent use of coercion, through the Native Authorities, to secure compliance with rural development policies in a number of districts generated widespread rural discontent and, by loosening the people's acceptance of their chiefs, opened the way for TANU to establish a claim to their loyalty and support. Even more important, the attempt to introduce racial parity in the legislature and to secure representation for the minority communities in the district councils provided TANU with an issue of great emotional force around which to rally its support throughout the country.

The unpopularity of these policies, along with the comparative freedom to organize, were important aids to the growth of TANU and therefore were also important contributions to the effectiveness of the transfer of power in Tanganyika. But to claim this is hardly to claim evidence of any wisdom, foresight, or skill on behalf of the Tanganyikan government. For the first four and a half crucial years of TANU's life, the British intended to be entirely unhelpful to TANU. The Tanganyikan government dismissed Nyerere and his colleagues as "men of straw" and as agitators stimulated to action by outsiders; it refused to allow African civil servants, including teachers, to join political parties, thus preventing a high proportion of the educated population of Tanganyika from joining TANU; it sought to revive the position of the chiefs so that they could serve as local counterweights to TANU and, collectively, could be alternative spokesmen for African interests; it promoted the revival of tribal loyalties in an open indulgence in "divide and rule"; it banned TANU from a number of districts, often on thin grounds; it encouraged the district commissioners to carry the political fight against TANU directly to the people; and it instigated the establishment of a progovernment party, the United Tanganyika party.

In regard to TANU—as in regard to the Africanization of the civil service, the use of coercion in rural development, and the composition of the legislature and of the district councils—the Tanganyikan government persisted

---

Conference, 1968; G. Andrew Maguire, *Towards "Uhuru" in Tanzania* (Cambridge, 1969); and the essays by Terence Ranger, John Iliffe, and Arnold Temu, in A. Temu and I. N. Kimambo, eds., *A History of Tanzania* (Nairobi, 1969). Since this chapter (and this footnote) was first written, a very fine volume has been published which includes, inter alia, a full and most perceptive history of nationalism in Tanganyika. This is John Iliffe's *A Modern History of Tanganyika* (Cambridge, 1979).

until very late in the day with policies that reveal a single-minded commitment to its own idea of what was in Tanganyika's interest. Very little it did in these important areas of policy was helpful to the transfer of power that was to begin in 1959.

The Final Transfer, 1959-1961[59]

The final dénouement in the tale of the British in Tanganyika was sudden and abrupt. Tanganyika's advance to independence, once it finally began, took place at a prodigious pace. The result was a timetable for the transfer of power in Tanganyika so telescoped as to make it quite a different process from the transfer in most other British colonies. Nigeria and Ceylon, for example, each had a period of thirty-eight years between the year in which some members of the legislature were elected for the first time and the final achievement of independence. In Jamaica the equivalent period was seventy-eight years, and in the Gold Coast it was thirty-two years. In contrast to this, there were a mere thirty-nine months between the first national elections in Tanganyika and December 9, 1961, the date on which Tanganyika became independent. Even more relevant is the fact that Nigeria had nine years of responsible government before achieving independence, while Ghana had six years, Ceylon, seventeen years, and Jamaica, nine years. In contrast to these, the period of responsible government prior to independence in Tanganyika lasted only nineteen months.

The speed of this process may primarily be explained by the factors which led to the British decision, late in 1959, to bring to an end their colonial rule throughout Africa as rapidly as possible.[60] Within the Tanganyikan experience there was ample evidence that it was a wise decision. In the years 1956-58 TANU rapidly grew in strength. The firm governmental hold on the direction of change was severely threatened: the various compulsory rural development projects had to be abandoned because of popular resistance; the chiefs resisted the government's effort to line them up solidly on its side and instead began individually to secure a cordial relationship with TANU; the eleven district councils which had been induced to accept non-African members had to be disbanded, again because of mass opposition; the United Tanganyikan party was overwhelmed in the elections of 1958 and February 1959, and thereafter all

59. These years are treated more fully in Claggart Taylor, *The Political Development*, chap. 7; Cranford Pratt, *The Critical Phase*, chap. 3; and Iliffe, *Modern History of Tanganyika*, pp. 552-76.

60. This decision is discussed, for example, in David Goldsworthy, *Colonial Issues in British Politics, 1945-61* (Oxford, 1971).

thirty elected members accepted Nyerere's leadership in the Tanganyika Elected Members Organization. In October 1958 Turnbull conceded that racial parity in the legislature should be replaced by majority rule, and in March 1959 he abandoned parity in his appointment of elected members to the Executive Council.

Perhaps it was this later decision that was the moment of truth for the British in Tanganyika. Turnbull had wanted to maintain a racial balance in his first appointments to the Executive Council. Nyerere refused to cooperate, insisting that a clear majority of those first appointed be African. For a brief time it was possible that there might be a direct confrontation on this issue. The word went out to the district headquarters to prepare for a period of conflict with TANU. Wire meshing was affixed to land-rover windows and plans were made for the evacuation of white women and children. But even as this planning was going on, it became absolutely clear to most officers that they could not contain a TANU-led campaign of open opposition for long. The "Indian dimension" was finally recognized in Tanganyika. Turnbull conceded to Nyerere's demand, and multiracialism in Tanganyika was finished.

The strategy which Turnbull followed at this time was, very belatedly, that recommended by Creech Jones and Cohen more than a decade earlier. Major concessions were made to African nationalism in the hope that this step would win an extended period of cordial partnership between colonial power and nationalist party. As a consequence of this strategy, the British expected, in mid-1959, to remain in Tanganyika until 1970.[61]

At this point the colonial administration underwent a surprising upturn in its morale. After October 1958, and even more after March 1959, TANU swung its influence behind the government, securing a higher level of mass cooperation with its rural policies than had been experienced for over a decade. There was suddenly a new vision within the Colonial Service—the vision of a Tanganyika that would be independent in the immediate future and in which, under African political leadership, the British administrators could get on with the pursuit of the policies they had long felt were needed. The emergence of this vision coincided with the British decision, usually dated sometime in late 1959, to move out of Africa as swiftly as possible.

The British decision to grant independence in 1961 is best seen as a modification of the earlier strategy rather than as an abandonment of it. The Tanganyikan government hoped it had found a political leadership which

61. Michael Blundell reports that this was the decision of the East African governors meeting in London at that time with Lennox-Boyd, the new secretary of state. Michael Blundell, *So Rough A Wind* (London, 1969), pp. 261–62.

would accept a major dependency on Britain. It hoped that British interests and objectives in Tanganyika would be better served by a rapid advance to independence than by an effort to extend colonial rule. This was no dark design that had long guided British planning on Tanganyika; it had been stumbled upon in 1959 once the British discovered the quality of Nyerere's leadership. Moreover, they acclaimed it openly. It was, for John Fletcher-Cooke, deputy governor, a "Grand Design." As he saw it, it had these central features: large numbers of British officers would remain in Tanganyika, the importance of the economic contribution of non-Africans would be recognized, and Nyerere's leadership would keep the "disruptive element in check."[62]

Conclusions

No doubt it was the euphoria of these few years and the cordial style of Turnbull and Nyerere which explain the widely prevalent view that the British executed the transfer of power in Tanganyika with particular success. This is surely a shallow judgment. The vision of the "Grand Design" according to which the British would continue to run Tanganyika under TANU leadership had as little basis in political reality as the multiracial policies that had preceded it. The Grand Design began to disintegrate even before independence. Serious tension developed between TANU and the British concerning the financial components of the independence settlement. More fundamental still, the members of the Colonial Service in Tanganyika made clear how tentative and self-centered their commitment to Tanganyika was by the arrangements upon which they insisted regarding their pensions and their compensation for "loss of career."[63]

After independence the inadequacy and political unreality of the "Grand Design" quickly became apparent. A long, dependent relationship with Britain was a political nonstarter in Tanganyika. Within days after independence, Nyerere resigned as prime minister. He remained president of TANU and began the long search for more creative policies and institutions than those he had inherited. A close and subordinate relationship with Britain was too high a price for a leadership determined to play a significant role in the liberation of southern Africa. By December 1965 Tanganyika's relations with Britain were in serious disarray. Diplomatic relations had

62. In his statement to the U.N. Trusteeship Council in June 1960, quoted in "United Nations Visiting Mission to Trust Territories in East Africa, 1960. Report on Tanganyika," *Trusteeship Council Official Records, Twenty-Sixth Session* (14 April–30 June 1960), supplement no. 2. (New York: United Nations Organization, 1960), p. 60.

63. The evidence for this harsh judgment is discussed in my *The Critical Phase*, pp. 98–103.

been broken. Aid negotiations had been canceled, and Tanganyika began its search for a range of international links that would be more compatible with its commitment to liberation, and with its determination after 1967 to achieve a greater measure of national self-reliance and a transition to a socialist society.

The transfer of power in Tanganyika was bound to be difficult. The poverty of the country, the scarcity of trained persons, the fragility of national loyalties, the inexperience of the nationalist leadership, and the untested character of the nationalist movement, all made difficulties inevitable. However, it is clear that the policies pursued by the Tanganyikan government during the years from 1949 through 1958 tended to increase these difficulties rather than to lessen them. Little can be claimed on behalf of the policies of the British in Tanganyika during the transition to independence except that they could have been worse and that, when it was finally decided in London that it must hand over power rapidly, the Colonial Service in Tanganyika did it with style.

11. The Impact of Ethnic Demands on British Decolonization in Africa: The Example of Uganda

GRACE S. IBINGIRA

So long as it was not certain that the nonwhite global empires of Great Britain would become independent states, diverse ethnic groups in most African dependencies were disposed to join hands in nationalistic parties or movements to assail colonial rule, sometimes content to leave their ethnic differences and potential conflicts in abeyance. But once the British colonizers took the decision to disengage and hand over power to indigenous leaders, the focus of these diverse groups within each colony shifted dramatically. It became almost irrelevant to attack the colonizers, because they had for a variety of reasons manifestly decided to pull out. The preoccupation of many local leaders consequently became how to ensure a secure place for their respective groups after independence was attained. This could best be done by each group, separately or in alliance with others, attempting to influence the crucial stages in the transfer of power, which involved, among other things, the shaping and defining of national institutions and the exercise and sharing of political power on which all else would depend. The decade of the 1950s remains memorable for the intensity with which these diverse ethnic groups in most British colonies attempted to attain such objectives. But it is worth remembering that this dramatic rise of ethnic demands and fears was largely a result of the very nature of how the colonies had originally been created and then governed.

Because the partition and colonization of Africa took place primarily for the benefit of European powers, the interests of indigenous peoples had often been irrelevant, at best secondary. Little thought, therefore, was given to the creation of relatively more homogeneous colonies. Within most of them were gathered diverse ethnic groups which may, for centuries past, have lived in and operated independent social systems with no regard for their compatibility. Thus, it was common to find societies ruled by centralized monarchies like the emirates of the north and the Yoruba of the west in Nigeria, the Ashanti of Ghana, or the Baganda of Uganda, living within common borders with societies that knew no central authority or that administered themselves through heads of extended families or clans, like the Ibo of eastern Nigeria or the ethnic groups north of the Nile in Uganda. Moreover, no thought had been given to the fact that within a colony European rulers might have gathered together inveterate enemies from long and incessant wars of precolonial history. It followed, therefore, that the whole imperial process had created artificial colonies, each containing ethnic groups that were widely diverse and sometimes incompatible or historically hostile to one another.

To compound the complexity of this circumstance, once such heterogeneous groups had been lumped together within a single colony, the effort to give them a shared sense of belonging, the experience of a common destiny, was totally inadequate, if not often absent. From the perspective of the colonizers, however objectively unjust otherwise, it made good sense to keep the natives divided. In that way they were more easily governable, as within the colony each group retained much of its precolonial identity and thus continued to be systematically kept from an effective, all-embracing consciousness, which, in a joint effort with others, could threaten imperial rule.

There are abundant examples of how indigenous ethnic groups were systematically denied a central focus that would have cultivated better, more tolerant interethnic relations.[1] Ghana, for instance, had been ruled by Great Britain for over a hundred years, and yet it was not until 1952, only five years before independence, that the first African-led government embracing most groups, under Kwame Nkrumah, came into being, and exercised, even then, only a limited measure of political power. In Nigeria, the most populous and diverse African state, the situation was perhaps even worse. Although the northern and southern parts of the country had been united by Lord Lugard in 1914 to form Nigeria, the two remained separate entities until Governor Richards' constitution nearly a half-century later. The first African government to experience and exercise any measure of political responsibility for the whole country was not formed until 1956, under Prime Minister Tafawa Balewa, when the country had only four years to go before independence. The situation in Uganda was comparable. British rule had lasted sixty-eight years, but the very first countrywide general election was held only one year before independence,

1. For some accounts of these thwarted interethnic relationships, see: for Ghana, Kwame Nkrumah, in *Gold Coast Legislative Assembly Debates*, July 30–Nov. 16, 1956, col. 19 (Accra, 1956); for Uganda, G. S. K. Ibingira, *The Forging of an African Nation* (New York, 1973), chap. 4; and for Nigeria, Kalu Ezera, in *Constitutional Developments in Nigeria* (London, 1960).

in 1961. The first African government to exercise substantial political power, under Benedicto Kiwanaka in 1961, was defeated the following year. The successor regime, under Milton Obote, was experiencing and exercising political power and responsibility for the first time when independence was only six months away, in October 1962. No wonder, therefore, that even nationalist parties which agitated for independence were decisively influenced by or rooted in ethnic group loyalties, despite rhetoric to the contrary.

Having thus been denied participation in overall unifying national institutions which, more than anything else, would have diminished ethnic particularism, most groups felt they had to protect their communal identities in the final constitutional arrangements before independence. In the circumstances, it seemed to them too risky and illogical to entrust their fate to largely untried nationalist leaders, many of whom invariably came from other, perhaps even historically hostile, ethnic groups.

But whatever had been the sins or prevarications of the colonial power, once a decision had been made to decolonize, it was pursued in relative earnest. Yet smooth transition to independence was to be frustrated, delayed, or threatened by the intensity and particularism of both majority and minority ethnic groups within most British colonies, as they vied for advantage and self-preservation. The last stages of decolonization were thus to be significantly affected and influenced by these ethnic dynamics. Uganda provides a good illustration of why and how this happened.

Partly because of domestic and external forces, but also because of the rise of local nationalism, Great Britain set out seriously to prepare a voluntary liquidation of almost all her colonial possessions after the Second World War. As was the case in other colonies, such preparations in the protectorate of Uganda involved, among other things, sustained reforms in the institutions of the future state and the promotion of increasing indigenous participation in such i stitutions on both national and local levels, however belatedly.

The initial effort to reform the Legislative Council had begun with the modest step of the colonial governor nominating three African members to it in 1946.[2] This was followed by more rapid and increasingly Africanized enlargements of this council in the 1950s under the dynamic leadership of a reform-minded governor, Sir Andrew Cohen. He had been among the

2. On the growth of the Legislative Council in the decade of the 1950s leading to independence, see Ibingira, *Forging of an African Nation*, chap. 3. K. Ingham's *The Making of Modern Uganda* (London, 1958) remains a useful text on its early development.

prime movers at the Colonial Office who had urged the decolonization of Africa. Now, as governor of Uganda, he had the opportunity to implement the process he had helped to initiate. In 1954 and 1957, the Legislative Council was enlarged, bringing in more Africans from most ethnic groups of the protectorate, while at the same time its ratio of expatriates and other non-Africans was correspondingly reduced. In 1958 the first direct elections in the protectorate were held on a qualitative franchise, though for only twelve seats representing the Eastern, Western, and Northern provinces. As the legislative arm of the council expanded, so was its executive side transformed. In 1956, Governor Cohen turned this colonial executive council into a ministerial system with a cabinet, laying the foundations for a future cabinet system of government in an independent Uganda. To this first ministry he appointed three Africans.

One of the highlights of these reforms was the appointment of a constitutional committee in 1958 to review Uganda's progress and recommend the next major constitutional steps to take on the road to self-government.[3] It was headed by a British civil servant but its membership was overwhelmingly African. Its recommendations, which were to spur the largest ethnic group toward secession, constituted a landmark in the protectorate's political and constitutional history. They firmly established that Uganda was to remain a single country with a unicameral parliamentary system of government representing every region in the protectorate and elected on a universal adult franchise.

Parallel with these reforms at the national level, corresponding reforms were undertaken in local governments. Hitherto, the colonial administration had divided the protectorate into districts for the purpose of local government. Where, as was the majority of cases, an ethnic group was sufficiently large to constitute a viable local government unit, it was designated a district by itself. Such was the case with Busoga, Teso, Acholi, Lango, Ankole, and Bunyoro, for example—and, on a larger scale, the kingdom of Buganda. Where several neighboring groups were too small, they were grouped together to form the local government district, as was the case with Kigezi, Toro, Bukedi, West Nile, and Karamoja. Not only had these local government units been kept relatively separated from one another in order to stifle the rise of unified nationalism, but within themselves they were quite unrepresentative of the communities they were supposed to serve. Their first reform came in 1949 with the formal establishment of district councils for all local governments. In 1955, further reform was introduced to make them more representative of their com-

3. See *Report of the Constitutional Committee* (Entebbe, Uganda, 1959).

munities and able to shoulder relatively more responsibility for local affairs than hitherto, even though more could have been done.

Contemporaneous with these colonial reforms were the birth and growth of nationalist parties, which for the first time sought to articulate the political aspirations of Ugandans as a whole rather than any particular ethnic group.[4] The postwar political changes that had brought the independence of India and Pakistan were not lost on local aspiring politicians. It was thus no accident that the first nationalist party, the Uganda National Congress (UNC), had been formed in 1952, directly inspired, as the name indicated, by the India National Congress. Several other political parties sprang up in the 1950s. The most significant of these were the Democratic party (DP), formed in 1954; the Uganda Peoples Union (UPU), formed in 1958; and the Uganda Peoples Congress (UPC), which had resulted from a merger of UPU and a faction of UNC. Although these parties could not be regarded as having mass followings (like the Convention Peoples party in Ghana or the Tanganyika African National Union in what was then Tanganyika), and although they came to the political scene relatively late, nevertheless they played the part of providing a nationalist vanguard of a sort to demand independence and a faster pace of decolonization. They published manifestos and organized countrywide meetings to propagate their views of why and in what form independence should be attained for the protectorate.

The UNC, UPU, and later the UPC (and to a lesser extent the DP), which were represented in the Legislative Council from the mid-fifties, grasped opportunities provided by membership to make the council a platform for nationalist demands.

All these efforts by the colonial power to reform and democratize local and national institutions in preparation for self-government, combined with and partly spurred on by rising local nationalism, produced a momentum that was clearly destined for the protectorate's independence. Governor Cohen felt confident enough to remark in 1956, for example, that in his judgment the most important achievement of the country during the last five years had been "the real progress made in giving responsibility to Africans in all the main spheres of public life." "A new atmosphere" had been created in the country, he declared, and the aim of all colonial efforts, "the building up of the country towards the goal of self-government in the future," was now "clearly understood."[5]

4. For a short history of Ugandan political parties of this period, see D. A. Low, *Political Parties in Uganda, 1949–62* (London, 1962). See also F. B. Welbourn, in *Religion and Politics in Uganda, 1952–62* (Nairobi, 1965), and Ibingira, *Forging of an African Nation*, chap. 7.

5. In *Proceedings of the Legislative Council, 1956*, 36th sess., p. 51.

But the governor had omitted something fundamental of which he knew. Precisely because these combined forces ineluctably led to British withdrawal, the process had become the primary catalyst for the dramatic rise of fears, demands, and obstructions among some ethnic groups because they felt insecure and uncertain about their identity in an independent Uganda. These fears were expressed with varying intensity by both large and small groups, by the monarchial peoples of the lacustrine kingdoms as well as peoples north and east of the Nile. But they were at their peak in the kingdom of Buganda, which formed the largest ethnic group (16 percent of the population) and was the most developed region of the protectorate. The intensity with which such fears were assiduously expressed and the attempts of the colonial power to allay them were significantly to influence the pace of decolonization and the nature of the national institutions that Great Britain bequeathed to Uganda on independence.

Buganda Separatism

When the British first came to the areas which comprise present-day Uganda during the latter part of the last century, they had been deeply impressed by the relatively advanced nature of the centralized kingdom of Buganda. Partly because of this local capability and partly because, as the most powerful kingdom strategically situated close to the source of the Nile it provided a logical ally, the British had decided to make this kingdom the base for their acquisition, expansion, and development of what later became the *Uganda* protectorate—clearly named after this kingdom. In this way, *Buganda* had become the heart of *Uganda*, the preeminent region from which most significant developments in the whole protectorate generally emanated.[6] Because of this history, and partly because colonial rule consistently discouraged meaningful unifying experiences with other groups, the Baganda, more than any other group, regarded themselves as a separate nation. As soon as colonial rulers and local nationalists combined to prepare the way for a unified independent Ugandan state, therefore, the traditional government of this kingdom responded with increasing alarm and resistance.[7]

Buganda had defended its identity as early as the 1920s and 1930s, when there had been talks at the Colonial Office about federating the British East African colonies. But it was from the early 1950s that its resistance in-

6. See the lucid account of this by D. A. Low and R. C. Pratt, *Buganda and British Overrule* (London, 1960).

7. See Ibingira, *Forging of an African Nation*, pp. 115 ff., for a full account.

creased in direct proportion to the preparations for British disengagement. In 1953, pursuing the goal of being a distinct, separate nation apart from the rest of the protectorate, the kingdom's government had made two demands of British authorities: first, that Buganda affairs no longer be handled by the Colonial Office, which dealt with matters of all colonies, but should be transferred to the Foreign Office. This was to indicate that Buganda was not a colony pure and simple, but a protected state whose monarch, Kabaka (King) Mutese I, had invited British protection, which was formalized in a treaty with his successor in 1893. This would mean recognizing Buganda as a foreign state, though protected, distinct from the rest of the protectorate. The second demand was that the British authorities work out a timetable for Buganda's evolution to its own separate independence. Both demands were rejected by the British government. Governor Cohen demanded, in turn, that the Kabaka retract these demands. He refused. Cohen then summarily deposed and deported Mutese to the United Kingdom, in the hope that those who remained in his government would be more compliant to imperial wishes. But the governor had miscalculated. The humiliation of their ruler caused such outrage among the Baganda, unifying and heightening their loyalty to the deposed Kabaka to such an extent, that the British authorities were forced to reinstate him two years later.

To appease the Baganda further, the colonial authorities granted Buganda more autonomy under a new Anglo-Buganda agreement in 1955. But rather than diminishing, Buganda's fears of its integral membership within a future unified Ugandan state were to increase. A series of steps were consequently taken intended to nullify the unity of Uganda and the British efforts to decolonize the protectorate as a single state.

The first step taken by the Buganda kingdom's government was to discredit, cripple, and if possible, to destroy central Uganda-wide institutions, particularly the Legislative Council. As the embryo of a future sovereign legislature, it was viewed by the Baganda with great apprehension as being endowed with a future capability to whittle away Buganda's powers, or—worse still—to destroy the kingdom. The fiery speeches made by members of the council from other groups attacking Buganda's efforts to go it alone simply reinforced these fears. To the majority of Baganda, the natural successors to British power were the indigenous local governments, of which theirs was the most outstanding. This seemed a natural result of indirect rule, which had given each ethnic group the illusion that it was separate from the rest. Yet it fatally overlooked the unifying aspect of colonial rule which theoretically tied all the diverse peoples inextricably together. Nevertheless, the Baganda were committed. Although in 1955 they had demanded direct elections to the Legislative Council in 1958, when that time arrived they did an about-face and thwarted the holding of these first direct, unified elections in the country within their kingdom. The ever-desired result was to make the elected council unrepresentative and therefore unqualified to take important decisions on Uganda's future, while the kingdom negotiated its own arrangements for independence.

The second strategy in Buganda's plan was to cripple or destroy the young nationalist political parties. This was to deny the Legislative Council a firm political base among the people and consequently to weaken or discredit it. Because this kingdom had been the center of national development, it followed that most of the early nationalist political parties began here: the UNC, the DP, and other lesser parties were originally Buganda-based and led. The kingdom's government now moved ruthlessly to intimidate and silence them, which it succeeded in doing to a large extent. When the colonial government overruled and rejected all Buganda's major demands and ordered the first countrywide general election on a universal adult franchise in 1961, the Buganda government responded by launching an effective boycott of registration of voters in Buganda in 1960 and the election that followed in 1961. So effective was the boycott, enforced as it was with threats of bodily harm or destruction of property, that only about 3 percent of the potential electorate registered, and even fewer voted.[8] These actions by the largest and most developed ethnic group not only detracted from the nationalist drive for faster decolonization, but it unwittingly denied Buganda a role which it had seemed in historical terms eminently qualified to play—namely, to provide nationwide leadership in moving Uganda to independence.

Along with these steps to diminish the influence of the Legislative Council, the Buganda government simultaneously launched vigorous efforts to persuade the British to grant them separate independence. Thus, in 1958, the Buganda Lukiko sent a lengthy memorandum to the queen seeking termination of the agreements by which their kabaka in the last century had invited British protection. Although British authorities rejected the request, in early 1960 yet another memorandum expressing similar terms was sent—and was similarly turned down. Meanwhile, in 1960, the kingdom's government set up a constitutional committee to negotiate Buganda's separate independence. The committee undertook lengthy and inconclusive negotiations with colonial officials, who totally rejected the idea of dividing up Uganda before independence.

Buganda now tried to seek allies among the other local and traditionally led districts in the protectorate, particularly the smaller western kingdoms

8. Welbourn, *Religion and Politics*, tables 1, 2, and 3.

of Ankole, Bunyoro (despite historical enmity between the two), Toro, and the district of Busoga in the east. If these could join in demanding substantial autonomy on independence, it might ensure a loose federation with a weak central government; in this way the traditional identity of each group would be assured. On Buganda's initiative, therefore, the leading ministers of these kingdoms' governments promoted and held joint meetings with the principal local government officials from the rest of the country to sell the idea. What came to be called the Conferences of Katikkiros (premiers of kingdoms) and Secretaries-General (of nonkingdom areas) became fashionable from early 1960. But even in this effort Buganda soon became relatively isolated. While its friends among the kingdoms especially wanted some autonomy, none could support any bid for unilateral independence or excessive decentralization of power that might endanger the unity of its own state after independence.

Still, British resistance, supported by articulate and often angry response from Legislative Council members from other ethnic groups, as well as from the conferences of local leaders, convinced the Baganda more than ever that their future security and identity lay in attaining independence on their own. In October 1960 they sent another lengthy memorandum to the colonial secretary, more despearately insisting on their demands and threatening secession. Fear of their future countrymen was clearly the crucial motivation. They observed: "Public pronouncements made on various occasions by people likely to be leaders of a future Uganda are not conducive to the idea of unity as Her Majesty's Government envisages it. In order to avoid another 'Katanga' in this country immediately after Uganda's independence, Buganda has decided and is determined to go it alone."[9]

Though irritated and frustrated, British authorities were not deterred in their preparations for independence. Thus, the colonial secretary announced a four-point timetable for major constitutional changes while the deadlock with Buganda continued. First, there was to be an initial countrywide registration of voters on a universal adult franchise in 1960. Second, before general elections in 1961, he would appoint a relationships commission to make recommendations on the best form of government for a future independent Uganda, including Buganda. Third, a general election to the Legislative Council in early 1961 would follow. Finally, after the general elections a constitutional conference would be held in London in 1961, representative of all parts of Uganda, including Buganda, to consider

9. The Buganda case for separate independence was comprehensively published in a booklet, *Buganda's Independence* (published by Buganda Government, 1960); see p. 30.

the recommendations of the Relationships Commission. This conference would also be attended by the elected members of the new Legislative Council.

Because this timetable had far-reaching implications, the Baganda opposed it strenuously. They frustrated the registration of voters for the 1961 general elections. Now, for the first time, they proposed to waive their demand to secede if the colonial secretary was prepared to make a commitment in advance of all these constitutional steps that Buganda would have a *federal relationship* vis-à-vis the future central government of Uganda, whatever the future form of government was to be for the rest of the country. Since the constitutional conference would be dominated by non-Baganda from the Legislative Council who had already demonstrated hostility to Bugandan demands, they feared there would be little chance for concessions unless the colonial secretary committed British authorities in advance. But he rejected this demand. As a result, Buganda now submitted a detailed constitutional plan of its own for separate independence.[10] When this was also rejected, the Buganda Lukiko, on December 31, 1960, declared their kingdom an independent separate state, thus seceding amid a highly emotional atmosphere. This was an empty claim, however, because the kingdom had no means of implementing it. Governor Crawford promptly rejected it and demanded that Buganda continue as part of the protectorate. This Buganda bid to secede had finally, or temporarily at least, been successfully resisted. But there was no doubt that it had been a major obstacle in the process of decolonization during the last decade of colonial rule. It influenced the future form of government and the character of national institutions which the British were to bequeath to independent Uganda.

Fears and Demands of Other Ethnic Groups

Although most attention was focused on Buganda separatism in the period under review, it would be misleading to conclude that other groups in the protectorate did not share similar fears for their identity after independence. Such fears and resulting demands manifested themselves at different levels and took different forms among the rest of the heterogeneous peoples.

First, there were the kingdoms of the western region—Ankole, Bunyoro, and Toro—and the district of Busoga in the east. Because they were smaller and poorer than the kingdom of Buganda, they could not

10. Ibid.

aspire to secession, which they firmly opposed. But they were generally assiduous in their demand for a federal relationship with the central government, which would guarantee the positions of their traditional rulers and assure their governments a measure of meaningful administration in local matters. While on the one hand they opposed Buganda's extravagant demands, on the other they allied with it to maximize the force of their demands for federalism. Even Bunyoro, which had a historic grievance against Buganda, could not oppose this general stance for federalism.

The nonmonarchical peoples of the country could not help reacting against what they considered a common position of the kingdoms. They became apprehensive that if independence were to come on the terms demanded by the kingdoms, particularly Buganda, their own future would be undermined and threatened. Thus, West Nile, Bugisu, Kigezi, Karamoja, and Lango—while conceding the necessity for constitutional safeguards for the kingdoms—vigorously argued for a strong, unitary central government, which alone could assure equality and fair play for all. Others, like Acholi and Madi, argued alternatively that if Uganda was to be a federal state, then the federation should be on a provincial basis of east, west, north, and Buganda, as a method of forestalling Bugandan domination by creating regional units of government comparable in both size and population.

To attain their objectives, these diverse groups outside Buganda conducted their efforts on two levels: first, through their local government leaders, who by the mid-fifties were fairly influential; second, through their representatives among the nationalist political parties that had come into existence, particularly the UNC, DP, UPU, and later, the UPC. It is significant to note how these parties, which outwardly espoused nationalistic and pan-African views, could in reality be clearly influenced by the dynamics of these ethnic hopes and fears. Ethnicity influenced the fundamental thinking of the majority of the diverse peoples of the protectorate more decisively and consistently than did nationalist parties. The first political party, the UNC, was not formed until 1952, when the protectorate had had a functioning administration for about half a century. But ethnic identity was as old as the groups themselves, often stretching over centuries of existence. No wonder, therefore, that even while the nationalists demanded independence for Uganda as a united country, most of them consistently defended or respected the stand generally taken by their respective groups to protect their identity. It was because of this, for example, that nationalist leaders from kingdoms in all these parties supported federalism for Uganda, while their counterparts from the rest of the country preferred more centralized government.

In addition to these demands, there were others from minority ethnic groups who, as independence approached, increasingly asked to be given their own local administrations in order to avoid perpetual domination by majority ethnic groups in the same administrative unit. The most famous was the demand made by the Banyoro inhabitants of several counties annexed to Buganda by the British as a reward for their assistance in conquering Bunyoro, whose ruler, Kabarega, had defied British colonization. These so-called lost counties constituted one of the emotional and thorny issues of the colonial legacy, in which most of the protectorate supported the demand of Bunyoro to have these counties returned to it before independence. Yet there were other ethnic communities whose fears could not be resolved by the creation of separate local administrations because they were scattered or too small. Such were the Bamba and Bakonjo of the kingdom of Toro, the Sebei of the Eastern Region, and the immigrant Asian community that had largely built and dominated the commercial life of the protectorate. Whatever formulae British authorities were to devise for independence, therefore, had to be designed to allay the fears of these diverse groups.

The Federal Solution

Despite its decentralization under indirect rule—which gave the impression of federalism—the Uganda administration had been unitary in nature from its inception. In the face of Buganda's demands for federalism, successive British authorities had asserted this. Indeed, in 1953 Sir Andrew Cohen, in a joint memorandum with the kabaka of Buganda, had declared, "The Uganda Protectorate has been and will continue to be developed as a unitary state."[11]

In 1957, in the face of further demands, the governor had rejected these ethnic, centrifugal tendencies: "if excessive demands are made, demands which appear to encroach on the rights, responsibilities, functions or revenues of the central government of the future, it is our duty as trustees for that government to resist such demands."[12]

But because of the persistence and intensity of Buganda's desperate bid to secede, Great Britain could no longer be certain of the suitability of the unitary solution. When the Relationships Commission gathered evidence in Uganda in 1960, it fed these fears with this observation: "The prospect that the country might disintegrate and suffer miseries like the Congo had

11. In *Proceedings of the Legislative Council, 1952–53,* 32d sess.
12. In *Proceedings of the Legislative Council, 1956,* 36th sess., p. 1.

suddenly become a real source of anxiety. . . . Against this background the hypothesis of a unitary state could no longer be taken for granted."[13] After careful consideration the commission recommended some form of federalism. Its findings therefore altered Uganda's last phase of colonial rule from a commitment to a unitary form of government to a compromise of semifederalism. They formed the basis for the constitution on which the protectorate was to attain self-government in 1961 and independence one year later.

It took two fully representative constitutional conferences in London, in 1961 and 1962, to draw up the final compromises that met most of the important demands of the diverse ethnic groups. The outcome can be summarized in accordance with how the respective powers of government were divided:[14] (1) What Buganda received in return for dropping its demand to secede; (2) what the other groups received to allay their fears; (3) the authority of the central government.

Buganda

This kingdom was granted exclusive powers to legislate and generally to deal with matters which it had considered peculiarly its own and which had spurred its demands to secede.[15] Foremost among these were the Kabakaship—the institution of monarchy—including everything that pertained to it. No longer would it be possible for a future Ugandan central government legally to determine the fate of the Buganda throne as Governor Cohen had done in 1953 when he desposed and deported the Kabaka. To ensure and protect the viability and strength of its traditional government, Buganda further received exclusive powers to legislate for its own public service and on all matters relating to its traditional and customary institutions. To support its substantial administration, it was also assured of some independent sources of revenue from taxation, although ultimately the Uganda government was to exercise significant financial control over it.

The Buganda system of Mailo land tenure was preserved and put beyond the control of the central government. More for prestige purposes than for substantive gain, a Buganda high court was created by constitutional fic-

13. *Report of the Uganda Relationships Commission*, paragraphs 79–82, entitled "The Choice before the Country" (Entebbe, Uganda, 1961).

14. See details in *Report of the Uganda Constitutional Conference*, Comnd. 1523 of 1961 (London: H.M. Stationery Office, 1961). For the details of these constitutional provisions, see Ibingira, *Forging of an African Nation*, chaps. 7 and 8.

15. Detailed in the Constitution of Buganda as Schedule 1 to the Uganda Independence Constitution, 1962, and its exclusive legislative powers, as part 1 of Schedule 7 of same constitution.

tion, when in fact all its judges were exclusively under the control of the central government. In addition to all this, the kingdom was granted authority to administer an extensive range of public services. Of more immediate concern, the Buganda Lukiko was given the option of electing its members to the Uganda parliament as an electoral college instead of sending them directly from parliamentary constituencies. In this way, the kingdom hoped to maintain an effective whip on its representatives at the national level. Together with other provisions imposing restrictions on the mode of generally amending the Uganda constitution, Buganda fears seemed at last to have been effectively put to rest, and the kingdom fully participated in the preindependence elections of April 1962 and joined UPC to form the coalition government that led the protectorate to independence on October 9, 1962.

Concessions to the Other Groups

The western kingdoms and Busoga were given exclusive powers to control all matters relating to their traditional rulers, similar to what Buganda had obtained for the Kabakaship.[16] But for practical purposes most of their powers and competence were very similar to what each of the other districts of the protectorate received. There was an increased number and level of services which these local governments were now permitted to administer for their respective peoples after independence. In general, no substantial group felt cheated of its colonial inheritance; none felt its future compromised by these arrangements, which had now been embodied in the independence constitution, except for a small number of minorities in the kingdom of Toro, the Bamba and Bakonjo peoples, who still clamored for separate administration.

The National Government

The framers of the Uganda independence constitution had been very representative of all the significant ethnic groups. The resulting constitution was designed not only to cater to them individually but to provide national unifying institutions that would hold the state together against centrifugal tendencies. The central government had therefore been endowed with sufficient—indeed, exclusive powers—over defense, internal security, and external affairs, most important finance matters such as currency and banking, the legal system and administration of justice (subject to relatively

16. For the detailed provisions for the constitutions of Ankole, Bunyoro, Toro, and Busoga, see Schedules 2–5 of the Uganda Independence Constitution, 1962; and see Schedule 8 to this constitution for their exclusive powers.

minor powers of Buganda customary courts), together with executive authority to enforce the Uganda constitution. It controlled and directed virtually all important spheres of economic and social development, including such fields as agriculture, animal husbandry, commerce and industry, education, health, and community development.[17]

But at the insistence of most framers of this independence compromise, certain provisions were entrenched in the constitution to safeguard, so far as was then possible, against excessive abuse of power by the national government. These general provisions were as strongly solicited by each group as its own local demands. Thus, the national legislature was restricted in the manner in which it could independently alter the Uganda constitution. For example, it could not legislate abolition of the option of indirect elections for Buganda's twenty-one representatives to the National Assembly; it could not alter the content of Buganda's executive authority; it could not vary provisions relating to the police forces of Buganda and Uganda; it was denied power to make alterations in the sources of Buganda's financial provisions; nor could it change the privileges of the Kabaka *unless* the legislative assembly of Buganda (Lukiko), by a resolution of not less than two-thirds of all its members, signified its consent that such an act of parliament touching on these matters should have effect in Buganda. The general provisions against adverse constitutional acts relating to the integrity of the other kingdoms were similar.[18]

To cater to every citizen, especially to those particular groups who were either too small or too dispersed to warrant a granting of separate powers, a detailed charter of human rights was embodied in the independence constitution guaranteeing basic freedoms for all.[19] A characteristic of these basic freedoms was that Uganda politics were multiparty on independence, each of the three parties enjoying solid support of some section of the country. To ensure against bad government, the diverse peoples were assured a constitutional right to vote in a periodic general election every five years to renew or to revoke the mandate of the postindependence governments. The independence of the juidiciary was assured.[20]

Finally, parliament could not alter the provisions of the constitution unless such amendment had been supported on second and third reading of

17. For the matters in which Parliament had exclusive powers to legislate, see Schedule 7, part 2, to the Uganda Independence Constitution. See also chapters 5 and 6 of this constitution.

18. See these sections of the Independence Constitution: 43, 77(2), 80, 81, 107(1), 124, 5(4).

19. Chapter 3 of the Uganda Independence Constitution.

20. Under chap. 9 of the Uganda Independence Constitution.

its bill by votes of not less than two-thirds of all members of the National Assembly. Only under such arrangements was it possible to secure the cooperation of all the heterogeneous nationals in accepting a shared destiny in a single state on independence. Undoubtedly, therefore, the diversity of ethnic groups and the consequent demands had been instrumental in determining the character of the final institutional legacy of British colonial rule.

The Colonial Bequest

The first five years of independence in Africa were characterized by a widespread repudiation of most of the political and institutional arrangements which the colonial rulers had evolved after 1946 and bequeathed to the new states on independence in the late fifties and early sixties. When the nationalist leaders refused to honor these arrangements, it was invariably on the alleged grounds that they protected, perpetuated, or encouraged centrifugal tendencies among different ethnic groups which threatened the unity of their young states. But pertinent questions persist with increasing urgency about these developments in the light of nearly two decades of independence for black African states. To what extent, for example, were the arrangements and compromises under which colonial rulers transferred power to African nationalists defective? In what ways were the alternatives imposed by independence leaders better suited to the realities of their heterogeneous states? What has happened in Uganda since independence is a typical illustration from which we may seek answers to these basic questions.

It is true that the colonial legacy had defects; but these were largely historical. The grave fundamental errors of colonialism had been committed not so much during the preparations and negotiations for the transfers of power in the 1950s and early 1960s but at the time of colonization, which had forcibly brought such diverse, sometimes incompatible, peoples together and then denied them meaningful participation in unifying economic activity and public service during the greater part of colonial rule. But the independence arrangements on the whole, in spirit if not always in letter, logically reflected the realities of this colonial history and the diversity of the peoples. Once the colonial power had clearly decided to disengage, it had presided over the final arrangements to transfer power with a relative impartiality which, regrettably, was never equaled, less still exceeded, by the nationalist leaders after they took power, despite much rhetoric to the contrary.

The UPC, under Prime Minister Milton Obote, could only form the independence government in coalition with the Buganda traditionalist party of Kabaka Yekka (KY). In the free and fair general elections that preceded independence, the UPC, though the largest single political group, had been outvoted by the combined supporters of KY and DP by nearly two to one. But within less than two years of independence Obote had dismissed KY from the alliance, having obtained a parliamentary majority through defections which did not necessarily reflect a swing in popular support. In February 1966 Obote, single-handedly and without any constitutional powers, suspended the Uganda constitution and usurped all the executive powers of the state. In April 1966, in a parliamentary session surrounded by armed troops, he formally abrogated the independence constitution and imposed a revolutionary one that parliament had neither read nor debated. Stunned and frightened by this overwhelming display of naked power, parliament rubber-stamped its approval.[21] Prime Minister Obote now declared himself the executive president of Uganda endowed with immense executive powers.

He argued that the constitutional arrangements bequeathed by the British "divided the country so much that there is no government that will ever be able to govern." The new revolutionary constitution, on the other hand, treated "Uganda as one united country . . . under one parliament, one government, one people." In 1967, a new Republican constitution was enacted, vesting Obote with practically absolute power to govern the state without any meaningful institutional safeguard against abuse of presidential powers. For example, a preventive detention law was enacted under which thousands of citizens from all walks of life could be, as they were, detained without trial on a mere allegation by the police and Obote's intelligence unit, called the General Service. The president was further given powers to legislate by statutory instrument, thus detracting from the authority of parliament, the most representative institution.[22] He could revoke and reform government departments and local administrations at will. He was vested with powers to appoint, promote, or dismiss all public officers of state. The Republican Constitution abolished kingdoms and all the concessions they had won, which were embodied in the independence constitution. To clinch this absolute power, no presidential action, however gravely wrong, could be questioned in a court of law.

The end result of this ruthless, monolithic concentration of power was the exact opposite of what Obote had hoped to achieve. Instead of becom-

21. Reported in *Uganda Parliamentary Debates*, vol. 59 (15 April 1966), p. 15. This was Obote's most authoritative statement of why he abrogated the Independence Constitution.

22. By Sec. 64 of the Republican Constitution, 1967.

ing more unified, the majority of the heterogeneous peoples became increasingly apprehensive about their security and survival: the repudiation of the independence constitution had been a unilateral abrogation of the only fundamental contract that had voluntarily brought all the nationals to independence in a single state. The Baganda, who had for so long sought to defend their identity, were now driven to revive the movement toward secession from the rest of the country, which Colonel Idi Amin, then a trusted army commander, crushed ruthlessly in May 1966, and which resulted in the loss of some thousands of largely innocent lives. The Kabaka, Mutesa II, fled and later died in exile in London. Other diverse groups, even those nominally represented in the UPC, felt cheated and threatened by this extreme concentration of power. General elections, which had promised citizens an avenue to control governments, were eliminated in practice though constantly paid lip service. Thus, in all of Obote's nine years of UPC government there was never a single parliamentary election. In a parliament of eighty-two elected members, as many as nineteen seats were vacant, several over many years as a result of deaths, resignations, or detentions. Yet, pressed as he was, Obote would never permit by-elections for fear his opponents might win. At the time of his overthrow, not only were principal leaders of the opposition, like the first prime minister Ben Kiwanuka, in detention without trial, but 50 percent of the cabinet on independence were in jail without trial, too—including Obote's cofounders of the UPC and leading nationalists.

Because many groups felt threatened and were denied recourse to any institutional redress, some now sought remedies outside the law. If the president could not be removed by a hostile vote in parliament or at the polls, then he had to be overthrown or eliminated by force, however hazardous the undertaking. Consequently, threats to Obote's security and regime rose in direct proportion to the increase of his monopoly of power. In 1969, immediately after the UPC meeting that banned other parties and imposed ill-understood economic measures, an attempt on his life made by the Baganda missed narrowly. He was shot in the mouth and a hand grenade thrown at him failed to explode. Scores of innocent people were shot at random by security men in the temporary chaos that followed.

Some Baganda elders now sought to outflank Obote by cultivating the friendship of his trusted army commander, Idi Amin, and having done so, by seeking to incite him to topple Obote, promising him massive popular support in return. The division that afflicted civilian political life inevitably invaded and affected the armed forces on which Obote, having lost popular political support, now largely depended. It is said by some that Amin overthrew him in January 1971 to save himself from Obote's disciplinary measures for embezzling army funds. This reason for the overthrow of Obote is as artificial as it is an oversimplification. At most, Amin's embezzlement was a catalyst. The country was already fundamentally destined for a revolution, because the majority of the population was not prepared to tolerate self-imposed autocratic rule indefinitely.

It is true that after independence the government of the Buganda kingdom had become difficult at times. But at no time, contrary to popular misconceptions, did the Buganda government defeat or frustrate any major policy of the UPC administration. In areas where they claimed excessive powers, such as more police strength or greater financial resources, the dispute was properly submitted to the high court for adjudication and the central government's preeminence was constitutionally upheld. Until it was dismissed from the coalition in August 1964, the Buganda KY party never voted against any important lawful UPC government measure. Public records attest to this. Indeed, in 1963 a joint committee to strengthen working relationships between the UPC national government and Buganda was set up by Obote and the kingdom's government. The author was a member representing the UPC on that committee and had been appointed by Obote. Yet when the committee made practical recommendations to eliminate intergovernmental frictions or misunderstandings, Obote simply ignored them, although the Baganda had accepted them. Secretly he had decided to acquire autocratic powers, by force if necessary; the fact that his impatience and lack of cooperation revived and promoted Buganda's primordial fears was immaterial. To Obote these revived fears, together with Buganda's well-known history of bids for secession, would provide the perfect cover and pretext for seizing absolute power; publicly he proclaimed the necessity for drastic measures to save the integrity of the state.

It is axiomatic that concessions to ethnic diversity, when carried too far, weakened the state and threatened it with disintegration. In principle, therefore, it was proper for independence leaders to resist those situations where any one group sought to disrupt the unity of the state. Yet, more often than not, when those diverse groups took recourse outside the law, thus threatening national unity, it was invariably because they had been unduly provoked and driven by an autocratic leader to do so, as the example of Uganda shows. Indeed, it is true that, generally speaking, the experience of many African states shows they were happier and more internally harmonious during the first few years of independence, when the basic compromises according to which independence had been granted were still operational. The origins of major domestic upheavals in most of these states can be directly traced to the efforts of the ruling government to repudiate or violate those compromises in a ruthless, winner-take-all manner.

It had been the belief of Obote, as it was of many other leaders, that once recognition of ethnic diversity was institutionally abolished and power was completely centralized, the concept of national unity among the diverse nationals would be enhanced, whereas ethnic consciousness would be correspondingly diminished. Yet the contrary was the case. In the first place, while he preached national unity and urged others to submerge their identities, the national leader was visibly relying on and promoting his ethnic kindred beyond what they were entitled to in the state. The result was that the other groups invariably became more acutely conscious of their own ethnic characteristics, feeling the need to emphasize how different they really were from those he trusted and favored. Consequently, among several of the nationalist and even the military leaders, there was a basic misunderstanding of the power and durability of the type of ethnic identity that had influenced the last decade of colonial rule.

When Idi Amin, as commander of the army, overthrew his former friend and collaborator Obote in January 1971 to establish a military regime, his subsequent conduct showed that he had learned little or nothing about the fundamental causes of Obote's fall, of which he was the immediate instrument.[23] Dramatic evidence of this was the fact that he believed the best way to meet the fears and demands of some ethnic groups was simply to liquidate those groups. Accordingly, he directed extensive massacres of Langi and Acholi, the two ethnic groups identified with the deposed president; indiscriminate official murder was visited on every other group that expressed apprehension about their future; and the Baganda, who could not forget that Amin had been Obote's willing tool to slaughter them in 1966, once more met with repression and insecurity.

Idi Amin became absolute ruler, whose word was literally law, and more power emanated from him than had ever come from Obote. Yet, this excessive centralization and attendant constant appeals for unity merely divided Ugandans more than they had ever been, as they thought more about the security and identity of their respective groups. This reaction was heightened by the glaring fact that the head of state was brutally and shamelessly establishing a hegemony over the country on the basis of his

23. For instructive accounts of the nature of the Amin regime, see the following three books: David Martin, *General Amin* (London, 1974); Thomas and Margaret Melady, *Idi Amin Dada, Hitler in Africa* (Kansas City, Mo., 1977); Henry Kyemba, *A State of Blood* (London, 1977); and G. S. K. Ibingira, *African Upheavals since Independence* (Boulder, Colo., 1980), chap. 12.

ethnic group (aided by religion), which comprised less than 1 percent of the national population. Amin then proceeded to declare himself president for life and therefore irremovable by peaceful means. Predictably, several attempts were made from within his own army to overthrow him. When Tanzania waged war against him for having invaded its territory, the majority of his troops refused to fight, being keenly aware of how detested he had become. So Amin was overthrown in April 1979. In both the civilian and the military governments that have led Uganda since independence, therefore, there has been an appalling failure to understand accurately the strength and persistence of ethnic consciousness and how to deal with it in such a way as to mold a common destiny for the heterogeneous peoples.

A study of the history of older nations reveals the durable nature of this phenomenon of ethnicity. For example, after more than 100 years of common nationhood between the English- and French-speaking peoples of Canada, the French community's bid to become a separate nation is at its strongest today. In Belgium, the survival of Walloons and Flemings as distinct peoples after more than a century and a half of common citizenship is well known. In Great Britain, where the English, Scots, and Welsh have shared a rich and common experience for three centuries, the Scottish and Welsh demands for local autonomy are as strong and persistent as they ever were. In all these countries the answer to ethnic diversity has not been attempts to legislate or shoot groups out of existence. It has been, rather, to promote measures of fair play and equal treatment in order to give each group a sense of shared belonging and common destiny. It is significant that even among monolithic powers like the Soviet Union and Yugoslavia sound policy recognized the necessity to come to terms with the power and fundamental nature of ethnicity. For this reason, both those Communist nations have federal constitutions permitting particular groups some autonomy in matters that are peculiarly their own, without compromising the integrity of the nation as a whole.

One can therefore draw the conclusion, for Uganda in particular and for many African states in general, that neither a stroke of the pen nor expanded repressive security forces are likely to provide desirable lasting solutions to meet the problems, demands, and needs of the ethnic diversity with which the last phase of British colonial rule tried to come to terms in Africa. This is all the more true because ethnicity, and the identity it confers, date from time immemorial, or are so regarded by particular groups, while the state structures in which nationals were gathered by colonial rule are of relatively recent origin and have at times been discredited by the repressive autocracy of some rulers. Those who have sought absolute power have often persuasively argued that it is precisely because ethnic identity is such a deep-rooted, divisive characteristic that it threatens the very foundations of the state if it is not curbed or eliminated by strong-arm measures. The refutation of this lies in the postindependence African experience of many states, which has overwhelmingly demonstrated that to seek to suppress fundamental characteristics like ethnicity is no less threatening to the state. The effort at the national level, therefore, should be a perpetual quest to balance the interests of the whole with those of the parts in the hope of attaining a measure of workable relationships devoted to securing a relatively harmonious, united country.

In retrospect, then, one can further conclude that the political and institutional arrangements through which the British transferred power to Ugandans had, to a large extent, been designed to ensure national harmony by bequeathing to most groups a sense of security and a place for their identity in the new state. But these arrangements collapsed for two main reasons. First, they had been devised so late that the diverse nationals had little time to operate them themselves and to adjust to their checks and balances under the objective eye of an impartial overseer. Second, with so little experience and legitimacy behind them, the new institutions and political framework could not withstand a postcolonial regime bent on seizing power—absolute power—at all costs, when the compromises precluded it. It is important to state again that the basic cause of the collapse was not attributable to an inherent unsuitability for holding heterogeneous peoples together in relative peace. Whatever shortcomings these arrangements had, they were a very small price to pay for the prized goal of national harmony and relative stability for which the country now so deeply yearns, and without which any talk about economic and social progress by the incumbent government is hollow and meaningless.

12. *Precipitous Decolonization: The Case of The Belgian Congo*

JEAN STENGERS

In July 1955 a Belgian figure of the first rank in the world of journalism and letters, Louis Dumont-Wilden, presented a paper to the Académie des Sciences Morales et Politiques at Paris, of which he was a member. It was entitled "Une réussite coloniale: le Congo Belge."[1] Dumont-Wilden wrote, "The Belgian Congo is the most prosperous and tranquil of colonies, the one whose evolution is the most peaceful and normal." This was the unanimous judgment of that time: the Congo, with its firmly established colonial regime, where no significant political reform was contemplated in the near future, and where the Africans were apparently not demanding any change in the regime, seemed to be a calm and happy land.

In January 1959 the Belgian government announced the first measures that were to lead to decolonization. Hardly had these measures taken shape when, in December 1959, Belgium promised the Congo its independence the following year. On June 30, 1960, independence was proclaimed.

This brief chronological reminder permits us to perceive the two essential problems presented by the Congo case: why was there, for so long a time, such complete political stagnation without the slightest augury of decolonization; why, then, an emergency decolonization of such stupefying rapidity?

In studying the former problem, one must above all examine the decade 1946–55.

These ten postwar years were, for the Congo, a period of intense economic development. All the economic indicators were triumphal.[2] The volume of mining production—the backbone of the country's development—increased by more than 60 percent in ten years. Copper output went from 144,000 to 235,000 tons. Industrial growth was even

1. *Revue des Travaux de l'Académie des Sciences Morales et Politiques*, 2d semester, 1955, pp. 12 ff.

2. See particularly "Dix années d'expansion économique au Congo belge, 1946–1955," in *Bulletin Mensuel de la Banque du Congo Belge*, February 1957; and *La Situation économique du Congo belge et du Ruanda-Urundi en 1955* (Brussels: Ministry of Colonies, 1956), passim.

more impressive: the volume of industrial production tripled between 1947–49 and 1955. Energy produced by hydroelectric generators quadrupled. External trade exhibited the same rise: the value of exports moved from an index of 100 to 388, and the value of imports from 100 to 553.

An attempt has been made to compute the change in national income. It is well known how risky such calculations are, particularly for countries with a high proportion of subsistence economy.[3] They nevertheless shed some light on the order of magnitude of growth. Between 1950 and 1955, it has been found that national income rose from 29 to 47 billion francs.[4]

To what extent did this economic development respectively benefit Europeans—both businesses and individuals—and Africans? The calculation here is still riskier. In any case, it can be stated that the Africans benefited handsomely. Doubtless, however, the gulf between their income and that of the Europeans remained enormous. In 1955 the total volume of remuneration of Congolese employees—more than a million persons—barely exceeded the overall volume of the expatriate Europeans' salaries—some 20,000 persons. The ratio between the average wage of a black and of a European was in the order of 1 to 40. (This is, of course, an average, with all the distortion of reality involved in any average: it does not, for example, permit us to estimate the great difference between the wage of a black clerk in the city and that of a laborer on a plantation.) While the gap remained exceedingly wide, the black was nevertheless making progress; his income, and consequently his standard of living, were rising considerably.

Efforts by the government and the companies in the social domain, along with efforts throughout the colony in the medical and public health field, also had definite, and sometimes spectacular, repercussions on the condition of a large part of the Congolese population.

All this represents movement—and progress—from the economic and social standpoint. It is therefore all the more striking to turn one's attention to other areas where all was stagnating, or changing very slowly. Slowness in the training of an African intellectual elite, the even greater slowness in the training of black leaders, the total absence of planning—even of simple foresight—with respect to decolonization, the silence of the blacks, who

3. See particularly P. Leurquin and L. Baeck, "Revenu national et économie dualiste," *Zaïre*, April 1956, pp. 339–50.

4. "Produit national, revenu national et dépenses nationales au Congo belge en 1955," *Bulletin de la Banque Centrale du Congo belge et du Ruanda-Urundi*, October, 1956; see also C. Carbonelle, "L'Evolution du revenu national du Congo de 1950 à 1955," *Belgique d'Outremer*, February 1957.

demanded nothing along that line: all these factors were, on the surface, ill-assorted companions of development. I shall review these various elements one by one.

The first, which generally conditioned the rest, was the delay in training intellectual elites—a delay that placed the Congo behind other countries with comparable economic development. One statistic sums up the essence of the problem: at the time of independence, in 1960, the Congo had only sixteen university graduates in any field. Among these sixteen there was not a single doctor of law, not one engineer, nor one physician. The first Congolese to obtain a university degree was Thomas Kanza, who took a "licence" in psychological science at the University of Louvain in 1956.[5]

During these years, as yet marked by political calm, two universities were nevertheless founded in the Congo: the Catholic University of Lovanium, near Leopoldville, in 1954, and the National University at Elizabethville in 1956. At first, however, they had only a small number of Congolese students, considering the size of the country. In 1956–57 there were still fewer than one hundred at Lovanium.

Why this scarcity? It is easy to trace its immediate cause: the dearth of classical secondary education and instruction in the humanities that normally leads to the university. For a long time such education, for the Congolese, simply did not exist. The postprimary studies available to blacks were merely vocational (often, indeed, excellent: good clerks and mechanics were produced and, at a higher level, even good medical and agricultural assistants) or else junior, and later senior, seminary studies. Among the postindependence leaders there were several who had had to "pretend to want to become priests" in order to attend junior seminaries—the only secondary-level studies accessible to them. But neither such studies nor vocational training led to the university.

This phenomenon (the lack of classical secondary education, which meant that there were no university candidates) had its root in a very simple fact: the educational sector had long been left to the missions.

The missions—both Catholic and Protestant, but with a Catholic majority—enjoyed a virtually absolute monopoly in the field of education until 1946. All schools in the Congo were either mission schools or schools staffed by missionaries. The first breach in this monopoly, opened in 1946,

5. See his autobiographical work, *Conflict in the Congo* (Harmondsworth, 1972). Note, however, that in 1947 an unrecognized mulatto, Brother Clement-Maria da Souza, had entered the Congregation des Frères des Ecoles Chrétiennes and completed studies in pedagogical science at the University of Louvain.

was only a limited one: a liberal Minister of Colonies, Godding, then created the first secular schools; but these were intended for Europeans.[6] It was not until 1954, with the arrival of another liberal, Auguste Buisseret, at the Ministry of Colonies, that a decisive turning point was reached: Buisseret established official secular education for blacks, and it rapidly achieved a substantial expansion.

So long as they were permitted freedom of action—enjoying, it must be emphasized, large government subsidies—the missionaries followed a policy of which the priorities quite naturally coincided with their own role and vocation.[7] Their first priority was to make education an instrument for the evangelization of the masses. This implied the development of primary education, and in fact it was in this direction that the major missionary effort was exerted. It was, at least statistically, a successful one. In 1955 it was announced that 10 percent of the Congo's population was attending school, while the percentage was only 7 percent in Ghana, 6 percent in India, and 3 percent in the French Equatorial African territories. Even if these figures were not completely convincing—they said nothing, for example, of the frequent mediocrity of instruction by native monitors—they demonstrated that the missionaries had in fact played their missionary role well in this field: they had carried the Gospel to the masses. On the eve of independence, one may consider that about 40 percent of the population belonged to Christian communities; of these, approximately four-fifths were Catholics, one-fifth, Protestants.

The missionaries' second priority was to train an African clergy—hence the proliferation of junior and senior seminaries. In 1948 there were already twenty-four junior seminaries in the Congo. As stated above, the first Congolese university graduate took his degree in 1956. But the first Congolese priest had been ordained nearly forty years before, in 1917. In 1956, when Thomas Kanza was the only individual in the category of university graduates, the African clergy had already reached the episcopal stage: the first Congolese bishop was consecrated in that year, at Kisantu. Upon

6. Beginning in 1950, a few blacks were, however, admitted to establishments intended for Europeans. But the admissions were of eye-drop size; in all the institutions in the Congo in 1953 there were as yet only 21 black students; in 1954 their number had risen to 75. *Rapport sur l'administration de la colonie du Congo belge pendant l'année 1953 presenté aux Chambres législatives* (Brussels, 1954), p. 135; report for 1954 in same series, p. 132.

7. Until shortly after the Second World War the educational subsidies were limited to "national missions," which were substantially identical to the Catholic missions. The Protestant missions, which with one or two exceptions were considered "foreign missions," were not subsidized. This policy was altered in 1946 by Minister Godding, who extended the subsidies to all the missions.

independence, in 1960, there were already more than six hundred Congolese priests.

The missionaries had yet a third duty: since the state granted them a monopoly, they were obligated to train the subordinate cadres which the state, and also the private sector, required. This was the role of vocational training.[8]

Primary education for the masses, seminary education at both junior and senior levels, and vocational education: once these great efforts were taken care of, the missionaries had hardly any additional resources—particularly human resources, since the number of teachers in their ranks had limits—to think seriously of classical, secondary education (except for Europeans). From their missionary (which is to say, religious) point of view, this was not a priority in any case; they therefore neglected it almost completely.

Nothing in the mentality of the colonial communities among which they lived, moreover, was of a nature to arouse their zeal in this regard. The classical colonist is most often quite hostile to "bookish" education for blacks, as he thinks that such education can only spoil them. To describe this mentality, the principle of "no elites, no troubles" is today frequently used. However, this formula, which was invented in 1960 (one does not find it earlier in Belgian colonial history) by critics of what they thought was Belgian policy, is not true to psychological reality. The formula's "no troubles" appears to mean "no political troubles." But at the time they were denouncing the dangers of book-learning, the Belgian colonials were thinking very little of the political aspect of the problem. The colonial order seemed so stable, so assured of the future, such a solid rock, that to speak of political dangers was to raise a virtually unreal hypothesis. The idea that the black was a big child, often a nuisance like all children, and that a type of education for which he was unsuited would make him a still greater nuisance by uprooting him and making him vain, runs like a leitmotiv among the colonials. This was stated, and incessantly repeated, in the Congo; the missionaries were not immune to the psychological contagion.

The first to break away from this mentality was the small group of Catholics who conceived and founded the University of Lovanium, and

8. Here we include in vocational training a number of schools which, while not placed officially in this category, were in fact primarily vocational training establishments. This, for example, was the case with the "écoles moyennes," whose purpose was defined as follows: "The 'école moyenne' is expected to provide instruction capable of ensuring to the students a satisfactory general education and effective preparation for occupying positions as junior employees in government offices." Belgian Congo, Service de l'Enseignement, *Organisation de l'enseignement libre subsidié pour indigènes avec le concours des sociétés de missions chrétiennes: Dispositions générales* (1948), p. 17.

they founded it in response to an ideal, not a need, since Africans capable of entering a university were extremely few. These men of faith—of faith in sharing the noblest intellectual values with the African—were at first quite isolated. Eminent university professors, notably those belonging to leftist circles, warned them against what they considered a dangerous illusion. "Any serious thought of creating universities for blacks in the Congo," one of them wrote in 1950, "will encounter insuperable obstacles. . . . University education requires an intellectual, moral, and social preparation that is far from being attained in the Belgian Congo." It could only be a "counterfeit" university.[9] Another such academe, also judging university education "premature," insisted particularly upon the impossibility of organizing medical studies. Training a physician, he wrote, requires "a body of abstract knowledge as yet inaccessible to the mind of the black, who has hardly yet emerged from a primitive civilization."[10]

The colonial administration was equally reticent, even hostile. Insofar as it finally became reconciled to Lovanium, and even supported it, it was because the administration perceived the university as a way to avert a political peril it feared above all others. The worst thing, in its eyes, would be to allow Congolese students to attend universities in Europe: the French and British examples demonstrated that there they would become dangerous revolutionaries. To forestall this risk,[11] it was better and wiser to create universities in the Congo itself, sheltered from extremist contagion. Thus, to the extent that it supported Lovanium, the administration calculated that the device of a Congolese university would prevent the growth of aspirations to be decolonized. That this calculation was mistaken—the

9. Paul Brien, "Quelques considérations sur l'orientation de l'enseignement aux indigènes," in the work *L'Enseignement à dispenser aux indigènes dans les territoires non autonomes: Colloque international organisé . . . en 1950* (Brussels, 1951), pp. 47–48. Brien, who had been a Communist senator in 1936 but later left the Communist party, was an eminent zoologist and biologist, and a professor at the University of Brussels.

10. Maurice Robert, *Contribution à la géographie du Katanga: Essai de sociologie* (Brussels, 1954), p. 95. Robert, a highly reputed geographer and geologist, was also a professor at the University of Brussels.

11. This fear was also expressed in Belgium by specialists in colonial matters. At a Social-Christian political meeting in Brussels in February 1956, Count d'Aspremont Lynden (who was to become Minister of African Affairs in 1960) exclaimed: "What will two blacks studying law in Brussels do when they return to the Congo? They will become agitators and troublemakers!" (*Le Soir*, Feb. 18, 1956: "Le P.S.C. d'Ixelles celèbre son 10e anniversaire"). The two students at the University of Brussels referred to by the speaker were Isidore Rwubusisi and Justin Bomboko. Only the former, as a matter of fact, was studying law. Justin Bomboko, who was to play a prominent political role after the Congo's independence, was studying policitcal science.

Africans who graduated from Lovanium proved to be perfectly good nationalists—is another story; it is the intention that is of concern here.

In the context of intellectual elites, the scarcity of university graduates and even, at a lower level, of holders of classical secondary-school diplomas must be stressed. This does not imply that a true elite can be defined simply in terms of diplomas. Patrice Lumumba, who had studied only nursing and was trained in postal work, was nevertheless an intellectual force. But among those who were called *évolués,* and who constituted the best-educated stratum above the mass of the people, there were, after all, few intellectuals of stature. Intrinsically first-rate men, furthermore, had little opportunity to demonstrate their ability: like others, they were restricted to subordinate functions. The European, in the 1950s, remained convinced that his political dominance corresponded to an overwhelming intellectual superiority. This gave him a quiet conscience. In his eyes it justified the fact that he still ruled the country practically by himself.

This leads to the second aspect of delay which, in a way that at first blush appears bizarre, economic and social development failed to extenuate—namely, the extreme slowness with which blacks were acceding to responsible posts and the slow training of black leaders. If one examines the administration, the army, and political organs during the years 1946–55, the findings are practically identical.

The administration. The three highest grades in the administration included not one Congolese. No Congolese held a higher rank than *agent auxiliaire.* This situation did not change until the second half of 1959. Then, through anxiety to "africanize" the civil service, two Congolese were named to the second highest grade, with the rank of *sous-directeur,* and four to the third grade, with the rank of *sous-chef de bureau.*[12] This placed six Congolese in the superior grades, as compared to more than 4,500 Europeans. In 1960, at the time of independence, the figures remained almost as low.

If Congolese were not promoted to any high-ranking post before 1959, it was for a very simple reason: they did not possess the requisite diplomas. To act in their favor in this respect would have been, in the eyes of the colonial authority, to engage in reverse discrimination, and so was out of the question. It would simply await the day when diploma-holders were at hand.

The Force Publique. The Congolese army (Force Publique) exhibited

12. V. Bindo-Albi, *L'Attitude politique des agents africains du secteur public avant l'indépendance du Congo* (University of Brussels: Mémoire de licence en sciences politiques, 1965), p. 90.

the same spectacle: in the upper echelons—at a time when the rank and file were all black—there was not a single African. About one thousand European officers and warrant officers commanded some twenty thousand black soldiers and noncommissioned officers. Here, too, there was no question of violating rules based on predetermined qualifications of Europeans and blacks, respectively.

African participation in political organs. Leaving aside the customary authorities, who above all were a part of the administrative mechanism and played no political role properly speaking, the balance sheet was quite short: a handful of Africans were appointed to the Conseil de Gouvernement and to the various Conseils de Province, purely consultative councils, where they were a small minority and played a minor role. That was all. It should, however, be added that one small reform was being blueprinted: a municipal statute was under discussion which would permit representatives of the residents of the large urban centers, both Europeans and Africans, to participate in governing the cities. The draft statute was published in 1948. It encountered difficulties—particularly because it raised the question of the respective weight to be assigned to Africans and Europeans—and the discussion of drafts and counterdrafts was not completed until 1957. The municipal statute's gestation thus lasted nine years.[13]

How can so completely negative a balance sheet in the political domain be explained? One cannot point to the obstacle of higher education, as in the case of the administration: diplomas were never required for politics. In the event, the lack of movement resulted from factors of force. The force of the Africans—their weight, so to speak—consisted in the legitimacy of their future rights: all leaders of Belgian politics recognized that in the democracy which would be gradually constructed in the Congo, democratic logic demanded that the blacks should, little by little, occupy the principal position. While awaiting the culmination of this evolution in the distant—very distant—future, however, they were not asking for anything; until 1955 no African political demand was to be heard. If it was possible to debate the municipal statute so leisurely and at such length, it was precisely because there was no pressure from the Africans to put it into operation.

While the Africans were holding their tongues, the Congo's white colonists, by contrast, were speaking: they were demanding political rights and participation in the country's government. The principal argument

13. Cf. M. de Schrevel, *Les Forces politiques de la décolonisation congolaise jusqu'à la veille de l'indépendance* (Louvain, 1970), pp. 375–91.

they advanced—and it was one which, objectively, was not without relevance—was that they possessed both the experience and the abilities needed to fulfill a political role. The blacks, they said, still lacked these qualities. The colonial authorities very firmly refused to accede to the colonists' requests; they did not wish to compromise the blacks' future rights by granting privileges to the whites. But how could they accelerate the political process for the blacks' benefit? To do so would be to place in the least capable hands something the blacks were not even asking for, while denying it to the most capable, who assuredly were asking for it. The situation was quite impossible.

To put it another way: a policy that foresaw future black demands, and gave political responsibilities to a certain number of them—who could be none other than the évolués—would have become conceivable only if dictated by a doctrine inspired by a vision of the emancipation of the Congolese people. But the most enlightened and liberal-minded theoreticians, in Belgium as well as in the Congo, were upholding a completely opposite doctrine; they regarded it dangerous, if a genuine democracy were to be built, to create a political class detached from the people before the masses were politically mature, because such a class might well abuse its powers and pave the way, not for democracy, but for domination by an oligarchy.

The vision of liberal minds was that of progressive political development through which the masses would be educated simultaneously with the training of leaders. Listen to Governor General Pétillon, speaking in 1956 to the Conseil de Gouvernement. "There is no real democracy," he said, "without two basic elements: first, a population capable of knowing wisely what it wants and, in this knowledge, organized in such a way that it can ascertain whether its leaders are carrying out its will correctly; second, elites capable of governing, that is, of enlightening the population respecting the country's higher interests and of implementing the policy chosen by the population." Political education of the people is thus indispensable if they are to fulfill their indispensable function of surveillance,[14] and that is obviously a long-range task. It must be approached by starting at the base—hence an initiative such as the municipal statute.

The prospect that political construction would be slow and long, even very long, did not worry the shapers of colonial policy; Belgium, they thought, had plenty of time before her in the Congo. This calm conviction was shared by all. Almost no voice was raised to question it before 1955. Congolese voices, to the extent they were heard, uttered no discordant

14. *Discours du Gouverneur General L. Pétillon* (Belgian Congo: Conseil de Gouvernement, 1956), p. 12.

sound. One évolué wrote in 1950: "We subjects of Belgium know and understand that it will require sixty or one hundred years, or more, before we shall be ready to be left to ourselves."[15] In 1956, again, even Patrice Lumumba was still asserting in a book he wrote at that time: "The day when the Congo has its own technicians in all fields, its doctors, agronomists, engineers, entrepreneurs, geologists, administrators, foremen, skilled workers . . . social workers, nurses, midwives: only then must we speak of independence and self-government, for then we shall be intellectually, technically, and materially strong enough to rule ourselves, should this be necessary." Therefore, Lumumba adds, only the future will tell when the Congo will attain "the more advanced degree of civilization and the required political maturity" that would permit it to be "raised to the ranks of self-governing peoples."[16] How could the Belgians doubt their conviction, when to all appearances it was shared by the Africans themselves? Political evolution would indeed require a great deal of time.

In these circumstances the colonial regime felt no need to hurry and was, furthermore, very little concerned with drawing up plans for the future. There was no question of planning for political emancipation, even in the mid-term. Governor General Pétillon, in his speeches, did outline a few attitudes—which in itself placed him in an avant-garde position—but these were after all simply attitudes, and his views were met with much indifference.[17] At the Ministry of Colonies in Brussels there was nothing. When M. Pétillon himself became Minister in 1958, he discovered that "nothing,

15. Antoine-Roger Bolamba, "Les Convoitises coloniales," *La Voix du Congolais*, February 1950, p. 64. On Bolamba, who was editor-in-chief of *La Voix du Congolais*, see P. Artigue, *Qui sont les leaders congolais?*, 2d ed. (Brussels, 1961), pp. 42–43.

16. Patrice Lumumba, *Le Congo, terre d'avenir, est-il menacé?* (Brussels, 1961), pp. 168, 205–06. On the conditions under which this book was written, see P. Salmon, "Une Correspondance en partie inédite de Patrice Lumumba," *Bulletin de l'Académie Royale des Sciences d'Outre-Mer*, 1974, pp. 359–68. On the question of Lumumba's sincerity in this work, see particularly the comments of R. Anstey in "Belgian Rule in the Congo and the Aspirations of the Evolué class," in P. Duignan and L. H. Gann, eds., *Colonialism in Africa, 1870–1960* (Cambridge, 1970), 2:215.

17. See L. A. M. Pétillon, *Témoignage et réflexions* (Brussels, 1967), pp. 139 ff; de Schrevel, *Les Forces politiques*, pp. 262 ff. M. Pétillon himself spoke to me of the lack of effect his statements had produced on the Congo's political orientation. "Even my provincial governors," he told me, "who were my closest collaborators, paid them little attention." In the same vein, one may cite the remarks of M. Van Bilsen in 1955, upon his return from a trip to the Congo: "With few exceptions," he said, "I met no white who was thinking about the political problem. I would even admit that it takes some courage to raise this question with them, for the most affable look upon you as a sort of complex-ridden armchair strategist, others as a meddling, dangerous progressive who could at any moment change into an agitator if you don't watch out." A. A. J. Van Bilsen, *Vers l'indépendance du Congo et du Ruanda-Urundi* (Brussels, 1958), p. 58.

not a single proposal, however minute" existed in his ministry concerning the basic future of the Congo.[18] In university circles, a few general ideas and proposals were occasionally discussed,[19] but they did not go beyond academic debate.

All this, in retrospect, may give an impression of lack of understanding. Were the Belgians so myopic that they did not see what was going on elsewhere in the world? Were they blind? Had they not observed the liberation movement that had swept all the European colonies in Asia? Were they unaware of the ferment in North Africa and the evolution underway in the British West African colonies?

The paradoxical fact is that the spectacle of unrest in the colonial world was one reason for the Belgians' confidence. Amid these strirrings, the Congo remained perfectly calm and tranquil: was that not proof that it constituted a genuine oasis? The Belgians did not hesitate to think so, since, collectively, they possessed an enormous superiority complex. They were convinced, as they themselves often said, that they had "found the right formula"—that is, a formula that guaranteed them against the miscalculations other colonizing countries had made. It consisted in improving the native's material condition to the point where he would not dream of the right to vote. That was the "formula": Keep the natives happy by looking after their welfare, their housing, and their health.[20] Look, it was said, at the broad smile on the faces of the Congolese; these are satisfied people, and because they are satisfied they will not permit themselves to be contaminated by the virus of nationalist demands. This Congolese smile—which in fact really did exist—had, for the Belgians, great psychological importance, however puerile it may appear: it gave them confidence in the success of their colonial rule.[21]

18. L. Pétillon, "Réponse à l'étude du comte de Briey sur la fin du Congo belge," *Civilisations*, 1968, p. 606.

19. See especially *Compte rendu des Journées interuniversitaires d'études coloniales organisées à l'Université Libre de Bruxelles les 29–30 decembre 1952* (Brussels, n.d.). See also these other studies: A. Sohier, G. Malengreau, and A. Morzorati, in *Problèmes d'Afrique Centrale*, 3d quarter 1951, pp. 172–74, 4th quarter 1951, pp. 269–78, and 4th quarter 1952, pp. 264–68; A. Rubbens, "Une organisation politique pour le Congo belge," *Revue Nouvelle*, June 15, 1952.

20. See, for example, a good definition of the "formula" in P. Deschamps, "L'Education démocratique d'un peuple," *Revue Générale Belge*, March 15, 1955, p. 777. Mr. Ronald Robinson has quite rightly emphasized that this concept was peculiar to the Belgians; the British, on the other hand, never believed that improvement of their material well-being would keep the Africans out of politics. Interview with Robinson in *Itinerario. Bulletin of the Leyden Centre for the History of European Expansion*, no. 1 (1977), p. 23.

21. One typical article: J. M. Domont, "Au Congo, le sourire des indigènes reflète le succès d'une politique sociale," *Problèmes d'Afrique Centrale*, 2d quarter 1955, pp. 95–103.

A further reassurance for the Belgians until 1955–56 was the fact, already mentioned but which must be reiterated and stressed, that the Congolese made no political demands on them. Nevertheless, the former were not, in these postwar years, silent, inert creatures. Quite a number of évolués made known their aspirations, their demands, and even their grievances. They expressed their views in a publication specially directed at them, the *Voix du Congolais,*[22] and also in the trade-union journals. Here one finds evidence of their preoccupations: they raised questions of wages, housing conditions, the conduct of education, the various forms of racial discrimination or even racial contempt, of which they had reason to complain; and they also wrote of the status they hoped to attain as évolués.[23] In the political field there was nothing, except the modest desire to achieve more substantial Congolese representation in the consultative councils. Nowhere appeared a political demand worthy of the name. In 1955, when King Baudouin undertook a visit to the Congo which proved a triumphal one—he was everywhere applauded by the Congolese in a virtually delirious fashion—he was accompanied by a caravan of journalists who took the occasion to question the Congolese about their aspirations. The complaints and demands they gleaned were still focused on the same objectives: wages, housing, racial discrimination, and so on. In the political field, nothing was voiced as yet.

Must one conclude that the évolués, and the Congolese population in general, accepted colonial domination as a fact without reacting against it? When one states such a conclusion today, it arouses the shocked indignation of all young Zaïrian intellectuals. In the eyes of contemporary Zaïrians two facts are beyond question, and have virtually the value of dogma: their fathers, they believe, never resigned themselves to submission; if they suffered so long in silence without raising their voices it was because they were paralyzed by the colonial system, which permitted them no political liberty.

22. On this publication, which appeared from 1945 to 1959, see D. Mpinda, "L'Analyse du contenu de *La Voix du Congolais,* 1945–1959," *Cahiers Congolais de la Recherche et du Développement,* Aug.-Sept. 1970, pp. 46–70; P. Ngandu Nkashama, "*La Voix du Congolais* et la prise de conscience des évolués," *Lectures africaines. Bulletin du CELRIA. Université Nationale du Zaïre* (Lubumbashi, 1972–73), 1:4–23; Eloko a Nongo Otshudiema, *Les Structures inconscientes de La Voix du Congolais, Cahiers du CEDAF,* nos. 2 and 3 (Brussels, 1975). Since the latter review was a publication of the Service d'Information du Gouvernement General, one must bear in mind that the freedom of expression of its contributors was circumscribed; on this point, see R. Anstey, "Belgian Rule in the Congo," p. 200, n. 1.

23. Cf. M. de Schrevel, *Les Forces politiques,* pp. 71–75, 95, 221 ff.; P. Demunter, *Luttes politiques au Zaïre: Le processus de politisation des masses rurales du Bas-Zaïre* (Paris, 1975), pp. 175–77.

This retrospective vision of the past on the part of a young nationalism is quite natural. It is nevertheless contrary to all that emerges from critical, calm examination of the testimony and the facts. Except among groups of limited size, such as the adherents of the Kitawala, the notion of the white man's superiority, and therefore of the legitimacy—or in any event the inevitability—of his dominance, had thoroughly permeated the minds of the Congolese and become a part of their mental universe. Fear, moreover, does not appear to have been the only obstacle, nor doubtless the major one, that deterred them from expressing their political aspirations for the future.

Beyond doubt, fear played its part for a long time, and long contributed to maintaining a silence that one may indeed describe as timorous. As a matter of fact, it was fear less of the gendarme than of the reaction of white society, whose crushing weight the blacks felt constantly. A contributor to *La Voix du Congolais* wrote in 1952: "Less than ten years ago, no black in the Belgian Congo would have dared to say exactly what he thought in his heart of hearts without incurring threats or contempt on the part of the whites. It was only after the establishment of *La Voix du Congolais* that the era of public complaint by Africans began. There are still some who dare not express their complaints, or do so insincerely, in a veiled manner."[24] When the complaints were against constituted authority, one may speak more confidently of fear of the gendarme. Patrice Lumumba wrote in 1956:

> It was not so long ago that every Congolese was imbued with the idea that the smallest disrespectful protest against the authorities would be punished. Even when a Congolese wished to call attention to unusual conduct by a junior government official, or to any other irregular situation, he often did not dare to do it. Even supposing that he wished to point out such a situation in the press, he often went no further than to write anonymously; all the journalists knew this, as they had received articles from Congolese recounting true facts, but unsigned. This anonymity was, and is, resorted to because of that fear, even by senior *évolués.*"[25]

When one turns to the years immediately preceding 1955–56, however, one may say that there were, in addition to overbearing authority and contemptuous whites, numerous men who were listening to Africa with sincerity and generosity. There was more than one European in whom the Congolese could confide and to whom they could, without fear, make

24. *La Voix du Congolais*, October 1952, p. 629.
25. Lumumba, *Le Congo, terre d'avenir*, p. 189.

known their aspirations; but the Congolese did not speak of political problems. A man such as M. Guy Malengreau, linchpin of the University of Lovanium, was at the center of a network of contacts permitting them to take the pulse of African society. Dealing at the end of 1952 with the problem of "native participation in political life," he pointed out that he was raising a question "to which those affected by it seem to be giving no attention."[26]

In addition to the possible inhibition due to fear, therefore, there were certainly other elements that can explain the prolonged political lethargy of the Congolese. There appear to be four essential factors.

First of all, was the question of intellectual training. The necessary compost in which political aspirations grow was long absent—namely, political thought itself. Political thought demands a certain conceptualization of political phenomena and a certain ability to use abstract notions and to reason from them; these were all things for which the Africans' education had in no way prepared them. The running of the state long seemed to them to be the Europeans' secret, just as curing illness was the doctor's. Over them were men who knew, whereas they felt they did not know. And so they kept silent.

Africans were all the less inclined to involve themselves in affairs of which the Belgians held the secret, or simply to ask to participate, because (and this is a second psychological factor) they had been taught that they owed everything to the Belgians. On this subject they had undergone an indoctrination that was tantamount to intellectual bludgeoning, and the indoctrination bore fruit. Take, for example, an article of 1949 in *La Voix du Congolais* by a rather well-known évolué, Antoine Omari, who was to become president of the Congolese Association of Friends of the Red Cross and to play a certain political role at the moment of independence.[27] It is an extraordinary text. Omari describes the abysses into which the Congolese were plunged before the whites' arrival:

> Idolatry and superstition governed all. Ignorance was hereditary. Hygiene was unknown. Epidemics were rife. Cannibalism was of daily occurrence. Undernourishment, due to unproductive methods of cultivation, was the lot of several regions. There were only footpaths to serve as communications routes. While the existence of some good customs must be recognized, it is appropriate to acknowledge that there was no

26. *Compte rendu des Journées interuniversitaires*, p. 23.

27. On Antoine Omari, see *Avenir Colonial Belge*, Sept. 9, 1953; *Courrier d'Afrique*, Oct. 9, 1953; Crawford Young, *Politics in the Congo: Decolonization and Independence* (Princeton, 1965), pp. 82, 404–05; B. Verhaegen, *Rébellions au Congo*, vol. 2 (Brussels, n.d.)

> rational law; this gave rise to innumerable conflicts and interminable internecine wars. . . . In short, we were a backward people, overwhelmed by all the evils of nature and remote from world civilization.

Thereupon, the Belgians came and everything changed. Omari enumerates their admirable accomplishments. As a concluding anthem he chants: "Belgium, to Thee all our gratitude, in Thee our unshakable confidence. We owe our all to Thee, thy tenth province through colonization."[28]

One must obviously allow for the element of flattery toward the master in such a text. But Omari doubtless believed a large part of what he wrote; from hearing it constantly said that the Congolese owed everything to their colonial masters, he likely ended up believing it. This is thus a case of successful indoctrination by the Belgians; one finds traces of it in writings by other évolués, including Patrice Lumumba.[29] Such sentiments among the subject people would obviously inhibit political agitation.

Perhaps the most important factor, however, is linked to a particular feature of the évolués' psychology. Their major ambition in the early postwar years was to become as nearly as possible like Europeans. The European represented an envied social model. The évolués aspired to resemble him and to arrive at a status whereby, in recognition of the degree of civilization they had attained, the multifarious forms of discrimination existing between them and the European would be relaxed. Their great hope, and their great concern, were for the "certificates of civilization" institutionalized by the colonial regime, by means of which they could secure personal rights; these were the *carte du mérite civil* and the *immatriculation*.[30] Through the *immatriculation* especially, which was the more important certificate, they hoped to obtain the same civil rights as the whites, access to the same means of transportation, education, and—beyond doubt the most essential thing—respect. The entire history of this period, for the évolués, is dominated by the history of the certificates. But, by making this their overriding concern, they obviously tended to set themselves apart from the masses and to stress the distance separating them from the non-évolués, who would not have a right to the same advan-

28. Omari, "Le Rôle civilisateur de Léopold II," *La Voix du Congolais*, December 1949, pp. 461–63.

29. See, for example, the article "Reconnaissance" by Ferdinand Wassa, *La Voix du Congolais*, January 1951, pp. 22–25. The theme is: "The Congolese people, oppressed by a chaotic regime and plunged into distress and desolation, received from God the signal grace of being saved by Belgium."

30. Among the many accounts which have been devoted to the subject, I would like to draw particular attention to those in Young, *Politics in the Congo*, and de Schrevel, *Les Forces politiques*, both cited above (nn. 27, 13).

tages; in fact, one frequently finds among them attitudes of contempt for those "ignorant and backward" masses.[31] There, in all probability, lies the principal psychological obstacle to the pressing of political demands. Such demands, if they are to mean anything, must imply that those who articulate them are acting as spokesmen for the people. The évolués were psychologically paralyzed; separating themselves deliberately from the mass of the people, how could they, in its name, speak a political language?

This obstacle was to be surmounted only when the great hopes aroused by the "certificates of civilization" had given way to disillusionment. Holders of the carte du mérite civil found out that very little, in practice, had changed in their condition. The few beneficiaries of immatriculation—only 116 heads of families at the end of 1955—were even more disappointed. Before being accepted for immatriculation, they had had to meet strict criteria (hence the small number selected); they had hoped to become really assimilated to the Europeans; but they still felt a whole series of discriminations weighing upon them. "Frankly speaking," wrote Lumumba (who was one of them) in 1956, "the *immatriculés* are deeply disappointed." Indeed, he explained, "despite his juridical status, his standard of living, his social position, and his real needs—needs inherent in the life of any civilized man—the Congolese *immatriculé* is, with rare exceptions, economically and socially assimilated to any other Congolese."[32] By this it is to be understood that his remuneration remained that of the ordinary Congolese, very far from that of the European. On the moral plane also the disenchantment was often bitter; the respect which the immatriculé had hoped to enjoy he gained only very partially. Most whites made it clear to him, often bluntly, that he was still an inferior, a black.

Like many other wounded and disappointed évolués, Lumumba turned his energies in another direction; instead of seeking to rise toward the level of the Europeans, he now sought to impose himself upon them by using political leverage which, this time, would be the people's leverage.

In order to understand the long political lethargy of the Congolese, a fourth important factor must still be taken into account: the lack of contact among the évolués at the national level. *La Voix du Congolais*, it is true,

31. Memoire submitted by the black évolués of Luluabourg in March 1944, in *Documents parlementaires, Chambre*, 1947–48, no. 662 (draft law containing the ordinary budget of the Belgian Congo for 1948; report rendered on behalf of the Commission des Colonies), pp. 32, 34. "The people living in the bush" were "still mostly backward," wrote Ferdinand Wassa in the article "Reconnaissance," cited above, note 2g. But in *La Voix du Congolais* one would think that such expressions were probably deleted or softened by the officials responsible for the publication.

32. Lumumba, *Le Congo, terre d'avenir*, pp. 66–69.

had contributors in all parts of the Congo; but for a long time this was the sole countrywide link among the évolués. Those in Leopoldville never had an opportunity to meet those in Elizabethville or Stanleyville, the circle of évolués in each city living without contact with those in other regions. When the évolués of the entire Congo met in Brussels, on the occasion of the 1958 International Exposition, in which they participated, when they first shook hands with each other was literally an unforgettable moment for many of them. This protracted lack of contact was also an inhibiting factor: how could one think in terms of nationwide politics when, even physically, one did not know how it felt to rub elbows in such a context?

The Africans' silence in the field of political demands lasted until 1956. In that year appeared the first manifesto written by Congolese, the first text expressing a nationalist spirit: the *Conscience Africaine*. It set in motion a movement that, exactly four years later, ended with the Congo's independence.

What was new in the situation to explain this entry of the Congolese upon the political stage? There was doubtless an evolution of minds (mentioned above in connection with the évolués' psychology) and also a maturing of thought among men who were reading more and more (Lumumba himself was a voracious reader) and were becoming better informed about what was happening in the world, and consequently were beginning to think in genuinely political terms. In addition, aside from these basic phenomena, there are three explanatory elements that date from precisely this time.

In the first place, a new Minister, Auguste Buisseret, took charge of the Ministry of Colonies in 1954. Buisseret was a liberal, but on colonial matters he was by no means advanced or liberationist. The Congolese nevertheless felt that with his arrival a new wind was blowing—the wind of liberty; many of them were soon to call him the "liberating minister."[33] For Buisseret dared to confront the power to which everyone theretofore had bowed and to which the Congolese, at least, felt themselves entirely delivered up: the power of the missions. Against the will of the missions, he dared to introduce secular education, which was desired by great numbers of Congolese. Here was a Minister, furthermore, who spoke a warm, brotherly language—that, one is tempted to say, of a French Radical-Socialist—and who, in Brussells, without making them go through administrative channels, listened to the grievances and requests of blacks as well as whites. This was something new which no one had seen before. Vis-à-vis the administration, the Congolese, knowing that they could now appeal

33. See R. Slade, *The Belgian Congo: Some Recent Changes* (London, 1960), p. 41; see also Lumumba, *Le Congo, terre d'avenir*, pp. 183–84, 212–14.

directly to Brussels (especially if they claimed to be liberals victimized by the misconduct of Catholic officials), breathed more easily. All this created a new atmosphere in which the Congolese felt more at liberty to express their political ideas as they became more clearly defined.

In the Congo itself, moreover—and this is also an important new factor—the Africans were being encouraged to engage in a certain form of political activity. The new education policy inaugurated by Buisseret in fact stirred up an extremely lively battle. The missions and Catholic circles launched a coordinated attack against the Minister and the lay schools. Leftists—liberals and socialists—meanwhile mobilized their forces to ensure the success of government instruction. A veritable war about schools took place. In this confrontation each side sought to recruit allies among the Africans and draw them into the battle. The missionaries mobilized the seminarians; some were even known to have had them recite prayers for Buisseret's death. Defending Buisseret, Lumumba wrote in 1956 that "a certain propaganda has been spread by irresponsible persons . . . to stir up the indigenous populations—particularly the évolué circles—against the government in power. That certain writings of an unspeakable insolence have been directed by some évolués to senior officials is ample proof of this. These are Europeans who are hiding behind blacks in order to foment difficulties for the government."[34] In the opposing camp, liberal and socialist circles also enlisted Congolese. The latter thereby learned a lesson from all this: if the Europeans were appealing to them, this meant that they constituted a political force in the eyes of the Europeans themselves. Their self-confidence and belief in their own capabilities emerged stronger from this battle.

Finally, the Congolese now had, for the first time, a definite source of inspiration for their country and their emancipation which they could use to perfect their political ideas, the *Plan de trente ans pour l'émancipation de l'Afrique belge*, published by M. Van Bilsen early in 1956.[35] Van Bilsen's thirty-year plan was in all respects an innovation, not only in its content but also because of the fact that it represented the first appearance of thought respecting the Congo based on a view of the world at large and integrating the Congo with it.

34. Lumumba, *Le Congo, terre d'avenir*, p. 189.

35. A Dutch version of this study had already appeared at the end of 1955 in *De Gids op maatschappelijk gebied*, December, 1955. The French text appeared in *Dossiers de l'Action Sociale Catholique*, February, 1956, and was reprinted in Van Bilsen's *Vers l'indépendance*, pp. 164 ff. See also Van Bilsen, "L'Avenir politique du Congo," *La Relève*, Jan. 28, 1956.

Curiously, the Belgians had been little affected by decolonization in the world, and as little affected by the hostility to colonialism that was making itself felt on the international level. The multifarious criticisms in the UN and other attacks on colonialism aroused much indignation among them but hardly intimidated them; they felt they had to react energetically and "defend our colonial accomplishment." That was the general watchword. As for the disturbances and collapses that had occurred in the Asian and in some African colonies, they, as has been shown, simply reinforced Belgian confidence because of the contrast presented by a calm and prosperous Congo.

As a result of Van Bilsen's study for the first time the perspective changed. A professor at the Institut Universitaire des Territoires d'Outre-Mer at Antwerp, he observed the "worldwide process of emancipation" of colonies and derived a diagnosis: the Congo could not escape it. The "liberation forces on the move in Africa" would make themselves felt in the Congo as they had elsewhere. It was therefore necessary to "prepare the stages of an ineluctable evolution." Van Bilsen proposed that emancipation be accomplished within thirty years in such a way as to arrive, at the end of that period, at a Belgo-Congolese federal union (he carefully avoided the word *independence*).[36]

To return to the *Conscience Africaine* manifesto, which dates from July 1956, a few months later, this text emanated from a small group of Leopoldville évolués who had had fairly good education—though not university education—and who were in contact with one or two Belgian professors at Lovanium, who served as their advisors.[37] "We are but a small group," they stated, "but we believe we may speak in the name of a large number, because we have deliberately confined ourselves to identifying and formulating the aspirations and sentiments of the majority of thinking

36. Van Bilsen evokes "the hope that lives in our hearts: to see the Belgium of our children and our grandchildren united to the Congo and Ruanda-Urundi." "In my opinion," he wrote, "the solution is to be found by contemplating a flexible confederation between Belgium on the one hand, and a gradually constructed great Congolese federation." *Vers l'indépendance*, pp. 176, 178.

37. Cf. de Schrevel, *Les Forces politiques*, pp. 322 ff., and M. D. Markowitz, *Cross and Sword: The Political Role of Christian Missions in the Belgian Congo, 1908–1960* (Stanford, 1973), pp. 146–48. The text of the manifesto, which appeared in the July–August 1956 issue of the periodical *Conscience Africaine*, is reprinted in J. Labrique, *Congo politique* (Leopoldville, 1957), pp. 252 ff., and in *Congo 1959: Documents belges et africains*, 2d ed. (Brussels, 1961), pp. 9–16. English translation appears in A. P. Merriam, *Congo: Background of Conflict* (Evanston, Ill., 1961), pp. 321–29.

Congolese." The manifesto's authors expressed themselves straightforwardly: as Congolese, they felt the "call of a nation," and they wanted "gradual, but total, emancipation" for their country.

However, they did want it, and this they emphasized, with Belgium's agreement:

> Belgium should not see any feeling of hostility in our desire for emancipation. On the contrary, Belgium should be proud that—unlike nearly all other colonized peoples—our desire is expressed without hate and without resentment. That is irrefutable proof that the Belgians' work in this country has not been a failure. If Belgium manages to realize the Congo's total emancipation in understanding and in peace, this will be the first example in history of a colonial enterprise culminating in complete success.

With respect to the pace of emancipation, the manifesto's authors referred with approbation to M. Van Bilsen's plan. "We have read that a thirty-year plan is being considered for the political emancipation of the Congo. While taking no stand on all of its elements, we believe that a plan of this sort has become a necessity. . . . The plan should express Belgium's sincere intention to lead the Congo to complete political emancipation within a period of thirty years."

The whole text was clearly nationalistic beyond any doubt, but moderate. The authors adorned their manifesto with a photograph of King Baudouin and concluded it by exclaiming: "Long live the Congo! Long live Belgium! Long live the King!"

Conscience Africaine was published at Leopoldville on July 1, 1956. As mentioned, it demanded emancipation within thirty years. Four years minus one day later, on June 30, 1960, the Congo became independent. And this comprises the second major problem posed by Belgian policy in Africa: why, after such a protracted immobility, was there a crash program of decolonization?

Essentially, the phenomenon placed on stage two groups of characters: the Congolese who had become nationalists, on the one hand, and Belgian policymakers on the other. The evolution of the former's attitudes, and the response of the second group, offer the key to the history of the years 1956–60. Among the Congolese, the acceleration of nationalist demands was prodigiously rapid. It occurred in two phases, first between 1956 and the end of 1958, and then after the beginning of 1959.[38] During the first

38. From a very voluminous bibliography, special mention should be made of the account by R. Lemarchand, *Political Awakening in the Belgian Congo* (Berkeley, 1964).

period the Congo remained perfectly calm. Public order was not threatened. It was still *pax belgica*, a *pax belgica* which meant that, from 1945 to the end of 1958, not one shot was fired in the Congo against the colonial order or in its support. But in évolué circles ideas came to a boil. Within two years the moderate, virtually pro-Belgian nationalism of *Conscience Africaine* gave way to the slogans of classical African nationalism: independence, liberation from colonialism and its chains.

The culmination of this first phase in the evolution of ideas is contained, to take a characteristic text, in the speech and program presented by Patrice Lumumba before a political meeting held at Leopoldville on December 28, 1958. Defining the objectives of the Mouvement National Congolais which he had founded shortly before, he exhorted:

> The Mouvement National Congolais has as its basic aim the liberation of the Congolese people from the colonial regime, and its accession to independence. . . . We wish to bid farewell to the old regime, this regime of subjection which deprives our nationals of enjoyment of the acknowledged rights of any human individual and any free citizen. . . . Africa is irresistibly engaged in a merciless struggle for its liberation against the colonizer. Our compatriots must join us in order to serve the national cause more effectively and to carry out the will of a people determined to free itself from the chains of paternalism and colonialism.[39]

It must be emphasized that this radicalization of demands between 1956 and 1958 was a purely ideological phenomenon that was produced without a political struggle in the true sense of the term. Most frequently, it is struggle that hardens the positions of those taking part. In the Congo between 1956 and 1958 discussions were held, speeches were made, programs were launched, but no struggle of any kind was organized against the Belgian regime. Ideas alone became heated.

The spectacle of Africa assuredly influenced the movement. This spectacle consisted, notably, of Ghana becoming independent in 1957; of General de Gaulle proclaiming in 1958 at Brazzaville, within earshot of the Congolese capital, that those who wished independence had only to take it. More than these external incitements, however, the most significant force brought into play was probably what one might call an internal dynamic of thought and expression. From the moment one pronounced the word *emancipation*, *independence* came naturally to the lips, and the great intoxication had begun—the eternal intoxication of liberty. Within a few months

39. *La Pensée politique de Patrice Lumumba: Textes recueillis et presentés par Jean Van Lierde* (Paris, 1963), pp. 18, 21.

this intoxication seized hold of men who felt their hearts swelling from their ability to utter these liberating words.

The intoxication intensified further in 1959 following a bloody episode which was brief but a decided turning point. The Leopoldville riots erupted in January 1959: the pax belgica was shattered; suddenly the black no longer smiled; a movement of violent anger, in fact less political than social and racial, aroused mobs—among them the numerous unemployed—who suddenly rebelled against the luxury of the white man's city and the Europeans' racial arrogance. The repression of the riots caused dozens of deaths. The Belgian government, in order to restore calm, decided to make a major gesture: not only did it announce a political reform program but itself pronounced the magic word *independence*.

The colonial power itself used the word; the political leaders seized upon it henceforth with veritable frenzy. Independence, of course; but "soon" was added and, increasingly, "immediately." Within the parties that sprang up one after another, launching manifestos and organizing congresses—a whole political life awoke and developed with remarkable rapidity—the slogan of immediate independence quickly came to dominate all others. Just as in the preceding phase, it was certainly the internal dynamic of political thought that operated above all: the more excited one became in speaking of independence and evoking the liberation that was going to change the lot of the Congolese, the more one wanted to seize these blessings quickly, immediately.

This radicalization of nationalist demands (which was, moreover, purely verbal; no party resorted to violent action) was located chiefly in the urban environment, where the évolués played the principal role. In the countryside, on the other hand, in at least one region of the Congo, 1959 witnessed another phenomenon which, although it would be an exaggeration to call it rebellion, ended at any rate in civil disobedience.

This disobedience made its appearance in the area of Lower Congo situated between Matadi and Leopoldville, which is entirely dominated by the ethnic party of the Bakongo, *the Abako*.[40] By the summer of 1959 the population of this region was largely beyond the colonial authority's reach; it no longer recognized any authority other than that of the *Abako* and its chief, M. Kasavubu, who was the object of a veritable cult. Upon his return

40. On the *Abako*, see particularly: *A.B.A.K.O., 1950–1960: Documents* (Brussels, 1962); B. Verhaegen, "Dix ans de nationalisme au Congo: Le cas de l'Abako," *Bulletin de l'Académie Royale des Sciences d'Outre-Mer*, 1971, pp. 195–205; L. Monnier, *Ethnie et intégration régionale au Congo: Le Kongo central, 1962–1965* (Paris, n.d.), pp. 49 ff.

from a tour of inspection in that district in August 1959, Vice-Governor Schöller addressed to the Minister an almost totally pessimistic report.

> "I have just been through the Cataract District between Thursday, August 6 and Monday, the 10th," he wrote. "All the persons I met were unanimously agreed that contact with the population on the political level has become impossible. Directives, advice, efforts at persuasion, attempts to institute a dialogue, everything that emanates from the administration, whether from Europeans generally or from Congolese considered to be collaborators with the whites, is rejected without discussion. They reply that a single thing counts: immediate independence; that there is only one person competent to decide anything: M. Kasavubu. . . . One is thus hardly likely to be wrong in asserting that all the country between Leopoldville and Banane is loyal to M. Kasavubu. . . . As a result of this development the position of the chiefs [i.e., the native chiefs] has become untenable; some, as a result, are openly espousing the cause of the extremists; others confess their total impotence. . . . We find ourselves, in fact, confronting a state of rebellion by a fraction of the population sufficiently large to annihilate any reaction on the part of the minority.[41]

Political radicalization of the urban centers, and semirevolt in an important rural area—that describes the posture of the Congolese, and that is what the colonial power was faced with.

The phrase "colonial power" was just used, but it is necessary to define here exactly who was to give the reply. Thus far, in speaking of Belgian policy, the referent has been the "colonial authority," which in fact shaped policy. This term served to designate both the Ministry of Colonies in Brussels, with its bureaus, and, in the Congo, the governor-general and the administration, all acting *grosso modo* along the same lines. In the reply that was to be made to Congolese nationalism, it was no longer a question of the colonial authority. The governor-general, the Belgian administration in Africa, and even the offices of the Ministry of Colonies in Brussels were to be practically short-circuited. The reply, or rather the successive replies,

41. *Congo 1959: Documents belges et africains*, pp. 128–30. Two months later, in October 1959, a report by the Congolese Sûreté stated: "In the Cataract district, the territorial and judicial personnel in general believe that no solution can be found for their problems except by recourse to a state of emergency, placing all powers in the hands of the military authority." F. Vandewalle and J. Brassine, *Les Rapports secrets de la Sûreté congolaise, 1959–1960* (Brussels, 1973), 1:163.

were to be drafted and decided upon by the Minister and a small group of policymakers of shifting composition but including metropolitan politicians and experts and a few colonial personalities acting in a personal capacity.[42] A handful of men, literally, decided the Congo's fate. The Belgian Parliament did nothing but follow along.

All the decisions, furthermore, were made in Brussels. Leopold II had created the Congo from his Brussels palace without ever going to Africa. It was unmade by a small number of policymakers, the majority of whom were from the metropole.

As for the above-mentioned "successive replies" to Congolese nationalism, three general phases may be distinguished.

The first phase was marked, in my view, by the persistent effects of the superiority complex that characterized the Belgians. They had long, and proudly, considered themselves model colonizers. Confronted with the new and unsettling fact represented by Congolese nationalism, they were determined to demonstrate their superiority. As noted previously, the *Conscience Africaine* manifesto quite cleverly invited them to do so. It stated, it will be recalled: "If Belgium manages to realize the Congo's total emancipation in understanding and in peace, this will be the first example in history of a colonial enterprise culminating in complete success." It was precisely to this flattering invitation that the policymakers responded.

Belgium, they thought, should show itself more intelligent than other colonial powers in the way it dealt with the nationalist phenomenon. Elsewhere, emancipation movements had been engaged in battle, and in the end—in Indochina as in Morocco, Tunisia, and the Netherlands Indies—the result was defeat of the colonial power, a defeat leaving catastrophe and often ruins in its wake. Profiting by these lessons, Belgium must avoid such errors. It must achieve what no one had until then conceived of or accomplished: emancipation brought about in friendship, without fighting those who desired liberty for their country, but, rather, extending to them a fraternal hand.

That was the principal idea of the policymakers. It found expression in the plan of a "working group" (its official name) appointed by the Minister and including, notably, three politicians who belonged to the country's three leading political parties. The group drafted its plan at the end of 1958.

The working group, which concluded its labors on December 24, 1958,

42. I believe I was the first to emphasize this particularly distinctive aspect of the Belgian decolonization. See Jean Stengers, "Notre nouvelle politique congolaise," *Le Flambeau*, 1959, pp. 457–58; also Stengers, "La Belgique et le Congo: Politique coloniale et décolonisation," *Histoire de la Belgique contemporaine, 1914–1970* (Brussels, 1974), pp. 422–23.

outlined a detailed program of decolonization that was to culminate in Congolese self-government. It proposed that Belgium's fundamental objective be henceforth stated in these terms: "Belgium intends to establish in the Congo an autonomous state enjoying a democratic regime with respect for human rights and African values." The group made clear which reforms were to be introduced first as the foundations for democratic institutions. "When this development is complete," its report stated," Belgium will offer to the residents of the Congo the choice, which they will exercize in perfect liberty, between complete independence, implying separation from Belgium, and an association of which the conditions would be discussed by authorized representatives of the two communities." The group's members hoped, of course, that the future decision would be for association.[43]

"Future," but when? The report mentioned no precise time-frame for the evolution it outlined. One of the strongest criticisms of the Van Bilsen plan had been that, by fixing a time period in advance, it deprived emancipation policy of all flexibility and any possibility of adapting to reality. The members of the working group took care not to act in the same way. But there can be no doubt about their thought: they considered that decolonization would be a long-term process. Van Bilsen's thirty years certainly seemed to them a minimum. They remained faithful to the basic idea of liberal-minded theoreticians: evolution must be gradual.

The working group's report was published during the second half of January 1959.[44] By that time it had already been partially overtaken by events. The Leopoldville riots had led the Belgian government to introduce an important new element into the response to Congolese nationalism: the promise of independence. This was the second phase.

The Leopoldville disturbances produced stupefaction and confusion in Belgium as well as the Congo. They were a sledgehammer blow. The image of the Congo with which one had lived—that of the happy black with the broad smile—suddenly dissolved in blood. Those who until then had spoken with authority concerning the Congo were completely disoriented. The time was right for a man of strong character to impose his views.[45]

That man was the new Minister for the Congo (use of the title "Minister of Colonies" had been discontinued), Maurice Van Hemelrijk. The only

43. *Rapport du Groupe de Travail pour l'étude du problème politique au Congo belge* (*Documents parlementaires, Chambre*, 1958–1959), pp. 18–20.

44. The parliamentary document in which it appears (see preceding note) is dated January 20, 1959.

45. G. H. Dumont, "Positions et affrontements antérieurs à la Table Ronde belgo-congolaise, 1945–1960," *Liber Amicorum August De Schryver* (Ghent, 1968), pp. 376–77.

gesture that could restore the climate of understanding with the Africans, in Van Hemelrijk's judgment, was the promise of independence. On the night of January 11–12, during a dramatic confrontation, Van Hemelrijk brandished the threat of his resignation; and he won.

A government declaration made public on January 13, 1959, consequently stated: "Belgium intends to organize in the Congo a democracy capable of exercizing the prerogatives of sovereignty and of deciding upon its own independence." The king, in an address delivered the same day, expressed himself more directly still,[46] declaring that: "Our resolve today is to lead the Congolese populations to independence in prosperity and peace, but without either baneful delays or ill-considered precipitousness." Thus, on both sides the magic word of independence had been advanced.

Did this mean that the working group's proposals, and particularly their spirit, had been abandoned? Not at all, for the march to independence, as in the working group's report, was conceived as a gradual one. When the king described the prerequisites for independence, and said: "Independence is inconceivable except in conditions where there are solid and well-balanced institutions, experienced administrative staffs, firmly-established social, economic, and financial agencies in the hands of proved technicians, and a population with the intellectual and moral training without which a democratic regime is but mockery, delusion, and tyranny," it is clear that he was describing requirements whose realization would take time.

How much time? On the question of time the government declaration and the king's speech were equally silent. Early in 1959, the Minister for the Congo was repeatedly pressed to reply to this question; he never wavered from an extreme reticence. His reticence and prudence certainly stemmed from the fact that within the government itself expectations remained quite vague. Some, in private conversation, mentioned a period of fifteen years as a possibility. In any event, all responsible parties had in mind an extended period.

Leap ahead from January 13 to October 16. M. De Schryver, Van Hemelrijk's successor at the Ministry for the Congo, announced in an official statement: "The road to independence is open, and the political emancipation of the Congo which will lead to it is now entering a decisive phase of execution." The Minister gave the detailed timetable to be fol-

46. His address had not, in fact, suffered the fate of the governmental declaration; the latter had been edited by a drafting committee of which certain ministers had insisted that the promise of independence should not be too direct. Cf. Dumont, "Positions et affrontements," p. 377.

lowed: elections, by universal suffrage, in the territories and communes in December 1959; immediately afterward, organization of provincial institutions; in 1960, the installation of a Congolese government and of two legislative assemblies for the entire Congo; preparation by the legislative assemblies at their first session of a "first version of a permanent constitution" for the Congo—which would lead straight to independence.[47] This amounted virtually to emancipation within four years. From a long transition period one had shifted to a brief one.

Two months after announcing this plan, De Schryver made a new declaration on December 15, 1959. The peoples of the Congo must know, he said, "that in 1960 an independent regime in that country will be an accomplished fact."[48] This meant independence the following year. In actual fact, at the Belgo-Congolese round-table conference which met early in 1960, the date of independence was set for June 30, 1960. This puzzling shortening of the interim period, which transformed the march into a race, and finally the granting of immediate independence, constitutes the third and last phase of the response to African demands.

The mystery disappears, however, if one takes into account the logic of the system the policymakers had chosen and of which they became the prisoners. Their initial choice, which continued to govern their entire policy, was to achieve emancipation in friendship with the Congolese, without struggle. Now in the Congo during 1959 there appeared a whole series of important political leaders, and also parties dominant in several regions of the country, who declared that without immediate independence there would be a struggle: no collaboration with Belgium, they declared, would be possible. How could the Belgian leaders contemplate such a struggle? If they entered into it, the very raison d'être of their policy would vanish; nothing would remain of it except its disadvantages. The system's logic therefore demanded that, if any sense were to be preserved in the policy adopted, an understanding be achieved with the Congolese parties and their leaders. The price, in the end, was the one the Congolese nationalists themselves had fixed. Payment of this price was placement of what came to be called the "Congolese bet"[49]—that is, essentially, a bet on friendship.

47. *Congo 1959*, pp. 192–97 (n. 37 above).

48. *Annales parlementaires, Chambre*, session of Dec. 15, 1959, p. 10.

49. The term *bet* was used for the first time, it would appear, by Minister De Schryver in a speech on May 28, 1960. "If we have a little luck," he said, "we shall have won the independent Congo bet." M. De Schryver made quite clear what the essential stake in the bet was: "friendship," by which one would endeavor to bring about emancipation, "instead of prolonging what could well be a period of suffering for the Congolese and for the Belgians." Report in *Revue Congolaise Illustrée*, July 1960, p. 15.

To the virtually implacable logic of the system was added another equally decisive element: the Belgian government's inability to adopt any policy involving the use of force.

If one sought to maintain Belgian authority in the Congo, order had to be restored in the region of the Cataracts, which had, as we have seen, virtually passed into the hands of the *Abako*. Indeed, a region so important, even vital, to the country's communications because the Matadi-Leopoldville railway passed through it could not be left to rot. Only an operation relying on military force could produce results. But in order to ensure success, it would be necessary to count not only on the Congolese Force Publique but also, if need be, on metropolitan troops. But here the government ran up against an insurmountable obstacle; public opinion would not tolerate the engagement of Belgian troops in operations to maintain or restore order in the Congo. To Congolese nationalists on one hand, and to metropolitan policymakers on the other, as stated above, a third actor had to be added to the cast, one who did not express himself clamorously but nevertheless played a massive role: Belgian public opinion.

From early 1959 on, Belgian opinion dejectedly, almost mutely, but quite clearly, approved the policy of the outstretched hand toward Congolese nationalism. What was clear in any case was that it wanted no resort to force. It wanted no Algerian policy; the French example served as a powerful deterrent. The government therefore knew that if it proposed to send Belgian soldiers to fight in the Congo it would encounter resistance so fierce that it could not be surmounted—the more so as the resistance movement would be led with determination by the Socialist party, which at the time was the principal opposition party. This would be tantamount to suicide on the government's part. In view of the inability to contemplate an energetic solution, only one possible course remained, that of concessions.

Did the influence of international factors make itself felt in this march toward independence, which had become a race? The example offered by other colonial countries of what ought not to be done did act, as has been shown, upon the policymakers and then on public opinion. In this respect, the Algerian war was the major bugaboo. But that is as far as international factors went. No more than in the preceding phase—the calm phase—did leaders of opinion permit themselves to be overawed by anticolonial currents in the world: Belgium's policy would be conducted on its own, without much concern for noise from outside. There is nothing, besides, to suggest that the Belgian government received from foreign countries counsel of the sort it would have responded to. Belgium's great Western allies, it seems, observed with astonishment, and even some dismay, the spectacle of a country long famous for its colonial immobilism suddenly taking the bit in its teeth. The bit was peculiarly and exclusively Belgian.

In this Belgian phenomenon one might have expected that the forces which had traditionally dominated the country's colonial policy would have continued to carry great weight. One thinks immediately of the renowned triology: the administration, the church, and the large companies. Colonial Congo had lived to a great degree in this triple grasp. It is striking that in the course of decolonization these traditional forces now stood aside and played only a minor role.

As has been seen, the administration was short-circuited in the decision-making process. It passively observed the institution of a policy it disliked or even roundly disapproved of. Speaking of the Ministry of Colonies in Brussels, Minister Van Hemelrijk said early in 1959 (in private, of course), "My subordinates are almost unanimously against me." In the Congo itself, ill-humor and a feeling of impotence combined to produce a profound discouragement.[50] One of the few initiatives of the administration in 1959–60 was the attempt to encourage "moderate" political parties, even, eventually, itself inspiring their formation;[51] these parties, although they achieved some success in a few regions, in reality exerted no influence in the country's political life.

The church, for its part, held carefully aloof, confining itself to giving its approval, in statements of principle, to the idea of emancipation. Its great preoccupation, palpably, was henceforth to avoid any identification with the colonial power in order to avoid being itself decolonized.

But the most extraordinary case is certainly that of the large colonial companies. It is difficult to conceive how they failed, in the crucial hours, to employ their exceptional strength, which made them literally masters of the colony's economy. The fact nevertheless is there, confirmed by all the testimony. Disoriented, surprised by the unexpected nature of events they had not prepared themselves for, they remained passive. The very consciousness of their economic power doubtless explains their attitude in part: whatever the Congo's political fate, were they not assured of staying there? Their principal preoccupation in dealing with the development of

50. Crawford Young states it quite accurately: "What is particularly striking about the final phases of Belgian rule in the Congo was the very small role played by the administration. After the departure of Pétillon, the administration had no voice in the cabinet—the new Colonial Minister, Van Hemelrijck, quickly came into bitter conflict with Leopoldville. In the last months of Belgian rule in the Congo, the once proud and all-powerful administration became increasingly demoralized and ineffectual, discredited in the eyes of both the nationalists and the metropolitan government. Decolonization became strictly an affair to be arranged between Brussels and the nationalists, with Leopoldville a silent, sullen spectator." *Politics in the Congo*, p. 478.

51. See, for example, for the Maniema, B. Verhaegen, *Rébellions au Congo* (Brussels, n.d.), 2:78 ff.

Congolese political life was not to favor certain parties as the administration was doing, but to ensure for themselves, if possible, the good will of all. In September 1959, Sûreté reports pointed out that the "Société Générale, without openly involving itself. . . is authorizing its branches to give subsidies, eclectically, to associations and parties in the cities as well as in the bush."[52] A few months later the Sûreté observed what this "eclecticism" consisted of: "The companies are irrigating the parties without discrimination so as to secure friends among the future leaders."[53] Money was given to everyone. This was the case in Katanga, it may be noted, as elsewhere. At the time of Katanga's secession, the big companies linked their fate to that of Moïse Tshombé and his party, Conakat. But before secession they had been just as generous to parties opposing Conakat; they were covering all bets.

The last group that might have been expected to act to influence events, but who were practically missing from the decolonization process, were the colonists. During the era of the great calm in the colony they had advanced certain political demands but had not established political organizations properly speaking. From this point of view, consequently, they had not in practice advanced beyond the Africans. When the Congo suddenly awoke to political life, it was too late for them to form their own parties, which would necessarily have been white parties: a white party appearing at that juncture amidst the African parties would have been a target more than anything else. There remained the possibility of influencing, even of guiding, certain African (or perhaps interracial) groups. Of the various efforts in this direction, the only one that produced results of any significant importance was the aid given to Conakat. While one may thus conclude that a certain colonist influence entered into the secession of Katanga, which came after independence, the colonists' preindependence role was almost negligible. At the round-table conference early in 1960 that settled the terms of independence, the Europeans in the Congo had not a single representative; their absence accurately reflected their real impotence.

In a general way, one may say that, in the decolonization of the Congo, the different pressure groups that one would assume normally to have asserted themselves remained strangely inert. A prominent socialist member of Parliament, M. Pierre Vermeylen, deplored the fact. In order to function well, Vermeylen insisted, Parliament needs to feel pressures from outside; even if it resists them, they serve to inform, instruct, and oblige it to think. In the Congolese affair, he added, the Chambers were

52. Vandewalle and Braissine, *Les Rapports secrets de la Sûreté*, 1:144.

53. Ibid., 2:114.

left to their own devices by the traditional pressure groups; this, in Vermeylen's judgment, was "disastrous."[54]

How to explain this phenomenon? Essentially, by the fact that those who disliked the new policy could sign their misgivings but were unable to propose a different policy. Any possible alternative to the government's policy implied, in one way or another, the application of force. To speak of it directly was to provoke public opinion, no one dared to do so. The attitude of Belgian public opinion, as can also be seen here, was the major paralyzing agent which stifled any possibility of effective reaction to nationalist demands. In the Congo the protagonists of Congolese independence were the Patrice Lumumbas and the Kasavubus; in Belgium the protagonist was, more than anyone else, the man in the street.

54. P. Vermeylen, "Le Parlement," *Res Publica* (1961), pp. 9–10.

13. *Portugal and Africa: The Last Empire*

KENNETH MAXWELL

Portuguese claims to Guinea-Bissau, Mozambique, and Angola extended back to the fifteenth century, but the geographical delineation of these territories and modern economic exploitation of their natural resources were more recent. Portugal's African empire, more than the Portuguese ever cared to admit, was an empire by default, consisting of regions that more powerful competitors during the halcyon days of imperialism could not agree to divide among themselves. Angola and Mozambique, no less than the Belgian Congo or the Rhodesias, were creations of the nineteenth-century scramble for Africa.[1]

From the beginning, moreover, Portuguese overseas expansion had been a cosmopolitan affair. Portugal provided the men, rarely the capital. Lisbon's possessions in southern Africa, with their vital rail and port facilities, were intimately linked to the vast interlocking mining, financial, commercial, and industrial complex of southern Africa. There, British, Belgian, German, French, and South African interests have jostled, combined, and competed since the 1890s. This international penetration was not to disappear once the Portuguese had gone. In fact, it was likely to intensify, particularly if Western and South African interests felt threatened.

Portugal was the last European power in Africa to cling tenaciously to the panoply of formal domination. This was no accident. For a long time Portugal very successfully disguised the nature of her presence behind a skillful amalgam of historical mythmaking, claims of multiracialism, and good public relations.[2] But as the late Amilcar Cabral, founder of the libera-

1. On nineteenth-century Portuguese colonialism, see: J. Hammond, *Portugal and Africa 1850–1910*; James Duffey, *Portugal in Africa* (Cambridge, Mass., 1962); and René Pelissier, *Résistance et révolte en Angola (1845–1961)*, 3 vols. (privately printed, 1976). Also David Abshire and Michael A. Samuels, eds., *Portuguese Africa: A Handbook*, Center for Strategic and International Studies, Georgetown University (New York, 1969).

2. The most prominent proponent of the theory of "luso-tropicalism" was the Brazilian sociologist Gilberto Freyre, who published his influential *O mundo que o português criou* [The world the Portuguese created] in Rio de Janeiro in 1940. Freyre argued that Portuguese

tion movement in Guinea-Bissau, said, "Portugal could not afford neocolonialism."[3] Economic weakness at home made intransigence in Africa inevitable. It was precisely through the exercise of sovereignty that Portugal was able to obtain any advantages at all from its "civilizing mission." These advantages were very considerable: cheap raw materials, large earnings from invisibles, the transfer of export earnings, gold and diamonds, protected markets for her wines and cotton textiles.

The problem was that this sovereignty limited the options of decolonization. Portugal faced real losses if control of her African territories were to end, and these would be difficult to sustain without major social and economic changes at home—changes which, for political reasons, the Salazar and Caetano dictatorships were not prepared to contemplate.[4] The consequence of this situation, however, denied Lisbon the chance for a clean

---

tolerance and assimilation of tropical values distinguished them as pioneers of modern tropical civilizations. The focal point of the ideology of luso-tropicalism was the notion of the unique nonracism of the Portuguese colonizer. For a discussion and demolition of his theory, see: Gerald Bender, "The Myth and Reality of Portuguese Rule in Angola: A Study of Racial Domination" (Ph.D. diss., University of California, Los Angeles, 1975). See also Charles Boxer, *Portuguese Society in the Tropics: The Municipal Councils of Goa, Macao, Bahia and Luanda, 1510–1800* (Madison, Wis., 1965), and his *Race Relations in the Portuguese Colonial Empire 1415–1825* (Oxford, 1963). In this latter book Boxer had challenged the theory with irrefutable historical evidence and was thoroughly vilified by the Salazar regime for having done so. There was nevertheless difference in Portuguese colonial practice from that, say, of the British, and there is a need for a thorough and unbiased account of the whole question of Portuguese colonalist mentality and myth which will strike a balance between a wholly materialist explanation espoused by scholars such as Bender or the wholly mythic interpretation espoused by the more fervent supporters of Salazar.

3. See especially Amilcar Cabral, *Unité et lutte*, 2 vols. (Paris, 1975). António Oliveira Salazar (1889–1970) dominated Portugal from soon after the military coup of 1926 which overthrew the 1st Republic. He was succeeded by Marcello Caetano (1906–1980) in 1968 following his incapacitation. Caetano was overthrown by the military coup of April 25, 1974.

4. There are several good accounts of Salazar and his system. The best ones in English are: Hugh Kay, *Salazar and Modern Portugal, A Biography* (New York, 1970), which is written from a sympathetic perspective, and António de Figueiredo, *Portugal, Fifty years of Dictatorship* (London, 1975), which is written from the point of view of the opposition. On corporatism in Portugal, see Philippe C. Schmitter, *Corporatism and Public Policy in Authoritarian Portugal* (London and Beverly Hills, Calif.: Sage Publications, 1975), and Lawrence S. Graham, *Portugal: The Decline and Collapse of an Authoritarian Order* (London and Beverly Hills, Calif.: Sage Publications, 1975). The most comprehensive coverage in English is by Howard J. Wiarda, *Corporatism and Development: The Portuguese Experience* (Amherst, Mass., 1977). Salazar's own view can be seen in António de Oliveira Salazar, *Doctrine and Action, Internal and Foreign Policy of the New Portugal 1928–1939* (London, 1939), and Oliveira Salazar, *Como se levanta um Estado* (Lisbon, 1977). A good overview of the Salazar and Caetano period is Manuel de Lucena, *A evolução do sistema corporativo portugues*, 2 vols. (Lisbon, 1976).

exit. There was precious little room, for example, to manufacture the sort of commonwealth-style departure which had enabled some other European powers to cushion the end of empire by leading their peoples to think that nothing was altered while at the same time beguiling the former colonies into believing that everything was new. Such a plan was actually laid out in General António de Spínola's *Portugal and the Future* (Lisbon, 1974). But this "Lusitanian Federation" was twenty years too late.

Intransigence in the defense of empire, even if it had a certain logic from the Portuguese point of view, was sustained only at very great cost. During the decade and a half when the world's attention was focused on Southeast Asia, a bitter struggle had been going on in Portuguese Africa. By 1974 over a million Portuguese had seen service overseas. One of every four adult males was in the armed forces. In Africa, a 200,000-strong Portuguese army facing defeat in Guinea-Bissau found itself severely pressed in Mozambique and stalemated in Angola. It was the junior officers of the bloated and demoralized military establishment who finally toppled the Caetano regime. A coup d'etat was the only way they could see to end the colonial wars they had spent most of their professional lives fighting. If they opened a Pandora's box in the process, it was partly because the difficulties that would follow the collapse of Portuguese rule in Africa had been accumulating for years.

The white settler population had grown rapidly in the 1960s, especially in Angola. By 1974 it numbered some 350,000 only 20 percent of whom had been born there. For the most part the new settlers were peasants with minimal education and few skills. Despite some expensive government attempts to establish white agricultural settlements, almost all the poor whites ended up in cities, where they dominated commerce and semiskilled jobs to the exclusion of Africans.[5]

Elsewhere in the continent, the 1960s had produced much disillusionment with the venal regimes and military cliques that dominated many of the newly independent states. With time and experience, therefore, the ideological content of the anticolonial struggle was refined, and it moved beyond nationalism to a more explicit Marxian critique of dependency and its mechanisms. In the Portuguese colonies in particular, these issues were

5. On numbers of white settlers in Angola on the eve of decolonization, see Gerald Bender and Stanley P. Yoder, "Whites on the Eve of Independence: The Politics of Numbers," *Africa Today* 21 (Fall 1974), pp. 23–37. Bender and Yoder give minimal figures; the Portuguese colonial authorities gave maximum figures. It should be noted that the Portuguese population increased by 10 percent between 1974 and 1980 as a result of the flight of settlers from the African territories during the process of decolonization. Estimates placed Portugal's population at 8,200,000 in 1974 and at over 9,000,000 by 1980.

paramount in the thinking of the liberation movements. In part this was because of the peculiarities of Portuguese colonialism, and in part because of the accelerating penetration of large-scale foreign capital into the region after 1965.

The liberation movements that emerged in the Portuguese colonies differed in many ways from the earlier nationalist movements in the other former European colonies which had achieved independence during the late 1950s and 1960s. With the important exception of Holden Roberto's Frente Nacional de Libertação de Angola (FNLA), the issue in Portuguese Africa—for Partido Africano da Independeñcia de Guiné and Cabo Verde (PAIGC) in Guiné, the Frente de Libertação de Moçambique (FRELIMO) in Mozambique, and the Movimento Popular de Libertação de Angola (MPLA) in Angola—was as much neocolonialism as it was nationalism. Led by the late Amilcar Cabral and Aristides Pereira in particular, the PAIGC combined European revolutionary theory and Asian experience to create a party self-consciously fitted to the special geographical, social, and economic conditions of Guiné. The PAIGC called for emphasis on "the people," for "re-Africanization" of cultural life, and for social action and economic reconstruction to take place through constant discussion, example, and demonstrated benefits at the local level. It wanted to "modernize" the tribal culture, but to do so within the history and conditions of Guiné. In Angola, Agostinho Neto, the president of MPLA, spoke of "a dual revolution, against traditional structures which can no longer serve them and against colonial rule." In Cabral's view, the "petty bourgeoisie," who had already achieved some education and modern skills but had no real part in colonial power, had become "the revolutionary vanguard."[6]

This intensification of ideological consciousness was perhaps inevitable. The issues in Portuguese Africa were, after all, real and not theoretical, and were fortified daily in an armed struggle which the rest of Africa, with the exception of Algeria, had not experienced. It was also inevitable that the liberation movements—PAIGC in Guinea-Bissau, FRELIMO in Mozambique, and the MPLA, FNLA, and UNITA in Angola—developed their own heterogeneous international contacts, arms suppliers, and dip-

6. On liberation movements, see: Ronald H. Chilcote, *Emerging Nationalism in Portuguese Africa* (Stanford, 1972); John A. Marcum, *The Angolan Revolution*, 2 vols. (Cambridge, Mass., 1968, 1976); Basil Davidson, *The Liberation of Guiné: Aspects of an African Revolution* (Harmondsworth, 1909); idem, *In the Eye of the Storm* (Harmondsworth, 1972). There is some useful comparative perspective in Kenneth W. Grundy, *Confrontation and Accommodation in Southern Africa: The Limits of Independence* (Berkeley and Los Angeles, 1973), especially chapters 5 and 6, and in Richard Gibson, *African Liberation Movements* (Oxford, 1972).

lomatic supporters: Algeria, Cuba, the Soviet Union and Eastern Europe, China, Scandinavia, Western church groups—even, during the early 1960s, the United States. Since those movements most strongly influenced by Marxian analysis—PAIGC, FRELIMO and MPLA—saw the struggle with Portugal as only part of their problem, and because they focused on what they believed to be the realities of economic power rather than its vectors, a latent hostility to the West, especially Western Europe, was built into their philosophy. It was a distrust only encouraged by the surreptitious aid the Western powers gave to Portugal in Africa, aid that increased as the end neared.

Portugal's imperial pretensions had always been compromised by the fact that for most of its history Portugal itself was little more than a dependency of others.[7] This situation received every encouragement from Portugal's commercial and administrative leaders, who were content to act as front men for enterprising foreigners, or to see Portugal's bloated and incompetent bureaucracy supported by the legal and extralegal kickbacks paid for by the passage of goods through the nation's ports. The arrangement relieved both businessmen and government of the more strenuous and potentially disturbing task of constructing a modern industrial society. But it also created severe, if disguised, internal social and economic tensions that surfaced when the structures of authority collapsed, as they did before the military coup of 1926 that eventually brought Salazar to power, and again when the regime he created fell in 1974.

Before the 1974 coup, a conflict had emerged within the large Portuguese monopolies which dominated key parts of the internal and African market between those which favored internal development along European lines—and those which wanted to develop Portugal's African wealth. In fact, the conflict appeared more straightforward than it was. The sort of solution proposed by General Spínola after the 1974 coup and attempted by Caetano in the early seventies was to remove the worst rigidities of the corporate state but to continue to give the monopolists special protections in the interest of efficient large-scale production. Not all of the monopolists themselves were convinced that liberal capitalism was the answer, especially if it involved a compromise with the nationalists in Africa or any relaxation of the institutional intervention of the Portuguese state in order to protect their interests. Salazar's longtime foreign minister, Franco

7. See especially S. Sideri, *Trade and Power, Informal Colonialism in Anglo-Portuguese Relations* (Rotterdam, 1970). Also: Mariam Halpern Pereira, *Assimetrias de crescimento e dependência externa* (Lisbon, 1974); William Minter, *Portuguese Africa and the West* (New York, 1972); and idem, *Imperial Network and External Dependency, The Case of Angola* (Beverly Hills, Calif.: Sage Publications, 1972).

Nogueira, and the Espirito Santo interests saw any compromise with liberal demands as suicide—especially demands for compromise in Africa. Nogueira, in fact, on one occasion observed that if Portugal lost Africa, it would "immediately be absorbed by Spain." But, as Nogueira well knew, if Portugal for most of her history had been in danger of being absorbed by anyone, it was Great Britain. Like several other former Portuguese foreign ministers, between leaving his official position and taking over the direction of the Espirito Santo bank, he served his stint as chairman of the board of the Benguela Railway, the main outlet from the Katanga and Zambian copper belts to Lobito Bay in Angola, owned by the British-based Tanganyika Concessions.

The Portuguese empire was thus supported by economic linkages that combined an almost mercantilist restrictiveness with complex networks representing the interests of Western European, North American, and South African capital. Though it was not always apparent on the surface, the pressures to hold on to Portuguese Africa and to protect European capital in Portugal itself were closely interconnected. As long, that is, as the Portuguese government showed no willingness whatsoever to negotiate a settlement with the African Nationalists.

The regional context of Portugal's colonies was also extremely important, since multiple interconnections tied both Mozambique and Angola to every aspect of the explosive situation in Central and southern Africa.[8] In South Africa itself no one doubted that the Portuguese colonies represented a breakwater against the tide of majority rule. In 1974 Angola had the largest white population in the continent outside of South Africa, and the de facto alliance of South Africa, Rhodesia, and Portugal against insurgency in southern Africa merely confirmed the obvious. The burden the Portuguese bore on South Africa's behalf, however, was very considerable indeed: an army of 150,000 in Africa in 1974 (60,000 in Angola alone); and defense expenditures of $425 million in the early 1970s, while South Africa, with a gross national product three times that of Portugal, spent about the same amount ($448 million). With the Portuguese gone, the South African defense budget tripled, standing at $1,332 billion for 1975–76. And on March 31, 1976, military spending was raised by another 40 percent "to meet increased threates on the borders."[9]

Angola shares a long border with Namibia; any developments that ad-

8. For useful economic and geographical background on Angola and Mozambique, see William A. Hance, *The Geography of Modern Africa*, 2d ed. (New York, 1975), pp. 484–509.

9. See *World Military Expenditures and Arms Control 1967–1976*, U.S. Arms Control and Disarmament Agency, Publication 98 (Washington, D.C.: G.P.O., July 1978. Also *The Military Balance 1974* (London: International Institute for Strategic Studies).

versely affected the South African position in Namibia were of special concern to the upholders of white supremacy in Pretoria. There were three reasons for this. First, the control of the territory by the Pretoria regime rests on dubious legality. Namibia, a former German colony, was a mandated territory of the League of Nations, administered by South Africa, a situation perpetuated after World War II by United Nations trusteeship. In December 1974, however, a unanimous decision of the United Nations Security Council (reaffirmed at the end of 1975) called for a South African withdrawal with United Nations assistance.[10] Second, the system of labor control and mobilization and the racial and social inequalities in Namibia represent in cruder and exaggerated terms the South African system itself. Intertwined in the exploitation of the mineral wealth of the territory are the same corporate and international business interests that dominate enterprise in southern Africa as a whole.[11] Third, the frontier of Namibia is vulnerable to incursion and potential border disputes in a way that the boundaries of South Africa proper are not.

Namibia has been the scene of labor unrest among the Ovambo migrant workers, whose tribal homeland abuts Angola along much of the central area of the frontier. Two-fifths of the Ovambo in Namibia are, in fact, from Angola. Some 12,000 Ovambo workers throughout Namibia participated in the 1971 strike. To the west, the South African-financed Cunene hydroelectric scheme, begun after a 1969 agreement with Portugal, was intended to provide cheap power to the mines and urban centers in Namibia, among which the Rossing uranium development is one of the most important. All the Cunene dams are in Angola, but its powerhouse is in Namibia.

10. On Namibia, see John Dugard, *The Southwest Africa/Namibia Dispute, Documents and Scholarly Writings on the Controversy between South Africa and the United Nations* (Berkeley and Los Angeles, 1973).

11. For background on South African corporate networks, see Richard L. Sklar, *Corporate Power in an African State: The Political Impact of Multinational Mining Companies in Zambia* (Berkeley and Los Angeles, 1975). Consolidated Diamond Mines, for instance, one of Namibia's major corporations, is a wholly owned subsidiary of De Beers; it accounted for a staggering 53 percent of the group's total profits in 1974. De Beers is, in turn, an associated company of the giant South Africa-based Anglo-American Corporation. Copper and lead are mined by the Tsumeb Corporation, owned by Amax and Newmont Mining (American) in association with Selection Trust (British) and the Union Corporation (South African). Uranium deposits in Namibia are exploited by British-run Tinto Zinc (which holds 54 percent of the equity in the Rossing uranium mine), in association with the French multinational Total, West Germany's Urangesellschaft, and the South African Industrial Development Corporation. The Rossing mine became the world's largest producer by 1977. A substantial interest in Rio Tinto Zinc is held by Charter Consolidated Ltd., the principal corporate associate of Anglo-American in the United Kingdom. In 1970, 42 percent of Rio Tinto Zinc's profits came from the Palabora, its copper mine in the northeast Transvaal.

And to the east, adjacent to the valley of the upper Zambesi and Cuando rivers, the narrow Caprivi strip of Namibia brings Angola, Rhodesia, Zambia, and Botswana into close juxtaposition. This region provided a corridor for guerrilla activity in Rhodesia, Namibia, and Angola itself. During the mid-1970s, the South-West African Peoples Organization (SWAPO) from bases in southern Angola supported insurgency in the Caprivi strip and into Ovamboland. This, in turn, provoked stepped-up activity by the South African army all along the frontier with Angola.

The decolonization of Angola was thus of special concern to the South African government. But Angola was no more isolated from its African neighbors to the north and east than it was from the white-ruled territory to the south. Basic sectors of the transportation network of Angola are indispensable links in the infrastructure of all southern Central Africa. Both Zaire and Zambia depend for essential imports and exports on the ports and railways of Angola. The 896-mile-long Benguela Railway connects the mineral-rich heart of the continent—Shaba (formerly Katanga) in Zaire and the copper belt in northern Zambia—to the Angolan Atlantic port of Lobito. Copper and cobalt mined as a by-product account for between 94 and 96 percent of the value of Zambian exports, and copper accounts for 60 percent of Zaire's export earnings. In 1973 Lobito handled 320,000 tons of Zaire manganese ore and 200,000 tons of copper. All alternatives to the Benguela route involve major physical and political difficulties. For Zaire, the alternative is expensive transshipment by rail and river via Matadi. Matadi itself is vulnerable to reprisal from northern Angola; the town lies several miles up the Zaire estuary, with Angola's border running along the bank of the river almost to the port. Zambia until the late 1960s had used the railway through Rhodesia to the ports of Mozambique, but this was closed following disputes with the white settler regime of Ian Smith. The Chinese-built and Chinese-financed TanZam railroad, running 1,000 miles from Kapiri Mposhu in the copper belt to the Tanzanian port of Dar es Salaam, was unable to carry sufficient capacity to offset the loss of the Benguela route, and in addition the port facilities at Dar es Salaam were congested.

The Benguela Railway is 90 percent owned by the British firm, Tanganyika Concessions Ltd. (TANKS). The Paris branch of Lazard Frères, the New York investment house, is one of the largest stockholders in TANKS, which in turn has large interests in Rhodesia and South Africa. Both Zaire and Zambia had been involved in Angolan politics. President Mobutu of Zaire was the major supporter of Holden Roberto's FNLA; and Roberto, to solidify his Zairian connections, had married Mobutu's sister-in-law. President Kaunda of Zambia had supported the MPLA and had allowed it to use Zambia as a base for guerrilla activities in eastern Angola after 1966.

Kaunda also supported Jonas Savimbi in 1966, until some of his UNITA guerrillas attacked the Benguela Railway and Savimbi was unceremoniously expelled from Zambia, thereafter subsisting within Angola without much outside support.

The complex interrelationships in the region and the danger of escalating conflicts were thus intrinsic to the geographical location of Portugal's African empire. The process of decolonization was thus bound to be an extremely complex, dangerous affair, with racial, economic, and ideological overtones that reached far beyond the boundaries of Portugal and her African territories.

Portugal had been a member of NATO since 1949, though Salazar at the time had been careful to state that Portugal's participation in it did not signify acceptance of what he regarded as the vague and wordy invocations of liberal and democratic principles stated in its charter. The Iberian-Atlantic Command Headquarters of NATO (IBERLANT) has its offices just off the main road from Lisbon to Cascais, overlooking the narrow entrance to the Tagus estuary. NATO fleets frequently rendezvous off Portugal's coasts or periodically anchor before the elegant eighteenth-century Lisbon waterfront to disgorge thousands of sailors for shore leave. In fact, a NATO fleet had been in the harbor on the evening of the April 1974 coup and had slipped anchor and quietly put out to sea as the first rebel tanks reached the waterfront.

A major policy review of U.S. relations with southern Africa had taken place early in the Nixon administration. An interdepartmental group established to review U.S. African policy options had reported to the National Security Council in the summer of 1969 that "the outlook for the rebellion (in Portuguese Africa) is one of continued stalemate: the rebels can not oust the Portuguese and the Portuguese can contain but not eliminate the rebels." Nixon had promised Franco Nogueira, the Portuguese foreign minister, that he intended to rectify the errors in past U.S. dealings with Portugal, and he had confirmed that promise in private correspondence. He was true to his word. In 1970 the United States began to move closer to both Portugal and South Africa. Export-Import Bank facilities were extended in Portuguese colonies and the covert aid which had previously gone to Holden Roberto's FNLA in Angola was curtailed, while in Mozambique aid to the elements within FRELIMO that were considered "pro-Western" was stopped.[12]

12. See National Security Council Interdepartmental Group on Africa Study in Response to National Security Study Memorandum 39: South Africa. Secret AF/NSOG 69-8, August 15, 1969, p. 56. None of the quotations from this document is from section 4, which presented policy "options." They are all from parts of the study which provided supposedly reliable information on which policy should be based. This memorandum was published as *The*

Direct U.S. economic interests in Portugal were relatively small, $193 million of investments at the beginning of 1974, the largest belonging to General Tire and ITT. In Africa the economic stake was more important, especially that of Gulf Oil in the Cabinda enclave, a small territory separated from the rest of Angola to the north of the mouth of the Congo River. Yet nowhere in Portugal or in what was Portuguese Africa, apart from Cabinda, did there exist the clear-cut type of U.S. corporate interests that were threatened by the socialist government of Chile, for example. Moreover, the interdepartmental group's report to the National Security Council in 1969 was unequivocal on the "national security" argument. Referring not only to the Portuguese territories but also to the whole of southern Africa, the report stated: "Our policy positions in southern African issues affect a range of U.S. interests. None of the interests are vital to our security, but they have political and material importance."

It was not direct American interests that were involved but large European interests tied into the southern African mining complex (a source of vital raw materials and bullion), as well as the strategic and economic routes around the Cape used by the tankers that carry almost all of Europe's oil supplies from the Arabian Gulf. The importance of these factors to the stability of Western Europe had a strong influence on Washington's policies toward Africa and conditioned the American response to the collapse of Portugal's African empire.

The particular problem in the case of Portugal was that NATO began to find the notion of "pluricontinental Portugal," the idea that Portugal was an intercontinental country with European and African provinces (the central ideological—or mystical—tenet of the Salazarist African policy), to be a very convenient fiction just at the time when the whole edifice was about to collapse. NATO's charter excluded it from the South Atlantic, but U.S. and European navy circles, in response to the growing Soviet naval power, had been voicing criticism of this stipulation for a number of years. After 1970, the United States Navy made increasing use of Mozambique and Angolan ports, mainly to avoid any "embarrassment" by visits to South Africa itself. Increasing interest was shown in the port of Nacala in Mozambique which, with the proper technical facilities, could contain the entire U.S. Seventh Fleet. In mid-1973, the Supreme Allied Command Atlantic (SACLANT) at

Kissinger Study of Southern Africa, edited and introduced by Mohamed A. El-Khamas and Barry Cohen (Westport, Conn., 1976). For fuller background, see John Marcum, *The Angolan Revolution*, 2 vols. (Cambridge, Mass.: MIT Press, 1976), and Gerald J. Bender, "Kissinger and Angola: Anatomy of Failure," *American Policy in Southern Africa* (Washington, D.C., 1978), pp. 65–143.

Norfolk, Virginia, on instructions from the NATO Defense Planning Committee (a committee of the NATO defense ministers), began contingency planning for air and naval operations in defense of South Africa. SACLANT carried out surveys of the state of communications, airfields, and ports of Portugal's Atlantic islands and African colonies. U.S. Secretary of State Henry Kissinger, while visiting Lisbon in December 1973, had promised sophisticated ground-to-air missiles "red-eye missiles," and other equipment to Portugal for use in Africa, a commitment which contradicted previous U.S. policy.[13]

The fact that the United States during the Nixon presidency had chosen to move closer to the white minority regimes in southern Africa, and to Portugal, just as the whole situation was about to be transformed as a result of the coup in Lisbon, carried over into a predisposition by the Western allies of Portugal after the fall of Caetano to link up with discredited cliques in Portugal and in Africa, and hence shut out the possibility of forming new alliances with the individuals or political movements the Portuguese dictatorship had opposed. It had been shortsighted to have allowed this to happen while the Portuguese empire remained intact. Once Portugal's authority collapsed and the advantages the West enjoyed as a function of good relations with the colonial power were lost, to persist in such relationships was sheer folly. Accurate intelligence about, and good contacts with, the liberation movements were more essential than ever. Unfortunately for the West, the advantage of good contacts and good intelligence now rested with the West's geopolitical rivals.

It need not have been so. Ironically, on the very day the Caetano regime was overthrown in Lisbon, Agostinho Neto, leader of the Popular Movement for the Liberation of Angola (MPLA) was in Ottawa. The Canadian government had changed its policy regarding nonmilitary aid to the liberation movements in Portugal's African colonies, and Neto had come to encourage this promising development in a leading Western country. He next went to London, where he met with members of the government and Labour party officials, and to Sweden, where the MPLA had long been supported by the Swedish International Development Agency and the Social Democratic party. On May 2, 1974, through the good offices of

13. This contingency planning was confirmed by a senior State Department official in December 1974. Linwood Holton, Assistant Secretary of State for Congressional Relations, to Honorable Charles Diggs, Chairman, Subcommittee on Africa, Foreign Affairs Committee. U.S., Congress, House, Foreign Affairs Committee, Subcommittee on Africa, *Review of State Department Trip through Southern and Central Africa* (hearing), 93d Cong., Dec. 12, 1974, pp. 153–54.

Father Houtard of the University of Louvain, Neto met secretly in Brussels with Mario Soares, the Portuguese Socialist leader, who only five days before had returned triumphantly to Lisbon from his exile in Paris.[14]

Between 1973 and 1975, the MPLA also received substantial support from the Danish International Development Agency. In 1963 Neto had tried to interest Washington in the struggle against Portuguese colonialism but had been rebuffed. In 1964, through Alvaro Cunhal, secretary-general of the Portuguese Communist party, Neto entered into direct contact with Moscow. Neto's 1963 overture to the Americans had come too late, because the United States had already set its priorities in the Angolan struggle and had chosen its friends. During two important years between 1960 and 1962, while Agostinho Neto had been imprisoned by the Portuguese, the Kennedy administration had taken a stand critical of Portuguese colonialism and had established a covert working relationship with nationalist forces in Angola. But then, under pressure at home, and simultaneously faced with the chaotic situation in the Congo and the intrusion of cold-war struggles into that conflict, the Kennedy administration had backed down. The withdrawal had a variety of causes: Western Europe, a campaign financed by the Portuguese government and orchestrated in the media by the New York public relations firm of Selvage and Lee (a task taken up in the late 1960s by Downs and Roosevelt), political pressure exerted by Portuguese-Americans in Kennedy's backyard in Boston, a series of "spontaneous" anti-American demonstrations organized by the Salazar government in Lisbon and Luanda, and above all a threat to refuse renewal of the United States lease on theLajes base in the Azores.[15]

The relationships between the United States and Portugal had always had a special cast to them as the result of the Azores base. And one of the most peculiar aspects of the U.S. role in Portugal and Portuguese Africa is that the Azores base not only contributed to the longevity of Portugal's African empire, but also, because of the economic consequences of the U.S. use of that base to resupply Israel in 1973, became one of the most important immediate causes of the coup d'etat of April 25, 1974, which brought about its demise.

Between the 1940s and the 1970s, there had been a succession of quite distinct turning points, particular moments when a variety of possibilities

14. For Soares's contacts with Neto, see Mario Soares, *Quelle révolution* (Paris, 1975).

15. On the Kennedy period, see Minter, *Portuguese Africa and the West*, and also the excellent paper by Richard Mahoney based on documents declassified under the Freedom of Information Act, "The Kennedy-Salazar Skirmish over Portuguese Africa," unpublished paper presented at 2d International Conference on Modern Portugal, held in Durham, N.H., June 1979.

and options existed in the situation on all sides—in Portugal, in the United States, in Europe in general, in South Africa—that might have helped produce some change in Portugal's intransigent stance in Africa. But on each occasion when a "window for change" occurred, Portugal, rather than compromising in the face of the inevitable, instead took a more stubborn stance. And on each occasion the Azores were an ingredient in the equation.[16]

Between 1944 and 1947 in Portugal, for instance, there was hope among those opposed to the Salazar dictatorship that a process of democratization would follow the end of the war and the victory of the Allies. Within Portugal there was a good deal of political mobilization. The Roosevelt administration in the mid-1940s, moreover, had espoused a very strong anticolonialist position. So strong, in fact, that the British Colonial Office took the American policy seriously enough to initiate planning for a "transfer of power" in their own African colonies. The Portuguese had to be aware of this as well. The Salazar regime itself was compromised. It was a regime with the trappings, less muted at this time than they became afterward, of national socialism and of Italian fascism. The regime, therefore, was far from comfortable in a democratic world. This was also the period when the Cold War had not yet begun, so that anti-Communist arguments exploited so effectively later on by Salazar did not yet have credibility.

The complication for the United States and its allies in the 1940s and the opportunity for Salazar was the Azores settlement. Salazar brilliantly manipulated the forces at play in a situation. During the war, the British, in order to combat German naval activity in the Atlantic, had been quite prepared to seize the Azores if Salazar had persisted in denying them bases in the islands, and this option was also discussed privately by U.S. policymakers. Indeed, an ultimatum was given to Salazar by the British. In the negotiations which brought the United States into the Azores agreement, initially under the auspices of the British, however, a critical conces-

16. For background on the Azores agreements, see J. F. Sweeny, "The Luso-American Connection 1941–45," unpublished paper presented to 2d International Conference on Modern Portugal, Durham, N.H., June 1979; see also Kay, *Salazar and Modern Portugal*, and Minter, *Portuguese Africa and the West.* For Nogueira's views, see Franco Nogueira, *Diálogos interditos: A política externa portuguesa e a guerra de Africa* 3 vols. (Lisbon 1979–80), vol. 1. The "Anderson Plan" is discussed by Michael A. Samuels and Stephen M. Haykin in "The Anderson Plan: An American Attempt to Seduce Portugal out of Africa" *Orbis* (Fall, 1979), pp. 649–669. For the original negotiations between the U.S.A. and Portugal, George F. Kennan, *Memoirs: 1925–1945* (Boston, 1967) and his dispatch, Lisbon, 19 February 1943, 740.0011 EW 1939/28173. National Archives, Washington, D.C. Also J. K. Sweeny, "Portugal, the United States and Aviation, 1945." *Rocky Mountain Social Science Journal* ix (April 1972), pp. 77–83.

sion was made which committed the United States to respect the territorial integrity of the Portuguese territories. This concession was the first break in the anticolonial position espoused up to that time, and was the starting point for many of the problems which were to bedevil U.S. policy with respect to Portugal and Portuguese Africa thereafter.

Once the territorial integrity of the Portuguese empire had been assured and linked to access to the Azores bases, the one moment when a conjunction of favorable circumstances existed internally and externally had passed. By the late 1940s the Cold War had begun, and for the next twelve years or so, which brought with them Portugal's entrance into NATO, the United Nations, and "respectability" within the Western community, the Portuguese took full advantage of the fear of communism within the United States and Western Europe.

The second period when important options for change existed occurred between 1958 and 1962. Internally, the election campaign of General Humberto Delgado in 1958 had led to large-scale popular mobilization, and the regime was shaken by disgruntlement within the military. There were favorable external conditions, too, between 1958 and 1961; it was the grand period of African independence, with former British and French colonies stampeding toward nationhood. The Kennedy administration, which took office in 1960, adopted an activist policy in Africa, going so far as to give help to Holden Roberto and Eduardo Mondlane, as well as maintaining liaison via the CIA with disaffected generals in Portugal itself. But by 1962–63 the moment when the possibility of change existed again passed. Salazar thwarted the military plot against him, a major motive of which had been the military's reaction to his intransigent position on Africa. The various opposition pressures in Portugal faltered. In 1962 the attack on the army barracks at Beja by a group of military and civilian dissidents was quite clearly identified in the minds of the CIA as being Communist-influenced, a concern which had not been preeminent in their minds even a year or two years before. The Congo, the Bay of Pigs episode, the Cuban Missile Crisis, had all hardened people's attitudes. Again, the possibilities had been lost. Admiral George Anderson, the U.S. ambassador in Lisbon during the mid-sixties, devised an ingenious scheme to "buy" Portugal out of Africa, but the plan was a foregone failure because the possibilities of change had slipped away again and old intransigence dominated Portugal's position.

There was another dramatic period of open options—1968 and 1971. A combination of internal and external factors again existed to create a "window for action." The internal factors were the incapacitation of Salazar and the accession of Caetano, with a great deal of hope for change, bringing as he did younger, more European-oriented, modern people into the government and the National Assembly. It was hoped that they might be able to effect some change both internally and externally. Caetano himself hoped for some liberalization of colonial policies, and had been identified by the CIA as a potential leader at the time of the 1961 plotting against Salazar, had that plot succeeded. The irony is that in this case the external factors changed. In Washington, the Nixon administration concluded, at the precise point when in Portugal some pressure might have produced results, that (as the National Security memorandum puts it) "the Portuguese are in Africa to stay." This period ends with the murder of Amilcar Cabral in 1973, which foreclosed any possibility of a negotiated settlement with the PAIGC. The "liberals" in Portugal had already resigned from the National Assembly in Lisbon, wiping out the possibilities of liberal reform in Portugal and an orderly disengagement in Africa.

Given the background of pressures from Washington, the irony of the final period from 1974 to 1976 is that when, as a result of the April 1974 coup, the Portuguese eventually recognized that decolonization was inevitable, the United States received the Spínola regime with great caution. Spinola's, in fact, was precisely what the United States had been pressing for in its more enlightened moments for thirty-four years—a liberal, capitalist, modern, Europe-oriented regime, promoting a slow, moderate transition in Africa. Yet, because the United States was petrified, in fact panic-stricken, over Communist participation in Spinola's government, it gave no support until it was too late and Spinola was in exile.

Portugal's long delay in following her European neighbors in coming to terms with African nationalism had another consequence. In the 1940s the Soviet Union and its clients had no possibility of involvement in African affairs; by the 1960s the Soviets were an element, but a marginal one; by the 1970s the Soviet Union's capacity to influence events in Africa was substantial. The role of the United States had also grown with time. The arrival of the United States and the USSR on the African scene in fact marked a broader shift in international power. Africa had already become a focus of intense rivalry between them in the early 1960s, in the former Belgian Congo. In the Portuguese territories, however, during the decade between 1963 and 1973 neither great power pushed hard for major changes in the status quo. Soviet aid for the liberation movements in the Portuguese territories was modest in scale—much less than either the Portuguese claimed or the liberation movements wanted; and the same can be said for what Western support the Portuguese managed to squeeze out of their

NATO allies.[17] General Spínola, in his book *Portugal and the Future*, concluded that neither the West nor the East seemed to have any real interest in bringing the conflict to a resolution one way or the other.

This situation began to change marginally in the 1970s. In early December 1970, after Portugal launched a small amphibious attack by some 350 soldiers on Conakry, Guinea, intended to overthrow the government of President Sekou Touré and assassinate the leaders of PAIGC, the Soviet Union dispatched a group of naval combatants to the West African waters to deter similar adventures.[18] The raid had been planned by General Spínola in hope of striking a decisive blow against both his enemy within Portuguese Guiné and his enemy's sanctuary in Guinea Conakry. Like the Bay of Pigs, the whole affair misfired, objectives were not taken, and the expedition was a disaster for the Portuguese. Yet by revealing the vulnerability of Guinea-Conakry to Portuguese intervention, the result was a quiet escalation of outside support from Sekou Touré and the PAIGC from non-African countries—Cuba and the Soviet Union. Castro had been personally interested in the PAIGC since Amilcar Cabral's participation in the 1966 Havana Tricontinental Conference of African, Asian, and Latin American leaders. By the late 1960s, the Cubans had assumed responsibility for several PAIGC training camps in Guinea and Senegal and were entering Portuguese Guiné with guerrilla raiding parties. General Spínola claimed in September 1971 that each PAIGC operations unit was led by Cuban officers. The Soviets, after the initial dispatch of a destroyer from the Mediterranean fleet in late 1970, had by September 1971 stationed a Soviet destroyer, tank landing ship, and oiler permanently in the Conakry area. The Nixon administration had also been asked by Sekou Touré for assistance after the Portuguese raid on Conakry, but Nixon was strongly, if surreptitiously, committed to the Portuguese cause. The White House and the State Department, in fact, imposed a news blackout on the Soviet role in Guinea in the interests of maintaining a working relationship with both Guinea and Portugal. Only when the Soviet navy used Conakry for long-range reconnaissance missions during the 1973 Middle East war was word of Soviet military activity in Guinea leaked by the Pentagon. In 1973, partly to offset setbacks in Egypt, the Soviets began providing sophisticated

17. Portugal received 280 million dollars-worth of arms transfers between 1967 and 1976. Most of it came from France: 121 million dollars-worth. Fifty million dollars-worth came from West Germany, and only 30 million dollars-worth from the United States.

18. For an excellent discussion of this episode, see the chapter "Naval Diplomacy in West African Waters" in Stephan S. Kaplan, *Diplomacy of Power: Soviet Armed Forces as a Political Instrument* (Washington D.C. *Brookings Institution*, 1981), pp. 519–69.

ground-to-air missiles to the PAIGC. At the end of the year, again partly for reasons that related to superpower interest in the Middle East, Kissinger promised sophisticated weapons to the Portuguese.

In southern Africa, the experience of the early 1960s was to have important ramifications for later U.S. reactions to the process of decolonization. The choice made by the Kennedy administration in 1960 of Holden Roberto as a recipient of covert American aid was a bold measure placing Washington's support behind an armed insurrection against the government of one of its NATO allies. At the time Roberto was supported by the then two most radical independent African governments—those of Kwame Nkrumah in Ghana and of Sekou Touré in Guinea. He was in many respects a protégé of the American Committee on Africa.[19] Despite the later withdrawal of Washington's support and the Nixon-Kissinger decision in 1970 to move closer to Lisbon and the white minority regimes in southern Africa, these early connections remained. When in 1974 Portugal's position in Africa disintegrated, the alliances forged in the early Kennedy years surfaced almost unaltered as if nothing had happened during the the intervening fifteen years.

Washington, on the other hand, was suspicious of Agostinho Neto, who had a long record of arrests for political activity. He had been imprisoned while a medical student in Portugal, first in 1951 and again between 1955 and 1957. He returned to Angola in 1959 and was arrested a year later in his consulting room in Luanda, flogged in front of his patients, and deported to the Cape Verde Islands. International protests led to his transfer to Lisbon, where he was incarcerated and later placed under house arrest. In 1962 he escaped from Portugal and resurfaced in Leopoldville (now Kinshasa). In December 1962 he became president of MPLA.[20]

Neto, born in 1922, the son of a Methodist pastor, received his higher education in Portugal at Coimbra and Lisbon universities on a scholarship from American Methodists. He graduated as a doctor of medicine in 1958. He worked for a time as a gynecologist in Lisbon slums and married a Portuguese woman. In background, he was from that very small group of so-called *assimilados* (about 1 percent of the Angolan population), a designation used by the Portuguese for those Africans deemed sufficiently "civilized" to be granted the rights of Portuguese citizenship, insofar as those rights existed under the Salazarist dictatorship. Neto was also a dis-

19. See chapter 3 above (Hollis R. Lynch).
20. On MPLA and Neto, see Marcum, *The Angolan Revolution*.

tinguished poet in Portuguese. A collection of his works, entitled *Sagrada esperana* (Sacred hope), banned in Portugal by the dictatorship, was eventually published in Lisbon after the April 25 coup and became a best-seller.

During the late 1940s Agostinho Neto was a central committee member of the youth section of the United Democratic Movement in Portugal (MUD), a broad antifascist coalition within which the Portuguese Communist party was an important element. Several other future leaders of the liberation movements in Portugal's African colonies were also active in MUD, among them Amilcar Cabral (PAIGC) and Marcelino dos Santos (FRELIMO). MUD was also a testing ground for many of those who emerged in civilian leadership roles in Lisbon after April 25, 1974, most notably the Socialist leader, Mario Soares, a member of the Communist youth organization between 1943 and 1947. If Neto's connections in the anti-Salazar underground made him suspect to Washington (as indeed such connections made Mario Soares until the April 1975 Portuguese elections revealed him to be the main democratic bulwark against communism), they were to stand him in good stead in Portugal after the April 25 coup. Unlike Holden Roberto, leader of the Zaire-based FNLA, who had spent less than two years in Angola in his whole life, and almost no time in Portugal, Agostinho Neto knew the Portuguese Left from the inside.

The MPLA itself was never a monolith. Among the groups in its genealogy was the Angolan Communist party (ACP), and the MPLA's union organization was affiliated with the Prague-based World Federation of Trade Unions. In essence, however, the MPLA was a broad coalition, and it was led by a strong but often divided cadre of radical and Marxist intellectuals. The centrifugal tendencies within it were so strong that they seriously weakened its effectiveness and on several occasions threatened to destroy it altogether. Toward the end of the 1960s, there had been a movement to form within the MPLA a disciplined and ideologically pure party organization; this movement intended to mobilize the broadest possible support, while at the same time the party provided a politically reliable cadre for leadership positions after the end of the war. But this seems to have increased rather than diminished contention, and during the early 1970s Neto's position was challenged by two major competing groups. The first was associated with Mario de Andrade, a founding member of the MPLA and former member of the ACP, but later seen to prefer a Chinese orientation. The second was led by one of the MPLA's most successful field commanders, Daniel Chipenda, a former professional soccer star then considered closer to Moscow.

In early 1974, President Julius Nyerere of Tanzania, concerned that the MPLA's internal struggles had so weakened its ability to fight the Portuguese that Lisbon had been able to shift 10,000 troops from Angola to face FRELIMO's 1973 offensive in Mozambique, had persuaded China to provide technical assistance to the MPLA's Zaire-based rival, Holden Roberto's FNLA. The Chinese had already had considerable success in Mozambique, where they had aided the reorganization of FRELIMO following the setbacks and internal splits that racked the movement after the 1969 assassination of Eduardo Mondlane, FRELIMO's president. The division between the factions became so severe that by 1974 Neto's survival as president of the MPLA seemed problematical, and he was reinstated in the presidency at the MPLA conference in Lusaka in mid-1974 only at the insistence of Kenneth Kaunda. The MPLA, however, enjoyed exclusive relations with the major liberation fronts in Portuguese Guiné and Mozambique. Neto's personal relations with the leaders of both PAIGC and FRELIMO went back to his student days in Lisbon, and they had been fortified by a formal structure of mutual consultation among the three movements since 1961 (CONCP). Amilcar Cabral, president of PAIGC, while working as an agronomist on a sugar estate in Angola, had in fact been a founding member of the MPLA. Neto himself, since the assassinations of Mondlane (1969) and Cabral (1973), had enjoyed the prestigious and dangerous distinction of being the last of the founding leaders of the liberation movements in Portuguese Africa. Because of this, there was never any doubt about who, in the event of dispute, the other newly independent Portuguese colonies would recognize as the legitimate aspirant to the government in Luanda.

All three movements also had long-standing formal relationships with leading members of the nonaligned Afro-Asian and Latin American Solidarity Organization, founded in Havana in 1966. Some of Cabral's most important statements of revolutionary theory were delivered at the Havana conference. Cabral observed then that the Cuban revolution "constitutes a particular lesson for the national liberation movements, especially for those who want their national revolution to be a true revolution." There was never any mystery about these views, or about the fact that ideological affinity had been translated into concrete aid.[21] The establishment of diplomatic ties between Zaire and China in late 1973 and the decision of the Chinese to train the FNLA in 1974 had galvanized Soviet concerns about Chinese objectives in Africa. The Soviets had consistently supported the

21. At the time of the Lisbon coup, the CIA was attempting to exchange Captain Pedro Peralta, a Cuban captured by the Portuguese in Guinea, for Lawrence K. Lunt, an American businessman held in Havana. Peralta was elected to the central committee of the Cuban Communist party in late 1975, and represented Cuba at the declaration of the Peoples' Republic of Angola in Luanda on November 11, 1975.

national liberation movements: support for the MPLA went back to the 1958; and despite a cooling of the Soviet relationship with Neto in the early 1970s, Soviet support throughout went to one or the other of the MPLA's factions. Soviet long-term strategy placed considerable emphasis on Angola, since its geopolitical position promised to give a sympathetic regime there considerable influence in Zaire—a primary object of Soviet interest since Soviet intervention in the early 1960s, as well as a vital link to Zambia, Namibia, and South Africa itself.

The lines of conflict and alliance in Portugal and Africa were thus clearer in fact than they appeared to be on the surface. When the Armed Forces Movement (MFA) overthrew the decrepit dictatorship in Lisbon because of exhaustion by colonial wars, the pressure of economic problems at home, and irritation with an unbending autocracy, the repercussions of their actions were almost bound to be startling. Portugal was a NATO ally, anachronistic and at times embarrassingly stubborn, but nevertheless an ally that had no doubt whatsoever on which side it stood in a bipolar world. The United States, because of the intimacy of relationships with the dictatorship, was unsettled by change in Portugal and especially unprepared for the sometimes bewildering reversals and turmoils that were the immediate consequences of the coup. And the United States, unlike its geopolitical rivals, had next to no relationships with the old clandestine opposition in either Portugal or the African territories.

In the first months after the April 25, 1974, coup d'etat in Lisbon, the young officers of the Armed Forces Movement stayed very much in the background, preferring to remain as anonymous as possible. This did not mean they had any desire to see the fruits of their victory taken away from them. In a conversation with David Martin of the London *Observer*, Major Victor Alves commented pointedly that the problem with the coup of 1926 was "that although the soldiers knew what they did not want they did not know what they did want. They had no program." In 1974 Major Alves's coordinating committee had already rectified the error of their predecessors. The problem was how the program that existed was to be interpreted and by whom. The question of interpretation was especially acute concerning the issue which had been largely responsible for causing the coup d'etat in the first place: the wars in Africa.

The MFA's ambiguous phrases about colonial policy and the "need of a political not military solution" had been if anything, gross understatements. The MFA program and General Spínola's book in fact set out positions so diametrically opposed that they contained seeds for a conflict that could be resolved only by the victory of one over the other. The nature of the revolution disguised for a long time the seriousness of the divergences within the new regime, and in particularly the degree to which the young officers who had made the coup were intensely political men. But the conflict staked out at the beginning was at its heart a conflict between revolutionary and evolutionary change in Europe and between immediate decolonization and gradual disengagement in Africa. Major Vitor Alves, however, regarded Spinola's federative scheme, outlined in his book *Portugal and the Future,* as "his personal dream." Yet during his first months in office Spinola spoke privately of a timetable for decolonization over "a generation or so," during which time the people "would be given democracy and equipped to choose."[22]

The major economic monopolies stood at the center of the conflict between Spinola and the MFA. Because of the nature of their interests, pan-national and international in scope, the problem of the economic system in Portugal and the nature of decolonization were two sides of the same coin.[23] The greatest of the monopolies, Jorge de Melo's Companhia União Fabril (CUF) was a vast conglomerate of 186 enterprises, built up around a near monopoly of the tobacco market, but long diversified into chemicals, shipbuilding, fertilizers, soap, textiles, mining, cellulose, refining, insurance, real estate, tourism, and restaurants. In addition to numerous joint ventures with foreign multinationals, CUF was linked through the Banco Totta Aliança into a vast spider's web of international interests, with connections to all the southern African giants—De Beers, Union Minière, and Standard and Chartered (15 percent of which was owned at the time by Chase Manhattan). CUF's stockholders' equity in 1974 was almost $537 million, and its assets at least $2.5 billion.

Dr. Miguel Quina, son-in-law and heir to the Count of Covilha, headed a group containing at least sixty companies. The Quina empire had large interests in southern Africa, three banks (Borges e Irmão, Banco Crédito e Industrial, Banco do Alentejo), and interests in insurance, plastics, tires with General Tire and Rubber (Mabor, which in Angola had a ten-year

22. For Spinola's own account of this period, see António de Spínola, *Pais sem rumo: contributo para a história de uma revolução* (Lisbon: Scire, 1978). For other analyses of the first year of the revolution, see: Robin Blackburn, "The Test in Portugal, "*New Left Review*, vols. 87–88 (September–December 1974); Paul M. Sweeny, "Class Struggles in Portugal," *Monthly Review*, vols. 26 and 27 (September–October, 1975); Michael Harsgor, "Portugal in Revolution," *The Washington Papers*, Center for Strategic and International Studies, Georgetown University (Beverly Hills, Calif.: Sage Publications, 1976). Also Kenneth Maxwell, "The Thorns of the Portuguese Revolution," *Foreign Affairs* (January 1976), pp. 250–70, and Kenneth Maxwell, "The Transition in Portugal," Working Papers no. 81, Latin American Program, The Wilson Center, Smithsonian Institution, Washington D.C., 1981.

23. See Maria Belamira Martins, *Sociedades e grupos em Portugal* (Lisbon, 1973).

monopoly), civil construction, textiles, fishing, oil in Angola, data processing, newspapers (*Diario Popular, Journal do Comerico*, part ownership in *Primeiro de Janeiro*), and marketing and advertising with J. Walter Thompson (Latina Thompson Associados).

The Espírito Santo group, whose chief administrator was Franco Nogueira, Salazar's former foreign minister, with twenty of its major companies directly administered by members of the Espírito Santo family, comprised the Banco Espírito Santo e Comercial, insurance (Tranquilidade), large agricultural holdings in Africa, pulp paper in Angola, petroleum in Angola in Association with Belgium Petrofina (Petrangol), cellulose, tires (with Firestone), telecommunications, and tourism (ITT-Sheraton). Espírito Santo was associated with the First National City Bank of New York in Africa (Banco Inter Unido). Antonio Champalimaud's empire contained banking (Banco Pinto e Sotto Mayor), a cement monopoly, the national steel monopoly, stock ranching in Angola, insurance, paper, and tourism.

The magnates, like General Spínola, regarded the retention of the African territories, even in the short run, as essential to their proposals for the development of Portugal. The economic relationship with Portuguese Guiné was of little importance. The Cape Verde Islands lying off it were of more interest to NATO than to Portugal, and geopolitical and psychological factors do more to explain Portuguese intransigence in West Africa than do economic motivations.

The stakes in Mozambique and especially in Angola, however, were very high indeed. With Portugal's own chronic trade deficits and economic depression already affecting the remittances from Portuguese abroad and from tourism, the large surplus from the African territories would be painful to lose. In 1973 such earnings represented as much as 5 percent of the gross national product, about $540 million. All the cotton of Mozambique was exported to Portugal and 99.7 percent of its sugar, both at well below world prices. At the same time, the wages of the Mozambique miners working in South Africa were converted into gold shipments to Lisbon—in effect a hidden subsidy to the Portuguese war effort, since the bullion was valued at the official rate of $42.20 an ounce instead of the world market price that rose to nearly $200 an ounce in 1974. During the three years before the coup, the official value of this gold amounted to at least $180 million.

The colonies also provided protected markets for Portuguese textiles, wines, and processed foods. The transfer of private funds and profits from the overseas territories showed a net worth of over $100 million in favor of Portugal over the last two years of the Caetano regime. And there was the immense potential of the rapidly expanding and booming economy of Angola, with its oil, iron ore, diamonds, coffee, fishing, and tropical cash crops.

But to retain Mozambique and Angola even in the short term meant to continue the war the MFA had made the coup to end. Many officers of the MFA, who had all fought in Africa, were totally opposed to a solution that merely changed the terms of the game. They did not believe that Portugal as a whole benefited from retaining the African territories. Nor did they think, even in the improved international climate following the coup, that the Portuguese army could sustain the holding operation necessary if Spinola's model was to work. "We have no desire to construct a neocolonial community," one of them told Jean Daniel of *Nouvelle Observateur*, "we are interested more in the formation of a Socialist interdependence, and that only to the extent that our brothers in Guiné, Mozambique, and Angola accept, desire, and demand."

The political solution for Africa the MFA was talking about thus signified much more than the type of autonomy within a Lusitanian Federation which Spinola foresaw. As the bulletin put out by the MFA explained with some bluntness: "Those who benefited from the war were the same financial groups that exploited the people in the metropolis and, comfortably installed in Lisbon and Oporto or abroad, by means of a venal government obliged the Portuguese people to fight in Africa in defense of their immense profits."

In Guiné, Mozambique, and Angola the liberation movements always made a careful distinction between the Portuguese people, on whom they counted for support, and the dictatorial government that was trying to crush them. PAIGC, MPLA, and FRELIMO had all feared from the first that a political revolution in Portuguese Africa could still leave them in a condition of neocolonial dependence on Lisbon, and on the European economic interests to which Lisbon was tied and for which it sometimes acted as agent. The emergence of "Third World" notions within the military establishment of their enemy, as well as the growing de facto alliance between the radical wing of the MFA and the Communists was, therefore, watched by the Marxist movements in Africa with considerable interest. It provided them with a wedge to speed up the process of decolonization and guarantee that, where competing nationalist groups existed, those which enjoyed long-time connections with the old Portuguese clandestine opposition such as the MPLA would receive special consideration.

At intimate part of these shared understandings between the MFA and the African movements was a deep hostility to liberalism, both political and economic; for the conundrum that the Portuguese have never been able to resolve is this: whenever economic and political liberalism are wedded, orthodoxy in one makes the other hollow. The advent of individual liberties during the nineteenth century also threatened to remove the few traditional protections the poorer classes had against economic exploitation. The adoption of free trade, a policy that favored the strong expanding industrial powers of northwestern Europe, threatened a country like Portugal with total subjection. Hence the old oligarchies could always reclaim the mantle of "nationalism" despite the fact that it had been their own subjection to foreign interests that had often caused their overthrow in the first place.

The point is not merely esoteric, for it is important to an understanding of the philosophy of the MFA during its apogee between July 1974 and November 1975. It explains the quiet influence in MFA publications of historians and activists such as Piteira Santos and José Tengarrinha, scholars of the period of the 1820s when Portugal, struggling simultaneously to fend off anticolonialism in Brazil and to maintain a liberal constitution at home, succumbed to decades of civil strife. The distrust of liberalism also helps to explain the importance of the combination of eclectic Marxism and nationalism in the MFA's philosophy. As a consequence, there existed the basis for convergence between the PAIGC, MPLA, and FRELIMO on the one hand and the MFA on the other. This unique, if temporary, alliance between the colonialist officer corps and its opponents was made possible both by the timing and the special circumstances of the liberation movement struggles and by the backwardness of Portugal which the MFA officers so resented. The alliance was bound to be temporary because, whereas the liberation movements had clear objectives, the MFA did not. Moreover, the liberation movements were committed by necessity to a permanent condition—national independence—while the MFA's commitment, important as it was, remained a commitment to a process that would end once the colonies were free. Nevertheless, temporary though it might be, the momentum which the convergence of views between former enemies brought to the internal politics of Portugal and to the timetable of decolonization in Portuguese Africa proved to be irresistible.[24]

24. There are several important works on the origins of the MFA, as well as accounts by the leading participants in the movement. The best overview can be found in: Avelino Rodrigues, Cesario Borga, and Mario Cardoso, *O Movimento de capitaẽs e o 25 de Abril: 229 dias para derrubar of fascismo* (Lisbon, 1974); *Insight on Portugal* (by the Insight Team of the *London Sunday Times*) (London, 1975); Otelo Saraiva de Carvalho, *Alvorada em Abril* (Lisbon, 1977); Diniz de Almeida, *Origins e Evolução do Movimento de Capitaẽs* (Lisbon, 1977); George Grayson, "Portugal and the Armed Forces," *Orbis* 19 (Summer 1975): 335–78. See Mario Moreira Alves, *Les Soldats socialistes du Portugal* (Paris, 1975), and Douglas Porch, *The*

In the first year of the revolution three crises moved Portugal decisively to the left and Portuguese Africa equally decisively toward independence. They appeared as a series of sometimes lengthy struggles in which political tensions in Portugal, developments in Africa, and external pressures, both overt and covert, combined to force major confrontations.

Each crisis in Lisbon was connected with critical moments in the negotiations in Africa, where the liberation movements combined military pressures with diplomatic inducements to allow them a free hand. In Mozambique especially, FRELIMO stepped up its fighting while arranging local cease-fires. The MFA in Africa was already acting with a large degree of autonomy, each colony having a different MFA organization linked only informally to the others and, through Captain Vasco Lorenço, to the coordinating committee of the MFA in Lisbon. These arrangements prefigured independence, and they allowed a great deal of flexibility in local arrangements with the guerrillas.[25]

In Portuguese Guiné, local peace came long before its recognition in a formal settlement. The circumstances of that settlement are extremely revealing. In May 1974, Spinola's friend and Council of State member, Colonel Almeida Bruno, went to London with Foreign Minister Mario Soares to negotiate with the PAIGC. When they failed to make a deal in June, a decisive shift took place. The negotiations moved out of the European orbit and shifted to the secret diplomacy carried out in Algiers by Major Melo Antunes of the MFA. (Melo Antunes replaced Soares as foreign minister in March 1975). A settlement was finally arranged at the end of July, but only after a new cabinet had been installed with an idealistic Communist sympathizer, Brigadier General Vasco Gonçalves, as premier and after the MFA had consolidated its military power in Portugal by setting up a security force, COPCON (the Operational Command for the Continent, organized July 8, 1974), under the effective command of Otelo Saraiva de Carvalho, the military mastermind of the April 25 coup who also became commander of the Lisbon military garrison.

Portuguese Armed Forces and the Revolution (London, 1977). Alves and Porch take differing views as to the importance of the African experience, Alves giving it a primary role in stimulating the MFA's radicalism, Porch arguing against the importance of Africa as a radicalizing influence. Porch, however, exaggerates his case, and the disagreement in this author's view is more to do with chronology than substance. The African component was vital to explain the process of politicization, not its ultimate outcome, about which Porch, by stressing the strength of the corporate identity of the officer corps, is undoubtedly right. Both authors draw heavily on my articles written at the time for the *New York Review of Books* 21, no. 10 (June 17, 1974): 16–21; 22, no. 6 (April 17, 1975): 29–39; 22, no. 9 (May 29, 1975): 20–30.

25. For a useful view of the MFA of this period, see Diniz de Almeida, *Asencsão, apogeu e queda do MFA* (Lisbon, 1976).

This was a crucial blow to Spínola's power, perhaps the most important one: the MFA and its leftist allies in Lisbon were able to make an African settlement that he could not, as it sustained a momentum toward African independence that he opposed. Similar crises erupted over Mozambique in August and September of 1974 and over Angola from January to March 1975. Both were complex, but in each case the settlements shored up the power of the MFA and allowed it to drive from power the moderate and conservative forces in Lisbon that wanted to hold on to Portuguese Africa or slow the pace of decolonization.

Developments in Guiné were central to what happened in Portugal over the summer of 1974. A tiny, poverty-striken territory with small economic and only indirect strategic importance, it was central to the drama. No other colony could have been a more poignant symbol to mark the end of Europe's imperial adventure. More than five hundred years before it was discovered by Portuguese mariners in search of a sea passage to the Guinea coast in order to capture control of the commerce in gold and slaves that previously reached Europe from West Africa along Saharan caravan routes. Edging around the difficult African littoral at Guinea, they found the systems of winds and currents which opened the way to the New World, the Cape of Good Hope, and the Indian Ocean. In a sense it had all begun where it ended.

For the Portuguese, the war in Guiné was a patent absurdity, but for reasons of precedent and presitge it could not be abandoned. The conflict tied down a vast army in proportion to the population, yet toward the end Portuguese troops were restricted to enclaves, coexisting in the same small territory with a state that had already declared its independence. It was a war where the head of the Portuguese government, Marcello Caetano, could tell the country's leading general, Antonio de Spinola, then military commander in Guiné, that he preferred defeat to a negotiation that might provide a precedent for Mozambique and Angola. More than anything else this comment by Caetano drove Spinola to opposition.[26]

After the 1974 coup in Lisbon, the liberation movements had long-time supporters in influential places who proved to be highly effective allies. Spinola's views of a Lusitanian commonwealth were totally inappropriate to the real situation in which Portugal found herself. The armies in Africa

26. For accounts of General Spinola's accomplishments in Guinea, see António de Spínola, *Linha de acção* (Lisbon, 1970). Also see Al Venter, *Portugal's War in Guinea-Bissau* (Pasadena, Calif., 1973) and Lars Rudebeck, *Guinea-Bissau, A Study of Political Mobilization* (Uppsala, 1974). For accounts of the war from the side of the PAIGC, see Basil Davidson, *The Liberation of Guiné* (Baltimore, 1969). Marcello Caetano's own account of the meeting with Spinola is in *Depoimento* (Rio de Janeiro, 1975).

were simply unwilling to act in any way which prolonged their stay in the overseas territories. Brazil, a supposed partner in Spinola's concept, had decided to cut her losses and make her own approaches to the new Portuguese-speaking states emerging in Africa. Brazil recognized Guinea-Bissau on July 18, one week before Spinola himself made his declaration of July 27, that Portugal would begin an immediate transfer of power in its African colonies. By then, 84 countries had already recognized Guinea-Bissau.[27]

Amilcar Cabral, founder of the PAIGC, held an important place in Third World mythology. In a desperate bid to split his movement and vitiate his cause, the Portuguese secret police (PIDE) and its sinister friends killed Cabral on January 10, 1973, thereby making him one of independent Africa's most important martyrs. Cabral had also been a serious internationalist, who had gained the support of the independent African states, established close relations with Castro's Cuba, and was well-known and respected among the nonaligned nations. These connections proved vital in 1974. It was insufficiently appreciated at the time that the decolonization of Guinea-Bissau and Mozambique was a quiet triumph for African and nonaligned diplomacy. While Kissinger muttered about the Portuguese Communist party (PCP) and sought to stir up right-wing opposition in Portugal, a strenuous secret diplomacy was laying the basis for settlements with both PAIGC and FRELIMO. The diplomacy that arranged them emanated largely from Algiers and from Lusaka in Zambia. The process of making the settlements helped to bring Spinola down.

The underlying reasons for this African success were that Washington and Western Europe could not distinguish the forces at play in the Portuguese situation; they blundered into associations with groups so intransigent that they were doomed to help destroy the very solution that the United States and its NATO partners dearly wished to arrange. No such misjudgment took place within the liberation movements. They, after all, knew the Portuguese, appreciated their strengths, and were aware of their weaknesses. They knew the leaders involved—some of them only too well—and above all they knew that real power in Portugal was held by the MFA leaders and that a tacit alliance with them could be made against Spinola. These connections had decisive impact in Angola, recognized by all sides as the most difficult and most important test of Portugal's intentions. Several of the factors that contributed to MPLA's weakness as a

27. For Brazilian policy I have relied on "Palestra proferida na Escuela Superior da Guerra por Italo Zappa," May 31, 1976. For the texts of the independence agreements and related materials, see Orlando Neves, comp., *Textos históricos de Revolução*, 3 vols. (Lisbon, 1974–76).

guerrilla organization proved to be sources of strength in the different circumstances which emerged after the Lisbon coup. The MPLA's urban intellectual and cosmopolitan leaders had always strongly opposed tribalism and racism, and had enjoyed long-term relationships with the old antifascist opposition in Portugal, especially the Communists. *Assimiliados*, mulattoes, and whites had from the beginning found places in its higher echelons. The MPLA enjoyed wide support from urbanized Africans, who tended, whatever their ethnic or linguistic backgrounds, to form a distinct group in relation to the rural majority. MPLA had always had difficulty appealing beyond this base, especially in the FNLA-dominated Bakongo backlands of the north. MPLA support was concentrated, however, in the strategically located central zone of the country, along the 263-mile railway from Luanda to Malange, among the 1.3 million Kmbundu-speaking peoples, one of Angola's four main ethnic-linguistic groups. MPLA support was almost monolithic among the African population of Luanda and in its teaming slums (*musseques*). But above all, the MPLA enjoyed exclusive relations with the major liberation fronts in Portuguese Guiné and Mozambique, both of which by the autumn of 1974 had successfully negotiated settlements with the Portuguese.

Angola was always close to the center of the struggle between General Spinola and the Armed Forces Movement during the first turbulent months following the Lisbon coup. Outmaneouvered in July 1974 in the agreement with PAIGC over Guinea-Bissau, and thwarted in early September over Mozambique, Spinola attempted to retain personal control of the Angola negtiations.

The Spinola plan for Angola depended heavily on the collaboration of President Mobutu of Zaire. On September 14, 1974, Spinola flew to the island of Sal in the Cap Verde archipelago and met secretly with President Mobutu. Spinola's formal proposals for an Angolan settlement, which were made public at this time, envisioned a transitional two-year period during which a provisional government would be formed of representatives from the three nationalist groups (FNLA, MPLA, and UNITA), together with representatives of the major ethnic groups and the white population. Elections would follow for a constituent assembly, with the franchise based on universal sufferage. The private understanding reached between Mobutu and Spinola at Sal remained secret but was based on their common desire to see MPLA neutralized, and if possible eliminated. Vice Admiral Rosa Coutinho, Portuguese high commissioner in Angola, who had not been informed of the meeting, described the objectives later as being "to install Holden in first place, with Chipenda and Savimbi at his side, and to eliminate Neto." Spinola, when insisting that no negotiations take place with the MPLA, said of Neto, "He receives his orders from Moscow."

Like so many of Spinola's projects, his plans for Angola were not without shrewdness. In 1974, the Portuguese military was under less pressure in Angola than in either Guiné or Mozambique. At the time Spinola met with Mobutu, there were still 60,000 Portuguese troops in the colony, and beyond that an extensive paramilitary network. The secret police (PIDE/DGS) continued to operate in Angola under the authority of the chief of staff, and were renamed the police of military information (PIM). Like the MPLA, Holden Roberto's FNLA had not yet agreed to a cease-fire, and in terms of the military struggle, the FNLA was by far the most formidable opponent of the Portuguese army. Mobutu was the obvious person to deal with, since Roberto depended entirely on Zairian support and certainly could not function without it. Jonas Savimbi of UNITA had already agreed to a cease-fire in June and opened negotiations with a variety of white civilian and business groups. UNITA in mid-1974 consisted of less than a thousand trained guerrillas (probably closer to four hundred) with ancient and inadequate weapons. Savimbi appears to have enjoyed covert "protection" from Portuguese military intelligence and PIDE for some years, the objective being to split nationalist groups along tribal lines in eastern and southern Angola following the early successes of MPLA penetration into these regions after 1966.

On August 8, 1974, moreover, four hundred MPLA militants meeting in Lusaka had split three ways: 165 delegates supporting Neto; 165, Chipenda; and 70, Mario de Andrade. Chipenda's group represented the major fighting force of the MPLA within Angola proper, and Chipenda himself had been elected president of MPLA at a rump session of the conference. Chipenda, despite his temporary role as a Moscow protégé, had also at various times been a protégé of almost all the outsiders who had fingers in the Angolan pie, including, it would seem, the Portuguese secret police. At any rate, both Spinola and Mobutu regarded Chipenda as persuadable, given the right inducements. The scenario laid out between them at Sal was thus not entirely implausible, and shortly after his meeting with Spinola, General Mobutu attempted to persuade both Julius Nyerere of Tanzania and Kenneth Kaunda of Zambia of the merits of the project.

The plan failed, however, and for reasons that lay in Lisbon as much as in Luanda. On September 30, 1974, Spinola resigned from the presidency, having failed in his attempt to bypass the MFA and the Communists by a popular appeal for support from "the silent majority." Between October 1974 and January 1975, effective power in Portugal was in the hands of the MFA. It strengthened its hand by forming a broader-based group to oversee its affairs called the Committee of Twenty, and by constituting an assembly, the so-called Assembly of Two Hundred, to act as a quasi-legislative body where major policy issues could be discussed. During these five critical months, the MFA remained united in its commitment to immediate decolonization, since all the diverse leftist elements within the movement agreed on the need for a rapid disengagement from Africa. The ascendency within the movement of its leftist elements also brought the Portuguese authorities ideologically closer to the MPLA than to either of the MPLA's two competitors. The period was a critical one because it allowed the MPLA to recuperate from its mid-1974 nadir. Above all, it allowed Agostinho Neto a breathing space to reestablish leadership over his badly divided movement.

Not least of the elements working in the MPLA's favor during these months was the aid the movement received from the Portuguese high commissioner in Luanda between July 1974 and January 1975, Vice Admiral Rosa Coutinho, soon dubbed by the white settlers the Red Admiral. Rosa Coutinho had a pathological hatred of the FNLA and made no secret of the fact that he regarded President Mobutu as a "black fascist." The most important result of Rosa Coutinho's intervention was to thwart a key element in the Mobutu-Spinola plan—the substitution of Agostinho Neto. Although the Andrade faction was reintegrated into the MPLA during the latter part of 1974 (friction reemerged after the MPLA's victory in early 1976), Chipenda, despite a brief reapproachement, was expelled from the MPLA in November.

The temporary resolution of the MPLA's internal squabbles, however, provided a basis for settlement. Under the patronage of President Boumediene, Agostinho Neto and Major Melo Antunes met in Algiers between November 19 and 21, 1974, and negotiated a cease-fire agreement. A week later, the FNLA and the Portuguese made a similar agreement in Kinshasa. The Organization of African Unity (OAU), which had at different times recognized both FNLA and MPLA as the sole legitimate nationalist spokesmen for Angola, now extended last-minute recognition to Jonas Savimbi's UNITA. In early January 1975, the three nationalist leaders, Roberto, Neto, and Savimbi, came together under the chairmanship of Jomo Kenyatta in Mombasa. They agreed to mutual recognition and the speedy opening of negotiations on Angolan independence with the Portuguese government.

On January 10 the negotiations were moved to the Algarve in Portugal. The leaders of the three movements and their delegations met with the Portuguese government at the heavily guarded Penina Hotel, and by January 15 had thrashed out a delicately balanced and highly precarious agreement. Leading the Portuguese side were General Costa Gomes, who had replaced General Spinola as provisional president of Portugal the previous September; Mario Soares, the foreign minister; Major Melo Antunes; and the high commissioner, Admiral Rosa Coutinho.

The settlement, which became known as the Alvor Agreement, set the date for Angolan independence at November 11, 1975. During the transitional period, the country would be administered by a coalition government composed of the three nationalist groups and the Portuguese. The transitional administration would be headed by a presidential college of three, each "president" representing one of the three movements. Lisbon's high commissioner was to control defense and security and to "arbitrate differences." Each movement and the Portuguese would hold three posts in the cabinet. A national army was to be formed, the movements contributing 8,000 men each, while the Portuguese retained a 24,000-man force in the country until independence. The Portuguese troops would be withdrawn by February 1976. Elections for a constituent assembly were to be held prior to independence. Meanwhile, the three movements agreed to place a freeze on their January 1975 military positions.

The settlement was no mean achievement. It had been brought about preeminently by the MFA, then at the height of its power and prestige. Agostinho Neto, president of the MPLA, paid the Armed Forces Movement a quiet tribute at the end of the Alvor meeting, which was little noted at the time but was extremely significant in its implications. He called the MFA "the fourth Liberation Movement."

Until January 1975, the rapidly moving situation in Africa contributed to the dramatic shift to the left in Portugal. Events in Europe and in Africa coincided in a manner which strengthened the radical forces in each region. After March 1975, these circumstances were dramatically reversed. One of the keys to the implementation of the Alvor Agreement, which had established the date, November 11, and the framework for Angolan independence, was the MFA's ability to control the situation until the transfer of power could take place. The intrinsic problems in Africa were formidable enough. But the weaknesses of the MFA, and its inability to fulfill its side of the bargain, also doomed the settlement. The MFA, even as late as January 1975, remained a mystery to many both inside and outside Portugal. Above all, it appeared much more united and formidable than in fact it was.

Agostinho Neto was, as always, especially sensitive to the political situation in Portugal. Unlike Holden Roberto and Jonas Savimbi, who left Portugal quickly once the agreements had been signed in Janaury, Neto remained in MFA-ruled Portugal, traveled extensively throughout the country, and had lengthy meetings with political and military leaders. It was a critical time in Portugal. The euphoria that followed the fall of the old regime was passing. January 1975 saw a fundamental change in the atmosphere, a beginning of the long struggle between the Communists and the Socialists; and within the military itself conflicts were developing—indeed had already developed—which would later split the MFA into warring factions. As shrewd and well-informed a politician as Neto must have seen the storm warnings; they were not hard to recognize. Thus, while the ink on the Alvor Agreement was barely dry, the forces that would undo it were already gathering.

Those who enjoyed fishing in troubled waters found much sport in Portugal's last African colony. Between November 1974 and January 1975, some ten thousand FNLA troops moved into the northeast of Angola, occupying the northern Uíge and Zaire districts and forcing out all MPLA and UNITA rivals. The Portuguese, their soldiers unwilling to become involved in armed confrontation, had virtually abandoned the frontiers. Behind the FNLA regulars came thousands of refugees, returning to the lands they had abandoned in the aftermath of the bloody rural uprising in 1961. As a result, thousands of Ovimbundu workers on the coffee estates were expelled from the region, and some sixty thousand fled south to their tribal homelands on the central highlands.

On the crowded Benguela-Bie plateau in southern Angola there were serious social and racial tensions too. The Portuguese army's counterinsurgency measures had uprooted thousands of peasants, concentrated them in "secure" village compounds, and in many cases opened up their lands to white settlers. In the capital, Luanda, the tension that had remained after serious racial clashes of the previous summer was aggravated by the arrival in February 1975 of heavily armed contingents from the rival nationalist movements.

The uneasy standoff between these factions lasted only until March when, coincident with the *intentona* by Spínolista soldiers in Portugal, widespread fighting broke out between the MPLA and the FNLA in the Angolan capital. In Caxito, to the north of the capital, the FNLA rounded up MPLA sympathizers and shot and mutilated them. It was the old nightmare of massacre and reprisal that had been a constant theme in the long Angolan struggle. To the massive internal ebb and flow of people and refugees was now added a mass exodus abroad. First to leave were Cape Verdians caught beteen the rival African movements and deprived of their role as intermediaries and small tradesmen. Then followed the exodus of whites. In Lisbon the airport began to fill with large boxes, crates, tattered suitcases, dejected huddles of old women and young children, and the heavy humid smell of Africa, as the settlers returned. First the official jargon referred to them as the "dislocated"; then, the "returned." But they were refugees, and several hundred thousand of them poured into Portugal from Africa throughout the summer. Their arrival was a rude awakening for many of those army officers who a few months before had been speaking naively about a Socialist commonwealth. In consequence, the process of decolonization—which, as it interacted with the internal situation in Portugal, had done so much to propel the country to the left in the months following the coup—now faltered.

The decolonization process, therefore, which until March had helped cement the MFA's internal solidarity became, after March 1975, a major irritant and divider as the situation in Angola proved increasingly intractible and as outsiders intervened there at will. There had also been an unforeseen consequence of the March nationalizations in Portugal which subtly altered attitudes toward Africa. The state, by taking over the banks and industries which had been the core of the oligarchy's power, also assumed responsibility in the former overseas territories for vast assets. Ironically, the revolutionary governments held a more important economic stake in Angola than had the governments of the old regime. After March in Angola, it was obvious to all that the Portuguese could not contain outside intervention or control internal security, both obligations which Portugal had assumed under the Alvor accords, and any pretense at a bipartite transitional government collapsed. There was open fighting in Angola, and in Portugal, too, the military factions were beginning to eye each other ominously. The initiative that had rested in the hands of the revolution for almost twelve months was gone.

The rapidly deteriorating situation in Angola was especially dangerous because it opened up opportunities for interference by outsiders which had not existed to the same degree in either the case of Guinea-Bissau or Mozambique. In Angola, three nationalist groups, all battle hardened, each with strong ethnic roots, competed with each other as much as they did with the Portuguese. The movements in Angola had regional bases: the FNLA in the northeast of the country; the MPLA in the western center and Luanda; and UNITA in the central highlands. The zones of influence were not clearly demarcated, however, and clashes between the rival movements were frequent. Fragmentation and rivalry within each organization was also common. In February 1975, Neto forced out Daniel Chipenda, who had been a key element in the Mobutu-Spínola stratagem to circumvent Neto's leadership the previous year. His removal was thus hardly surprising; but Chipenda, leader of the "Eastern Revolt," had been one of the more successful field commanders the MPLA possessed, and was the only prominent non-Mbundu or non-Meztizo leader in the MPLA.

The schisms among and within the national liberation movements in Angola were partly ethnic, partly regional, partly the result of Portuguese colonial policy. The Salazar regime had ruthlessly rooted out nationalists, the educational system in the territory was woefully inadequate, and years of clandestineness, exile, and infiltration had left psychological scars. Each of Angola's main ethnolinguistic communities was represented by a political movement and a guerrilla army. The FNLA was rooted in the 700,000-strong Bakongo community of northern Angola. After a bloody rural uprising in 1961 and the subsequent brutal repression vented on the Bakongo by the Portuguese, over 400,000 Bakongo refugees had crossed into Zaire, where they lived among kinsmen. The FNLA, led by Holden Roberto, was deeply embedded in the Zairian political system and enjoyed sanctuary and support from President Mobutu. In 1973, the FNLA received military assistance from the Chinese. The movement was militarily strong but politically weak, and its leadership personalistic. UNITA, rooted in the two million Ovimbundu of the central Berguela plateau, was led by a former Roberto aide, Jonas Savimbi, charismatic, Swiss-educated son of a Benguela railroad worker. After the Lisbon coup UNITA had made overtures to the Angolan whites, who provided it with important support until the white presence and power collapsed as settlers fled from Angola in increasing numbers during 1975.

The MPLA's roots were the 1.3 million Mbundu (Kimbundu-speaking) people of Luanda and its hinterland. Denied bases in Zaire, the MPLA had operated from headquarters in Congo-Brazzaville, conducting military incursions in Cabinda, the oil-rich enclave, and in the grasslands of eastern Angola. The MPLA's leadership was urban, leftist, and racially mixed, with strong popular support from the rural Mbundu and the city slum-dwellers. The leader of the MPLA, Agostinho Neto, like Roberto but unlike Savimbi, owed his survival largely to outside support. The MPLA had been the exclusive recipient of Soviet and East European aid, and the MPLA had long been close to the Portuguese left. The Liberation Committee of the OAU, assessing the strengths of the three movements in early 1975, found that UNITA enjoyed the most support and the MPLA the least, with the FNLA falling somewhere between them. The OAU at the time (early 1975), like the Portuguese and the Soviets, supported the idea of a coalition government.

Partly as a consequence of the factionalism within and among the liberation movements in Angola, the Portuguese had been much more successful there from a military point of view than they had been in either Guinea-Bissau or Mozambique. With the exception of UNITA, which in 1974 was a very poorly armed and small organization, each of the other nationalist movements, the FNLA and MPLA, were as much coalitions of exiles as they were effective insurgency forces. This was, of course, in striking contrast to both PAIGC in Guinea-Bissau or FRELIMO in Mozambique—movements which had formidable offensive capacity, controlled large areas of territory, and had developed rudimentary administrative structures. Angola had, in 1974, the largest white population in Africa outside South Africa, and whites almost totally dominated Angola's agricultural, transportation, and administrative infrastructures. It was partly as a result of these differences from the other territories that Angola took on the importance it did when Lisbon's inability to control the decolonization process became apparent.

The speed with which the transfers of power to PAIGC and FRELIMO took place during 1974, therefore, proved to be deceptive precedents when it came to the complexities of the Angolan situation. Kissinger claimed after the event that the United States did not oppose the accession to power by "radical movements" in Guinea-Bissau and Mozambique. This is only partly true: the United States, in fact, was extremely disturbed about the consequences of the independence of the Cape Verde Islands under the auspices of the PAIGC, and there is evidence that it did contemplate support for anti-FRELIMO movements in Mozambique. It was not the lack of desire but lack of capacity that prevented the United States or anyone else from interfering with the decolonization process in either country. The rapidity of the process, the recognition by the Portuguese Armed Forces Movement of the necessity to deal exclusively with PAIGC and FRELIMO, and the firm action of the Portuguese in suppressing diversionary attempts, meant that in each situation, because the liberation movements and the Portuguese army worked in close collaboration, the opportunity for any effective interference never arose. In Angola, no single movement had the capacity to act with the effectiveness of either PAIGC or FRELIMO, and by the time Angolan decolonization became the prime order of business, the Portuguese were so divided among themselves that they, too, were unable to provide any consistent or effective opposition to the rapid internationalization of Angola's crisis.

Angola, moveover, with a population of about five and a half million, was different in other important ways from all the other Portuguese territories. It was immeasurably rich in natural resources (oil, diamonds, iron) and agricultural production (cotton, coffee, sisal, maize, sugar, tobacco). Unlike all the other territories, Angola had a favorable trade balance with the rest of the world and a firm basis for real independence. Yet the whole structure of Angola was so dominated by and dependent upon whites that the rapid deterioration of the security situation, the burgeoning and at times bloody confrontations between the three nationalist movements, soon created panic among them. After March 1975, as the Angolan whites began to stream out of Angola, they took with them almost everything that made the system of government and the economy work, throwing an already confused situation into chaos. Angola, by the summer of 1975 in fact, had the misfortune to recreate some of the worst characteristics of two previous African crises, the Congo and the Algerian war, combining militarized, battle-hardened nationalists with an environment where the mechanisms which made society function had almost totally collapsed.[28]

The importance of stressing this chaos in Angola is to point out the contrast it presents to the situations which had transpired in much of the rest of Africa in the period of decolonization. Almost everywhere—except, perhaps, for the Congo, Algeria, and Guinea Conakry—the transfer of power occurred with the acquiescence (albeit sometimes reluctant) of the colonial powers; and in consequence, disruption in administration and in the economies had been surprisingly small. The experiences of outside powers in their relationships with the new African states were therefore not appropriate to the situations that had developed in Angola. There, new circumstances required new policies, which would have to be formulated within an international environment that had itself changed dramatically since 1962.

The decolonization of Angola was of special concern to the South African government, even more than the rapid withdrawal of the Portuguese from Mozambique. In Portugal's east African colony there was very little South Africa could do to influence the outcome once it became clear in September of 1974 that the Portuguese military in the colony, under the leadership of Admiral Vitor Crespo, would tolerate no interference with the smooth transfer of authority to FRELIMO. An independent Mozambique, however, even if ruled by a Marxist government, would be extremely vulnerable to South Africa and economically dependent on the goodwill of Pretoria.

28. On Angola in this period, see: Ernest Harsch and Tony Thomas, *Angola: The Hidden History of Washington's War* (New York, 1976); Jim Dingeman, "Angola: Portugal in Africa," *Strategy and Tactics*, no. 56 (May/June 1976); Colin Legum and Tony Hodges, *After Angola: The War over Southern Africa* (New York, 1976); Gerald J. Bender, "Angola, the Cubans, and American Anxieties," *Foreign Policy*, no. 31 (Summer 1978), pp. 3–33: John A. Marcum, "The Lessons of Angola," *Foreign Affairs* 54, no. 3 (April 1976): 407–25; Kenneth Adelman and Gerald J. Bender, "Conflict in Southern Africa: A Debate," *International Security* 3, no. 2 (Fall 1978): 67–122; Gerald J. Bender, "Kissinger and Angola: Anatomy of Failure," *American Policy in Southern Africa* (Washington, D.C., 1978), pp. 65–143; and John Marcum, *The Angolan Revolution*, vol. 2 (which deals with this period); Robert Moss, "Castro's Secret War Exposed," *The Sunday Telegraph* (London), Jan. 30, 1977, Feb. 6, 1977, Feb. 30, 1977; Gabriel García Marquez, "Operation Carlota: Cuba's Role in Angolan Victory," *Cuba Update*, Center for Cuban Studies, no. 1 (New York, April 1977). This is an excerpted account based on the original in Spanish published in Mexico. A good overview is Arthur Jay Klinghoffer, *The Angolan War: A Study in Soviet Policy in the Third World* (Boulder, Colo.: Westview Press, 1980).

Mozambique and South Africa were bound together by a mutual dependency. Much of Mozambique's foreign earnings depended on the use of its port and rail facilities by South Africans and the earnings of Mozambique workers in the South African gold mines. South Africa relied on Mozambique for more than 25 percent of its mining labor force and needed the energy that would come from the Cabora Bassa dam. South Africa's own ports were overcongested. The South African government also hoped that good relations with FRELIMO would discourage any aid to guerrillas in Zululand and the eastern Transvaal. In Angola, by contrast, South Africa could exert very little economic leverage over any nationalist government in Luanda, and because of Namibia, South Africa was vulnerable where its own position was weakest. The temptation to interfere militarily was thus very great, and on the surface seemed to be relatively risk-free, given the divisions between the nationalist movements in Angola and South Africa's own logistical advantages.

The South African response to developments in Angola had thus to rely more on military capabilities than economic suasion. The defense posture which South Africa's military strategists had adopted during the 1970s therefore set important conditions to South African options in Angola. While Dr. Vorster, the South African prime minister, had been talking of "detente" with neighboring black nations, he had also been rapidly building up the South African defense forces. South African military strategists, meanwhile, increasingly evoked the Israeli precedent of swift preemptive action, a doctrine that in the South African context was called "hot pursuit." Ironically, "hot pursuit" was first used against Kenneth Kanunda of Zambia in 1971 as a result of clashes in the Caprivi strip, when Botha, the South African defense minister, threatened to "hit him so hard he will never forget." The doctrine of "hot pursuit" was used to justify the first armed South African incursions into Angola in the summer of 1975. The "defense" of the Cunene Dam complex in Namibia's border was used to justify the first permanent installation of South African regular forces inside Angola in early August 1975.

The deteriorating situation within Angola was also of concern to Zaire and Zambia. The closure of the Benguela railway over the summer of 1975 as a result of hostilities in Angola could not have come at a worse time for both countries. Each was in deep political and economic trouble—mainly, though by no means exclusively, as a result of the dramatic drop in world copper prices. Zaire, with an external debt of some $600 million, faced a chronic debt service problem and began in July 1975 to fall behind in obligations to its international bankers, among them the Export Import Bank, First National City Bank, Chase Manhattan Bank, and Continental Illinois. Its foreign exchange reserves were sufficient for only about three weeks' imports. For Zambia the economic problems were no less acute. The decline in copper prices had made the industry totally unprofitable, since the cost of production surpassed the market return. The result was to reduce the country's foreign earnings to nil. The social impact of this economic condition was very serious indeed. Copper exports had sustained an exceptionally high level of trade. In addition, 40 percent of direct government revenues came from the mining sector, and a large part of the food supply was imported from outside the country.

It was these complex interrelationships in the region which made the escalating conflicts in Angola so dangerous. But it was the Zaire connection which entrapped the United States in the Angolan crisis and revived the old plan that General Spínola and President Mobutu had concocted the previous September.

In Zaire the special sensitivity to President Mobutu's desires and his effectiveness in promoting them had five causes. First, through late 1974 and 1975 Zaire was facing a major economic crisis, one result of which was to give the viewpoints of the international financial community, especially in the United States, France, and Belgium,[29] unusual weight where Zairian affairs were concerned. Second, Mobutu possessed some very influential private lines of communication with Washington, and by using them succeeded in circumventing and neutralizing realistic assessments of the situation being made by many experienced African specialists within the intelligence community and the State Department.[30] Third, by the end of the summer of 1974, Mobutu had already preempted the strategy to be followed by the West, providing the FNLA with a privileged access to sources of Western support. This was an inevitable consequence of acting in Angola through Zaire. Over the years, the FNLA had become little more than an extension of Mobutu's own armed forces, and Holden Roberto, the leader of the FNLA, was a man linked to Mobutu by marriage and obligated to him for many past favors. Fourth, Zaire played a key role in the overall structures within which the Nixon administration had sought to organize its international relationships. Recognition of the limits to the United States's power and ability to engage herself worldwide was the original rationale

29. Excellent accounts of the tense negotiations over Zaire's debt and economic problems can be found in Nancy Bellieveau, *Institutional Investor* (March 1977), pp. 23–28, and Crawford Young, "Zaire: The Unending Crisis," *Foreign Affairs* (Fall 1978), pp. 169–85.

30. On private lines of communication and their impact on Zairian-U.S.-Angolan relations, see Bruce Oudes's reports in *Africa Contemporary Record*, ed. Colin Legum (New York: Africana Publishing Company), especially vol. 7 (1974–75), pp. A87-A101, and vol. 8 (1975–76), pp. A118–A126.

underlying the Nixon doctrine—in effect, a policy of selective involvement in building up friendly states in important regions.[31]

The fifth reason for the deference accorded to Mobutu's schemes was that, despite the fact that Zaire had been accorded a prime place in U.S. relationships with Africa during the 1970s, top policymakers in Washington remained largely ignorant about what was happening there. The reason for this ignorance had much to do with the personal style of the most influential U.S. policymaker of the period, Henry Kissinger. The problem well into the summer of 1975 was not that Kissinger gave Zaire and Angola too much attention but that he gave them too little. He held Africa, Africans, and African specialists in low esteem, and they had been frequent butts for his jokes and humiliations. Moreover, between 1974 and 1976 there were four different assistant secretaries of state for African affairs, and two of them were forced out within less than a year for warning Kissinger that he was creating a debacle in Africa. Portuguese Africa, moreover, had been something of a Nixon specialty. The Spinola-Mobutu decolonization plan, in fact, had its roots in the Nixon-Spinola summit held on June 19, 1974, in the Azores, when Spinola had painted an extraordinary picture for Nixon of Communist subversion in Europe and Africa.[32] But Nixon was out of office

31. See "U.S. Policy on Angola," *Hearing before the Committee on International Relations, House of Representatives, 94th Congress, 2nd Session, January 26, 1976* (Washington, D.C.: G.P.O., 1976), p. 13. Also see "Security Supporting Assistance for Zaire," *Hearing before the Subcommittee on African Affairs and the Subcommittee on Foreign Assistance of the Committee on Foreign Relations, U.S. Senate, 94th Congress, 1st Session, October 24, 1975* (Washington, D.C.: G.P.O., 1975), p. 32. Also Kenneth Maxwell, "A New Scramble for Africa," in *The Conduct of Soviet Foreign Policy*, ed. Erik Hoffman and Frederick Fleron, Jr. (Hawthorne, N.Y.: Aldine Publishing Co., 1980), pp. 515–34.

32. For Spinola's own account of this episode, see de Spínola, *Pais sem rumo*. See also Stephen R. Weissman's testimony before the Committee on International Relations, January 26, 1976 (see n. 30), and his book, *American Foreign Policy in the Congo 1960–1969* (Ithaca, N.Y.: Cornell University Press, 1974), as well as John Stockwell, *In Search of Enemies: A CIA Story* (New York: W. W. Norton and Company, 1978). There has been much speculation about what was discussed between Spinola and Nixon at their June 19, 1974, Azores meeting. The two men met alone with only an interpreter present, and officials on both sides were left in the dark as to the topics covered. Spinola has now given his version of the conversation in *Pais sem rumo*, pp. 158–68. Also see Stephen R. Weissman, "CIA Covert Action in Zaire and Angola: Patterns and Consequences," *Political Science Quarterly*, vol. 94, no. 2 (Summer 1979). For background on Cuba's role in Africa, see: Nelson P. Valdes, "Revolutionary Solidarity in Angola," *Cuba and the World*, ed. Cole Blasier and Carmelo Mesa-Lago (Pittsburgh, 1979), pp. 87–117; William M. Leo Grande, "Cuba-Soviet Relations and Cuban Policy in Africa," *Cuban Studies* (Pittsburgh, January 1980), pp. 1–48; Carla Anne Robinns, "Looking for Another Angola: Cuban Policy Dilemmas in Africa," *Working Papers Number 38* (Latin American Program, Wilson Center, Smithsonian Institution, Washington, D.C.).

within two months, and Spinola only survived in his until the end of September. It should have been obvious that there was a debilitating weakness in an enterprise which had inherited its rationale from a dead colonialism, which sought to exercise power through informal influence over tenuously controlled clients, and where European predecessors who had possessed the formidable advantages of long local experience and formal sovereignty had just failed.

One major result of these circumstances was that, when eventually top U.S. policymakers began taking a serious direct interest in what was happening in Central Africa, it was largely as a result of the direct and serious measures the Soviet Union was taking to counteract the all-too-obvious attempts by Zaire to exclude the MPLA and Neto from the fruits of the victory which they, with Soviet encouragement, had fought twenty years to achieve. But by then, with respect to Africa the United States was already trapped within a framework of alliances, assumptions, and barely comprehended past failures from which it was difficult to escape. The salience given in Washington to the fact of Communist support for the MPLA served to cover up the fact that the roots of escalation lay in actions in which the United States had been indirectly involved (and after January 1975, directly, when the CIA reactivated its connection with Holden Roberto) through her Zairian client. The African dimension became almost irrelevant in the process. As Helmut Sonnenfeldt, counselor in the State Department and Kissinger's closest advisor on Soviet affairs, explained later, the United States "had no intrinsic interest in Angola as such." But "once a locale, no matter how remote and unimportant for us, becomes a focal point for Soviet, and in this instance, Soviet-supported Cuban military action, the United States acquires a derivative interest which we simply cannot avoid."[33]

Preoccupation with Soviet intentions, therefore, overwhelmed the warnings that were pouring in from, among others, the U.S. consul in

33. Helmut Sonnefeldt, "American-Soviet Relations: Informal Remarks," *Parameters, Journal of the U.S. Army War College,* vol. 6, no. 1, pp. 15–16 (an article adapted from an address given before the 22d Annual National Security Seminar at the U.S. Army War College, June 3, 1976). On Soviet policy, William E. Griffith, "Soviet Power and Policies in the Third World: The Case of Africa," p. 152; *Adelphi Papers,* one hundred fifty-two, "Prospects on Soviet Power in the 1980's" (International Institute for Strategic Studies, London, 1979), pp. 39–46; "The Soviet Union and the Third World: A Watershed of Great Power Rivalry," *Report to the Committee on International Relations, House of Representatives, by the Senior Specialists Division, Congressional Research Service, Library of Congress,* May 8, 1977 (Washington, D.C.: G.P.O. 1977). Also Colin Legum, "The African Crisis," in *America and the World 1978* (*Foreign Affairs* Special Edition, 1979), pp. 633–51.

Luanda, an interagency task force, and two assistant secretaries of state for African affairs on the inside; from such respected African specialists as John Marcum and Gerald Bender on the outside; and from Senator Dick Clark in the Congress—all of whom argued that unless a broad-based political strategy aimed at conciliating the factions in Angola was substituted for the attempt to favor some at the expense of others, the United States was doomed to face escalating demands with no certainty of success. Doomed indeed to help create a situation where the resolution of the conflict would come through military means, with the United States unprepared and incapable of acting to aid the very forces it had egged into the conflict. At no time, until too late, did the United States give any serious thought to what a purely military solution to the Angolan crisis would involve, so great was the belief that the old and trusted formula of clandestineness, mercenaries, and cash would still work as they had in the past. By the time it became obvious that this was not enough, the only alternative power with the capacity and desire to intervene was South Africa, which was the last thing the West or the anti-MPLA nationalists should have permitted to become obvious. South African intervention at a stroke undermined the Western groups' credibility in African opinion, overwhelmed the doubts that many African states (Nigeria in particular) had about the MPLA and its friends, and made large-scale Soviet and Cuban assistance to Neto respectable.

The Soviets, who have long memories, had their own special reasons for being sensitive to the role of Zaire in the Angolan crises. Zaire had been the scene of Soviet humiliation during the early sixties. It had been precisely because of the unhappy Soviet experiences in places like the former Belgium Congo that the Soviet Union embarked on a major buildup in long-distance support capacity to prevent the reoccurrence of such a humiliation. The Soviets, who had only been able to provide Lumumba with sixteen transport planes and a few trucks in 1960, were able in 1975 to provide Agostinho Neto with $200 million in military assistance by sea and air, to establish an air bridge with some 46 flights of Soviet medium and heavy air transports, and to airlift in Soviet IL-62's a sizable part of the 11,000 Cuban combat troops sent into Angola during this period.[34]

In late October 1975, the remnant of the old Spinola-Mobuto plan went into operation. The U.S.-backed Zairian forces moved from the north, as did a combined operation from the south by Portuguese right-wing extremists, South African regulars, and a motley collection of UNITA, FNLA

34. *Strategic Survey 1978* (International Institute for Strategic Studies, London), p. 13.

auxiliaries, and Daniel Chipenda. When these forces attempted to take Luanda before November 11, 1975, much to their surprise they came up against Cuban regulars flown in during the previous weeks in old Britannia transport planes at Agostinho Neto's urgent request. The West's hodgepodge forces thus failed to prevent the MPLA from declaring the independence of Angola under their exclusive auspices in the Angolan capital on November 11.

The Soviet Union's intervention in aid of Lumumba in 1960, despite its small size and dubious results, had neveretheless been an important turning point. It had marked the first use of transport aircraft in a crisis situation outside the immediate Soviet bloc countries. The creation of the West African naval patrol in late 1970 in order to protect Conakry, and indirectly to protect the headquarters of the PAIGC, was also an important step in the Soviets' increased willingness to support clients militarily and to take risks on their behalf. Large-scale Soviet airlift capacity had been much in evidence during the 1973 Middle East war, when the Soviets had made 934 flights to Arab nations, delivering 15,000 tons of material in addition to the much larger tonnage shipped by freighter. The U.S. airlift by C-5 and C-141 to Israel via the Azores in the same period had comprised 568 flights and delivered 23,000 tons of supplies. The Middle East experience, however, had given the Soviets much greater confidence in their ability to influence events successfully in the Third World. In April 1974, Marshal Grechko said that "at the present stage, the historical function of the Soviet armed forces is not restricted merely to their function in defending the motherland and other socialist countries. In its foreign policy activity, the Soviet state actively and purposefully opposes the export of counterrevolution and the policy of oppression, supports the national liberation struggle, and resolutely resists imperialist aggression in whatever distant region of the planet it may appear."[35]

In 1975, direct Soviet aid to the MPLA began in the form of arms deliveries by sea and air via Brazzaville; in March, Russian cargo planes began delivering military equipment, which was later transshipped to Cabinda or Luanda; in April, some hundred tons of arms were delivered, in chartered Bristol Britannias, from Dar es Salaam to MPLA-controlled airfields in central Angola. Two Yugoslavian freighters unloaded weapons in Angola, followed by two East German vessels and an Algerian one. In April, Paulo Jorge of the MPLA visited Cuba in search of specialists to assist with the

35. For a balanced account of the outside intervention in the Angolan war, see Colin Legum chapter in Kaplan, *Diplomacy of Power*, pp. 570–637.

sophisticated equipment now arriving from the Soviet Union and Eastern Europe which the MPLA's own forces were not yet trained to handle.[36]

Cuban military men knowledgeable enough to use sophisticated equipment were beginning to take part in combat operations by the late spring of 1975. Cuban "advisers" were involved in the fighting at Caxito at the end of May, an engagement where the first tanks were used by the MPLA. In May and June, some 230 Cuban military advisers established training camps at Benguela, Cabinda, Henrique de Carvalho, and Salazaro. All these early Cuban arrivals entered via Congo-Brazzaville. By mid-August, UNITA found its units facing Cubans at Lobito. In July the MPLA approached the Soviets for a Soviet troop presence in addition to military training experts. The Soviets balked at the suggestion as being too provocative and advised the MPLA to seek such assistance from Cuba. In early August a MPLA mission visited Havana to urge Castro to supply them with troops. In mid-August Castro authorized the logistical planning necessary to mount the sea- and airlift of troops, equipment, and supplies across the Atlantic to Angola. The operation was a complex one, involving the simultaneous arrival in Angola of troops from Cuba and armaments from the USSR.

The East Germans and the Soviets were also active between mid-August and November. Twenty-seven shiploads of military equipment and forty supply missions by Soviet AN-22 military cargo planes were unloaded at Brazzaville, to be transshipped to Angola before independence. The number of Soviet military advisers in Angola reached two hundred. The East Germans had, since 1972, enjoyed a military cooperation agreement with Congo/Brazzaville—the first such agreement between the GDR and an African country. Brazzaville had been the center of the MPLA's activities prior to the Alvor settlement and up until the time when the MPLA leadership moved to Luanda in February 1975. The East Germans, like the Cubans, had an important collaborative role in the "counterimperialistic" strategy of the Soviets and, also like the Cubans, the GDR's security forces were subordinated to the KGB apparatus. The East German SED party chairman, Honecker, reported to the party congress in May 1976 that "in

36. See the excellent accounts by Tony Hodges, "How the MPLA Won," and Colin Legum, "The Role of the Big Powers," in *After Angola: The War over Southern Africa*(London: Rex Collins, 1976); Charles K. Ebinger, "External Intervention in Internal War: The Politics and Diplomacy of the Angolan Civil War," *Orbis* (Fall 1976), pp. 669–99; as well as the firsthand report by Stockwell, *In Search of Enemies*, and Nathaniel Davis, "The Angola Decision of 1975: A Personal Memoir," *Foreign Affairs* (Fall 1978), pp. 109–24. On South Africa's intervention, see Robert S. Jaster, South Africa's Narrowing Security Options (Adelphi Papers no. 159, IISS, International Institute for Strategic Studies, London, 1980).

view of the present relationship of forces . . . the GDR's mission in Africa and the Third World was thoroughly substantial." In Angola in 1975, East Germany supplied heavy weapons and other war material to the MPLA, military instructors, pilots for the ports of Luanda and Lobito, and medical personnel. The GDR's state security service provided training for the MPLA's own security and intelligence services.

The crisis in Angola escalated in July. On July 18, the United States decided to step up support to the anti-MPLA forces. The "40 committee" (the high-level interagency policy group that advised the president on covert action and to which the CIA was responsible) authorized $14 million in covert assistance to be paid in two instalments to the FNLA and UNITA (a sum increased to $25 million in August and $32 million in November). A week before, on July 14 in Angola, the MPLA had expelled its rivals from Luanda. By taking the offensive, it had by October seized control of twelve of the sixteen district capitals of Angola. In July, Zaire sent a commando company and armored car squadron across the border into Angola and into combat. Daniel Chipenda had flown to Namibia in June to meet in Windhoeck with General Hendrik van den Bergh, chief of the South African Bureau of State Security (BOSS). South Africa's support for the FNLA seems to have begun in July and its support for UNITA, in September. In mid-August two Zairian paratrooper companies joined the action in support of the FNLA. At the same time, regular South African troops occupied the Ruacana and Calacque pumping stations and the Cunane Dam complex. In September, Soviet 122-millimeter rockets were used for the first time in fighting north of Luanda. These so-called Stalin-organs sent the FNLA and Zairian regulars into a panicky retreat. Three Cuban merchant ships left Cuba for Angola in early September after urgent appeals from the MPLA, which now feared a large-scale South African invasion augmented by U.S. assistance, via Zaire, to the FNLA and UNITA. The Soviets had abandoned the idea of a political coalition in March; they were now portraying the FNLA and UNITA in their propaganda as "splintists" and describing the war in Angola not as a "civil war" but as a "war of intervention." Unfortunately for Angola, the war was both a civil war and a war in which outside intervention occurred on a massive scale. The Chinese, looking on from their vantage point in Zaire, decided to cut their losses. On October 27, 1975, they withdrew all their military instructors from the FNLA.

By November, the Portuguese army in Angola was a helpless bystander. The last official Portuguese representative, Commandor Leonel Cardoso, and his staff scuttled quietly away from Luanda the day before independence. In fact, at the moment independence was declared in Luanda, the MPLA held little more than the capital and a strip of central Angola inland toward Shaba.[37] South African advisers and South African antitank weapons had helped to stop an MPLA advance on Nova Lisboa (Huambo) in early October. Nova Lisboa was the center of UNITA strength and the site of a declaration of an independent state (the "Social Democratic Republic of Angola") by UNITA and FNLA on November 11. By October, the South Africans had helped turn the tide in the south against the MPLA. A South African-led combat group (Zulu) with armored cars and mortars had traveled four hundred miles from the Namibia border in two weeks, overwhelming the MPLA and Cubans in Benguela and Lobita, thus seizing control of the terminal of the Benguela railroad. In central Angola, a second South African combat unit ("Foxbat") with a squadron of armored cars had moved five hundred miles north toward Luanda and inflicted a severe defeat on the Cubans at Bridge 14 (North of Santa Combo), killing over two hundred of them as well as two hundred MPLA troops. North of Luanda, the FNLA and Zairian troops had again reached Caxito, within a short drive of the capital.

A big Cuban buildup started on November 7, when 650 combat troops were flown to Angola via Barbados and Guinea-Bissau. On November 27, a Cuban artillery regiment and a battalion of motorized and field troops landed on the Angolan coast after a sea crossing of twenty days. The Soviets had meanwhile deployed a naval force in Angolan waters which provided protection to the ships unloading and transshipping arms from Pointe-Noire (Congo) to Angola. Soviet military transports were airlifting reinforcements and arms from late October. The Russians provided MIG-21's, T-34 and T-54 tanks, armored personnel carriers, antitank and SAM-7 missiles, rocket launchers, and AK-47 automatic rifles, in addition to the 122-millimeter rocket launchers, which proved totally effective against the Zairians in particular. (After October, it was said that Zairian regulars went into battle driving in reverse, the better to drive away again when threatened by the Stalin-organs' awesome power.) The Soviet and Cuban intervention was decisive. It saved the MPLA and their regime, and it profoundly altered the balance of power in southern Africa.

U.S. Secretary of State Henry Kissinger, like the South Africans, was shaken by the scale of the Soviet and Cuban response. The CIA's Angolan task force at CIA headquarters at Langley had been so confident of success

37. For some interesting and well-informed comments on this aspect, see "The Battle for Angola," by Robert Moss, editor of the *Economist's* confidential *Foreign Report*, November 12, 1975, pp. 1–6. Moss was in southern Angola with the South Africans and was one of the best-placed observers to know their thinking on this question. Also see comments by Cord Meyer, *Facing Reality: From World Federalism to the CIA* (New York 1981). Cord Meyer was the CIA station chief in London over this period.

by the Zairian and South African regulars, that on November 11 the members had celebrated Angolan independence with wine and cheese in their crepe-paper decorated offices. The arrival of Soviet and Cuban ships and planes at Pointe-Noire and Brazzaville was observed by U.S. intelligence surveillance, but the unloading of troops had taken place at night, and strictly imposed discipline during the sea voyage concealed the presence of troops. Not until November did the CIA realize that 4,000 Cuban combat troops were deployed in Angola, a figure which had grown to 15,000 by January 1976. By February 1976, the combined Soviet-Cuban sea- and airlift had transported 38,000 tons of weapons and supplies to Angola. Although South African foreign policy had consistently played up the Communist threat to Africa, it had clearly not given serious attention to the consequences of a strong conventional Communist military presence in the form of some 20,000 Cuban troops. Although South Africa lost only 43 dead in Angola of its over 2,000 troops deployed there, it had by the end of 1976 concluded that, for military and political reasons, it was not in a position to take on a superpower. As a result of press leaks in the fall, the United States was effectively removed from the Angolan competition on December 19, 1975, when overwhelming majorities in both Houses of Congress banned covert aid to the FNLA and UNITA. The OAU, in response to the fact that South African intervention had become public knowledge in November, swung from its former neutrality to support of the MPLA as the legitimate government of Angola. South African intervention was especially decisive in the case of Nigeria, the MPLA going so far as to send captured South African prisoners to the OAU meeting in Lagos to prove that South African regulars were in fact involved in the Angolan fighting.

Throughout the Angolan civil war the West had found itself at cross purposes. French objectives were not the same as those of the Americans. The Portuguese whom the Americans supported in Angola were the same groups they opposed in Portugal. South Africa, while useful as a source of intelligence, was a disaster as an ally in conflict.

Two of the major multinationals in Angola showed themselves more than willing to work with the MPLA. Diamang, which held diamond concessions in the Lunda area, had for some years employed former Katanga gendarmes, who had fled to Angola following the collapse of the succession movement in neighboring Katanga during the mid-1960s, as its own private security force. With encouragement and financial support from sympathetic Portuguese officers and with Diamang's acquiescence, the gendarmes, an effective fighting force, had joined with the MPLA's depleted military units in 1975; they were important in the defense of Luanda in November. The Katangans were bitter enemies of Zairian President

Mobutu, the main outside supporter of the MPLA's rivals, Holden Roberto and the FNLA. The other multinational was Gulf Oil, which after the transitional tripartite government collapsed in July 1975, continued to pay its royalties to an administration in Luanda which to all intents and purposes was composed of the MPLA alone. Kissinger intervened to stop these payments for a time in November, but Gulf paid the royalties into escrow, and the MPLA later collected the $100 million in question with interest.

The West's position was also fundamentally flawed by the failure to provide any clear objectives for its actions other than the negative one of denying the MPLA victory. What sort of Angola, for example, did they think a FNLA/UNITA victory would create? The South Africans seem to have been thinking of setting up some sort of buffer state in the central south of the country. Zaire seems to have coveted Cabinda. The MPLA, in contrast, stood firm with the concept of a unitary state; they held the capital, and their main source of ethnic support lay in a broad belt at the heart of the country. So conscious, in fact, was Neto of the risks of Balkanization implicit in the FNLA/UNITA offensive, that on the day of Angola's independence he refused to cut the celebratory cake for fear that it would be a bad omen for the division of Angola. Several likely allies were also noticeably absent from the Western lineup: Brazil, for example, which had been among the first to recognize the Neto regime, and Israel, which, despite Kissinger's entreaties, had the good sense for once to keep clear of the conflict.

As to the scale of aid, it is very difficult to find accurate figures. Kissinger has repeatedly used the $200-million figure as representing the value of arms transfer from the Soviets to the MPLA in 1975. Other sources place the figure at $300 million; the U.S. arms control agency says $190 million. United States aid prior to the prohibition by Congress was in the region of $32 million, but investigators from the House Select Committee on Intelligence discovered this figure was based on bookkeeping devices that grossly underestimated the value of the arms provided. But arms imports to Zaire, over the period of the civil war, rose to $126 million in 1976 as compared with a mere $27 million the year before. The Chinese also provided support directly to FNLA, and permitted Chinese arms held by the Zairian army to be released to them also. France and Britain are estimated to have committed the equivalent of several million dollars each to Angolan operations, and the South African defense expenditures rose to nearly 19 percent of all public expenditures (1,711.7 million Rands 1977–78) to accommodate the costs of intervention in Angola, the actual expenditures exceeding the budget estimates by some 228.7 million Rands. There was also considerable support from government and private sources for Portuguese right-wing forces that were active with UNITA and the South Africans in the south of Angola in 1976–76 and in the north with the FNLA during the same period. Further funds were also later available in Europe to recruit mercenaries. And some part of the monies which various NATO governments poured surreptitiously into Portugal in 1975 went to protect Western objectives in Africa. It seems likely, therefore, that in toto these diverse subventions from Western sources matched, and may even have surpassed, the $200-million figure the Soviets spent. The problem in any case was not how much was spent on armaments but the quality of the soldiers who used them.[38]

The end of Portugal's rule in Africa had far-reaching international consequences. In sourthern Africa it was very soon apparent that the position of the white minority govenrment in Rhodesia was no longer tenable; and within five years of the independence of Angola, Rhodesia emerged as the independent black-ruled nation of Zimbabwe, something Ian Smith, the former Rhodesian prime minister vowed would not happen within a century. The fiasco of South Africa's intervention in the Angolan war shook Pretoria's confidence, awakened the African townships, and dramatized the isolation of the apartheid regime.

The active involvement of the two superpowers and their clients in the Angolan imbroglio set precedents for future adventurism in Ethiopia and Afghanistan. American secretary of state, Henry Kissinger, called Angola one of "the decisive watersheds" in Soviet expansionism in the Third World.[39] One major result of the manner in which Portuguese decoloniza-

38. These figures are pieced together from Mark M. Lowenthal, "Foreign Assistance in the Angolan Civil War," in appendix 3 to "Mercenaries in Africa," *Hearing before the Special Subcommittee on International Relations, House of Representatives, 94th Congress, 2nd Session, August 9, 1976* (Washington, D.C.: G.P.O., 1976), from *World Military Expenditures 1967–1976*, and *Strategic Survey 1977* (London: International Institute for Strategic Studies, 1977), p. 27. The best brief accounts of the role of the various European countries in Africa can be found in *Africa Contemporary Record* (New York), (ed. Colin Legum, especially vol. 7 (1974–75) and vol. 8 (1975–76).

39. U.S. Secretary of State, Henry A. Kissinger, in a speech on February 3, 1976, stated that "for the first time in history the Soviet Union could threaten distant places beyond the Eurasian land mass—including the United States. . . Angola represents the first time that the Soviets have moved militarily at long distances to impose a regime of their choice. It is the first time that the United States has failed to respond to Soviet military moves outside the immediate Soviet orbit. And it is the first time that Congress has halted national action in the middle of a crisis" (*The Washington Post*, February 16, 1976). He repeated this view more starkly in an interview published in *Encounter* (November 1978). "Had we succeeded in Angola there would have been no Ethiopia. The situation in southern Africa would be entirely different, and I think this was one of the decisive watersheds" (p. 12). Also see "Statement by Hon. Henry A. Kissinger, *Hearings before the Subcommittee on African Affairs, U.S. Senate,*

tion had occured was a weakening of detente. The irony for Portugal was that, once it was all over and the formal ties of empire were gone, little remained but the cultural links which Portugal had spent so much time touting but so little time cultivating.

The decolonization of Portuguese Africa was also fundamentally influenced by its timing. The last empire ended within an international environment quite different from that which saw the end of the French, British, or Belgian colonies. By the 1970s the West was weakened and divided in comparison with the preeminence of its power and influence during the earlier postwar decades. Within Portuguese Africa the equivocation of the West's relationship with Portugal—more influenced by the desire to protect strategic assets in the North Atlantic, especially in the Azores, than with the smooth transfer of power in Portugal's African territories—limited the West's options. Time and again the Azores' issue preempted American and Western European pressure for change in Portugal's colonial policy; and in the end, especially during the year when Portuguese Africa moved swiftly toward independence, the West and Portugal paid a heavy price for the Azores connection.

The delay in decolonization and the long wars in the Portuguese colonies also helped to produce a very different type of nationalist movement in Portuguese Africa—one more explicitly Marxist in ideology, more militant in action, and, in the case of Angola, more dependent on external support from Soviets, Cubans, and Eastern Europeans. No less important had been another change: the ability and capacity of the Soviets and their friends to influence events to their own advantage in Africa.

In the final analysis, the furtive scuttling away of the Portuguese from Luanda in November 1975 was of more than passing significance. A whole epoch was drawing to a close, ending a relationship between Europe and Africa which, for better or worse, had profoundly influenced both continents for a half a millennium.

94th Congress, 2nd Session, January 3, 4, 6, 1976 (Washington, D.C.: G.P.O., 1976). For the contrary "regionalist" argument, see Gerald J. Bender, "Angola, the Cubans, and American Anxieties," *Foreign Policy*, no. 31 (Summer 1978), pp. 3–33, and John A. Marcum, "The Lessons of Angola," *Foreign Affairs* 54, no. 3 (April 1976): 407–25. The violence of the debate can be seen in Kenneth Adelman and Gerald J. Bender, "Conflict in Southern Africa: A Debate," *International Security*, vol. 3, no. 2 (Fall 1978).

14. *Misconceived Dominion: The Creation and Disintegration of Federation in British Central Africa*

PROSSER GIFFORD

As we look back at the years 1945–63 in British Central Africa from the perspective of the late 1970s, we can sense in ways denied to contemporaries the irony of the Federation as a construct for the transfer of power from metropolitan to local control. One of the few advantages historians have is the opportunity to assess the unintended and unanticipated consequences of past action and past thought. The attempt in this chapter will be to present concisely what contemporaries thought they were doing, and then as best I can to trace out the causal linkages to the actual course of events. The assumptions made in London in the early 1950s about the future of the peoples of the territories then called Nyasaland, Northern Rhodesia, and Southern Rhodesia continue to retain a significance equal—but quite different in nature—to that attributed to them by contemporaries. We can now read the "Great Debate" over colonial policy which preceded the establishment of the Central African Federation in 1953 with some of the same frisson for truths glossed over or half-comprehended that we feel when we read the debates that took place one hundred years earlier concerning Irish Relief after the potato famine.

We are helped immeasurably to achieve perspective on the years following the Second World War by recent historical scholarship on the precolonial period and the early years of settlement. The work of Charles van Onselen, Robin Palmer, Ian Phimister, Laurel van Horn, Maud Muntemba, Leroy Vail, and others has laid a crucial foundation for our understanding of the years after 1923.[1] The detailed argumentation of their

1. Charles van Onselen, *Chibaro: African Mine Labour in Southern Rhodesia 1900–1933* (London, 1976); Robin Palmer, *Land and Racial Domination in Rhodesia* (Berkeley, 1977); Robin Palmer and Neil Parsons, eds., *The Roots of Rural Poverty in Central and Southern Africa* (Berkeley, 1977), which contains essays by Ian Phiminster, "Peasant Production and Underdevelopment in Southern Rhodesia, 1890–1914," Laurel van Horn, "Agricultural History of Barotseland, 1840–1914," Maud Muntemba, ". . . Economic Change in the Kabwe

studies makes undeniable the depth and kind of knowledge which Africans had about colonialism in Central Africa from the outset. Africans *knew*, not from books or from missionary education, but from experienced suffering, disease, and degradation. They realized from the 1890s that the central struggle was over rights to land in Southern Rhodesia; some of them had lived through the growth and then the discriminatory closure of market opportunities in agriculture. They knew the conditions of squalor, disease, inadequate pay, and varying forms of fiscal coercion which accompanied labor in the mines; they knew directly the network which connected areas as distant as Barotseland and Nyasaland with the mines of Southern Rhodesia and South Africa. They knew the enforced discipline of the compound and the hierarchy of mines which had its apex in Johannesburg. They did not know, but they suspected, that benefits alleged to derive from colonial investment, such as the Nyasaland railways, were in fact financed by a disproportionate levy of taxes on villagers whose produce never benefited from such transportation.[2]

Firsthand knowledge of these realities helps to explain why African spokesmen and women expressed repeatedly before commissions and boards, in tribal and political associations, through pamphlets and deputations, skepticism and disbelief in European pronouncements or assurances.[3] More clearly than many European settlers and many British legislators, Africans who had experienced what white Rhodesians had done, could make the distinction between promises—even noble and admirable promises—and results. How, they wished to know, would the new society being built benefit them? Access to education and to economic advancement could indeed bring real benefits, but there was much in the record to suggest systematic discrimination and a calculated attribution of in-

---

Rural District of Zambia, 1902–70," and Leroy Vail, "Railway Development and Colonial Underdevelopment: The Nyasaland Case"—among others. Essential for an understanding of the African perspective on Southern Rhodesia is the work of Terence O. Ranger, *Revolt in Southern Rhodesia 1896–7* (London, 1967), *The African Voice in Southern Rhodesia 1898 to 1930* (London, 1970), and *Aspects of Central African History*, chaps. 6 and 9 (London, 1968).

2. Leroy Vail, "Railway Development and Colonial Undevelopment: The Nyasaland Case," in Palmer, ed., *Roots of Rural Poverty*, pp. 365–95, argues that the railway prevented the Protectorate Government from acting on "all the good intentions aimed at developing a solid, peasant-based agriculture in the country" (p. 375).

3. The best sustained analysis of African reactions is T. O. Ranger, *The African Voice in Southern Rhodesia*. See also Robin Palmer's discussion of the Morris Carter Land Commission evidence in *Land and Racial Domination*, pp. 176–78.

feriority.[4] These conditions made any shared, nonracial vision of the future difficult, almost impossible.

A second line of inquiry which helps to put our topic in perspective examines the place of Rhodesia in British policy. Martin Chanock argues that British policy toward the Rhodesian settler was never formulated for its own sake—Rhodesia was always viewed from London as a counterpoise: to the rise of Afrikanerdom in the Union of South Africa after 1910, or, after 1945, to the rise of African paramountcy in the north.[5] As a result, the settlers in Rhodesia were permitted "a role their strength did not warrant"—because they were thought to embody a promise of imperial predominance. Rhodesia "developed its political identity in a reaction against both British Liberalism and Afrikaner nationalism between 1910 and 1923."[6] Chanock's desire "to put the southern perspective back into Rhodesian history" is as important for us as van Onselen's *Chibaro*, because the entirely unwarranted political strength of the small white Rhodesian population is otherwise inexplicable. That the costs of such myopia are high hardly needs ampler proof than the disintegration which threatened civil war as a prelude to the birth of black Zimbabwe. Both in 1923 and in 1953, crucial events in Rhodesia were shaped in the shadow of South Africa.

A third line of scholarship since 1963 that provides a context for the examination of the years of the Federation derives from detailed economic studies of development, and of "the development of underdevelopment." Colin Leys's *Underdevelopment in Kenya* suggests by silent analogy a series of pointed questions to be asked of Rhodesia.[7] From a different ideological perspective, the work of Robert Baldwin and Robert Bates on the limited "multiplier effect" of the Northern Rhodesian and Zambian copper industry in stimulating other kinds of growth provides a needed corrective to the largely unexamined economic premises which underlay

4. See, for example, L. H. Gann's analysis of Charles Mzingeli's decision to join the ICU, in *A History of Southern Rhodesia: Early Days to 1934* (London, 1965), p. 270, and Ranger's analysis of the responses of various African associations to the Land Apportionment Bill in 1929, "African Politics in Twentieth-Century Southern Rhodesia," in *Aspects of Central African History*, pp. 210–45, at 226–27.

5. Martin Chanock, *Britain, Rhodesia and South Africa 1900–45: The Unconsummated Union* (New York, 1977).

6. Ibid., p. 256.

7. Colin Leys, *Underdevelopment in Kenya: The Political Economy of Neo-colonialism 1964–1971* (Berkeley, 1974).

arguments for federation.[8] That the rural responses to industrialization are, in many parts of independent Zambia, limited to migration or political protest makes starkly clear the importance of industrial and economic structures created in colonial times and the enormous inertia inherent in the continued operation of these systems. The years 1945–60 become the more important because they gave rise to the institutions which constituted the colonial legacy to independent nations. Zambia and Malawi had to build on the institutions of a dismantled federation—institutions which had never been intended for and were not designed to support independent states. This is a special instance, or an instance of a special kind, of the development of underdevelopment.

Having reflected a bit on the lenses through which we now view historical experience, we will look first at the postwar years from 1945 to 1953, the years which led—not at all inexorably and with much passionate contention—to the Central African Federation.

The foundations upon which federation was built were laid in Southern Rhodesia during the 1930s. Without either the territorial segregation of the Land Apportionment Act of 1930 or the political power of Godfrey Huggins and his United party, founded in 1934 and reelected overwhelmingly in 1939, the initiative for and the shape of association between the three territories would have been different. Whether the differences would have been considerable enough to provide recognition of African needs and African political aspirations, or whether they would more likely have prevented the push toward federation, must remain speculative questions. But the inadequacies of the Southern Rhodesian land settlement and the power of European politics in Southern Rhodesia were both real and clear by the beginning of the 1939 war.

The division of land in Southern Rhodesia went back to the Coryndon Commission of 1914–15, which, because it never contemplated the expropriation from Europeans of lands originally taken in Charter times, really ratified the claims of earlier European pioneers.[9] The principle on which the 1914 commission operated was that Africans would be gradually assimilated into a European way of life, and that the need for reserves

8. Robert E. Baldwin, *Economic Development and Export Growth: A Study of Northern Rhodesia, 1920–60* (Berkeley, 1966); Robert Bates, *Rural Responses to Industrialization: A Study of Village Zambia* (New Haven, 1976). See also Richard L. Sklar, *Corporate Power in an African State: The Political Impact of Multinational Mining Companies in Zambia* (Berkeley, 1975), esp. chap. 4.

9. R. Palmer, *Land and Racial Domination*, p. 109.

would diminish. This was almost exactly the opposite of the premise which provided the basis for the work of the Morris Carter Land Commission ten years later (1925), but the latter could not, even with different premises, obviate the landed legacy of the Coryndon group. The Carter Commission moved firmly in the direction of segregation, seeking the establishment of Native Purchase Areas adjacent to established native reserves. The theory was to provide land for individual purchase and development by Africans but away from the main European areas, and away also from the roads and railways that could make direct African competition with subsidized European agriculture possible. When the Land Apportionment Act finally came into effect on April Fool's Day, 1931, "the country's 48,000 Europeans (of whom only 11,000 were settled on the land) were given an average 1,000 acres per head of population."[10] The Europeans had more land than the approximately one million rural Africans, while about 6 million acres of European land within 35 miles of railway transportation "lay unoccupied and wholly undeveloped."[11] Despite the fact that in 1925 almost all witnesses (government, missionary, and African as well as settler) who spoke to the commission had favored possessory segregation, by the Second World War views had again changed.

> Africans were becoming increasingly vocal and critical of a land policy which squeezed them from their homes, moved them to distant areas which were generally inhospitable and far from markets, and offered in exchange a few purchase areas of exceedingly dubious value. Indeed by the late 1930s so notorious were Southern Rhodesian land policies, that migrant workers from Nyasaland and Northern Rhodesia had already decided that they wanted nothing to do with any proposed amalgamation of the three territories.[12]

The political climate of the 1930s was shaped initially by the Depression and by the exaggerated fears it generated of African competition and "poor whitism." In Southern Rhodesia the political climate was also shaped by Dr. Godfrey Martin Huggins, an English stockbroker's son, an able and highly qualified surgeon, who in 1932 "objected to the idea of Africans enjoying the same political rights as white men, and . . . called for amalga-

10. Ibid., p. 186.

11. Ibid., p. 185. "In 1976, 3 million acres of European farming land was not being used at all." "A Rhodesian National Farmers' Union study of 1977 reported that 30% of all [European] farms were insolvent." *Africa News* 14 (April 14, 1980); 7.

12. Ibid., p. 230.

mation with the north."[13] Huggins took over the leadership of the Reform party, won election in September 1933, and a year later received support for the formation of a United party, "so that the country might secure stable government over the next five years."[14] The United party won the election in November of 1934, taking 24 out of the 30 seats. "Effective opposition was at an end. Huggins ran the country, and his personality was to dominate the next two decades of its history."[15]

The structure of the government of Southern Rhodesia aimed at providing for Europeans a level of service and a style of life comparible to that of a Western European nation. But it "rested only on the financial and human resources of a small white community in a relatively poor and undeveloped country."[16] Because Great Britain in 1923 had turned over the control of local Southern Rhodesian politics and of African political advance to an almost entirely white electorate, that party stayed in power which managed at once to serve the wishes of the white electorate without sounding as overtly racist as the Afrikaners to the south.

> [E]very available artificial means was employed, from taxes and pass laws to the Industrial Conciliation Act and the Grain Marketing Act, to squeeze from the country a standard of life which would increase the European population and make it secure. The African population was cleared from the bulk of the best land; by the recruitment of African labour from a very wide area beyond the country's borders, wages were kept to a minimum which made possible enterprises which would not otherwise have paid; the European economy was insulated in every way possible from African competition, skilled employment being reserved for European artisans, paying markets for European farmers.[17]

Huggins understood these realities, although he came close to losing power in 1946 when the opposition Liberal party won only one less seat than his United party.[18] He was quick, however, to capitalize on the course of events in South Africa. The victory of Malan's Afrikaner Nationalists in the May 1948 election meant that any strengthening of Rhodesian ties with the south "would be at the price of Afrikaner dominance." Since the white

13. L. H. Gann, *A History of Southern Rhodesia*, p. 294.

14. Ibid., p. 309.

15. Ibid., p. 311. For an informative and highly readable account of Rhodesian events from Huggins's perspective, see L. H. Gann and M. Gelfand, *Huggins of Rhodesia: The Man and his Country* (London, 1964).

16. Colin Leys, *European Politics in Southern Rhodesia* (Oxford, 1959), p. 57.

17. Ibid., p. 290.

18. Ibid., p. 139.

opposition to him in Southern Rhodesia was associated with the South African element, Huggins lost no time in calling an election. He "won a large working majority,"[19] partly on the plank of amalgamation with the north as the only viable option for Southern Rhodesia. He was in a strong position to make use of the South African "threat" as an inducement to the growing but still small group of whites in Northern Rhodesia to consider amalgamation as well as a justification for British consent to reconsider some grouping of territories in Central Africa.[20] Because both British political parties had made clear their opposition to amalgamation, a meeting of the settlers in the Northern Rhodesian Legislative Council and Southern Rhodesian amalgamationists in Lusaka in October 1948 agreed to proceed with the idea of federation. "Huggins was not enthusiastic." "But he was persuaded that this was a formula which the British government might be induced to accept and which could be interpreted so as to give the real substance of power to the central government, which would be controlled by Europeans."[21]

While the consistency of Huggins's policy from 1934 and the purposefulness of his continual pushing of the British government in 1949, 1950, and 1951 are comprehensible, what happened to alter the antiamalgamation perspective in London? The Colonial Office, or at least some colonial officers, had been steady and persuasive before the Second World War about the necessity of advancing African interests in Northern Rhodesia and Nyasaland, and the need to see these territories pointed toward a future different than that of the white south. These perceptions were sustained into the postwar years. As one of many examples, I cite the handwritten note by A. B. Cohen on a draft letter of October 30, 1947, concerning the possibility of closer cooperation in defense matters between the three Central African territories: "Further, Southern Rhodesia policy in relation to their African population is in material respects at variance with the policy followed by the Governments of Northern Rhodesia and Nyasaland."[22]

Earlier that same year, in May 1947, Cohen, as assistant undersecretary of state for African affairs, had submitted his department's secret document

19. Colin Leys and Cranford Pratt, *A New Deal in Central Africa* (London, 1960), pp. 12, 13.

20. There has been a long history of the idea of amalgamation or federation in Central Africa. It is best described by Robert I. Rotberg, "The Federation Movement in British East and Central Africa 1899–1953," *Journal of Commonwealth Political Studies* 2 (1964): 141–60.

21. Leys and Pratt, *A New Deal*, p. 14.

22. CO537/2516, successive drafts of a letter to Major Lord Douglas Gordon, October 30, 1947.

urging a rapid transfer of power to African elites, based upon the assumption that African territories would have attained full responsibility for local government within a generation.[23] Why, at the moment when constitutional and political advance was being advocated for Africans in West Africa, would the Colonial Office countenance an apparently retrograde policy in Central Africa? If African access to the franchise had become the key to "democratization from below" in West Africa, why was not African political advancement seen as potentially crucial also in Central Africa? One year after Cohen's document, Huggins was publicly advocating the closure of the franchise to Africans in Southern Rhodesia and their removal from the common roll. In June 1948 this was part of the platform on which he campaigned successfully.[24] After the election, Huggins discussed his policy with the British government. The policy "was not implemented as, in 1949, Imperial officials discouraged him, while in 1950 as a concession to gain Federation, he dropped these proposals, writing to the Minister of Justice, Mr. Beadle, in London to request instead the raising of property and wage qualifications."[25] The contrast between Southern Rhodesian and Colonial Office policies toward an African electorate could hardly be more stark.

Unfortunately, the papers are not yet open which would reveal how two courses of action so potentially contradictory could be pursued simultaneously. Ronald Robinson speculates:

> Cohen's scheme for transferring power in Central Africa from 1948 to 1951 proved less fortunate. It is said that he naively believed better constitutions can improve human nature; if there is any truth in this claim, it is to be found in the bargains that his plan for federating the two Rhodesias and Nyasaland offered the settler leaders. By conceding considerable local authority to the white minority he hoped at best to persuade them to share power with the black majority; at worst, to stop the spread of apartheid from South Africa into the British dependencies.[26]

The fear of the spread of South African doctrine and influence seems to have been a powerful motive when viewed from London. This fear, com-

23. Ronald Robinson, "Sir Andrew Cohen: Proconsul of African Nationalism (1909–1968)," in L. H. Gann and Peter Duignan, eds., *African Proconsuls* (New York, 1978), pp. 353–64, at 358.

24. Claire Palley, *The Constitutional History and Law of Southern Rhodesia 1888–1965* (Oxford, 1966), p. 245.

25. Ibid.

26. R. Robinson, "Cohen," p. 361. See also David Goldsworthy, *Colonial Issues in British Politics 1945–1961* (Oxford, 1971), p. 53, where, relying on an interview with Griffiths, he writes: "It was Cohen's advocacy that decisively influenced Griffiths."

bined with the hope (which the history of South Africa since 1910 should have dimmed) that political generosity on the part of the imperial government might induce emulation by the local white Rhodesian regime, provided the emotional context for optimisim about federation. From Southern Rhodesia, however, federation was seen in 1949 as simple expediency, and the Victoria Falls conference of unofficials in February "produced a federal draft scheme reflecting Sir Godfrey's political aims of amalgamation and his franchise views. It proposed a House of Representatives, from which Africans would be excluded, and suggested that minimal powers be given to the Territorial legislatures."[27] The assumptions of the Colonial Office planners and the Southern Rhodesian government led in opposite directions.[28]

In retrospect, the differences of policy seem incontrovertible. But through three changes in Colonial Secretary between 1949 and 1953 (Creech-Jones, Griffiths, Lyttleton),[29] several meetings of officials,[30] and a series of command papers,[31] these differences became muted. It was hoped that Northern Rhodesia might be a positive influence on Southern Rhodesia, that a multiracial state might avert the worst excesses of either white or black nationalism, that a larger federal unit would be more viable economically, and that a federal scheme (others were being designed for

27. Palley, *Constitutional History*, pp. 334–35.

28. Evidence of these differences is the deadlock of the Victoria Falls Conference in September 1951. "[I]t was typical of the whole exercise that the provisions in the Plan which Huggins most wished to alter were the very provisions to which Griffiths attached most importance." Goldsworthy, *Colonial Issues*, p. 221.

29. Arthur Creech Jones, Under-Secretary of State for the Colonies, 1945–46, Colonial Secretary, 1946–50; James Griffiths, Minister in Labour government, 1945–51, Colonial Secretary, 1950–51; Oliver Lyttelton (Lord Chandos, 1954), Colonial Secretary, 1951–54.

30. Conference of unofficials, February 1949, Victoria Falls; Conference of Officials of the Three Central African Territories, the United Kingdom Government, and of the Central African Council, March 1951, London; Conference of Officials at Victoria Falls, September 1951; unofficial conference in London, January 1952; Lancaster House Conference, April and May 1952; Carlton House Terrace Conference, London, January 1953.

31. The most important were:

Cmd. 8233 Central African Territories: Report of the Conference on Closer Association (1951)
Cmd. 8235 Central African Territories: Comparative Survey of Native Policy (1951)
Cmd. 8411 Closer Association in Central Africa: Statement by His Majesty's Government (1951)
Cmd. 8573 Southern Rhodesia, Northern Rhodesia, and Nyasaland: Draft Federal Scheme (1952); Cmd. 8671 Report of the Judicial Commission; Cmd. 8672 Report of the Fiscal Commission; Cmd. 8673 Report of the Civil Service Preparatory Commission
Cmd. 8753 Report by the Conference on Federation Held in London in January 1953 (1953)
Cmd. 8754 The Federal Scheme for Southern Rhodesia, Northern Rhodesia, and Nyasaland Prepared by a Conference Held in London, January 1953 (1953)

Nigeria, the West Indies, East Africa) would provide time for the component units to evolve a common policy. The newly elected Conservative government, in November 1951, decided to proceed with the federal idea. "On the 21 November 1951, Mr. Oliver Lyttleton, the Colonial Secretary, announced governmental approval of the principle of federation of the Central African Territories."[32] From this point forward, Griffiths, as the Labour party's chief spokesman on colonial matters, gradually pulled further away from the Conservative government's position, finally leading the divisions over Central African policy which marked the crucial parliamentary debates of March through July of 1953.[33]

The differences between Imperial and Southern Rhodesian points of view did not seem muted to Africans. African opposition to federation began early; they had anticipated settler enthusiasm for amalgamation and resisted it during the interwar years. Explicit African objections to federation were apparent to Arthur Creech Jones when he visited Northern Rhodesia and Nyasaland in April 1949, and to Griffiths and to Gordon Walker in September 1951, when they toured Southern Rhodesia.[34] African objections grew louder and more pointed. In April and May 1952, African delegates from the northern territories boycotted the Lancaster House Conference to make unambiguous their desire not to be associated in any way with federation.[35] Behind the objections of official delegates lay a variety of protests, with near unanimity in the Nyasaland and Northern Rhodesian countryside. Even in Southern Rhodesia there had been signs of African protest (although not then related to federation) in 1945 and 1948, with a revival of the Reformed Industrial and Commercial Workers' Union (ICU) and a show of African trade unionism.[36] On the issue of federation, Africans in Southern Rhodesia were more cautious; potentially, they had something to gain by association with the African policies of the northern territories. Africans in the north, on the contrary, felt they had nothing to gain and much to lose. In December 1952, the hostility toward the government of the African Representative Council in Northern Rhodesia became marked.[37] Despite the explanations of the Native Affairs Department

32. Palley, *Constitutional History*, p. 336.

33. Goldsworthy, *Colonial Issues*, p. 219.

34. For the Creech Jones visit, see Robert I. Rotberg, *The Rise of Nationalism in Central Africa* (Cambridge, Mass., 1965), p. 226; for Griffiths and Gordon Walker, see Goldsworthy, *Colonial Issues*, pp. 219–20.

35. Palley, *Constitutional History*, p. 338.

36. Ranger, *The African Voice*, p. 230.

37. David Mulford, *Zambia: The Politics of Independence 1957–64* (Oxford, 1967), p. 33.

and meetings of the African provincial councils during the first half of 1953, at the meeting of the African Representative Council on July 22, 1953,

> the Africans stood firm in their opposition to Federation. A motion deploring the decision taken by the British Government to implement the Federation against the expressed opinion of Northern Rhodesia's overwhelming indigenous population and calling for an all-African conference on the subject was passed unanimously... nearly every speaker expressed loss of confidence in the Government and considerable antagonism towards Central Africa's Europeans.[38]

In the Nyasaland Legislative Council, both African and missionary voices in December 1951 "urged the British government not to default upon its historic promise to transfer authority in the Protectorate only to Africans."[39] By late June 1952, Harry Nkumbula told a large crowd at a Congress meeting in Mapoloto Township, near Lusaka, "The only safeguard [for] an African is self-government in which the African will play a predominant part in determining the destinies of his fellow men."[40] For those who cared to listen, it was apparent that many shades of African opinion in Northern Rhodesia and Nyasaland—traditional chiefly councils as well as the emerging African political parties—were deeply and vocally hostile to federation. Why, then, was federation implemented?

The answer lies in London. Cabinet papers for the period remain closed. We do not yet know with certainty the blend of strategic decisions, financial decisions, or "kith and kin" sympathies which drove Conservative policymakers. What we do have is the series of parliamentary debates on the proposed Federation, and a close analysis of the pros and cons used in argument suggests much of political and constitutional substance. During 1952 and 1953 there were seven sustained debates about the creation of the Central African Federation. The first three came during the course of debates on supply, on March 4, April 29, and July 24, 1952.[41] With increasing clarity, argument came to focus on the relationship between the proposed constitution and African rights. First, ought the Federation to be

38. Ibid., p. 35, relying on the African Representative Council Proceedings, July 22, 1953.

39. Rotberg, *The Rise of Nationalism*, pp. 238–39.

40. Ibid., p. 243.

41. Great Britain, *Parliamentary Debates*, House of Commons, 1951–52, vol. 497, cols. 208–334, March 4, 1952; vol. 499, cols. 1233–98, April 29, 1952; vol. 504, cols. 773–882, July 24, 1952. The first of these debates led to a division during which the Conservatives accused the Opposition of "trying to kill their own child." A division was avoided in the third, which was acknowledged at the time to be "an act of statesmanship on the part of the Labour Party."

imposed when African opinion, particularly in the two northern territories, was in large part hostile to it? Second, were the proposed safeguards included in the draft constitution adequate to prevent the use of the federal political machinery from discriminating against Africans, or, to phrase the same concern differently, adequate to prevent the long-term hegemony of whites in the federal government? Third, how could there be any assurance of African political advance in the federal parliament when the draft constitution gave a predominantly white legislature control over its own franchise rules and required a two-thirds majority to change them? Speakers, primarily on the Labour side of the House, expressed grave concern over "a shutting down of the scope and hope of African political advancement,"[42] and asked in a variety of ways: "What is the urgency?"[43] Was it not possible to seek federation more slowly and do it in such a way as to obtain African consent?

A variety of other important points were developed, beginning with the recognition by many speakers that the House of Commons stood in these debates as a legislature for Central Africa where Africans were almost entirely unfranchised. Those favorable to federation argued that the creation of a multiracial state was critical for the future of the Commonwealth, for the preservation of the British connection. Southern Rhodesia, it was asserted, could not stand alone—it would go either north or south. Without political federation there would not be the confidence or the economic scale to attract outside financing for development. The real racial fears of both black and white could only be ameliorated, it was argued, in conditions of economic prosperity: "Sufficient wealth must be produced to raise the African's level of living and his standards of health and education without, at the same time, lowering the standard of life that is required for maintaining the white civilisation."[44]

On the Conservative side, in addition to great reliance upon alleged economic prosperity which the Federation would bring, Lyttelton and many of his colleagues argued that the Labour government had, when in office, made a commitment to the federation idea and that now, in opposition, they were making a party issue out of resistance to the federal scheme.[45] But as David Goldsworthy demonstrates, neither the align-

42. Gordon Walker, July 24, 1952, col. 780.

43. Clement Davies, July 24, 1952, col. 811; Sir Leslie Plummer, col. 840: "What is the busting rush about it?"

44. Frederic Harris, col. 843.

45. See, for example, Oliver Lyttelton, Viscount Chandos, *The Memoirs of Lord Chandos: An Unexpected View from the Summit* (New York, 1963), pp. 369–70. His whole treatment of the issue seems superficial and tendentious.

ments nor the situations were simple, static, or easy to characterize. Griffiths, who clearly emerged as Labour's most articulate critic of federation, "explicitly decided against dividing in the debates of April and July 1952."[46] Yet he and many others had been consistent in their insistence that commitment to the idea of federation was contingent upon African acceptance of the actual proposals.

In July of 1952, 199 members of the Labour party in Parliament had signed a motion urging the government to frame for Kenya a "policy which will permit Africans, and in particular African cooperatives, to own land in the highlands."[47] Labour was attuned to African opinion, and its opposition to Central African policy hardened as the passage of time made clearer the fact that African opinion about the proposed Federation was being ignored. Griffiths had apparently hoped that the African leadership in Northern Rhodesia and Nyasaland would raise alternatives to the proposed Federation, alternatives which might be palatable. But the few suggestions that were raised were not heard. Worse, the Conservative government, as a result of the conference of officials in January 1953, conceded in the draft constitution to Huggins's objections and weakened the constitutional safeguards against discriminatory legislation.[48] Griffiths, still not condemning federation in principle, moved in the first ratification debate (March 24, 1953) to disapprove "on the two grounds, by now familiar, that the safeguards were inadequate and the scheme was being imposed."[49] These remained the fundamental bases of Labour opposition through all the final stages of the parliamentary debate to the vote on approval of the Federal Constitution Order in Council on July 27, 1953.[50]

With strong Labour opposition domestically and with overwhelming African skepticism or rejection in the two northern territories, why did the Conservative government press ahead with federation? Although I cannot yet fully document my views, I believe that the principal reasons were three: a political judgment that this was the only means to retain substantial influence over the future course of European-controlled Southern Rhodesia; a strategic judgment that the Federation would provide a base for British and Commonwealth forces in southern Africa, should that ever be necessary; and an economic judgment that economies of scale and a

46. Goldsworthy, *Colonial Issues*, p. 218.

47. Ibid., p. 214.

48. Ibid., pp. 224–25.

49. Ibid., p. 225. Great Britain, *Parliamentary Debates*, House of Commons, 1952–53, vol. 513, cols. 658–802. Griffiths's remarks are at col. 676.

50. Great Britain, *Debates*, House of Commons, 1952–53, vol. 518, cols. 899–962. Upon division, the Order in Council was voted 288 in favor and 242 opposed.

European-managed infrastructure would lead to rapid economic development. If I am correct in my suppositions, it is worth noting that none of the three judgments turned on African opinion; someone giving these three aspects priority would believe that African opinion is tractable and that changes in it would follow upon the structural alterations made inevitable by federation. Only those concerned fundamentally with political participation or with the societal distribution of economic benefits would take care to look closely at the probable long-term effects upon Africans of the proposed federal structure.[51] To those who had no such concerns, the Colonial Secretary could say, in an after-dinner speech to the British Africa Club on June 30, 1953, before the Federation was officially in being, "That Federation, both politically and economically, will be of immense benefit to the three Central African territories is, I believe, an established and unshakable fact."[52]

That political and economic progrsss would result from federation was clearly an unshakable Conservative opinion. But there was remarkably little fact.

> Given the extent to which the economic case has been emphasised, one would expect that it had been made a subject for thorough investigation, and that a detailed assessment of the prospective economic effects would have been made and published before the decision in favour of Federation was made. This is not the case. In all the published reports, discussions and debates which preceded the establishment of the Federation, there is no comprehensive—or even remotely adequate—treatment of the economic issues. It is repeatedly taken for granted that the economic benefits of Federation are too obvious for detailed argument to be necessary, or alternatively that they have been fully discussed in some other context. In fact, neither of these things is true.[53]

What those who used the argument of an augmented economy apparently meant was that the political stability which they predicted for the Federation would induce greater confidence among outside investors, leading in turn to greater outside investment of capital, greater capacity to borrow, an increased European immigration into the Federation, and a higher rate of internal reinvestment.

51. For example, one can consult the arguments made by the small group of specialists within the Colonial Bureau. See Goldsworthy, *Colonial Issues*, p. 228.

52. Ibid., p. 242.

53. Arthur Hazelwood and P. D. Henderson, *Nyasaland: The Economies of Federation* (Oxford: Blackwell, 1960), p. 18.

During the first four years of the Federation, these unexamined hypotheses were in fact largely confirmed in practice, or so it seemed. The high prices for copper on the international markets meant high tax returns from the Copperbelt, which the federal fiscal arrangements redistributed from Northern Rhodesia to the benefit of Southern Rhodesia and Nyasaland. The largest share went to Southern Rhodesia, as did most European immigration and the largest share of the Federation's loan expenditures.[54] It is worth remarking once again that the need for or extent of African participation in these benefits did not occasion any hard analytical thinking; it was assumed that a growing economy would provide more jobs and (ultimately) better wages. Federal development plans for capital expenditure did not reflect, for instance, an attempt "to give special consideration to Nyasaland because of its poverty and economic backwardness."[55] By far the largest share of investment was in Southern Rhodesia, which reflected the preponderance of its European population—both in numbers and in its control of federal political structure. "In no year was less than 54 per cent of the total [financial investment in the Federation] invested in Southern Rhodesia, and in some years Southern Rhodesia's share exceeded 60 per cent."[56] This pattern held in both private and public investment, but it was perhaps most noticeable, because "not readily explicable in terms either of raw material or of market orientation,"[57] in the concentration of manufacturing.

> The value of manufacturing output increased during the federal period by nearly £ 30 mn in Southern Rhodesia compared with an increase of only £ 9 mn in the other two territories together. The encouragement of manufacturing industry was an important element in the economic policy of the federal government, and throughout the federal period this policy in effect meant that much the greater part of the expansion in manufacturing took place in Southern Rhodesia.[58]

It must have seemed from the perspective of Europeans in Southern Rhodesia in 1956 that the Conservative arguments of 1952 were proving to be true in practice. New investment from outside the Federation was high, as was the reinvestment of earnings by companies within. There had been a

54. Arthur Hazelwood, "The Economics of Federation and Dissolution in Central Africa," in Hazelwood, ed., *African Integration and Disintegration* (London, 1967), pp. 185–250.

55. Hazelwood and Henderson, *Nyasaland*, p. 58.

56. Hazelwood, "The Economics of Federation," p. 202.

57. Ibid., p. 203.

58. Ibid.

commercial and residential building boom accompanying a large influx of Europeans to Southern Rhodesia. Productivity had increased and wages had gone up for both black and white workers (though there was still an enormous disparity between them). The federal government's revenues were high, which meant that there was much money for educational and agricultural services to the non-African population allocated by the constitution to the federal, rather than the territorial, government. And African protest had apparently died away, or at the least was relatively ineffective been 1953 and 1956. In fact, in Southern Rhodesia during the first three years of federation there was heady progress in both political participation and the lifting of racial discrimination for a few middle-class Africans.

> After the apparent show of strength with the All Africa Convention [1951] the various trade unions and political associations almost fell into abeyance while their leaders tried again to work from within. "By 1955 only Mzingeli was still active. The Bulawayo branch of the ANC kept going after Federation, but mostly as a social organisation running concerts. . . . Everyone else was rushing to join multi-racial organisations, imbued with the new spirit of partnership and believing it would change their whole lives and bring equality." . . . African politics in Rhodesia has always had to choose between resistance and participation. . . . This was the golden age of participation.[59]

In 1956, then, the economic prosperity of the European electorate, the muted criticism or even participation of some of the more articulate Africans, the political myopia of the majority of European voters, and the political ambitions of Roy Welensky, now federal prime minister, for the rapid attainment of Dominion status for the Federation, led white Southern Rhodesians and the Federal government to a serious miscalculation. The mistake they made was in the event to prove fatal to their hopes for the Federation.

In retrospect there can be no doubt that the crucial decision which transformed the prospects of the Federation and provided African

59. Terence O. Ranger, "African Politics in Twentieth-Century Southern Rhodesia," in Ranger, ed., *Aspects of Central African History* (London, 1968), pp. 210–45, at 238. The quotation is an adaptation from Nathan Shamuyarira, *Crisis in Rhodesia* (London, 1965; New York, 1966), p. 39. See also Kenneth Kaunda, *Zambia Shall Be Free* (London, 1962), p. 60: "During 1954, I realized that some constructive thinking would have to be done if Congress were going to hold together. People were saying that now Federation had become an accomplished fact, we could never break it and therefore we had no reason to continue our fight."

nationalists with both an urgent cause and an explicit timetable was the revision of the federal constitution in 1957. This was the third proposed revision of franchise arrangements under the federal constitution: the first was in Nyasaland in 1955, the second in Southern Rhodesia in 1956—and in some ways they are all of a piece.[60] But it was clearly the Constitution Amendment Act of 1957, designed to enlarge the Federal Assembly and to alter its franchise qualifications, that made European conceptions of democracy and European political ambitions unambiguously transparent. The plan was to enlarge the assembly from 35 to 59 members, to create two classes of voters ("ordinary" and "special"), and by various complex requirements to enforce cross-racial voting between the two electoral rolls. The effects of these provisions have been analyzed in many places,[61] and the most astute observer of European politics in Southern Rhodesia puts the matter thus:

> The outside observer must not make the mistake of supposing that these provisions represent a wholesale fraud on the part of the European political leaders who have been responsible for them, and who have put them forward in the name of 'partnership'. To do this would be ungenerous and it would also miss the important point. These franchises, like the Europeans' approach to changes in the colour bar, fit logically into the same interpretation of 'partnership'; they are aimed to give a stringently restricted measure of political participation to an African middle class.[62]

The proposed constitutional amendment was reviewed by the African Affairs Board, which had been built into the federal structure as a safety valve against discriminatory legislation. The board had only once used its power to declare a measure discriminatory—in pointing out that the Defense Regulations of 1956 made no provision for promoting Africans to commissioned rank—and in that instance the legislation had been altered.[63] The board then objected to the constitution amendment bill as discriminatory and referred it to the British Parliament on two grounds: that enlarging the assembly diminished the value of African representation

60. Palley, *Constitutional History*, pp. 308–09, 403 ff.

61. Perhaps most thoroughly in ibid., pp. 384–400. For a sense of the emotional impact of the changes, see Guy Clutton-Brock, *Dawn in Nyasaland* (London, 1959), p. 116: "Of the 91,767 voters on the Federal General Roll, only 1,164 are African."

62. Colin Leys, "'Partnership' as Democratisation," chapter 10 in Colin Leys and Cranford Pratt, *A New Deal in Central Africa* (London, 1960), pp. 109–17, at 114. The best analysis of European political behavior through 1956 is Colin Leys, *European Politics in Southern Rhodesia* (Oxford, 1959), a seminal book which continues to provide the basis for understanding European politics into the UDI years.

63. Palley, *Constitutional History*, pp. 386–87.

in defiance of understandings undertaken at the creation of the federal constitution in 1953; and that the proposed electoral requirements meant in practice that the eight African representatives added to the enlarged assembly under the new franchise arrangements would be primarily dependent upon European votes.[64]

Because the board made its objections explicit, the issues surrounding the amendment were squarely before Parliament when it debated the measure on November 25, 1957. The debate was lengthy (lasting from 3:30 P.M. to 9:55 P.M.), generally of high quality, and led to a division which the Conservative government won 301 to 245. Once again the responsibility of the British Parliament for the course of events in Central Africa became focused and unambiguous. All the essential questions were asked; Griffiths was again pointed and articulate in opposition:

> if the Government carry out their intention, the message that goes to Africa—this is how it will be interpreted—is that the African Affairs Board, upon which the Africans have rested for their safeguards. has on the first occasion that it has sought to protect them been set aside by Her Majesty's Government. That is the crucial issue.[65]

Lennox-Boyd in response felt compelled to deny that there was any "deal" involved with the Federal government:

> there is no commitment whatever by anyone, except to hold in 1960 the review of the Constitution by the five Governments for which the Constitution itself provides and, in the course of that review, to consider—I repeat "consider"—a programme for the attainment of such status as would enable the Federation to become eligible for full partnership in the Commonwealth.[66]

Griffiths was of course correct. Parliament's action signaled to the perceptive Africans in Northern Rhodesia and Nyasaland that less than three years remained before a review of the federal constitutional arrangement, that the push for Dominion status was aggressive and open, that the African Affairs Board was ineffective, and that Parliament would defer to the asserted interests of the federal government. Nineteen sixty would clearly be the year of decision.[67] African political advance in the northern territories

64. Ibid., pp. 392–96.

65. Great Britain, *Parliamentary Debates*, House of Commons, 1956–57, vol. 578, November 25, 1957, col. 922.

66. Ibid., cols. 925–26.

67. This is the title of a book by Philip Mason, *Year of Decision* (London, 1960). The importance of these years is amply demonstrated by the spate of books published between 1958 and 1960 that offer critical analyses of federation: M. W. Kanyama Chiume, *Nyasaland*

would have to be assured before 1960 if Africans were to have sufficient influence to counter proposals for Dominion status on essentially Southern Rhodesian terms. What options were there? For those fundamentally opposed to federation the options had been reduced to two: political activism on the ground and hard-headed criticism of the real benefits of federation by analysts in Britain. The political battle needed to be engaged both in the Federation and in Parliament, where it would ultimately be decided. From 1958 to 1960 the initiative was taken by African nationalists in Nyasaland and Northern Rhodesia.

Although African nationalist activity had slowed during 1954 and 1955 in Northern Rhodesia and Nyasaland, opposition to the Federation, resentment over its imposition, and outrage at its professions of "partnership" (in the face of such segregated public facilities as post offices) continued. The threatened change in the federal constitution catalyzed the rather haphazard arrangements of the African National Congresses in both territories into more organized and systematic activity. In late March 1957, Masuako Chipembere, one of four members of Congress elected to the Nyasaland Legislative Council a year earlier under the changes resulting from the legislation of 1955, wrote to Dr. Hastings Banda in London that the Nyasaland Congress badly needed new leadership. Dr. Banda, increasingly suspicious of a deal between the federal government and the Conservative party, urged the two Nyasaland African members to resign from the Federal Parliament. When they refused to do so, they were expelled from Congress in August 1957—"a decisive victory for the militant left wing, led by Chipembere and Chiume."[68] By December 1957 the critical importance of the next two years was undeniable, and Dr. Hastings Kamuzu Banda decided to return from London to lead the anti-Federation fight in Nyasaland. He landed at Chileka Airport, near Blantyre, on July 6, 1958, and on August 1, at the annual meeting of Congress, was elected

---

Speaks (London, 1959); Edward M. Clegg, *Race and Politics: Partnership in the Federation of Rhodesia and Nyasaland* (London, 1960); Guy Clutton-Brock, *Dawn in Nyasaland* (London, 1959); Thomas R. M. Creighton, *The Anatomy of Partnership* (London, 1960); Cyril Dunn, *Central African Witness* (London, 1959); Thomas M. Franck, *Race and Nationalism: The Struggle for Power in Rhodesia-Nyasaland* (New York, 1960); Richard Gray, *The Two Nations: Aspects of the Development of Race Relations in the two Rhodesias and Nyasaland* (London, 1960); A. Hazelwood and P. D. Henderson, *Nyasaland: The Economics of Federation* (Oxford, 1960); C. Leys and C. Pratt, *A New Deal in Central Africa* (London, 1960); Colin Morris and Kenneth Kaunda, *Black Government?* (Lusaka, Zambia, 1960); Clyde Sanger, *Central African Emergency* (London, 1960); G. Michael Scott, *A Time to Speak* (London, 1958); Ndabaningi Sithole, *African Nationalism* (London, 1959); Shirley Williams, *Central Africa: The Economics of Inequality* (London, 1960).

68. John G. Pike, *Malawi: A Political and Economic History* (New York, 1968), pp. 141 and 135–172 passim.

president-general with a hand-picked cabinet of militants, including Chipembere, Chiume, Dunduzu Chisiza, Rose Chibambo, and Chalaluka.[69]

In Northern Rhodesia the spring and summer of 1956 brought an outbreak of boycotts against European and Asian shops and a series of "rolling strikes" on the Copperbelt which appeared to bring the African National Congress under Nkumbula's leadership and the African Mine Workers Union under Lawrence Katilungu closer together.[70] Europeans were alarmed and the government instituted a proceeding in Mufulira against four ANC officials over the boycotts. But the tactic backfired, because the magistrate "acquitted all the accused and declared that he had no hesitation in saying that the boycotters had sufficient justification for their action. There was no evidence, he said, that the boycott had been organized to force recognition of Congress. The evidence showed that its object was to redress the grievances of the African consumer."[71] This was a great psychological victory for Congress, and it strengthened the more aggressive members of the party, whom Kenneth Kaunda increasingly represented. Kaunda had thrown himself into organizing work for Congress after his release from prison in March 1955. By October 1956, at the party's annual conference he stressed dedicated leadership, party organization "and the Federal Government's increasingly open campaign for dominion status by 1960."[72]

> The shift in African nationalist thinking which emerged full-blown in 1957 had clearly begun in 1956. At first it was restricted to a mere handful of A.N.C. leaders. Gradually they built up branch organizations and began consolidating the party's more militant elements. For the next eighteen months the build-up continued, slowly but steadily, until in October 1958 the split occurred which produced Kaunda's Zambia African National Congress (Z.A.N.C.).[73]

Thus, in December 1958, when both Kaunda and Banda went off to the All-African Peoples Conference in Accra, they were the nuclei of strong militant parties in both territories dedicated to the prevention of a Central African Dominion. Kaunda stayed in Accra for a month after the conference ended; he had produced a fifteen-page memorandum against federation

69. Ibid., p. 143, and Rotberg, *The Rise of Nationalism,* pp. 268–70 and 286–89. See also Griff B. Jones, *Britain and Nyasaland* (London, 1964), pp. 236–37.

70. David C. Mulford, *Zambia, The Politics of Independence 1957–64* (Oxford, 1967).

71. Kenneth Kaunda, *Zambia Shall be Free* (London, 1962), p. 77.

72. Mulford, *Zambia*, pp. 62–63.

73. Ibid., p. 63.

and against the Benson Constitution in Northern Rhodesia, and he "succeeded personally in winning Nkrumah's esteem."[74] For both Banda and Kaunda the Accra conference gave outside support to their convictions that time was short and action necessary.

Others, too, were beginning to perceive increasing tension. For both chiefs who were Native Authorities and for some members of the Colonial Service, it became increasingly necessary to take sides—one could not support both the Federation and the nationalists. One contemporary observer wrote:

> Most of the officers of the Nyasaland Protectorate Government did not like the Federal solution, the way it was reached, nor its present trend. They have little faith in the future of Federation, but few will be there to endure its results. They are under orders . . . to press the merits of Federation upon an unwilling population and to make it work. With considerable discomfort and manifest irritation at being harried by the African members in the Legislative Council, they make conscientious efforts to carry out their duties in the face of what they know to be a betrayal of the people who for half a century have put their trust in them. . . .[75]

By the spring of 1959 the Benson Constitution was being bitterly disputed in Northern Rhodesia and a state of emergency had been declared in Nyasaland. Authority was eroding. On March 2, Banda and one hundred and twenty members of Congress were arrested and taken to detention in Southern Rhodesia; on March 11, ZANC's leaders were arrested and rusticated to remote areas. All the registered branches of ZANC were declared illegal; yet despite the fact that polling took place in Northern Rhodesia on March 20, 1959, the results were a disaster for the Benson Constitution. Africans were quick to perceive the disproportionate effects of European votes in constituencies returning Africans. More important, "Z.A.N.C. had been bestowed suddenly with an element of martyrdom, which set its leaders distinctly apart from and well above all other Northern Rhodesia nationalists."[76]

Changes in the perspective from London considerably accelerated. The Labour party refused to accept the Colonial Secretary's explanation of events in Nyasaland, and as a result, a commission under Judge Devlin was appointed to inquire into the facts. The commission produced its report, largely written by E. T. (Sir Edgar in 1973) Williams, then Warden of

74. Ibid., pp. 80–81.
75. Guy Clutton-Brock, *Dawn in Nyasaland* (London, 1959), pp. 133–34.
76. Pike, *Malawi*, p. 147; Mulford, *Zambia*, pp. 95, 98–99, 101.

Rhodes House, Oxford, in the astonishingly short time of fourteen weeks.[77] The Devlin Report was critical of the autocratic methods of the Nyasaland government and concluded that evidence for a "murder-plot" was insufficient to justify the action taken.[78] Although the Cabinet "rejected the Devlin Report's main condemnatory passage and gave Lennox-Boyd solid support in the House," the situation in Nyasaland was clearly one of several in Africa which led to a major shake-up in Conservative colonial policy after Macmillan was returned in the October elections with a large majority.[79] Iain Macleod took over as Colonial Secretary, and in early November he described in Parliament his inheritance: "In the colonial territories at the present time, there is a state of emergency which has lasted seven years in Kenya; there is a state of emergency which has lasted seven months in Nyasaland; there are persons in Northern Rhodesia living in restriction by order; and there is rule in Malta by the Governor instead of by normal processes. Here clearly are my first tasks."[80]

Macleod's policies were quickly perceived to be different. He made vital concessions to the Africans in Kenya, and he drafted the final instructions to the Monckton Commission, which arrived in the Federation in February 1960 to take evidence bearing upon the future of the Federation. It is no coincidence that in the same month the "Rhodesia Lobby" came into existence in London, backed by expensive public relations materials designed by Voice and Vision and paid for by Welensky's federal government.[81] The lobby was fighting to preserve European interests in the Federation and the older Conservative view of what was "right" in the "kith and kin colonies." Macleod, on the other hand, sought to avoid bloodshed and wanted to extricate Britain from those conditions where armed conflict might inevitably lead to lengthy, costly, unwinnable involvement.[82] The gusts of African nationalism had led to Macmillan's "wind of change."[83]

After the passage of almost twenty years, a rereading of Sir Roy Welensky's autobiography, *4000 Days*, together with the Monckton Commission

77. Cmnd. 814, *Report of the Nyasaland Commission of Inquiry* (July 1959). See Pike, *Malawi*, p. 148.

78. *Report*, pp. 84–86.

79. Goldsworthy, *Colonial Issues*, pp. 365 and 34–35; Pike, *Malawi*, pp. 150–51.

80. Goldsworthy, *Colonial Issues*, p. 362, quoting speech in House of Commons, Nov. 2, 1959.

81. Patrick Keatley, *The Politics of Partnership* (Harmondsworth, 1963), pp. 446–51.

82. Goldsworthy, *Colonial Issues*, p. 363.

83. The phrase was first used by Prime Minister Macmillan in Accra, Ghana, on January 9, 1960. His use of it again in Cape Town, South Africa, on February 3, 1960, signaled "something of a watershed in African affairs." See Harold Macmillan, *Pointing the Way, 1959–61* (London, 1972), pp. 124, 156.

Report (September 1960) illuminates several of the critical dynamics of the final years of federation. The commission, which Sir Roy had fought, and over whose membership he tried to exercise some control through the Rhodesia Lobby in London, wrote in the end a reasonable and even modestly creative report. The essence of its findings was that federation should be preserved, but under a different name and with reshaped instrumentalities. The reshaping should reflect more accurately what the commission members took to be the original purposes and originally intended division of functions. They recommended that a number of important areas (roads, prisons, health, non-African agriculture) become territorial rather than federal subjects; that the territorial civil services be appropriately augmented by transfers of federal civil servants; that bills of rights governing individual constitutional rights be inserted in the federal constitution and made actionable in both federal and territorial courts; that the power of Parliament to legislate for the Federation be retained. On the question of secession, the commission recommended that the constitutional Review Conference discuss the issue, that secession be permitted under certain conditions, and that Her Majesty's Government determine the wishes of the inhabitants of a territory with respect to secession. The commission recommended explicitly that "Her Majesty's Government should declare as soon as possible that further constitutional advance toward full self-government will be made in the near future in Northern Rhodesia."[84]

The design of these recommendations was to make the federal structure more equitable and more responsive to the needs of its inhabitants. Had similar recommendations been made in 1956, the Federation might then have evolved into a flexible and durable structure. But by 1960 attitudes had hardened. Kaunda, in *Black Government*, a published discussion between him and Colin Morris, explained why he refused to give evidence to the commission:

> the terms of reference are so narrow as far as Africans are concerned that by participating in the giving of evidence before this Commission we would be accepting the idea of Federation, i.e. the terms of reference are concerned with affecting improvements to the Federation. . . . we link our demand for the break-up of the Federation with the demand for a new Constitution for Northern Rhodesia.
>
> The year is 1960 and the sands of time are running out. We are clinging

84. Cmnd. 1148, *Report of the Advisory Commission on the Review of the Constitution* of Rhodesia and Nyasaland (presented to Parliament by the prime minister, October 1960), pp. 47–62, 114, 92–94, 79–89, 116–18, 109; 100–05, 119–20; 113.

> desperately to our Protected Status in Northern Rhodesia. It is the knowledge of what will happen at the Federal Constitutional review that drives us to demand Self Government this year on the basis of one man one vote.[85]

Given these assumptions, the recommendations of the commission were a pleasant surprise, as was the adjournment without conclusion of the Federal Review Conference held in London in December 1960—a pleasant surprise at least for the African nationalist parties in Nyasaland and Northern Rhodesia. Not, clearly, for Sir Roy Welensky and the federal government.

On first reading, Sir Roy's *4000 Days* appeared to be a straightforward, if somewhat blinkered, presentation of this case. Upon reflection, however, one recognizes the deliberate omissions and partiality in the way the account is put together. They reveal a good deal about the reasons for federal dissolution. There is, for example, no acknowledgment that the Southern Rhodesian constitution and the Federal franchise changes of 1956–57 were the triggers which set off the explosive political events in both Nyasaland and Northern Rhodesia. African political activity is presented as a new phenomenon, sparked largely by disaffected radicals and completely separate from the historical realities of colonial government. The issue of consent, which Welensky views as absolutely critical for the European population of Southern Rhodesia, is regarded as impractical idealism with respect to the African populations of the two northern territories, not to mention Southern Rhodesia. When he speaks of "the population," he usually means the white European population. Thus, in his view, which directly contradicts the preamble of the federal constitution, Britain gave a virtual promise of the attainment of Dominion status and of the continuance of the Federation, regardless of the opinion of the majority of the inhabitants who live under its jurisdiction. By this curious line of reasoning, Sir Roy finds dissent illegitimate, the question of secession taboo, and the existence of the Federation itself not a reviewable issue. On this basis, he asserts that Britain's recognition of a different set of emergent realities is a breaking of faith. The chaos which followed independence in the Congo (July 1, 1960) confirmed Sir Roy in his views that African nations are incapable of self-government and that outside intervention—whether by the United Nations, the United States, or the Soviet Union—is deeply threatening. He

85. *Black Government? A Discussion between Kenneth Kaunda and Colin Morris* (Lusaka, Zambia, 1960), pp. 83, 86.

calls his discussion of these events "Katanga Tragedy" and seeks the secession of Katanga from the Congo with the same passion that he denies secession to either of the northern territories in the Federation.[86]

In a chapter of this scope there is not space to give equal attention to the individual views of many others whose perspectives serve as a corrective to Welensky's. Any detailed history of the Federation years, however, must take account of a number of individual testimonies concerning the effects of the years between 1955 and 1960 on their personal faith in federation. They are largely odysseys of increasingly radical departure from the hopes—multiracial hopes—of the early 1950s. The accounts are by Africans: Lawrence Vambe, B. Vulindlela Mtshali, Nathan M. Shamuyarira; by white observers and actors who came to the Federation as clergy or as journalists: Colin Morris, Leslie Charlton, Cyril Dunn, and Patrick Keatley; even by old and distinguished white settlers, such as Sir Stewart Gore-Browne.[87] In the aggregate these accounts are powerful antidotes to the racial and political myopia afflicting the Federal government. No system could simultaneously sustain a passionate defense of democratic rights for the ruling minority and a daily humiliation of the unenfranchised majority.

The course of events following the adjournment sine die of the Review Conference in December 1960 can be succinctly summarized. In early 1961 there was a constitutional conference in Salisbury on the Southern Rhodesian Constitution.[88] The 1960 agreement on a more advanced constitution for Nyasaland was implemented in 1961; in 1962 it was announced that Nyasaland would have full internal self-government by 1963, and in May 1962, Butler indicated he would appoint advisers to examine the consequences of secession for Nyasaland.[89] After three sets of proposals in February 1961, June 1961, and March 1962, a new constitution was announced for Northern Rhodesia, under which, at the end of October 1962,

86. Sir Roy Welensky, *4000 Days: The Life and Death of the Federation of Rhodesia and Nyasaland* (London, 1964). The Katanga discussion is in chaps. 9 and 10, pp. 209–66.

87. Lawrence Vambe, *From Rhodesia to Zimbabwe* (Pittsburgh, 1976); B. Vulindela Mtshali, *Rhodesia: Background to Conflict* (New York, 1967); Nathan M. Shamuyarira, *Crisis in Rhodesia* (New York, 1966); Leslie Charlton, *Spark in the Stubble: Colin Morris of Zambia* (London, 1969); Harry Franklin, *Unholy Wedlock: The Failure of the Central African Federation* (London, 1963); Cyril Dunn, *Central African Witness* (London, 1959); Patrick Keatley, *The Politics of Partnership* (Harmondsworth, 1963). For Gore-Browne, see the full and sympathetic biography by Robert I. Rotberg, *Black Heart: Gore-Browne and the Politics of Multiracial Zambia* (Berkeley, 1977). Gore-Browne's decision to join UNIP in March–April 1961 is treated on pp. 314–15.

88. James Barber, *Rhodesia: The Road to Rebellion* (London, 1967), pp. 68–90.

89. Palley, *Constitutional History*, p. 677.

UNIP won a surprisingly conclusive victory.[90] In mid-December 1962, "Mr. Butler announced that the United Kingdom Government would permit Nyasaland to secede from the Federation." A similar permission was decreed for Northern Rhodesia on March 29, 1963.[91] Meanwhile, late in 1962, elections in Southern Rhodesia under its new constitution had resulted in the defeat of the United Federal party and a marked swing to the right with a victory of the Rhodesia Front party.[92] The Federation of Rhodesia and Nyasaland (Dissolution) Order in Council was approved by both Houses of Parliament on December 17, 1963, and the Federation ceased to exist on January 1, 1964.[93]

Thus far the facts. These changes were accomplished after much shuttling back and forth between the Federation and London, a good deal of complex constitution-mongering, a certain amount of violence and intimidation under cover of political campaigning, conclusive electoral victories by Congress in Nyasaland and UNIP in Northern Rhodesia, growing distrust between the white Southern Rhodesian electorate and British officials, and intense arguments over who should get the spoils upon dissolution of the Federation.[94] Knowing the outcome of the Federal experiment, we are in a position to ask a question which contemporaries could not: what were the effects of the Federation as a device for the transfer of power from British to African rulers?

The Federation had never been intended as a way to transfer power to three separate governments, so the unfortunate nature of the results is not surprising. On the positive side, it can be acknowledged that political authority was transferred in Nyasaland and Northern Rhodesia with relatively little violence and without massive disruption caused by emigration or the internal migration of components of the population. The need to demonstrate widespread popular antipathy to federation had resulted in two reasonably well-organized mass parties led by Banda and Kaunda, each of whom had diverse popular support from a variety (but not all) of the tribal

90. David C. Mulford, *The Northern Rhodesia General Election 1962* (Nairobi, 1964), pp. 19–30, 147–48.

91. Palley, *Constitutional History*, p. 678.

92. Barber, *Rhodesia*, pp. 147–68.

93. It was announced in the House of Commons on June 18, 1963, that the governments concerned had agreed to attend a conference to arrange the dissolution of the Federation. See Hazlewood, "Economics," pp. 228–49, for a discussion of dissolution.

94. A particularly important point was the division of the armed forces. "When the detailed negotiations were completed, Southern Rhodesia had acquired one of the strongest defence forces in Africa." Barber, *Rhodesia*, pp. 173 ff.

groups in their respective countries. But to win elections is not to run a government, and neither country had trained African civil servants or technical specialists in even modest numbers.

The constitution-mongering of the years 1961–63 had markedly different effects in Northern and Southern Rhodesia. This is not surprising, given the fact that the Southern Rhodesian white electorate was essentially in control of any attempt to widen the franchise in the south. Welensky fought with every technique he knew to try to maintain control as well of the franchise in the north. But Macleod and his advisors had their own purposes—to widen the franchise significantly in the north and to require both African and European candidates to attract some support from the other group—and they managed to achieve them.

The constitutional negotiations in Southern Rhodesia in 1961 and those in London in 1961 and early 1962 concerning Northern Rhodesia, which provided the foundations for national elections in both territories in 1962, had markedly different effects. The cause of the differences lay in the fact that the negotiations over the Northern Rhodesian Constitution took place under circumstances where the shaping initiative still lay with Her Majesty's Government. In contrast, London had no leverage over Southern Rhodesia, which was to become clear to all by 1965. Although Sir Edgar Whitehead, under the stimulus of the 1961 constitutional arrangements, did try to reach out to African voters and, through an appeal for their increased registration, attempt to change somewhat the complexion of the Southern Rhodesian electorate, the result was politically disastrous. White attitudes hardened; white fear of fundamental changes (for instance, in the Land Apportionment Act) was played upon; Africans boycotted the elections; white voters shifted to the right, elected the Rhodesian Front, and virtually eliminated the United Federal party.[95]

The cleverness of the constitutions promulgated by Macleod for multiracial areas was that they required voters of one race to at least attend to candidates of other races. This strategy worked moderately well in East Africa and Northern Rhodesia as a temporary expedient between minority government and majority rule. Whatever their failings as constitutions—they were much too complex to provide a foundation for independent nations—they did accustom minorities to rapid transition and a new political frame of reference. The speed of political change in Northern Rhodesia from 1961 through 1964 almost exceeded the capacity of Kaunda's emerging national party-turned-government to absorb. In Southern Rhodesia no

95. Ibid., pp. 147 ff.; Mtshali, *Rhodesia*, pp. 123 ff.; Shamuyarira, *Crisis in Rhodesia*, pp. 148 ff.

initiative from outside the country could change attitudes or rearrange the political structure. The white electorate resisted constitutional change for almost twenty years, and then acceded only after several years of increasingly bitter and costly civil war.

In a period of ten years, the Federation had made possible—although such was certainly not its original design—a transfer of political power to independent nations in Malawi and Zambia. The transfer was effected without violence of a major kind, and the circumstances of political opposition had required in both countries that the emerging nationalist organization grow from the grass roots. Despite the fact that the end result was directly contrary to the explicit hopes of 1953, why is it not another fortunate example of muddling through?

The question is difficult to answer because there are no "controls," no comparable examples purposely set on another course. What would have happened if in 1953 policymakers had determined that in ten years' time Malawi and Zambia should become independent nations? How much would have been different? One hopes that the differences would have been significant. But the experience of West African colonies suggests obliquely that many of the fundamental problems would have remained: Malawi and Zambia would still have reached independence desperately short of trained civil servants and technical staff, with largely undifferentiated economies, with serious wage differentials, and an archaic and underutilized African agricultural sector.

Did federation make things worse? Did it put fetters on Malawi and Zambia which might not otherwise have been there? By strengthening Southern Rhodesia, diversifying its economy, concentrating much of the capital development of the Federation there, and bolstering the confidence of its white political regime, the Federation decreased the bargaining power of the two northern territories when they had to deal with the commercial, manufacturing, and transportation sectors of the Southern Rhodesian economy. Most of the large Southern Rhodesian firms were controlled by boards with Southern Rhodesian or South African sympathies, and the early years of UDI gave the Rhodesian government a chance to put these sympathies to the test. Northern Rhodesia suffered during the years of federation a net drain of seventy-seven million pounds, money which could not be spent on the diversification of its economy or the development of its African agriculture.[96] Thus, paradoxically, federation

96. Hazlewood, "Economics," table h on p. 210, showing Federal revenue minus Federal expenditure by territory for each year of the Federation. This calculation does not take account of the distribution of the Federal debt, which again probably discriminated somewhat against Northern Rhodesia (pp. 239–40).

prepared Southern Rhodesia better to attempt independence, while making Zambia more vulnerable to Southern Rhodesian economic manipulation. The extent of Zambia's dependence has been recounted and analyzed in several studies which show the high economic and political costs imposed on her new institutions by the situation in Rhodesia.[97] Malawi gained financially from federation, although nowhere near proportionately to her population. Neither African education nor African agriculture, the two areas of Malawi's greatest need and greatest comparative advantage, received under federation resources comparable to their structural importance. Still, it is not easy to argue that Malawi would have been demonstrably better off, or would have built a better general infrastructure, had there been no Federation. Unlike Northern Rhodesia, Malawi did not suffer a diversion of resources to the other two territories.

Federation appears to have confounded its designers in almost every respect. It resulted in Malawi and Zambia becoming independent, probably making them politically stronger and economically weaker than they would otherwise have been had they reached independence directly as Colonial Office territories. Conversely, Southern Rhodesia, which Britain had wished to restrain from going its own way under an archaic colonial constitution, reached the end of the federal years with a greatly strengthened economy and a more entrenched minority political regime. The northern territories did not gain economically from federation, which had been one of the reiterated arguments at the outset. Southern Rhodesia showed none of the alleged ameliorative effects on its racial and political policies from close association with its northern neighbors, which initially had been the other strong argument. At least, these had been the arguments used in London. In Salisbury, as we have seen, the arguments had always been somewhat different: federation was viewed as a poor second to amalgamation with Northern Rhodesia, and the aim of the exercise was to strengthen white political power in the race for Dominion status. On balance, the arguments made in Salisbury seem to have been a good deal more realistic—so, at least, the white Rhodesians thought when they decided in November 1965 not to go either north or south but to declare their own independence, mouthing a parody of the American Declaration of 1776.

But the white settlers' confidence was illusory. The paramountcy of African interests, which Sidney Webb (as Lord Passfield) had declared for East Africa in June 1930, *was* inevitable over time. By the 1970s all but the most myopic had realized that European rule in Africa was a relatively brief

97. Richard Hall, *The High Price of Principles: Kaunda and the White South* (London, 1969); Jan Pettman, *Zambia: Security and Conflict* (Lewes, Sussex, 1974); William Tordoff, ed., *Politics in Zambia* (Berkeley, 1974), especially the essay by Richard Sklar on pp. 320–62.

historic phase, which had disappeared with almost the same suddenness that it had appeared in the 1880s. When a man who had been publicity secretary of the National Democratic party and secretary of its Harare branch in 1960 was elected prime minister of Zimbabwe in 1980,[98] only South Africa remained as the Great Anomaly.

By insisting on federation, the Conservative governments in London had greatly complicated Her Majesty's Governments' task of achieving an honorable extrication from British Central Africa. After the independence of Malawi and Zambia, Britain no longer had the political will or the military capability to impose majority rule on Southern Rhodesia. She did not even have the economic strength to carry the costs incurred by Zambia in abiding by British principles. Only a sustained armed insurrection from bases outside Rhodesia, combined with substantial support in the Rhodesian countryside, provided Britain in the end with the leverage to achieve a settlement equitable to the majority of Zimbabwe's inhabitants. The federal legacy was finally undone by African arms.

The final irony is that the policies which improved and diversified the Southern Rhodesian economy during federation, and which made possible further diversification and self-sufficiency in the early yers of UDI, may redound to the ultimate benefit of Zimbabwe. The last black nail in the coffin of federation would be that Zimbabwe turns north to seek new associative arrangements with Zambia and Mozambique.

98. Barber, *Rhodesia,* p. 60, where he quotes Mugabe: "One man, one vote is not a parrot cry. It is the cry of the African will, determination and their demand for the restoration of the motherland" (from the *Daily News,* July 5, 1960).

15. *The Parting of the Ways in South Africa*

LEONARD THOMPSON

After the most abundant deposits of diamonds and gold in the world were discovered in southern Africa in the last third of the nineteenth century, the entire region became a far more integral part of the world economy than the territories in tropical Africa, and the black[1] as well as the white inhabitants of the region began to be incorporated into a modern industrial system. By the 1940s, Western culture had made more pervasive inroads into the African societies of southern Africa than those farther north. In 1946, for example, 53 percent of the African population of South Africa were Christians, 35 percent of the Africans over seven years old could speak English or Afrikaans, 28 percent of the Africans over ten could read and write, and 36 percent of the African men over fifteen were engaged in mining or industrial occupations.[2] All these figures increased quite rapidly throughout the later 1940s and the 1950s. The Colored and Asian communities were even more thoroughly integrated into the white-controlled political economy. Moreover, some blacks had been involved in political activity in a Western system ever since parliamentary institutions were created in the Cape Colony in 1854. Mohandas K. Gandhi launched an Indian Congress in Natal in 1894, Dr. Abdullah Abdurahman founded a

I am grateful to the editors and other members of the Bellagio conference for constructive suggestions, and also to members of the Yale-Wesleyan Southern African Research Program who made many effective criticisms of an early draft of this chapter—especially Heribert Adam, William Foltz, Hermann Giliomee, Stanley Greenberg, Thomas Karis, Richard Ralston, and Newell Stultz—and also to Robert Rotberg.

1. The South African population is officially classified as "White," "Colored," "Asian," and "Bantu." In 1960 the total was nearly 16 million and the proportions were: White 19.3%, Colored 9.4%, Asian 3.0%, Bantu 68.3%. In this chapter, I modify South African usage in two respects: I use the word *African* to designate people and confine the word *Bantu* to their languages; and I use the word *black* to include all the three subject groups in South Africa.

2. Union of South Africa, *Union Statistics for Fifty Years* (Pretoria, 1960), pp. A-14, 21, 22, 29, 33.

Colored political organization in Cape Town in 1902, and the African National Congress was inaugurated in 1912.

During the first four decades of the twentieth century, the South African regime was not alone in practicing racial discrimination. Vast political, social, and economic disparities between people of European origin and others were standard features throughout most of Africa, much of Asia, and also the United States; and these practices were buttressed by theories of racial inequality. During the 1940s and 1950s, however, the situation began to change everywhere but in southern Africa. Subject races asserted their dignity and demanded political and economic rights; Europeans—victors and vanquished alike—were seriously weakened by the Second World War, and the Nazi excesses shocked them into revising their racial attitudes. Consequently, the European empires were dismantled in Asia; the British, the French, and eventually the Belgians introduced substantial reforms leading toward outright independence in their African colonies, and Jim Crow began to falter in the United States. In South Africa, on the other hand, the white population, greatly outnumbered by blacks, believed that its own survival depended on the maintenance of racial discrimination, and many Afrikaners assumed that the reports of Nazi atrocities were wartime propaganda. Consequently, although black South Africans organized a series of political campaigns with the object of persuading the white authorities to move in the same direction as the rest of the world, many of the rights that they had previously possessed were whittled away, and the structure of South African society became more rigidly racial than any the world has known.

These, then, were the years of the parting of the ways between South Africa and the rest of the world.[3] By the early 1960s, when black regimes were installed or were on the verge of being installed in most of the territories of tropical Africa and desegregation was making strides in the United States, in South Africa a white regime had eliminated all black participation in the authoritative political system, had banned the major African political organizations, and had devised elaborate, efficient, and indeed ruthless, techniques for modernizing racial domination,[4] giving black South Africans the choice between accommodating to permanent subordination or resorting to violence and revolution. The purpose of this chapter is to describe and explain this process.

3. But see chapters 13 and 14 of this work for the former Portuguese territories and for the erstwhile members of the Central African Federation.

4. *Modernizing Racial Domination: The Dynamics of South African Politics* is the title of a perceptive work by Heribert Adam (Berkeley and Los Angeles, 1971).

Secondary Colonialism in South Africa

The basic explanation of South Africa's failure to keep in step with the rest of the world lies in the history and structure of South African society. Commentators have described the South African situation as constituting "domestic" or "internal" or "settler" colonialism.[5] The term "secondary colonialism" is more appropriate because it places the situation in historical perspective. In all European colonies, society was racially stratified. Some of the preconditions for secondary colonialism existed in those colonies which contained sizeable communities of European origin established as settlers in the midst of more numerous indigenous populations. The transition from primary to secondary colonialism occurred when, voluntarily or involuntarily, the metropolitan government ceased to administer the territory and political power passed into the hands of the local white community.

Wherever the European population was numerous in Africa, it exerted an inordinate influence over the administration during the primary colonial era and resisted the transfer of power to members of the indigenous majority as that era drew to a close. The cases of Algeria and Kenya, as well as Angola and Mozambique, are conspicuous examples, but only in Rhodesia and South Africa did secondary colonial regimes come into power. In Rhodesia, Great Britain took the crucial step of granting responsible government to a predominantly white electorate in 1923, but the transition was completed as recently as 1965, by unilateral action in defiance of world opinion. In South Africa, the transition began in the nineteenth century, and it was completed during the period when racial inequality was still endorsed and practiced by the European powers and the United States. Consequently, the South African state was legitimate at birth, whereas Rhodesia never won international recognition.

With its temperate climate, its freedom from tropical diseases of man and beast, and its strategic location, the Cape Colony became a colony of settlement in the same century as New England and Virginia. Long before the colonial era opened in most of tropical Africa, Great Britain began to devolve political authority on local communities in the Cape Colony and Natal, where representative institutions were created in the 1850s. These legislatures acquired control over the executive branches of government in 1872 and 1893 respectively, and the system known as responsible government was also instituted in the former Boer republics in 1907 and 1908, paving the way for the formation of the Union of South Africa in 1910. From

5. Ibid., p. 2.

the first, the Union had a great deal of de facto autonomy in external as well as internal affairs. In 1934 the South African parliament removed the last vestiges of British overrule. Thus, before the Second World War precipitated the thrust toward independence in tropical Africa, South Africa was a sovereign, independent state.[6]

In the early stages of this process of devolution of power, responsible British statesmen declared that race should not be a criterion for participation in local politics. A clearcut assertion that British intentions were not discriminatory came from Lord Stanley, Colonial Secretary, who, authorizing the annexation of Natal in 1842, instructed the governor of the Cape Colony "that there shall not be in the eye of the law any distinction of colour, origin, race, or creed";[7] and when the Cape and Natal parliaments were created in the 1850s, the vote was theoretically available to any man who possessed certain economic qualifications. In practice, however, white men dominated the political systems of both colonies from the outset and, while maintaining a legal facade of nondiscrimination, they used their powers to curtail the numbers of black voters by various devices. In Natal, for example, all people who were subject to "Native Law"—that is to say, nearly all the African population—were disqualified. Consequently, in 1909 whites formed about 23 percent of the population and had 85 percent of the votes in the Cape Colony, and in Natal whites formed only 8 percent of the population and had 99 percent of the votes; and no black person ever sat in the parliament of either colony.[8] Moreover, the constitutions that the British government provided for the Transvaal and the Orange River Colony (Orange Free State) in 1907 and 1908 reinstituted the absolute political color bars that had existed in the Boer republics. The South African constitution which white South African politicians then hammered out in a national convention, and the British parliament enacted in 1909, provided that the colonial franchise qualifications should remain in force until amended by the Union parliament, and that only white men should be eligible to sit in that parliament.[9] Thus Great Britain transferred power to the local white population and instituted a system of secondary colonialism.

The differences between primary and secondary colonialism are fundamental. The rulers of a secondary colonial state are an entrenched local oligarchy, whereas a primary colonial regime is run by officials who are responsible to a distant government. In a secondary colonial state all the members of the ruling oligarchy have clear economic as well as political

6. The classic analysis of this process is in W. K. Hancock, *Survey of British Commonwealth Affairs*, vol. 1: *Problems of Nationality 1918–1936* (London, 1937).

7. Stanley to Sir George Napier, Dec. 13, 1842, C.O. 49/36, Public Record Office.

8. L. M. Thompson, *The Unification of South Africa 1902–1910* (Oxford, 1960), pp. 109–12.

9. Ibid., pp. 212–26.

interests in maintaining the system, whereas only particular sections of the electorate of a metropolitan state perceive that they derive advantages from primary colonialism. The maintenance of a colonial system is but one of the many concerns of a metropolitan government, and it is negotiable. In South Africa, the secondary colonial situation makes maintenance of the system the most vital concern of the government. The norms of Western political democracy—one man one vote, and one vote one value—are regarded by the white oligarchy as a prescription for suicide.

Reactions to Conquest before the Second World War

By 1939 South Africa dominated the entire southern part of the continent. The mandated territory of South West Africa, the three territories administered by the British High Commissioner, the self-governing colony of Southern Rhodesia, and Portuguese Mozambique were all heavily dependent on South Africa—virtual satellites.[10] Moreover, the South African state bore heavily upon its people; legislation had proliferated and the bureaucracy had expanded. Secondary colonialism was a far more intensive form of government than primary colonialism.

In varying degrees, the African as well as the Colored and Asian inhabitants of South Africa were incorporated in subordinate roles in the white-controlled capitalist economy. Overt compulsion—a frequent occurrence in earlier years—was no longer necessary. The effects of land shortage and taxation, orchestrated by a vast labor recruiting network for the mines, were sufficient for the purpose. Consequently, the indigenous peoples of South Africa had experienced a more complete disruption of their way of life than those farther north. They were no longer self-sufficient farming communities, nor did they have the opportunity to accommodate to the market economy by becoming peasant producers of cash crops in addition to their food.[11] In seven-eighths of the country they could own no land: some were labor tenants on land owned by white farmers; others, often in defiance of the pass laws, were residents of African "locations" adjacent to industrial towns. The majority retained rights in sub-subsistence landhold-

10. Larry W. Bowman, "The Subordinate State System of Southern Africa," *International Studies Quarterly* 12, no. 3 (September 1968):231–61.

11. Colin Bundy, "Emergence and Decline of a South African Peasantry," *African Affairs* 71 (October 1972):369–88, and Leonard Thompson, *Survival in Two Worlds: Moshoeshoe of Lesotho, 1786–1870* (Oxford, 1975), pp. 190–96, show that some African communities in the region did temporarily become peasantries in the nineteenth century, but that they were reduced to sub-subsistence production and dependence on migrant labor by the early twentieth century. Kenneth Vickery's unpublished work on the plateau Tonga of Northern Rhodesia (Zambia) shows that that community did become a peasantry in the 1930s. There is no similar case south of the Zambezi.

ings in the reservations that were the remnants of their precolonial territories and survived by sending out members of their families as migrant workers to earn wages in the white areas.

The greatest industries were still the gold, diamond, and coal mining industries of South Africa which, in 1939, employed 408,706 African men from every part of the region on contracts varying from between six to eighteen months, and housed them in compounds separate from the local community. Africans showed remarkable skill in adapting to this shuttle existence. Nevertheless, the social effects were disastrous. Families were constantly being broken up; from some reservations, more than half the men of working age were absent at a time. Moreover, white employers, workers, and politicians acted on the assumption that the reservations provided Africans with a basic livelihood, so that it was not necessary to pay migrant laborers substantial wages. Throughout the region, black workers were always subordinated to whites in the workplace and earned far less money. In the gold-mining industry, for example, the difference was twenty to one.[12] White power and wealth were buttressed by differential social services and discriminatory laws. There were excellent, heavily subsidized schools and medical services for whites; those for blacks were greatly inferior. Africans were obliged to carry passes in white areas; most Africans were excluded from the industrial bargaining system; and it was unlawful for them to strike. Moreover, the government applied a "civilized labor" policy, providing the most unsuccessful whites with well-paid, sheltered employment, so that blacks bore the full burden of unemployment. And in 1936 the African voters in the Cape Province were removed from the common voters' roll. Instead, they were given the right to elect three white people to represent them in the House of Assembly, and Africans in all provinces were able indirectly to elect four white senators. A Natives Representative Council was also created, but without being given any effective powers.[13] White fears that black power might escalate within the established system were thus allayed.

12. On the gold-mining industry, see Francis Wilson, *South African Labour in the Gold Mines 1911–1969* (Cambridge, 1972), and *Migrant Labour in South Africa* (Johannesburg, 1972). For a doctrinaire, neo-Marxist analysis, see Frederick A. Johnstone, *Class, Race and Gold: A Study of Class Relations and Racial Discrimination in South Africa* (London, 1976). African labor in the Rhodesian gold-mining industry is dealt with from the neo-Marxist viewpoint much more perceptively by Charles vanOnselen, in *Chibaro: African Mine Labour in Southern Rhodesia 1900–1923* (London, 1976).

13. On the structure of South African society before 1948, see Social and Economic Planning Council Report no. 13, *The Economic and Social Conditions of the Racial Groups in South Africa, U.G. 53–'48* (Cape Town, 1948). There is a summary of "Principal Legislative Measures affecting Race Relations (1909–1948)" in Muriel Horrell, *Legislation and Race Relations*, rev. ed. (Johannesburg, 1971), pp. 1–8.

Despite all this, South African society did not become completely polarized before the Second World War. With primary colonialism still entrenched in the rest of Africa and much of Asia, and blacks still subordinated in North America, there was no foreign model to inspire radical change in South Africa before the Russian Revolution, and even then, although a Communist party of South Africa was founded in 1921, it had little impact.[14] Moreover, black South Africans were far from united. History, custom, and law created numerous ethnic barriers, not only between Africans and Asians and Colored people, but also within each of these communities—for example, between Xhosa and Zulu and Sotho. Class divisions were also developing within each black community; the majority of the more successful blacks were ambiguously poised between their resentment of the deprivations they experienced as blacks and their desire to use their existing opportunities to master Western skills and raise their living standards. This was even the case among Africans. Nearly all the clergy, teachers, and nurses who formed the bulk of the emerging African bourgeoisie had been educated in mission schools. Most of them continued to respect the Christian ethic and the social and political norms purveyed by their mentors, and to accept the advice of those few whites who were sensitive to their problems and who arranged interracial contacts in organizations such as the Joint Councils of Europeans and Natives.[15]

Consequently, before the Second World War the principal black political organizations were sectional in scope, reformist in objective, and nonviolent in method. African political activity within the imperial system originated among the qualified voters in the Cape Colony in the 1880s, and the Union-wide African National Congress (ANC) was founded in 1912. Until the Second World War it was led by mission-educated professional men. Of the five ANC presidents of that period, four had had higher education in England or the United States, two were ordained clergymen in orthodox Christian denominations (Congregational and Methodist), two were teachers, and one was a lawyer. Except for the brief presidency of Josiah T. Gumede (1927–30), who inclined toward socialism, they aimed at reforming the system from within and achieving full equality for Western-educated people like themselves and progressive extensions of the fran-

14. On the Communist party of South Africa, see A. Lerumo (Michael Harmel), *Fifty Fighting Years: The South African Communist Party 1921–1971* (London, 1971), H. J. and R. E. Simons, *Class and Colour in South Africa, 1850–1950* (Harmondsworth, 1969), and Edward Roux, *Time Longer than Rope: A History of the Black Man's Struggle for Freedom in South Africa*, 2d ed. (Madison, Wis., 1964).

15. Leo Kuper has reported that similar attitudes were dominant as late as the early 1960s; see his *An African Bourgeoisie* (New Haven, 1965). For the 1920s and 1930s, see W. M. Macmillan, *My South African Years* (Cape Town, 1975).

chise to the rest of the population, following the British precedent. The implication was that South Africa would eventually become a culturally homogeneous, nonracial, liberal democracy. They sought to achieve their objectives through propaganda and constitutional pressure. They sent deputations and petitions to the white authorities in Pretoria and Cape Town, and also to London and, in 1919, to Versailles, protesting existing racial laws and practices and criticizing racial bills that were before parliament, from the land legislation of 1913 to the scheme that was eventually enacted in 1936. However, the ANC did not stem the racist tide; it merely waged a series of unsuccessful rearguard actions. During the 1930s the organization was moribund. It had few members and was ridden with personal and ideological disputes.[16]

There were also sporadic attempts to organize black industrial workers. African mineworkers on the Witwatersrand went on strike in 1920; the government suppressed them ruthlessly. In the mid-1920s, the Industrial and Commercial Workers Union of Africa (ICU), under the leadership of Clements Kadalie, an immigrant from Nyasaland (Malawi), established branches throughout the country and enrolled many thousands of Africans; but in 1928–29 it collapsed as rapidly as it had grown.[17]

Many Africans sublimated their frustrations in religious activity. African Christians had begun to separate from their parent white-controlled churches in the 1880s. By the 1930s there were hundreds of separatist churches, which provided leadership roles that were denied to black clergy in the orthodox churches, as well as psychological and cultural alternatives to the pursuit of European norms and the acceptance of European dogmas.[18] The government was wary of these organizations but did not normally interfere with them. An exception occurred in 1921, when police attacked members of the millenarian Israelite sect who had refused to move from land they were occupying at Bulhoek, near Queenstown, Cape Province, killing 163 Africans and wounding 129.

16. Thomas Karis and Gwendolen M. Carter, eds., *From Protest to Challenge: A Documentary History of African Politics in South Africa, 1882–1964*, 4 vols. (Stanford, 1972–77). Volumes 1–3 are collections of documents in chronological sequence, with substantial introductory essays by Sheridan Johns III, Thomas Karis, and Gail M. Gerhart, and volume 4 contains "Political Profiles" of 333 personalities. For the period before 1939, see also the works listed in n. 14 above, and Peter Walshe, *The Rise of African Nationalism in South Africa: The African National Congress, 1912–1952* (London, 1970).

17. Clements Kadalie, *My Life and the ICU*, ed. Stanley Trapido (London, 1970).

18. Bengt G. M. Sundkler, *Bantu Prophets in South Africa*, 2d ed. (London, 1961), and *Zulu Zion and Some Swazi Zionists* (London, 1976).

THE TRANSITIONAL PERIOD, 1939–1948

During and immediately after the Second World War there was a distinct trend toward black-white polarization in South Africa. Black expectations were raised by external events: the Japanese demonstration of European vulnerability; the egalitarian, populist element in Allied propaganda, epitomized in the rolling phrases of the Atlantic Charter and the preamble of the Charter of the United Nations; and the beginning of substantial reform in the British and French territories in tropical Africa.

The government contributed to these rising expectations. Prime Minister Jan Christiaan Smuts publicly admitted that "segregation has fallen on evil days," and justified continued white leadership in terms of the concept of Christian trusteeship.[19] He also played a leading part in drafting the United Nations Charter. Jan Hendrik Hofmeyr, his heir presumptive, pointedly reminded the public that the time comes when a ward reaches maturity, implying that trusteeship meant that Africans should eventually participate fully in the central political process.[20] The Social and Economic Planning Council, appointed by the government, revealed that South African society consisted essentially of a rich and powerful white minority and a poor and powerless black majority, and that the reservations were far too small to sustain their inhabitants; and early in 1948 a government commission reported that "the idea of total segregation is utterly impracticable" and that the process of urbanization of the African population was inevitable and irreversible.[21]

However, the government did little to fulfill these expectations. It did initiate social welfare benefits for certain blacks and increased the grants for black education, but at far lower rates than for whites. Moreover, it applied new segregation measures to Asians and Colored people; it did scarcely anything to meet the housing needs of the thousands of Africans who were flocking to the cities and were obliged to live in tin shanties in squatter camps; and it violently suppressed a series of African strikes, notably a strike by 70,000 mineworkers in 1946. The acid test of the 1936 legislation, which Prime Minister J. B. M. Hertzog had regarded as a "solution" of the "Na-

19. W. K. Hancock, *Smuts: The Fields of Force 1919–1950* (Cambridge, 1968), p. 475.

20. Alan Paton, *Hofmeyr* (London, 1964).

21. Union of South Africa, *Social and Economic Planning Council Report No. 9: The Native Reserves and Their Place in the Economy of the Union of South Africa: U.G. 32/1946* (Pretoria, 1946) and *Report of the Native Laws Commission, 1946–48: U.G. 28/1948* (Fagan Report; Pretoria, 1948). See also Howard Brotz, *The Politics of South Africa: Democracy and Racial Diversity* (Oxford, 1977), which contends that Fagan had the key to a peaceful transition in South Africa.

tive problem," was the fate of the Natives Representative Council (NRC). In its annual sessions the NRC made measured criticisms of the effects of racial discrimination in South Africa and offered judicious advice; but the government ignored it. By 1948, the NRC was virtually on strike to demonstrate its own frustration.[22]

Faced by the growing gulf between their condition and their expectations, a new generation of black leaders sought more effective methods of protest. In 1943, the annual ANC conference adopted a statement of *Africans' Claims in South Africa* that cited the Atlantic Charter and set out a bill of rights calling for the abolition of all discriminatory legislation, redistribution of the land, African participation in industrial collective bargaining, and universal adult suffrage.[23] In the same year a group of young professional Africans, including Anton Lembede, Nelson Mandela, Walter Sisulu, and Oliver Tambo, soon to be joined by Robert Sobukwe, founded a youth league as a pressure group in the ANC, stressing the need for African self-reliance and unity. In 1945, ANC delegates attended the Pan African Congress in Manchester, England. Nevertheless, the ANC was still a small organization with essentially middle-class membership, and it had no mature plan of action, when Dr. D. F. Malan's Afrikaner Nationalists and their allies won the 1948 general election.[24]

The Parting of the Ways

The 1948 general election was the most important domestic political event that accelerated the polarization between white and black inside South Africa and also between South Africa and the world beyond its borders. Some commentators have implied that the policy of the Afrikaner National party which came into power in 1948 has been little more than an "elaboration of the existing system."[25] They have pointed to the undoubted facts that South Africa was already a castelike society, with power and wealth concen-

22. Margaret Ballinger, *From Union to Apartheid: A Trek to Isolation* (New York, 1969).

23. Karis and Carter, *From Protest to Challenge*, 2:209–23.

24. Besides the numerous documents by Africans in Karis and Carter, vol. 2, see: Albert Luthuli, *Let My People Go: An Autobiography* (London, 1962); Jordan Ngubane, *An African Explains Apartheid* (New York, 1963); and I. B. Tabata, *The All African Convention: The Awakening of a People* (Johannesburg, 1950); also Mary Benson, *South Africa: The Struggle for a Birthright* (New York, 1969).

25. Martin Legassick, "Gold, Agriculture, and Secondary Industry in South Africa, 1885–1870: From Periphery to Sub-Metropole as a Forced Labour System," in Robin Palmer and Neil Parson, eds., *The Roots of Rural Poverty in Central and Southern Africa* (London, 1977), p. 191.

trated in white hands, that previous governments had intended to keep it that way, and that many of the laws passed by the Nationalists had roots in earlier legislation. However, such facts do not sufficiently explain subsequent events. Before the 1948 election, there were many gaps in the racial laws and great regional variations in custom where the laws were silent. Furthermore, although the United party government was dismayed by the wartime escalation of African urbanization, it was both too confused and too sensible to try to reverse major historical processes.

In contrast, dogmatic intellectuals were associated with the party that came into power in 1948—fervent apostles of a secular religion derived from Calvinism. They insisted that ethnic groups, not individuals, are the most meaningful human entities; and they were sure that they possessed the key to the solution of the country's problems—a solution that would ensure white survival, and especially the survival of the Afrikaner nation, for all time, and a solution that would also be just for all concerned. A mere continuation of United party policy would be disastrous, for it was not checking the flood of Africans into the white areas. A radical reconstruction of South African society was essential. The races were to be completely separated from one another, biologically and territorially; each would be able to develop along its own lines in its own area; and white people should have exclusive and absolute control of the white area for all time. Even though this reconstruction might produce hardships for some during the period of reconstruction, the end would justify the means.[26]

A principal architect of this solution was Dr. G. Cronjé, whose *'n Tuiste vir die Nageslag* (A Home for Posterity), published in 1955, was a blueprint for apartheid.[27] Its master builder was Hendrik Frensch Verwoerd, minister of Native affairs (under D. F. Malan and J. G. Strijdom from 1950 to 1958) and then prime minister until he was assassinated in 1966. By the end of 1960, many of the bricks were in place, as a result of a mass of complex legislation enacted by an increasingly submissive parliament. Laws created a population register to fix the racial category—and with it the rights—of every South African, prohibited marriages between whites and blacks, and extended the existing prohibition of extramarital sexual relations between whites and Africans to include sexual relations between whites and Asians

26. Writing from inside knowledge, W. A. deKlerk, in *The Puritans in Africa: A Study of Afrikanerdom* (Harmondsworth, 1976), emphasizes the gulf between the ideology and practice of previous South African governments and those of the National party governments of Malan and his successors. So does T. Dunbar Moodie, in *The Rise of Afrikanerdom: Power, Apartheid and the Afrikaner Civil Religion* (Berkeley and Los Angeles, 1975).

27. Published in Stellenbosch. Also, G. Cronjé, *Regverdige Rasseapartheid* [A just racial separation] (Stellenbosch, 1947).

or Colored people. Absolute white control of the sovereign political machinery was assured by laws abolishing the representation of Africans in parliament, repealing earlier legislation that would have provided parliamentary representation for Asians, and removing the Cape Colored voters from the common roll and giving them the right to elect four white representatives to parliament (who were destined to be eliminated in their turn in 1970). Laws also abolished the Natives Representative Council, grouped the African population into eight (later ten) "national" units, and delegated powers in the reservations to a hierarchy of Bantu Authorities, consisting mainly of chiefs who were appointed by and responsible to the central government. Other laws authorized the executive to divide the towns and cities into uniracial residential and business zones and to reserve any type of work for workers of specified racial groups. Increasingly severe regulations limited the right of Africans—women as well as men—to reside in the urban areas and empowered officials to "endorse out" all Africans deemed to be "idle" or "undesirable." Gaps in the existing industrial laws were closed, to ensure that no African man or woman should be a member of a trade union that was entitled to take part in collective bargaining under the industrial conciliation system.

The educational system was drastically restructured. The Bantu Education Act transferred African schools from the provinces to the central government, removed subsidies from mission schools, and made it unlawful to conduct a school unless it was officially registered and subject to government regulations, with the result that by 1960 nearly all African school education was conducted in government schools according to government plans by teachers who were civil servants. To round out its domination of the black educational system, the government also excluded blacks from the established universities and created and strictly controlled five colleges for Colored, Asian, and three ethnic categories of African students. Legislation also outlawed the Communist party and authorized the executive to declare any other organization to be unlawful if it was "satisfied" that it was pursuing any of the aims of communism, which was defined in extremely broad terms.[28]

Initially, the Supreme Court was a moderating influence. It upset several administrative orders on the ground that they were technically invalid and, where statutes were imprecise or ambiguous, it applied principles derived from common law. But step by step parliament restricted the

28. Succinct summaries are in Muriel Horrell, *Legislation and Race Relations: A Summary of the Main South African Laws which Affect Race Relationships* (Johannesburg, 1963), 1966 and 1971 eds.

latitude of the judiciary. Besides passing amending legislation to eliminate loopholes, it enacted new laws providing that separate amenities need not be equal and prohibiting the courts from issuing interdicts that suspended the application of various types of administrative orders to Africans. Moreover, after the Appellate Division of the Supreme Court had disallowed legislation purporting to remove the Colored voters from the common roll in the Cape Province, because it had not been enacted in accordance with the special procedure laid down in the constitution, the Nationalist party achieved its purpose by passing laws to pack the Senate with its nominees and to enlarge the Appellate Division. Thus, while the United States judiciary was actively promoting desegregation, the power of the South African judiciary was being curtailed by a mass of racial legislation and by the assertion of parliamentary supremacy. The doctrine of legal positivism had always been influential in South African legal circles; it provided the theoretical underpinning for the emasculation of the courts.[29]

Even so, some of the essential goals of Cronjé's blueprint were not achieved. There were no territories that could conceivably become "national homes" for the Colored and Asian communities; the African reservations remained scattered lands that amounted to less than one-eighth of the area of the country and were quite incapable of producing a livelihood for the African population; and, despite the influx controls, the de facto African population of the urban areas continued to increase and the market economy continued to depend on cheap black labor. By the time of the 1960 census, over eight million Africans—more than half the African population of the country—were in the "white" areas outside the reservations. Pretoria was the only town or district in the country where white people formed a majority. Whites amounted to only one-ninth of the total population of the "white rural areas" and one-third of the total population of the towns and cities. The dynamics of territorial integration were not being reversed: they were being accentuated. Consequently, the utopian vision that had inspired Afrikaner intellectuals in the first flush of their 1948 victory had faded by 1960. The South African government was blatantly determined to preserve Afrikaner identity and power, and resorted to sophistries to account for its actions. It was obvious to objective observers, foreign as well as domestic, that grand apartheid as conceived by Cronjé was a fantasy.[30]

29. Geoffrey Marshall, *Parliamentary Sovereignty and the Commonwealth* (Oxford, 1957); Albie Sachs, *Justice in South Africa* (Berkeley and Los Angeles, 1973); A. S. Mathews, *Law, Order, and Liberty in South Africa* (Berkeley and Los Angeles, 1972).

30. Leonard M. Thompson, *Politics in the Republic of South Africa* (Boston, 1966), pp. 44–46. I have drawn on this book for several other passages in this section.

Numerous white professional people repeatedly criticized the actions of the Nationalist government, pointing to the enormous gulf between the theory and the practice of apartheid, to the continuous increase in the number of Africans in the white areas, to the absence of any adequate substitute for participation in the political system for Coloreds and Asians, and to the ever-increasing harshness of the methods employed to maintain white supremacy. Between them, they built up an impressive critique of conditions in South Africa. They were influential in the English-language universities, churches, and press; in addition, there were a number of courageous Afrikaner critics. Amid the barrage of verbal criticism, one may note the blunt declaration of Professor Philip Tobias of the University of the Witwatersrand that "science provides no evidence that any single one of the assumptions underlying South Africa's racial legislation is justified"; Anthony Delius's brilliant verse satire, *The Last Division,* which mocked the leading politicians and their ideas; and the overwhelming evidence of the degrading conditions in the African townships outside Johannesburg in Father Trevor Huddleston's *Naught for your Comfort.*[31]

The most dramatic episode in the white reaction was the manner of the death of the seventy-two-year-old Geoffrey Clayton, archbishop of Cape Town and head of the Anglican church in South Africa. A profoundly conservative churchman, after great anguish he composed a letter to the prime minister saying that, if parliament passed a bill including a clause limiting the right of churches to admit Africans to services in white areas, he and his fellow bishops would be "unable to obey it or counsel our clergy and people to do so." Clayton signed the letter on the morning of Thursday, March 17, 1957. That afternoon, alone in his study, he died of a heart attack.[32]

Effective political action was a different matter from verbal criticism. The whites who were elected to parliament by Africans under the 1936 legislation (three in the House of Assembly and four in the Senate) argued cogently but unavailingly against each successive racial bill.[33] The War Veterans Torch Commando had a brief and exciting career in 1951–53, before it shattered on the rocks of racism. The Black Sash, a women's organization, devised methods of political protest that were original but soon lost their sting. In 1953, whites founded a Liberal party, and in 1959 eleven members of Parliament seceded from the United party on a matter of principle and formed a Progressive party. But none of these organiza-

31. Philip V. Tobias, *The Meaning of Race* (Johannesburg, 1961), p. 22; Anthony Delius, *The Last Division* (Cape Town, 1959); Trevor Huddleston, *Naught for Your Comfort* (London, 1956).

32. Alan Paton, *Apartheid and the Archbishop: The Life and Times of Geoffrey Clayton* (Cape Town, 1973), pp. 275–81.

33. Ballinger, *From Union to Apartheid.*

tions threatened the Nationalists' hold over the electorate. The Liberal party never won a seat in a white constituency, and the Progressive party was reduced to a single seat in the 1961 election.[34] The Nationalists increased their strength in the House of Assembly from 70 seats out of 153 in 1948 (when they were dependent on an alliance with the short-lived Afrikaner party), to 94 out of 159 in 1953, 103 out of 159 in 1958, and 105 out of 159 in 1961.[35] Moreover, the programs adopted by the Liberal and Progressive parties did not include straightforward, unambiguous provisions for both universal suffrage and the redistribution of wealth. Consequently, black South Africans had no reason to expect that their liberation would come from within the established political system.

Protest and Resistance to Apartheid

Black South Africans continuously opposed the imposition of apartheid. But the existence of a secondary colonial state made black emancipation immensely more difficult to achieve in South Africa than elsewhere. During the 1950s blacks were beginning to break down the barriers of segregation in the southern United States. In most parts of anglophonic and francophonic Africa, blacks were advancing toward independence by appealing to their rulers' moral scruples as well as by organizing political demonstrations. Blacks made no such headway in South Africa, where the white oligarchy had the will and the means to overcome external and internal opposition and concentrate on maintaining white supremacy.

There were other formidable obstacles to black liberation in South Africa. Suspicion and hostility were endemic between the African, Asian, and Colored communities. In 1949, for example, more than a hundred people, most of them Asians, were killed in communal riots between Africans and Asians in Durban. There were also deep cleavages within each subordinate caste. Classes and cultures were quite sharply differentiated among the Asians and the Colored people. Among Africans, especially rural Africans, ethnic rivalries were still potent—for example, rivalries between Nguni and Tswana-Sotho, the two major linguistic groups, and also within each linguistic group, as between Xhosa and Mfengu. White penetration and domination had created further cleavages among Africans. Permanent residents of the reservations, permanent farm workers, permanent townspeople, and migrant laborers had different interests. There was a broad distinction between conservatives and modernists. Despite many

34. Janet Robertson, *Liberalism in South Africa: 1948–1963* (Oxford, 1971); also Paton, *Hofmeyr*.
35. Kenneth Heard, *General Elections in South Africa, 1943–1970* (London, 1974).

exceptions, conservative Africans were for the most part illiterate, rural, or migratory, and either members of Zionist sects or non-Christians, while modern Africans were likely to be educated, urban, and members of orthodox Christian denominations. Poverty constituted the greatest obstacle of all. Most blacks were so preoccupied with the daily struggle to acquire food and shelter that they had little time or energy for political activity. Consequently, black leaders faced immense obstacles in trying to create movements dynamic enough to reverse the racist tide in South Africa, even though all the members of all three subordinate castes experienced severe deprivations and indignities.[36]

The government intensified blacks' problems. It was able to impose a considerable amount of ideological control through its monopoly of the radio and manipulation of the educational system. Through the Bantu Authorities system, it employed African chiefs as its local officials in the reservations and channeled the political rewards of Africans to the periphery.[37] When blacks did engage in resistance politics, they were liable to be reported on by informers and deprived of their livelihood by imprisonment, or simply by being "endorsed out" of the towns or banished from the reservations where they were known. Thus, poverty was compounded by insecurity. It was a terrible decision for a man to put his livelihood and the livelihood of his dependents at risk by becoming involved in resistance activities. Moreover, whites had a monopoly on modern weapons: blacks were not permitted to possess firearms and did not in fact obtain many. It is therefore not surprising that even though the police had no compunction in resorting to violence when they deemed it necessary, they did not have to do so very often.[38]

Notwithstanding these obstacles, the level of resistance to apartheid was quite remarkable during these years.[39] The main organ of resistance was

36. For outstanding examples of autobiographies revealing the realities of life for Africans in South Africa, see Ezekiel Mphahlele, *Down Second Avenue* (Garden City, N.Y., 1971), and Naboth Mokgatle, *The Autobiography of an Unknown South African* (Berkeley and Los Angeles, 1971).

37. On the use of chiefs as government agents and their loss of popular legitimacy, see Govan Mbeki, *South Africa: The Peasants' Revolt* (Harmondsworth, 1964); also, for an example of official treatment of an upstanding chief, see Albert Luthuli, *Let my People Go* (London, 1962), pp. 119–24.

38. Albie Sachs, "The Instruments of Domination," and Heribert Adam, "Internal Constellations and Potentials for Change," in Leonard Thompson and Jeffrey Butler, eds., *Change in Contemporary South Africa* (Berkeley and Los Angeles, 1975); Walshe, *Rise of African Nationalism*, chap. 14.

39. For an admirable summary, see Muriel Horrell, *Action, Reaction, and Counteraction: A Brief Review of Non-White Political Movements in South Africa*, 2d ed. (Johannesburg, 1971).

the ANC, revitalized since 1943 by the Youth League. In 1949, the annual ANC conference adopted a Programme of Action that called for "freedom from White domination and the attainment of political independence"; rejected the policy slogans that were being used by the United party opposition as well as the Nationalist government—"segregation, apartheid, trusteeship, or White leadership which are all in one way or another motivated by the idea of White domination"; and committed Congress to boycotts, strikes, and civil disobedience.[40] During 1952, while white South Africa was celebrating the three hundredth anniversary of the founding of the settlement at the Cape by Jan van Riebeeck, the ANC and the South African Indian Congress mounted a passive resistance campaign. By the end of that year, the ANC membership had climbed toward the unprecedented height of a hundred thousand, and over eight thousand people had been incarcerated for "defying unjust laws"—most of them Africans, but also Asians and handfuls of Colored and white people. By then, however, forty people, including six whites, had been killed in riots in Port Elizabeth, Johannesburg, and other towns and, although the campaign organizers claimed that the government had instigated the disturbances, the government held the organizers responsible and, with an overwhelming majority of the white electorate solidly behind it, introduced legislation placing drastic new curbs on passive resistance.[41]

The next major campaign was organized by a National Action Council, comprising representatives of organizations of each of the four racial groups in the South African lexicon: the ANC, the South African Indian Congress, the South African Colored Peoples' Organization, and the white Congress of Democrats. The ANC was the senior partner in the planning and execution of the campaign. The idea emanated from Professor Z. K. Matthews, a veteran member of the ANC and a distinguished scholar, who had recently returned from a year's appointment as a visiting professor in the Union Theological Seminary in New York. Throughout the country, local groups collected lists of grievances and appointed delegates to a "Congress of the People." On June 26, 1955, nearly three thousand delegates (mostly Africans, but including 320 Asians, 230 Colored people, and 112 whites) met in a field at Kliptown near Johannesburg and adopted a "Freedom Charter" that had been drafted by a committee of the organizing council. The preamble of this document read:

40. *Karis and Carter, From Protest to Challenge,* 2:337–39.

41. Luthuli, *Let My People Go,* pp. 106–32; Leo Kuper, *Passive Resistance in South Africa* (London, 1956); Karis and Carter, *From Protest to Challenge,* 2:403–508.

> We, the people of South Africa, declare for all our country and the world to know:
>
> That South Africa belongs to all who live in it, black and white, and that no government can justly claim authority unless it is based on the will of the people;
>
> That our people have been robbed of their birthright to land, liberty and peace by a form of government founded on injustice and inequality;
>
> That our country will never be prosperous or free until all our people live in brotherhood, enjoying equal rights and opportunities;
>
> That only a democratic state, based on the will of the people can secure to all their birthright without distinction of color, race, sex or belief;
>
> And therefore, we, the people of South Africa, black and white together—equals, countrymen and brothers—adopt this FREEDOM CHARTER. And we pledge ourselves to strive together, sparing nothing of our strength and courage, until the democratic changes here set out have been won.[42]

The government responded by passing fresh repressive laws, making a series of police raids to collect documents, and, in December 1956, by arresting 156 persons, including the leaders of the organizations forming the National Action Council, and charging them with high treason in the form of a conspiracy to overthrow the state by violence and replace it with a state based on communism. After a preliminary hearing that lasted over a year, ninety-two of the accused were indicted. The defense material included an analysis by Thomas Hodgkin, a British expert on African nationalism, who described the language of the Freedom Charter as essentially that of "Rousseauian democratic nationalism—an ideology which Communists regard as petty bourgeois, romantic, utopian," and explained that it was similar in both language and ideas to comparable documents issued by nationalists in tropical Africa, though somewhat more moderate.[43] Eventually, Mr. Justice Rumpff, the presiding judge, interrupted the defense presentation, and on March 29, 1961, he announced a unanimous verdict of not guilty. Scrupulously respecting the South African tradition of legalism, limited though it was by a vast accumulation of statutes and the doctrine of legal positivism, Rumpff found that it had not been proved

42. Karis and Carter, *From Protest to Challenge*, 3:205. On the Congress of the People and the Freedom Charter, besides Karis and Carter, 3:3–270, see Benson, *South Africa*, chap. 18, Luthuli, *Let My People Go*, chap. 15, and Edward Feit, *South Africa: The Dynamics of the African National Congress* (London, 1962), chaps. 3–5.

43. Karis and Carter, *From Protest to Challenge*, 3:64.

that the ANC had adopted a policy to overthrow the state by violence, nor that the ANC was a Communist organization. Nevertheless, the prolonged trial on a capital charge had a deterrent effect on opponents of the South African system.[44]

The failure of the passive resistance campaign of 1952, the Congress of the People campaign of 1955, and other efforts of the period brought a long-simmering dispute within the ANC to the boil. There were those who agreed with Albert Luthuli (president-general from 1952 onward), Nelson Mandela (deputy president from 1952 until he was banned in 1953), and Oliver Tambo (secretary-general from 1954 to 1958 and then deputy president), that the ANC should continue to seek the cooperation of other bodies, to confine itself to nonviolent methods, and to strive to create a nonracial democracy in South Africa. Others contended that the alliance with the Indian, Colored and white congresses had weakened and distracted the ANC, that there were excessive Communist influences in each congress, and that the ANC leadership had not lived up to the 1949 Programme of Action. What they wanted was a pure African movement, "without interference from either so-called left-wing or right-wing groups of the minorities who arrogantly appropriate to themselves the right to plan and think for the Africans."[45] Such a movement should use whatever means were necessary for the emancipation of the African majority.

> We aim, politically, at government of the Africans by the Africans, for the Africans, with everybody who owes his only loyalty to Afrika [*sic*] and who is prepared to accept the democratic rule of an African majority being regarded as an African. We guarantee no minority rights, because we think in terms of individuals, not groups.[46]

Failing to wrest control of the ANC, the frustrated minority seceded in 1959 and founded the Pan Africanist Congress (PAC). Its leaders were younger than the ANC leaders. The PAC president was Robert Sobukwe, who was born in the eastern Cape Province in 1924, educated at Fort Hare college, and, since 1954, was a language teacher in the University of the Witwatersrand. The national secretary was Potlako Leballo, who was born

44. On the treason trial, see ibid., pp. 344–49 and 579–626; Luthuli, *Let My People Go*, chap. 18; Benson, *South Africa*, chap. 20; and Lionel Forman and E. S. Sachs, *The South African Treason Trial* (London, 1957).

45. Inaugural Convention of the PAC, opening address by Robert Sobukwe, April 4, 1959, Karis and Carter, *From Protest to Challenge*, 3:515.

46. Ibid., p. 516.

in Basutoland in the same year as Sobukwe and had been chairman of the ANC branch in Orlando township near Johannesburg since 1954.[47]

Attempting to keep the initiative, the ANC planned a new campaign against the pass laws—the crux of the system of labor exploitation. This campaign was to have started on March 31, 1960, but the PAC forestalled the ANC, announcing that a nationwide, nonviolent defiance of the pass laws was to take place on March 21. The response was not great, except in the Cape peninsula and the Vereeniging area of the southern Transvaal, where several thousands of Africans presented themselves at police stations without passes, inviting arrest. At the police station at Sharpeville, near Vereeniging, the police resorted to shooting at such a crowd, killing 69 Africans (most of whom were shot in the back as they ran away) and wounding 178 others. Both the ANC and the PAC called for a day of mourning a week later, and there were widespread stoppages of work, especially in Cape Town, Johannesburg, and Port Elizabeth. On March 30 a vast crowd of Africans, estimated to number 30,000, marched to the center of the city of Cape Town, near the Houses of Parliament, which were in session.[48]

The government struck back fiercely. It defused the Cape Town crisis by deceiving Philip Kgosana, the young and inexperienced leader, into believing that concessions would be made if he persuaded the crowd to disperse; and then, when the people had gone home, it arrested Kgosana. The government also declared a state of emergency under the Public Safety Act of 1953; it detained 11,279 Africans, 90 Asians, 36 Colored people, and 98 whites under emergency regulations; and it outlawed the ANC and the PAC. It jailed another 6,800 Africans for pass law and other offenses, while the police beat up hundreds of Africans and compelled them to return to work.[49]

During the next few years, the government perfected its system of controls. By 1964, parliament had provided the executive branch with devastating statutory powers. It could declare any organization unlawful. It could ban any person from attending any meeting, and imprison anyone for publishing anything that was ever said or written by such a person. It could

47. On the founding of the PAC, see ibid., pp. 307–25 and 498–555; Luthuli, *Let My People Go*, chap. 18; and Gail M. Gerhart, *Black Power in South Africa* (Berkeley and Los Angeles, 1978).

48. Muriel Horrell, comp. *Days of Crisis in South Africa* (Johannesburg, 1960); Karis and Carter, *From Protest to Challenge*, 3:329–35; Luthuli, *Let My People Go*, pp. 217–23; Benson, *South Africa*, chap. 23.

49. Karis and Carter, *From Protest to Challenge*, 3:335–44; Luthuli, *Let My People Go*, pp. 223–28; Benson, *South Africa*, chap. 23.

arrest anyone and hold him in prison indefinitely, without access to lawyers; the courts were expressly debarred from intervening in such cases. The crime of sabotage, carrying penalties from five years' imprisonment to death, was defined to include giving encouragement to anyone to commit "a wrongful and wilful act" damaging "any property of another person or of the State."[50]

Armed with such authority, the government suppressed the last remnants of overt resistance. For a while, three underground groups committed numerous acts of defiance, but they came nowhere near to threatening the stability of the state. *Poqo* (meaning Pure or Alone), derived from the PAC, was broken by mid-1963; *Umkonto we Sizwe* (The Spear of the Nation), derived from the ANC, collapsed after the police staged a coup in July 1963, arresting seventeen men in a house near Johannesburg; and in 1964 they arrested most of the members of the African Resistance Movement, which consisted mainly of young white professionals and students. Nearly all who evaded seizure or escaped from detention fled the country, with the result that by the end of 1964 scarcely any active revolutionaries remained at large in the Republic.[51]

This ended an entire phase of overt opposition to the racist order in South Africa. Previously, virtually all African leaders of the resistance had been wedded to peaceful methods. Now they concluded that liberation could only be achieved by violence. As Nelson Mandela informed the court in 1964, when he stood trial on charges of attempting a revolution by violence:

> I, and the others who started the organization (*Umkonto we Sizwe*), did so for two reasons. First, we believed that as a result of Government policy, violence by the African people had become inevitable, and that unless responsible leadership was given to canalise and control the feelings of our people, there would be outbreaks of terrorism which would produce an intensity of bitterness and hostility between the various races of this country which is not produced even by war. Secondly, we felt that without violence there would be no way open to the African people to succeed in their struggle against the principle of White supremacy.
>
> . . . Our problem was not whether to fight, but was how to continue the fight. We of the ANC had always stood for a non-racial democracy, and we shrank from any action which might drive the races further apart than they already were. But the hard facts were that fifty years of non-

50. Horrell, *Legislation and Race Relations.*
51. Horrell, *Action, Reaction, and Counteraction.*

violence had brought the African people nothing but more and more repressive legislation, and fewer and fewer rights.[52]

THE EXTERNAL FACTOR[53]

Opponents of the regime who fled South Africa found much that was encouraging in the international scene. By 1960, a gulf was opening up between the values that continued to prevail in South Africa and those that were becoming dominant elsewhere; and as the news of the killings at Sharpeville spread around the world, the structure of South African society became the object of widespread obloquy. Practice was moving in the same direction as ideology. Both the superpowers favored transferring political power to members of the indigenous societies, and all the primary colonial powers except Portugal were dismantling their empires.

Soon after the 1948 election, the Nationalist government had begun to remove the remnants of the imperial past—creating an exclusively South African national flag and anthem, abolishing appeals to the Privy Council, slashing aid to British immigration, and reducing the advantages that British immigrants possessed over others for acquiring South African citizenship. The consummation of this major goal of Afrikaner nationalism came in 1961 when, following a referendum in which only whites could vote, South Africa became a republic. But this final step in the elimination of primary colonialism from South Africa had a corollary that isolated the successor regime. Facing criticism of apartheid from new members, Prime Minister Verwoerd withdrew South Africa's application to remain in the Commonwealth as a republic. That left the country without participation in any international alliance or association except for the United Nations and some of its agencies.

There, too, South Africa's status was in jeopardy. Even in the time of Smuts, the UN had placed South Africa on the defensive, criticizing its racial policies and refusing to allow it to incorporate South West Africa. Thereafter, the verbal attacks on South Africa became more and more vehement, as the effects of apartheid became more widely known and more Asian and African nations became members of the UN. In 1963, the Gen-

52. Karis and Carter, *From Protest to Challenge*, 3:772, 776

53. Basic references are: James Barber, *South Africa's Foreign Policy 1945–1970* (London, 1973); Sam C. Nolutshungu, *South Africa in Africa: A Study in Ideology and Foreign Policy* (Manchester, 1974); Dennis Austin, *Britain and South Africa* (London, 1966); and Jack E. Spence, *Republic under Pressure* (London, 1965), and "South Africa and the Modern World," in *The Oxford History of South Africa*, ed. Monica Wilson and Leonard Thompson (Oxford, 1971), 2:477–527.

eral Assembly (by 67 votes to 16, with 23 abstentions) asked all member states to break off diplomatic and commercial relations with South Africa; and the Security Council (by 9 votes to none, with France and Britain abstaining), "being convinced that the situation in South Africa is seriously disturbing international peace and security," called on all states "to cease forthwith the sale and shipment of arms, ammunition of all types and military vehicles to South Africa."[54]

But rhetorical speeches and high-sounding resolutions are one thing, effective action quite another. Initially, the Nationalist government had been adamantly opposed to the movement toward independence in tropical Africa and, like its predecessors, had tried to persuade Britain to allow South Africa to incorporate the High Commission Territories. During the early 1960s, however, it accommodated to the decolonization of tropical Africa and to the forthcoming independence of Lesotho, Botswana, and Swaziland. There was only one great absolute in South Africa's policy. As Prime Minister Verwoerd put it in 1965, "Our motto is to maintain white supremacy for all time to come over our own people and our own country, by force if necessary."[55]

That left considerable scope for manoeuver. Before 1960, the Nationalist politicians had insisted that the reservations were destined to remain inside South Africa and subordinate to its government for all time. Then, however, with decolonization taking place in tropical Africa and unprecedented African resistance occurring in the South African towns, Prime Minister H. F. Verwoerd and his colleagues began to prepare their electorate for the possibility that the reservations might eventually become a series of independent states. In their internal propaganda, they emphasized that vital white interests would not be jeopardized; the Bantustan governments would be obliged to cooperate because they would continue to be economically dependent on South Africa. In their foreign diplomacy, they described their policy as decolonization, comparable with the policies of Britain, France, and Belgium. In fact, there were fundamental differences between the process that South Africa initiated in the early 1960s and the process of decolonization in tropical Africa. In the tropical empires, African nationalism was an autonomous movement, uncontrolled by the colonial power; and, as it progressed, each British colony, each French territory, and the entire Belgian Congo became an undivided independent state. In South Africa, too, the autonomous African national movement was as extensive as the boundaries of the existing state and sought black participa-

54. United Nations General Assembly, *A/5497/Add.1* (1963), pp. 3–5 and 28–29.
55. Barber, *South Africa's Foreign Policy*, p. 137.

tion in the government of the entire country; whereas what was actually happening was that a series of small territories, each of them fragmented, was beginning to be excised from the rest of the country as a pretext for depriving Africans of a right to any such participation. Moreover, no colonial power manipulated the process of decolonization to anything like the extent to which the South African government manipulated the demission of formal political authority in the Bantustans. The tentacles of neocolonialism were never as suffocating as the tentacles of secondary neocolonialism. Under South African laws of 1951 and 1959, giving administrative powers to chiefs in the reservations, many popular chiefs had been removed and potential collaborators had been promoted—events that evoked widespread peasant resistance, especially in the Transkei, where a state of emergency was proclaimed in 1960. In 1963, parliament passed a law giving the Transkei a limited measure of self-government, with a constitution that had been drafted by white civil servants and endorsed by a committee headed by Kaiser Matanzima, who had been elevated to a senior chieftainship in the face of strong local opposition. The Transkei acquired a legislature containing 64 ex officio chiefs, 45 elected members, and an executive responsible to that legislature. During the election, the emergency regulations prevented Matanzima's opponents from campaigning effectively; nevertheless, they won a large majority of the elective seats. However, with the support of the majority of the ex officio members, Matanzima became prime minister. Sixteen years later, with the 1960 emergency proclamation still in force, South Africa would grant formal independence to the Transkei, under Kaiser Matanzima. Such was the prototype for the process of "decolonization" in South Africa.[56]

Despite the growing gulf between the political trends in southern Africa and elsewhere, the South African economy continued to expand at an exceptional rate throughout the 1950s and again, after a pause following Sharpeville, in the ensuing decade.[57] During the 1960s, especially, South Africa attracted large-scale and profitable trade and investment from conti-

56. On the "Bantustans," see John Hatch, et al., eds., "South Africa's Bantustans," *Third World* 2, no. 6 (1963), passim; Govan Mbeki, *South Africa: The Peasants' Revolt* (Harmondsworth, 1964); Gwendolen M. Carter, Thomas Karis, and Newell M. Stultz, *South Africa's Transkei: The Politics of Domestic Colonialism* (Evanston, Ill., 1967); Muriel Horrell, *The African Homelands of South Africa* (Johannesburg, 1973); Lawrence Schlemmer and Tim J. Muil, "Social and Political Change in the African Areas: A Case Study of KwaZulu," in Leonard Thompson and Jeffrey Butler, eds., *Change in Contemporary South Africa* (Berkeley and Los Angeles, 1975), pp. 107–37; Jeffrey Butler, Robert I. Rotberg, and John Adams, *The Black Homelands of South Africa* (Berkeley and Los Angeles, 1977); and Newell Stultz, "What's Wrong with Transkei Independence," *Plural Societies* (Spring, 1977), pp. 17–34.

57. D. Hobart Houghton, *The South African Economy*, 2d. ed. (Cape Town, 1967).

nental western Europe, the United States, and Japan, as well as Great Britain.[58] Also, as British power waned, South Africa became the dominant power throughout the entire southern African region.[59] As James Barber has written:

> Whatever their views of apartheid, the states which traded with South Africa, whether economic giants like the United States or poor, undeveloped countries like Malawi, had a stake in retaining a prosperous South Africa. Here the South Africans were able to make a telling point. They argued that a *prosperous* South Africa could only be achieved by a *politically stable* South Africa and this in turn implied accepting the *status quo* which provided both the prosperity and the stability.[60]

South African propaganda also influenced many foreigners by presenting South Africa as a bastion of the free world against communism, and equating opponents of apartheid with Communists. Consequently, the western powers, Japan, and, on occasion, independent African states outside as well as inside the southern African region ignored the General Assembly's resolution calling for a general commercial and diplomatic boycott, and some of them—France most persistently—also ignored the Security Council's arms embargo.

As was to be expected, the southern African resistance movement received its most emphatic support in tropical Africa. Southern African representatives attended the All-African Peoples' Conference in Ghana in 1958, and the liberation of the rest of the continent became a major objective, and the principal cement, of the Organization of African Unity, founded in 1963. Tanzania provided a headquarters for the Liberation Committee of the OAU and facilities where southern Africans received military training with weapons and instructors from the Soviet Union, the People's Republic of China, and other Communist countries. The Kaunda government, too, allowed bases to be used in Zambia after it became independent in 1964.

After Sharpeville, black South African leaders shed the illusions that had previously frustrated their efforts. No longer did they assume that they could start a process of genuine deracialization in South Africa by nonvio-

58. Ruth First, Jonathan Steele, and Christobel Gurney, *The South African Connection: Western Investment in Apartheid* (London, 1972).

59. Christian P. Potholm and Richard Dale, eds., *Southern Africa in Perspective: Essays in Regional Politics* (New York, 1972); Timothy M. Shaw and Kenneth A. Heard, eds., *Cooperation and Conflict in Southern Africa: Papers on a Regional Subsystem* (Washington, D.C., 1976); and Bowman, "Subordinate State System of Southern Africa."

60. Barber, *South Africa's Foreign Policy*, p. 201. Italics in the original.

lent methods. Nor did they expect to be able to bring down the South African regime in a single blow, such as a general strike. Rather, they began to plan a war of liberation, knowing that, before they could effectively penetrate the Republic itself, it would be necessary to decolonize the buffer territories—Angola, Mozambique, Rhodesia-Zimbabwe, and South West Africa-Namibia, as well as the High Commission Territories. This may have been a realistic appraisal of their problem. But the implementation of their strategy was delayed and bedeviled not only by numerous factors beyond their control, such as the chronic weaknesses and divisions among and within the newly independent African states, but also by their own internal cleavages. Throughout history, exile groups have been notoriously prone to feuding. The South African exiles (and those from the other countries in the region) were no exception. The ANC and the PAC leaders were hostile to one another, and cleavages developed within each organization. These divisions had complex causes. Ethnic and class factors probably played a part; so did ideological differences that went back to the early history of the ANC but were exacerbated by the Sino-Soviet dispute; and personal rivalries certainly became extremely serious.[61]

Consequently, by the mid-1960s, when the Pretoria government appeared to have crushed the internal resistance, it could also look with some complacency, if not pleasure, at the external situation.

Conclusion

In tropical Africa, liberation from primary colonialism was a process of cooperative interaction between primary colonial regimes and Western-educated African subjects, in the context of rapidly changing global as well as local conditions. The European withdrawal from tropical Africa was just as unpremeditated and abrupt as the European conquest had been a century earlier. The major wars of liberation were fought elsewhere—in Indonesia, Indochina, and Algeria. Except in Kenya, where the presence of a white settler community created some of the characteristics of a secondary colonial situation, not much blood was shed in tropical Africa before the European governments decided to abdicate in favor of local politicians who had only recently announced that independence was their goal. The crucial precedent occurred in India. In the Gold Coast soon after 1947, in the face of a few riots and rallies by the new Convention Peoples party, Great

61. Richard Gibson, *African Liberation Movements: Contemporary Struggles against White Minority Rule* (London, 1972); Gerhart, *Black Power in South Africa*.

Britain began to transfer power, thus starting a process that rapidly gathered a momentum which only the Portuguese regime could resist—and then only by incurring serious and eventually intolerable strains.

In South Africa, the actors and the power relationships were quite different. From Pretoria and Cape Town, Soweto and Langa, tropical Africa seemed to be remote and exotic. South Africa's rulers regarded European decisions to decolonize tropical Africa as signs of moral as well as material weakness. Having only encountered blacks as subjects and servants, they were convinced that the incoming regimes in tropical Africa would be incapable of running their countries efficiently. And although black South Africans did devise several ingenious campaigns and conduct them courageously, the dice were loaded heavily against them; while their sympathizers within the authoritative system—the white liberals and socialists—were too few and most of them too half hearted to have any substantial impact on policy. So the government easily crushed the resistance, clapping the leaders into jail or driving them into exile and outlawing their organizations.

By the early 1960s, experience had shown that South Africa was not a society that could be deracialized by the means that were being employed in either tropical Africa or the United States, because the structure of South African society was fundamentally different. Unlike the whites in tropical Africa, South African whites had become a large, deeply entrenched, self-perpetuating community; and unlike those in the United States, they were only a fraction of the total population. The leaders of the dominant Afrikaner faction believed that the only way to ensure their survival was to maintain their monopoly of political power, and Dutch Reformed clergy continued to assure them that group survival was their God-given task. For their part, African leaders such as Mandela and Sobukwe, who were incarcerated in Robben Island, and Tambo and Leballo, who were in exile, considered that they had exhausted the possibilities of nonviolent pressures upon a regime that lived by violence. Therefore, they concluded, the system itself lacked legitimacy, and force was the essential instrument for its destruction.

Throughout the 1960s and the early 1970s, however, the white South African regime was to remain strong and inviolate. Internal polarization, black votes in international organizations, and changing Western norms were offset by the attraction of the South African economy to Western investors and the immersion of the United States in Vietnam. The effects of the parting of the ways would become more evident in the mid-1970s, with the decolonization of the Portuguese territories, the escalation of guerrilla warfare in Rhodesia, South Africa's ill-judged invasion of Angola, and the rise of black consciousness and development of sustained resistance in Soweto.

Although the government responded to the resurgence of internal unrest with intensified suppression, violent revolution was not necessarily the outcome. Perhaps the South African situation differed so profoundly from a primary colonial situation that the racial line would eventually be superseded by cross-cutting alliances, and the black middle classes would perceive themselves as beneficiaries of a modified and stabilized, but not revolutionized, society.[62]

62. This analysis has been developed most effectively by Heribert Adam. See his *Modernizing Racial Domination*. See, too, Heribert Adam and Hermann Giliomee, *Ethnic Power Mobilized: Can South Africa Change?* (New Haven, 1979), and Leonard Thompson and Andrew Prior, *South African Politics* (New Haven, 1982).

16. *From Colonization to Independence in French Tropical Africa: The Economic Background*

JEAN SURET-CANALE

At the end of August 1945, after the capitulation of Japan ended the Second World War, all the French possessions in tropical Africa remained subject to the colonial regime as established at the end of the nineteenth century and early in the twentieth. Fifteen years later, by the end of November 1960 (when the independence of Mauritania was declared), all these territories (except Djibouti and the Comoros, and Réunion, which was now a *département* of France) had gained their independence.

What role did economic factors play in this evolution that was to lead fifteen territories (a total of fourteen on the continent: French West Africa, French Equatorial Africa, Togo, and Cameroun; and, in the Indian Ocean, Madagascar) from their colonial status to political independence?

This is the question we seek to elucidate. Together with the economic facts, we shall take into consideration their social dimension, which cannot be separated from them. In order to understand what happened between 1945 and 1960, a few words will be said on what occurred before and after.

The Trade Economy ("Economie de Traite")

The continental block of these French possessions, contiguous across the Sahara with French North Africa, was impressive in geographic extent; but on the whole it was poor and sparsely populated, and the Saharan desert formed the major part of its area. The coastal enclaves, principally British, were wealthier and more densely populated; Nigeria alone had at least as many, and probably more, inhabitants than the entire continental complex administered by France (in about 1946 there were less than 25 million inhabitants in French West Africa, French Equatorial Africa, Togo, and Cameroun put together).

Development was insignificant. According to Frankel,[1] less than 6 percent of investments in Africa had been made here where 19 percent of the continent's population lives; per capita investment was two pounds sterling, as compared with fifty-six pounds in South Africa.

To take private investments alone, according to another source whose data approximately coincide with Frankel's, we find that half of these (48.5 percent) were in sectors not directly productive (commerce alone, 39 percent; banking, real estate.)[2] This commercial preponderance is even more marked if we consider the value of shares distributed on the stock market of the companies operating in French tropical Africa: 63 percent of the total in 1946.[3]

This preponderance of commerce, which was chiefly a seasonal one governed by the marketing of annual harvests, and which was still locally called by the old word *traite*, led the geographer J. Dresch,[4] followed by the economists,[5] to suggest the designation *économie de traite*, or "trade economy," for the economic system then prevailing in these territories.

The term calls to mind the slave "trade," ("traite des esclaves") and it expresses aptly the survival of methods inherited from a past age. As a matter of fact, trade in slaves had given way in the nineteenth century to trade in products, designated at first by the term *troque* ("barter").[6] Even if there was some continuity from one system to the other, however, the twentieth century's trade was something other than the nineteenth-century barter.

In the first place, trade economy was indissolubly connected with seizure of territorial possession and with the establishment in depth of colonial domination. The latter made it possible to eliminate the local middlemen—the coastal tribes, the half-breed "traders" in the godowns—for the benefit of European commerce. This commerce, moreover, was able to function only through administrative pressure and intervention; "politics" was involved here as an integral part of the economic system, in the form of the colonial administration's arbitrary power with respect to a

1. S. H. Frankel, *Capital Investment in Africa* (Oxford, 1938).

2. Jean Suret-Canale: *Afrique Noire occidentale et centrale*, vol. 2: *L'Ere coloniale* (Paris, 1964).

3. P. Valdant, in *Marchés coloniaux*, March 23, 1946, p. 269.

4. J. Dresch, "Les Trusts en Afrique Noire," *Servir la France* (Paris, 1946), p. 30; and "Sur une géographie des investissements de capitaux: l'Exemple de l'Afrique Noire," *Bulletin de l'Association des Géographes Français*, March–April 1946, pp. 59–64.

5. Notably, M. Capet, *Traité d'économie tropicale: Les Économies d'Afrique Occidentale française* (Paris, 1958).

6. Cf. Henri Brunschwig, "La Troque et la traite," *Cahiers d'Etudes Africaines* 2, no. 7 (1962): 339–46.

"subject" population deprived, not only of civil rights and sovereignty, but also of usual guarantees of personal liberties. (The *indigénat* regime allowed the administration to impose penal sentences—imprisonment or fines—by simple administrative decision, and also permitted the practice of forced labor). The introduction of a capitation tax to be paid in cash helped force the peasant to gather or cultivate the products in demand in European commerce, in order to earn the required money; the administration intervened to enforce delivery of these products (by obligatory deliveries, or by forced cultivation of the "commander's field"), and fixed prices at levels agreeable to commerce (administered prices), substantially lower than those current among the "natives" when the products moved in domestic trade.

Extortion, pure and simple, was hidden behind the mask of "commerce." The system is often praised as more "humanitarian" than the settlement of colonists on the land: the peasant was not deprived of his land. But one notes above all that this system was more economical: it required no investment aside from the provision of a few transport routes, which forced labor, moreover, took care of for the most part. It simply required of the peasant, in addition to his labor and the area of land devoted to agriculture and other subsistence activities, additional effort and extension of the cultivated area, without technical change or improvement; the result was ridiculously low productivity and a grave threat to the balance of nature. This was of little importance to the commercial companies, which within the framework of this system realized very high levels of profit on an extremely meager amount of capital risk.

The influence of the commercial houses upon the administration and the high level of profits are explained by a second element, new as compared with the nineteenth-century "barter": the monopolistic character of this "trade" commerce. In French Equatorial Africa, which represents a separate case, this was a legal monopoly in the hands of concessionary companies (1899–1929);[7] in French West Africa it was a de facto monopoly which emerged before the end of the nineteenth century. There was monopoly in the sense that a small number of companies (or commercial houses) had control over the great share of external commerce and were able to agree among themselves (and with the administration) in setting prices and economic policy.

It is unimportant here that at first these houses or companies were not an

7. Cf. C. Coquery-Vidrovitch, *Le Congo au temps des grandes compagnies concessionnaires (1899–1930)*(Paris, 1972); and G. Mazenod, *La Likouala-Mossaka: Histoire de la pénétration du Haut-Congo (1878–1920)*(Paris, 1970).

integral part of the large capitalist French financial system (they were, instead, a few family houses from Bordeaux, Marseille, and Lyon, and a few Parisian promoters with official connections). The integration did in fact take place, but rather late—in the 1920s.

These two features—the decisive nature of the recourse to political authority, resulting from the colonial partition; and the monopolistic character of the dominant companies—makes the trade economy something entirely different from a simple, anachronistic continuation of methods inherited from the nineteenth century (even though, in reality, it did preserve some anachronistic features). It fits perfectly into the contemporary imperialist system as defined by Lenin (after other writers) in 1916.[8]

The trade economy is exclusivist: any intrusion of competitors, or any alternative methods of exploitation, would jeopardize its functioning and the resulting profits. Hence this "trade" commerce was to interpose itself as an obstacle, insofar as circumstances permitted, to any tendency toward "modernization."

At the base of a pyramidal structure of principal agencies, counting-houses, and subagencies, the trading station, a branch of the company (and occasionally a few middlemen: Europeans, Lebanese, Greeks, very rarely Africans) collected the local products furnished by the native peasantry. (For a long time these were mainly gathered products, such as tropical rubber; but from the first there were also cultivated crops.) In exchange were distributed shoddy goods, imported items of small value called "trade goods"—cotton textiles, hardware, alcoholic beverages, sugar, and so on.

The traditional modes of production, and the corresponding forms of social organization, were thus, on the surface, left intact by the trade economy. At the same time, it transformed them and managed them for its own profit. That is why the trade economy, in our view, cannot be explained in terms of a "dual" economy, nor of "articulation" between a (dominant) capitalist mode of production and a (dominated) precapitalist one.[9] In reality there was a very rapid integration into the capitalist mode of production in its contemporary form, which is that of imperialism, of economic and social forms inherited from the past. Their function now became, not to ensure tbeir own reproduction, but to contribute in their specific fashion to the reproduction, of the overall capitalist system, while

8. Lenin, *L'Impérialisme, stade suprême du capitalisme,* published in Petrograd, 1917; French translation in *Oeuvres* (Moscow, 1960), 22: 201–327.

9. I differ here from the interpretations proposed, for example, by P. Ph. Rey, *Colonialisme, ńeo-colonialisme et transition au capitalisme, l'exemple de la COMILOG au Congo-Brazzaville* (Paris, 1971), and C. Meillassoux, *Femmes, greniers et capitaux* (Paris, 1975). See my review in *La Pensée,* no. 194 (August 1977), pp. 130–31.

leaving exclusively to the account of the "traditional" producer the costs of production as well as the cost of his own maintenance (subsistence).

The system is thus basically characterized by the assessment of a rent in kind from the producer. Therein it is fundamentally distinct from colonial systems based on the introduction of capitalist-type enterprises (colonists' farms or plantations, mining, and so on) characteristic of Algeria or South Africa. Naturally, this does not imply the total exclusion of the second variant of colonial exploitation (based on the imposition of a rent in the form of labor) from the former; at most there is only a relative incompatibility.

From the beginning certain forms of forced labor, "requisitions" of manpower, were employed, belonging to the second "variant." But they were long used almost exclusively by the administration and for public works purposes (roads, railways, official buildings). Only in special cases were they used in production (in the forestry industry in Gabon; later, in the 1930s, on European plantations in limited coastal areas of Guinea, Ivory Coast, and Cameroun). Even in Madagascar, where the colonist community attained significant size at an early date,[10] trade economy was dominant.

There were few, or no, modern plantations, and almost no mining. The relative size of investments in 1940 (18 percent for plantations, 7.5 percent for mines) should not deceive us: many of the "investments" on the account books represented aborted ventures or simply dummy enterprises designed to cover up stock-market swindles.

Processing industries were insignificant (a few oil presses in Senegal, which in 1937–38 processed the equivalent of 3 percent of the volume of peanut exports; a textile mill in Ivory Coast; the first brewery built in 1938 at Dakar).[11] Infrastructure was confined to a few ports or wharves, a few railroads into the interior (meter gauge or 60 cm.), and laterite trails.

The Political and Economic Turning Point of 1946: The "Aid" Myth

On the morrow of the 1939–45 war, the economic and political contexts, in any case inseparable even though their operation sometimes exhibits contradictory aspects, intervened to induce the most significant changes

10. Cf. René Gendarme, *L'Economie de Madagascar* (Paris, 1963), pp. 126–34 (note the map); and P. Boiteau, *Madagascar, contribution à l'histoire de la nation malgache* (Paris, 1958), p. 224.

11. J. Suret-Canale: "L'Industrie en A.O.F. au lendemain de la deuxième guerre mondiale," "Revue Economique de Madagascar (Antananarivo), nos. 3–4 (1968–69), pp. 27–56.

French tropical Africa had known since the dawn of the colonial era.

One may, indeed, identify the precursors of these changes in the 1930s: relaxation of political repression and the timid awakening of trade-union activity at the time of the Front Populaire, on the political level; the outlines of a fuller development of Africa's resources hitherto held in reserve, within the framework of the economic integration of the empire, made necessary by the Depression (customs protection and price supports for export commodities; an increase in the number of European agricultural colonists so as to ensure the supply of bananas, coffee, and so on, to the French market without foreign exchange cost; major construction projects financed by the Maginot Loan).[12]

With the approach of war all this was abruptly suspended. The relative isolation of the French possessions during the war, the intensive resort during this time to the worst methods of traditional colonization, both in the territories that joined Free France and those that remained obedient to Vichy until 1942, made the rupture during the years 1944–46 much more noticeable than in the British possessions.[13]

Let us first examine the political context, which is the more flagrant. The Allies' victory was achieved in the name of the right of peoples to self-determination, in itself a negation of the colonial principle. The excesses attending the use of classical colonial methods during the war (forced labor, obligatory delivery of products, arbitrary administration) had created an explosive situation. Although they were in the victors' camp, the colonial powers, and most particularly France, emerged from the war weakened. The aspiration for thoroughgoing change of a democratic and social nature which manifested itself in Africa coincided with the same aspiration in France, with the advance of the Socialist and Communist parties that was the continuation of the Resistance movement. And finally, the first disturbances of the colonial system in Asia had their repercussions in Africa.

All this, together with the political awakening stimulated by the first elections in 1945 and 1946, in which former "subjects" were permitted to vote (even though the vote was at first confined to only a tiny minority of them) led to the passage by the First Constituent Assembly, early in 1946, of the Lamine Guèye and Houphouët-Boigny laws that put an end to the

12. J. Suret-Canale, *Afrique Noire*, 2: 361–69.

13. In his contribution, David K. Fieldhouse suggests that, for British Africa, the change should be dated from the 1930s. For French Africa, C. Coquery-Vidrovitch ("La Mise en dépendance de l'Afrique Noire: Essai de périodisation, 1800–1870." *Cahiers d'Etudes Africaines*, 16 [1976]: 7–58), suggests dating the change between 1930 and 1936; while this may be justified, the allegedly decisive nature of the years 1940–45 is unconvincing.

indigénat regime and to forced labor, and made citizens of the former subjects.

In the economic field, circumstances (France and Europe were in ruins) led to plans for a more systematic and rational development of resources which the trade economy had theretofore left fallow. Now the war had left the paltry infrastructure of the Black African countries in parlous condition. In order to extract the indispensable raw materials from these countries it was necessary to embark upon a massive modernization effort: to create the necessary modern infrastructure (energy, transport facilities); to bring up to date, more particularly to mechanize, production processes, an indispensable condition for any substantial rise in the level of production in view of the low efficiency and limited size of the population and the political impossibility of resorting, as before, to forced labor.[14]

To accomplish these goals capital was needed. But private capital demanded immediate, assured, and high profits; in the circumstances it could not be relied upon, at least before conditions of profitability and security had been created. In the first instance, consequently, the investment effort had to be made by the public sector. Until then, such investment in the colonies had depended exclusively on local taxation, and to a lesser extent on borrowing, since the law (*Loi de finances* of April 13, 1900, Article 33) prohibited any recourse to the metropole's budget to meet the colonies' needs. Now the financial capabilities of the colonies (which rested primarily upon the natives) were limited, and could not be appreciably increased without untoward political results. Another solution thus had to be found.

The means had, in fact, already been discovered—the same means that had to be used in France, devastated by the war: massive resort to public investment; "planning," but conceived in a manner quite different from Soviet planning, which at that time enjoyed wide prestige. In a liberal, that is, capitalist, system there could be no question of mandatory planning; it could only set up guidelines, using the allocation of public credits as the motivating instrument to attain the proposed objectives.

Investment being incompatible with the annual cycle of budget processes, a block allotment of funds would be made from the budget to a Fonds de Développement Économique et Social (FDES), exempt from rigorous budgetary and parliamentary supervision, which could be used to finance multiyear plans. The first of this type was the Monnet Plan,

14. These arguments are set forth at length in an editorial in *Marchés coloniaux*, no. 31 (June 15, 1946), p. 578. Cf. J. Suret-Canale, *Afrique Noire*, vol. 3: *De la colonisation aux indépendances* (Paris, 1972), pp. 98–103. The data which follow are taken from this work.

adopted in 1946. On the model of the system established in the metropole, a Fonds d'Investissement et de Développement Economique et Social des Territoires d'Outre-Mer (FIDES) was created, and the corresponding plans were drawn up.

During the time it took for the bureaucratic machine to set itself in motion, however, the political and economic circumstances had changed appreciably.

First, on the political level, beginning in the summer of 1946 a colonialist reaction occurred, which intensified with the onset of the war in Vietnam, expulsion of the Communist ministers, the repression in Madagascar (1947), and the progress of the Cold War. No one dared to propose reconsideration of the 1946 laws; but an effort was made to circumvent them, in the political field by administrative rigging of elections, and in the economic field by continued use of forced labor wherever the local relationship among forces permitted.

In the economic field, conditions of short supply ended by 1949 and the specter of glutted markets reappeared, although markets were, in the event, to expand rapidly notwithstanding recessions. To the need for raw materials of concern in 1946 (little thought was given to any but the traditional, agricultural raw materials) the Cold War added a strategic consideration: in case of a "Red" invasion of Europe, Africa might serve as a refuge and, with the help of the United States, as a springboard for reconquest. It would then be important to have available the industrial bases necessary for arms industries. It is this argument which, initially at least, led to the first effort to develop mineral resources, an idea that had not been contemplated at the outset.[15]

What was the balance sheet of this policy of investment and modernization by the end of the period? Most of the credits were devoted to infrastructure (electric generating plants, ports, airports, dieselization of railroads, improvement of road networks). This absorbed 65.96 percent of the credits under the first plan, 45.82 percent under the second. "Social" investments, on the other hand (health, education), unprovided for in 1946, took on substantial importance (15.76 percent for the first plan, 19.46 percent for the second). These investments responded, for the most part, to political demands (in 1945 the proportion of children in school in French West Africa was not above 5 percent; full secondary education existed only at Dakar and Saint Louis), but also to economic demands (the increased

15. Arguments set forth particularly in J. Chardonnet, *Une Oeuvre nécessaire: L'Industrialisation de l'Afrique* (Paris and Geneva, 1956).

need for personnel possessing at least a minimum of qualifications and the necessity for a work force "ready to go").

On the other hand, the goal of modernizing production was not, or was only very partially, achieved. Mechanization hardly went beyond handling cargo in the ports and logging (with particular efficiency in the latter case). In agriculture, which absorbed most of the credits allotted to production (18 percent in the first plan, 34.72 percent in the second), methods were little changed. The agricultural investments were mostly ineffective since, especially under the first plan, they were devoted principally to large operations entrusted to state or mixed companies (arrangements for rice-growing, mechanized cultivation of peanuts) which ended as fiascos. Agricultural production rose more slowly than foreseen, more rapidly for new crops (coffee production in Ivory Coast quadrupled between 1938 and 1956) than for the traditional ones (Senegal did not equal its prewar record peanut crop until 1957).[16] In fact, growth in production was achieved much more by extending the area cultivated than by technical improvements.

Industrialization developed, but not in the field contemplated in 1946, which was calculated to enhance the value of exportable commodities. Industries of this type (except for vegetable oil pressing) remained the least developed because of the veto by metropolitan industrialists who, for example, closed the French market to products of tropical wood veneer and plywood plants in Ivory Coast and Gabon. Import-substitution industries exhibited the greatest expansion—food products, textiles, construction materials, and so on—and, above all, mining. FIDES contributed little (at least directly) to industrial investment, which did not mean that state financing did not play a role here also, at least in the mining industry. This was done through other channels, the operations of state agencies such as the Overseas France Bureau of Mines (Bureau Minier de la France d'Outre Mer-BUMIFOM), the Atomic Energy Commission (CEA), or the Petroleum Research Bureau (BRP), which assumed charge of prospecting and infrastructure. These same agencies participated in the capitalization of enterprises, as did the Caisse Centrale de la France d'Outre-Mer (CCFOM), which also furnished loans. Between 1946 and 1957, of 31.25 billion CFA francs provided by CCFOM to 249 overseas enterprises (excluding North Africa) in the form of loans or equity capital, more than 25 billion went to four large African mining enterprises (Manganese of Gabon, Alumina of Guinea, Phosphates of Sénégal and Togo), to the Edéa aluminum foundry (Cameroun—using local hydroelectric power from the

16. *Afrique Noire*, 3: 388.

Sanaga River) and, outside Africa (the apportionment figure is not available), to Nickel, a company of the Rothschild group (New Caledonia).

In short, public investments in French Black Africa may be put at 820.9 billion 1960 CFA francs, excluding social investment, as compared with 120 to 160 billions in private investments. These figures alone give a measure of the size of the public effort relative to that of private investors.

The recourse to massive investment of metropolitan funds was, as noted above, something new. Only a few years passed before the export of capital (chiefly public, from the metropole) came to be called "aid." By the 1960s this terminology was extraordinarily fashionable, "aid to underdeveloped countries" being put forth as the key to "development." (The expressions "Third World," "underdeveloped" countries, and later "developing" countries date from the same period.) It was not until the 1970s that the term "aid," and the idea it embodied, became matters of general dispute.[17] Meanwhile they served as the basic justification for the practice whereby exploitation of colonies by the metropole (admitted more or less vaguely from an allegedly remote past) was replaced by a generous and disinterested "aid" that justified, in return, the preservation of the metropole's political tutelage (until 1958–60), and the acceptance of certain constraints, along with the "gratitude" of the recipient populations. Some even complained that the situation alleged to exist by the opponents of colonialism had been reversed: the metropole had become the milk-cow of its former colonies.[18] The journalist Raymond Cartier gave his name to the doctrine of aid to underdeveloped countries, denouncing prodigality toward unworthy and ungrateful recipients, not so much in order to bring about a systematic refusal of "aid" (which he denied), as to establish the legitimacy of the economic and political [corollaries to counterparts implied by] aid—on which point he was in accord with many avowed adversaries of *cartiérisme*.[19]

But what did this "aid" in reality mean?

It must be determined, first, to what extent the credits were really invested in the country to which they were allocated or spent there for public-interest purposes. Part of the FIDES credits was spent directly in France or repatriated in the form of profit margins for firms participating in the operations, for salaries of European personnel returning to France, or for the cost of studies conducted in France. The economist J. Lecaillon

17. Cf. particularly Tibor Mende, *De l'aide à la recolonisation: Les leçons d'un échec* (Paris, 1972).

18. A thesis expounded, notably, by Jean Ehrhardt, *Le Destin du colonialisme* (Paris, 1957).

19. Raymond Cartier, articles in *Paris-Match*, April 11 and 18, 1956.

estimated in 1954 that, of the expenditures under the first four-year plan, 15 percent of the counterpart value actually remained in Africa.[20] A distinction must next be made between productive, or potentially productive, investments and operating expenses or those related to sovereign functions. Furthermore, it must not be forgotten that the FIDES credits involved an obligatory counterpart of local financing, ultimately from the African peoples themselves: out of public investments totaling 820.9 billion CFA francs of 1960 for the period 1946–60, 569.8 had been provided by the metropole and 251.1 by the local budgets.

Finally, one needs to know in whose interests these investments were made and who profited by them, at least in the first instance: the African peoples? or the firms (virtually all of them French) active in the various sectors of the economy?

Survival of Trade Economy

The total French private capital invested in the zone under consideration (excluding Madagascar) at the end of 1958 was distributed approximately as follows:

	End of 1958	*1900–1940*
Commerce, banking, insurance	37.6%	45.0%
Processing industries		
Construction and public works	27.6%	13.1%
Public services		
Mining	24.5%	7.5%
Agriculture and forestry	8.8%	30.8%
Transportation	1.4%	3.6%

While the precision of these figures should not be overestimated, they give an accurate idea of relative proportions, and some lessons can be drawn from them.[21]

The preponderance of commerce, and thus of the trade economy, has hardly been challenged. As will be shown, its structures had evolved. But it was commerce that was the principal beneficiary of the development of

20. J. Lecaillon, "Le Financement des pays sous-développés: L'Exemple des territoires dépendants de l'O.E.C.E.," *Revue de Science et de Législation Financières*, April–June 1952, pp. 408–23; "L'Intégration de l'Union Française dans l'Union Européenne et les enseignements de la théorie économique," *Annales africaines* (Dakar, 1954), pp. 19–48; "Les Incidences économiques et financières du Code du travail des Territories d'Outre-Mer," *Revue de Science et de Législation Financières* (1954), pp. 688–715.

21. *Afrique Noire*, 2: 207, and 3: 388–92.

external trade marked by moderate, but appreciable, progress in exports, and by a considerable rise in imports, as the following table shows:

Total Imports of French West Africa, Togo, Cameroun, and French Equatorial Africa[22]
(Millions of tons)

	1938	*1949*	*1959**
Condensed milk	1.5	3.1	14.75
Rice	47.4	38.7	186.7
Sugar	23.1	32.5	123.2
Wine and spirits	15.2	30.9	53.7

*Does not include Guinea

Must this be taken as evidence of growth and prosperity? It is by no means a safe conclusion. The trend reflects above all the pervasive growth of the mercantile economy, the decline of the traditional subsistence economy, and increasing urbanization. There had been across-the-board progress in trade (at least in certain regions) simultaneously with impoverishment and the gradual ruin of the nuclear, or patriarchal, family resting on the subsistence economy which was the basis of the system. To draw a parallel, indeed, if agricultural production increased (although in lesser proportion), the increase took place partly to the detriment of the food crops traditionally raised: hence, in part, the rising imports of rice.

The expansion and diversification of commerce did not call into question the preponderance of the old trading companies; at most they had to make room for a few new companies, notably those specialized in technical materials, direct subsidiaries of similarly specialized groups in France, or direct subsidiaries of manufacturing firms (for example, in the field of construction materials, DAVUM and Brossette-Valor, sales agencies linked to French steel-making consortiums).

The form of the trade economy was nevertheless changing. The "factory," a bazaar where agricultural products were bought and a little of everything was sold, was no longer the sole, nor even the dominant, trade process. It did not disappear, of course; in coastal areas like Ivory Coast or Cameroun, where agricultural production expanded remarkably, the network of factories increased in both breadth and depth; the same phenomenon could be observed in regions previously little touched by trade, such as Chad.

However, where the local items traded embraced only a sampling of low-quality and low-value products in limited and fluctuating quantities, as

22. According to the annual reports of the Comité Monétaire de la Zone Franc, 1953–60.

dictated by climatic and economic conditions (local varieties of cotton, shea products, kapok, and coconut products), and where only administrative pressure preserved the obligation to deliver produce at very low prices, a retrenchment took place in the trading companies' network, as in Congo-Brazzaville and Upper Volta. In order to solve their monetary problems, the people were now obliged to emigrate either to the coastal plantations (Upper Volta) or to the urban centers (Congo).

Even where the trade persisted in its traditional form most of the large companies began to disengage from retailing, to the benefit of middlemen, either Lebanese (already present at the end of the nineteenth century) or (and this was a new phenomenon) Africans, who rented existing factories no longer profitable enough to justify the presence of a European agent, or simply assumed management of them. Alternatively or simultaneously, the Lebanese or African middleman became a freight carrier. In either case, the trading company kept control of him by advancing trade goods or a truck, or both, which he contracted to pay for with the agricultural products he collected. He henceforth assumed all the risks; the trading companies retained the wholesale business, along with most of the profits.

In the cities (the territorial capitals principally) the factory-bazaar tended to give way to more modern and more attractive types of business. Here, in any event, it was a question not of buying (the city produced nothing for export) but of selling. Urbanization, and the growing number of European and African civil servants who absorbed a constantly increasing share of income and thus offered opportunity for the largest volume of business, led to the development and diversification of urban commerce. For day-to-day consumption it was the large "Prisunic"-type department store launched in France in the 1930s (self-service stores were to appear only in the 1960s, after independence). The sort of merchandise sold changed: the "trade goods" intended for a peasant clientele were now replaced by foodstuffs and household items of European type like those sold in similar stores in France. For more specialized products, there were the luxury shops (couture, and so on, chiefly for European customers) and technical installations (construction materials, motor vehicles, electric appliances. industrial and household refrigeration, and so on).

There was appreciable industrial progress, as indicated by the ratio of investment mentioned above. The isolation of French West Africa during the war, under the Vichy regime, had already stimulated the birth of various industries designed to make up for dwindling imports or to reduce the volume of exportable products in view of the scarcity of maritime cargo space. Many of these industries (fish canneries, for example) did not survive the return of abundance in the 1950s. On the other hand, infrastructural works stimulated on-the-spot manufacture of some necessary but bulky products of which the transportation cost exceeded the cost of production (cement, prestressed concrete members, and so on). The expansion of the market resulting from the flow of FIDES credits, and the slow growth of exports, tended to encourage the enlargement or the founding of local industries in sectors where the lower cost of labor could compensate for adverse factors such as the small scale of production, the weak level of technical competence, the absence or scarcity of supporting technical services such as maintenance, and so on.

This progress was neither uniform nor consistent. The most stubborn opposition to this industrial development did not come from the trading companies but from French industrialists anxious to protect their market. The case of the lumber-processing industry has already been mentioned. The Senegalese peanut-oil factories continued to expand, processing an increasing percentage of the crop (nearly 50 percent), although restraints were imposed by the metropolitan oil producers. (Strict quotas were imposed on entry of the Senegalese product to the French market; it should, moreover, be emphasized that this was raw oil that had to be refined before consumption.) Similarly, until 1956 the professional flour-milling and sugar associations in France opposed the creation of similar industries in Africa which might deprive them of a captive market.

In short, the balance sheet is a modest one. Except for oil-pressing, there was little progress in processing export products: a few cotton gins in the producing areas (this is, properly speaking, conditioning rather than processing); sawmills in the forested zones; two cocoa-butter factories processing material rejected for export; three plants canning fruit juice and pineapples (Guinea and Ivory Coast); and a few fish canneries, which reappeared after 1954 on the Cap Vert Peninsula. At best, these "industries" represent treatment processes without which export of the materials would be difficult or impossible.

Import-substitution industries exhibited more substantial growth: breweries and bottling plants for carbonated beverages; textile mills using local cotton; shoe factories (a monopoly of Bata, the former Czech firm now headquartered in Canada); Grands Moulins de Dakar (1955); Sucrerie de Jacob, in the Congo (1957); and so on.

In sum, all these industries, whether for import or export, fell within the existing "trade" pattern. Far from jeopardizing the trade economy, they became perfectly integrated with it and strengthened the hold of the commercial companies over the economy rather than threatening it. Thus it is not surprising that the entrepreneurs of these industries were very often the large trading companies themselves, in association with technically specialized firms. Even when the trading companies did not share in the capitalization of the industrial firms, the latter (with some exceptions, including Bata) did not have their own sales networks, and for the distribution of their products were obliged to contract with the commercial companies, which found it profitable.

The location of these industries confirms this integration: although Dakar lost its virtual monopoly as the only industrial center, nearly all these industries, especially the import-substitution ones, were situated in the seaports. In French West Africa, Abidjan developed into a rival to Dakar, but between them they provided two-thirds of French West African industrial production. In Cameroun, Douala accounted for 75 percent of processing industry capacity. In French Equatorial Africa, Port-Gentil and Pointe-Noire accounted for two-thirds.

The most radical innovation in the economy during the first fifteen postwar years was the rise of extractive industries and the use of hydroelectric resources. The relative progress of private French investment in this sector does not accurately reflect its importance. It has been seen, indeed, that these industries represented a very important share of public investment (in the order of one-third of registered capital, and far more for actual disbursements). Furthermore, there was substantial foreign (namely, non-French) participation in these industries (American, British, and so on), amounting to approximately one-third or one-half of the registered capital.

The private capital involved here is entirely different from that invested in the traditional trading companies, at least before 1960. Involved on the French side were the "operating" industrial groups (Usinor for iron ore of Kaloum, later that of Mauritania), financial groups interested in metallic raw materials (Rothschild for Kaloum and Mauritanian iron, and Gabon's manganese and uranium), the large diversified financial groups (the Banque de Paris et des Pays-Bas for Senegal's phosphate and Gabon's petroleum).

The massive presence of foreign capital, which did violence to the colonial principle of maintaining a private preserve, was something new. There had indeed been exceptions to the rule: Bata, already mentioned, and especially the subsidiaries of the Anglo-Dutch Unilever group in the trade; Unilever's presence, however, had its counterpart in the presence of French companies (Compagnie Française de l'Afrique Occidentale and Société Commerciale de l'Ouest Africain) in the British West African colonies. It was early evidence of the tendency toward internationalization of capital that was to come into full flower after 1960. The scale of these mining enterprises, the large capital and outlets required, and the need to limit risk necessitated this opening to foreign capital. Its participation was therefore accepted, even sought after, on condition that control by the French private interests was not challenged. As additional protection, a specially tailored law passed by the French Parliament permitted French stockholders, even if they held a minority of stock, to retain their position of control by means of preferred stock carrying the right to a multiple vote—an arrangement maintained, curiously enough, after the African states became independent.[23] Foreign participation, moreover, was desired for political reasons: this was affirmed in 1958 by the present director-general of the Banque de Paris et des Pays-Bas (then *chef de cabinet* of the Minister of Overseas France), who deemed it "desirable that foreign capitalists, and eventually even foreign States, should, together with the French capitalists and State, wish to see the Overseas countries develop in a calm atmosphere, and evolve peacefully."[24]

Mining economy differs fundamentally from trade economy. The former, of course, is also confined to exporting raw materials, or materials processed enough only to facilitate transport. But it does not induce a compensating current of imports: these are reduced to a minimum (industrial material and the raw materials required for extraction and treatment of ore; consumer products for the personnel, especially the relatively numerous European personnel—often as many as one-third of the employees, at least at first—who enjoyed most of the purchasing power).

Above all, mining enterprise remained alien to the country's economy. It was a typical enclave, a state within the state, not only because of its economic power but also because it operated in isolation from the host country, with its own towns, its own commissary, and eventually its own railways and ore-loading port. It did not become integrated with the country's human substance as the trade economy did, even though the latter did so in response to an external economic need. It employed only a limited number of locals (a few hundred, two or three thousand in extreme cases), for the most part as unskilled laborers representing a small volume of wages. Its contribution to the country was further reduced by the fact that it invariably enjoyed a privileged tax position. Its effect on the local economic and social environment, far from acting as an exemplary showpiece of development, in general powerfully contributed to discouraging traditional activities, agricultural or others, by the attraction of higher wages

23. Law of February 1957, reestablishing for the benefit of "certain overseas companies" the multiple vote abolished by French legislation of 1933.

24. Pierre Moussa, *Les Chances économiques de la communauté franco-africaine* (Paris, 1957), p. 191.

(though still modest in absolute value) and of the resulting parasitism (domestic service, commerce, and so on).[25]

Economic Integration and Uneven Development

With the aforementioned exceptions (Unilever and shares in mining) French black Africa remained a market reserved to the metropole's capital, state or private. To this characteristic, which Lenin noted as typical of contemporary colonialism, must be added the two inherited from the older form of colonialism: the market reserved for the metropole's manufactures, and the market confined to supplying the metropole with food or industrial raw materials. Relatively unaccentuated until the 1930s (particularly in the field of imports: the trading companies, even the French ones, obtained their trade goods mainly from Manchester), these characteristics became more prominent between 1946 and 1960. The crisis and depression of the 1930s had already strengthened protectionism within the empire; with recovery from the consequence of the war (after 1949) it was reinstated and even intensified. The cement of this integration now became membership in the franc zone. Within the zone transfers were unrestricted; through various intermediate agencies, including the Comité Monétaire de la Zone Franc, it was ultimately the Banque de France that allocated foreign exchange to cover import licenses, the proceeds from the sale of overseas products being paid into a common pool of foreign currencies.

After 1945, of course, French tropical Africa had a separate monetary unit, the CFA franc; but its parity with the French franc did not vary after 1948, and it was in reality simply a local designation for the same currency, the CFA franc and the "métro" franc being freely convertible at par. From one point of view, the influx of French private and state capital ("aid") balanced the outflow of revenues such as company profits and the repatriated earnings of Europeans.

African products enjoyed a privileged distribution status in France. A whole arsenal of measures (quotas, subsidies, price-support funds, "pairing,"[26] and so on) ensured their sale on the French market at preferential prices, above those on the world market. But the surcharges benefited chiefly the exporting firms, while the producers derived only a small

25. On this subject, see my study, "Fria, un exemple d'industrialisation africaine," *Annales de Géographie* (1964), pp. 172–88.

26. Pairing: the obligation for an importer to purchase a specified quantity of products inside the franc zone in order to obtein a license to import a corresponding quantity of the same products from outside the franc zone. The procedure had been instituted in the 1930s.

advantage—smaller still since, in the other direction, French merchandise enjoyed a still higher surcharge. In 1953 the surcharge was estimated at 12.5 billion "métro" francs for the metropole and 35.2 for the overseas territories; in 1956, 15.9 and 25.2 billions, respectively.[27]

The foregoing suffices to shed light on the accentuation and strengthening of the "colonial" nature of the African economies—"colonial" in the specific sense of the contemporary imperalist era's colonialism, which began at the end of the nineteenth century: domination by the metropole's monopolistic financial capital, represented principally by large trading companies, of which three alone controlled nearly two-thirds of the external commerce;[28] the activating role of capital exports (now principally public capital); and the confinement of the territories to the role of furnishing raw materials to the metropole and providing an outlet for its manufactures.

Without disregarding the importance of the development of the mining industry (after all, of a purely colonial type), which attained its ultimate scale only after 1960, this expansion of the colonial economy took place within the framework of the trade economy. The principal effect of the massive investment in infrastructure (ports, highways) was to make possible an increase in volume and geographic depth of the trade, by opening to it regions that had previously remained relatively somnolent because of their remoteness and absence of a means of access.

Doubtless, the most striking example is the rapid development of Ivory Coast, into which several factors entered: the opening of the port of Abidjan (1951), a secure outlet of large capacity as compared with the old wharves at Port-Bouët and Grand Bassam; the opening of roads; the clearing of woodlands, facilitated by the widespread use of mechanical equipment; and the organization, finally, of a massive immigration of labor from Upper Volta. Ivorian coffee production thus rose from 10,000 tons in 1937 to 144,000 in 1960; it represented 26.2 percent of French West African exports in 1956, as against 33.8 percent for peanuts (the 1938 proportions were respectively 5.5 percent and 45.1 percent).

By contrast, in Upper Volta, in which a retrenching commerce had lost interest, the trade diminished. Upper Volta became a manpower reserve whose monetary resources were provided chiefly by remittances from migrant laborers, including soldiers enlisted in the French army.

27. Ehrhardt, *Le Destin*, chap.2; Moussa, *Les Chances économiques*, pp. 76–84.

28. According to "quotes" set by the administration, on the basis of prewar levels of imports, during the years 1941–48. The proportion remained approximately the same.

Already apparent before 1940 between the coast and the interior, the disparity in development between exploited areas either near the coast or adequately provided with means of access and fertile soils, and neglected areas reduced to the role of manpower reservoirs, became more marked. Uneven development was similarly reflected in the swelling of the urban population, fed by the exodus from the countryside, and in a concentration of income in the cities, of which the effects on commercial procedures have already been described. None of this, including uneven development, is absent from the analysis produced by Lenin in 1916.[29]

State Monopoly Capitalism

A single new element must be added to this analysis: the new role of the state: its pervasive intervention in economic mechanisms, most particularly at the investment level. As has already been noted, this is a phenomenon in no way typical of the colonial sphere but which enters into a general transformation of monopoly capitalism's structures. The first manifestations of this transformation appeared during the Depression of the 1930s and became widespread just after the Second World War. State intervention in economic mechanisms was not itself a new phenomenon, especially in the colonies; the role of administrative intervention in the functioning of the trade economy has been shown above. What is new is the inability of monopoly capital to ensure its own maintenance and growth while ensuring the indispensable level of profits, either by market mechanisms or by agreements among monopolists. This inability led it to accept, and even to invite, pervasive involvement by the state, not only at the level of regulation (customs, currency management, and so on) and of certain important public services, but also in processes of production and exchange themselves, notably at the investment level.

This process was to continue and intensify after independence. In order to understand the significance of the period 1946–60 in the economic field, one must pursue the investigation into the period 1960–77. Indeed, while 1960 marked a rupture in the political domain, it did not do so in the economic domain; there was simply a continuation (and in some cases an acceleration) of the movements and trends already observable in the preceding period, and one can thus perceive more clearly where some of these were leading. In this sense there was no "neocolonial" economy—unless one gives this expression the purely indicative meaning of postcolonial economy.

29. Lenin, *L'Impérialisme*, p. 324.

Increasing Concentration of Capital

As stated above, the integration of the large commercial companies and high financial capital dates from the 1920s. For nearly half a century they were controlled by the same interest groups: Marseilles shipowners and industrialists for the Compagnie Française de l'Afrique Occidentale (CFAO); Lyon and Swiss interests for the Société Commerciale de l'Ouest Africain (SCOA); the Bordeaux houses, closely linked to Protestant high finance and its principal organ, la Banque de l'Union Parisienne; and, between the two World Wars, the Unilever group that absorbed the old Manchester commercial firms (John Holt, Hatton and Cookson, Ollivant, and King). In the 1960s several important changes occurred, tending toward a more intimate incorporation among the dominate groups of the French financial oligarchy. These changes were part and parcel of the concentration operations conducted during the de Gaulle era, designed to deal with the consequences of internal competition within the Common Market and of its anticipated extension (with the entry of Great Britain).

Only the most outstanding of these changes will be noted here. On the one hand, there was the merger and absorption in 1963–66 of most of the Bordeaux firms into the OPTORG company, a subsidiary of the Banque de l'Union Parisienne (BUP), and then, in 1966, the absorption of BUP by the Financière de Suez. Along with OPTORG, Suez inherited other properties subordinate to BUP, notably the SCAC–SOCOPAO (Société Commerciale d'Affrètements et de Commissions and Société Commerciale des Ports de l'Afrique Occidentale), specialized in maritime transit but with interests in various industrial enterprises. On the other hand, the Banque de Paris et des Pays-Bas took control of SCOA in 1968; "Paribas" already had control of many business affairs in Africa (public works, the agri-industrial sector, and so on) and had interests in various mining enterprises (see above).

Survival and Extension of State Monopoly Capitalism Mechanisms

All the principal agencies for the intervention of French state monopoly capitalism were maintained, albeit with some changes of title. The Banque de France and the Comité Monétaire de la Zone Franc (in which a few berths were granted to representatives of the new states) preserved their powers intact. When devaluation overtook the French currency, and therefore the CFA franc, the African chief of state heard about it like everyone else, by the radio or press: he was neither consulted nor forewarned. FIDES became FAC (Fonds d'Aide et de Coopération), the Bureau Minier de la France d'Outre-Mer became the Bureau de Recherches Géologiques et Minières (BRGM), the CCFOM became CCCE (Caisse Centrale de Coopération Economique), and so on.

French agencies, however, were no longer the only ones in the field. Foreign state capital had become diversified and internationalized. Diversification was not necessarily linked to political independence, although the latter contributed to it. It resulted from obligations under the Treaty of Rome (1957), predating independence, creating Europe's "Six." Organs of the European Economic Community (European Development Fund and European Investment Bank) were now side by side with the FAC and CCCE, with somewhat analogous functions. Moreover, the World Bank (IBRD) and its subsidiary the Société financière internationale (SFI) whose activity had been limited before 1960, were now operating on a large scale, notably in mining enterprises and certain large infrastructural works. There was also participation, although relatively modest, by similar agencies of the Federal Republic of Germany (Kreditanstalt für Wiederaufbau, Deutsche Entwicklungsgesellschaft) and the United States (USAID).

Another innovation clearly resulted from independence: outside capital (chiefly French) was more and more associated with the nation's public capital, or channeled through it, both in its traditional and in its newer functions. It is true that the role of the new nation's public sector is in many respects a contradictory one. For the moment, suffice it to say that in most cases it simply effects a transfer of functions—and obligations—from the French state to the national state. Extension of the nation's public sector thus corresponds to the assumption of responsibility for more and more numerous and varied activities indispensable to the efficient operation of the economy, and therefore to the operation of foreign monopoly capitalism and maintenance of its high profits. These activities no longer concern infrastructure alone but production and commerce as well; indispensable to the economy, they are considered insufficiently profitable by private capital and, in the circumstances, are left to the state or transferred to it. As for state participation in private business (particularly industry), it is willingly accepted, and sometimes requested, by private capital as a guarantee against possible future demands by employed personnel or intrusion of future competitors. Furthermore, the priority given to industrialization as an indication of "development" has led the African states to renew or increase the customs and other tax privileges accorded to foreign industrial, agri-industrial, and mining enterprises. That is the purpose of the various "investment codes" adopted by the new states, often under direct pressure from monopolist firms and the international agencies that serve them (the IBRD, and others).

In processing industries, which remain largely confined to import-substitution and partial transformation of export products, the commonest form of entry by public capital is the "supporting" participation referred to above. If the prospects of profit are low, it may take the form of state enterprise, private capital retaining de facto control by providing its "technical assistance"—at burdensome cost, of course. Here, technological control takes over where financial control leaves off.

In agriculture, the large mechanized-cultivation operations undertaken by state agencies or companies, or mixed entities (Office du Niger, and so on), had failed. Public involvement in agriculture thereafter developed along other lines existing before 1960 only rarely or in embryo. In the 1930s, following a model borrowed from the Belgian Congo, cotton growing had been introduced in Oubangui-Chari (Central African Republic) and Chad on the initiative of private concessionary companies holding a state monopoly of the purchase and ginning of cotton, with the responsibility of providing a "framework" for the local peasantry's cultivation. This system entered into the forced-labor structure; each taxpayer had to sow and cultivate one *corde* (about 4,900 square meters) under the supervision of monitors, the "cotton-boys." A mixed company with a state majority share, la Compagnie Française pour le Développement des Fibres Textiles (CFDT) continued and expanded this procedure in North Cameroun before independence, and later, after 1960, throughout western Africa. Various French companies, public or mixed, adopted this method under the name of *encadrement* or "promotion" of various export crops: Société d'Assistance Technique et de Coopération (SATEC) for peanuts in Senegal; Bureau pour le Développement de la Production Agricole (BDPA), and so forth. Gradually (not until 1974 for the CFDT), the French public companies were replaced by similar national agencies that were performing the same role but were themselves incorporated in the former mother-companies' "framework," which provided them technical assistance; the transformation thus amounted merely to a change of label.

In liaison with specialized French research institutes established on the spot in the 1940s, these national agencies assumed responsibility for furnishing selected seeds, agricultural machinery, and fertilizer for pest control, and for providing the producer a "framework" of European and African "promoters" charged with ensuring that the cultivation methods recommended by the experts were followed.

In reality, the "independent" African peasant was forced, as in the past and now often on a larger scale, to cultivate export crops that were not of his own choosing but were in demand in the developed countries. Even where the old constraining devices of the colonial era have disappeared (as a matter of fact, there is much evidence that these constraints persist: Chad has written into law, with corresponding penal sanctions, the obligation to raise cotton, which had in practice never been discontinued, notwithstanding the 1946 law), the African peasant has no choice: in order to obtain the cash necessary to pay his taxes and buy indispensable manufactured goods, he can only raise the crops for which a "framework" and market outlets exist, even though their cultivation pays him little. In this sort of "state métayage" investment is provided by the state (or states: those providing "aid," and the national states), which compensates the intermediary companies or agencies by contract; expenses are, by and large, shifted onto the producer himself as, for example, where equipment or fertilizer is advanced on credit, for which servicing charges are deducted from the total value of the harvest delivered by the producer.

This system leads to involvement of the state, or its agencies, at the marketing level. The private cotton companies and the CFDT had already been accorded a purchasing monopoly. After 1960, nearly everywhere the collection of export agricultural products was entrusted gradually to state offices or companies, sometimes with participation from the private sector if the business was profitable. The trading companies abandoned product collection to state offices or specialized companies (trade in harvested products by the CFAO, which represented 50 percent of its business volume in 1945, fell to 0.5 percent in 1970–71; for SCOA, from 24 percent in 1952–53 to 10 percent in 1963–64 and 4.3 percent in 1970–71).[30]

The result was that the traditional trade of the factories, reduced to the sale of manufactured goods, was deprived of half its volume of business and was no longer profitable except in a few fostered regions such as those in Ivory Coast and Cameroun. The disengagement of the commercial companies from the bush trade, already begun in the 1950s, was to become total.

Retail trade in the bush was thereafter left to small African middlemen. When it was not profitable enough to interest private business, it was taken over by state or mixed firms, which usually operated at a loss and thus assumed a "social" character.

The large commercial companies were nevertheless not slowing down, as their regularly increasing volume of business and profits demonstrates. They retained their dominant position at the level of wholesale and external trade; they kept, and enlarged, their profit-making activities: shops and

30. The above data concerning the years 1970–77 are taken from my *thèse d'Etat*, "Géographie des investissements et problèmes du développement en Afrique tropicale d'influence française."

special services in the capitals and large centers (automobiles, machinery, electrical appliances, refrigeration, construction materials, machines, and materials for public works, and so on) and large stores (where open shelving and self-service now appeared). These companies retained and expanded their participation in import-substitution industries, priding themselves on their contribution to "industrialization." As for state trading, they continued their participation in the case of mixed companies, and in general supplied it with goods and "technical assistance"; thus they kept their advantages without risk while leaving to the state the eventual deficit of a "public welfare" commerce. The trade economy, both in its traditional form and in its modified form of the years 1946–60, now belonged to the past.

Regional imbalances became more marked through the concentration of activity and investment in the urban centers, mining zones, and the rich agricultural areas, while the others were increasingly abandoned and relegated to the role of reserves of migrant labor. Migration, heretofore to the rich coastal countries, began to expand to Europe also (notably to France by Senegalese, Malians, and Mauretanians from the Senegal valley).

In the industrial field, the early 1970s witnessed the appearance of a new type of industry: a handcraft industry using imported materials intended for re-export (textiles in Ivory Coast and Togo; the industrial free port at Dakar). Copied from the Far Eastern example (South Korea, Hong Kong, Singapore), this involves unalloyed exploitation of cheap hand labor that might be described as "emigration within the household." The recession of the past few years, however, does not permit prediction of a substantial expansion in this field.

International interdependence, whose aspect on the level of state capital has been mentioned, is equally manifest in the field of private investment and foreign trade. The provisions of the Treaty of Rome, and also the juridically independent status of the new states, no longer permit maintenance of a "private preserve." At the same time, continued membership in the Franc Zone, and the cooperation agreements concluded between France and the new states upon their independence, limit opportunity for penetration by foreign influences other than French. The result is that the French positions, both in private investment and in commerce, have weakened, without, however, losing their preponderant character.

In 1970–71, for the large commercial enterprises (those with a volume of business exceeding 200 million CFA francs), the share of French private capital in Congo-Brazzaville represented 57.27 percent of investment and 60.8 percent of business volume; in the Central African Republic, 65.09 percent of investment and 60.87 percent of business. It must be kept in mind that the largest non-French foreign enterprise, Unilever's subsidiary La Société Commerciale du Kouilou-Niari, was present in these two countries before independence. For the same year, among about a thousand industrial enterprises listed in the thirteen continental states of French-speaking tropical Africa (Guinea excluded), French capital represented 64.6 percent of the capital invested (British, 11.39 percent; American, 8.58 percent; West German, 4.82 percent).[31]

In foreign trade, members of the Franc Zone remained the leading partners everywhere except Guinea; their share nevertheless declined from 60–70 percent around 1958 to 30–40 percent in about 1970.[32]

Social and Political Evolution

Until 1946, colonialism and the trade system had generally worked in the direction of breaking down the social differentiations inherited from the precolonial era: liquidating the former aristocracies or reducing them to the level of canton chiefs; eliminating the nascent commercial bourgeoisies, the middlemen of the nineteenth-century "barter"; and ending slavery, less to comfort the slaves than to rescue their masters from a life of "ease and sloth"[33] and oblige all to work as hard as possible for the greater profit of the colonists. For political reasons, however, this evolution remained confined within certain bounds. To keep control of the people, colonialism needed intermediaries. It was thus led to maintain the chieftaincy system, while reducing it to a subordinate role, and to adapt itself to certain precolonial structures (including slavery), particularly in the regions least penetrated by the trade economy (the Sahara and Sahel areas, Fouta-Djalon, and so on). It had meanwhile created a new social stratum in the form of the African civil service, which was similarly limited to subordinate functions. The slow but persistent diffusion of the money economy among the rural masses had progressively undermined the traditional patriarchal structures, encouraged a growing independence of youths with respect to their elders, and fostered the differentiation in wealth and income between the pauperized masses and the notables.[34]

There was, however, evolution in other directions also. First among these was the irremediable decline of chieftaincy, which seemed more and

31. Lenin, *L'Impérialisme,* p. 324.

32. Reports of the Comité Monétaire de la Zone Franc (1961–75).

33. R. Cuvillier-Fleury, *La Main d'oeuvre dans les colonies françaises de l'Afrique occidentale et du Congo* (Paris, 1907), p. 31.

34. *Afrique Noire,* 2: 79–92; R. Barbé, *Les Classes sociales en Afrique Noire: Economie et politique* (Paris, 1964).

more an anachronistic institution, and whose role during the "war effort" period had profoundly discredited it. In vain did the administration redouble its efforts to "modernize" and preserve an institution it still regarded as an indispensable mechanism. The popular revolution of 1956–58 in Guinea against the chiefs, which culminated at the end of 1957 in the abolition of chieftaincy ratified by the colonial officials, is both significant and instructive in this regard.[35]

Meanwhile, however, to some degree new strata of "modern" intermediaries were coming into being, induced both by economic evolution and by political necessity. First, there were the growing number of subordinate African civil servants and their aspiration to more senior positions. This stemmed from economic and social development itself, and from the increasing role played by the state apparatus. It is from among these évolués—who had received a European education in the schools (under the colonial system, entering a French school signified a desire to enter the public service)—that the new political elites were to be recruited, those who became members of the territorial councils and deputies in Parliament within the framework of the 1946 institutions. Evolués were also to provide cadres for the colonial order's "opposition" (including trade-union leaders), while the administration endeavored to effect the transfer of the most prominent among them from the former to the latter category. This represented the broadening of a policy already followed before 1946 within the smaller framework of the *communes de plein exercice* in Senegal.

On the other hand, growth in the volume of exchanges and the partial retrenchment of the trading companies' networks led to the appearance of a stratum, as yet narrow and penurious, of small African merchants and freight carriers, a development previously obstructed for political reasons, under the pretext that the Africans lacked honesty and commercial ability and implemented in practice by systematic denial of credit. They made a place for themselves, still quite modest, alongside the theretofore privileged intermediaries, Lebanese and others. Middlemen for the trading companies, as well as being their debtors, played no independent role and were confined to the function of "micro-compradors."

Only in plantation agriculture, and chiefly in Ivory Coast (to a lesser extent in Senegal), did a class appear before 1960 in French black Africa that was really deserving of the name "bourgeoisie." The abolition of forced labor in 1946 allowed that region equal access to manpower, reserved until then for the European colonists. In Ivory Coast, European planters pro-

35. Suret-Canale, "La Fin de la chefferie en Guinée," *Journal of African History* 7, no. 3 (1966): 459–93.

vided one-third of the coffee harvest in 1939–40; by 1953, the area of their plantations had diminished by nearly half, and they occupied only 4.5 percent of the total planted acreage (as compared with more than 25 percent in 1940), even though the latter had tripled in size.[36] Elsewhere, even when European production did not fall in absolute terms, it diminished in relative value, to the benefit of African planters; thus, in Cameroun, "European" coffee production rose from 3,430 to 4,080 tons between 1954 and 1957, but African production rose from 5,500 to 11,520 tons. Similarly, also in Cameroun, banana production in 1946 was 96 percent European in 1946, but became more than half African in the 1950s (56 percent in 1955, 70 percent in 1957).[37] It is true that in 1957–58 there were still large numbers of African planters in the forested regions of Ivory Coast who used family labor primarily, hiring wage earners only as a supplement. But from this mass there emerged a minority, between 8,000 and 10,000 planters, cultivating more than ten or twelve hectares and permanently employing more than five employees.[38]

Another consequence of economic evolution was the progressive increase in the number of salaried workers. For French West Africa, their number increased from 129,000 in 1934 to 241,700 in 1947 and 404,550 in 1957. This represented between 1.6 percent (Niger) and 19.3 percent (Ivory Coast) of the active male population. It should, of course, be made clear that in Ivory Coast half the work force consisted of immigrant agricultural laborers. The high figures for the Congo (28.1 percent of the active male population) and Gabon (29.6 percent)—still for the year 1957—must be interpreted in the light of the large numbers who were holdovers from forced labor requisitions rather than proletarians properly speaking; these were contract laborers in logging operations, more than a third of the work force in Gabon.

On the other hand, it is the expansion of commerce, transportation, public works, and state agencies that explains the increase in the work force, rather than expansion of industry and mining, which were only small-scale employers: one-eighth of the total in Senegal, one-tenth in Cameroun, one-seventeenth in Ivory Coast. The proportion of salaried workers in public service was generally high, especially in the more backward regions (66 percent in Niger, 68 percent in Upper Volta). But it should not be concluded that all these were in the category of "civil servants," strictly speaking; many were laborers in the true sense of the

36. *Afrique Noire*, 3: 219.
37. Ibid., pp. 220, 223.
38. Barbé, *Les Classes sociales*, p. 37.

term—workers on the railways, in the ports, and in the official public works agencies, linemen in posts and telecommunications, and so on. From them were often recruited the most militant elements of the trade-union movement.[39]

It remains true that in 1958–60 social differentiation and polarization were as yet little developed within the African population. The contradiction setting the general mass of the people against foreign imperialism far outweighed the internal contradictions that were only just beginning to arise. This explains, notwithstanding the important role played by the unions, the absence of political organizations based on class, and the quest for "universality" by the organizations that were founded. Furthermore, it explains the attempts made to erect theories on the absence of classes in black Africa.

It is risky, and often wrong, to try to think of social differentiations and their political expression in terms of "social stratification," which, even in developed capitalist countries, never represents more than an approximation. This is the more true in the African case, as "modern" social differentiations intersected and interacted with those inherited from precolonial society (or their ideological survivals). Above all, one must observe the developing polarization and the contradictory lines of force that resulted from it.

Politically, the colonial power continued to rely on the chiefs, who (with a few exceptions) were the more devoted, as they owed to it their very survival. This reliance sometimes succeeded, as in Niger where, opposing the Bakary Djibo government which had called for a "no" response to the constitutional referendum, the administration in 1958 obtained a "yes" majority thanks to the chiefs' assistance. But the contrary example of Guinea shows that this social support was becoming more and more precarious. The colonial power consequently had to seek support from new privileged strata.

In Ivory Coast the basis for such support was provided by the planter bourgeoisie, which coincided in part with the social group derived from the chieftaincy, whose "rights" to land and to the "customary" use of manpower (forced labor, in other words) had at an early date permitted the establishment of extensive plantations. Between 1944 and 1946, nevertheless, it had formed the spearhead of the anticolonial movement, the nucleus of the Rassemblement Démocratique Africain (RDA), by launching the slogan of

39. Ibid., pp. 66–73; H. d'Almeïda-Topor, "Recherches sur l'évolution du travail salarié en A.O.F. pendant la crise économique 1930–1936," *Cahiers d'Etudes Africaines* 16 (1976): 103–17.

abolition of forced labor. This slogan responded to a popular demand but also to class interests, inasmuch as these placed the bourgeoisie in intense competition with the European colonists for access to labor. Once the demand was met, the planters' militancy evaporated. At the end of 1950, following their leader Houphouët-Boigny, they moved bag and baggage into the opposing camp.

Ivory Coast, however, was an exceptional case. Elsewhere the bourgeoisie, or the nascent petite bourgeoisie, lacked the breadth necessary to play such a role, and the contradictions setting it against its colonial competitors and masters tipped the scales, at least until independence; it followed and supported the anticolonial movement, like the Union des Populations du Cameroun (UPP), and sometimes even led it, like the Ewe bouregoisie with Sylvanus Olympio and the Comité d'Unité Togolaise (CUT).

The colonial power strove to make the new "elite," emerging from the civil service provided with political sinecures, the successor to the declining chieftaincy. This was a fragile structure, as it was numercially weak and lacked its own distinct economic base; but these features made it all the easier to control.

On the other side of the barricade, what were the social forces supporting the anticolonial movement? Study of the activities of the more radical political movements that played a decisive role in events, such as the Parti Démocratique de Guinea, an RDA affiliate, or the Union des Populations du Cameroun (although the latter was to be dismantled and crushed by repression after ten years of struggle), yields some elements of the answer.

The earliest role was played by the urban masses mobilized by the unions. The majority of these were affiliated with the French CGT (the "Christian" or "believers" unions affiliated with the CFTC and the Force Ouvrière unions—chiefly European—seemed like government-sponsored unions); their leaders were civil servants, as were the leaders of the opposition political movements. Union action followed an anticolonialist logic rather than a "class" logic in the narrow sense: employers were principally European firms and individuals, and the colonial state. Demands were aimed for the most part at abolishing racial discrimination in the field of wages and working conditions. That is why union actions received support from the broadest strata of the urban population, including African merchants.[40] The strikes in 1952 and 1953, for passage of the Code du Travail

40. Cf. our study "The French West African Railway Workers' Strike, 1947–1948," in Peter C. W. Gutkind, R. Cohen, and J. Copans, *Labor History in Africa*, Sage Series on African Modernization and Development, vol. 2 (Beverly Hills, 1978).

Outre-Mer (which had been buried since 1946 in parliamentary committee files) and then for its implementation, gave considerable impetus to the pressing of labor demands and to the strikes that proliferated after 1953, particularly during the years 1956–60, which assumed a more and more obvious political significance. In Guinea, Cameroun, and Niger it was the union movement that provided political movements with leaders of radical stripe (Sékou Touré, Saïfoullaye Diallo, Ruben Um Nyobe, and Bakary Djibo).

When political movements, solidly supported by this urban base, succeeded in winning over the peasant masses (in Guinea, by mobilizing them against the chiefs), the dynamics of forces altered in their favor, permitting these movements to assume power (Guinea, Mali) or to impose their demands (independence and reunification in the case of Cameroun, although the movement that had imposed them was later crushed). Their cadres were recruited from older-generation African civil servants—those already on the rolls in 1946—just as, elsewhere, cadres of movements and organizations obedient to the administration came from the same source. Students returning from France—the new generation, since students were not sent to France before 1946—were much less closely linked to the popular masses than their elders; they played a more limited role than is now sometimes claimed, even though it was they who created the Parti Africain de l'Indépendence, to which historic credit is due for raising, for the first time, the question of independence.[41]

In short, independence appears to be the result of popular struggles sweeping along with them, in varying degrees, most of the components of the African population, with the exception of a few quite restricted categories. Until 1957 these struggles advanced only democratic and anticolonialist objectives—implementation of the 1946 laws and the constitution, and genuine equality for the new "citizens"—without raising the question of independence. The impossibility of pursuing these struggles to a successful conclusion within the colonial framework, and evolution in the international environment—notably, the progress of national liberation struggles in other regions of the world, particularly in Asia and North Africa—placed the question of independence on the agenda at the end of the period.

The French government and its colonial administration strove to the end to maintain the colonial principle—that of French sovereignty—by making partial concessions. In this sense, and notwithstanding the interpretations

41. It may be noted in passing that its founder, Majhemout Diop, is nevertheless a representative of the older generation, a former student at the Ecole William Ponty.

that have been adduced after the fact, neither the Loi-Cadre of 1956 (placed in effect in 1957 and giving the territories "government councils" proceeding from, and responsible to, elected assemblies) nor the "Community" proposed by the 1958 de Gaulle constitution (giving the former territories the status of states and a limited sovereignty) had the objective of preparing the way for independence, but were intended to obstruct it. Evidence of this is the treatment meted out to Guinea, which dared, in 1958, to say no and to opt for an independence that had, in the end, to be granted to all in 1960.

Once independence was gained, it was greeted as a victory even by those who had neither desired nor sought it. It was not obtained without combat, even if (with the exception of Cameroun) the combat did not take the extreme form it did elsewhere. But it is true that the international context (the Algerian war, which placed the opening of a "second front" south of the Sahara out of the question) played a decisive role in the concession. It was granted in this region because, on the side of colonial imperialism, it was thought that the dependent relationship could be preserved in other ways. In fact, with few exceptions (notably Guinea), the independent regimes did perpetuate the colonial situation in other ways, replacing the former colonialism with neocolonialism.

As the euphoria of independence disappeared, internal contradictions were not long in emerging. The political secretary of the Union Soudanaise-RDA (Mali) could accurately say, in 1962;

> All countries in the world which have undergone foreign or colonial domination have seen battle fronts drawn, often of a heterogeneous nature, within which conflicts of interest were suppressed because of the overriding priority of the struggle, whether or not by force of arms, for national liberation. But once foreign domination disappears, the social problems stemming from these conflicts of interest reappear sooner or later, even if national sentiment and the nation-building phase temporarily blur them or delay their practical manifestations.[42]

After 1960 these contradictions continued to develop in the same direction as between 1946 and 1960, without qualitative change. The economic transformations described above have culminated in a relative consolidation of the agrarian bourgeoisie (where it exists) and, more particularly, of the commercial strata, for which the trading companies' retreat has left a vacant space but a position that remains subordinate. In general, these

42. Idrissa Diarra, "Rapport d'activités et d'orientation," Fifth Congress of the Union Soudanaise R.D.A., Bamako, pp. 88–99. Cited in Barbé, *Les Classes sociales*, p. 5.

strata, bourgeois in the proper economic meaning of the term, have not played a decisive role as the animating force of the new regimes. The outstanding feature of the independent era is undoubtedly the emergence of a bureaucratic stratum, born of the former African civil service, which has in part taken the place of the former European functionaries. Rather than acceding to "power," it serves the same function as its predecessors, of management for the benefit of foreign interests. It takes advantage of its administrative and political functions in order to build private fortunes (commissions from government-managed markets, real-estate concessions, membership on the boards of directors of certain companies). But its economic role remains secondary, and in any case subordinate. Traditions against ostentation and favoring redistribution make it difficult for its members to accumulate wealth, but when they do it goes to France or Switzerland.

Conclusion

When one considers the economic evolution of French-influenced tropical Africa between 1946 and 1960 along with its contemporary, postindependence extensions, and not neglecting the social, political, and ideological components of this evolution, it seems impossible to explain either in terms of decolonization or of the transfer of power.

The word *decolonization,* at least in France, is loaded with ambiguity. One may certainly construe it in the "neutral" sense of transition from colonial status to that of juridical independence. In practice, however, the use of the term connotes a certain idea of the way in which this process took place. The imperalist powers, it is thought, once having colonized, suddenly changed their policy and deliberately "decolonized." Some consider this a generous and disinterested program (the approach of a certain de Gaullist mythology which credits the General with such clear-sightedness); whereas to others it was proof of a diabolical perfidy, since the purpose of decolonization was better to exploit the dominated peoples.[43]

I believe I have shown that imperialism deserves neither this excessive honor nor this insult. The empires did not deliberately decide upon decolonization, did not desire it, and did not really prepare for it. It simply happened, and measures that today appear to constitute preparatory steps toward independence in fact never intended to lead to it, as Jean Stengers has rightly demonstrated (see chap. 12), but, on the contrary, meant to

43. This could be concluded from certain judgments in the preface to Colin Leys, *Underdevelopment in Kenya* (London, 1975).

raise an obstacle to it by granting partial concessions calculated to preserve the essence of imperialism.

What we are in fact witnessing on the global scale (for in this domain one cannot consider Africa in isolation) is a bitter, complex, and continuing struggle between imperialism (that is, high international monopolistic capital and the states that serve it), on the one hand, and, on the other, all those forces that are objectively in contradiction to imperialism: the socialist countries, the laboring classes (and more generally the working masses), and the national liberation movements of those peoples subjected to imperialist exploitation. In French tropical Africa this struggle reached a first culmination around the year 1960, with the collapse of a traditional colonial system badly shaken since 1945, partly because of external factors (essentially, the Algerian War). The result, in most cases and in forms that varied according to the forces emerging in the respective countries, has been that imperialism has fallen back upon indirect methods of domination which do little to alter economic realities. But this neocolonialism was called into question from its birth by avant-garde groups, including, in some cases, those at the state level (Guinea, Mali until the military coup d'état, Congo in 1963, and more recently Benin and Madagascar). Today it is increasingly challenged and finds itself considering more and more often the socialist alternative as the only guarantee of authentic independence.

The common characteristic of the experiments we are concerned with here has been to embark simultaneously upon changes in political structure—more or less extensive nationalizations aimed at eliminating the direct presence of foreign imperialism, and measures intended to inhibit or prevent the formation of a local bourgeoisie—and upon a struggle within the system on which they are still dependent, in order to thwart broader economic and political pressures by relying on the socialist countries and playing rival empires off against one another. Such a policy is often laden with ambiguities, even leaving aside "socialist" countries in name only, of which Senghor doubtless offers the most typical example. These ambiguities, which are attributable to the effects of internal social and political struggles, to setbacks, and sometimes to outright failures (as in the case of Mali), can exist as long as the question, "Which will win, capitalism or socialism?" continues to be raised within the country itself. None of these states is in fact "socialist" in the strictly objective sense of the term, which assumes the preponderance in the country's economy of collective ownership of the essential means of production.

Among West African countries, Guinea has undoubtedly carried the experiment the furthest: the "modern" economy—commerce, banking, industry, infrastructure—is totally nationalized there except for the two principal enterprises in the mining sector (Alumina of Fria and Bauxites of Boké), owned by mixed companies in which the Guinean state (with 49 percent of the capital and a guaranteed 65 percent of the earnings) is associated with the international aluminum and bauxite trusts; these provide most of the country's foreign exchange revenues. Meanwhile, a stubborn struggle is taking place to impede the formation of a local bourgeoisie, crowned in 1975 by the total prohibition of private commerce (except for the sale or resale of local products in the markets), a measure that may seem economically aberrant but whose sociopolitical motives are clear.[44] At the same time, despite various efforts (agricultural production cooperatives in 1960–62, production brigades within the framework of "local revolutionary authorities" in the villages), agriculture still remains the domain of the small private producer.[45]

Must these efforts be considered negligible, even simply as dust in the eyes?[46] That is apparently not the opinion of the imperialist forces, as is shown by the numerous attempts made (with success in Mali and, beyond our purview, in Ghana) to get rid of these "troublesome" regimes. Adherents of orthodox liberalism and certain economists who claim to be Marxists have not failed to emphasize the economic failure of these experiments. Certainly, in terms of capitalist growth and profitability one cannot speak of "success," even if it is noted in passing that economic and financial pressures, to say the least, have been among the means of dissuasion most widely used by the capitalist environment. These experiments are nevertheless "contagious," and are a threat to the neocolonialist regimes. In sociopolitical terms, they apparently represent a success.

The very fact that such experiments are being undertaken, and are persisting, demonstrates that they respond to a need—a need that runs afoul of the privileged minorities' desire for comfort but which, in the absence of a social base comparable to that of more developed countries, draws strength from a profound aspiration toward national dignity and from a refusal to accept dependent status regardless of the immediate material conse-

44. Cf. A. Sékou Touré, "La Révolution et la guerre de classes: Charte de la Révolution du 16 fevrier 1975," in *Horoya* (Conakry), special issue of Feb. 16, 1975; and opening address at the May 5, 1975, session of the Central Committee of the Parti Démocratique de Guinée, *Horoya*, May 4–10, 1975.

45. Ibid., and *Horoya*, Aug. 31–Sept. 6, 1975.

46. Such is the case with Samir Amin, who sees in African "socialist" experiments (his quotation marks) nothing more than an "impasse" reflecting the "myopic vision of a small bureaucracy of the ex-colonial State"; *L'Afrique de l'Ouest bloquée* (Paris, 1971), p. 255. In the same vein, see his earlier work, *Trois Expériences africaines de developpement: Le Mali, la Guinée et le Ghana* (Paris, 1965).

quences. Sékou Touré's message in his 1958 address in reply to General de Gaulle—"We prefer poverty in liberty rather than opulence in slavery"—still rings out loud and clear, although it is too seldom heard by outside observers who have never lived in a colonized situation.

Its echo is heard, even in the neocolonial countries, particularly since the 1974 OPEC crisis as reflected in the disruption of OCAM, that relay device to perpetuate French influence now reduced to redundancy by the desertion of its members, in the nationalization of mining enterprises in Mauritania and Togo, in protests against the monetary regime, and in the withdrawal of Mauritania from the Franc Zone (initiatives of which the long-range results, in Mauritania's case, are placed in doubt by its involvement in the Sahara war).[47]

Of course, imperialism is not lacking opportunities to retrieve the situation. A withdrawal to new positions and to new formulae for neocolonial control has been anticipated and is beginning to take place. This is the "new international order" as conceived in the West, a sort of insurance policy covering the rights of the strongest in the name of "economic imperatives" and international solidarity. In other words, iternational agreements are to take the place of the discredited bilateral agreements; economic exploitation is to continue, no longer by means of the direct presence of foreign companies, but through control of markets and of technology exercized by means of "technical assistance." In the end, the question will be settled in the political, not the economic, arena. And that is why it is questionable whether the argument advanced by some,[48] who assert that socialism can triumph in the Third World countries only at the price of total isolation and severing of all relations with the capitalist market, corresponds to reality. This situation, which was imposed upon, not chosen by China (at one time), Korea, Vietnam, and Cuba, is hardly conceivable in the case of the African mini-states, whose artificial frontiers are so impossible to police. For the former countries, isolation involved as many difficulties (for example, boycott) as advantages. It would be absurd to regard it as a necessary step in the process toward socialism. It would be equally absurd to encourage countries starting down this path to confine themselves to a primitive technology on the pretext of thus escaping technological blackmail. This,

47. To obtain financial and military support from France in its conflict against the Polisario Front, Mauritania was forced to agree to indemnify the former stockholders of MIFERMA (Mines de fer de Zouérate) on draconian conditions: $90 million, of which $40 million was to be paid within two months, the remainder in five years. *Marchés tropicaux et méditerranéens*, Feb. 6, 1976, p. 312.

48. This is the thesis of Samir Amin in *L'Accumulation a l'échelle mondiale* (Paris, 1970), p. 43.

one may observe, is precisely the advice now being liberally handed out by certain international agencies (whose socialist orientation is not discernible) who counsel such countries to play host to the industries that require a high percentage of unskilled labor rejected by the developed countries.

The choice is not between access to the international market and an isolationist policy, nor between advanced technology and primitive technology; the choice is between an economic and technological policy that meets the requirements of the imperialist firms and one that meets the requirements of independent, self-centered development. Orthodox liberalism and one form of neo-Marxism both, in fact, fall victim to a sort of "economism," a unilateral determinism, forgetting that, while society's economic base (which is different from "economics" in general) plays a determining role in the course of history in the *final instance* (which excludes any unilateral determinism), the class struggle at the international level (which must be conceived in terms of polarization, not social stratification), states, politics, and ideology—all are involved as constituent elements of economic realities. That was Marx's point of view, and it is absolutely alien to any "economic fatalism"; otherwise, it would be difficult to understand how he could have ended up appealing for revolutionary action and concluding that "men make their own history" (though not in just any way whatever, or in whatever circumstances).[49]

However summarily these considerations have had to be presented within the limits set for this chapter, they lead back to the question raised at the beginning of the study: what role did economic factors play in the historical process that led the former colonies of French tropical Africa to political independence?

If one insisted upon a unilateral economic determinism, this process would remain strictly incomprehensible, for what took place in the economic field, until 1960 and beyond for most of the countries concerned, was an accentuation of "colonialist" features: increasing and continuously perfected integration and subordination to the great imperialist powers' economies—namely, their large companies—to their profit objectives, and thus to their aim of exploitation. Unilateral determinism would have to conclude that political dependence had to be reaffirmed and intensified, and that independence would therefore be incongruous (an argument often used between 1946 and 1960 under the euphemism "interdependence").[50]

49. Scrutiny from this point of view of the theses advanced by a certain number of "neo-Marxist" economists would obviously deserve more extended treatment.

50. Particularly by Ehrhardt, *Le Destin*; Moussa, *Les Chances économiques*; and R. Hoffherr, *La Cooperation économique franco-africaine* (Paris, 1958).

But this determinism is not unilateral; the "development of underdevelopment," to use A. G. Frank's phrase, produces contradictory effects. On the social and political plane it produces social, political, and ideological forces which are self-destructive:—in Marx's words, "their own gravediggers."

Independence entered into the logic neither of economic development, narrowly conceived, nor of the colonialist tutors' intentions. It asserted itself as a consequence of the dialectic of history—that is, of history's contradictory development; it was (and still is) the stake in a rearguard action on the part of imperialism in which phases of resistance alternate with phases of concession and retrieval. From this point of view, history has not ended: it is just beginning.

17. *Decolonization, Development, and Dependence: A Survey of Changing Attitudes*

DAVID FIELDHOUSE

We are all slaves of our place in history, and it is probably too soon to write anything about the two decades after 1945, when the colonial empires in Africa ended, which is likely to carry conviction a hundred years from now. The main difficulty is not lack of source material, though that is a serious one, but the fact that we do not know what happened afterward; or rather, we do not know what happened over a long enough period to validate any particular hypothesis about whether decolonization was a good or a bad thing from the standpoint of the once-colonial countries. Hindsight is, after all, critical to any worthwhile verdict on colonization, because it can only be judged by its fruits. Gibbon built the vast construct of his *Decline and Fall of the Roman Empire* on the belief, firmly held by virtually all Europeans for many centuries before he wrote, that the end of the Roman Empire had been one of the great disasters of human history. Indeed, the very terminology of European historiography, which uses concepts such as "the Dark Ages" and "the Renaissance," shows how fundamental this assumption has been. This was the long-term verdict of history, but it may well not have been conventional wisdom in the period of the decline of the Roman Empire. Must we not assume that somewhere in the abandoned empire there was an indigenous ruler who, in the style of Kwame Nkrumah, assured his subjects that since they had successfully sought the political kingdom, all else would now be added unto them?

It is not my concern to consider when and why this retrospective change of heart took place. Nor do I necessarily accept the premise that the fall of Rome brought unrelieved loss to her former subjects. I am even prepared to accept the ingenious argument put forward in John Strachey's *The End of Empire*[1] that the Roman Empire had become technologically muscle-bound by its social and economic structure, so that progress eventually

1. London, 1959.

became contingent on a fundamental socioeconomic change. My aim is simply to establish the starting point of my argument: that what one thinks of imperialism, colonialism, and their demise is very largely a function of time and place; that our perspectives are still too short to justify any convincing verdicts or forecasts; and that it is in any case likely that fashions among historians of decolonization will change as time makes it possible to see new aspects of the process and its consequences.

This caution is more than usually necessary when dealing with the economic aspects of any period of modern imperial or postimperial history, because conventional approaches to the subject have changed so fast that a historian who busies himself with laboriously trying to discover what happened in one small corner of the colonial or ex-colonial world is in danger of finding, when he has at last assembled his material, that the whole intellectual landscape has changed while his eyes were fixed on his sources. This matters, not because the historian should concern himself with every transient historiographical fad, but because it is part of his business to attempt to answer the questions currently being asked. If he attempts to ignore the challenge of contemporary theorists, he is in danger of being seen as some academic Rip van Winkle who wakes up after twenty years mumbling answers to questions posed so long ago that no one knows what he is talking about. One must, therefore, try to keep pace with the questions but answer them with decent reticence.

Yet even if the student of decolonization constantly reformulates the questions he is attempting to answer he is still left in an insoluble dilemma. It has always been one of the special features of the historiography of imperialism that supporters and critics of empire alike have made sweeping generalizations about its economic consequences, few of which could satisfactorily be verified or disproved by concrete evidence available at the time. Hackluyt in the later sixteenth century and mercantilist writers such as Davenant and Defoe a century later predicted vast benefits from empire which no one has ever successfully quantified. In 1776 Adam Smith argued that formal empire involved losses to the metropolitan states, but neither he nor any one else has ever measured these. In the age of "the new imperialism" Hobson and the neo-Marxists made far-reaching allegations about the economic causes and consequences of the new colonialism in Africa which are still a matter of debate seventy years later.

It is, therefore, not surprising that most of the literature on the economic aspects of decolonization in modern Africa should be cast in the same prophetic mold, or that the questions asked could not be answered by any historian at present. Two of these are particularly important and exceptionally difficult to answer. First, whether the metropolitan states chose to end formal colonial rule during these two decades because they then for the first time felt confident that the European economic stake in Africa would be safe without a continued political presence. Second, whether the consequence of decolonization for the new states is or will be unprecedented affluence or continued poverty. The first question cannot be answered with any confidence yet because neither the public nor the private papers of those directly involved in the decision-making process are yet generally open to historians, though by now enough information has been leaked or gleaned for a reasonable preliminary picture to be sketched.[2] But the second question remains almost totally unanswerable. There are short-run indications of trends on which forecasters avidly pounce; but no one will be able to give a historically acceptable answer for several decades, when medium-term developments can be examined. Until then, the hypothecators will hold the field almost unchallenged, just as those who explained "the new imperialism" in unqualified and unquantified economic terms were able to do from the 1900s to the 1950s.

The aim of this chapter is, therefore, not to answer but to pose questions: or, more precisely, to survey some of the contrasting attitudes to the economic causes and consequences of decolonization before, during, and after the event. The value of doing this is that it underlines the variety of concepts in play and how these have evolved over time. At the end an attempt will be made to sharpen the issues still in dispute and to underline those issues on which future historians with sufficient evidence at their finger tips will have to make up their minds.

Though some might dislike the bedfellows allotted to them, commentators on the economic prospects and consequences of decolonization since the 1940s can arbitrarily be divided into two groups and labeled "optimists" and "pessimists." The line of demarcation is not primarily chronological, for there were people of both persuasions at all times. Nevertheless, there are grounds for saying that optimism was predominant until some time in the 1960s, but that the pessimists then broke through and held the initiative in the early 1980s. It is, therefore, reasonable to begin this survey with the optimists, who fall into two quite different categories, linked only by a common belief after about 1940 that the "backward" colonial territories of Africa could achieve real economic development. As to how and why this was to happen the two sides disagreed fundamentally. The first, notably

2. The publication, after this chapter was written, of D. J. Morgan's *The Official History of Colonial Development*, 5 vols. (London, 1980) has provided much valuable new evidence on this question and on other topics discussed here.

imperial administrators and imperialist politicians, believed development would and could take place because the colonies were part of a now beneficent empire and because they were confident that European rule would last long enough for the foundations of economic growth to be firmly laid. Those on the other side took a diametrically opposed view. They were optimistic precisely because after 1945 they at last saw the possibility that alien rule, which they regarded as a major obstacle to economic development in Africa, would be ended within the foreseeable future. For them the end of empire would mark the start of growth. Let us consider each group in turn, starting with the imperialists. For reasons of space, consideration will be given mainly to the British case, with only a short comment on French official attitudes to colonial development after 1945.

In British official circles, awareness of the need to undertake economic development in the African colonies seems to have grown up only in the later 1930s, and adoption of the development idea was perhaps symbolized by the confidential report made to the Colonial Office in 1940 by Lord Hailey.[3] Behind this, and largely accounting for the new concern with colonial development as an end in itself rather than as a means to benefit the British economy, lay the terrible experience of the 1930s. Early in that decade most public development schemes had had to be put aside because colonial revenues could not afford to service the loans required, even with imperial help provided under the 1929 Colonial Development Act; and very little new private investment took place before the war because low export prices for commodities and the consequential reduction in the domestic market for industrial products inhibited foreign capital. This standstill, coupled with evidence of intensified poverty in many colonies, generated in London a bad imperial conscience, possibly for the first time since before 1914. By 1940 the Colonial Office had responded by reorganizing itself, and also the Colonial Service, to plan and execute economic development projects; and the Colonial Development and Welfare Act of 1940 promised a substantial increase in British grants and loans after the war. Thus the era of colonial economic development by state initiative had been officially born, though the infant was kept under wraps until the war was well over and Britain had resources available to give substance to the new idea.

The age of official optimism lasted from the early 1940s well into the 1960s. It would be impossible here to trace its evolution, but four important though often contradictory aspects must be noted. First, the British

3. The following account relies on J. Michael Lee, *Colonial Development and Good Government* (Oxford, 1967).

characteristically refused to think in terms of overall plans or central control. Although much more British money was made available by the British Treasury than would have seemed conceivable in the 1930s—perhaps £506 million in grants and loans between 1946 and 1964[4]—its use depended on planning by the individual colonial governments. Since these usually lacked men qualified to plan economic development as a whole, their projects, even when obligatorily formulated as ten-year plans, tended to resemble highly diversified shopping lists. This led naturally to a second feature of official development policy—its emphasis on "infrastructure" rather than the means of production. State enterprise in colonial Africa had always concentrated on transport, education, health, electricity supplies, agricultural improvement, and so on; and although a lot more money was now available, it was for the most part spent on more of the same things. Hence, of the expenditure approved in the ten-year development plans to 1950, 21 percent was allocated to communications, 43 percent to social services, and only 26 percent to what was broadly described as "economic potential."[5] The rest of the field was left almost entirely to private enterprises.

It is true that several colonies set up local development boards or corporations, for example, the Nigerian Local Development Board, the Gold Coast Corporation, and the Kenya Industrial and Commercial Development Corporation. It is also true that these and similar organizations invested in or lent money to a wide variety of local productive enterprises, partly to stimulate indigenous local entrepreneurs, partly to gain a share in the profits of European-owned businesses. Some even took an active part in running manufacturing enterprise. But these were marginal to governmental economic activity. For the most part, colonial development continued until the end to imply a partnership between a state which provided as much behind-the-scenes stimulus as it could afford and a private sector which invested and produced as much as it found profitable.

The third and paradoxical aspect of this approach to African development after 1940 was that, for the first decade and more, there was a real danger that colonial development would be made a tool of metropolitan welfare. This had been the underlying assumption of most imperialists in the 1920s and the motive behind the 1929 Colonial Development Act. In 1940 Hailey had emphasized the importance of burying this concept; yet during the war and the postwar currency crisis, British officialdom slid rather too easily

4. For the basis of this calculation, see my paper "The Economic Exploitation of Africa," in Prosser Gifford and Wm. Roger Louis, eds., *France and Britain in Africa* (New Haven, 1971), p. 632.

5. Lee, *Colonial Development*, p. 113.

into assuming that the war was being fought in the interests of colonial subjects as much as of those in Britain, so that all could be called on to make sacrifices. This gave rise to the wartime Produce Control Boards in Africa, which after 1945 often became permanent Marketing Boards with far-reaching economic consequences for those territories.[6] More serious, the war produced bulk-buying of tropical commodities by the Ministry of Food at prices which tended to subsidize the British consumer at the expense of the colonial producer. After 1945 these attitudes and practices were carried into the postwar world, ironically by a Labour government pledged to work for the welfare of the colonial peoples. Ministry of Food contracts with the colonies continued well into the 1950s. Control of colonial money supply by the various currency boards seemed designed to force the colonies to lend Britain the large sums required to be lodged in sterling securities as cover for their coin and note issues at very low rates of interest.[7] The sterling area hard-currency pool appeared to deny dollars to those colonies which earned them, and Britain tightly restricted supplies of scarce commodities such as cement and steel. Most notorious, though merely an extension of these assumptions, was the Tanganyika groundnut scheme, on which, so the then Minister of Food, John Strachey, told men working on the project, "depends more than any other single factor whether the harassed housewives of Great Britain get more margarine, cooking fats and soap in the reasonably near future."[8]

Nothing did more to discredit the motives of British officialdom in promoting economic change in Africa; and critics might well argue that if imperial economic integration of this kind had proved more successful, Britain would have been less ready to decolonize. Fortunately for both parties, the government's admission in 1951 that the groundnut scheme was a failure also marked the beginning of the end of this postwar neomercantilism, and during the next decade the Conservative government gradually wound up most of the bulk-buying and other schemes which had attempted to harness colonial production to British needs. In the end the only important metropolitan organization that continued to play an active

6. See, for example, Peter T. Bauer, *West African Trade* (Cambridge, 1954), and Gerald K. Helleiner, *Peasant Agriculture, Government, and Economic Growth* (Homewood, Ill., 1966).

7. For surveys of British currency systems, see W. T. Newlyn and D. C. Rowan, *Money and Banking in Colonial Africa* (Oxford, 1954), and A. R. Conan, *The Sterling Area* (London, 1952). For French policy, see François Bloch-Lainé, *La Zone Franc* (Paris, 1956), and Michel Leduc, *Les Institutions monétaires Africaines, Pays Francophones* (Paris, 1965).

8. Quoted S. A. Haque Haqqi, *The Colonial Policy of the Labour Government* (Aligarh, U.P., 1960), p. 211. On the scheme as a whole, see S. Herbert Frankel, *The Economic Impact on Under-developed Societies* (Oxford, 1953).

role in the colonies was the Colonial (later Commonwealth) Development Corporation, established in 1948.[9] The CDC eventually played a valuable role in establishing and running a wide range of productive ventures in the colonies and ex-colonies, assessing opportunities from their standpoint rather than that of Britain or the corporation itself as a business enterprise. But it always operated on a relatively small scale, and until 1959 was hamstrung by its legal inability to raise money on the open market as well as borrow from the British government.

These were significant features of the British approach to economic development in Africa. But the most important single reason why the official classes were optimistic, indeed confident, that they could get development under way successfully was that they believed they knew the right way to do so and had ample time to carry the thing through. Behind the piecemeal and self-help approach already mentioned there lay a profound belief that the key to successful modernization lay in progressively restructuring African society but not making abrupt or radical changes. The roots of this idea lay far back in the missionary past, but it had recently received strong support from anthropologists such as Malinowski and a vast amount of commissioned "social research" undertaken during and after the war. All emphasized the importance of evolution rather than revolution, of helping "primitive" peoples to move at their own pace along lines pioneered by Europeans. In political terms, after 1945 this meant evolving new and more liberal forms of local and even central government in the African colonies from existing traditional authorities or legislative councils. In economic terms, it implied helping Africans to improve production techniques gradually and to take their first steps as industrial or commercial capitalists—for example, by milling cotton seed in Uganda or taking over the middleman functions previously performed by the big trading companies in West Africa. This was believed to be the only safe way for Africa to develop: there were no short cuts to growth or modernization.

In retrospect, it now seems incredible that in the early 1950s the British official mind still believed that there was time to carry through the economic development of Africa by this means and at this very slow speed. Yet it was so, and British optimism about African prospects can only be understood as resting on the assumption that, as one senior official put it, they had "an infinity of time." This, in turn, underlines the essential point that British development policy was not seen in the context of decolonization at

9. The best account of its activities is in Sir William Rendell, *The History of the Commonwealth Development Corporation* (London, 1976). See also Morgan, *Official History of Colonial Development*, vols. 2 and 4.

all. Lee has emphasized that the basic assumption of the 1940s was that "power could only be transferred legitimately if it were given to an experienced ruling class," one, moreover, which "had a faith in good government" as the British construed this term.[10] Given the almost total absence of modern forms of representative government and the virtual exclusion of Africans from the higher levels of the civil and military services in the later 1940s, this implied that independence might take place in the 1970s or 1980s, almost certainly not before. It follows that the British did not decolonize when, and because, they had restructured the economies of their African colonies to the point at which formal rule could safely be withdrawn. Modernization as they understood it had scarcely begun when the empire was wound up.

This is not the place to consider when and why the timetable was changed so radically: Lee suggests that it was in the mid-1950s, culminating in decisions taken in 1959. The important point so far concerning British attitudes to African economic and social development is that colonialism was unable to carry through that policy of social and moral reform in which officialdom had placed its hopes. Withdrawal thus forced the British into a new form of optimism—that the succeeding regimes would, given sufficient technical and financial assistance, be able and willing to carry through the process the British had begun, and along essentially the same lines. This, of course, was a forlorn hope. Imperialists may have believed that they had time to spare, but the new rulers of Africa knew that they had not. Political pressure to produce quick economic results would have forced them to innovate even if their own inclinations had not. During the 1960s those who had once run the African empire and believed in their mission to develop it continued to proclaim their faith in the will and ability of the new rulers to carry on the old policies. They preached the importance of aid and the value of Commonwealth links. But as the new regimes one by one adopted totally different policies and evolved political styles which did not conform to the traditional concept of "good government," optimism waned and the rhetoric was muted. By the 1970s few of the one-time rulers of empire seemed to retain any hope that decolonization would result in the type of economic and social development they had projected, and many covertly joined the ranks of the pessimists.

On the other side of the channel, French officials also seem to have become optimistic about the future of Francophone Africa in the mid-1940s. Their ideas and policies cannot be described in detail, but essentially the French approach to colonial development was highly structured,

10. Lee, *Colonial Development*, p. 195.

legalistic, and centralized, and French aid cost a lost more than that of Britain.[11] Above all the system aimed without embarrassment at making French colonial and ex-colonial territories closely integrated with France and the European Economic Community (EEC). In this they were remarkably successful, and hence to Frenchmen decolonization might well seem merely one step along an already planned route leading the African territories to development by means of close cooperation with metropolitan capitalism. For the same reason, contemporary Marxists and later dependency theorists were prone to argue that decolonization had done little or nothing to reduce the dependence of Francophone Africa on the capitalist metropolis.

The second general category of optimists had only two things in common—their optimism about the economic potential of Africa and their belief that the end of colonialism was either necessary or at least not harmful to economic development. This miscellany of people could be considered under many heads, but for practical purposes they can be divided into three: the colonial nationalists, European humanitarians, and the development economists. Let us consider, before looking at each approach in turn, why all of these tended to regard colonialism as a bar to effective development.

The main reason was, of course, that the record seemed proof that the institutions of empire were an obstruction to progress in that they subordinated the colonial interest to that of the metropolis and metropolitan capitalism. Despite the high promises held out by British and French politicians and publicists from the beginning of the twentieth century, most colonial economies seemed to have stagnated. The volume of trade had indeed increased in many parts of Africa in the 1920s, and this reflected larger production of many existing export staples and the establishment of new trades. But the ground won had been more than lost in the early 1930s, with disastrous social and economic consequences; and it was now widely accepted that there was a secular deterioration in the terms of trade between Africa (among other primary producing countries) and the developed world which was intrinsic to this economic relationship. Thus, insofar as colonialism had based its claims to foster colonial economic growth on expanding the commodity export trade through an open econ-

11. For contemporary analyses and prescriptions, see Bloch-Lainé, *La Zone Franc*; J.-J. Poquin, *Les Relations économiques extérieures des pays d'Afrique Noire de l'Union Française, 1925–1955* (Paris, 1957); Leduc, *Les Institutions monétaires;* P. F. Gonidec, *Droit d'Outre-Mer*, 2 vols. (Paris, 1959).

omy, the 1930s seemed to discredit the whole system. The generation of Europeans and Africans who were most vociferous critics of empire in the 1940s and 1950s had mostly grown to maturity in that terrible decade after the slump, and few of them waited to see whether post-1945 developments would affect this initial judgment.

Economic failure in the African empires prompted investigation of the instruments of imperial economic policy, and few of these withstood scrutiny. Tariff policy was a first target. In so far as it was protectionist and preferential (as in most of French Africa and to a lesser extent in British South, Central, and East Africa), it was criticized as deliberately benefiting the metropolis at the expense of the subject peoples. Whereas Africans were forced to pay more for privileged French or British imports than they would have paid for Japanese or other goods, there was little or no compensating preference for their commodity exports to the metropolis. Conversely, the free-trade colonies of British West Africa complained that industrial development there was virtually impossible because of the lack of protection for "infant industries" and the imposition of revenue duties on imported raw materials and intermediates. Monetary policy also seemed designed to obstruct economic growth. By the 1930s all European currencies were fiduciary, and governments had begun to use money supply as an instrument of economic policy. But until the eve of independence, all British African colonies were virtually gold-based, because the colonial sterling exchange system forced them to cover their issues with sterling securities. For their part, French colonial currencies were tied to the metropolitan franc, though after 1940 the CFA franc used in colonial Africa had a different value. By the early 1940s critics in Britain were pointing out that these currency systems not only denied the colonies the freedom to use money supply as a countercyclical device but had a positively deflationary effect—an unforgivable offense to men still concentrating their attention on how to defeat deflation. Thus, a generation which had just adopted Keynes's *General Theory* as economic gospel inevitably regarded conservative imperial policies on money, together with the absence of colonial central banks and the foreign monopoly of commercial banking in the colonies, as evidence that economic growth was held back by archaic metropolitan attitudes.

Indeed, from the standpoint of the 1940s and 1950s there were few aspects of imperial policy in colonial Africa that seemed acceptable to advanced thinkers. Systems of government largely excluded Africans, and those who were allowed into the hallowed circle were the least progressive—traditional chiefs in British Africa, official administrators in French Africa. Their function was to confirm and collaborate, not to decide or act. To the growing number of educated Africans, and also to their liberal allies in Europe, such limitations seemed by the 1940s not only to deny Africans human rights but also to weaken the political will of the subordinate society to struggle for economic growth. Educational policy also was thought to be far too limited in the numbers taught and the level they could attain. Medical facilities were totally inadequate. Transportation policy was hamstrung by the precedence given to those railways which linked the ports with the areas producing export commodities. Taxation was regressive, putting most of the burden on the poor through import duties and hut or poll taxes rather than on income or corporate taxation. Yet all these were part of that infrastructure which, so the imperial administrators claimed, had to be developed as the seedbed for broader economic growth. If these things were done incompetently, it was not surprising that the colonial governments seemed unable or unwilling to draw up serious plans for economic growth. They thought small and piecemeal: a bridge here, a wharf there, a few more miles of road or rail. But where was anything to compare with Russia's five-year plans and collectivization or even America's New Deal? The logical conclusion was that neither imperial government nor their capitalist allies seriously wanted to see Africa developed. Presumably, both preferred that it should continue to supply cheap raw materials and a captive market. Colonialism thus meant indefinite stagnation and possibly even immiserization.

So much seems to have been common ground among those various groups in Europe, America, and Africa who were demanding the end of empire in the 1940s and 1950s as a prerequisite to economic development. This is not the place to consider whether their analysis of cause and effect was correct, though one evident weakness was to assume that imperial policies and results characteristic of the slump and the Second World War would necessarily be typical of the postwar period. The important fact is that each group was optimistic about the future economic development of Africa precisely because they believed that present ills were primarily the result of colonialism. Pull that tooth and the pain would disappear. Let us examine in more detail how each of the groups defined above regarded the opportunities of decolonization.

The nationalist politicians had no doubt that the end of formal empire would lead to immense and immediate progress of all kinds. Kwame Nkrumah's much quoted advice to fellow Africans who had still to achieve independence to "seek ye first the political kingdom and all else shall be added unto you" was accepted by very many without reservations. Correctly interpreted, of course, this did not mean that independence would make everyone rich. The underlying truth was that the end of alien rule would give the new rulers control of all the available instruments for creating wealth. With the charisma to which only the founders of a new country can aspire, supported by the political organizations they had forged in the struggle against the imperialists, men such as Nkrumah, Kaunda, Nyerere, Houphouët-Boigny, Sékou Touré, and Kenyatta were in an immensely stronger position to undertake radical reform than any colonial government before them or, for that matter, than their successors would be later, when the novelty of independence had worn off. Certainly this was the conventional view of most foreign observers of widely differing political standpoints in the 1950s and early 1960s, and in principle at least it would be difficult to show that it was false.[12] Conversely, if the more optimistic of these early expectations have since been disappointed, the question must be whether they were unrealistic from the start or whether the promise was stunted by forces which only became significant after independence was achieved.

The second group of optimists about the prospects after decolonization was less homogeneous, and their optimism was generally short-lived. They were the liberal humanitarians and moderate socialists of Europe and America, people like Fenner Brockway, who had been advising African nationalists for many years, Dame Margery Perham, who had done as much as anyone in the thirty years after 1930 to act as a watchdog for colonial interests, and John Strachey, a liberal social democrat on the left of the Labour Party.[13] These and many others who had criticized various aspects of formal empire believed that decolonization was not only morally necessary but also that it provided an opportunity for a radical new departure; and, while fully aware of the many serious obstacles to progress, they seemed to have no doubt that if the developed world gave sufficient help, African independence could lead to African opulence. Thus Strachey, writing in 1959, could borrow the current ideas of the development economists. To achieve growth the new states would have to undertake an immense task of social engineering, destroying "peasant agriculture" and replacing it by "a new agricultural system which will produce more food with a far smaller labour force," and "putting the millions of ex-peasants thus released on the work of building the basis of an industrial system." The result would be that, "if . . . the efforts of the peoples of the underdeveloped world are well directed and successful, and if their self-discipline

12. There is a vast literature on African nationalism. See, for example, Thomas Hodgkin, *Nationalism in Colonial Africa* (London, 1956), and Basil Davidson, *The African Awakening* (London, 1955).

13. See, for example, Fenner Brockway, *The Colonial Revolution* (London, 1973); Margery Perham, *The Colonial Reckoning* (London, 1961); Strachey, *The End of Empire*.

and capacity for self-denial holds firm, their absolute standard of life will be slowly rising." To accelerate this growth and to check the tendency toward a widening gap between rich and poor countries, all that was needed was for the rich countries to "provide that relatively small but decisive quantity of capital which will overcome the initial inertia of economies which have been virtually static for millennia. What has to be provided is the 'assisted take-off,' without which the underdeveloped world can never under democratic institutions get under way at all."[14] Such was the innocent faith of contemporary idealists who, in that first dawn of independent Africa, could still believe that to be free was heaven.

Their optimism was, of course, to a large extent based on the work of the third and last category of generally anticolonial optimists to be considered here, the professional economists. These were, by the later 1940s, for the first time seriously applying the standard tools of economic analysis to the problems of the undeveloped—or, as they were euphemistically called, "less developed" or "developing"—countries. Most economists tended to be critical of colonialism because they accepted (some without sufficient question) the fact that the colonial powers were unable or unwilling to apply the proper economic policies in the colonies. Conversely, they can be called optimists because most believed that their science provided the key to developing even the least promising country. By the late 1940s an increasing number of economists were developing methods for analyzing the causes of poverty and prescribing remedies for it, and in the next decade "development economics" became a major academic industry. Special research institutes were established; academic practitioners came to be in great demand throughout the world; and international organizations set up major research and propaganda institutions such as the Organization for European Cooperation and Development and the United Nations Commission on Trade and Development. The age of faith in growth had been born.

Not all its priests, of course, preached the same dogma, nor were their theologies equally sophisticated.[15] Possibly the best known, because it was

14. Strachey, *The End of Empire*, pp. 310, 312, 316.

15. The literature is, of course, too extensive to list. Some of the better known and most influential books were: W. Arthur Lewis, *Theory of Economic Growth* (London, 1954); Gunnar Myrdal, *Economic Theory and Underdeveloped Regions* (London, 1957); Ragnar Nurske, *Patterns of Trade and Development* (Stockholm, 1959); Walt Rostow, *The Stages of Economic Growth* (Cambridge, 1960); S. David Neumark, *Foreign Trade and Economic Development in Africa* (Stanford, 1964); Hla Myint, *The Economics of Developing Countries* (New York, 1965); Ian Little and Jim Mirrlees, *Manual of Industrial Project Analysis in Developing Countries*, vol. 2 (Paris, 1969); Ian Little, Tibor Scitovsky, and Maurice Scott, *Industry and Trade in Some Developing Countries* (London, 1970).

evocatively written, general study that laymen could understand was W. W. Rostow's *The Stages of Economic Growth* (1960), which argued broadly that every economy could "take off" into "sustained growth," provided a defined level of investment could be reached and maintained. Rostow held that many less-developed countries would need considerable external aid to achieve this rate of investment; but an essentially optimistic strand in his argument was that the new states of Africa and Asia were following known and proved paths toward affluence: Britain, Europe, and North America had passed that way before, and where they had gone Africa and the rest could go also.

Rostow was acting as a publicist. At the other end of the spectrum were a multitude of detailed reports, often made by visiting experts or teams of specialists at the invitation of African governments, who analyzed specific local conditions and made broad policy recommendations. One of the earlier and better known of these was the *Report on Industrialisation and the Gold Coast* made by W. A. Lewis in 1952 at the invitation of Nkrumah, who had just become the first prime minister of the colony, and published as a government paper in Accra in 1953. The *Report* is valuable not only because it had a considerable influence on Gold Coast policies up to about 1961, but more generally because it sets out sober arguments of considerable force which, in the event, few newly independent governments could afford to accept. The concluding paragraphs are as follows.

> *Conclusions and Recommendations*
>
> 252. Measures to increase the manufacture of commodities for the home market deserve support, but are not of number one priority. A small programme is justified, but a major programme in this sphere should wait until the country is better prepared to carry it. The main obstacle is the fact that agricultural productivity per man is stagnant. This has three effects. First, the market for manufactures is small, and is not expanding year by year, except to the extent of population growth; consequently it would take large subsidies to make possible the employment of a large number of people in manufacturing. Secondly it is not possible to get ever larger savings out of the farmers, year by year, to finance industrialisation, without at the same time reducing their standard of living; hence industrialisation has to depend on foreign capital, and large amounts of capital for this purpose could be attracted only on unfavourable terms. And thirdly, agriculture, because it is stagnant, does not release labour year by year; there is a shortage of labour in the Gold Coast which rapid industrialisation would aggravate.
>
> 253. Number one priority is therefore a concentrated attack on the

system of growing food in the Gold Coast, so as to set in motion an ever increasing productivity. This is the way to provide the market, the capital, and the labour for industrialisation.

254. Priority number two is to improve the public services. To do this will reduce the cost of manufacturing in the Gold Coast, and will thus automatically attract new industries, without the government having to offer special favours.

255. Very many years will have elapsed before it becomes economical for the government to transfer any large part of its resources towards industrialisation, and away from the more urgent priorities of agricultural productivity and the public services. Meanwhile, it should support such industrialisation as can be done on terms favourable to the country. That is to say, it should support industries which can be established without large or continuing subsidies, and whose proprietors are willing to train and employ Africans in senior posts. Because industrialisation is a cumulative process (the more industries you have already, the more new industries you attract) it takes time to lay the foundations of industrialisation, and it would be wrong to postpone the establishment of any industry which could flourish after a short teething period.

That *Report* was characteristic of the hopeful but cautious early 1950s. A quarter of a century later much of the general optimism had been dissipated by the apparent inability of successor governments to achieve sustained growth by these methods. This left the way open to the pessimists, who could claim that the hope had always been an illusion under capitalist conditions. Yet classical development theory of this type has not in any sense been discredited. A series of studies made in the 1960s under the aegis of OECD (Organization for Economic Cooperation and Development), which included Brazil, Mexico, India, Pakistan, Taiwan, and the Philippines, and whose findings were summed up in a single volume by Little, Scitovsky, and Scott, *Industry and Trade in Some Developing Countries* (London, 1970), made it clear that where development strategies had failed it was almost always because of incomplete or improper application of essentially sound general principles: for instance, excessive protection of local industry, obstructive bureaucratic controls, political weakness, overemphasis on industrial investment at the expense of the agricultural sector, corruption, and so on. Although these studies did not include any African country, because they were designed to concentrate on economies in a slightly more advanced state than any tropical African countries had then reached, their prescriptions and warnings are equally relevant to Africa in the 1980s.

One factor more than any other divided the optimistic economists already considered from the pessimists still to come, and that was their contrasting view of the role of the state in the process of economic growth. To both, of course, state action was fundamental; but whereas the optimists were prepared to believe that the governments of independent Africa and Asia, once free from colonialism, could and probably would adopt enlightened policies in the public interest, the pessimists almost without exception denied this possibility. The reason was, of course, that most of the pessimists were Marxists, who had never accepted that governments in developed countries pursue policies in the general interest as contrasted with what benefits capitalists, and who have consistently refused to believe that liberal democratic regimes in less developed countries have either the power or the will to stand up to international capitalism. African independence must therefore inevitably result in continued exploitation of the masses within each society and of the less developed country as a whole by international capitalism. These general beliefs have not changed substantially over the period covered by this survey; but because there has been a very significant change in the style and sophistication with which it is expressed, a somewhat artificial distinction will be made here between pessimistic Marxists writing before the early 1960s and the rapidly expanding cohorts of those writing since the later 1950s, who have developed still more pessimistic concepts of underdevelopment and dependence.

The early Marxist writings on imperialism are too well known to require exposition; but it is necessary to emphasize that these left large conceptual gaps which contemporary underdevelopment theorists are attempting to fill. From the early days of the twentieth century, those who took part in the great socialist debate over the nature of imperialism set out to demonstrate that the impact of the capitalist West on the less developed world must be fundamentally harmful. The difficulties they encountered were, of course, that there was no clear theory of colonialism in Marx's writings, and that much of what he did say could be construed to mean that, while foreign capital would exploit and destroy, it would also stimulate growth. In an overquoted passage written in 1853 about India, Marx predicted that "the railway system will become, in India, truly the forerunner of modern industry"; and in somewhat obscure language he seemed to imply that this would lead to the restructuring of the Indian economy, the emergence of a "hindoo" bourgeoisie, and so eventually to a cumulative cycle of reproduction.[16] Rudolf Hilferding also was prepared to admit in 1910 that foreign

16. S. Averini, ed., *Karl Marx on Colonialism and Modernisation* (New York, 1969), p. 136.

capital might generate rapid economic development in less developed countries and that the subject peoples, once given the means of achieving their own liberation through industrialization, would attempt to throw off alien rule, compelling capitalism increasingly to use force to maintain physical control.[17] Rosa Luxemburg, writing in 1913, had no doubt that foreign capital would exploit native peoples; but her *Accumulation of Capital* was long regarded as heretical by orthodox Marxists. And unfortunately, Lenin, in his *Imperialism: The Highest Stage of Capitalism* (1916) failed to provide an authoritative ruling on the issue.

Later Marxists thus had considerable difficulty in establishing a proper approach to the impact of imperialism in the less developed world. Paul Sweezy's *The Theory of Capitalist Development*, first published in 1942 and long regarded as a standard exposition of correct Marxist-Leninist views, could do little more than project the conventional life cycle of capitalism in Europe into the colonial situation. He did, however, add two concepts. The first, taken from the standard historiography of Indian nationalism, was that industrialization destroyed "handicraft producers." This caused "a swelling of the ranks of the peasantry, increased pressure on the land, and a deterioration of the productivity and living standards of the agricultural masses," an assumption clearly based on dogma rather than Indian history. Second, and consequentially, "the colonial economy stagnates, and living conditions for the great majority of the people tend to become worse rather than better. All classes of the colonial population, with the exception of the landlords and few relatively small groups which are in effect agents of imperialist rule, are therefore thrown into the struggle for national independence." Beyond that point Sweezy could not go because he had no model: there had been no successful rebellion in a European possession in modern times by 1942. He therefore had to use his imagination. The colonial bourgeoisie would lead the struggle to independence in alliance with the "colonial working class." But the bourgeoisie would not be able to make up its mind whether finally to break with its imperialist allies, so the working class, in alliance with "the more advanced sections of the peasantry" take the lead, and the colonial nationalists make common cause with the workers in the more developed world.[18]

That was as far as Sweezy's vision could take him. He had pinpointed several of the most commonly held Marxist assumptions about the impact

17. Rudolf Hilferding, *Das Finanzkapital* (**1910**), *Marx-Studien* (Vienna, 1923), 3: 386–407.

18. Paul M. Sweezy, *The Theory of Capitalist Development* (1942; London, 1946), pp. 326–28.

of capitalism in the colonies—notably the immiserization argument—and had emphasized the dilemma of the indigenous bourgeois, torn between his nationalism and his class interest, which was to form a fruitful theme in later left-wing thought. But the absence of a comprehensive rationale of decolonization until the later 1950s or early 1960s meant that Marxist historians of Africa had to make do with a limited range of not very relevant general dogmas and to interpret African history along lines more suited to Europe. Their main tools were monopoly capitalism, extraction of surplus value, the use of force to exploit indigenous commodity resources, unequal development, and the pauperization of the indigenous artisan and peasant classes, to which some added the principle of the adverse terms of trade between more and less developed economies. As handled by Jean Suret-Canale in his masterly pioneering work, *Afrique Noire: L'Ere Coloniale*,[19] the general conclusion was that colonialism had meant the immiserization of the continent. West Africa was dying of declining fertility resulting from exploitative production of unsuitable export crops, lack of productive capital, adverse secular trends in the terms of trade, heavy taxation of the poor, and the activities of foreign monopoly capital. Salvation lay in industrialization and the use of agricultural techniques specifically adapted to African conditions, neither of which was conceivable under colonial rule. But Suret-Canale is a historian rather than a theorist, and it is impossible to deduce, from that work at least, whether, writing at the end of the colonial era, he had much hope that an independent Francophone Africa would be able to provide itself with the tools for sustained growth.

It is, in fact, reasonable to suggest that until some point in the late 1950s, Marxists had not yet developed a mature critique of the long-run impact of monopoly capitalism on the peoples of the less-developed world. Franz Fanon's *Peau Noire, Masques Blancs*, which discussed the dependency complex of colonized peoples, came out in 1952, but his much more influential *Les Damnés de la Terre* was not published until 1961.[20] Marxists were agreed that colonialism meant exploitation by monopoly capitalism supported by state power, but so far there was little attempt to distinguish the character of this exploitation in the colonies from that in Europe and America. The workers were workers, the peasants, peasants, and a black bourgeois virtually interchangeable with his opposite number in Europe. The eventual revolution would come as a joint or parallel effort by all these classes. Few, if any, theorists were concerned with what would happen if

19. Paris, 1964. Published in English as *French Colonialism in Tropical Africa* (London, 1971).

20. Published in English as *The Wretched of the Earth* (London, 1965).

nationalist revolutions were successful in ending formal colonial rule but did not lead almost immediately to socialist revolutions. Evidence of what this intermediate condition might be like was in fact accumulating in India and other parts of Asia where this situation had developed after 1947, but it was not until the 1960s that serious studies of the long-run consequences of foreign capital operating in independent ex-colonial countries became available.[21]

The way was therefore open for a new and far more comprehensive approach to the whole problem, one that would analyze the dependence of postcolonial societies on foreign monopoly capital. Who can claim parentage is a matter of debate; but 1957 has a fair claim to being the year of birth, for it saw the publication both of Gunnar Myrdal's *Economic Theory and Underdeveloped Regions* and of Paul Baran's *The Political Economy of Growth.*[22] What characterized these writers and books was not so much any particular new element or dogma—indeed, almost every specific idea in this whole canon of underdevelopment theory can be traced back to some earlier source—but the fact that they began to take a total view of the relations between less and more developed states, and evolved explanatory hypotheses that embraced all aspects of economic, social, and political life. Myrdal, for example, described a process of cumulative polarization between those countries which industrialized first, and the rest, in which the developed countries exploited the less developed by destroying their handicrafts, removing their accumulated wealth, and forcing them to provide the raw materials needed by foreign industry at prices held artificially low by monopoly capital. Because he rejected the Marxist-Leninist view that a substantial capital investment was actually made in these poor countries, Myrdal could also discount any possibility that the poor countries could make real economic progress; and by ignoring the distinction between formal colony and economic dependency, he could generalize his hypothesis throughout the entire world, applying it as much to ex-colonies as to countries still under alien rule.

Baran also took a total view of the nature of underdevelopment. Its origin he ascribed, in conventional neo-Marxist terms, to the historical process whereby Europeans used an accidental and temporary power advantage to remove a great deal of their accumulated wealth from countries such as India, to destroy indigenous systems of manufacture, and to force the natives to produce primary export commodities. Thereafter, although

21. See, for example, Michael Kidron, *Foreign Investment in India* (London, 1965).

22. New York, 1957. Colin Leys, *Underdevelopment in Kenya* (London, 1975), suggests on page 4 that Baran "has good claims to be regarded as the most influential founder of contemporary 'underdevelopment theory.'"

some of the locally generated economic surplus was diverted into genuine investments, such as communications, this only stimulated the mercantile capitalists and indigenous bourgeoisie with strong vested interests in protecting the existing economic system, who used their wealth to maintain high standards of living rather than to make fruitful investments in local industry. Locally generated capital did not, therefore, lay sufficient foundations for sustained economic growth. On the other hand, Baran went on to reject the traditional Marxist belief that foreign capitalists had made a substantial investment of "surplus" European or American capital in backward countries. In fact, he wrote, "The increase of Western assets in the underdeveloped world is only partly due to capital exports in the strict sense of the term; it is primarily the result of the reinvestment abroad of some of the economic surplus secured abroad."[23] Hence the backwardness of the underdeveloped world as a whole was due to an imposed inversion of the normal laws of capitalist accumulation—initial assets stolen and current surplus misapplied. This state of things, Baran concluded, was perpetuated by the indigenous comprador class, bolstered by the foreign imperialist states and encouraged—perhaps even compelled—to maintain military establishments sufficient to repress revolutionary tendencies. In this way, international monopoly capitalism could secure its economic stranglehold over the rest of the world without the cost or inconvenience of maintaining formal colonial empires.[24]

In 1957 Baran's arguments were still tentative, and the style of his book showed little advance over earlier Marxist writings—being diffuse, prone to fall back on rhetoric, and vague about actual developments in the less developed world. He may also not have been the first to emphasize these themes. Yet here one can find, at least in embryo, the basic elements of what was to become the dominant attitude of the 1970s toward economic development after the end of colonialism, which gave a new and specific content to the term *underdeveloped* as the concrete outcome of the activities of international capitalism in the less developed world. I do not propose to trace the evolution of these ideas in detail, nor do I pretend to have read more than a sample of the swelling literature on underdevelopment. A short comment is, however, warranted on the significance of the Latin American contribution to these concepts in the 1960s, followed by a more careful analysis of how Colin Leys has recently interpreted the theory and applied it to the historical evolution of Kenya.

It is significant that it was Latin Americans who eventually brought

23. Baran, *Political Economy*, p. 179.
24. Ibid., passim, esp. pp. 140–62, 178–84, 249–64.

Marxist theory on underdevelopment down from the highly theoretical level at which it had tended to float since the days of Lenin and applied it to the facts of Latin American history. An obvious reason is that Latin America provided the only evidence available in the 1950s and 1960s of the long-run economic performance of one-time European colonies after they had achieved independence (apart, that is, from the United States, which suggested very different conclusions on the potential consequences of foreign investment in a developing country). To allot credit for particular ideas to one author or another is dangerous; but it would appear that from 1966 to 1969 three men in particular helped to clarify the concept of underdevelopment to the point at which it could be adopted and adapted to the analysis of decolonization in Africa. The first was Celso Furtado, who published *Development and Underdevelopment* in 1964. His basic point, which was a refinement of arguments already found in Baran and others, was that "underdevelopment" was not a negative condition—namely, the comparative absence of development—but a concrete and potentially permanent condition into which some (though not all) less developed countries had been forced by the activities of international capital. According to Furtado, the essential feature of underdevelopment was a "dualistic economy," consisting of a "capitalist wedge" driven into a surrounding precapitalist economy. This resulted in a "hybrid structure" and a "static equilibrium" at a low overall level, with substantial transfers of profit overseas and very little impact of capital on the mass of the precapitalist parts of the domestic economy.

Furtado emphasized the need for "autonomous theorization" about the economic history of Latin America along these lines, and it was an attempt by André Gunder Frank to relate these themes to Chile and Brazil that first made him a leading exponent of dependency theory. In *Capitalism and Underdevelopment in Latin America*,[25] Frank picked up and restated points previously made by Baran and others: "My thesis is that these capitalist contradictions and the historical development of the capitalist system have generated underdevelopment in the peripheral satellites whose economic surplus was appropriated, while generating economic development in the metropolitan centers which appropriate that surplus—and, further, that this process still continues." He went on to demonstrate that this process in Latin America was not recent or even postcolonial, but as old as European colonization there. This led to the conclusion that "economic development and underdevelopment are not just relative and quantitative. . . . [They] are relative and qualitative, in that

25. (1967; London and New York, 1969). References are to this edition.

each is structurally different from, yet caused by its relation with the other."[26]

Two years later T. Dos Santos published an article whose English title was "The Crisis of Development Theory and the Problem of Dependence in Latin America."[27] In this, while criticizing some aspects of Frank's arguments, he took the basic concept of dependence one stage further; indeed, his definition remains widely accepted in the 1980s. "Dependence" was "not the 'external factor' which it is often believed to be" but, as another writer had put it, "a fundamental element in the interpretation of our history." Latin American economic development was different from that of Europe because its dualistic character "neither permitted nor stimulated full development of capitalist relations of production but rather based itself upon servile forms of work or slavery."

Dependence, therefore, was a perpetuation of what might have been a transient stage of economic development. It was "a *conditioning situation* in which the economies of one group of countries are conditioned by the development and expansion of others. . . . Dependence . . . is based upon an international division of labour which allows industrial development to take place in some countries while restricting it in others, whose growth is conditioned by and subjugated to the power centers of the world." It followed that "if dependence is a conditioning situation, then it establishes the possible limits of development and of its forms of dependenct countries." Nevertheless, a fatalistic standpoint was wrong. All dependent situations are concrete and specific and may change either in the direction of different forms of dependence (for example, from mercantile to financial and industrial) or toward genuine independence, which could be achieved by breaking off relations with the capitalist world altogether, as China had done. Thus the future lay in the hands of those who lived in the dependent countries. "'External' domination, in a pure sense, is in principle impracticable. Domination is practicable only when it finds support among those local groups who profit by it." And consequently, "the only solution would be [for a country] to change its internal structure—a course which necessarily leads to confrontation with the existing international structure."

Since 1969 dependency theory has come a long way, and in particular many attempts have been made to apply and adapt it to African situations. Some idea of the variety of problems to which it has been applied is given by the collection of essays edited by Peter C. W. Gutkind and Immanuel

26. Frank, *Capitalism and Underdevelopment in Latin America*, pp. 3 and 8.

27. Reprinted in Henry Bernstein, ed., *Underdevelopment and Development* (Harmondsworth, 1973), pp. 57–69.

Wallerstein called *The Political Economy of Contemporary Africa*, which includes a useful bibliographical essay by Chris Allen.[28] These and similar studies make it very clear why those who accept the assumptions of dependency theory are incurably pessimistic about the economic and social consequences of decolonization in Africa. It would be impossible here even to summarize the specific arguments currently in play on this theme, but to demonstrate the way in which one specialist in East African history can apply, and if necessary modify, these basic assumptions, I propose to summarize the central argument put forward by Colin Leys in his book, *Underdevelopment in Kenya*.

Leys's restatement of dependency theory can be summarized as follows.[29] The relations between Europe and the rest of the world were at all times uneven, and Europeans took what they wanted by force, using, variously, influence or formal rule as required to protect their activities.[30] The effect, either way, was the extraction of Baran's "actual surplus" by the metropolis and the creation of "new relations of production in the periphery countries, based on their progressive exposure to, and domination by, capitalism." A most important by-product was the emergence of new indigenous strata or classes which in course of time became sufficiently powerful to make it unnecessary for the imperial powers to continue direct rule. This was one of the criteria for decolonization: the other was that primitive accumulation (through annexing the fruits of precapitalist production) had given way to capitalist accumulation, "in which the apparently 'natural' forces of the market for labour are sufficient to ensure that the surplus is appropriated by the capitalist." Once the colony had thus been made a peripheral extension of the imperialist economy, the metropolitan state could safely withdraw its legions and pull down the flags, leaving behind its indigenous allies as the agents of international monopoly capital to ensure that the actual surplus continued to be exported. That was the point at which Britain, France, and other countries felt able to put an end to formal empire in Africa.

From the standpoint of this chapter, the important consequential question is, of course, whether these mechanisms of imperialist control were so effective after decolonization that the African states remained both "dependent" and "underdeveloped." Leys's analysis of why this was to be expected is as follows. First, the monopoly of the commodity export trade

28. Beverly Hills, Calif., 1976, pp. 291–313.

29. Leys, *Underdevelopment in Kenya*, pp. 8–27.

30. Compare the well-known phrase in Gallagher and Robinson, "The Imperialism of Free Trade," *Economic History Review*, 2d ser. 6, no. 1 (1953), "trade with informal control if possible; trade with rule where necessary."

previously held by international capital (predominantly the multinational companies) is safeguarded by their monopoly of know-how in the international markets. Second, although local industry might be expected to break through into full-scale production after independence with the help of tariffs and state encouragement of many kinds, genuinely autonomous industrialization is commonly held back by three factors.

First, the limited markets provided by small territories seldom offer scope for more than one modern plant making any particular product, and these often existed under European ownership before independence. Second, such new industries as are set up are usually owned by foreign firms, because they alone possess the capital and skills required to take advantage of official stimulation of industrial investment. This type of factory, moreover, typically makes the same products under the same brand names as these foreign firms previously imported. They seldom develop new products, and because they tend to import raw materials or intermediates rather than developing production of local substitutes, their activities have limited backward linkages into the local economy. Such practices merely reinforce the "external orientation" of local industry; and of course foreign ownership of the capital involves continued export of the "actual surplus," which is thus lost to the local economy. Finally, because industrialization undertaken by foreign firms with sufficient capital or borrowing facilities at their disposal usually results in capital-intensive factories, these will employ relatively few Africans (though they will be comparatively well paid); and this in turn limits the value of industrial employment as a source of demand for other local products.

For all these reasons, decolonization is likely to make little difference to the local African economy, which remains fundamentally dependent as a satellite of international capitalism. Although per capita incomes may rise in absolute terms, the gap between these and incomes in the developed countries widens. Thus the result of decolonization is that "the society has been 'locked into' its subordinate role in the international economy by new means."

So far this is an orthodox statement of contemporary dependency theory, but Leys is too good a historian to believe that every aspect of it is relevant to African conditions.[31] He has, for example, reservations about the meaning of "neocolonialism" and thinks that too many liberal exponents of dependency concepts refuse to face the fact that reformist measures may be ineffective. But his most important reservation is that, as a historian, he cannot accept that a theory intended to rationalize the failure of certain

31. Leys, *Underdevelopment in Kenya*, pp. 18–27.

societies—notably those in Latin America—to develop economically in the past can be regarded as an infallible blueprint of what will happen in Africa in the future. In particular he suggests that underdevelopment theory does not furnish convincing grounds for claiming that no "third world" country can ever become an "advanced" and relatively autonomous capitalist country.

This is a very important reservation, which is reinforced by his earlier rejection of the commonly held theory that there has been a secular and inevitable deterioration in the terms of trade against underdeveloped countries; and he argues that, in principle at least, the monopoly of international commodity markets and industrial technology by which the imperialists continue to exert their control could be thrown off or weakened by the underdeveloped states.[32] In short, Leys rejects some of the more deterministic aspects of current theory, particularly those which are predictive; but he accepts its central premise that, so long as the alliance between foreign capitalism and the indigenous bourgeoisie holds firm, a less developed country will be unable substantially to change its character or break through the constraints imposed by foreign monopoly.

This, of course, deals only with the theoretical introduction. The bulk of Leys's book is concerned to demonstrate historically, first, how the postindependence dependence of Kenya evolved during the thirty odd years before 1963, the key argument being that Africans were persuaded to preserve both the existing white-settler mixed farming system and also the rights of private property; and, second, how after decolonization foreign capital worked out a modus vivendi at the expense of the Indian petty bourgeoisie and the African proletariat. He concludes that in the 1970s Kenya provides a clear example of a dependent sovereign state, yet he maintains that the country contains an internal dynamic which makes this situation unstable. There is an inherent tension, on the one hand, between foreign capital, which would like to see some income redistribution so as to widen its local market, and the indigenous bourgeoisie, which does not wish to endanger its privileges; and, on the other hand, between that indigenous elite and the mass of the underprivileged. The fact that Kenya in the 1970s seemed locked into a stable position as a satellite of international capitalism is no guarantee that the balance of forces that made this stability possible will outlast even the life span of the successor regime which had made it possible.[33] Here at last is pessimism about the consequences of decolonization tinged with optimism.

32. Ibid., pp. 11–12, 18–19.
33. Ibid., pp. 254–73.

With so many contrasting interpretations of the causes and consequences of decolonization to consider, how should the historian proceed? He is faced with two main problems: first, the comparative invulnerability of general theories, such as that on underdevelopment, to specific evidence; second, the shortness of the historical perspective and the consequential lack of evidence on the medium- to long-term consequences of the end of formal empire. To illustrate the first difficulty, it would be quite possible to dispute Leys's account of the process of decolonization in Kenya by demonstrating that neither international nor resident European capitalists felt any great confidence in the early 1960s that their interests would be safe under any then predictable form of successor state. They certainly did not, so to speak, give the British government the green light to withdraw. But even the assumption that they might have acted in this way and that the British government timed withdrawal accordingly is vulnerable, because it implies a degree of rationality on the part of the metropolitan government and a degree of correspondence between them and the multinationals which almost certainly did not exist. To say that they did is mere speculation. Yet although such criticism may give satisfaction to the positivist historian, it is unlikely to impress those who believe in underdevelopment theory. Just as defenders of the original Leninist explanation of the partition of Africa have done in the past, they are likely to fall back on the position that such details are unimportant: it is the consequential situation that really matters, and this is fully consistent with the speculative interpretation already given. This is the invariable dilemma of the historian whose facts prove ineffective against the armor of a priori assumption.

Reassessment of the economic consequences of decolonization is still more difficult because, although some of the facts of the decolonizing process are now available, little can be said with any confidence about its outcome. The time-scale is too short and such information as is available is largely inconclusive. For example, very little work has yet been done on the activities of foreign companies, their relations with successor governments and with the indigenous bourgeoisie, the consequences of public and private participation in their equity, the impact of import substitution on other parts of the local economy, and so on.[34] But again, it is the

34. Anothy G. Hopkins' *An Economic History of West Africa* (London, 1973), which is probably the best attempt yet made to tell a coherent story of regional development to the end of the colonial period in any part of Africa, reflects, as its author remarks, the limitations of the existing historiography. Three particularly useful studies among many others now appearing are: Walter Birmingham, I. Neustadt, and E. N. Amaboe, eds., *A Study of Contemporary Ghana*, vol. 1: *The Economy of Ghana* (London, 1966); Peter Kilby, *Industrialisation in an Open Economy* (Cambridge, 1969); and Samir Amin, *Le Développement du Capitalisme en Côte d'Ivoire* (Paris, 1967).

interpretation of trends that is so difficult. For example, on the face of the evidence a number of new states have prospered through continuing and expanding their existing systems of commodity production for export. The Ivory Coast has often been held up as an example; yet Samir Amin, while admitting that things had gone well so far, concluded that "in 1970 [its] capacity for independent financing was practically nil."[35] And so one could move round the continent, finding always that evidence of industrial or agricultural development was in fact misleading because these countries were still dependent on foreign capital and skills rather than on genuinely autonomous initiative. In short, because any number of swallows do not make a conceptually satisfactory summer, the historian finds himself quite unable to come to grips with those who argue that decolonization has not in itself begun to solve the problems of underdevelopment in Africa.

Yet it would be cowardly to end on an entirely agnostic note. If the substantive question cannot or should not yet be answered, it is at least reasonable to consider which of the four early projections of the probable consequences of decolonization seems likely to prove most accurate in the light of existing evidence; and also what measuring rod the economic historian half a century from now is likely to find most useful in explaining what actually occurred.

In the early 1980s two at least of the projections made in the 1950s and 1960s appear always to have been unrealistic. First, the somewhat paternalistic assumption made, or at least expressed, by so many imperial politicians and administrators, that postcolonial Africa governments would and could continue successfully along the lines hurriedly laid down in the previous decades quickly proved false. Systems of government changed very quickly and the successor states soon discarded the economic and fiscal conservatism of the colonial period. In the British case at least, hope that the new states would continue to link their economies with that of Britain and operate within a Commonwealth context was also disappointed. Anglophone Africa quickly learnt the value of shopping for aid and making trading deals outside the Commonwealth, the sterling area, and even the capitalist world; though most Francophone states (with the exception of Guinea and, briefly, Mali) remained closely attached to the French monetary system and the European economy. Thus the too convenient assumption that decolonization would make little difference to the economic policies and external orientation of the African colonies is now discredited. The new states have opted for speaking roles on the world stage rather than walk-on parts in a neoimperialist drama.

Nor, on the other hand, have the more pessimistic assumptions of the

35. Samir Amin, *Neo-Colonialism in West Africa* (Harmondsworth, 1973), p. 177.

old-time Marxist-Leninists proved entirely correct. Foreign investment has certainly flowed into the new Africa, and the international corporations have increased their stake there. But much of the new investment consisted of undistributed profits made in Africa itself; and this simultaneously strikes a blow at the concept of surplus capital vegetating in the hands of "finance capital" until it could find investment opportunities in the less developed world, and at the assertion that foreign capital was keen to transfer all the actual surplus it could extract from Africa. More important, the dual forecast of immiserization and the formation of revolutionary cadres of workers and peasants has also proved largely false. The terms of trade have not moved consistently against commodity exports; national products and even per capita incomes have improved as often as they have remained static or declined; and there is little sign that African capitalism is generating replicas of a revolutionary proletariat. So it is not surprising that few latter-day Marxists write of Africa in the apocalyptic terms conventionally employed by their predecessors in the 1940s and early 1950s.

We are, therefore, left with the two more sober alternatives offered by the conventional development economists and those who formulated underdevelopment theory. Both, in fact, apply similar criteria to the problems resulting from decolonization: what is the best method by which a less developed country can increase its national and also per capita income; how can it become "autonomous" in the sense that development capital is generated within the local economy and not inevitably borrowed from outside? Where they differ is over the predictable utility of particular means to these ends. On the whole the conventional development economists have insisted that capitalism does offer Africa and other countries a satisfactory road to true development. While pointing to the desirable goal of adequate local capital formation, they hold that borrowed capital, even if owned by a multinational, is beneficial if properly applied; and the two most important tests of its proper application are whether the project can operate successfully without large protection for an indefinite period and whether the host government imposes sufficient controls on the operations of the foreign owners of the capital, including regulation of the type and volume of its production and reasonable taxation of its profits. On such assumptions it can still legitimately be argued that an African host country stands to gain by having the use of capital it could only have provided for itself after a long period of accumulation and probably with considerable sacrifice by the mass of the producing and consuming public. On the other hand, while optimistic, the development economists issue warnings: there is no shortcut to affluence; the potential benefits of investment, whether foreign or local, can easily be squandered by incautious policies; in the last resort everything depends on the ability and honesty of the local government.

On this last point at least there is agreement between liberal economists and Marxist proponents of underdevelopment theory; and their fundamental disagreement therefore stems from the basic lack of confidence held by the second group in the character of postcolonial African governments. As has been seen, the key assumption underlying most underdevelopment theory is that the governing and capitalist classes in less developed countries are virtually identical and are concerned with promoting their own interests rather than those of the country as a whole. Because they stand to gain from the activities of foreign control, whether as politicians and bureaucrats taking bribes, as capitalists cooperating in business ventures, or as managers in foreign enterprises, they do not judge development and investment plans as disinterested patriots. And in so far as they constitute an indigenous bourgeoisie resembling that of Europe, they are in any case accumulating capital at the expense of their own working class and peasants, capital which they seldom employ in nationally useful local enterprises. If Marxists distrust the ability and intentions of governments in advanced capitalist countries they have even stronger grounds for claiming that only a political and social revolution can bring about better government in the less developed countries of Africa.

In the last resort, then, it seems that there is common agreement that the economic consequences of decolonization will depend on the role of governments in Africa and that the point at issue turns on contrasting assessments of the will and ability of the governments that inherited power after decolonization to use and control foreign capital. On the second of these it is already safe to say that sovereign states, however small and poor, can, if they wish, effectively control the operations of even the largest multinational. My own work on Unilever in Africa has shown that this representative of international capitalism accepted that its activities in independent Africa were entirely conditioned by the policies adopted by the host governments, and that while Unilever would negotiate, it would not and could not dictate. The record also shows that there, and in all other less developed countries, a resolute government can determine what goods a foreign company may make, what raw materials it must use—whether local or imported—what prices it may charge, what proportion of the equity in the local company must be held by the local government or citizens, what proportion of the management must be indigenous, and what sums may be remitted overseas by way of dividends, royalties, service fees, or repatriation of capital. In short, subject to the sanction that excessive constraints may persuade a multinational not to invest or to write off its investment and withdraw, host governments have effective control over foreign entrepreneurs operating in sovereign African states. In this fundamental respect, Kwame Nkrumah and the optimistic African nationalists of the 1950s were absolutely correct.

There remains the character of the host government and its will to pursue the national interest rather than that of the individuals, classes, or social strata who compose and support it. It is here that the short record of the past fifteen years gives some credibility to the assertions of proponents of underdevelopment theory, such as Leys. Ironically, it also justifies the view of most British and French imperialists of the 1940s and 1950s (though not the limited steps they then took to meet the problem) that a considerable time would be necessary before their African colonies would be capable of providing "good government" on the lines of Western social democracy. The regrettable fact is that the eventual transfer of power in colonial Africa—by marked contrast with that in South and Southeast Asia—came before the indigenous peoples had had the experience or training necessary if they were to meet the needs of autonomous nation states. They had virtually no experience of representative democracy, for almost all their experience was with a benevolently despotic colonial civil service. They had not grasped the principle that in a democracy the majority must use its power in the general interest—not that of individuals, groups, or regions—and must tolerate the interests of minorities. They lacked established institutions of local and central government through which the collective will could express itself. They also lacked experienced politicians and administrators comparable with those who took control in South Asia when the British withdrew. In addition, the geographical areas which had been convenient administrative units under imperial rule were not necessarily viable as nation states or autonomous economic organisms: indeed, Amin has concluded of Francophone West Africa that "any attempt at a 'development policy' within such narrow limits as those set by the economic areas characteristic of the states in this region is bound to fail."[36] Thus, through no fault of their own, many (though not all) of the new states of postcolonial Africa at the time of their political independence were not "nations" as the West understood the term. The optimism expressed by so many European imperialists stemmed either from muddled thinking or dishonest rhetoric.

It is, therefore, not surprising that the governments of such states should, in the early decades of their existence, have been weak, unsure of

36. Ibid., p. 273.

themselves, and vulnerable to the well-meaning but not always judicious advice given by European friends, the pressures of interest groups at home, and the seductive investment proposals made by foreign capitalists and governments. Some continued established patterns of economic activity and found that these did not produce results quickly enough to satisfy their domestic supporters. Others broke for the open, undertaking vast investments on borrowed money and without sufficiently careful investigation, only to find that they very soon ran out of resources and were virtually bankrupt. Nor is it surprising that failure often discredited infant systems of democratic government and resulted in coups and military rule. It is clear, also, that the great age of industrial investment by multinationals in tropical Africa began only with decolonization, when successor governments, anxious to expedite economic development and so fulfill the promises incautiously made before they achieved power, were ready to pay far too high a price to international capital in terms of protective duties, tax holidays, guarantees of freedom to import foreign materials, and so on. Nothing did more to discredit liberal systems of government in Africa than this postindependence bonanza.

All this gives initial credibility to the arguments of those pessimists who claim that decolonization merely transferred power to self-seeking minority groups in Africa who depended for the means of sustaining their power on financial and military support from the capitalist West, and that Africa thus joined Latin America as a continent of comprador regimes. Where the conventional historian must part company with them is their consequential proposition that neither good government nor economic development has taken or can take place until a fundamental sociopolitical revolution has occurred. Here Marxist historicism mars their logic. Because such conditions appear to have existed for long periods in Latin America, there is no guarantee that they will continue there, or in Africa, in the future. How much credence should, in fact, be given to a system of historical analysis which has denied for a century that the proletariat of Europe and North America could ever benefit from capitalism? More important, how certain is it that only the replacement of "Bonapartist" governments, as Leys has described the government of Kenya, by a system of totalitarian social democracy will produce economic plenty? To assert this is to deny the ability of Africans to strike and maintain a judicious balance between the forces competing within each country and between their own countries and the capitalist world. The fact that few have achieved either objective during the first two decades after decolonization is no ground for rejecting the possibility that it may happen in the future.

It seems likely, therefore, that when the economic consequences of colonialism come eventually to be assessed in the light of sufficient time elapsed and evidence available, the verdict will turn not so much on the influence of international capitalism as on whether indigenous African systems were able to master the problem of providing "good government," and whether they could do this without adopting the techniques of totalitarian socialism. In the early 1980s the fundamental difference of opinion about future prospects lay between those who believed that the contradictions said to be inherent in underdevelopment could not be resolved unless each African state underwent a socialist revolution and then broke completely with international capitalism, and those who hoped that Africans would be able to solve their undeniable economic and social problems without totally rejecting the liberal values of Western civilization. The outcome remains entirely open, for there is no model which sufficiently duplicates African conditions: Europe, America, and Japan are little use to the optimists, nor Russia, China, or Latin America to the pessimists. The historian who believes in the autonomy of the historical process can safely predict only that the patterns of African economic and political development will be unique to Africa.

18. Decolonization in French, Belgian, and Portuguese Africa: A Bibliographical Essay

DAVID E. GARDINIER

Introduction

This essay surveys the literature which contributes to an understanding of decolonization in French, Belgian, and Portuguese Africa. It concentrates on the period from the early 1940s through the early 1960s in French and Belgian Africa and through the 1970s in Portuguese Africa. It also includes references to French Somaliland and the Comoro Islands through their independence in the late 1970s.[1]

The term *decolonization* was apparently first used in 1932 by Moritz Julius Bonn in the *Encyclopedia of the Social Sciences*, and has been widely employed since the 1950s to describe the emancipation of Asia and Africa from foreign control.[2] Decolonization may be defined in a restricted sense as the process by which the Asians and Africans gained self-government and independence from their colonial rulers. Involved in this mainly political process were African reactions and responses to colonial rule, which led to anticolonialist and nationalist movements, as well as to outside pressures (that is, elsewhere in Africa, in other colonial empires, and in the international political system, including the United Nations) which had an impact on the course of developments in colonial lands. These external elements helped to form the larger context within which the transfer of power took place. Decolonization may also be broadly defined as the

1. The volume *France and Britain in Africa*, ed. Prosser Gifford and Wm. Roger Louis (New Haven, 1971) contains my chapter, "French Colonial Rule in Africa: A Bibliographical Essay" (pp. 787–902), along with a bibliographical list that includes additional works (pp. 903–50). That chapter surveyed most of the literature on decolonization in French Africa published through 1971. To avoid duplication, the present essay concentrates upon works published subsequently or not included there.

2. For further details, see my article, "Decolonization," in Joseph Dunner, ed., *Handbook of World History* (New York, 1967), pp. 268–72.

process by which Africans and Asians remove all vestiges of external control at the economic, cultural, and psychological levels as well as at the political level. In this broader sense, they acquire the power to make the decisions that affect their lives and allow them to be authentically themselves.

This essay gives primary attention to the literature on decolonization in the restricted sense of the term. But it also contains references, particularly in the French case, to decolonization in the broad sense. For the French policy of *coopération* may be seen as a means of ultimately lessening African dependence and thereby leading to another stage in the transfer of power. It may also be viewed, though, as a means of perpetuating the kind of dependence which stifles further decolonization or, even worse, increases dependence and thereby reverses the process of decolonization. This essay therefore includes the major literature on the postindependence relationships involving aid and assistance from the three European states to their former African territories. Lack of space makes it impossible, however, to consider the vast literature that deals with broader questions of the postindependence relationships, particularly the economic ones, between Europe and Africa.[3]

French Africa

The 1970s have seen the appearance of important studies by D. Bruce Marshall and Paul Clay Sorum on decolonization in all of French Africa.[4] Marshall's *The French Colonial Myth and Constitution-Making in the Fourth Republic* (1973) studies the thinking that produced the constitutional arrangements for the overseas countries during the Fourth French

3. For guides to the sources on French Africa, see pp. 888–97 of my previous bibliographical essay (1971). The historiographer of French Black Africa, Belgian, and Portuguese Africa is also fortunate to have *A Bibliogrpahical Guide to Colonialism in Sub-Saharan Africa* (1973), by Peter Duignan and Lewis Gann of the Hoover Institution of Stanford University. In addition to being a mine of information about archives, research libraries, serials, and reference works, it has factual summaries of the most important works on colonial rule that were available through June 1972. Secondarily, there are references to the quality or importance of some of the works and to the ideological tendencies and backgrounds of their authors. Valuable guides to more recent printed sources are David L. Easterbrook, "Bibliography of Africana Bibliographies, 1965–1975," *Africana Journal* 7, no. 2 (1976): 101–48, and "Bibliography of Africana Bibliographies, 1975–1976," ibid. 8, no. 3 (1977): 232–42.

4. Writers in French on decolonization in French Africa have employed that term since the early 1950s, when Henri Labouret publicized it through a volume entitled *Colonisation, colonialisme, et décolonisation* (1952). But they seem to use the expression "transfer of power," which derives from British colonial experience, only when discussing the political evolution of the British territories. It is then translated literally as "transfert de pouvoir."

Republic. The "colonial myth" is his expression for the belief on the part of the elite that the links between France and the colonies were indissoluble. This idea prevented them from forming a loose union that would provide their colonies with a good deal of local autonomy and structures capable of evolution without violence. After discussing the historical components of the colonial myth between the eighteenth and twentieth centuries, Marshall examines the ambivalent and often contradictory character of the Brazzaville proposals, which envisioned the advancement of the African territories only within a framework controlled by the metropole. He then focuses on the constituent assemblies of 1945–46, in which the French established institutions leading to frustration and conflict rather than orderly decolonization. He blames Georges Bidault, Charles de Gaulle, and the Communist party in particular, for the shortcomings of the constitution of October 1946, which brought the overseas people neither freedom nor equality, and was therefore bound to falter.

In *Intellectuals and Decolonization in France* (1977), Paul Clay Sorum shows the failure of the intellectual critics of French colonial policies to transform the beliefs of most of the political elite that France had a humanist colonial vocation and that France's greatness required the continuation of empire. His work is valuable in showing the connections between the intellectuals' views on Indochina, North Africa, and Black Africa. Sorum did not investigate the positions of Communist intellectuals, whom he sees, along with their party, as standing outside the political process from May 1947 onward. But other scholars have begun to publish some of their findings about the views and actions of the Communists. Irwin Wall (1977) indicates that during the Fourth Republic the Communist party argued for the maintenance of links between France and Africa, but on a reformed and liberal basis; for the Communists feared that African independence would lead to the intrusion of American imperialism and the establishment of Fascist regimes. Wall has also explored the attitudes of the French Communists toward the Algerian war (1977). Roger Kanet (1976) discusses the relationship between the French Communist party and African nationalists, including the RDA, between 1945 and 1950. He points out the very limited and indirect influence of the Soviet Union on Black Africa in this period. Raoul Girardet, *L'Idée coloniale en France, 1871–1962* (1972) contains useful discussions on the evolution of French thinking on colonial matters, including the ideas of the Communists after 1940.

The past decade has seen the publication of several very useful surveys of French or European colonial rule. Among them are Xavier Yacono, *Histoire de la colonisation française* (1969); Jean Miège, *Expansion européenne et décolonisation de 1870 à nos jours* (1973); Henry Wilson,

The Imperial Experience in Sub-Saharan Africa since 1870 (1978); and Raymond Betts, *Tricouleur* (1978). Unfortunately for our purposes, their sections on decolonization are either very brief or contain little that is new. Far more useful for understanding decolonization is Yacono's *Les Etapes de la décolonisation française* (1971), which indicates the failure of both the Fourth and Fifth republics to define clear policies of colonization or decolonization, with the resultant shifts, inconsistencies, and confusion. Yacono in this work treats the decolonization of the French Empire from the centenary of the French landing in Algeria to the independence of Algeria. He analyzes the impact of the world depression of the 1930s and the Second World War on the undermining of the colonial system. He notes that in Africa the French transferred power to bourgeois nationalists who possessed varying degrees of mass support. Finally, Yacono contends that in 1958 President de Gaulle did not consider the total independence of Algeria inevitable. He arrived at this conclusion only in the light of subsequent events, and then probably not until 1961.

Two German studies treat the juridical evolution of the French African territories. Helmut Konrad Weinbuch, *Entkolonisierung und föderales Prinzip im Spiegel der Franzosischen Gemeinschaft* (1968), discusses the federal principles and juridical theories involved in the transformation of the French Union and Community. N. Scherck, *Dekolonisation und Souveräntität* (1969), examines the postindependence relationships and insists on the continued large-scale dependence upon France of the former French territories. He makes a distinction between legal sovereignty and actual independence in such areas as international politics, economics, and culture. He provides a good review of the transition from the French Union to the Community and then to coopération, giving much attention to the various agreements and treaties.

Black Africa

The decolonization of French Black Africa is the subject of an extensive literature, the largest part of which was produced during the events themselves or shortly thereafter. In particular, there are two large clusters of writing, the one on the reforms made between 1944 and 1946 and the other on the changes from 1958 to 1961. There is a smaller amount of writing which looks at the entire period from the Second World War through independence or through the postindependence era of coopération. During the late 1960s and 1970s important research on particular aspects of colonial rule and decolonization has taken place. Most of this research has been the work of European and American scholars, for the majority of French-educated African historians have tended to investigate periods for which archival records are available, whereas their social scientist colleagues have been examining contemporary issues. As for sources, very few archives are as yet open for the period since 1945, and not many more new materials became available during the 1970s. Some recent studies have utilized interviews with personalities involved in decolonization who are now willing to talk more freely than they were in the early 1960s, or collections of private papers whose contents are no longer so controversial.

Jean Suret-Canale's third volume on all of French Black Africa, *Afrique noire occidentale et centrale: De la colonisation aux indépendances (1945–1960)*(1972), like its predecessors, is written from a doctrinaire Marxist perspective and almost exclusively employs French sources. Its sections on the political awakening from 1944 to 1946 have particular value because of the author's presence in Africa at this critical juncture. Its sections on the economic evolution of French Black Africa in the period of decolonization are the most detailed and comprehensive available. Their value is enhanced for those who do not share the author's viewpoint by their massive data and exhaustive French documentation.

Dorothy Shipley White, in an article on General de Gaulle and the decolonization of Black Africa (1976) and in *De Gaulle and Black Africa: From the Empire to the Community* (1979), employs interviews with the General's associates and family, as well as other political figures, to ascertain the evolution of his thinking. White concludes that the Free French leader played an important personal role in the inclusion of liberal reforms for Black Africa at the Brazzaville Conference and that Governor-General Félix Eboué much influenced him in this direction. Brian Weinstein's biography, *Éboué* (1971), which also relies on interviews and the governor-general's private papers, seems implicitly to support this latter conclusion. White discusses the very real role de Gaulle played in securing various reforms benefiting Black Africa between 1944 and 1946. She sees his influence as much more positive in this period than does Bruce Marshall (cited above). She contends that the dismantling of the French Union between 1958 and 1961 occurred much more rapidly than it would have otherwise, and with less difficulty for the French nation, because of the immense prestige and political wisdom of the General.

The 1970s have seen a good deal of important writing on French economic involvement in Africa, both during the colonial period and since independence. Some of this writing deals with both periods and also encompasses various British territories. For example, Samir Amin, *L'Afrique de l'Ouest bloquée: L'Economie politique de la colonisation, 1880–1970* (1971), studied European-African economic relations in French West Africa and Ghana from 1880 to 1970. For French West Africa he found that the French had made virtually no investment in improving the technology of production during the post-1945 period. Instead, they had emphasized the development of processing and other light industries. Consequently, since independence there has been some growth in a few countries but no genuine development. Most of the former French states have had chronic deficits in balance of payments and have remained dependent on France for budget subsidies and investment capital. A. G. Hopkins, *An Economic History of West Africa* (1973), includes the era of decolonization in an analysis of British and French territories since 1800. Between 1945 and 1960 the economies of these states underwent substantial modifications, the chief of which centered upon the expansion of the public sector, the transfer of commercial and political power to Africans, and the beginnings of modern industry. By 1950, the colonial powers were seeking to placate the Africans yet to safeguard the future of expatriate business interests through arrangements that aided metropolitan well-being. By the late 1950s, most African leaders had come to understand the great difficulties in fundamental reordering of their economies and thus remained moderate nationalists rather than radical ones. As far as French West Africa was concerned, Hopkins concludes that the modifications in the economies of the various territories integrated them more closely with the French economy. This situation helps to explain why only Guinea opted for immediate and complete independence in September 1958. Hopkins also contends that the federation of French West Africa was dismantled primarily because the wealthiest state, the Ivory Coast, did not wish to continue to subsidize the poorer states.

The Marxist economic historian, Catherine Coquery-Vidrovitch, in cooperation with a team of investigators at the University of Paris, has been studying Franco-African economic relations from the nineteenth century through the 1970s. She has so far published several important articles on different aspects of their findings, including some that encompass the era of decolonization. A first article attempts to periodize 1800–1970 on the basis of dependency (1976); a second deals with imperial ideology and development policy between 1924 and 1975 (1976); and a third treats the impact of the two largest French commercial firms in West Africa between 1910 and 1965 (1975). The Coquery team has also published some of the results of their investigations of the impact of the world depression of 1930 on the economies of French Black Africa in a double issue of the *Revue française d'histoire d'outre-mer* (1976) and in an article by Coquery (1977) on the changes in French colonial imperialism during the 1930s. These latter writings throw much light on the weakening of the French system as a result of the depression and on the main characteristics of the colonial economy as it existed at the start of the Second World War. The researches of the Coquery team involve reference to contemporary economic theories and use of econometrics, whereas those of Suret-Canale (cited above), and Thompson and Adloff, are more in the tradition of economic geography. Virginia Thompson and Richard Adloff, noted American specialists on Francophone Africa, have prepared a chapter in the fourth Duignan and Gann colonialism volume (1975) on French economic policy in Black Africa during the colonial period. Though mainly descriptive, their account contains much useful data.

The Cameroonian scholar, Georges Ngango, *Les Investissements d'origine extérieure en Afrique noire francophone: Leur statut et incidence sur le développement* (1973), deals with French economic activities throughout Black Africa since the First World War. He treats the policies of Albert Sarraut and of FIDES as well as postindependence developments. Michel Leduc, *Les Institutions monétaires africaines des pays francophones* (1965), provides a history of monetary institutions in French Black Africa and a detailed analysis of those of the eras after the Second World War and after independence through 1965. Because of the separate monetary arrangements for independent Guinea and Mali, Leduc devotes separate chapters to them. The study shows the ways in which most of the former French states remained linked to France and dependent on her. Guinean scholar Aguibou Yan Yansané (1976) treats Franco-African financial relations in the mid-1970s in historical perspective.

At the time of independence, France signed agreements with all of the African states (except Guinea) and Madagascar to provide financial and technical aid and assistance in the form of funds and personnel in such areas as defense, foreign affairs, economic development, currency, education, and culture. These new relationships formed part of the French policy called coopération, for which a body of doctrine, official and unofficial, soon developed. The initial agreements, which were negotiated for five years and were renewable, stayed in effect during the presidency of de Gaulle and began to undergo revisions in the direction of greater African control under Presidents Pompidou and Giscard d'Estaing. Detailed information on the first cooperation agreements and French aid is found in two official publications of *La Documentation Française:* "La Coopération entre la France, l'Afrique Noire d'expression française et Madagascar" (1966), and "Le Service de la coopération culturelle, scientifique et technique avec les Etats francophones africains et malgache: Bilan et perspectives" (1971). An officially sponsored study, *Les Accords de coopération entre la France et les Etats africains et malgache d'expression française* (1964) by Maurice Ligot analyzes the juridical framework for aid. A briefer study by Jacques Vaudiaux, *L'Evolution politique et juridique de la coopération franco-africaine et malgache* (1971), carries the account into the Pompidou era. These two studies, like the two reports, are more descriptive and explanatory than critical. Taken as a whole, they indicate that France had a single aid policy for the African states and Madagascar. They show the very large role which France continued to play in the affairs of these countries during the first decade after independence. They reveal the details concerning the powers not transferred or exercised jointly by France and the African states.

The brief study by the American political scientist, Richard Robarts, *French Development Assistance: A Study in Policy and Administration* (1974), has particular value because of its coverage of coopération through 1974, its careful descriptions of aid mechanisms, and its objectivity. Robarts points out that the policy of coopération implied equality between France and the other states. It was a policy that viewed all of the countries of the *Tiers Monde* as a whole, with France perceived as a liberating agent in a bipolar world.

Robarts treats the policy in historical perspective from the de Gaulle presidency to the start of that of Giscard d'Estaing. He shows its ad hoc character until the aftermath of Algerian independence with the formulation of principles in the Jeanneney Report: *La Politique de coopération avec les pays en voie de développement* (1963). He discusses at length the Gorse Report of 1971, which called for fundamental reform of the administrative structure for development assistance. The Pompidou regime never published the Gorse Report, thus indicating that it did not intend to adopt its recommendations. Robarts clearly analyzes the *crise de coopération* of 1970–72, in which the various African states and Madagascar requested revision of the agreements to give them greater control and flexibility. President Giscard reoriented coopération on the basis of the Abelin Report of 1975 (*La Politique française de coopération*), which emphasized multilateral aid, public-private cooperation, and the necessity for further Africanization of personnel.

Also useful for understanding the early years of cooperation is *French Aid* (1966) by the British scholar, Teresa Hayter. Two American political scientists, Morton Schwab in his brief *The Political Relationship between France and Her Former Colonies in the Sub-Saharan Regions since 1958* (1968), and Edward M. Corbett, in *The French Presence in Black Africa* (1972), show the very real French involvement in Africa in the decade after formal independence. Though Corbett's work is far more detailed than Schwab's, it provides neither a comprehensive statement of continuing African links nor a full-scale analysis of these relationships in historical perspective. The Zaïrian scholar, Kabongo-Kongo Kola, has reviewed

Franco-African relations in *Traité des rapports franco-africains* (1972). Yvon Bourges, the French Minister for Cooperation, briefly stated official policies during the Pompidou era (1971). Richard Joseph, a West Indian political scientist (1976), the French journalist Claude Wauthier (1972), and Jean Suret-Canale (1974), all criticize French aid policies as neocolonialism.

The largest category of French aid has been in the field of education. With French aid and assistance, most African states have retained French educational models and have even incorporated the latest French reforms. They have acquired a system of higher education and have greatly expanded enrollments at all levels. The most important single study of aid to education is André Labrousse, *La France et l'aide à l'éducation dans 14 Etats africains et malgache* (1971), which covers the 1960s. Further information on French involvement is found in David Gardinier's article on education in the states of Equatorial Africa (1974) and in the various country articles in Asa Knowles, ed., *International Encyclopedia of Higher Education*, 10 vols. (1977). The extensive literature on coopération in education is reviewed in David Gardinier's bibliographical essay on education in the Equatorial African states (1972). The association of French-language universities promoted by France is discussed by Olivier Duhamel (1976), and various aspects of cultural cooperation are reviewed by Philippe Leymarie (1976).

While the largest part of French aid has been bilateral through the mechanisms of coopération, other French aid has been multilateral through the European Development Fund of the European Economic Community and through agencies of the United Nations. Daniel Vignes, *L'Association des Etats africains et malgache à la CEE* (1970), provides a useful collection of documents on this topic. Willy Leonard (1971) treats Madagascar's ties with the EEC between 1958 and 1968. I. William Zartman, *The Politics of Trade Negotiations between Africa and the European Community* (1971), treats the period from the convention implementing the Treaty of Rome through the Yaoundé Convention of 1971. His work includes the Maghreb and former Belgian possessions as well as the former French Black African territories. Zartman updates his study in certain respects in a subsequent article (1976). Jacques Bourrinet, *La Coopération économique eurafricaine* (1976), deals with the first two decades of EEC relations with Africa.

As part of its policy of treating the Black African states as an ensemble, France promoted postindependence ties among them. Lynn Krieger Mytelka (1974) deals with the evolution of the various regional organizations in former French West Africa and French Equatorial Africa, as does a book by Abduh Jalloh, *Political Integration in French-Speaking Africa* (1973).

Various Communist nations have established relations with the former French states and have granted them aid and assistance. Works that show the characteristics of these ties and, in some cases, their impact upon African relations with France, include: Helen Desfosses Cohn, *Soviet Policy towards Black Africa* (1972); Robert Levgold, *Soviet Policy in West Africa* (1970); Bruce Larkin, *China and Africa, 1949–1970* (1971); and Alaba Ogunsanwo, *China's Policy in Africa, 1958–1971* (1974), which also includes Algeria.

Various works published during the past decade on individual countries have made contributions to our understanding of particular aspects of decolonization and the transfer of power. Jacques-Louis Hymans, *An Intellectual Biography: Leopold Sedar Senghor* (1971), provides detailed information about the intellectual and cultural influences on the Senegalese leader and his political career through 1970. The British sociologist, Rita Cruise O'Brien, *White Society in Black Africa: The French of Senegal* (1972), deals with the position of the French settler community at Dakar in the twentieth century. While the work provides useful information about the changing characteristics of the French population, including the arrival of many *petits blancs* after 1945, particularly during decolonization, it fails to utilize the theoretical literature on plural societies. O'Brien (1971) also discusses French technical aid to Senegal in the decade after independence. Babakar Sine, former president of the Federation of Students of French Black Africa (FEANF), treats the socioeconomic evolution of Senegal in his *Impérialisme et théories sociologiques du développement* (1975). Adrian Adams (1974) and Sally N'Dongo, *La 'Coopération' franco-africaine* (1972), examine the problems of the many thousands of Senegalese workers in France whose presence results from French colonialism.

Bertrand Fessard de Foucault (1973) has treated the foreign relations of Mauritania since independence, including those with France. Grégoire Addra, *L'Aide extérieure au Mali* (1971), deals with the economic and social effects of postindependence aid. An American economist, William I. Jones, *Planning and Economic Policy: Socialist Mali and Her Neighbors* (1976), focuses upon the reasons for the failure of the socialist experiment of Modibo Keita between 1961 and 1966. His book provides a useful resumé of precolonial and colonial economic history and the events preceding independence. It includes insightful comparisons of the post independence economic evolution of Mali and neighboring Francophone states. R. W. Johnson's chapter on French imperialism in Guinea (1972) discusses the demise of the European planters and trading companies after independence but the survival of the mining companies which had been installed only after the Second World War. The French sociologist, Claude Rivière (1974), has discussed Guinean political parties before independence. Sylvain Soriba Camara, *La Guinée sans la France* (1976), is a Guinea scholar's account of Franco-Guinean relations from the rupture of October 1958 through the 1970s, including the attempts to establish a new relationship during the early 1960s. Though accurate, it contains neither new facts nor fresh analyses.

The dissertations of Jean-Noël Loucou, *La Vie politique en Côte d'Ivoire de 1932 à 1952* (1976), and of Raymond Guillaneuf, *La Presse en Côte d'Ivoire: La Colonisation, l'aube de la décolonisation, 1906–1952* (1975), throw additional light on Ivorian political evolution under colonial rule, including the repression of the RDA in the late 1940s and early 1950s. M. Landraud (1978) treats the administration of justice during the colonial period. The elegiac biography, *Félix Houphouet-Boigny: L'homme de la paix* (1975) by Paul-Henri Siriex, includes a discussion of the Ivorian president's role in decolonization and postindependence relations with France. F. O. Alalade (1976–77) has provided a useful bibliography on Franco-Ivorian relations since independence. Virginia Thompson's *West Africa's Council of the Entente* (1972) deals more thoroughly with developments in the Ivory Coast and with other council members since independence than with the council itself. The council's evolution is treated more extensively in A. Manouan's long article (1975). Bastian A. den Tunden, *Ivory Coast: The Challenge of Success* (1978) discusses the post-1960 economic expansion and diversification of the agricultural sector, including French involvement. Bonnie Campbell (1975) examines the economic and political impact of the development of the cotton textile industry with European assistance.

For Benin (formerly Dahomey), the Israeli political scientist, Dov Ronen's *Dahomey between Tradition and Modernity* (1975), includes the eras of decolonization and independence. Ronen shows the three-way geographical and ethnic divisions that have contributed to political instability and military rule there. Martin Staniland (1973) emphasizes how the three regionally based parties accommodated their tactics to the rapid expansion of the electorate between 1951 and 1956. J. Beynel (1973) has dealt with the transition to self-government and independence in terms of the national representative institutions.

Niger has been the subject of several important articles. The Norwegian historian, Finn Fuglestad, deals with Djibo Bakary's motivations in urging a negative vote on the French Community in 1958 (1973) and the transfer of official French support from traditionalist to modernist parties between 1948 and 1960 (1975). Three French authors discuss Niger's first decade as an independent state, including its relations with France. Alain Faujas (1971) focuses on foreign policy; Jean-Claude Luc (1971), on the economy; and Gilbert Comte (1971), on political evolution, including the period of self-government from 1957 to 1960.

A number of works deal with several of the West African countries. Lansine Kaba, a Guinean historian, in *The Wahhabiyya: Islamic Reform in West Africa* (1974), deals with a Muslim reformist movement that was both antitraditionalist and anticolonialist during the period 1945 and 1958, including its political activities. Joseph-Roger de Benoist, *La Balkanisation de l'Afrique occidentale française* (1976), discusses the consequences of the failure of the French West African states to maintain or refashion the federation. Two chapters in J. F. Ade Ajayi and Michael Crowder, eds., *History of West Africa*, vol. 2 (1974), should be noted. One by Crowder discusses the Second World War. Another by Crowder and Donal Cruise O'Brien on French West Africa, 1945–60, emphasizes the precedence which the future of the federation took in the leaders' thinking over the question of independence. They also point out the very large extent of economic and administrative dependence upon France even after formal independence in 1960. *The End of Colonial Rule in West Africa* (1979) by John Hargreaves focuses upon the British territories but includes comparisons with the French.

For the former trusteeship territories, Samuel Suka Adabra, in *Les Autorités traditionnelles et le pouvoir politique moderne au Togo* (1973), shows the evolving situation of the traditional chiefs under colonial rule and independence. He treats the various attempts to define their status, including the postindependence moves by the dominant party to diminish their role in administration. D. E. K. Amenumey (1975) has discussed the general elections of April 1958 in the Autonomous Republic of Togo; and the *Revue française d'études politiques africaines* (January 1976) reproduces the text of the white book on reunification of the two Togolands. Richard A. Joseph, *Radical Nationalism in Cameroun: Social Origins of the U.P.C.* (1977), throws additional light on the socioeconomic origins of the Union des Populations du Cameroun and its rebellion, as well as on the role of the French settlers in the territory's post-1945 political evolution. Joseph contends that the French destroyed the authentic nationalists and transferred political power to antinationalists who still control the country two decades later in alliance with French neocolonialists. The French political scientist Jean-François Bayart (1972) has discussed Cameroon's foreign relations between 1960 and 1971, including relations with France.

Moving on to the Equatorial states, Gilbert Comte (1973) reviews the period 1960 to 1973 in Gabon, including relations with France and French involvement in the economy. H. Bertrand, *Le Congo: Formation sociale et mode de développement économique* (1975), reveals the profound contradictions between socialist theories and the neocolonial socioeconomic realities in the People's Republic. Pierre Philippe Rey, a French Marxist scholar, in *Colonialisme, néo-colonialisme et transition au capitalisme: Exemple du COMILOG au Congo-Brazzaville* (1971), treats the role of a large European-financed mining enterprise in the eras of decolonization and independence. The Congolese scholar Martial Sinda, in *Le Messianisme congolais* (1972), shows the political impact of religionationalist movements such as that centered around André Matsoua in the postwar evolution of the Congo. René Gauzé, *The Politics of Congo-Brazzaville* (1973), deals with the period from 1946 to 1962. Gauzé was a civil servant in Equatorial Africa from 1950 on, and from 1958 to 1962 headed the *sûreté* at Brazzaville. He has much to say of interest about the attempts to form a new union of Equatorial states after the demise of the federation and about the transition to independence. In the same volume, Virginia Thompson and Richard Adloff provide a detailed account of the Congo's political evolution from 1962 to 1972, including relations with France, which, however, is lacking in analysis. Pierre Kalck, a longtime French civil servant in the Central African Empire, devotes half of his *Histoire de la république centrafricaine* (1974) to the period 1945–66—that is, up to the arrival in power of Jean-Bedel Bokassa. Kalck provides new information on the impact of the Second World War and the role of the settlers in the country's political evolution. Jacques Serre (1975) reviews the six years of the government of President David Dacko (1960–66), which he personally observed while serving at the National School of Administration in Bangui.

The rebellion in Chad has led to a large literature of articles, much of it inaccurate, incomplete, or so partisan as to be of little scholarly value. The recent exceptions to this generalization are Edmond Jouve (1978), which treats the Tombalbaye and Malloum regimes, and Rob Buijtenhuijs (1978), which places postindependence developments in historical perspective.

For Madagascar, Nigel Hesseltine discusses the political evolution leading to independence in his general history, *Madagascar* (1971). The first history of Madagascar by a Malagasy, *Histoire de Madagascar* (1972) by Edouard Ralaimihoatra, provides useful data on the insurrection of 1947, a topic to which J. Tronchon devotes an entire book, *L'Insurrection malgache de 1947* (1974). Tronchon's work, which rests on extensive interviewing, places the events within their larger political context and concludes that they were definitely part of a nationalist movement. Articles by Francis Koerner (1971) and Pierre Kalck (1973) have also reviewed these events. Kalck throws light on the role of Malagasy Protestants in the nationalist movement. Koerner (1970) has also dealt with the impact of decolonization on the European plantations in the northern coastal regions. Philippe Hugon (1974) has treated Madagascar's economic evolution since independence. Georges Ramamonjisoa (1973) has reviewed Madagascar's renegotiation of its cooperation agreements with France in the early 1970s.

Two small French possessions, the Comoro Islands and French Somaliland, did not achieve independence at the same time as the other Black African territories and Madagascar. The Comoro Islands, minus Mayotte, which remained French, declared its independence unilaterally in 1975 and was immediately deprived of the French financial and technical aid that had allowed its economy and administration to function viably. An article by Laurie Wiseberg and Gary Nelson (1977) is the best source in English for reviewing these and subsequent developments. Earlier, in English, André Bourde (1969) had discussed the political evolution of the Comoros during the 1960s, including the activities of the exile-based liberation movement called MOLINACO. In French, the starting place for an understanding of decolonization in the Comoros is Thierry Flobert, *Les Comores: Evolution juridique et socio-politique* (1977), which treats the political evolution from the Second World War. He includes the international dimensions and the role of the United Nations. There is a large number of articles on the Comoros in French, the most useful of which are those by Said Kemal on the Mahorais separatists of Mayotte (1977); Jean Charpentier on the referenda of 1974 (1976); Jacques Binet (1976); and Louis Favoreu and Jean-Claude Maestre (1975); and André Vallier (1977).

French Somaliland became the French Territory of the Afars and Issas in 1967. At independence a decade later, it took the name Republic of Djibouti. *Afars et Somalis: Le Dossier de Djibouti* (1971) by Philippe Oberle is especially useful for the decade under the *loi-cadre* institutions, 1957–66. Yassin El Ayouty (1969) dealt succinctly with the referendum of 1967, which led to a greater degree of self-government for the territory. Robert Saint-Veran's *A Djibouti avec les Afars et les Issas* (1977) contains information on the transition to independence. Maurice Barbier, *Le Comité de décolonisation des Nations Unies* (1974), reviews the UN discussions on the territory during the 1960s. Articles recommended for comprehending the developments between 1967 and 1975 leading to independence are those in English in the UN publication, *Objective: Justice* (Summer 1977); Said Yusuf Abdi (1977 and 1978); Edward Morgan (1978); W. Sheldon Clarke (1977–78), which contains a long bibliography; and in French, those by Georges Malecot (1977); Pierre Chauleur (1977); Philippe Leymarie (1976,

1977, 1978); R. Pascal (1974); René Benezra (1975); André Nolde (1976); and Benoît Vazeilles (1976).

Literary portraits often provide valuable insights into the historical process. Dorothy S. Blair, *African Literature in French* (1976), is the most comprehensive and detailed guide to authors from the former French and Belgian territories and to works published through 1974.

French North Africa

Most of the writing during the 1970s which contributes to an understanding of decolonization in the countries of French North Africa is the work of Europeans and Americans. Comparatively few Algerians, Tunisians, and Moroccans have published scholarly studies on this period. British historian Michael Brett's historiographical article on the colonial period (1976) points out the preoccupation of French scholars with what went wrong with the French colonial regimes, and when it went wrong. Brett notes that the third edition of Charles-André Julien's *L'Afrique du Nord en marche* (1972) reproduces the original text (1952) but appends a critical bibliography that reveals the issues in French North African scholarship during the intervening decades.

Among those works dealing with all three North African countries are two studies of the Jewish minorities. André Chouraqi, *La Saga des juifs en Afrique du Nord* (1972), includes a discussion of the impact of decolonization upon the Jewish populations, which saw the departure of most of Algeria's 160,000 Jews for France and Israel between 1955 and 1962. He explains the circumstances under which large sections of the Jewish communities in Tunisia and Morocco remained. Doris Bensimon-Donath, *L'Intégration des juifs nord-africains en France* (1971), deals with the North African Jews who settled in France. The American political scientist, Mark Tessler (1978), has compared the status of the Jews who remained in Tunisia and Morocco with that of the Arabs in Israel.

There is also a sizeable analytical literature on the formation of political elites in the three countries, which shows how the different colonial experiences helped to create different types of leadership in the era of decolonization and after independence. Two studies published under the auspices of the Centre de Recherches Economiques et Sociales du Maghreb (CRESM) are Lhachmi Berrady et al., *La Formation des élites politiques maghrébines* (1973), and M. Teitler et al., *Elites, pouvoir et légitimité au Maghreb* (1973). A work edited by Elbaki Hermassi, *Leadership and National Development* (1973), carries the perspective on elite formation back into the precolonial period and forward into the present. It shows how colonial influences penetrated older social and political structures to produce distinctive institutions and processes during decolonization and since independence. Hermassi (1971) shows in what ways the institutions of the colonial regimes in the three North African countries helped to shape postindependence institutions.

The French North African countries have also been treated in studies dealing with the Arab Muslim world. A work edited by P. J. Vatikiotis, *Revolution in the Middle East* (1972), has chapters on Algeria, Tunisia, and Morocco by French specialists. In *L'Orient Second* (1970), French sociologist Jacques Berque develops further some of the themes he presented in *Dépossession du monde* (1964) and takes up some new ones. The best case studies and examples in his work deal with North Africa. Berque employs the methodology of historical sociology with many anthropological influences. He analyzes the meaning of decolonization in the Arab Muslim world and its repercussions on the former colonized and colonizers. Decolonization, he declares, means not only national independence and economic reconstruction but also redefinition of the self, individual and collective. The independent state needs to find authenticity—that is, to rediscover a collective identity rooted in historical continuity but not necessarily in tradition. It needs to find a route to technological advancement and economic progress while retaining a continuity within itself, a difficult but not an impossible task.

Algeria

Algeria has been the subject of the bulk of historical writing on French North Africa during the past decade. Jean-Claude Vatin's *L'Algérie politique: Histoire et société* (1974) represents a major effort to reexamine the entire colonial period in terms of its impact upon the Algerian Muslim majority. To this end he undertakes a thorough historiographical discussion of previous writing and thereby forces a thoughtful reconsideration of the stereotypes held by previous specialists in the colonial period. On the basis of his reexamination, Vatin argues that 1962 saw the rebirth of an Algerian nation that had existed before 1830. It took the Algerians until after the First World War, in his opinion, to begin the reversal of the setback of 1830. The contest against colonial domination and exploitation which gained headway after 1919 culminated in the colonial revolution that led to independence. According to Vatin's thesis, decolonization begins with the First World War and then enters a much accelerated stage during and after the Second World War.

Several scholars who have been studying various aspects of the decolonization of Algeria have published some of their results in article form. Charles-Robert Ageron has treated the role of Ferhat Abbas in the Muslim political awakening during the Second World War (1975) and French opinion about the Algerian war (1976). A. Nadir has examined the place of the Muslim reformists in the war of national liberation (1975), and Redouane Ainad-Tabet has interpreted the incidents at Sétif in May 1945 (1972).

A large part of the literature on Algeria has concerned the colonial revolution and its aftermath, including its origins in French colonial policies and practices, and Algerian reactions and responses. Students of these subjects are fortunate to have a review article by Guy Pervillé (1977) which discusses 148 books in French on the Algerian war that were published between independence in 1962 and mid-1977. His study also analyzes a dozen unpublished French theses and *mémoires* and refers to a dozen or so nontranslated books and dissertations in English and German. It provides valuable information about the backgrounds and viewpoints of the authors. Pervillé concludes that the bulk of the literature in French on the Algerian war consists of *témoignages* and narratives composed from a definite viewpoint (for example, settler, Gaullist, FLN) rather than of scientific studies. According to Pervillé, the two best accounts of the war in terms of accuracy and completeness are Pierre Beyssade, *La Guerre d'Algérie, 1954–1962* (1968), and Philippe Tripier, *Autopsie de la guerre d'Algérie* (1972). Beyssade was educated as a lawyer and Tripier as an officer at St. Cyr; both graduated from the Centre des Hautes Etudes Administratives Musulmanes (CHEAM) in Paris. Beyssade was a civil servant in Algiers from 1945 to 1955, whereas Tripier held a military command there after service in Indochina. Even more detailed than Tripier's 700-page account are the four volumes of *La Guerre d'Algérie* (1968–71) by the perceptive journalist, Yves Courrière, who interviewed many FLN figures, including Belkacem Krim, in the course of the conflict. The British writer, Alistair Horne, interviewed many of the Algerian, Tunisian, and French participants and observers for his recent detailed study, *A Savage War of Peace, Algeria 1954–1962* (1977). A massive German work, *Frankreichs Algerienkrieg* (1974) by Harmut Eisenhans, also employed extensive interviewing and German documentation as well as French.

Several important studies on the FLN have appeared during the 1970s. Mohammed Harbi, *Aux origines du FLN* (1975), is a participant's account of the split within the MTLD that gave rise to the Centralist faction, which started the rebellion, and the Messalist faction, which opposed the conflict and continued to look to Messali Hadj for direction. Harbi's viewpoint is more favorable to the Messalists than to the Centralists. His work provides a very useful analysis of Algerian society between 1945 and 1954 and the political context from which the FLN sprang. In *Insurgency and Counter-Insurgency in Algeria, 1954–1958* (1972), Alf Andrew Heggoy, a

Norwegian-American who was born and grew up in Algeria, argues that the French adapted themselves well militarily to the FLN rebellion. By mid-1956 they had regained the initiative, but by the same time the nationalists had won Muslim Algerian opinion over to the FLN cause. Though the rebels had lost the military struggle by 1958 in Heggoy's opinion, by shifting emphasis to the political aspects of the struggle they were able to win the war. In addition to providing valuable analyses of the tactics of the insurgents and French counterinsurgents, Heggoy's work has much value for comprehending the course of the revolution after May 1958, as well as of events after independence. Martha Crenshaw Hutchinson, *Revolutionary Terrorism: The FLN in Algeria, 1954–1962* (1978), discusses the FLN's use of terrorism as a political strategy and as an integral part of the nationalist struggle against French colonialism. She explains the successes and failures of terrorism in obtaining popular support, destroying the French presence, gaining international recognition, and maintaining the discipline and morale of the revolutionary organization. Hutchinson contends that France, by concentrating on the military rather than the political aspects of the rebellion, failed to prevent the FLN from gaining effective control of the Algerian population. Henry I. Jackson, *The FLN in Algeria: Party Development in a Revolutionary Society* (*1954*-1965)(1977), argues that the FLN did not create a centrally organized structure that could become the basis for a single-party system after independence. His study has particular value for showing the conditions that brought Ahmed Ben Bella to power and later led to his downfall. Hutchinson's conclusions about the FLN seem to square well with Heggoy's findings, while Jackson's arguments support William Quandt's, in *Revolution and Political Leadership: Algeria, 1954–1958* (1969), that the revolution did not create a single cohesive elite but a pluralistic series of elite factions.

Other important works on the war include Peter Geismar, "De Gaulle, the Army, and Algeria: The Civil-Military Conflict over Decolonization" (Ph.D. diss., Columbia University, 1967), and Régine Goutalier, *L'OAS en Oranie* (1975). The latter treats an aspect of the conflict in the western third of Algeria, which contributed to the massive departure of the settlers. Bernard Tricot, *Les Sentiers de la paix, Algérie, 1958–1962* (1972), provides the best discussion of the Evian accords. Robert Buron, the chief French negotiator at Evian, in *Carnets politiques de la guerre de l'Algérie par un signataire des Accords d'Evian* (1965), discusses some of the aspects of the settlement that were not implemented, in part because of the actions of the Secret Army. Jacques Ribs, *Indemnisation* (1971), treats compensation to settlers who lost properties through departure or confiscation.

There is an extensive literature on the policies and practices of the

French Communist party and the Algerian Communist party in relation to Algerian nationalism and the revolution. Most of these works are analyzed in an extended review by François Alexandre in the *Annuaire de l'Afrique du Nord* (1976). Alexandre points out the very real tensions produced among European Communists by the conflicts between Marxism and French nationalism, and among Marxism, Algerian nationalism, and Islam for the Muslim Communists. For the best discussions of these matters, one should consult Jacob Moneta, *Le Parti communiste français et la question coloniale* (1971), and Emmanuel Sivan, *Communisme et nationalisme en Algérie, 1920–1962* (1976). Not reviewed by Alexandre is a recent work written from a Marxist perspective, *La Question coloniale et la politique du Parti communiste français* (1977), by Grégoire Madjarian. An American historian, Irwin M. Wall (1977), has explored the attitudes of the French Communists toward the Algerian war.

Among the various works which examine decolonization on a broader scale than the war or the revolution is *The French Stake in Algeria, 1945–1962* (1978) by American political scientist Tony Smith. Smith focuses on the French colonial consensus concerning Algeria, a product of the Third Republic and the Second World War, whose support extended from the far Right to the socialist Left, to explain why the Fourth Republic had such a hard time relinquishing control to Algeria, even in the face of the breakdown of the colonial system. Smith credits General de Gaulle, who in 1944–46 was largely responsible for France's retention of the empire as a means of keeping its international rank, for making relinquishment in 1962 seem, not a humiliation, but a reaffirmation of its civilizing mission. Smith sees the French settler community and the colony's weak economic structure as the chief reasons for the failure to create integrative links between Algeria and the metropole; he does not mention the religious and cultural differences between the North African Muslims and Europeans as a major factor. Raoul Weextsteen, *Colonisation, décolonisation et structures urbaines: Une ville d'Algérie, Blida* (1974), provides a case study of the impact of colonial rule and decolonization on a city near Algiers. *La Naissance et la reconnaissance de la république algérienne* (1972) by Abdelmadjib Belkherroubi deals with the juridical aspects of decolonization and the formation of the Algerian state. Though useful, the study might have been more valuable if the author had employed more of the available sources. Recent years have seen the appearance of several important works on economic development and social change. Adbellatif Benachenhou, *Formation du sous-développement en Algérie: Essai sur les limites du capitalisme, 1830–1962* (1976), contends that the absence of an indigenous bourgeoisie to develop the economy after independence left only the options of state capitalism or socialism. Benachenhou's work contains much valuable data, including statistics not found elsewhere. Maurice Brogini, *L'Exploitation des hydrocarbures en Algérie de 1956 à 1971: Etude de géographie économique* (1973), is an indispensable reference for the role of petroleum and natural gas in the evolution of Algeria, including their political dimensions. Brogini concludes that under colonial rule hydrocarbons made no contribution to development in Algeria. Independent Algeria changed the structures so they would aid development and founded Sonatrach to administer the oil wealth. But even by 1971 hydrocarbons were not yet integrated into a program of industrialization.

Marnia Lazreg, an American-educated Algerian sociologist, has written *The Emergence of Classes in Algeria—a Study of Colonialism and Socio-Political Change* (1974). She shows in what ways the French presence led to a restratification of the Muslim population and to what extent her findings verify or modify current social theories. She concludes that Marx's class analysis does not take account of colonial formations, in particular their ethnic and national characteristics. She contends that the Algerian revolution saw the defeat of Algerian bourgeois elements and the transfer of power to radical elements of the petite bourgeoisie who sought alliance with technocrats in order to promote rapid industrialization. David C. Gordon, *Women of Algeria: An Essay on Change* (1968), shows that the involvement of women in the Algerian revolution did not lead to an improvement in their condition in a Muslim society. Once independence was achieved, a traditional reaction scuttled the advances they had started to make. Fadéla M'rabet, *Les Femmes algériennes et Les Algériennes* (1969) deals with the evolving status of women in recent decades. Alf Andrew Heggoy has written several important articles on colonial education in Algeria, which he personally experienced, including the cultural conflicts (1973), Arab education (1975), and the French army's role during the revolution (1973).

One of the legacies of the French presence in Algeria is the several hundred thousand Algerians living and working in France. Malek Ath-Messaoud, an Algerian sociologist, and Alain Gillette, a French jurist, have collaborated on *L'Immigration algérienne en France* (1976). Their work is a valuable reference and synthesis in historical perspective, which shows how Arab emigration was, above all, a response to French colonization and colonialism.

Frantz Fanon's ideas and theories, which were derived in part from his Algerian experience, continue to be the subject of important articles. Irene Gendzier, the biographer of Fanon, (1976) examines his psychology of colonization and decolonization as expressed in *A Dying Colonialism*. In particular, she analyzes his views on the extent to which oppression in a colonial setting can transform the psychology of both colonizer and colonized, affecting both their self-image and relations. B. Marie Perinbam (1973) has compared Fanon's theories on the revolutionary peasantry with the realities of the Algerian experience, while Paul Beckett (1973) has looked at the gaps and contradictions between his theories on decolonization and the Algerian situation.

L'Algérie politique: Institutions et régime (1975), by Jean Leca and Jean-Claude Vatin, forms a sequel to Vatin's study of the previous year (discussed above). Their sociopolitical analysis shows the kind of "administrative state" which was transferred into Algerian hands through independence. Another work that deals with the postindependence institutions and relations in terms of their roots in the colonial and decolonizing eras is *L'Algérie indépendante: Idéologie et Institutions* (1974) by Bernard Cubertafond. A left-wing French journalist couple, Gérard Chaliand and Juliette Minces, in *L'Algérie indépendante* (1972), express disappointment that the Algerian revolution did not lead to what they considered a genuine socialist regime. Their analyses seem to confirm Marnia Lazreg's conclusion that Algeria in the early 1970s still possessed capitalist structures and mainly socialist aspirations.

Finally, for the understanding of Franco-Algerian relations since 1962 there is a growing literature. *French International Policy under de Gaulle and Pompidou: The Politics of Grandeur* (1974), by Edward A. Kolodziej, ably places postindependence relations within the larger context of France's Third World role. A long chapter in the dissertation of Robert Adler Mortimer, "Foreign Policy and Its Role in Nation-Building in Algeria" (Columbia University, 1968), deals with the first five years after independence, while Jean Offredo, *Algérie: Avec ou sans la France?* (1973), and Nikolai Ivonovich Kirei, *Algeria and France, 1962–1971* (1973), cover the first decade.

Tunisia and Morocco

During the past decade, there has been only a small amount of scholarly writing on decolonization and the transfer of power in Tunisia and Morocco. Two Tunisian scholars have examined aspects of their country's political evolution after 1940. Mustapha Kraiem has written of labor-union activities in the year following the ousting of the Axis armies (1974) and the events of 5 August 1947 at Sfax (1977). Mohnsen Toumi has discussed the place of the Neo-Dstour party in the nationalist movement (1974). A Jewish Tunisian, Elie Cohen Hadria, who played a prominent role in the Socialist party from the 1920s, has published his recollections in *Du protectorat français à l'indépendance tunisienne: Souvenirs d'un témoin socialiste* (1976). Jean Poncet, *La Tunisie à la recherche de son avenir* (1974), and Reinhardt Bloz, *Tunesien: Wirtschaftliche und soziale Strukturen und Entwicklung* (1976), treat the economic and social evolution of independent Tunisia, including the transformation of the role of the French settlers and economic interests.

For Morocco, Robin Bidwell's study of French administration in the tribal areas, *Morocco under Colonial Rule* (1973), suggests that indigenous political institutions continued to function below the surface of the colonial regime, to which the nationalists were an exotic addition. Thus decolonization touched only a tiny portion of the population. Henri Marchat (1971) has explored the roles of France and Spain in the protectorate regime. Hervé Bleuchot, *Les Libéraux Français au Maroc, 1947–1955* (1974), Félix Nataf, *L'Indépendance du Maroc, témoignage d'action (1950–1956)*(1975), and Sheridan Nichols (1976) have all treated French liberals in Morocco during decolonization—the first two as observers and political activitists. William Hoisington (1974) has studied the role of French businessmen in the same period. Leon Borden Blair has pursued his research on the impact of the American armed forces on Moroccan nationalism (1972) and has examined the role of the American vice-consuls in all of North Africa during the Second World War (1973).

Belgian Africa: The Congo

In the wake of the Congo's precipitous course to independence and the subsequent crisis, the Institute of Race Relations in London commissioned two British historians to undertake the general studies of Leopoldian and Belgian rule which are still the best introductions to the subject in English. Ruth Slade prepared *King Leopold's Congo* (1962), and Roger Anstey, *King Leopold's Legacy* (1966). The title of Anstey's study not only indicates that it is a sequel to Slade's; it also emphasizes the real extent to which Leopoldian policies created the problems with which Belgium had to deal and the institutional structures through which it was to govern the country. Anstey sees Belgium as a reluctant colonial power which lacked a colonial tradition; it sought to correct abuses and yet hoped to profit from its new acquisition. Belgian policies formulated by the early 1920s remained stable through the 1950s, despite the changed conditions created by the industrialization, urbanization, and production of an elite or évolué class to which colonial rule had contributed. In Anstey's view, these changes should have led to a reformulation in policies at least by the end of the Second World War. But significant changes came only at the end of the 1950s, and then too late to deal with the forces of decolonization. Anstey's and Slade's studies, taken together, allow us to see the decolonization of the 1950s and the transfer of power within a perspective that encompasses the precolonial period and both the Leopoldian and Belgian phases of the colonial period.

Ruth Slade also published a brief study, *The Belgian Congo*, in 1960 under the auspices of the IRR. It focused on African discontent with colonial rule, particularly from 1954 onward, and the Belgian responses that led to the Declaration of January 1959. Early in 1961 the book was reissued with a long chapter by Marjorie Taylor covering the events between early 1959 and independence in June 1960. Also helpful for understanding Belgian rule is still another brief work published under the auspices of the IRR, *Belgian Administration in the Congo* (1961) by Georges Brausch. Brausch was an anthropologist and colonial administrator who served between 1954 and 1957 as an advisor to the Liberal colonial minister, Auguste Buisseret. This work shows, among other things, how metropolitan politics hindered orderly steps toward decolonization and ultimately undermined the authority and morale of the colonial authorities during the critical transition to independence between late 1958 and mid-1960.

Congo, Background of Conflict (1961), by American anthropologist Alan P. Merriam, illuminates the political awakening, with emphasis on the various political formations and their leaders as well as on the Belgian background for relinquishing authority. By far the most interesting sections today are those dealing with the impact of the country's political evolution at the national level upon the village in eastern Kasai Province, where Merriam did fieldwork during 1951–52 and 1959–60, and upon the Lumumbist stronghold of Stanleyville.

In *Political Protest in the Congo* (1967), an American political scientist, Herbert Weiss, focuses on the Parti Solidaire Africain (PSA), which was formed by non-Bakongo elements in Leopoldville in reaction to the ethnic exclusiveness of the Alliance des Ba-Kongo (ABAKO). The PSA also had Centralist and Socialist tendencies. Though the PSA leadership included many different ethnic groups, its mass support came from the rural areas of the Kwilu and Kwango districts of the Leopoldville Region. Weiss observed on the spot that Belgian colonial rule had touched the lives of these rural residents more profoundly than had French rule in West Africa and British rule in East Africa, both areas he had previously studied. His findings help to explain the inability of the colonial or postindependence regimes to control the masses in the rural Leopoldville region and elsewhere in the Congo between 1959 and 1964. Rural anarchy in 1959–60 and the widespread rebellions in 1963–64 offer proof for Weiss of the existence of the kind of revolutionary peasantry and rural radicalism which earlier interpreters of the decolonization process in Asia and Africa, such as Rupert Emerson of Harvard University, had denied.

René Lemarchand's *Political Awakening in the Belgian Congo* (1964) provides some of the most lucid analyses and precise data available for understanding the Congo's political evolution through independence and Katangan secession. Lemarchand's main objective was to analyze the causes of political fragmentation in Congolese politics. To this end he examined in historical perspective the socioeconomic settings from which the political formations came and the subsequent political forces that gave them shape. He analyzed in much detail the varied geographical and ethnic impacts of Belgian rule and their consequences for social mobilization.

Lemarchand concluded that the several types of distinct institutions through which Belgian acculturative influences were projected—the colonial administration, the large companies, the Christian missions—tended to inhibit rather than to promote the development of a national consciousness and a national loyalty. Furthermore, the heterogeneous nature of Belgian national culture, with its French/Flemish, republican/royalist, Christian/secular cleavages, fostered a situation in which so-called national symbols tended to be identified with subcultures rather than with a genuinely national culture. As a result of these various factors, independence for the Congolese masses ultimately came to mean the eviction of Belgian interests rather than a common striving toward the construction of a viable nation-state.

In *Politics in the Congo: Decolonization and Independence* (1965), political scientist Crawford Young sought to analyze the emerging Congolese political system in terms of nation-building, a theme popular in the 1960s. Young concluded that Belgium created a formidable colonial structure but refused to begin political adaptations to changing conditions, especially needed after 1945, until the entire system began to disintegrate. This situation made the transfer of power (and Young employs the term) peculiarly difficult. The Belgian plan for transfer in June 1960 involved a new set of African-run political institutions but retention of a Belgian-run bureaucracy and the Belgian-officered army. The rapid breakdown of this system in July 1960 tragically revealed the greatest weakness of Belgian rule: the failure to give the Congolese access to administrative and military positions of importance. Thus the Congolese elite that came into being was in the lower ranks, regional without national ties, and sheltered from the impact of the world outside the Congo. It was ill-prepared to fulfill its new political roles.

The Belgian political scientist, Michel de Schrevel, taught at the University of Lovanium in Kinshasa at the time of the publication of his case study of the political problem of decolonization, *Les Forces politiques de la décolonisation congolaise à la veille de l'indépendance* (1970). Using the methodology of political sociology, he analyzed the roles played by the various political forces in the Congo and elsewhere in moving that country toward independence through January 1959.

De Schrevel's work is especially good for the influence of metropolitan politics on developments in the Congo, particularly from 1954 on. He notes that emancipation of the Congo was undertaken above all at the level of the Ministry of the Colonies, not by the Belgian parliament and government, and not by the colonial administration. Like Crawford Young, de Schrevel concludes that the lateness and inadequacy of Belgian plans for decolonization had disastrous effects.

Another Belgian political scientist, Paule Bouvier, in *L'Accession du Congo belge à l'indépendance* (1965), also using the methodology of political sociology, sought to isolate the main factors of the social, economic, and political conjuncture which conditioned the manner in which the Congo acceded to independence, and to show their interrelationships in the course of events through the end of 1962. Michel Merlier, in a work completed less than two years after independence, *Le Congo de la colonisation belge à l'indépendance* (1962), used Marxist-Leninist categories to analyze the Belgian colonial system, the agrarian question, the formation of the urban "proletariat," the impact of the missions and the rise of messianic movements, and the political evolution leading to independence.

Still another Belgian political scientist, Jules Gérard-Libois, has provided a very detailed account of the *Katanga Secession* of 11 July 1960 to 14 January 1963 (1966). Gérard-Libois, who taught at Lovanium, was present in the Congo for much of the period and was able to hold interviews and to obtain unofficial materials as well as the usual published sources. Appendixes to the volume contain relevant documents.

Professors Gérard-Libois and Benoit Verhaegen were involved in the collecting and editing of important documents for the period 1959–61. Under the direction of these Belgian political scientists, the Centre de Recherche et d'Information Socio-Politique (CRISP) in Brussels published *Congo 1959*, *Congo 1960* in three volumes (the third containing annexes and biographies of Congolese leaders), *Congo 1961*, and *ABAKO, 1950–1960. Documents* (1962). Pierre Artigue published a most useful reference work, *Qui sont les leaders congolais?* (2d ed., 1961), which contains the biographies of eight hundred Congolese leaders. He describes the political role of all of them and gives personal and education information about the most important ones.

Antoine A. J. Van Bilsen is a Belgian scholar who taught in the mid-1950s at the Institut Universitaire des Territoires d'Outre-Mer and at the Institut Supérieur de Commerce de l'Etat at Antwerp. There he came to see the evolution of the Belgian Congo and Ruanda-Urundi in a Pan-African and global context. Through newspaper and journal articles he tried to educate his fellow countrymen to the need to change their colonial policies, in particular to prepare the Africans to run their own affairs. In 1956 he formulated a *Thirty-Year Plan* for the emancipation of the Congo, which subsequently became the basis for the *Manifesto* of the Conscience Africaine written by évolué elements in 1956. Van Bilsen later became an advisor to Kasavubu and the ABAKO during the Round Table Conference. Thus his writings are the work of both a scholar and an active participant. Two collections of his essays and articles were subsequently published and form a valuable source for the evolution of his thinking and the understanding of the events from 1954 to 1961: *Vers l'indépendance du Congo et du Ruanda-Urundi* (1958) and *L'Indépendance du Congo* (1962).

The Belgian historian, Georges-Henri Dumont, attended all of the sessions of the Round Table Conference of January–February 1960. He taped many sessions and obtained the complete stenographic records of the remainder, as well as the government, party, and delegation documents. The last quarter of his *La Table ronde belgo-congolaise* (1961) contains the texts of some of the most important documents. The bulk of Dumont's study consists of a detailed interpretive account of the conference situated within both its metropolitan and its African contexts.

Walter J. Ganshof van der Meersch was a distinguished Belgian professor of law and practicing attorney before the Court of Cassation. Between 15 May and 20 July 1960, he served as Ministre Chargé des Affaires Générales en Afrique. The report he made to the government concerning his period of service led to the writing of *Fin de la souveraineté belge au Congo* (1963), which treats in great detail the last six weeks of Belgian sovereignty in the Congo. The work contains many important documents and a useful chronology. It has details on the legislative and provincial elections, the parties, the setting up of the new political institutions, the formation of the Lumumba government, and the mutiny of the Force Publique.

Témoignage et réflexions (1967) is another important work by a participant. Léon A. M. Pétillon was a career officer in the Colonial Service from 1929 to 1958. He assisted Pierre Ryckmans before becoming governor-general of the Congo between late 1951 and July 1958 and then Minister of the Colonies from July to November 1958. In 1952, Pétillon was responsible for the concept of the Belgian-Congolese Community, in which he tried, with ministry support, to put relations on a better basis. Approximately one-quarter of this book contains addresses and writings from the period of his governor-generalship and ministerial post.

Useful for the interpretation of events from 1959 through the mid-1960s are the transcripts of fourteen radio and television broadcasts edited by Pierre de Vos, in which noted Belgian politicians, civil servants, and scholars participated: *La Décolonisation: Les Evénements du Congo de 1959 à 1967* (1975).

A British scholar working under the auspices of the Royal Institute of International Affairs, Catherine Hoskyns, composed a detailed account of the events in the Congo between January 1960 and December 1961, *The Congo since Independence* (1965). It is especially useful for an understanding of the international dimensions of the Congo crisis of July 1960 and after; an appendix contains the texts of the various UN resolutions on the Congo. Also valuable for the international dimensions is *Mission for Hammarskjold: The Congo Crisis* (1976) by Rajeshwar Dayal, the Indian diplomat who headed the UN mission in the Congo from early September 1960 to March 1961 as Secretary-General Dag Hammarskjold's special representative. Dayal presents a detailed account of UN involvement in the crisis from its beginnings through the death of Hammarskjold in September 1961. His volume is primarily a defense and a justification of the secretary-general's actions and secondarily of his own. It nevertheless has much merit because of Dayal's access to hitherto unused sources and its valuable portraits of Lumumba, Kasavubu, Mobutu, and especially Hammarskjold.

Patrice Lumumba (1925–61) wrote *Le Congo, terre d'avenir—est-il menacé?* during 1956–57, but it was not published until after his death. British journalist Colin Legum, author of *Congo Disaster* (1961), wrote a useful introduction to the English translation, *Congo, My Country* (1962). Given the lack of freedom of expression in the Congo in the mid-1950s, it is hard to know to what degree Lumumba censored himself in expressing his ideas about the future of the Congo and its relations with Belgium. But if one takes him at face value, in 1957 he still accepted the notion of a Belgian-Congolese community and advocated reforms of the colonial system rather than its abolition. After Lumumba's murder, the Belgian Jean Van Lierde edited his speeches and writings between 1958 and 1961 (*La Pensée politique de Patrice Lumumba* [1963]). They were published by *Présence Africaine*, with a long polemical introduction by Jean-Paul Sartre that places Lumumba's career in its historical context as perceived from the far Left in France. An English translation did not appear until 1972. These two works, when read in conjunction with *Conflict in the Congo* (1972) by the Zairian diplomat and political scientist Thomas Kanza, allow one to see the historical importance of Lumumba and his tragic role in the crisis that killed both him and Hammarskjold. Kanza knew Lumumba well and remained loyal to him without being blind to his shortcomings.

Charles-André Gilis, a Belgian civil servant, provides a most useful biography of the Congo's first president, *Kasa-Vubu au coeur du drame congolais* (1964). Moise Tshombe is interpreted from the perspective of the Cold War by the American political scientist Anthony Bouscaren. His *Tshombe* (1967) provides a healthy antidote to the studies which are hostile to the secessionist leader. It has much useful information about Tshombe's connections with American interests and supporters. What are said to be the authentic memoirs of Tshombe were published in Belgium in 1975. Perhaps the most valuable sections of Edouard Bustin's *Lunda under Belgian Rule* (1975) are those on the period 1945–65, and in particular the ones on Tshombe and his relationship with Conakat, the secessionist movement, and the traditional Lunda authorities.

The study of the political evolution of the Congo has taken precedence over that of the economic evolution. But in the late 1960s the Marxist Belgian historian Jean-Philippe Peemans began to publish the results of his investigations of the colonial economic system. *Diffusion du progres économique et convergence des prix* (1968) dealt with the period 1900–60, and a chapter in 1975 discussed the role of the colonial government in the accumulation of capital during roughly the same period. Then, in the early 1970s, another economic historian, Bohumil Jesiewicki, began to publish important articles on the colonial system and its social consequences (1972 and 1976). In 1968 a team of scholars headed by Michel Norro examined the postindependence economic evolution in the light of the colonial period, in *Indépendance, inflation, développement: l'Economie congolaise de 1960 à 1965*. Then, in 1975, Peemans reviewed the economic and social evolution of Zaïre since independence in the same perspective.

In the field of social history, Marie-Louise Martin, *Kimbangu: An African Prophet and His Church* (1975), adds little new on the prophet himself but much on the development of his church after this death in 1951. Martin, who headed the Ecole de Théologie Kimbanguiste at Kinshasa, shows how the church gained toleration and then recognition by the Belgian administration.

The question of postindependence cooperation between Belgium and its former territories has been the subject of several books and many articles. Among the most important are: the volume of Baudouin Piret, *Aide de la Belgique aux pays sous-développés* (1972); the long study by J. Brassinne on the Congo (1968), which contains many important documents in its appendixes; Brassinne's study on military cooperation (1972); and brief general articles by Jean Eloy (1972) and Viviane Michel (1975).

A review of the article literature that has appeared in the past decade indicates that Belgian, American, and Zaïrian scholars are turning their attention to the transformations of the colonial period in specific regions and among particular ethnic groups (Jan Vansina, 1972, and Thomas Turner, 1973); to the appearance of resistance groups and anticolonial political elites in the periods before the late 1950s (Benoît Verhaegen, 1971a and 1971b; Bakonzi Agayo, 1974; and Mulamba Mvuluya, 1974); and to the impact of Belgian colonial education (Pierre Erny, 1974, and Kekwakha Kinenge Kimena, 1974). Zaïrian scholars are still giving more attention to precolonial periods than to the colonial period, it would appear, and the eras of colonial rule and decolonization are still mainly the province of Europeans and Americans.

Rwanda and Burundi

In addition to the Congo, Belgium administered portions of German East Africa, which it acquired as a result of the First World War as the mandate, and later trusteeship, territory of Ruanda-Urundi. These areas achieved independence in 1962 as separate states called Rwanda and Burundi.

Wm. Roger Louis's *Ruanda-Urundi, 1884–1919* (1963) is a definitive study of these lands, and includes imperial competition, German administration, the First World War, and the peace settlement of 1919 that assigned them to Belgium. There does not seem to be a single detailed study of Belgian administration and League supervision of the mandate. One must look to various works on the mandates system, Belgian policies in Africa, and general histories of the two states to establish the main lines of Belgian policies and practices and their impact upon the Africans. Similarly, one must turn to general works on trusteeship and Belgian policies to understand the role of the UN in the supervision of Belgian administration.

The noted anthropologist Jacques Maquet, in his *The Premise of Inequality in Rwanda* (1961 English trans. of the 1954 French text), analyzes the respective roles of the ruling Tutsi and the subject Hutu in the society of the Rwanda kingdom. In 1959, Maquet's *Elections en société féodale* discusses the first elections in which the entire adult male population was eligible. He provides a detailed analysis of the elections, the places of the candidates in their societies, and the impact on the territory's ethnic problem.

Under the auspices of CRISP, F. Nkundabenzi edited *Rwanda politique* (1961), which contains documents from the period 1956–61. Many of them related to the political changes connected with the breakdown of the Tutsi-dominated society in the face of the voting strength of the Hutu majority. The volume terminates with the proclamation of the Republic on 28 January 1961 and the international reactions to this action. The Institut

Royal des Relations Internationales in Brussels in 1963 published a very detailed survey of Rwanda and Burundi, including documentation from official sources, in its journal, *Chronique de politique étrangère* 16, nos. 4–6 (July–November 1963).

Only after independence did original works begin to appear in English on the era of decolonization. John B. Webster, bibliographer of Syracuse University's East Africa Program, published two mimeographed studies, *The Constitutions of Burundi, Malagasy, and Rwanda* (1964) and *The Political Development of Rwanda and Burundi* (1966). The first contained the texts of the new states' constitutions, annotated and translated into English, while the second outlined their political evolution from precolonial times through independence. But only with the appearance of René Lemarchand's monumental *Rwanda and Burundi* (1970) was there a detailed account of the era of decolonization, including the transfer of power into African hands. His focus, however, was on neither of these phenomena but on the revolutions in both states which destroyed the power of the Tutsi ruling minorities, including the monarchies, and gave more power to elements from the Hutu majorities. The revolution in Rwanda took place between 1959 and 1961, with Belgian blessings; but in Burundi it was mainly after independence. Using the analytical tools of sociology and political science, Lemarchand explains and interprets these developments, placing them in a historical context that includes both the precolonial and colonial periods.

Ian Linden, *Church and Revolution in Rwanda* (1977), shows the extensive penetration by the Catholic church in Rwanda during the twentieth century, which after 1945 saw younger Belgian missionaries shifting support from the Tutsi clergy toward the Hutu priests. This situation ultimately placed most of the church's leadership on the side of the revolution of 1959–61 but left the institution itself deeply divided.

Recent research on colonial rule and decolonization relevant to our topic includes Gaetan Feltz's interpretive article (1971) and study of the civil war in Rwanda, *Les Causes et conséquences de la guerre civile au Rwanda* (1973); Helen Codere's study of social change in Rwanda between 1900 and 1960, *The Biography of an African Society* (1973); Warren Weinstein's monograph on decolonization in the two states, *The Patterns of African Decolonization* (1973); Baudouin Paternostre de la Marie, *Le Rwanda* (1972), a Rwandan's view of the twentieth century; and Pierre Erny's articles on colonial education (1974–78).

After independence, Rwanda and Burundi received aid from Belgium and developed new ties with the Common Market, France, and former French African territories. Maurice Ligot has described coopération between Rwanda and France (1964). C. Reuss has treated Belgian aid to Burundi (1969), and Warren Weinstein military aid from 1961 to 1973 (1973). International Monetary Fund, *Survey of African Economies*, vol. 5: *Botswana, Lesotho, Swaziland, Burundi, Equatorial Guinea, Rwanda* (1973), contains data on the postindependence economic evolution.

The most useful bibliographies for both territories are found in Webster and Lemarchand, cited above. In addition, for Burundi, there is a detailed one in the *Historical Dictionary of Burundi*, by Warren Weinstein (1976), and in an article by Simon Nahayo (1971–72); the dictionary also has a valuable chronology of political events. For Rwanda, the *Rwanda Area Handbook*, ed. Richard F. Nyrop (1969) has a general bibliography, and Laurent Nkusi has prepared a specialized one on the Kinyarwanda (1977).

Portuguese Africa

Prior to the outbreak of the nationalist rebellions in Angola, Mozambique, and Portuguese Guinea in the early 1960s, the study of Portuguese colonial rule was largely confined, outside of Portugal itself, to a small number of scholars writing in English. Among them, James Duffy of Brandeis University has provided the most useful works for understanding the policies and practices of the Salazar regime. His *Portuguese Africa* (1959) concentrates on Angola and Mozambique since the fifteenth century, while his briefer *Portugal in Africa* (1962) includes materials on the other Portuguese territories as well. The key aspects of the New State's policies, according to Duffy, were the assimilation of individual Africans who had adopted a Portuguese life-style, insistence on the Africans' obligations to work as a means of becoming "civilized," tighter control of the colonial administration and economy from Lisbon, and the subordination of the interests of the African territories to those of metropolitan Portugal. Duffy concludes that Portuguese rule brought very few material benefits to the Africans and a good deal of exploitation. He contends that Portugal never consciously attempted to create a Western-educated elite who might collaborate in administering the territories; rather, it intended that the Portuguese should remain in charge indefinitely and should continue to hold even many subordinate positions.

Duffy sees the Salazar regime as laying the philosophical, administrative, and economic foundations in the late 1930s and early 1940s for the programs of European settlement of the late 1940s and 1950s. He contends that the Second World War had relatively little impact on Portuguese Africa or on Portuguese policies. Only when Salazar sought to have Portugal enter the United Nations did he recognize the growing strength of international anticolonialism by revising the constitution of 1951 to make the African territories "overseas provinces," and therefore beyond the surveillance of the United Nations.

Duffy's *Portugal in Africa* was written in the wake of the Angolan rebellions of 1961. It is far more critical than his earlier books of the abuses and lack of benefits under Portuguese rule. The work contains additional material on education and economic development, including the stepped-up European settlements in Angola and Mozambique. But like its predecessor, it concentrates on the gap between theory and practice, between the rhetoric and the reality, of Portuguese colonialism. Neither work presents much information about the African responses to Portuguese rule. This gap is ably filled by the works of Ronald Chilcote, a political scientist from the University of California at Santa Barbara, who is also a specialist on Brazil.

Chilcote's *Portuguese Africa* (1967) provides the best single introduction to African nationalism in Angola, Mozambique, and Portuguese Guinea. The work relates the nationalist movements to ethnic and cultural factors as well as to the policies of Portuguese rule. It portrays the struggles as a conflict between African and Portuguese nationalisms. The study terminates with an excellent twelve-page bibliographical essay. In 1972, Chilcote edited a monumental collection of 2,500 nationalist documents (*Emerging Nationalism in Portuguese Africa*); 179 of the most important of these, on the origins, organization, leadership, and ideology of the various groups, are translated into English. The editor provides capsule histories of each party and other reference aids.

Also useful for understanding the postwar evolution of the Portuguese empire, the appearance of nationalist movements, and international pressures, is *Anti-colonialismo, marxismo y Portugal* (1967) by Richard Pattee of the Université Laval. Pattee's work has special value for the United Nations dimension, which is the focus of two brief works, *The Portuguese Territories and the United Nations* (1963), commissioned by the Carnegie Endowment and written by Patricia Wohlgemuth, and *The United Nations and Portugal: A Study in Anti-colonialism* (1963) by Franco Nogueira. Dr. Nogueira was a former foreign minister of Portugal. The complete account of the Portuguese territories before the United Nations' Decolonization Committee from 1961 on is found in Maurice Barbier's massive *Le Comité de décolonisation des Nations Unies* (1974), which also contains a large bibliographical essay on UN involvement in decolonization during the 1960s.

Among general works, one must also mention *Portuguese Africa; A Handbook* (1969), edited by David Abshire and Michael Samuels, for it provides the most comprehensive introduction to the Portuguese territories, including the nationalist movements and their international dimensions. Despite a certain lack of understanding of African cultures in Abshire's sections, and a viewpoint that is more sympathetic to the Portuguese than to black nationalists, it is nevertheless a mine of useful information.

Gerald Bender, a political scientist at UCLA who has specialized in Angola, and Allen Isaacman, a historian of Mozambique, have collaborated on a chapter on the historiography of those countries (1976). Through the inclusion of Portuguese Guinea in a very long note, they have provided a most valuable introduction to the literature published between 1932 and 1975 on Portuguese rule, the nationalist movements and rebellions, and the transitions to independence. For Angola their essay is complemented by the bibliographical articles of René Pélissier (1976) and Carlos Serrano (1977), and for all territories by that of Michael Flores (1974). *Guinea-Bissau and Cape Verde Islands: A Comprehensive Bibliography* (1977) by Joseph M. McCarthy cites the extensive article literature as well as books.

Angola

Right after the beginning of the rebellion in Angola, the Reverend Thomas Okuma, a Hawaiian-American who served for eight years as a Congregational missionary there, wrote *Angola in Ferment* (1962), giving the outlines of Portuguese policies and the conditions that led to the revolt. Some of the best documented and most incisive criticisms of Portuguese rule in the Institute of Race Relations' *Angola, A Symposium: Views of a Revolt* (1962) also came from English-speaking Protestant missionaries, a group whom the Portuguese blamed for inciting the rebellion and against whom they undertook reprisals. Over the next dozen years there appeared a score of semischolarly and journalistic accounts of the origins and course of the rebellion. Bender and Isaacman list these titles and mention their viewpoints. Among the most important are *Guerra em Angola* (1968) by Hélio Felgas, who served as governor of the Congo District in northern Angola during 1961, and *La Guerre en Angola: Etude socio-économique* (1971) by Mario de Andrade and Marc Ollivier. The MPLA leader Andrade analyzed the causes of the rebellion from a Marxist perspective. He argued that Portugal was able to counterattack effectively because of Western and capitalist support. William Minter, *Portuguese Africa and the West* (1972), emphasizes the involvement of American interests in Angola.

The best scholarly work on the Angolan revolution is John Marcum's sociopolitical analysis, *The Angolan Revolution*, 2 vols. (1969 and 1978). Practically every publication subsequent to 1969 has drawn upon its first volume. Marcum is an American political scientist who has done fieldwork in Angola and Zaïre, where many of the rebels were based, at various times since the late 1950s. He provides an extremely detailed, heavily documented analytical account of the colonial revolution against Portugal; the rivalries of the major nationalist groups (two up to 1965 and three thereafter) which culminated in a civil war in 1975; and the involvement of foreign powers in that war. The study includes a discussion of the unsuccessful Cabindan separatist movement. It shows the external ties and tensions of the MPLA, FNLA, and UNITA; the tensions within them and among them; as well as the geographical, cultural, ethnoracial, and ideological bases for the various cleavages. The sections on the involvement of the United States, South Africa, Cuba, and the Soviet Union contain strong criticisms of American tactics and the role of Secretary of State Henry Kissinger.

The outbreak of the rebellion in Angola in 1961 turned scholarly attention not only to the origins of the nationalist movements but also to previous resistance against Portuguese rule and earlier African and settler anticolonialist groups. On these topics the French historian of Lusophone Africa, René Pélissier, has published two related works: *Les Guerres grises: Résistance et révoltes en Angola (1845–1941)*, 2 vols. (1977), and *La Colonie du minotaure: Nationalismes et révoltes en Angola (1926–1961)*(1978). Pélissier collaborated with another historian of these same themes, Douglas Wheeler of the University of New Hampshire, in a general history, *Angola* (1971). Therein Wheeler deals with the development of political consciousness by the *assimilados* and settlers from the 1880s to 1961, and Pélissier with the origins and course of the rebellions of the 1960s. Wheeler argues that between 1922 and 1930, first the republican governor, Norton de Matos, and then the New State crushed the assimilado and settler anticolonialists, thereby giving Angola a generation of classic colonial rule without effective anticolonial pressures. The New State allowed only official assimilado groups, which provided an outlet for African grievances, both elite and mass, but lacked the means to secure genuine reforms. Thus Angolan nationalism emerged only during the 1950s, with the formation of new and clandestine groups of assimilados, ethnic separatists, and settlers.

Gerald Bender, *Angola under the Portuguese: The Myth and the Reality* (1978), is the first work to deal with the entire period of Portuguese rule, including its termination. As part of his main theme of showing the wide gap between the theory and the reality of Portuguese rule, Bender examines the role of Lusotropicalism in the formulation of policies and legislation affecting racial interaction, the goals of these policies, and their local implementation from the late fifteenth century until independence in 1975. In this connection, the work provides the most thorough discussion yet available concerning Portuguese settlements and their roles in race relations. Bender demolishes the Lustropical myth that the Portuguese were constructing a harmonious multiracial society in Angola along lines supposedly developed earlier in Brazil, in which the African masses were gradually assimilating European culture and life-style. He shows that official settlement schemes in the 1950s and 1960s placed only a few thousand Portuguese in rural Angola at the cost of one hundred million dollars and the often brutal dispossession and victimization of thousands of Africans. The bulk of the 335,000 Europeans in Angola in 1974 had arrived since the outbreak of the rebellion. Only 6 percent of them had gone beyond the fourth grade, and only 1,200 were practicing a profession or skilled trade. The vast majority were unskilled poor whites concentrated in the towns. The civil war of 1975 left only thirty to forty thousand of them in Angola.

At the time of the rebellion, only 1 percent of the Angolans had become sufficiently Portuguese through education and employment to be considered assimilados. Further evidence of the tiny impact of Portuguese culture upon the Angolans is contained in the studies of German sociologist Franz-Wilhelm Heimer, *Educacão e sociedade na áreas rurais de Angola*, 2 vols. (1972). Using survey research techniques, Heimer found that only 1 percent of adults and 2 percent of the children outside the large towns used Portuguese in daily conversation. Most of them knew nothing of Portuguese history or geography. Heimer also edited *Social Change in Angola* (1973), which contains his own chapter on education, economics, and social change in rural Angola, and Gerald Bender's on planned rural settlements between 1900 and 1968, as well as other useful contributions on economic and social developments, mainly in the twentieth century.

Portuguese rule came to an end in Angola in the wake of the April 1974 military revolution in Lisbon. *Portugal e o futuro* (1974) by General António de Spínola had an important part in influencing the armed forces' intervention, through the argument that military responses could not end the rebellions in Africa and that only a political solution could bring peace. Douglas Porch, *The Portuguese Armed Forces and the Revolution* (1977), shows the role of the colonial wars in creating the military movement that brought down the Salazar-Caetano regime. Porch's work has greater accuracy and historical perspective than a comparable study by the sociologist Rona Fields, *The Portuguese Revolution and the Armed Forces Movement* (1976).

There is a very large article literature on the Angolan civil war and its aftermath, including its African and international dimensions. Among the most important ones by African specialists are: Basil Davidson (1976 and

1977); Franz-Wilhelm Heimer (1976a and 1976b); René Pélissier (1974 and 1975); Lewis Gann (1975); Kenneth Adelman (1975); Mohammed A. El-Khawas (1977); Gerald Bender (1976a and 1976b); Christopher Stevens (1976); Nkwelle Ekaney (1976); Alain Chevalerias (1976); Wolfgang Boge (1975); and Nathaniel Davis (1978). American involvement in the Angolan civil war is treated by two members of the Socialist Workers' party, Ernest Harsch and Tony Thomas, *Angola: The Hidden History of Washington's War* (1976), and by the head of the CIA's Angolan task force, John Stockwell, *In Search of Enemies: A CIA Story* (1978). The economic aspects of the civil war and independence are discussed by Guy de Bosschère (1976) and Hugues Leclercq (1976). Finally, Phyllis Martin of Indiana University treated the unsuccessful separatist movement in Cabinda (1977), as did an unsigned article in the *Revue française d'études politiques africaines* (1977), "Le FLEC et le problème du Cabinda."

Mozambique

Fewer scholars have dealt with Mozambique than with Angola. Non-Portuguese historians have studied topics from the eighteenth and nineteenth centuries such as the Zambezi *prazos* and resistance to Portuguese rule rather than questions from the twentieth century. Even after the outbreak of rebellion in 1964, the three-sided nationalist struggle in Angola continued to attract far more attention than did the FRELIMO rebellion.

The head of FRELIMO between 1963 and 1969 was Eduardo Mondlane, an American-educated Mozambican sociologist who had served in the UN Trusteeship Division and had taught at Syracuse University. Prior to his assassination at Dar es-Salaam, he wrote *The Struggle for Mozambique* (1969), a lucid, well-organized account of the Portuguese policies that had produced the nationalist movement and rebellion. Thomas H. Henriksen (1978) points out that FRELIMO became Marxist only after Mondlane's death. It had been organized in 1962 to gain independence, not to restructure society in any particular mold. Henriksen also points out that the success of the indigenous Marxist revolution in Mozambique indicates that no particular preordained socioeconomic development was necessary. Dr. Mondlane was succeeded as head of FRELIMO by the Marxist-oriented Samora Machel, some of whose speeches and writings have been published as pamphlets (1975 and 1976). Most of the literature on FRELIMO—its origins, leadership, internal personal and ideological conflicts, differences with other Mozambican groups—is in article form. Among the most important are: Walter C. Opello (1975a and 1975b); John S. Saul (1973); Tony Hodges (1977) and A. Seegers

(1977). The linkages between FRELIMO resistance and earlier resistance to colonialism are the subject of articles by three historians, A. J. Williams-Mayers (1977), Allen Isaacman (1975), and Edward Alpers (1974).

The first history of Mozambique in English, *Mozambique: A History* by Thomas H. Henriksen (1978), provides detailed accounts of Portuguese colonialism and Mozambican nationalism in the twentieth century. Its sections on FRELIMO show the influence of Mondlane, Chilcote, and Hodges, as well as the author's own reflections on the movement both before and after independence.

Other books and articles on the origins, course, and results of the Mozambican revolution include those by a longtime British Protestant missionary, John Paul, *Mozambique: Memoirs of a Revolution* (1975), and a British Catholic missionary, Adrian Hastings, *Wiriyamu: Massacre in Mozambique* (1974). The latter focuses on a single incident in the decade-long colonial war. Brendan Jundanian (1974) deals with Portuguese efforts to regroup populations to contain the rebellion. The first years of the rebellion are treated from a Portuguese viewpoint in two works, Nuno Rocha, *Guerra em Moçambique* (1969), and Guilhermo de Melo, *Moçambique Norte—guerra e paz (réportagem)*(1969). An Italian writer, Cesare Bertulli, *Croce e spada in Mozambico* (1974), gives special attention to the position of the Roman Catholic church in the rebellion and its relations with the government and the guerrillas. Luis B. Serapiao (1974) deals in less detail with these topics but puts them in historical perspective. He indicates the support of the local Portuguese bishops for official policies until at least 1970 alongside opposition by many priests, both as individuals and in groups, during the 1950s and 1960s. Kerry Swift, *Mozambique and the Future* (1974), examines the Mozambican situation in the light of the April 1974 revolution in Lisbon and its international dimensions.

The transfer of power and the first three years of independence are ably treated in the Spring 1978 number of *Issue* under the editorship of Allen Isaacman. The articles by eight specialists, including several currently working in Mozambique to construct a socialist society, provide important current data and ample documentation. Other articles on the transfer of power include J.-P. Colin (1976), Robin Wright (1976), Charles Geshekter (1975), and John Saul (1974 and 1975). Allen Isaacman and Jennifer Davis (1978) have reviewed American policy toward Mozambique since 1945, including support for Portuguese rule well into the 1970s. Mario J. Azevedo (1978–79) has discussed the legacy of colonial education. *Le Monde*'s correspondent, Philippe Decraene, has dealt with the economy at the time of transfer (1974). Elaine Friedland has compared Mozambique with South Africa as examples of colonialist political economies. Very useful for understanding the Mozambican economy and society on the eve of independence is a study in German by Manfred Kuder, *Moçambique* (1975). Among earlier works of value on economic and social matters are Antonio Ferreira's study of migrant workers to South Africa, *O movimento migratorio de trabalhadores entre Moçambique e a Africa do Sul* (1963), and Mario de Carvalho, *Aagricultura tradicional de Moçambique* (1969).

Portuguese Guinea

Prior to the outbreak of rebellion in Portuguese Guinea in July 1961, the small amount of scholarly writing on the territory was in Portuguese and limited to nonpolitical fields such as economics and ethnography. The two best introductions to these subjects from this period are Avelino Texeira da Mota, *Guiné portuguesa* (1954), which has chapter summaries in English and French, and Amilcar Cabral's agricultural census of the mid-1950s, which was published in the *Boletim cultural da Guiné portuguesa,* vols. 9–11 (1954–56). Parts of this survey have been translated in Chilcote, *Emerging Nationalism in Portuguese Africa*, and in the UCLA periodical, *Ufahamu*, vol. 3 (1973). José Julio Gonçalves, *O Islamico na Guiné portuguesa: Ensãio sociomissionólogico* (1961), treats Islam in Guinea from a Christian missionary perspective. The presence of Islamic influences, the absence of Portuguese settlers and missionaries in most areas, and the small amount of economic development made the situation in Guinea very different from those in Angola and Mozambique.

During the early 1960s, as the PAIGC took over leadership of the rebellion and came to control large portions of the interior, journalists and political scientists from many European nations, including all the Scandinavian ones, made their way into the rebel-held territories in order to study developments on the spot. The three most useful journalistic accounts are: Gérard Chaliand, *Armed Struggle: With the Guerrillas in 'Portuguese' Africa* (1969 translation of the 1967 French text); Basil Davidson, *The Liberation of Guiné* (1969); and Al J. Venter, *Portugal's War in Guinea-Bissau* (1973). Chaliand, a French journalist, examined the inner workings of the liberation movement and the wider problems of guerrilla warfare in Africa. Davidson, A British journalist and longtime critic of Portuguese rule, had access to some of the PAIGC archives, which dated back to its founding in 1956, and to the complete writings of the PAIGC leader Cabral, with whom he had long discussions. Cabral's foreword to the book contains an attack on the theory of Lusotropicalism. Davidson shows that in the absence of very many settlers, forced labor was mainly for public projects. But the peasants were forced to cultivate groundnuts, which were marketed primarily for the benefit of Portugal through the monopolistic

Companhia União Favril. Davidson shows how the PAIGC passed from subversion against Portuguese rule, which led to Portuguese repression and in turn to the growth of peasant support, to the formation of a guerrilla army that controlled rural areas but was not yet able to assault the Portuguese-controlled towns effectively. In the countryside under its control, the PAIGC began to construct a decentralized socialist state based on peasant agriculture. Davidson notes that Cabral rejected the involvement of foreign advisors or volunteers and insisted that the Guineans undertake national reconstruction by and for themselves. Finally, Davidson's work places the rebellion within its larger African setting.

Lars Rudebeck is a Swedish political scientist who had studied political change in Tunisia before turning his attention to the struggle for liberation in Portuguese Guinea. He completed his *Guinea-Bissau* (1974) shortly before the April 1974 revolution in Lisbon led to Portuguese recognition of Guinea's independence. His work focuses on the political mobilization of the populations against colonialism for purposes of liberation and development. After examining the colonial system in Guinea and the Cape Verde Islands, Rudebeck looks at the PAIGC's ideology and concrete goals and then at the emerging social order that was being created by the party in the areas under its control. He shows how a restructuring of the African society was taking place concurrently with the struggle for liberation from colonialism. Jean-Claude Andreini and Marie-Claude Lambert, *La Guinée-Bissau* (1978), supplement Rudebeck's analyses on the evolving economic and social structures.

General António de Spínola served for several years as the commander-in-chief of the Portuguese armed forces in Guinea. *Por uma Guiné melhor* (1970) is a collection of his speeches, interviews, and communiqués, which shows the evolution of his thinking about the means of dealing with the rebellion. His *Linha de accão* (1971) contains further documentation on his views and actions.

The last stages of the colonial war and the transfer of power are treated in many articles: Jeanne Makedonsky (1974), Michael H. Glántz (1973), Basil Davidson (1974), and J. H. Moolman (1974). Other authors have dealt with the aftermath of independence and the reconstruction of the society and economy: Boniface Obichere (1975), Ronald Chilcote (1977), and Tony Hodges (1979).

The PAIGG leader, Amilcar Cabral, was assassinated before the achievement of independence. As the 1960s wore on, Africanists became increasingly aware that this *mestiço* agronomist was an analyst of the colonial situation and a theorist of national liberation and reconstruction of an importance probably equal to Frantz Fanon, with whom his ideas would soon be compared. Among the collections of his writings and speeches are: *Revolution in Guinea: Selected Texts* (1969); *Our People Are Our Mountains* (1971); *Guinée 'portugaise': Le Pouvoir des armes* (1970); *Alguns princípios do partido* (1974); and *Guiné-Bissau—nacão forjada na luta* (1974). The best place to start for an understanding of Cabral is Ronald H. Chilcote's biographical-bibliographical essay (1974–75).

Cape Verde Islands and São Tomé and Príncipe

The Cape Verde Islands, where the PAIGC was also organized, did not experience a colonial war but became independent as a separate state as a result of the revolution in Lisbon. Cape Verde did not unite with Guinea-Bissau as Cabral and other PAIGG leaders had intended, but has maintained close relations with it. The transition to independence and current political and economic problems in Cape Verde and in São Tomé and Príncipe, which also became an independent state, are discussed succinctly by Laurie Wiseberg and Gary Nelson (1977). Further information about a Libreville-based liberation movement there and about the political evolution to independence is found in articles by René Pélissier (1968, 1972, and 1975).

Supplementary Bibliography

Since the completion of this book and the bibliographical essays, the following books, articles, and theses which contribute to an understanding of decolonization have appeared. Where the title does not indicate the relevant contents, a notation has been added in brackets.

Abi-Saab, Georges. *The United Nations Operation in the Congo, 1960–1964*. Oxford, 1978. [The role of law]

Ageron, Charles-Robert. *Histoire de l'Algérie contemporaine, 1871–1954*. Paris, 1979.

———. *'L'Algérie algérienne' de Napoléon III à de Gaulle*. Paris, 1980.

Azevedo, Mario J. " 'A sober commitment to liberation'? Mozambique and South Africa, 1974–79." *African Affairs* 79 (1980): 567–84.

Ba, Abdoul Aziz. "L'Immigration des travailleurs sénégalais en France." *Revue juridique et politique*, 34 (1980): 198–271.

Baroudi, Abdallah. *Maroc. Emigration et impérialisme*. Paris, 1978. [Under the protectorate and since independence]

Bayart, Jean-François. *L'Etat au Cameroun*. Paris, 1979.

Bentahar, Mekki. "Les Arabes en France. Itinéraire migratoire." Thesis, University of Paris, 1978. 2 vols. [North African immigrants]

Bézy, Fernand. "La Transformation des structures socio-économiques à Madagascar (1960–1978)." *Cultures et développement* 11 (1979): 83–116.
Bidwell, Robin. *Guide to African Ministers*. London, 1978.
Blanchet, Gilles. "L'Evolution des dirigeants sénégalais de l'indépendance à 1975." *Cahiers d'études africaines* 18 (1978): 49–78.
Blussé, L.; Wesseling, H. L.; and Winius, G. D., eds. *History and Underdevelopment: Essays on Underdevelopment and European Expansion in Asia and Africa*. Leyden, 1980. Issued as *Itinerario* 5, no. 1 (1980): 1–160.
Boisson, Jean. *Ben Bella est arrêté—le 22 octobre 1956. Etudes et recherches historiques*. Cholet, 1978. [Important documents in the appendixes]
Bon, Daniel, and Mingst, Karen. "French Intervention in Africa: Dependence or Development?" *Africa Today* 27, no. 2 (1980): 5–20.
Bourgi, Albert. *La Politique française de coopération en Afrique, le cas du Sénégal*. Dakar, 1979.
Buijtenhuijs, Robert. *Le FROLINAT et les révoltes populaires du Tchad, 1965–1976*. Paris, 1978. [Colonial backgrounds]
Cabral, Amilcar. *Unity and Struggle. Speeches and Writings of Amilcar Cabral*. New York, 1979.
Campbell, Bonnie. *Libération nationale et construction du socialisme en Afrique (Angola, Guinée-Bissau, Mozambique)*. Montreal, 1978.
Chabal, Patrick. "National Liberation in Portuguese Guinea, 1956–1974." *African Affairs* 80 (1981): 75–100.
Chassey, Francis de. *Mauritanie 1900–1979 de l'ordre colonial à l'ordre néo-colonial entre Maghreb et Afrique noire*. Paris, 1978. [Economic and social aspects]
Cohen, William B. "Legacy of Empire: The Algerian Connection." *Journal of Contemporary History* 15 (1980): 97–123.
Collot, Claude, and Henry, Jean-Robert. *Le Mouvement national algérien. Textes, 1912–1954*. Paris, 1978.
Decalo, Samuel. "Chad: The Roots of Centre-Periphery Strife." *African Affairs* 79 (1980): 491–509.
———. "Regionalism, Political Decay, and Civil Strife in Chad." *Journal of Modern African Studies* 18 (1980): 23–56.
Decraene, Philippe. *Le Mali*. Paris, 1980. [Mainly since 1940]
Dianoux, Hugues Jean de. "La Guinée-Bissau et les îles du Cap-Vert." *Afrique contemporaine* 19 (January–February 1980): 1–16.
Dougherty, James J. *The Politics of Wartime Aid: American Economic Assistance to France and French Northwest Africa, 1940–1946*. Westport, Conn., 1978.

Fol, Jean-Jacques. "Le Togo pendant la deuxième guerre mondiale." *Revue d'histoire de la deuxième guerre mondiale* 15 (July 1979): 69–77.

Gardinier, David E. "France in Gabon since 1960." *Proceedings of the French Colonial Historical Society*, vols. 6–7 (1981–82): 65–67.

———. *Historical Dictionary of Gabon*. Metuchen, N.J., 1981. [Detailed bibliography; decolonization]

Gonidec, P.-F. *Les Systèmes politiques africains*. 2d ed. Paris, 1978.

Gran, Guy, ed. *Zaire: The Political Economy of Underdevelopment*. New York, 1979. [Essays on colonial backgrounds]

Harbi, Mohammed. *Le FLN, mirage et réalité. Des origines à la prise du pouvoir (1945–1962)*. Paris, 1980.

Halvorsen, K. "Colonial Transformations of Agrarian Society in Algeria." *Journal of Peace Research* 15 (1978): 323–44.

Harshe, Rajen. "French Neo-Colonialism in Sub-Saharan Africa." *India Quarterly* 36 (1980): 159–78.

Higgott, Richard. "Structural Dependency and Decolonisation in a West African Land-Locked State: Niger." *Review of African Political Economy* (January-April 1980), pp. 43–59.

Houbert, Jean. "Réunion—I: French Decolonisation in the Mascareignes." *Journal of Commonwealth and Comparative Politics* 18 (July 1980): 145–71.

Hugot, Pierre. "Le Vide politique du Tchad musulman." *Revue française d'études politiques africaines* (July–August 1979), pp. 27–40.

Isaacman, Allen. *A Luta Continua. Creating a New Society in Mozambique*. Binghamton, N.Y., 1978.

Jewsiewicki, Bohumil. "Le Colonat agricole européen au Congo-Belge, 1910–1960: Questions politiques et économiques." *Journal of African History* 20 (1979): 559–72.

Julien, Charles-André. *Le Maroc Face aux impérialismes, 1415–1956*. Paris, 1978. [Primarily the last decade of the protectorate]

Kagame, Alexis. *Un Abrégé de l'histoire du Rwanda de 1853 à 1972*. Butare, Rwanda, 1975.

Keita, Sidiki Kabélé. "Les Réalités coloniales en Guinée (1945–1958)." *Banda* (March 1977), pp. 14–23.

Kiraranganya, Boniface. *La Verité sur le Burundi*. Sherbrooke, Quebec, 1977. [Eye-witness account of decolonization]

Klein, Jean. "Un Episode de la décolonisation: La Guerre d'Algérie (1954–1962)." *Francia* 6 (1978): 64–45.

Klinghoffer, Arthur Jay. *The Angolian War: A Study in Soviet Policy in the Third World*. Boulder, Colo., 1980.

Machel, Samora. *Le Processus de la révolution démocratique populaire au Mozambique*. Paris, 1977. [His speeches, 1970–74]

Maestre, J. C. "L'Expérience révolutionnaire d'Ali Soilih aux Comores (1976–1978)." *Annuaire des pays de l'océan Indien* 4 (1977): 25–42.

Mensah, G. "The Process of Monetary Decolonization in Africa." *Utafiti* 4 (1979): 45–64.

Middlemas, Keith. "Twentieth-Century White Society in Mozambiue." *Tarikh* 6, no. 2 (1979): 30–45.

Mulier, Freddy. "La Coopération technique belge dans l'enseignement zaïrois." *Cahiers du CEDAF*, no. 1 (1979), pp. 2–69.

Munywzangabo, Corneille Munyampeta. "L'Internationalisation du conflit Hutu-Tutsi en Afrique interlacustrine." Mémoire, University of Paris, 1976.

Mutin, Georges. *La Mitidja: Décolonisation et espace géographique*. Paris, 1977.

Naylor, Phillip Chiviges. "Algeria and France: The Post-Colonial Relationship, 1962–1975." *Proceedings of the French Colonial Historical Society* 5 (1980): 58–69.

———. "French-Algerian Relations, 1962–1978." Ph.D. dissertation, Marquette University, 1980.

Peemans, Françoise, and Lefèvre, Patrick. "Les Sociétés coloniales belges: Archives et données bibliographiques (1885–1960)." *Cahiers du CEDAF*, no. 4–5 (1980), pp. 3–95.

Peemans, Jean-Philippe. "Imperial Hangovers: Belgium—The Economics of Decolonization." *Journal of Contemporary History* 15 (April 1980): 257–86.

Périllier, Louis. *La Conquête de l'indépendance tunisienne*. Paris, 1979. [Diplomacy of the last stages]

Samuel, Michel. *Le Prolétariat africain noir en France*. Paris, 1978. [Mainly Soninke from Senegal, Mali, and Mauritania]

Saumagne, Charles. *Journal et écrits* (*Tunisie, 1947–1957*). Nice, 1979. [Important for 1954–56]

Scalabre, Camille. "Deux Années d'indépendance à Djibouti." *Revue juridique et politique* 33 (1979): 331–36.

Serapiao, Luïs B., and El-Khawas, Mohammed A. *Mozambique in the Twentieth Century: From Colonialism to Independence*. Washington, D.C., 1978. [International aspects of liberation]

Shehim, Kassim, and Searing, James. "Djibouti and the Question of Afar Nationalism." *African Affairs* 79 (1980): 195–208.

Simon, Gildas. "L'Espace des travailleurs tunisiens en France: Structures et fonctionnement d'un champ migratoire international." Thesis, University of Poitiers, 1978. [Protectorate backgrounds of postindependence immigration]

Soret, Marcel. *Histoire du Congo, capitale Brazzaville*. Paris, 1978.

Udokang, Okon. "Portuguese African Policy—A Critical Re-Appraisal." *African Review* 6 (1976): 289–312.

Vail, Leroy, and White, Landeg. "The Struggle for Mozambique: Capitalist Rivalries, 1900–1940." *Review*, Fall 1979, pp. 243–76.

Yansané, Agibou Yan, ed. *Decolonization and Dependency: Problems of Development of African Societies*. Westport, Conn., 1980. [Essays on French West Africa]

———. "Monetary Independence and Transition to Socialism in Guinea." *Journal of African Studies* 6 (1979): 132–43.

———. "Some Problems of Monetary Dependency in French-speaking West African States." *Journal of African Studies* 5 (1978–79): 444–70.

French Colonial Officials in Africa

I. *French West Africa*

HIGH COMMISSIONERS

1940–43 Pierre Boisson
1943–46 Pierre Cournarie
1946–48 René Barthes
1948–51 Paul Bechard
1951–56 Bernard Cornut-Gentille
1956–58 Gaston Cusin

HIGH COMMISSIONER-GENERAL

1958–59 Pierre Messmer

Dahomey

GOVERNORS

1940–43 Léon Truitard
1943–45 Charles Assier de Pompignan
1945–46 Marc Laurent de Villedeuil
1946–48 Robert Legendre
1948 Jean Chambon
1948–49 Jacques Boissier
1949–51 Claude Valluy
1951–55 Charles-Henri Bonfils
1955–58 Casimir Biros

HIGH COMMISSIONER

1958–60 René Tirant

Guinea

GOVERNORS

1940–42 Félix Giacobbi
1942–44 Horace Crocicchia
1944–46 Jacques Fourneau
1946–48 Edouard Terrac
1948–50 Roland Pré
1950–53 Paul-Henri Siriex
1953–55 Jean-Paul Parisot
1955–56 Charles-Henri Bonfils
1956–57 Jean-Paul Ramadier
1958 Jean Mauberna

Ivory Coast

GOVERNORS

1939–41 Horace Crocicchia
1941–42 Hubert Deschamps

1942–43 Georges Rey
1943–47 André Latrille
1947–48 Oswald Durand
1948 Georges Orselli
1948–51 Laurent Péchoux
1951–52 Pierre Pelieu
1952–54 Camille Bailly
1954–56 Pierre Messmer
1956–57 Pierre Lami
1957–58 Ernest de Nattes

HIGH COMMISSIONERS
1959 Ernest de Nattes
1959–60 Yves Guéna

Mauritania

1936–42 Jean-Louis Beyriès
1942–44 Jean Chalvet
1944–46 Christian Laigret
1947–48 Lucien Geay
1948–49 Henri de Mauduit
1949–50 Edouard Terrac
1950–51 Jacques Rogué
1951–54 Pierre Messmer
1954–55 Albert-Jean Mouragues
1955–56 Jean-Paul Parisot
1956–58 Albert-Jean Mouragues

HIGH COMMISSIONER
1959–60 Pierre Anthonioz

Niger

GOVERNORS
1939–40 Jean Rapenne
1941–42 Maurice Falvy
1942–54 Jean-François Toby
1955–56 Jean-Paul Ramadier
1956–58 Paul Bordier
1958 Louis Rollet
1958 Don-Jean Colombani

HIGH COMMISSIONER
1959–60 Don-Jean Colombani

Senegal

GOVERNORS
1938–41 Georges Parisot
1941–43 Georges Rey
1943–44 Hubert Deschamps
1944–45 Charles Dagain
1945–46 Pierre-Louis Maestracci
1946–47 Oswald Durand
1947–50 Laurent Wiltord
1950–52 Camille Bailly
1952–53 Lucien Geay
1953–54 Daniel Goujon
1954–55 Maxime Jourdain
1955–57 Don-Jean Colombani
1957–58 Pierre Lami

HIGH COMMISSIONER
1959–60 Pierre Lami

Sudan

GOVERNORS
1938–40 Jean Desanti
1940–42 Jean Rapenne
1942–46 Auguste Calvel
1946–52 Edmond Louveau
1952 Camille Bailly
1952–53 Salvador Etcheber
1953 Albert-Jean Mouragues
1953–56 Lucien Geay
1956–58 Henri Gipoulon

HIGH COMMISSIONER
1959–60 Jean-Charles Sicurani

Upper Volta

GOVERNORS
1947–48 Gaston Mourgues
1948–52 Albert-Jean Mouragues
1952–53 Roland Pré
1953–56 Salvador Etcheber
1956–58 Yvon Bourges

HIGH COMMISSIONER
1959–60 Paul Masson

II. French Equatorial Africa

GOVERNORS-GENERAL
1939–40 Pierre Boisson
1940 Louis Husson
1940–44 Félix Eboué
1944–47 Ange Bayardelle
1947 Charles Luizet

HIGH COMMISSIONERS
1947–51 Bernard Cornut-Gentille
1951–58 Paul Chauvet
1958 Pierre Messmer
1958 Yvon Bourges

HIGH COMMISSIONER-GENERAL
1959–60 Yvon Bourges

Chad

LIEUTENANT-GOVERNORS
1939–41 Félix Eboué
1941–42 Pierre Lapie
1943–44 André Latrille
1944–46 Jacques Rogué

GOVERNORS
1946–49 Jacques Rogué
1949 Paul Le Layec
1950–51 Henri de Mauduit
1951 Charles Hanin
1951–56 Ignace Colombani
1956–58 Jean Troadec

HIGH COMMISSIONER
1959–60 Daniel Doustin

Gabon

LIEUTENANT-GOVERNORS
1938–40 Georges-Pierre Masson
1941–42 Victor Valentin-Smith
1942–43 Charles Assier de Pompignan
1943–44 Paul Vuillaume
1944–46 Numa Sadoul

GOVERNORS
1946–47 Roland Pré
1947–49 Numa Sadoul
1949–51 Pierre Pelieu
1951–52 Charles Hanin
1952–58 Yves Digo
1958 Louis Sanmarco

HIGH COMMISSIONER
1959–60 Jean Risterucci

Middle Congo

LIEUTENANT-GOVERNORS
1941–45 Gabriel Fortune
1945–46 Ange Bayardelle
1946 Christian Laigret

GOVERNORS
1946–47 Numa Sadoul
1947–50 Jacques Fourneau
1950–52 Paul Le Layec
1952–53 Jean-Jacques Chambon
1953–56 Ernest Rouys
1956–58 Jean-Michel Soupault
1958 Paul Dériaud

HIGH COMMISSIONER
1959–60 Gui-Noël Georgy

Ubangi-Shari

LIEUTENANT-GOVERNORS
1939–42 Pierre de Saint-Mart
1942–46 Henri Sautot

GOVERNORS
1946–48 Jean Chalvet
1949–50 Pierre Delteil
1950–51 Ignace Colombani
1951–54 Aimé Grimald
1954–58 Louis Sanmarco
1958 Paul Bordier

HIGH COMMISSIONER
1959–60 Paul Bordier

III. Madagascar

GOVERNORS-GENERAL
1939–40 Jules de Coppet
1940–41 Léon Cayla
1941–42 Armand Annet
1942–43 Paul-Louis de Gentilhomme
1943–44 Pierre de Saint-Mart
1944–46 Paul de Saint-Mart

HIGH COMMISSIONERS
1946–48 Jules de Coppet
1948–50 Pierre de Chevigné
1950–54 Isaac Bargues
1954–60 Jean Soucadaux

IV. Cameroons

HIGH COMMISSIONERS
1940 Philippe Leclerc de Hauteclocque
1940–43 Pierre Cournarie
1943–44 Hubert Carras
1944–46 Henri-Pierre Nicolas
1946–47 Robert Delavignette
1947–49 René Hoffherr
1949–54 Jean Soucadaux
1954–56 Roland Pré
1956–57 Pierre Messmer
1958 Jean-Paul Ramadier
1958–60 Xavier Torré

V. Togo

HIGH COMMISSIONERS
1936–41 Michel Montagné
1941 Léonce Delpech
1941–42 Jean de Saint-Alary
1942–43 Pierre Saliceti
1943–44 Albert Mercadier
1944–48 Jean Noutary
1948–51 Jean Cédile
1951–52 Yves Digo
1952–54 Laurent Péchoux
1955–57 Jean Bérard
1957–60 Georges Spénale

VI. French Somaliland

GOVERNORS
1938–40 Hubert Deschamps
1940 Gaëtan Germain
1940–42 Pierre Nouailhetas
1942 Christian Dupont
1942–43 Ange Bayardelle
1943–44 Michel-Raphaël Saller
1944–46 Jean Chalvet
1946–50 Paul-Henri Siriex
1950–54 Numa Sadoul
1954 Roland Pré
1954–57 Jean Petitbon
1957–58 Maurice Meker
1958–62 Jacques Compain
1962–66 René Tirant
1966–67 Louis Saget

HIGH COMMISSIONERS
1967–69 Louis Saget
1969– Dominique Ponchardier

VII. Comoro Islands

GOVERNORS
1947–49 Eugène Alaniou
1949–50 Marie-Emmanuel Remy
1950–57 Pierre Coudert
1957–60 Georges Arnaud
1961 Louis Saget

HIGH COMMISSIONERS
1961–63 Louis Saget
1963–66 Henri Bernard
1966– Antoine Columbani

Belgian Colonial Officials in Africa

I. Belgian Congo

GOVERNORS

1934–46 Pierre Ryckmans
1946–52 Eugène Jungers
1952–58 Léon Pétillon
1958–60 Henri Cornelis

II. Ruanda-Urundi

GOVERNORS

1932–46 Eugène Jungers
1946–52 Léon Pétillon
1952–55 Alfred Clays-Boúúaert
1955–62 Jean-Paul Harroy

Ruanda

HIGH REPRESENTATIVE

1962 Guillaume Logiest

Urundi

HIGH REPRESENTATIVE

1962 Edouard Hennequiau

Portuguese Colonial Officials in Africa

I. Angola

GOVERNORS-GENERAL/
HIGH COMMISSIONERS

1939–41 Manuel da Cunha e Costa Marquês Mano
1941–42 Abel de Abreu Souto-Maior
1942–43 Álvaro de Freitas Morna
1943 Manuel Pereira Figueira
1943–47 Vasco Lopes Alves
1947 Fernando Falcão Pacheco Mena
1947–55 José Agapito da Silva Carvalho
1956–59 Horácio de Sã Viana Rebêlo
1960–61 Álvaro Rodrigues da Silva Tavares
1961–62 Venâncio Augusto Deslandes
1962–66 Jaime Silvério Marquês
1966– Camilo Augusto de Miranda Rebocho Vaz

II. Cape Verde Islands

GOVERNORS

1931–41 Amadeu Gomes de Figueirido
1941–43 José Diogo Ferreira Martins
1943–49 João de Figueirdo
1949–53 Carlos Alberto Garcia Alves Roçadas
1953–57 Manuel Marques de Abrantes Amaral
1957–58 António Augusto Peixoto Correia
1958–63 Silvino Silvério Marquês
1963– Leão Maria de Tavares Rosado do Sacramento Monteiro

III. Mozambique

GOVERNORS-GENERAL

1938–40 José Nunes de Oliveira
1940–47 José Tristão de Bettencourt
1947–58 Gabriel Maurício Teixeira

1958–61 Padro Correia de Barros
1961–64 Manuel Maria Sarmento Rodrigues
1964–68 José Augusto da Costa Almeida
1968– Baltasar Rebêlo de Sousa

IV. Portuguese Guinea

GOVERNORS
1932–40 Luís António de Carvalho Viegas
1941–45 Ricardo Vaz Monteiro
1945–49 Manuel Maria Sarmento Rodrigues
1949–53 Raimundo António Rodrigues Serrão
1953–56 Diogo António José Leite Pereira de Melo e Alvim
1956–58 Álvaro Rodrigues da Silva Tavares
1958–62 António Augusto Peixote Correia
1962–65 Vasco António Martins Rodrigues
1965–68 Arnaldo Schultz
1968– António Sebastião Ribeiro de Spínola

V. São Tomé and Príncipe

GOVERNORS
1933–41 Ricardo Vaz Monteiro
1941–45 Amadeu Gomes de Figueirdo
1945–53 Carlos de Sousa Gorgulho
1953–57 Francisco António Pires Barata
1957–63 Manuel Marques de Abrantes Amaral
1963– António Jorge da Silva Sebastião

French governments and ministries from June 1943 to May 1957 are given in Prosser Gifford and Wm. Roger Louis, eds., *France and Britain in Africa* (1971), pp. 900–01.

ADDITIONAL FOURTH REPUBLIC OFFICIALS

Date	*Prime Minister*	*Foreign Affairs Minister*	*Overseas Minister*
June 11, 1957	Maurice Bourgès-Manoury	Christian Pineau	Gérard Jacquet
Nov. 5, 1957	Félix Gaillard	Christian Pineau	Gérard Jacquet
May 12, 1958	Pierre Pflimlin	René Pleven	André Colin
June 1, 1958	Charles de Gaulle	Maurice Couve de Murville	Bernard Cornut-Gentille

Fifth French Republic

Whereas the Fourth Republic assigned responsibility for the protectorates of Tunisia and Morocco to the Minister of Foreign Affairs, and for the Overseas Territories to the Minister for Overseas France, the arrangements of the Fifth Republic are more complex and have been revised on

French Fifth Republic Officials Pertaining to Africa (1958–1977)

Date	*President*	*Prime Minister*	*Foreign Affairs Minister*	*Ministers of Cooperation or State Secretaries of Foreign Affairs for Cooperation*
Dec. 21, 1958	Charles de Gaulle			
Jan. 8, 1959		Michel Debré	Maurice Couve de Murville	Robert Lecourt
Feb. 5, 1960				Jean Foyer
Apr. 14, 1962		Georges Pompidou		Pierre Pflimlin
May 15, 1962				Georges Gorse
Dec. 6, 1962				Raymond Triboulet
Jan. 20, 1966				Jean Charbonnel
May 8, 1967				Yvon Bourges
May 31, 1968			Michel Debré	
July 11, 1968		Maurice Couve de Murville		
June 15, 1969	Georges Pompidou			
June 22, 1969		Jacques Chaban-Delmas	Maurice Schumann	
July 6, 1972		Pierre Messmer		Pierre Billecocq
April 5, 1973			Michel Jobert	
May 9, 1973				François Deniau
May 27, 1974	Valéry Giscard d'Estaing	Jacques Chirac	Jean Sauvagnargues	Pierre Abelin
Aug. 27, 1976		Raymond Barre		Robert Galley

several occasions to reflect changes in the political relationships between France and Africa as well as in internal French politics.

The President of the Fifth Republic also headed the Community. Though the Community ceased to function in most respects after 1961, it continued to have a secretary-general, Jacques Foccart, under Presidents de Gaulle and Pompidou. President Giscard d'Estaing abolished the post. French relations with the independent African states have been handled by the Ministry of Foreign Affairs and either by a separate Ministry of Cooperation (May 1961 to January 1966, and again since May 1974) or by a State Secretariat for Cooperation attached to the Foreign Affairs Ministry (January 1959 to May 1961, January 1966 to May 1974). The Overseas Territories and Departments such as the Comoros and French Somaliland were administered at times by a Ministry of Overseas Departments and Territories and at others by a State Secretariat of the Interior Ministry.

MINISTERS OR STATE SECRETARIES OF
OVERSEAS DEPARTMENTS AND TERRITORIES

Jan. 8, 1959	Robert Lecourt
March 1962	Louis Jacquinot
April 1966	Pierre Billotte
June 1968	Joel Le Theule
June 1969	Henry Rey
June 22, 1969	Pierre Messmer
July 6, 1972	Xavier Deniau
Apr. 5, 1973	Bernard Stassi
May 28, 1974	Olivier Stirn

BELGIAN GOVERNMENTS AND MINISTRIES PERTAINING TO AFRICA

Date	*Prime Minister*	*Colonial Minister*
Feb. 11, 1945	Achille van Acker	Edgar de Bruyn
Aug. 1, 1945		Robert Godding
Mar. 14, 1946	Paul-Henri Spaak	L. Craey-Beeck
Mar. 31, 1946	Achille van Acker	Robert Godding
Aug. 1, 1946	Camille Huysmans	
Mar. 19, 1947	Paul-Henri Spaak	Pierre Wigny
Aug. 10, 1949	Gaston Eyskens	
June 8, 1950	Jean Duvieusart	
Aug. 15, 1950	Joseph Pholien	André Dequae
Jan. 15, 1952	Jean van Houtte	
Apr. 22, 1954	Achille van Acker	Auguste Buisseret

Date	*Prime Minister*	*Colonial Minister*
June 25, 1958	Gaston Eyskens	
July 13, 1958		Léon Pétillon
Nov. 6, 1958		Marcel van Hemelryck*
Sept. 3, 1959		Auguste de Schryver
Sept. 3, 1960		Harold d'Aspremont Lynden
Apr. 25, 1961–July 28, 1965	Théo Lefèvre	Paul-Henri Spaak*

*In November 1958, the Colonial Minister became Minister of Congo Affairs, and in April 1961, Minister of African Affairs.

Portuguese Prime Ministers and Colonial Ministers (1932–1975)

Date	*Prime Minister*	*Colonial Minister*
July 5, 1932	António Oliveira Salazar	
Jan. 19, 1936		Francisco Machado
Sept. 6, 1944		Marcelo Caetano
Mar. 3, 1947		Teofilo Duarte
Aug. 1, 1950		Sarmento Rodrigues
July 8, 1955		Raul Ventura
Aug. 13, 1958		Vasco Lopes Alves
Apr. 13, 1961		Adriano Moreira
Dec. 3, 1962		António Peixoto Correia
Mar. 18, 1965		Joaquim Moreira da Silva Cunha
Sept. 26, 1968–Apr. 25, 1974	Marcelo Caetano	*Minister of Interterritorial Coordination*
May 15, 1974	Adelino da Palma Carlos	António de Almeida Santos
July 17, 1974	Vasco dos Santos Gonçalves	
July 31, 1975		[left vacant]
Aug. 29, 1975	José Baptista Pinheiro de Azevedo	[left vacant]

Sources of Information for Officials

Bidwell, Robin, comp. and ed. *Bidwell's Guide to Government Ministers.* Vol. 1, *Major Powers and Western Europe, 1970–1971.* London, 1973.

Henige, David P., comp. *Colonial Governors.* Madison, Wis., 1970.

Europe-France Outremer. Paris, 1958–77.

Africa South of the Sahara. London, 1971–78.

Statesman's Yearbook. London, 1971–78.

Keesing's Contemporary Archives. London, 1974–75.

Ministère de Coopération, Centre de Documentation. "Historique du Ministère de la Coopération." Paris, n.d. Courtesy of Mlle. Edith Aujames.

19. *A Historiographical Perspective on the Transfer of Power in British Colonial Africa: A Bibliographical Essay*

A. H. M. KIRK-GREENE

The general literature on the transfer of power by Britain in Africa is still relatively sparse. The works to which attention might be invited are of limited value. Among the most illuminating are J. Strachey's *The End of Empire* (1959), C. E. Carrington's *The Liquidation of the British Empire* (1961), and W. M. Macmillan's *The Road to Self-Rule* (1959)—largely because they were written by, respectively, an intellectual of the decolonizing Labour government and two professors of imperial history. The alluringly entitled *Transfer of Power* (1960) by Sir Charles Jeffries, deputy under-secretary at the Colonial Office through much of the period, does not fulfill the hopes aroused by the title, whereas *British Policy in Changing Africa* by Sir Andrew Cohen (1959), a leading figure in the decolonizing process at the Colonial Office, does not tell nearly enough. D. K. Fieldhouse's overview, *The Colonial Empires* (1967), devotes only a brief epilogue to decolonization. W. P. Kirkman's *Unscrambling an Empire* (1966), and Colin Cross's *The Fall of the British Empire, 1918–1968* (1968)(the former by the colonial correspondent of the (London) *Times*) both take a general look at the dismantling of empire. James Morris's *Farewell the Trumpets* (1978) is a popular and superbly written account of the end of the British Empire. The collection of essays in the special issue of the *Journal of Contemporary History* on "Colonialism and Decolonization" (January 1969) fails to live up to expectations; on the other hand, Robin W. Winks's "On Decolonization and Informal Empire," *American Historical Review* 81 no. 3 (1976) is a substantial essay. By far the most satisfactory studies, within the limitation of their subtitles, are: Rudolf von Albertini's wide-ranging study *Decolonization: The Administration and Future of the Colonies, 1919–1960* (1971); Henri Grimal, *Decolonization: The British, French Dutch and Belgian Empires, 1919–1963* (1978); and J. M. Lee's more narrowly focused *Colonial Development and Good Government: A Study of The Ideas Expressed by the British Official Classes in Planning Decolonization, 1939–1964* (1967). Rupert Emerson has usefully placed what he calls the rise to self-assertion in its global context in his *From*

Empire to Nation (1960). The two most recent valuable contributions are: A. H. M. Kirk-Greene, ed., *The Transfer of Power: The Colonial Administrator in the Age of Decolonisation* (1979), and W. H. Morris-Jones and Georges Fischer, eds., *Decolonisation and After: The British and French Experience* (1980).

J. D. Hargreaves's *The End of Colonial Rule in West Africa* (1976) is a masterly overview, as is Crawford Young's important chapter, "Decolonization in Africa," in L. H. Gann and P. Duignan, eds., *Colonialism in Africa*, vol. 2 (1970). The parliamentary politics of decolonization are dealt with by D. Goldsworthy's *Colonial Issues in British Politics, 1945–1961* (1971) and some of the constitutional procedures in chapter 5 of D. A. Low's *Lion Rampant* (1973). The regular feature, "African Affairs at Westminister," in the quarterly *Journal of the Royal African Society* during the 1950s, provides a handy lead into *Parliamentary Debates*. For the Tories and colonial issues in Parliament, see Dan Horowitz's article, "Attitudes of British Conservatives toward Decolonization in Africa," *African Affairs*, vol. 69 (January 1970). Some of the issues in the British press on the transfer of power are reflected in the second volume of Margery Perham's *Colonial Sequence* (1970).

The dearth of analytical writing may be partly attributed to the chronological fragmentation of the transfer of power in Africa. In the Indian subcontinent a single dependency became two independent states at the same moment; in Southeast Asia the Dutch, like the British, were out of their major colonial possessions within a few years. The postwar process of the transfer of power in Africa started with the Sudan in 1956 and the Gold Coast in 1957. Though it was to reach a climax in 1960, when over a dozen African countries became independent, it continued through the mid-1960s (for example, in Gambia, Zambia, Botswana), and into the mid-1970s (Mozambique, Angola, Djibouti). With southern Africa dominating the late 1970s and Zimbabwe becoming independent in 1980, the process may well continue through the 1980s—already a quarter of a century beyond the independence of the Sudan and the Gold Coast.

The explanation may also lie in the changing interests of Africa's own scholars. Nationalism as it was transferred into political party structure and performance, then concern with the operation of the one-party state, and now the focus on the military as a form of government—these themes have tended to be the main subjects of investigation in the political history of emergent Africa. The first generation of Africans who wrote professionally about their own history preferred to deal with the qualities of the precolonial empires, the potential of oral history, the history of missionary activity, the questions of indirect rule, the imposition of colonialism and the local initiatives and responses to the colonial influence, and the religious and psychological structures.

Finally, there is the decisive circumstance that the Colonial Office records in Britain for the crucial period of 1939–45 were opened only from 1973. Two recent dissertations examine this recent period from the vantage point of the Colonial Office files: Curtis R. Nordman, "Prelude to Decolonization in West Africa: The Development of British Colonial Policy, 1938–1947" (Oxford, 1976); and Robert Pearce, "The Evolution of British Colonial Policy Towards Tropical Africa, 1938–1948" (Oxford, 1978).

If there is no consensus about the meaning of the phrase "the transfer of power," there is even less agreement about the more searching question of what *was*—indeed, what actually *could be*—transferred. The point being made here is that the differing nuances of the vocabulary, hitherto subsumed under the single rubric of the transfer of power, reflect deep differences about this phenomenon of decolonization. Nobody who has had firsthand experience of the events leading up to independence in Africa or who has made a close study of the constitutional or political idioms used in the transfer of power could be satisfied with the commonplace assumptions of uniformity. The "transfer of power" in British Africa of the 1950s was derivative from the "demission of sovereignty" in India a decade earlier; and both terms are paralleled in the United Nations' dictionary by the word *decolonization*—a term not coined until the 1930s and one that did not gain general currency until the 1950s. "Independence" could either be "granted" by the colonial power or "achieved" by the colonial dependency; *liberation* was a word peculiar to the colonial rather than the metropolitan set of mind, particularly in the violence of Algeria and Indochina. As late as 1957—the year of Ghana's birth—Lord Hailey's revised *African Survey* used *self-rule, self-determination,* and *self-government* indiscriminately, as contrasting terms to *responsible government* or *autonomy;* though in the same period *self-government, internal self-government, semi-responsible government, full self-government* and *full responsible self-government* might mean very different things to the constitutional experts of the Colonial Office. There is an implied difference in viewpoint whether independence is "granted" or "achieved," "won," "wrested," or "wrung"—or indeed, as some African historians prefer, "regained"; or, by contrast, in Churchill's view, the empire is "frittered away." This is not, as J. D. Hargreaves observes, just a quarrel over words: "The terms reflect different views of what has actually taken place, and attitudes taken towards present regimes in the successor States may depend on which view is adopted" (*The End of Colonial Rule,* p. 5). And when one comes—as few scholars yet have—to analyze the vocabulary of independence in African and Asian languages, one may well find significant nuances of expectation hidden in such quintessential catchwords as *uhuru, merdeka, swaraj, 'yanci, kwacha, ngwee, mulkin, kai,* and "free-dom."

As scholars begin to examine the Colonial Office files for the critical years of World War II, we can determine that it is no longer adequate to date the beginning of the end of empire from the post-1947 years. There are a number of documents which prove that the Colonial Office was seriously drafting plans for decolonization several years before signs of this policy became public. These include Lord Moyne's *Report on Disturbances in the West Indies, 1938–39* (not published in full until 1945, as Cmd. 6607); Lord Hailey's *Native Administration and Political Development in British Tropical Africa* of 1940 (not widely circulated even at the confidential level until 1944, and not published in its entirety until 1979) and his lectures delivered at Princeton in 1943 (*The Future of Colonial Peoples*); the booklet prepared by the British government's Empire Information Service and published by His Majesty's Stationery Office in 1944, *Origins and Purpose;* and the forward-thinking minutes, especially by Andrew Cohen, in the African Department of the Colonial Office from the early 1940s on. General knowledge of these developments had to await such official publications as the two milestone despatches from the Secretary of State for the Colonies to his African governors, one on Colonial Development and Welfare (dated the 12 November 1945, Cmd. 6713) and the other on Local Government (dated the 25 February 1947). These revolutions in British colonial policy revised the centuries'-old principle that no colony should cost the British Exchequer a penny, and through the introduction of elected representative institutions they sounded the death knell of the hallowed principle of "indirect rule" as the basis of African administration. These despatches also eased the first explicit acceptance by the Colonial Office of the principle set forth in the Watson *Report on the Commission of Enquiry into Disturbances in the Gold Coast* (Col. no. 231, 1948), that "the constitution and government of the country must be so reshaped as to give every African of ability an opportunity to help govern the country, so as not only to gain political experience but also to experience political power."

What were the metropolitan initiatives for the transfer of power in the 1940s and 1950s? What was the role of that potentially influential and occasionally impotent anticolonial pressure group, the United Nations? What was the African side of the decolonization equation? To deal with African influences last in this series of questions is to recognize that in the end they could assume primary importance.

For the sake of convenience, the scope of discussion in this essay takes the story of the transfer of power up to 6 March 1957, the date of independence for the first of Britain's modern colonies in tropical Africa, the moment when a country went to sleep as the Gold Coast and woke up as Ghana. While much of the bibliography for the period from 1939 to 1957 can be comfortably classified under the theme of "old melodies, new tunes," the impact of the transfer of power as a reality redefined certain aspects of the literature and gave rise to others totally without ancestry in the colonial period. For instance, the impact of foreign affairs has no roots in the colonial period other than as an adjunct of the foreign policies of the metropolitan powers. The literature on elections in Africa was unestablished until such works as W. J. M. Mackenzie and K. E. Robinson, eds., *Five Elections in Africa* (1960), and K. W. J. Post's *The Nigerian Federal Election of 1959* (1963). The Africanization of the bureaucracies and the concomitant growth of public administration—as distinct from colonial or "Native Administration"—are further phenomena quite new to the literature before the mid-1950s (see A. H. M. Kirk-Greene, "Public Administration and African Studies," in Christopher Fyfe, ed., *African Studies since 1945*, 1976).

In other cases, the subject matter of the literature is not so much fresh as redirected. Thus the earlier classical works on colonial administration, on "Indirect Rule" and "Native Administration" (for example, Lord Lugard's *The Dual Mandate in British Tropical Africa*, 1922; Margery Perham's *Native Administration in Nigeria*, 1937; A. H. M. Kirk-Greene's documentary *The Principles of Native Administration in Nigeria, 1900–1947*, 1965) tended after World War II to give way to constitutional history (for example, M. Wight, *British Colonial Constitutions 1947*, 1952, *The Development of the Legislative Council, 1606–1945*, 1946, and his *The Gold Coast Legislative Council*, 1947; Joan Wheare, *The Nigerian Legislative Council*, 1950; Kalu Ezera, *Constitutional Developments in Nigeria*, 1960) and to incorporate local government studies (for example, R. E. Wraith, *Local Government in West Africa*, 1953; F. G. Burke, *Local Government and Politics in Uganda*, 1964). For the first studies of latter-day nationalism and nascent political parties, see T. L. Hodgkin's *Nationalism in Colonial Africa* (1956) and his *African Political Parties*, (1961), and J. S. Coleman's *Nigeria: Background to Nationalism* (1958); for the first investigations of the transfer of power itself, David Kimble's *The Machinery of Self-Government* (1953), and David Apter, *The Gold Coast in Transition* (1955). The broader study of African society also developed, from anthropology's conventional ethnographic surveys to sociology's preoccupation with elites and urbanization (see P. C. Lloyd, *The New Elites of Tropical Africa*, 1966, and his *Africa in Social Change*, 1967; P. Gutkind, *The Emergent African Urban Proletariat*, 1974; INCIDI, *Development of a Middle Class in Trop-*

ical and Sub-Tropical Countries, 1956), and to political perspectives, such as Martin Kilson's and Lucy Mair's chapters on the new African elites in volumes 1 and 3 respectively of L. H. Gann and P. Duignan's *Colonialism in Africa* (1969–75). In the field of history, the shift can be described as the writing of Africa's history from a European vantage point to writing *African* history. Its significance in the context of the transfer of power has seldom been better expressed than by one of the pioneers of the new school of African history, K. O. Dike, in his article "African History and Self-Government" (*West Africa*, February 28, 1953).

The survey that follows is divided into four principal parts: (1) works about Britain in Africa as at 1939; (2) the metropolitan initiatives toward the transfer of power from 1940 onward; (3) the impact of the international forces on Britain's policy on decolonization; and (4) the African imperatives of independence. Short sections at the end of the essay treat the theme of the transfer of power in fiction, give a note on sources, and summarize "who was who" in the transfer of power.

1. The Influential Literature ca. 1939

What were the books that exercised an influence on and were cited by those concerned with British colonial policy toward Africa at the outbreak of World War II—not so much the standard literature on "imperialism" as on what was called "the colonial problem"? Such thinking was in the air, if not yet in either the official mind or the basic literature. Examples are the writings of concerned liberals, such as Leonard Woolf's *Empire and Commerce in Africa* (1920) and Joyce Cary's *The Case for African Freedom* (1941), or the arguments of such activist groups as the Fabian Colonial Bureau (Rita Hinden's *Plan for Africa*, 1941) and the Movement for Colonial Freedom (see Lord Brockway's autobiography, *The Colonial Revolution*, 1973).

Sir Frederick Lugard's *Dual Mandate in British Tropical Africa* (1922) bore a dual imprimatur: not only was this a study derived from the personal achievement of twenty-five proconsular years, it also carried the weight of world stature by virtue of Lugard's postgubernatorial appointment as Britain's permanent representative on the Mandates Commission. Twenty years later, as Margery Perham has shown in her introduction to the fifth edition (1967), *The Dual Mandate* was still a central text for any debate on African administration. At the new training courses for colonial administrators designed by Major (subsequently Sir Ralph) Furse at Oxford, Cambridge, and later London, Lugard's *Political Memoranda* (Kaduna 1906, Lagos 1919, London 1974) were also recommended reading until at least

1950. Lugard in the 1940s was no spent ghost from a proconsular past. His works were the texts at the center of any debate on African administration right up to the outbreak of World War II, when they were joined by Lord Hailey's encyclopedic *An African Survey* (1938).

Striking the balance between Colonial Office cum Government House theory (Lugard's instructions to his political officers were revised by Sir Donald Cameron in his famous series of "little brown books" issued from Dar es Salaam and Lagos) and the District Officer's practice, were Margery Perham's *Native Administration in Nigeria* (1937) and Lucy Mair's *Native Policies in Africa* (1936), though 1939 was perhaps too early for either to have established themselves as standard texts. "Indirect rule" was acclaimed by its devotees as the philosopher's stone of colonial administration. Humane, undestructive of native society, and in keeping with the attractive concept of trusteeship and tutelage sanctioned by the League of Nations' mandates system, it seemed to offer the best in the imperfect world of colonial administration. Its appeal even survived the periodic setbacks to its implementation, such as its failure in eastern Nigeria (on which see A. E. Afigbo, *The Warrant Chiefs*, 1972), as well as the occasional reassessments undertaken by its most influential advocate, Margery Perham (for example, "A Restatement of Indirect Rule," *Africa*, 1934; "Some Problems of Indirect Rule in Africa," *Journal of the Royal Society of Arts*, 1934).

The debate on indirect rule was not confined to West Africa. A wide-ranging discussion is that by Prosser Gifford, "Indirect Rule: Touchstone or Tombstone for Colonial Policy?" in Gifford and Louis, eds., *Britain and Germany in Africa* (1967); while there are a number of important studies dealing with particular areas: D. A. Low and R. C. Pratt, *Buganda and British Overrule* (1960), and the latter's chapter in D.A. Low and Alison Smith, eds., *History of East Africa*, vol. 3 (1976); H. F. Morris and J. S. Read, *Indirect Rule and the Search for Justice* (1972); P. F. Mitchell's article "Indirect Rule" in the *Uganda Journal* (1936); and W. G. A. Ormsby-Gore, *Chieftainship in Bantu Africa and Indirect Rule in British African Dependencies* (1942).

Indirect rule was never, to say the least, free from criticism. This, predictably, came from the colonial liberals in Britain like Leonard Woolf and the Fabian Bureau, and, although muted up to the 1945 Pan-African Congress, from African nationalists (see O. Awolowo, *Path to Nigerian Freedom*, 1946), and indeed, in the African press, which goes back much further (see the two outspoken editorials in the *Lagos Weekly Record*, 1919, reproduced as an appendix in A. H. M. Kirk-Greene, *Lugard and the Amalgamation of Nigeria*, 1968). Criticism also came from within the Colonial

Service itself (for instance, J. J. F. Fitzpatrick, "Nigeria's Curse—The Native Administration," *National Review*, 1924; A. V. Murray, "Education under Indirect Rule," *Journal of the Royal African Society*, 1935; and, above all, W. R. Crocker, *Nigeria: A Critique of British Colonial Administration*, 1936). As Michael Crowder has shown by use of the Nigerian archives, in his *Revolt in Bussa* (1973), indirect rule in incompetent hands could degenerate into maladministration far more rapidly than direct rule. Nor, in this assault upon the dogma of indirect rule from within, should one overlook the incisive criticisms of one of the most distinguished of Britain's colonial governors, Sir Donald Cameron, both in his *Principles of Native Administration* (1934) and in his trenchant memoirs, *My Tanganyika Service and Some Nigeria* (1939).

It is this mounting criticism of indirect rule from within official circles that allows us to move from the specific of colonial administration as a field practice to the general problem of Colonial Office policy. If discontented District Officers and recriminatory retired governors could be ignored, Lord Hailey could not. Onetime governor in the Indian Civil Service, Hailey wrote his authoritative *An African Survey* (1938) under the auspices of the Royal Institute of International Affairs and the Carnegie Corporation. The origins of this project (in Smuts's Rhodes Memorial Lecture delivered at Oxford in 1929) have been clearly traced by J. D. Hargreaves, in his 1973 presidential address to the African Studies Association (*African Research and Documentation*, 1973). Hailey had no qualms about attacking the prevalent idea that indirect rule was incompatible with self-government based on representative institutions. The assault upon the continuing viability of indirect rule as an administrative policy is, of course, only one of many themes of that magisterial work.

To Lugard's *Dual Mandate* and Hailey's *An African Survey* should be added Raymond L. Buell's *The Native Problem in Africa* 2 vols. (1928) as the third fundamental work of reference for the historian initiating himself into African studies. For more specialized work, see G. St. S. Orde Browne's *The African Labourer* (1933); R. R. Kuczynski's *Demographic Survey of the British Colonial Empire* (1948–49); C. K. Meek's *Land Law and Custom in the Colonies* (1946); on the economics of empire, S. H. Frankel's *Capital Investment in Africa* (1938) and Sir Alan Pim's *The Financial and Economic History of the Tropical African Territories* (1940), along with the earlier but solitary *The Economic Revolution in British West Africa* by A. McPhee (1926); and on the natural sciences, E. B. Worthington's *Science in Africa* (1938). The years each side of 1939 were indeed productive for colonial studies. The fact that so many volumes appeared within such a short space of time helps to underline that the "survey" tradition of the reference compendium was filling a practical need. One work which stands out beyond the compendium tradition is W. Keith Hancock's *Survey of British Commonwealth Africa* (1937–42), a monumental achievement in synthesis and analysis.

2. The Metropolitan Initiative after ca. 1940

Lord Hailey, who combined experience in Indian administration with expertise in African affairs, forms the bridge in the literature between prewar and postwar British colonial policy in Africa. We find in his writing the notion of the transfer of power in Africa beginning to take shape. Two of his post-1938 publications are of such central importance to this theme that they deserve to be closely studied.

The Future of Colonial Peoples comprises the lectures Hailey delivered at Princeton in 1943, as part of the British government's move to take some of the sting out of the American attack on any continuing imperial role after the war. In terms rarely heard before, Americans learned of a real breakthrough in British colonial policy, which now recognized the need to grant self-government to those areas already fitted for it, and to educate the others in the management of their own affairs. While this was the clearest public indication to date of this new approach in Whitehall, both Hailey and the Colonial Office had been thinking in these terms at least since 1940. In that year, as one result of *An African Survey* (1938), Hailey was commissioned to visit nearly all the British African territories and to take confidential soundings from their governments on what impact the war was likely to have on demands for constitutional change and political advance. His report was written in 1940–42 but circulated only to a restricted audience in 1944. Not until 1979 was the full report published for the first time (Hailey, *Native Administration and Political Development in British Tropical Africa*, 1979). It is a document that has yet to be fully appreciated for its shrewd and seminal qualities.

The three remaining Hailey contributions to British policy in Africa can be dealt with more summarily. His *Native Administration in the British African Territories* (1950–54, 5 parts) is to a limited extent an expurgated version of his 1940–42 confidential *Report*, updated by a further visit to Africa in 1948–49 to gather new data on provincial and native administration. In design, these volumes follow the descriptive, compendium surveys of the period just before the war. In content, they are the last of the major descriptive surveys, and they form an indispensable synthesis of British colonial administration at the field level. The next edition of *An African Survey—Revised 1956*, while it lived up to its title as an extensively revised work, has real limitations, already clear in its rejection—as late as 1957, the year of Ghana's independence!—of the term *nationalism* as applicable to the African scene. Of perhaps greater relevance to the theme of the transfer of power is Hailey's earlier discussion of Britain's new policy in the Royal Institute of International Affairs' *Colonial Administration by European Powers* (1947). There has as yet been no study of the life and work of Lord Hailey.

As the Colonial Office wartime records were opened, it became clear that the initiatives of Hailey (1938) and Moyne (1939) were muted rather than muzzled by the preoccupation of Britain's very survival. From 1943 onward, when the Secretary of State for the Colonies altered the emphasis from trusteeship to partnership and confirmed that Britain's policy was to guide all her colonial peoples toward self-government within the empire, the Colonial Office began to think no longer of Malcolm Macdonald's "generations or even centuries," but of decades. A significant turn came with the Labour party's landslide victory in the first postwar general election. A party now came to power which had won respect from Africans because of its overt sympathy with African political aspirations. Although the Labour party itself signally failed to include any promise of independence for Africa in its 1945 manifesto (see P. S. Gupta, *Imperialism and the British Labour Movement*, 1975, and S. A. H. Haqqi, *The Colonial Policy of the Labour Government, 1945–51*, 1960), it ushered in the era of Arthur Creech Jones, Colonial Secretary from 1946 to 1950. As a prominent figure of the Fabian Society, he held pronounced views (see the Fabian Colonial Bureau pamplet *Labour's Colonial Policy*, 1947; his own article in the *Yale Review*, 1949, entitled "British Colonial Policy—Current Scene and Outlook for the Future"; and his Cust Foundation Lecture, *The Future of the African Colonies*, 1951), and he was responsive to such arguments as those put forward in Rita Hinden's *Fabian Colonial Essays* (1945) and the bureau's *Downing Street and the Colonies* (1942) and their joint publication *Colonies and International Conscience* (1945).

Two milestone Colonial Office despatches were those on Colonial Development and Welfare (Cmd. 6713, 1945) and on Local Government (dated 25 February 1947). The initiative for political advance was now firmly that of Whitehall. To keep pressure on the Colonial Service leadership to move with the times, a conference of African governors was convened in 1947 and of unofficial members of Legislative Councils in 1948 (African no. 1176). The message was clear: the future was going to be more than the past updated. The new Colonial Office Summer School on African Administration at Cambridge (African no. 1173, confidential, London 1948) endorsed the substitution of a system of representative local government for the moribund one of indirect rule (see R. E. Robinson, "Why Indirect Rule Has Been Replaced by Local Government in the Nomenclature of British Native Administration," *Journal of African Administration* 2 [July 1950]: 12–15). Soon a younger generation of up-and-coming colonial top officials who could be expected to work with the emerging nationalist leadership were appointed in West Africa—men like Arden-Clarke and Dorman, Macpherson and Foot, and a little later Cohen himself, with the early Twining, the first of the East African radical governors. Finally, the Colonial Office established its own think-tank, the African Studies Branch (cf. Sir George Cartland, "Retrospect," and Ronald Robinson, "The 'Journal' and the Transfer of Power," *Journal of Administration Overseas* 13 [January 1974]) and converted its house *Bulletin* into an influential *Journal of African Administration*.

The reports of the various Colonial Office Summer Conferences held at Cambridge between 1947 and 1960 (thereafter Cambridge Summer Conferences) still have value. Among them, the most important were those of 1951 on African administration (African no. 1178), of 1957 on the place of chiefs in administration (African no. 1190), and of 1958 and 1961, both on local government (African no. 1193). The abundant literature on local government began with such early documentation as the unpublished report by E. J. Gibbons, "African Local Government Reform in Kenya, Uganda and Eastern Nigeria" (1949), and the Eastern Region of Nigeria White Paper "Memorandum on Local Government Policy," dated 16 June 1949, as well as with such major studies as L. Gray Cowan's *Local Government in West Africa* (1958) and R. E. Wraith's *Local Government in West Africa* (1964; revised in 1972 as *Local Administration in West Africa*). The central chapters of W. Tordoff, *Government and Politics in Tanzania* (1967) and Stanley Dryden, *Local Administration in Tanzania* (1968) both reveal the dynamism of the Tanzanian reinterpretation of local administration in the context of a transfer of power. Current research at African universities suggests that N. U. Akpan's *Epitaph to Indirect Rule* (1956), however important as an informed treatise, will in no way be the last word, even on Nigerian local administration.

Out of the massive literature on the localization of the bureaucracies, much of it in the form of reports, mention may be made to two good general studies, Richard Symonds, *The British and their Successors* (1966), and A. L. Adu's *The Civil Service in New African States* (1965).

Serious analysis of Africa's economies in the late colonial period did not really begin until after decolonization. D. K. Fieldhouse's *Economics and Empire, 1830–1914* (1973) stands out as an impressive study. A major collection of contributed essays is vol. 4 of *Colonialism in Africa*, edited by L.

H. Gann and Peter Duignan (1975), which may be read in conjunction with A. G. Hopkins's review article, "The Burden of Empire Building," *African Affairs* (January 1978). The most coherent account at the regional level is also by A. G. Hopkins, *An Economic History of West Africa* (1973). Of major significance, too, are the Hopkins articles on "Imperial Business in Africa"—the first on sources, the second on interpretation—in the *Journal of African History* (1976). West Africa is also examined with special reference to the controversial role of the marketing boards, in P. T. Bauer's *West African Trade* (1954). Notable economic studies relating to individual countries include Polly Hill, *Migrant Cocoa Farmers of Southern Ghana* (1963); K. D. S. Baldwin, *The Niger Agricultural Project* (1957); and R. Galletti, K. D. S. Baldwin, and I. Dina, *Nigerian Cocoa Farmers* (1956). In East Africa, research on economic history has been even more productive. E. A. Brett, *Colonialism and Underdevelopment in East Africa* (1973); R. M. A. van Zwanenberg, *An Economic History of Kenya and Uganda, 1800–1970* (1975); Cyril Ehrlich, "Some Aspects of Economic Policy in Tanganyika, 1945–1960," *Journal of Modern African Studies* (1964); R. D. Wolff, *The Economics of Colonialism* (1974); and Christopher Wrigley's chapter on changes in East African society in vol. 3 of the *Oxford History of East Africa*, are cases in point. The iconoclastic approach of Walter Rodney is clear in the title of his critique, *How Britain Underdeveloped Africa* (1973). The principal surveys of the currency systems are to be found in W. T. Newlyn and D. C. Rowan, *Money and Banking in British Colonial Africa* (1954) and A. R. Cenan, *The Sterling Area* (1952). The recent house histories by the two chief banks on the West Coast, Richard Fry, *Bankers in West Africa* (1976), and Sir Julian Crossley and John Blandford, *The DCO Story* (1975), add, like F. J. Pedler's history of the United Africa Company, *The Lion and the Unicorn in Africa* (1974), only a limited amount to our knowledge. In the latter context, D. K. Fieldhouse's new study, *Unilever Overseas* (1978), is far more informative.

British economic aid is more relevant to the 1960s than to the period of the 1940s and 1950s, but mention should be made of Sir William Rendell's *History of the Commonwealth Development Corporation* (1976) and of D. J. Morgan's excellent analysis of the integrally associated Colonial Development and Welfare acts, *Colonial Development* (1964). Further examinations of the Commonwealth Development and Welfare policy are to be found in D. Meredith, "The British Government and Colonial Economic Policy, 1919–39," *Economic History Review* 28, no. 3 (1975); G. C. Abbott, "A Re-examination of the 1929 Colonial Development Act," ibid. 24, no. 1 (1971); and E. R. Wicker, "Colonial Development and Welfare, 1929–1957: The Evolution of a Policy," *Social and Economic Studies* 7, no. 4

(1958). D. J. Morgan is about to publish his five-volume *The Official History of Colonial Development.*

3. The International Impact

This section separates the treatment of studies of bilateral foreign relations from studies of pressure groups at the international level such as the United Nations and, at a later date, the Organization of African Unity.

For a study of Anglo-American relations in their imperial context during the Second World War, with their crisis of America's demand for some form of international administration for the colonies, the most important work is Wm. Roger Louis, *Imperialism at Bay* (1977). J. A. Gallagher's Ford Lectures (1974), some of which touched on the same theme of America's refusal to countenance the continuation of a British empire after a war she had helped Britain to win, have not yet been published. On a broader canvas, Correlli Barnett's *The Collapse of British Power* (New York, 1972) hinted at Roosevelt's hostility toward Britain's imperial role in the postwar world, although twenty years earlier Chester Wilmot, in his *Struggle for Europe* (1952), had written from firsthand observation of Roosevelt's assault upon the colonial concept and the key it offers to an understanding of what really happened at Yalta. By the immediate postwar period, as America found the purity of her anti-imperialist stand tainted by the necessity to wage the Cold War in Europe, the focus had begun to shift to the importance of Anglo-Russian relations over the matter of empire and decolonization. Here *Soviet Light on the Colonies* (1944) by Leonard Barnes, a one-time Colonial Office official, is an important document. For the general background, see William Hardy McNeill's *America, Britain and Russia* (1953).

From 1947 onward, the colonial arena of the international focus changed to the United Nations. In view of the ineffectiveness of the League of Nations in Africa between the wars, skeptics may be forgiven for failing to see that the United Nations would exercise any great influence over colonial affairs. Despite the plea of British delegates that the anticolonial debate suffered from the syllogism of the "saltwater fallacy," the UN came more and more to be aligned with a vociferous and often effective decolonization lobby. A study of the voting patterns, such as that undertaken by T. Hovet in his *Africa in the United Nations* (1963), or by B. D. Meyers in his "African Voting in the UN General Assembly," *Journal of Modern African Studies* (1968), is instructive. Good studies of the demand for decolonization are to be found in such works as, on the one hand, *In Defence of Colonies* (1957) by Sir Alan Burns, who in 1947 had been Britain's first permanent representative on the UN's Trusteeship Council (no less than ten chapters in his book are devoted to "the general attack on British 'colonialism'"), and on the other, Yassin El-Ayouty's close study, *The United Nations and Decolonization* (1971), and Emil J. Sady's *The United Nations and Dependent Peoples* (1956). A major contribution to the literature on trusteeship, before the UN had got into its decolonizing stride, is H. D. Hall, *Mandates, Dependencies and Trusteeship* (1948). This was followed a few years later by R. N. Chowdhuri's *International Mandates and Trusteeship Systems* (1955). B. T. G. Chidzero's *Tanganyika and International Trusteeship* (1961), Victor T. LeVine's *The Cameroons, from Mandate to Independence* (1964), and Claude Welch's *Dream of Unity* (1966), are case studies of the growth of nationalism and the associated involvement of the UN in the independence movements of three mandated territories in Africa where Britain had a responsibility. Primary material of substantial value is to be found in the *Reports* of the UN triennial visiting missions to the trust territories (notably, that of the 1954 mission to Tanganyika, which called for a specific timetable for the transfer of power), along with the annual *Reports* by the administering authorities and the subsequent debates, motions, and petitions at the UN. Though the Organization of African Unity was not established until 1963 and so properly belongs to a different period, mention should be made of Z. Cervenka's chapter in K. Ingham, *Foreign Relations of African States* (1974) and his *The Unfinished Quest for Unity* (1977).

Decolonization cannot be divorced from the international dimensions of Pan-Africanism, at least from its rhetoric. The African—as opposed to the Caribbean—voice was not fully heard at Pan African congresses until the one held at Manchester in 1945 (see G. Padmore, ed., *History of the Pan-African Congress*, 1947; new ed. 1963). Its more recent voice has been well described by Ras Makonnen in his *Pan-Africanism from Within*, recorded and edited by Kenneth King (1973), whereas the most detailed account of the whole movement is that given by Imanuel Geiss, *Pan Africanism* (1974). An unrelenting commitment to Pan Africanism, of fundamental significance for the transfer of power, found its clearest expression in the closing words of the autobiography of one of the movement's most ardent promoters, Kwame Nkrumah: "Our task is not done and our own safety is not assured until the last vestiges of colonialism have been swept from Africa" (*Autobiography*, 1957, p. 290).

Decolonization was not always seen in the 1950s as a straightforward substitution of a separate nation-state for each colonial territory. Several ideas illustrate this point. One was the belief, however short-lived, that—to remodel a historic phrase in the history of the end of empire—there should be no decolonization without federation. Hence the plans to federate Nigeria and to establish the Central African, Malaysian, and the West Indies federations, and the moves to create a regional constitution in Ghana and in Kenya (if not for the whole of East Africa). The arguments have been admirably discussed in R. L. Watts, *Administration in Federal Systems* (1970), and, in an extensive bibliographical approach, in W. S. Livingston, *Federalism in the Commonwealth* (1963). As a device for the transfer of power, the record of failure speaks for itself. A second idea about imposing constitutional form on the process of decolonization was the no less abortive British plan to leave Tanganyika, Kenya, and maybe Uganda, as constitutionally entrenched multiracial societies (for the man-on-the-spot's view, see Philip Mitchell, *African Afterthoughts*, 1954, and Darrel Bates's biography of Lord Twining, *A Gust of Plumes*, 1972). The smaller territories constituted a third troubling situation. For Britain, most of these were outside Africa, The Gambia being a notable exception. Thought was given to a merger with Francophone Senegal, but this found little enthusiasm in The Gambia (see R. C. Bridges, ed., *Senegambia* (1974). The three High Commission Territories of Basutoland, Bechuanaland, and Swaziland raised difficult problems, because at one time incorporation into the Union had been argued as the sole viable solution to any eventual transfer of power (see Margery Perham and Lionel Curtis, *The Protectorates of South Africa* (1935).

4. The African Imperatives

The literature on African nationalism and on African political parties which negotiated, demanded, and inherited the transfer of power already outweighs that of the three previous sections. Because space is limited, I have described this literature in acceptedly summary fashion and organized it by region rather than by territory. A useful general reflection is Robert I. Rotberg, "African Nationalism: Concept or Confusion," *Journal of Modern African Studies* (1966).

By the late 1950s, case studies of individual African territories replaced surveys. The catalyst may be said to have been "politics." Many of the studies on the last years of nationalism and the final transfer of power portray an extensive interplay of historical and contemporary themes. Thus, studies dealing with African political history may take into account colonial policy, provincial administration, land and labor, the social culture of the principal ethnic groups, education and economics, political parties and leadership, the localization of the bureaucracy, and elections in the metropole as well as in the territory. In addition to politics, the development of universities in Africa in the 1950s led to the emergence of active local departments of history which tended to be "national" in their focus (Ibadan and Legon both made their mark early in the publishing world with their historical journals—for example, *Journal of the Historical Society of Nigeria*, *Transactions of the Historical Society of Ghana*, and their two highly respected *History Series*—while later Dar-es-Salaam was credited with having its own "school" of history—see the arguments by Donald Denoon and Adam Kuper and the riposte by Terence Ranger in *African Affairs* vol. 69 (1970), and vol 70 (1971). The perspective had now shifted from a Eurocentric to an Afrocentric one: "African history" could no longer be left in the care of amateurs, gifted or otherwise. It became the occupation of trained and fulltime scholars, few of whom in Africa, however, worked initially on the transfer of power (E. A. Ayandele's *The Educated Elite in the Nigerian Society*, 1974, is an exception). Rather, they did research on African history before or immediately after the colonial impact or else stimulated interest in its classical texts and traditions.

General

The two most influential studies on the then relatively new phenomenon of political party formation in Africa were G. Almond and J. S. Coleman, *The Politics of Developing Countries* (1960), and T. L. Hodgkin's *African Political Parties* (1961). Without these seminal studies, the understanding of the motivation, mobilization, and mechanics of African political parties in their quest for independence would have been a far slower process. The rapid increase of knowledge led to composite volumes with chapters by a number of specialists. These multichapter works include: Calvin W. Stillman, ed., *Africa in the Modern World* (1955); Charles Grove Haines, ed., *Africa Today* (1955); J. S. Coleman and Carl E. Rosberg, eds., *Political Parties and National Integration in Tropical Africa* (1964); the three volumes edited by Gwendolen Carter, *African One-Party States* (1962), *Five African States* (1963), and *National Unity and Regionalism in Eight African States* (1966); Robert I. Rotberg and Ali A. Mazrui, eds., *Protest and Power in Black Africa* (1970); *Colonialism in Africa, 1870–1960*, edited in five volumes by L. H. Gann and P. Duignan (1969–75); and the projected *Cambridge History of Africa*, of which only three volumes have been published (vols. 3–5, 1975–76). The eighth volume, to be edited by Michael Crowder, will cover the central period of decolonization. Neither of the twentieth-century volumes has yet (1980) appeared from the UNESCO project for the multivolume history of Africa: the one covering the transfer of power will be edited by Ali Mazrui.

West Africa

The transfer of power took place in West Africa a decade or so before that in East and Central Africa. In addition, larger numbers of secondary-school graduates and of home and overseas students meant that future West African historians were writing their theses an academic generation ahead of their colleagues on the other side of Africa. Thus the literature on the African initiative in the transfer of power is at its most substantial in the West African context. While there has been no standard *Oxford History* to balance those on East and South Africa, the gap has been more than adequately filled by J. F. Ajayi and M. Crowder, eds., *History of West Africa* (1971 and 1974), the second volume of which brings the story to 1960. The most relevant chapter to our theme is that by Olajide Aluko, "The Politics of Decolonisation in British West Africa, 1945–1960." Harry S. Wilson's *Origins of West African Nationalism* (1969) and Robert July's *The Origins of Modern African Thought* (1968) discuss the intellectual background. Thomas Hodgkin and Wilfred Whiteley each contributed an important article on the language of African nationalism to K. Kirkwood, ed., *St. Antony's Papers No. 10: African Affairs* (1961). Two further studies of the forceful semantics of African political expectations are Ali Mazrui, "The English Language and Political Consciousness in British Colonial Africa," *Journal of Modern African Studies* (1966), and Carol M. M. Scotton, "Some Swahili Political Words," ibid. (1965). K. W. J. Post's short but very useful *The New States of West Africa* (1964), and its excellent successor, John Dunn's *West African States* (1978), both offer an overview, while P. C. Lloyd's *Africa in Social Change* (1967), which draws most of its data from Nigeria and Ghana, provides insight into the tumultuous social processes.

No less influential for the whole of British African policy than it is for Ghana is the report of the Watson Commission, *Report of the Commission of Enquiry into Disturbances in the Gold Coast* (Col. no. 231, 1948). If forced to pick a date, this is perhaps when one would say that the actual transfer of power in Africa had its beginnings. The Watson Commission was followed by the Coussey *Report by the Committee on Constitutional Reform* (Col. no. 248, 1949), described by Hailey as "one of the most remarkable of the series of State papers in which the problems of government in British African territories has been discussed" (1957, p. 204). The analysis of nascent political party activity and its growth to political mobilization and the transfer of power was admirably set out in two early studies: James S. Coleman, *Nigeria* (1958), and David Apter, *The Gold Coast in Transition*

(1955; revised with new material, 1972). In the 1960s came further studies: Dennis Austin's excellent *Politics in Ghana, 1946–1960* (1964); David Kimble's profoundly researched *A Political History of Ghana* (1963), which, however, brings the story only to 1928; and Richard Sklar's *Nigerian Political Parties* (1963), unlikely ever to be excelled. B. J. Dudley's *Parties and Politics in Northern Nigeria* (1968) supplements the data on the Northern Region, on which C. S. Whitaker's *The Politics of Tradition* (1970) stands out as the best contribution; both, however, require a word of warning about reliability on proper names. A notable specialized example of the study of political parties is Maxwell K. Owusu, *Uses and Abuses of Political Power* (1970). H. L. Bretton, *Power and Stability in Nigeria* (1962) and, more objectively, J. Mackintosh, ed., *Nigerian Government and Politics* (1966), both reveal, in their identification of the weaknesses of the Nigerian system, much about the colonial legacy. K. W. J. Post's *The Nigerian Federal Election of 1959* (1963) is a major analysis of the last general election in Nigeria before the transfer of power. His *Structure and Conflict in Nigeria, 1960–1966*, with M. Vickers (1973), seeks, less successfully, to repeat the process for the first postindependence general election.

For the period leading up to the transfer of power in Sierra Leone, the best analysis so far is Martin Kilson's *Political Change in a West African State* (1966). John Cartwright has now followed his *Politics in Sierra Leone, 1947–1967* (1970) with a rewarding comparative study of the leadership of the Margai brothers, *Political Leadership in Sierra Leone* (1978). Christopher Fyfe's encyclopedic *A History of Sierra Leone* (1962) remains the standard work of historical reference for the period up to independence. The activities of that underestimated figure of prewar West African nationalism, I. T. A. Wallace-Johnson, have been brilliantly sketched in Leo Spitzer and LaRay Denzer's two-part article on the activities of his West African Youth League in *African Historical Studies* (1973) and in the latter's unpublished thesis (1967).

Autobiographies by the actors involved in the transfer of power make intriguing reading, often as much for what is omitted as for what is included. Kwame Nkrumah's autobiography (1957) is less revealing than could be wished. Among other nationalist leaders in West Africa, Obafemi Awolowo's *Awo* (1960) is, like Ahmadu Bello's *My Life* (1964), moderately rewarding, though less so than his polemical *Path to Nigerian Freedom* (1946). Neither goes beyond 1960, while Azikiwe's autobiography *My Odyssey* (1970) stops at 1947, just when the story becomes politically exciting. In *The Price of Liberty* (1973), K. W. J. Post and G. D. Jenkins provide a major portrait of a minor political figure of the decolonizing decade in

Nigeria, Alhaji Adelabu. Sir Charles Arden-Clarke, the popular terminal governor of the Gold Coast, wrote a short retrospective piece, "Eight Years in the Gold Coast" (*African Affairs,* vol. 57, 1958), as did his deputy R. Saloway ("The New Gold Coast," *International Affairs,* vol. 31, 1955), along with which may be read Richard Rathbone's article, "The Government of the Gold Coast after World War II," *African Affairs,* vol. 67 (1968), and his unpublished thesis on the transfer of power in Ghana (1968). Sir James Robertson's memoir, *Transition in Africa* (1974), is more informative on his Sudanese than his Nigerian years. The most revealing of the gubernatorial reminiscences is that of Sir Bryan Sharwood Smith (1969).

East Africa

The three-volume *Oxford History of East Africa* provides an impressive baseline for the colonial years in East Africa. While some of volume 2 (ed. Vincent Harlow and E. M. Chilver, 1965) is relevant to the themes covered here, it is volume 3 (ed. D. A. Low and Alison Smith, 1976) which provides the best coverage for a study of the transfer of power, taking the story up to Kenya's independence in 1963. The introductory essay by D. A. Low and J. M. Lonsdale, "Towards the New Order, 1945–1963," represents a notable conspectus. Prior to this, and still useful in a number of ways, the best single text was K. Ingham's masterly condensation, *A History of East Africa* (1962). On the economic side, more work has been done than for West Africa. In his *Colonialism and Underdevelopment in East Africa* (1973), E. A. Brett takes a critical view of the economic policies attaching to the British presence in the area, as does R. M. A. Van Zwanenberg, in his *Colonial Capitalism and Labour in Kenya 1919–1939* (1975). The final volume of the *Oxford History of East Africa* has no less than four chapters that focus on the region's economy, taking the analysis up to the transfer of power.

The literature on the decolonizing decades in East Africa reflects identifiable patterns. That on the Kenyan experience is characterized by a certain preoccupation with the twin themes of Mau Mau and racial bargaining. In the Tanzanian case, the wealth of political science writing on the experiment in socialism in postindependent Tanzania contrasts with the poverty of historical analysis, an imbalance likely to be redressed by the publication of John Iliffe's masterly *A Modern History of Tanganyika* (1979). For Zanzibar, the interest comes to life chiefly after the revolution of 1964, while for Uganda it is the parts (and especially the Bugandan one) rather than the whole that have been the main feature of the literature. In the last case, valuable data are to be found in such government reports as the Wild (1959) and Munster (1961) reports on the constitution and internal relationships, respectively. Two important articles appeared in the *Journal of African History* in 1968: J. M. Lonsdale, "Some Origins of Nationalism in East Africa," and T. O. Ranger, "Connexions between 'Primary Resistance' Movements and 'Modern Mass' Nationalism in East and Central Africa."

George Bennett's short *Kenya: A Political History* (1963) remains a small masterpiece and is invaluable for the period up to independence. The critical final election before the transfer of power has been examined by Clyde Sanger and John Nottingham in "The Kenya General Election of 1963," *Journal of Modern African Studies* (1964). There is little comparable for Tanganyika, where Claggett Taylor, *The Political Development of Tanganyika* (1965), H. W. Stephens, *The Political Transformation of Tanganyika* (1968), and I. N. Kimambo and A. J. Temu, *History of Tanzania* (1969), comprise the best of a somewhat limited choice, pending the appearance of Iliffe's major study. On the other hand, a number of particularly good localized studies exist on nationalism at the grassroots level: G. A. Maguire's *Towards 'Uhuru' in Tanzania* (1969), J. G. Liebenow's *Colonial Life and Political Development in Tanzania* (1971), Goran Hyden's *Political Development in Rural Tanzania* (1968), Joel Samoff's *Tanzania: Local Politics and the Structure of Power* (1974) and Roland Young and H. Fosbrooke, *Smoke in the Hills* (1960). Lionel Cliffe's article "Nationalism and the Reaction to Enforced Agricultural Change in Tanganyika," in L. Cliffe and J. Saul, eds. *Socialism in Tanzania* (1973) is an important statement on an issue that is crucial to the rise of nationalism in East Africa (see also R. L. Tignor's chapters on Kikuyu agriculture and the Kamba and Maasai stock problem in his *The Colonial Transformation of Kenya* (1976), along with J. Forbes Munro's *Colonial Rule and the Kamba* (1975).

Moving from the general to more specialized topics, Mau Mau—perhaps the nearest British Tropical Africa got to a colonial war once the era of initial conquest was past—emerges as a dominant feature of the literature on Kenya's final decade before the transfer of power. The importance—irrespective of the merits—of the publication of the official report by F. D. Corfield, *Historical Survey of the Origins of Mau Mau* (Cmnd. 1030, 1960) has never been denied, though no researcher should overlook the Kenyan students' riposte, *Comment on Corfield* (1960). *The Myth of Mau Mau* by Carl Rosberg and John Nottingham (1966) remains the most balanced account of the episode, while J. M. Kariuki, *Mau Mau Detainee* (1963), D. L. Barnett and Karari Njama, *Mau Mau from Within* (1966), and Bildad Kaggia, *Roots of Freedom* (1975), offer authentic inside views. Inevitably the literature has continued long after the event; see especially R. Buijtenhuijs's *Mau Mau Twenty Years After* (1973). In the same category, perhaps, are Ngugi wa Thio'ngo's stirring play put on the stage in Nairobi in 1972, *The Trial of Dedan Kimathi*, and his novels culminating in *Petals of Blood* (1977), as well as Bethwell Ogot's splendid essay "Revolt of the Elders," in his edition of *Politics and Nationalism in Colonial Kenya* (1972). From the other side, there are no less informative but subjective texts, such as the memoirs of Ian Henderson and P. C. Goodhart, *The Hunt for Kimathi* (1958); or of Fred Majdalany, *State of Emergency* (1962); or the objective, carefully compiled account by Anthony Clayton, *Counter Insurgency in Kenya* (1976). Because of the notorious "Hola affair," a critical factor in the British Cabinet's decision to transfer power to Kenya (see the Colonial Secretary's reference to it in Nigel Fisher, *Iain Macleod*, 1973), the official reports of how the eleven deaths took place in that corrective camp require inclusion here (Cmnd. 778 and 816, 1959). An extremely valuable bibliographical tool is that by Kennell A. Jackson and Marshall S. Clough, *A Bibliography and a Syllabus of Mau Mau* (1975).

Since much of the problem of how to transfer power in Kenya was bound up with Westminster's concern for the British settlers there, the literature on race relations and competition is of prime importance. For a view of how it all came about, superior accounts are to be found in Elspeth Huxley's biography of the arch-settler of them all, Lord Delamere, *White Man's Country*, 2 vols. (1935), and in M. P. K. Sorrenson's *Origins of European Settlement in Kenya* (1968). This is perhaps the best place to include a reference to Anthony Clayton and Donald C. Savage, *Government and Labour in Kenya, 1895–1961* (1974), a topic inseparable from settler considerations. The theme of racial bargaining is well treated in Elspeth Huxley and Margery Perham, *Race and Politics in Kenya* (1944), Donald S. Rothchild, *Racial Bargaining in Independent Kenya* (1973), and R. A. Frost's *Race Against Time* (1979). An astute account of the finale to the issue of racial bargaining in respect of Kenya's white settlers is given in G. B. Wassermann, *Politics of Decolonization: Kenya Europeans and the Land Issue, 1960–1965* (1976).

In Uganda the racial question was seen largely in terms of an Asian and not a European problem. Important studies of the Asian predicament include R. G. Gregory, *India and East Africa* (1971), Yash and Dharam Ghai, *The Asian Minorities of East and Central Africa* (1971), Hasu Patel, "Race, Class and Citizenship in Uganda, 1900–1972" (Ph.D. diss., UCLA, 1977), and, for a later period, Michael Twaddle, ed., *Expulsion of a Minority* (1975).

For an understanding of the political party process in East Africa, D. A.

Low's *Political Parties in Uganda 1949–1962* (1962), Cherry Gertzel's *Party and Locality in Northern Uganda, 1945–1967* (1974), and R. Cranford Pratt's *The Critical Phase in Tanzania, 1945–67* (1976) are major sources. Two theses, one by Margaret Bates, "Tanganyika under British Administration" (D. Phil., Oxford University, 1957), and the other by Marvin Lowenkopf, "Political Parties in Uganda and Tanzania" (M.Sc., University of London, 1961) may also be consulted. Cherry Gertzel's perceptive *The Politics of Independent Kenya* (1970) takes up the electoral story from G. Bennett and Carl Rosberg, *The Kenyatta Election* (1961); and in *The Anatomy of Uhuru* (1966) N. S. Carey Jones discusses why independence came when it did. For a later period, H. Bienen, *Kenya: The Politics of Participation and Control* (1974) serves well. One of the most original studies of decolonizing Kenya is Colin Leys's pessimistic anatomy of the postcolonial state, *Underdevelopment in Kenya* (1975). Henry Bienen's *Tanzania: Party Transformation and Economic Development* (1970), and L. Cliffe, ed., *One Party Democracy* (1967) offer valuable analyses of the political process on either side of the transfer of power. W. H. Friedland's *Vuta Kamba* (1969) is an account of the development of the trade-union movement in colonial and independent Tanganyika. The extensive literature on socialism and the *ujamaa* villagization schemes all relate to the postcolonial period.

When we turn to the actors involved in the transfer of power and the negotiations that led up to it in East Africa, we see that the literature is possibly stronger than that from West Africa. Much of Julius Nyerere's ample and highly quotable oratory belongs to the postindependence period: the evidence is abundant in his important collection of speeches, *Freedom and Unity* (1967), *Freedom and Socialism* (1968), and *Freedom and Development* (1973), as well as in his *Essays on Socialism* (1968). The unusual quality of Nyerere's leadership has attracted a wide range of biographical study, for example, William Edgett Smith, *They Run While We Learn to Walk* (1971), and John Hatch, *Two African Statesmen* (1976). Another insider's autobiographical work is Sophia Mustafa, *The Tanganyika Way* (1962). Judith Listowel's *The Making of Tanganyika* (1965), Darrel Bates, *A Gust of Plumes* (1972), and Cranford Pratt's *The Critical Phase in Tanzania, 1945–1958* (1976), all examine—from different viewpoints—the key relationship between the first premier and the penultimate colonial governor. There is no satisfactory full biography of Kenyatta (and in any case, it was his absence rather than his presence that was a force in the leading up to the transfer of power), but in compensation the autobiographies of such political leaders as Tom Mboya (of whom David Goldsworthy is currently working on a biography), *Freedom and After*

(1963), Oginga Odinga, *Not Yet Uhuru* (1967), and Michael Blundell, *So Rough A Wind* (1964), are all informative. Grace Ibingira's *The Forging of an African Nation* (1973) is the work of a scholar who was also a cabinet minister during the transfer of power in Uganda.

Central Africa

R. I. Rotberg's *The Rise of Nationalism in Central Africa, 1873–1964* (1965) looks at the move toward the transfer of power in two of the three component countries of the abortive Central African Federation—a political decision which, quite contrary to the British government's intentions, served as the ultimate catalyst to nationalism in Central Africa. There is no really satisfactory study of that failed Federation, and the several White Papers on its implementation—the Royal (Bledisloe) Commission, Cmd. 5949, 1939; Cmd. 8233–35, 1951; Cmd. 8573 and 8672, 1952; and Cmd. 8753–54, 1953, and those on its dissolution (e.g. Cmnd. 2093, 1963 and the Monckton Commission, Cmnd. 1148–51, 1960)—remain key documents for much of its understanding. The economic arguments have been well weighed in A. Hazelwood, *African Integration and Disintegration* (1967). H. D. Sills has a short piece on its final break-up in *African Affairs* (1974).

The nationalist movement in Northern Rhodesia has been documented in two close studies by D. C. Mulford, *The Northern Rhodesia General Election, 1962* (1964), and his *Zambia* (1967). A valuable comment from the African side is H. S. Meebelo, *Reaction to Colonialism* (1971). There are, too, some useful chapters on the preindependence period in W. Tordoff, ed., *Politics in Zambia* (1974). Kenneth Kaunda's autobiography, *Zambia Shall Be Free* (1962), constitutes an important insight into the nationalist experience.

Nyasaland has not fared so well in the literature on the nationalist prologue to the transfer of power. For anybody working on nationalism in Nyasaland it would be well to go back to the painstaking and illuminating analysis of the Chilembwe rising of 1915 presented in G. Shepperson and T. Price, *Independent African* (1958). Until the history of the Malawi Congress party now in the press is published, Z. D. Kadzamira, "Local Politics and the Administration of Development in Malawi" (Ph.D. diss., University of Manchester, 1974) is a far better source than the somewhat watered-down picture offered in B. Pachai, *Malawi: The History of the Nation* (1973) or the not very profound essays in R. J. Macdonald, *From Nyasaland to Malawi* (1975). One of the most revealing sources is the trenchant *Report of the Nyasaland Commission of Inquiry* (the Devlin Commission, Cmnd. 814, 1959). There is as yet no autobiographical contribution from the country's first head of state, though Philip Short has written a biographical study of Hastings Banda. Two unusual articles, in that they focus on the generally overlooked European reaction to African nationalism, are Robin Palmer's account of the Settlers and Residents' Association activities in Nyasaland between 1960 and 1963, in *African Affairs* (1973), and Alastair Ross's analysis of the role of the Capricorn Society in Tanganyika from 1949 to 1960, ibid. (1977).

Though Southern Rhodesia is well removed from the period of transfer of power covered by this volume (independence did not come until 1980), two bibliographical points deserve to be made. One is the signpost significance of such works as Colin Leys, *European Politics in Southern Rhodesia* (1959), and Cyril Rogers and Charles Frantz, *Racial Themes in Southern Rhodesia* (1962). The other is the far wider relevance of N. Sithole's thoughtful *African Nationalism*, 2d ed. (1968). While it is still (1979) premature to treat Rhodesia in the same vein as the other African states that qualify historiographically here under the rubric of the transfer of power, mention may be made of three studies: Claire Palley, *The Constitutional History and Law of Southern Rhodesia 1888–1965* (1966); Kenneth Young's *Rhodesia and Independence* (1969); and Robert C. Good, *U.D.I.: The International Politics of the Rhodesian Rebellion* (1973). See also two more recent contributions, Lord Blake's magisterial *A History of Rhodesia* (1977), and Elaine Windrich's *Britain and the Politics of Rhodesian Independence* (1978). Leaving aside at this stage of Rhodesian historiography the substantial quantity of partisan ephemera, one may nevertheless note the characteristic, posthumous *Rhodesia File* (1976) by Kwame Nkrumah.

South Africa

While accepting the vigorous African argument that it is premature to include South Africa in a volume dealing with the transfer of power between 1945 and 1960, the literature on that part of the continent is no less rich on the subject of nationalism. Nor can one afford to overlook the impact of the South African problem on the objectives and processes of the transfer of power in Central, East, and West Africa. Again, there was in that region, between 1930 and 1960, the controversial issue of the future of the three High Commission Territories of Basutoland, Bechuanaland, and Swaziland.

To take the last point first, the most useful examination of the arguments is to be found in M. Perham and L. Curtis, *The Protectorates and South Africa* (1935). Interesting contemporary insights are now available in Margery Perham's diary of the time, *African Apprenticeship* (1974). The transformation from protectorate to sovereign states has been discussed generally in R. P. Stevens, *Lesotho, Botswana and Swaziland* (1967), and, for Basutoland, in J. E. Spence, *Lesotho* (1968).

The second volume of *The Oxford History of South Africa, 1870–1966* (1971), edited by Monica Wilson and Leonard Thompson, constitutes a landmark in South African historiography. The chapter by Leo Kuper on African nationalism in the half-century from 1910 is complemented by that by René de Villiers on Afrikaner nationalism. The appearance of this *Oxford History* by no means superseded the value of Leonard M. Thompson's *Politics in the Republic of South Africa* (1966). Peter Walshe's *The Rise of African Nationalism in South Africa* (1971) is a well-documented history of the African National Congress from 1912 to 1952, the nationalist movement which also forms the theme of Edward Feit's earlier *South Africa: The Dynamics of the African National Congress* (1962). Richard Gibson's *African Liberation Movements* (1972) should also be mentioned. Muriel Horrell's *Action, Reaction and Counter-Action* (1963) confines itself to non-white political movements in South Africa. Edward Roux's *Time Longer Than Rope* (1948); I. B. Tabata, *The All-African Convention* (1950); Leo Kuper, *Passive Resistance in South Africa* (1956); Mary Benson's *South Africa: The Struggle for a Birthright* (1966); and Margaret Ballinger's *From Union to Apartheid* (1969), are all relevant to the consolidation of nationalist sentiment in South Africa. Nationalist autobiography is well represented by Albert Luthuli, *Let My People Go* (1962), Clements Kadalie, *My Life and the ICU* (1970), Ezekiel Mphalele, *Down Second Avenue* (1959), and Naboth Mokgatle, *The Autobiography of an Unknown South African* (1971). An outstanding documentary source is the ongoing series of volumes edited by Thomas Karis and Gwendolen M. Carter, *From Protest to Challenge* (1972–).

In the context of the impact the decolonization of Africa had on South Africa's international position, the basic reference volumes are J. E. Spence's *Republic Under Pressure* (1965), along with his chapter on "South Africa and the Modern World" in the *Oxford History*, and Dennis Austin's *Britain and South Africa* (1966). To these can now be added James Barber's *South Africa's Foreign Policy, 1945–1970* (1973) and S. C. Nolutshungu's impressive *South Africa in Africa: A Study in Ideology and Foreign Policy* (1975). The field of South Africa in international relations, along with that of South African politics in general, continues to expand at a rapid rate.

The bibliography of *The Oxford History of South Africa*, vol. 2, gives extensive coverage of the literature published up to ca. 1965. Further bibliographical guidance is to be found, for works published between 1960 and 1970, in Heribert Adam, *South Africa: Sociological Perspectives* (1971), and for those published between 1970 and 1974, in Leonard

Thompson and Jeffrey Butler, *Change in Contemporary South Africa* (1975). Shula Marks's chapter in C. Fyfe, ed., *African Studies since 1945* (1976), presents a useful survey of South African studies over the past thirty years.

5. The Theme of the Transfer of Power in Fiction

In keeping with the remarks made at the beginning of this essay, in fiction, too, Africa has not yet matched the quality of creative writing generated by the Indian experience of the transfer of power. So far there is nothing to set beside Paul Scott's superb *Raj Quartet* (*1967–1975*)—its final volume significantly entitled *A Division of the Spoils*—now rounded off with an epilogue, *Staying On* (1977). Nevertheless, African fiction can point to several novels which have the transfer of power as a tangential if not always a central theme. Conspicuous is Peter Abrahams's *A Wreath for Udomo* (1956). Nicholas Monsarrat followed his horror-story of the Mau Mau–style anticolonial uprising in his African protectorate of Pharamaul, *The Tribe that Lost its Head* (1956), with a scathing successor describing the territory's consequent independence and squalid decline, *Richer than All His Tribe* (1968), an unequivocal argument for the "too much too soon" school of decolonization. Robert Ruark's powerful *Uhuru* (1962) is in a similar gloomy vein, while Gerald Hanley's powerful *Consul at Sunset* (1951) is the story of a personal rather than an institutional withdrawal from colonial administration. James Ngugi's *A Grain of Wheat* (1967) has its climax in Kenya's Independence Day. By and large, most African novelists have preferred to write about the heady days of the eve of independence, such as Cyprian Ekwensi's *People of the City* (1954) and his *Jagua Nana* (1961), or Chinua Achebe's *No Longer at Ease* (1960); or about the problems associated with either the return of the Western-educated "has-been" and the resultant sociocultural predicament, like Mugo Gatheru's *Child of Two Worlds* (1964); or else with the seductive pleasures of those who inherited power and the socioeconomic problems of those who did not, as the metropolitan masters departed, for example, Chinua Achebe's *A Man of the People* (1966) and T. M. Aluko's *Chief The Honourable Minister* (1970), or Cameron Duodu's *The Gab Boys* (1967) and Onuora Nzekwu's *Blade among the Boys* (1962).

From expatriate novelists, Margaret Laurence's *This Side Jordan* (1960) and some of her short stories in *The Tomorrow-Tamer* (1963) capture the vibrant atmosphere of urban West Africa just prior to independence, while Elspeth Huxley's perceptive observations in such superior travelogues as *Four Guineas* (1954), *The Sorcerer's Apprentice* (1956), and *Forks and*

Hope (1964), or Negley Farson's comparable *Last Chance in Africa* (1949), all provide insights into Africa on the threshold of decolonization.

6. Sources

The modification of the "fifty-year rule" to that of thirty years for the closed period of Britain's official records, and the decision to open the archives for the period 1939–45 at a single moment, comprise two influential factors of the scholarly study of the prelude to decolonization. The situation in the independent African territories is different—sometimes more flexible, sometimes less so—in different capitals, and it would be unreasonable to expect that there will as yet be easy access for a scrutiny of the documents dealing with the delicate negotiations for the transfer of power. Some pertinent holdings are available in microfilm, for instance, the strong Kenyan collection at Syracuse University. The principal repository therefore remains the Colonial Office files in the Public Record Office, now at Kew Gardens. The PRO issues comprehensive sectional guides, notable among them being R. B. Pugh's *The Records of the Colonial and Dominions Offices* (1964). This is presently being updated by J. M. Lee.

Turning to private collections, the most notable advance over the list of personal papers described by H. Pogge von Strandmann and Alison Smith at page 761 in their historiographical chapter in Gifford and Louis, *Britain and Germany in Africa* (1967), is the Oxford Colonial Records Project archive (OCRP) in the Rhodes House Library. The scheme, which lasted from 1963 to 1972 and in its final years branched out into nearly a hundred tape-recorded interviews, has been described by J. J. Tawney, its director, in "Personal Thoughts on a Rescue Operation," *African Affairs* (1968), and now in more detail by Patricia Pugh, in her article in the *Journal of the Society of Archivists*, (1968). While not all of these ten thousand or so items are open, four handlists have been published by Rhodes House (Frewer 1968–71, Byrne 1978), and further descriptive checklists of the major collections may be consulted in the library. The Sudan archive is located at Durham University. The collection of private papers held by the Middle East Centre at St. Antony's College, Oxford, include those belonging to a number of officials who also served in Africa. Assistance from the National Register of Archives in tracing papers still in private hands may be usefully supplemented by reference to J. D. Pearson, ed., *A Guide to the Manuscripts and Documents in the British Isles Relating to Africa* (1971), and to D. H. Simpson, *Biography Catalogue of the Library of the Royal Commonwealth Society* (1961). At Oxford a new project extends the OCRP.

Britain's printed primary records on its colonial empire are extensive, in the official record of parliamentary proceedings (*Hansard*, covering verbatim the crucial debates in both the House of Commons and the House of Lords) and the voluminous output of Parliamentary Papers. This omnibus term covers special and annual reports laid before Parliament as well as the Blue Books and the numbered White Papers.

For secondary materials, the collections at Rhodes House and at the Institute of Commonwealth Studies, as well as the Bodleian Library, at Oxford, and in London at the Foreign and Commonwealth Office Library—where much of the singularly rich old Colonial Office library is still intact—and the libraries of the Royal Commonwealth Society, the Institute of Commonwealth Studies, and the School of Oriental and African Studies, are all invaluable. The International African Institute has transferred its library to Manchester University. The new Centres of African Studies often have unusual materials acquired or bequeathed and all deserve a careful visit. In regional terms, these centres have tended to specialize: West Africa at Birmingham University, southern Africa at York University, Central Africa (with much more besides) at Edinburgh University, and "development" at the Institute of Development Studies at Sussex University. The last-named institute publishes annually a useful Register of Research, and the Institute of Commonwealth Studies at London University produces an annual list of theses in progress which complements the continuing SCOLMA publications, *United Kingdom Publications and Theses on Africa* (1964–). Of outstanding importance to students of electoral behavior is Valerie Bloomfield, *Commonwealth Elections 1945–1970: A Bibliography* (1976). A. R. Hewitt's *Guide to Resources for Commonwealth Studies in London, Oxford and Cambridge* (1957) is badly in need of updating. Fortunately, *The Times* maintains its annual index. The Press Cuttings Section of the Royal Institute of International Affairs provides a notable service for the decolonizing decades. The BBC (and later ITV) archives are likely to be useful in connection with specific events that were covered in sound or on film. There is much United Nations material on decolonization in its various reports, especially in those originating from the Trusteeship Council.

Specialist African journals such as *African Affairs* (1901–), the *Journal of African History* (1960–), the *Journal of Modern African Studies* (1963–), and the *International Journal of African Historical Studies* (1968) are a source for articles on independent as well as colonial Africa. In the African countries themselves, the journals of the various historical societies, for example, the *Journal of the Historical Society of Nigeria* (1956–), *Kenya Historical Review* (1965–), *Odu* (1955–), *Sierra Leone Studies* (1963–), and *Transafrica Journal of History* (1971–), repay attention, as do their colonial predecessors, for instance, *Tanganyika Notes and Records*, *Sudan Notes and Records*, and *The Uganda Journal*. A useful vehicle in Britain has been the *Journal of African Administration*, (1949–80), subsequently renamed *Journal of Local Administration Overseas* (1963) and since 1966 called the *Journal of Administration Overseas*. Some relevant articles can also be found in the house journal of the Colonial Service, *Corona* (1949–62). A major bibliographical tool is Carole Travis, *Periodicals from Africa* (1977).

A WHO'S WHO OF THE PRINCIPAL OFFICEHOLDERS DURING THE TRANSFER OF POWER

Responsibility for Colonial Affairs in Britain; Colonial Governors; and the Heads of State and Prime Ministers of the African Countries and the Dates of Independence, ca. 1938–1965

Secretaries of State for the Colonies

1938 (May 16)	Malcolm Macdonald
1940 (May 13)	Lord Lloyd
1941 (Feb. 8)	Lord Moyne
1942 (Feb. 23)	Viscount Cranborne (later Marquess of Salisbury)
(Nov. 24)	Oliver Stanley
1945 (Aug. 3)	G. H. Hall (Later Viscount Hall)
1946 (Oct. 7)	Arthur Creech Jones
1950 (Mar. 2)	James Griffiths
1951 (Oct. 27)	Oliver Lyttelton (later Viscount Chandos)
1954 (July 30)	Alan T. Lennox Boyd (later Viscount Boyd)
1959 (Oct. 19)	Iain Macleod
1961 (Oct. 16)	Reginald Maudling
1962 (July 17)	Duncan Sandys (later Viscount Sandys)
1964 (Oct. 17)	Anthony Greenwood
1965 (Dec. 23)	Earl of Longford
1966 (Apr. 6)	Frederick Lee

The Colonial Office merged with the Commonwealth Relations Office on August 1, 1966, to form the Commonwealth Office. A further merger took place on October 17, 1968, resulting in a single Foreign and Commonwealth Office responsible to one Secretary of State.

On March 19, 1962, responsibility for the affairs of Northern Rhodesia and Nyasaland was transferred from the Secretary of State for the Colonies to the Home Secretary, Mr. R. A. Butler.

Permanent Under-Secretaries of State for the Colonies

1937 (Oct. 2)	Sir Cosmo Parkinson
1940 (Feb. 1)	Sir George Gater
(May 28)	Sir Cosmo Parkinson
1942 (Apr. 13)	Sir George Gater
1947 (Feb. 1)	Sir Thomas Lloyd
1956 (Aug. 20)	Sir John Macpherson
1959 (Aug. 20)	Sir Hilton Poynton

The post ceased to exist on July 31, 1966

A Calendar of Independence in the British Commonwealth

Former British dependent territories which did not join the Commonwealth on independence are enclosed in square brackets. New names assumed by countries at independence appear in parentheses.

1947 India; Pakistan
1948 Ceylon (Sri Lanka); [Burma]; [Palestine]
1956 [Sudan]
1957 Malaya; Gold Coast (Ghana)
1960 Nigeria; Cyprus; [British Somaliland]
1961 Sierra Leone; Tanganyika (Tanzania 1964); [Southern Cameroons]
1962 Jamaica; Trinidad and Tobago; Uganda; Western Samoa
1963 Zanzibar; Kenya; Sabah, Sarawak, Singapore (Federation of Malaysia), [Maldive Islands]
1964 Nyasaland (Malawi); Malta; Northern Rhodesia (Zambia)
1965 The Gambia
1966 British Guiana (Guyana); Bechuanaland (Botswana); Basutoland (Lesotho); Barbados
1967 [Aden](South Yemen)
1968 Mauritius; Swaziland; Nauru
1970 Tonga; Fiji
1973 Bahamas
1974 Grenada
1975 Papua New Guinea
1976 Seychelles
1978 Solomon Islands; Ellice Islands (Tuvalu); Dominica
1979 Gilbert Islands (Kiribati); Saint Lucia; Saint Vincent; Grenadines
1980 Southern Rhodesia (Zimbabwe)

A Calendar of Independence in Britain's African Colonies

(Foreign Office)	1956 (Jan. 1): The Sudan
West Africa	1957 (Mar. 6): Gold Coast (Ghana), including British Togoland
	1960 (Oct. 1): Nigeria, including Northern Cameroons
	1961 (Apr. 22): Sierra Leone
	1965 (Feb. 18): The Gambia
East Africa	1960 (June 26): British Somaliland (Somalia)
	1961 (Dec. 9): Tanganyika (1964 Tanzania, with Zanzibar)
	1962 (Oct. 9): Uganda
	1963 (Dec. 10): Zanzibar
	1963 (Dec. 12): Kenya
Central Africa	1964 (July 6): Nyasaland (Malawi)
	1964 (Oct. 24): Northern Rhodesia (Zambia)
	1980 (Apr. 18): Southern Rhodesia (Zimbabwe)
Southern Africa	1966 (Oct. 4): Basutoland (Lesotho)
	1966 (Sept. 30): Bechuanaland (Botswana)
	1968 (Sept. 6): Swaziland

Governors-General of the Sudan

1934 Sir Stewart Symes
1940 Sir Hubert Huddleston
1947 Sir Robert Howe
1954 Sir Knox Helm
Independence: January 1, 1956
Prime Minister: Ismail al-Azhari

Governors of the Gold Coast

1934 Sir Arnold Hodson
1941 Sir Alan Burns
1948 Sir Gerald Creasy
1949 Sir Charles Arden-Clarke
Independence: (as Ghana), March 6, 1957
Prime Minister: Kwame Nkrumah
Governor-General: Lord Listowel

Governors of Nigeria

1935 Sir Bernard Bourdillon
1943 Sir Arthur Richards
1948 Sir John Macpherson
1955 Sir James Robertson

NORTHERN NIGERIA
1954 Sir Bryan Sharwood Smith
1957 Sir Gawain Bell

WESTERN NIGERIA
1954 Sir John Rankine

EASTERN NIGERIA
1954 Sir Clement Pleass
1956 Sir Robert Stapledon
Independence: October 1, 1960
Prime Minister: Sir Abubakar Tafawa Balewa
Regional Premiers: Sir Ahmadu Bello (North)
Chief Obafemi Awolowo (West)
Dr. Michael Okpara (East)
Governor-General: Sir James Robertson

Governors of Sierra Leone

1934 Sir Henry Monck-Mason Moore
1937 Sir Douglas Jardine
1941 Sir Hubert Stevenson
1948 Sir George Beresford-Stooke
1953 Sir Robert Hall
1956 Sir Maurice Dorman
Independence: April 27, 1961
Prime Minister: Sir Milton Margai
Governor General: Sir Maurice Dorman

Governors of The Gambia

1936 Sir Thomas Southorn
1942 Sir Hilary Blood
1947 Sir Andrew Wright
1949 Sir Percy Wyn-Harris

1958 Sir Edward Windley
1962 Sir John Paul
Independence: February 18, 1965
Prime Minister: Sir Dauda Jawara
Governor-General: Sir John Paul

Governors of British Somaliland

1932 Sir Arthur Lawrance
1939 Sir Vincent Glenday
(1941 Under military administration)
1948 Sir Gerald Reece
1954 Sir Theodore Pike
1959 Sir Douglas Hall
Independence: (as Somalia), July 1, 1960
Head of State: Aden Abdulla Osman

Governors of Tanganyika

1934 Sir Harold MacMichael
1938 Sir Mark Young
1941 Sir Wilfrid Jackson
1945 Sir William Battershill
1949 Sir Edward Twining
1958 Sir Richard Turnbull
Independence: December 9, 1961
Prime Minister: Julius Nyerere
Union with Zanzibar as Tanzania: April 25, 1964

Governors of Uganda

1934 Sir Philip Mitchell
1940 Sir Charles Dundas
1944 Sir John Hall
1952 Sir Andrew Cohen
1957 Sir Frederick Crawford
1961 Sir Walter Coutts
Independence: October 9, 1962
Prime Minister: Milton Obote
Governor-General: Sir Walter Coutts

Governors of Kenya

1937 Air Chief Marshal Sir Robert Brooke-Popham
1940 Sir Henry Monck-Mason Moore
1944 Sir Philip Mitchell
1952 Sir Evelyn Baring (later Lord Howick)
1959 Sir Patrick Renison
1963 Malcolm Macdonald
Independence: December 12, 1963
Prime Minister: Jomo Kenyatta
Governor-General: Malcolm Macdonald

British Residents of Zanzibar

1937 Sir John Hall
1941 Sir Guy Pilling
1946 Sir Vincent Glenday
1952 Sir John Rankine
1954 Sir Henry Potter
1960 Sir George Mooring
Independence: December 10, 1963
Head of State: Sultan of Zanzibar
Union with Tanganyika as Tanzania: April 25, 1964

Governors-General of the Federation of Central Africa

1953 Lord Llewellin
1957 Earl of Dalhousie
Dissolution: December 31, 1963

Governors of Nyasaland

1939 Sir Donald Mackenzie-Kennedy
1942 Sir Edmund Richards
1948 Sir Geoffrey Colby
1956 Sir Robert Armitage
1961 Sir Glyn Jones
Independence: (as Malawi), July 6, 1964
Prime Minister: Dr. Hastings Banda
Governor-General: Sir Glyn Jones

Governors of Northern Rhodesia

1938 Sir John Maybin
1941 Sir John Waddington
1948 Sir Gilbert Rennie

1954 Sir Arthur Benson
1959 Sir Evelyn Hone
Independence: (as Zambia), October 29, 1964
Head of State: Kenneth Kaunda

High Commissioners of the High Commission Territories

1935 W. H. Clark
1941 Lord Harlech
1944 Sir Evelyn Baring
1951 Sir John Le Rougetel
1955 Sir Percival Liesching
1959 Sir John Maud
1963 Sir Hugh Stephenson
Post abolished: 1964

Resident Commissioners of Basutoland

1935 E. C. S. Richards
1942 C. N. Arden-Clarke
1947 A. D. Forsyth Thompson
1951 E. P. Arrowsmith
1955 A. G. T. Chaplin
1961 Sir Alexander Giles
Independence: (as Lesotho), October 4, 1966
Prime Minister: Chief Leabua Jonathan
Head of State: King Moshoeshoe II

Resident Commissioners of Bechuanaland

1937 C. N. Arden-Clarke
1942 A. D. Forsyth Thompson
1947 A. Sillery
1950 E. B. Beetham
1953 W. F. MacKenzie
1955 M. O. Wray
1959 Sir Peter Fawcus
1965 Sir Hugh Norman-Walker
Independence: (as Botswana), September 30, 1966
President: Sir Seretse Khama

Resident Commissioners of Swaziland

1935 A. G. Marwick
1937 C. L. Bruton

1942 E. K. Featherstone
1946 E. B. Beetham
1951 D. L. Morgan
1956 Sir Brian Marwick
1963 Sir Francis Loyd
Independence: September 6, 1968
Prime Minister: Prince Makhosini Dlamini
Head of State: King Sobhuza II

BIBLIOGRAPHY

Abbott, George C. "A Reexamination of the 1929 Colonial Development Act." *Economic History Review* 24, no. 1 (February 1971): 68–81.

Abdi, Said Yusuf. "Independence for the Afars and Issas: Complex Background: Uncertain Future." *Africa Today* 24 (January–March 1977): 61–70.

______. "The Mini Republic of Djibouti: Problems and Prospects." *Horn of Africa* 1 (April–June 1978): 35–40.

Abelin, Pierre. *La Politique française de coopération*. Paris, 1975.

Abi-Saab, Georges. *The United Nations Operation in the Congo, 1960–1964*. Oxford, 1978. [The role of law]

Abrahams, Peter Henry. *A Wreath for Udomo*. New York, 1956.

Abshire, David, and Samuels, Michael, eds., *Portuguese Africa: A Handbook*. London, 1969.

Achebe, Chinua. *A Man of the People*. London. 1966.

______. *No Longer at Ease*. New York, 1960.

Adabra, Samuel Suka. "Les Autorités traditionnelles et le pouvoir politique moderne au Togo." Thesis, University of Paris, 1973.

Adams, Adrian. "Prisoners in Exile: Senegalese Workers in France." *Race and Class* 16 (October 1974): 157–80.

Adam, Heribert. *South Africa: Sociological Perspectives*. London, 1971.

Addra, Grégoire. *L'Aide extérieure au Mali*. N.p., 1971.

Adelman, Kenneth. "Report from Angola." *Foreign Affairs* 53 (1975): 558–74.

Adu, A. L. *The Civil Service in New African States*. New York, 1965.

Afigbo, A. E. *The Warrant Chiefs*. London, 1972.

Agayo, Bakonzi. "Les Elites politiques de 1957 à Lubumbashi." *Cahiers zaïrois d'études politiques et sociales*. (October 1974), pp. 115–34.

Ageron, Charles-Robert. *L'Algérie algérienne de Napoleon III à de Gaulle*. Paris, 1980.

______. "Ferhat Abbas et l'évolution politique de l'Algérie musulmane pendant la deuxième guerre mondiale." *Revue d'histoire maghrébine*, (July 1975), pp. 125–44.

______. *Histoire de l'Algérie contemporaine, 1871–1954*. Paris, 1979.

______. "L'Opinion française devant la guerre d'Algérie." *Revue française d'histoire d'outre-mer* 63 (1976): 256–85.

Ainad-Tabet, Redouane. "Le 8 mai 1945: Jacquerie ou revendication agraire." *Revue algérienne des sciences juridiques économiques et politiques* 9 (1972): 1007–16.

Ajayi, J. F. A., and Crowder, Michael, eds. *History of West Africa*, vol. 2. London, 1974.

Akpan, N. U. *Epitaph to Indirect Rule*. London, 1956.

Alalade, F. O. "French-Speaking Africa-France Relations—A Critical Bibliographical Survey with Particular Reference to the Ivory Coast." *Current Bibliography of African Affairs* 9 (1976-77): 84-93.

Alexandre, François. "[Compte rendu de] Sivan (Emmanuel). Communisme et nationalisme en Algérie, 1920-1962." *Annuaire de l'Afrique du Nord* 15 (1976): 1295-1303.

Almond, Gabriel A., and Coleman, James S. *The Politics of the Developing Areas*. Princeton, 1960.

Alpers Edward. "Ethnicity, Politics and History in Mozambique" *Africa Today* 21 (Fall 1974): 39-52.

Aluko, Olajide. "The Politics of Decolonisation in British West Africa, 1945-1960." In Ajayi, J. F. A., and Crowder, Michael, eds., *History of West Africa*, vol. 2. London, 1974.

Aluko, T. M. *Chief the Honourable Minister*. London, 1970.

Alves, Mario Moreira. *Les soldats socialistes du Portugal*. Paris, 1975.

Amin, Samir. *L'Afrique de l'Ouest bloquée: l'Economie politique de la colonisation, 1880-1970*.Paris, 1971. Translated by Francis McDonagh as *Neo-Colonialism in West Africa*. Harmondsworth, 1973.

———. *Impérialisme et sous-développement en Afrique*. Paris, 1976.

Ammi-Oz, Moshe. "Les Impératifs de la politique militaire française en Afrique noire à l'époque de la décolonisation." *Revue française d'études politiques africaines* (February 1977), pp. 65-89.

Anderson, C. A. "Portuguese Africa: A Brief History of U.N. Involvement." *Denver Journal of International Law Policy* 4 (1974): 133-51.

Anderson, Perry. *Le Portugal et la fin de l'ultra-colonialisme*. Paris, 1963.

Andrade, António Alberto de. *História breve da Guiné portuguêsa*. Lisbon, 1968.

Andrade, Mario de, and Ollivier, Marc. *La Guerre en Angola: Etude socio-économique*. Paris, 1971.

Andreini, Jean Claude, and Lambert, Marie Claude. *La Guinée-Bissau*. Paris, 1978.

Anstey, Roger. *King Leopold's Legacy*. London, 1966.

Apter, David E. *The Gold Coast in Transition*. Princeton, 1955.

Ardant, Philippe. "Le Néo-Colonialisme: Thème, mythe et réalité." *Revue française de science politique* 15 (1965): 837-55.

———. "Vingt Ans de coopération culturelle et technique avec le Maroc: Echec ou réussité?" *Annuaire de l'Afrique du Nord* 14 (1975): 209-26.

Arden-Clarke, Sir Charles. "Eight Years in the Gold Coast." *African Affairs* 57, no. 226 (January 1958): 29-37.

Artigue, Pierre. *Qui sont les leaders congolais?* 2d ed. Brussels, 1961.

Ath-Messaoud, Malek, and Gillette, Alain. *L'Immigration algérienne en France*. Paris, 1976.

Atterbury, Mary Catherine. *Revolution in Rwanda*. Madison, Wis., 1968.

Augarde, Jacques L. "La Migration algérienne." *Hommes et migrations* 116 (1970): 7-161.

Austin, Dennis. *Britain and South Africa*. London, 1966.

———. *Politics in Ghana, 1946–1960.* London, 1964.
Awolowo, Obafemi. *Awo.* Cambridge, Eng., 1960.
———. *Path to Nigerian Freedom.* London, 1947.
Ayandele, E. A. *The Educated Elite in the Nigerian Society.* Ibadan, 1974.
Azevedo, Mario J. "The Legacy of Colonial Education in Mozambique (1876–1976)." *Current Bibliography of African Affairs* 11 (1978–79): 3–16.
———. "'A Sober Commitment to Liberation'? Mozambique and South Africa, 1974–79." *African Affairs* 79 (1980): 567–84.
Azikiwe, Nnambi. *My Odyssey.* New York, 1970.
Ba, Abdoul Aziz. "L'Immigration des travailleurs sénégalais en France." *Revue juridique et politique* 34 (1980): 198–217.
Baillet, Pierre. "Les Répatriés d'Algérie en France." *Notes et études documentaires,* nos. 4275–76 (March 29, 1976).
Baldwin, K. D. S. *The Niger Agricultural Project.* Cambridge, Mass., 1957.
Ballinger, Margaret. *From Union to Apartheid.* New York, 1969.
Barber, James P. *South Africa's Foreign Policy, 1945–1970.* London, 1973.
Barbier, Maurice. *Le Comité de décolonisation des Nations Unies.* Paris, 1974.
Barnes, Leonard. *Soviet Light on the Colonies.* Harmondsworth, 1944.
Barnett,Corelli. *The Collapse of British Power.* New York, 1972.
Barnett, Donald L., and Njama, Karari. *Mau Mau from Within.* London, 1966.
Barou, Jacques. *Travailleurs africains en France.* Paris, 1978.
Baroudi, Abdallah. *Maroc. Emigration et impérialisme.* Paris, 1978. [Under the protectorate and since independence]
Bates, Darrell. *A Gust of Plumes.* London, 1972.
Bates, Margaret. "Tanganyika under British Administration." D. Phil. thesis, Oxford University, 1957.
Bauer, Peter Tamas. *West African Trade.* Cambridge, Eng., 1954.
Baulin, J. "La Politique africaine de la Côte d'Ivoire: Accession à l'indépendance à la fin de la guerre civile du Nigéria." Thesis, University of Paris, 1974.
Bayart, Jean-François. *L'Etat au Cameroun.* Paris, 1979.
———. "La Politique extérieure du Cameroun (1960–1971)." *Revue française d'études politiques africaines* (March 1972), pp. 47–64.
Beckett, Paul A. "Algeria vs. Fanon: The Theory of Revolutionary Decolonization and the Algerian Experience." *Western Political Quarterly* 26 (March 1973): 5–27.
Belkherroubi, A. *La Naissance et la reconnaissance de la république algérienne.* Brussels, 1972.
Bello, Sir Ahmadu. *My Life.* Cambridge, Eng., 1964.
Benachenhou, Abdellatif. *Formation du sous-développement en Algérie: Essai sur les limites du capitalisme, 1830–1962.* Algiers, 1976.
Bender, Gerald. *Angola under the Portuguese: The Myth and the Reality.* London, 1978.
———. "La Diplomatie de Kissinger et l'Angola." *Revue française d'études politiques africaines* (June 1976), pp. 73–94.
———. "Kissinger in Angola: Anatomy of Failure." In René Lemarchand, ed., *American Policy in Southern Africa: The Stakes and the Stance,* pp. 63–144. Washington, D.C., 1978.
———. "Planned Rural Settlements in Angola, 1900–1968." In Franz-Wilhelm Heimer, ed. *Social Change in Angola,* pp. 236–79. Munich, 1973.

Bender, Gerald, and Isaacman, Allen. "The Changing Historiography of Angola and Mozambique." In Christopher Fyfe, ed., *African Studies since 1945: A Tribute to Basil Davidson*, pp. 220–48. London, 1976.
Bender, Gerald, and Lemarchand, René, eds. *American Policy in Southern Africa: The Stakes and the Stance*. Washington, D.C., 1978.
Benézra, René. "L'Accession des territoires portugais à l'indépendance." *Afrique contemporaine* 14 (January–February 1975): 9–24.
———. "Portugal, la fin d'un empire." *Afrique contemporaine* 14 (January–February 1975): 1–8.
———. "Le Territoire français des Afars et des Issas." *Afrique contemporaine* 14 (July–August 1975): 20–24.
Bennett, George. *Kenya, A Political History*. London, 1963.
———, and Carl Rosberg, *The Kenyatta Election: Kenya 1960–61*, London, 1961.
Benoist, Joseph-Roger de. *L'Afrique occidentale française de 1944 à 1960*. Dakar, 1978.
———. *La Balkanisation de l'Afrique occidentale française*. Dakar, 1976.
Bensimon-Donath, Doris. *L'Intégration des juifs nord-africains en France*. Paris, 1971.
Bentahar, Mekki. "Les Arabes en France. Itinéraire migratoire." Thesis, University of Paris, 1978. 2 vols. [North African immigrants]
Bernard, Guy. "Perspectives pour une sociologie dialectique de la décolonisation." *Canadian Journal of African Studies* 5 (1971): 33–43.
Berque, Jacques. *Dépossession du monde*. Paris, 1964.
———. *L'Orient second*. Paris, 1970.
Berrady, Lhachmi et al. *La Formation des élites politiques maghrébines*. Paris, 1973.
Bertrand, Hugues. *Le Congo: Formation sociale et mode de développement économique*. Paris, 1975.
Bertulli, Cesare. *Croce e spada in Mozambico*. Rome, 1974.
Betts, Raymond. *Tricouleur: The French Overseas Empire*. London, 1978.
Beynel, J. "Dahomey: De l'Assemblée territoriale à l'Assemblée consultative nationale." *Penant* 83 (1973): 456–76.
Beyssade, Pierre. *La Guerre d'Algérie, 1954–1962*. Paris, 1968.
Bezy, Fernand. "La Transformation des structures socio-économiques à Madagascar (1960–1978)." *Cultures et développement* 11 (1979): 83–116.
Bidwell, Robin, comp. and ed. *Bidwell's Guide to Government Ministers*. Vol. 1, *The Major Powers and Western Europe, 1900–1971*. London, 1973.
———. *Guide to African Ministers*. London, 1978.
———. *Morocco under Colonial Rule: French Administration of Tribal Areas, 1912–1956*. London, 1973.
Bienen, Henry. *Kenya: The Politics of Participation and Control*. Princeton, 1974.
———. *Tanzania: Party Transformation and Economic Development*. Princeton, 1970.
Binet, Jacques. "Les Comores au seuil de l'indépendance." *Afrique contemporaine* 15 (March–April 1976): 16–19.
Blair, Dorothy S. *African Literature in French*. London, 1976.
Blair, Leon Borden. "Amateurs in Diplomacy: The American Vice Consuls in North Africa, 1941–1943." *Historian* 35 (1973): 607–20.
———. "The Impact of Franco-American Military Agreements on Moroccan

Nationalism, 1940-1956." *Rocky Mountain Social Science Journal* 9 (January 1972): 61-72.
Blair, Patricia Wohlgemuth. *The Portuguese Territories and the United Nations.* New York, 1963.
Blake, Robert. *A History of Rhodesia.* London, 1977.
Blanchet, Gilles. "L'Evolution des dirigeants sénégalais de l'indépendance à 1975." *Cahier d'études africaines* 18 (1978): 49-78.
Bleuchot, Hervé. *Les Libéraux Français au Maroc, 1947-1955.* Aix, 1974.
Bloomfield, Valerie. *Commonwealth Elections 1945-1970: A Bibliography.* London, 1976.
Blume, Daniel et al. *La Politique de l'impérialisme français (1930-1958).* Paris, 1974.
Blundell, Michael. *So Rough a Wind.* London, 1964.
Blusse, L.; Wesseling, H. L.; and Winius, G. D., eds. *History and Underdevelopment: Essays on Underdevelopment and European Expansion in Asia and Africa.* Leyden, 1980. Issued as *Itinerario* 5, no. 1 (1980): 1-160.
Böge, Wolfgang. "Dekolonisation und amerikanisch Aussenpolitik. Eine Analyse der politischen Beziehungen Angola—U.S.A., 1945-1975." *Afrika-Spectrum* 10 (1975): 219-32.
Boisson, Jean. *Ben Bella est arrêté—le 22 octobre 1956. Etudes et recherches historiques.* Cholet, 1978. [Important documents in the appendixes]
Bolela, Albert Oscar. "Un Aperçu de la presse congolaise écrite par les noirs de 1885 à 1960." *Congo-Afrique* 11 (June 1971): 5-24.
Bolz, Reinhardt. *Tunesien: Wirtschaftliche und soziale Strukturen und Entwicklung.* Hamburg, 1976.
Bon, Daniel, and Mingst, Karen. "French Intervention in Africa: Dependence or Development." *Africa Today* 27, no. 2 (1980): 5-20.
Bony, Jacques. *La Formation de la Société ivoirienne.* Thesis, University of Paris, 1978.
Bosschère, Guy de. "L'Indépendance de l'Angola et son enjeu économique." *Présence africaine*, no. 2 (1976): 196-210.
———. *Perspectives de la décolonisation.* Paris, 1969.
Boudiaf, Mohammed. "La Préparation du Ier novembre 1954," *El-Jarida: Journal du parti de la révolution socialiste*, special no., November 1974.
Bourde, André. "The Comoro Islands: The Problems of a Microcosm." *Journal of Modern African Studies* 3 (1965): 91-102.
Bourges, Yvon. "La Coopération franco-africaine et malgache." *Revue de défense nationale* 26 (1970): 709-22.
———. *La Politique française d'aide au développement.* Paris, 1971.
Bourgi, Albert. *La Politique française de coopération en Afrique: Le Cas du Sénégal.* Dakar, 1979.
Bourrinet, Jacques. *La Coopération économique eurafricaine.* Paris, 1976.
Bousacaren, Anthony. *Tshombe.* New York, 1967.
Bouvier, Paule. *L'Accession du Congo belge à l'indépendance.* Brussels, 1965.
Brassinne, Jacques. "L'Assistance technique belge au Congo (juillet 1960—juin 1968)." *Chronique de politique étrangère* 21 (1968): 281-572.
———. "Douze Années de coopération technique militaire belgo-zaïroise." *Études africaines du CRISP* (Oct. 13, 1972), pp. 2-40.
Brausch, Georges. *Belgian Administration in the Congo.* London, 1961.

Brett, E. A. *Colonialism and Underdevelopment in East Africa.* London, 1973.
Brett, Michael. "The Colonial Period in the Maghrib and Its Aftermath: The Present State of Historical Writing." *Journal of African History* 17 (1976): 291–305.
Bretton, H. L. *Power and Stability in Nigeria.* New York, 1962.
Bridges, R. C., ed. *Senegambia.* Aberdeen, 1974.
British Government Empire Information Service. *Origins and Purpose.* Glasgow, 1944.
Brockway, Fenner. *The Colonial Revolution.* New York, 1973.
Brogini, Maurice. "L'Exploitation des hydrocarbures en Algérie de 1956 à 1971: Étude de géographie économique." Thesis, University of Nice, 1973.
Browne, G. St. J. Orde. *The African Labourer.* London, 1933.
Buell, Raymond, L. *The Native Problem in Africa.* 2 vols. Hamden, Conn., 1928.
Buijtenhuijs, Robert. "La Dialectique nord-sud dans l'histoire tchadienne." *African Perspectives* 2 (1977): 43–62.
———. *Le FROLINAT et les révoltes populaires du Tchad, 1965–1976.* Paris, 1978.
———. *Mau Mau Twenty Years After.* The Hague, 1973.
Burke, Fred G. *Local Government and Politics in Uganda.* Syracuse, 1964.
Burns, Alan Cuthbert. *In Defence of Colonies.* London, 1957.
Buron, Robert. *Carnets politiques de la guerre de l'Algérie par un signataire des Accords d'Évian.* Paris, 1965.
Bustin, Edouard. *Lunda under Belgian Rule: The Politics of Ethnicity.* Cambridge, Mass., 1975.
Cabral, Amilcar. *Alguns principios do partido.* Lisbon, 1974.
———. *Guineé-Bissau—Nação forjada na Luta.* Lisbon, 1974.
———. *Guinée 'portugaise': Le Pouvoir des armes.* Paris, 1970.
———. *Our People Are Our Mountains.* London, 1971.
———. *Return to the Source; Selected Speeches.* New York, 1973.
———. *Revolution in Guinea: Selected Texts.* London, 1969.
———. *Unity and Struggle. Speeches and Writings of Amilcar Cabral.* New York, 1979.
Caetano, Marcello. *Colonizing Traditions, Principles and Methods of the Portuguese.* Lisbon, 1951.
———. *Razões da presença de Portugal no Ultramar.* Lisbon, 1973.
Camara, Sylvain Soriba. *La Guinée sans la France.* Paris, 1976.
Cameron, Donald. *The Principles of Native Administration and Their Application.* Lagos, 1934.
———. *My Tanganyika Service and Some Nigeria.* London, 1939.
Campbell, Bonnie. *Libération nationale et construction du socialisme en Afrique (Angola, Guinée-Bissau, Mozambique).* Montreal, 1978.
———. "Neo-Colonialism, Economic Dependence, and Political Change: Cotton Textile Production in the Ivory Coast." *Review of African Political Economy* 4, no. 2 (1975): 36–53.
Carrington, C. E. *The Liquidation of the British Empire.* London, 1961.
Carter, Gwendolyn, ed. *African One-Party States.* Ithaca, N.Y., 1962.
———. ed. *Five African States.* Ithaca, N.Y., 1963.
———. ed. *National Unity and Regionalism in Eight African States.* Ithaca, N.Y., 1966.
Cartland, George. "Retrospect." *Journal of Administration Overseas.* vol. 13 (January 1977).

Cartwright, John. *Politics in Sierra Leone, 1947–1967.* Toronto, 1970.
Carvalho, Mario de. *A agricultura tradicional de Moçambique.* Lourenço Marques, 1969.
Cary, Joyce. *The Case for African Freedom.* London, 1941.
Centre de recherche et d'information socio-politique. *Congo 1959: Documents belges et africaines.* 2d ed. Brussels, 1965.
Cervenka, Zdenek. "Major Policy Shifts in the Organization of African Unity, 1963–1973." *Foreign Relations of African States,* edited by K. Ingham (April 1973), pp. 323–42.
———. *The Unfinished Quest for Unity: Africa and the OAU.* New York, 1977.
Ceulemans, Jacques. *Antoine Gizenga: Hier, aujourd'hui, demain.* Brussels, 1964.
Chabal, Patrick. "National Liberation in Portuguese Guinea, 1956–1974." *African Affairs* 80 (1981): 75–100.
Chalendar, Pierrette, and Chalendar, Gérard. "Considérations générales sur la décolonisation portugaise." *Revue française d'études politiques africaines* (October 1977), pp. 20–37.
Chaliand, Gérard. *La Lutte armée en Afrique.* Paris, 1967. Translated by David Rattray and Robert Leonhardt as *Armed Struggle in Africa: With the Guerrillas in 'Portuguese' Africa.* New York, 1969.
Chaliand, Gérard, and Minces, Juliette. *L'Algérie indépendante.* Paris, 1972.
Charpentier, Jean. "Référendums mahorais et hégemonie politique comorienne." *Revue française d'études politiques africaines* (June 1976), pp. 96–118.
Chassey, Francis de. *Mauritanie, 1900–1979 de l'ordre colonial à l'ordre néocolonial entre Maghreb et Afrique Noire.* Paris, 1978. [Economic and social aspects]
Chauleur, Pierre. "Incertitudes sur Djibouti." *Études* 346 (1977): 437–50.
Chevalerias, Alain. "La Guerre d'Angola et l'UNITA." *Comptes rendus trimestriels des séances de l'Académie des sciences d'outre-mer* 36 (1976): 303–24.
Chidzero, Bernard T. G. *Tanganyika and International Trusteeship.* London, 1961.
Chilcote, Ronald H. "Amilcar Cabral: A Bio-Bibliography of His Life and Thought, 1925–1973." *Africana Journal* 5 (1974–75): 289–307.
———, ed. *Emerging Nationalism in Portuguese Africa.* Stanford, 1969.
———. "Mozambique: The African Nationalist Response to Portuguese Imperialism and Underdevelopment." In Christian P. Potholm and Richard Dale, eds., *Southern Africa in Perspective.*
———. *Portuguese Africa.* Englewood Cliffs, N.J., 1967.
Chouraqui, André. *La Saga des juifs en Afrique du Nord.* Paris, 1972.
Chowdhuri, R. N. *International Mandates and Trusteeship Systems.* The Hague, 1955.
Chrétien, Jean-Pierre. "L'Enseignment au Burundi." *Revue française d'études politiques africaines* (April 1972), pp. 61–81.
Clarke, W. Sheldon. "The Republic of Djibouti—An Introduction to Africa's Newest State and a Review of Related Literature and Sources." *Current Bibliography of African Affairs* 10 (1977–78): 3–31.
Clayton, Anthony. *Counter Insurgency in Kenya.* Nairobi, 1976.
Clayton, Anthony, and Donald C. Savage. *Government and Labour in Kenya, 1895–1961.* London, 1974.
Cliffe, Lionel. "Nationalism and the Reaction to Enforced Agricultural Change in

Tanganyika." In L. Cliffe and J. Saul, eds., *Socialism in Tanzania*. Dar es Salaam, 1973.

———. "Western Economic and Political Involvement in Portugal and the Colonies." *Ufahamu* 4 (Fall, 1973): 145–65.

———, ed. *One Party Democracy*. Nairobi, 1967.

Codere, Helen. *The Biography of an African Society*. Brussels, 1973.

Cohen, Andrew. *British Policy in Changing Africa*. Evanston, Ill., 1959.

Cohen, William B. "Legacy of Empire: The Algerian Connection." *Journal of Contemporary History* 15 (1980): 97–123.

———, ed. *Robert Delavignette on the French Empire, Selected Writings*. Chicago, 1977.

Cohn, Helen Desfosses. *Soviet Policy towards Black Africa*. New York, 1972.

Coleman, James S. *Nigeria: Background to Nationalism*. Berkeley, 1958.

Coleman, James S., and Rosberg, Carl E., eds. *Political Parties and National Integration in Tropical Africa*. Berkeley, 1964.

Colin, J. P. "Le Mozambique un an après l'indépendance." *Politique étrangère* 41 (1976): 433–58.

Colin, Roland. "Mutations sociales et systèmes socio-éducatifs. Continuité et discontinuité en éducation. Le Cas du Sénégal." Thesis, University of Paris, 1977.

Collot, Claude, and Henry, Jean-Robert. *Le Mouvement national algérian. Textes, 1912–1954*. Paris, 1978.

"Colonialism and Decolonization." *Journal of Contemporary History*, vol. 4, no. 1 (January 1969).

Colonna, Fanny. "Cultural Resistance and Religious Legitimacy in Colonial Algeria." *Economies et sociétés* 3 (1974): 235–52.

Comte, Gilbert. "Treize années d'histoire nigérienne." *Revue française d'études politiques africaines* (December 1971), pp. 29–40.

———. "Treize ans d'histoire [Gabon, 1960–73]." *Revue française d'études politiques africaines* (June 1973), pp. 39–57.

Conan, A. R. *The Sterling Area*. London, 1952.

Coquery-Vidrovitch, Catherine. "L'Afrique coloniale française et la crise de 1930: Crise structurelle et genèse du sous-développement. Rapport d'ensemble." *Revue française d'histoire d'outre-mer* 63 (1976): 386–424.

———. "L'Impact des intérêts coloniaux S.C.O.A. et C.F.A.O. dans l'Ouest africain, 1910–1965." *Journal of African History* 16 (1975):595–612.

———. "L'Impérialisme français en Afrique noire: Idéologie impériale et politique d'équipement, 1924–1975." *Relations internationales* (Autumn 1976), pp. 261–82.

———. "La Mise en dépendance de l'Afrique noire. Essai de périodisation, 1800–1970." *Cahiers d'études africaines* 16 (1976): 7–58.

———. "Mutations de l'impérialisme colonial français dans les années 30." *African Economic History* (Fall 1977): 103–52.

Corbett, Edward M. *The French Presence in Black Africa*. Washington, D.C., 1972.

Corfield, F. D. *Historical Survey of the Origins of Mau Mau*. London, 1960.

Coulon, Christian. "Pouvoir maraboutique et pouvoir politique au Sénégal." Thesis, University of Paris, 1977.

Courrière, Yves. *La Guerre d'Algérie*, 4 vols. Paris, 1972.

Coussey Report by the Committee on Constitutional Reform (col. no. 248, 1949).

Couve de Murville, Maurice. *Une politique étrangère, 1958–1969.* Paris, 1971.
Cowan, Laing Gray. *Local Government in West Africa.* New York, 1958.
Crocker, Walter Russell. *Nigeria: A Critique of British Colonial Administration.* London, 1936.
Cross, Colin. *The Fall of the British Empire, 1918–1968*. New York, 1968.
Crossley, Julian, and Blandford, John. *The DCO Story: A History of Banking in Many Countries.* London, 1975.
Crowder, Michael. *Revolt in Bussa.* London, 1973.
Cubertafond, Bernard. *L'Algérie indépendante: Idéologie et institutions.* Paris, 1974.
Dash, Leon. *Get Off My Mountain.* Washington, D.C., 1977.
Davidson, Basil. "Angola: A Success That Changes History." *Race and Class* 18 (Summer 1976): 23–28.
______. "Angola since Independence." *Race and Class* 19 (Autumn 1977): 20–37.
______. *In the Eye of the Storm: Angola's People.* Garden City, N.Y., 1972.
______. *The Liberation of Guiné.* Harmondsworth, 1969.
______. "Victory and Reconciliation in Guinea-Bissau." *Africa Today* 21 (Fall, 1974): 5–22.
Davis, Nathaniel. "The Angola Decision of 1975: A Personal Memoir." *Foreign Affairs* 57 (1978): 109–24.
Dayal, Rajeshwar. *Mission for Hammarskjold: The Congo Crisis*. Princeton, 1976.
Debré, Jean-Louis. *Les Idées constitutionnelles du Général de Gaulle.* Paris, 1974.
Decalo, Samuel. "Chad: The Roots of Centre-Periphery Strife." *African Affairs* 79 (1980): 491–509.
______. "Regionalism, Political Decay, and Civil Strife in Chad." *Journal of Modern African Studies* 18 (1980): 23–56.
"Décolonisation et indépendance du Rwanda et du Burundi." *Chronique de politique étrangère* 16 (1963): 439–748.
Decraene, Philippe. *Le Mali.* Paris, 1980. [Mainly since 1940]
______. "Notes sur l'économie du Mozambique." *Revue française d'études politiques africaines* (September 1974), pp. 56–65.
Dejeux, Jean. "Connaissance du monde féminin et de la famille en Algérie—Essai de synthèse documentaire, 1947–1967." *Revue algérienne des sciences jurdiques économiques et politiques* 5 (1968): 1247–1302.
Denoon, Donald, and Kuper, Adam. "The 'New Historiography' in Dar es Salaam." *African Affairs* 69, no. 277 (October 1970): 329–49.
______. "The 'New Historiography' in Dar es Salaam: A Rejoinder." *African Affairs* 70, no. 280 (July 1971): 287–88.
den Tunden, Bastian A. *Ivory Coast: The Challenge of Success.* Baltimore, 1978.
De Schrevel, Michel. *Les Forces politiques de la décolonisation jusqu'à la veille de l'indépendance.* Brussels, 1970.
de Vos, Pierre, ed. *La Décolonisation: Les Evénements du Congo de 1959 à 1967.* Brussels, 1975.
Dianoux, Hugue Jean de. "La Guinée-Bissau et les îles du Cap-Vert." *Afrique contemporaine* 19 (January–February 1980): 1–16.
Dike, K. O. "African History and Self-Government." *West Africa*, Feb. 28, 1953.
Dos Santos, Edouardo. *Maza.* Lisbon, 1965.
Dougherty, James J. *The Politics of Wartime Aide: American Economic Assistance to France and French Northwest Africa, 1940–1946.* Westport, Conn., 1978.

Dryden, Stanley. *Local Administration in Tanzania*. Nairobi, 1968.
Dudley, B. J. *Parties and Politics in Northern Nigeria*. London, 1968.
Duffy, James. *Portugal in Africa*. Baltimore, 1962.
———. *Portuguese Africa*. Cambridge, Mass., 1959.
Duhamel, Olivier. "L'AUPELF et la coopération universitaire ou de la francophone au dialogue des cultures. *Revue française d'études politiques africaines* (February 1976): 30–59.
Duignan, Peter, and Gann. Lewis. *A Bibliographical Guide to Colonialism in Sub-Saharan Africa*. Cambridge, 1973.
Dumont, Georges-Henri. *La Table-Ronde belgo-congolaise*. Paris, 1961.
Dunn, John. *Modern Revolutions*. Cambridge, Eng., 1972.
———. *West African States: A Study in Comparative Politics*. Cambridge, Eng., 1978.
Dunner, Joseph, ed. *Handbook of World History*. New York, 1967. ("Decolonization" by David Gardinier, pp. 268–72.)
Duodu, Cameron. *The Gab Boys*. London, 1967.
Easterbrook, David L. "Bibliography of African Bibliographies, 1965–1975." *Africana Journal* 7, no. 2 (1976): 101–48; 3 (1977): 232–42.
Eastern Region of Nigeria White Paper. "Memorandum on Local Government Policy" (June 16, 1949).
Ehrlich, Cyril. "Some Aspects of Economic Policy in Tanganyika, 1945–1960." *Journal of Modern African Studies* 2, no. 2 (1964): 265–77.
Eisenhans, Harmut. *Frankreichs Algerienkrieg, 1954–1962*. Munich, 1974.
Ekaney, Nkwelle. "Angola: Post-Mortem of a Conflict." *Présence africaine* 2 (1976): 211–33.
Ekwensi, Cyprian. *Jagua Nana*. London, 1961.
———. *People of the City*. London, 1954.
El Ayouty, Yassin. "Referendum and Displacement of Population in French Somaliland, 1967." *Genève-Afrique* 8, no. 2 (1969): 47–53.
———. *The United Nations and Decolonization*. The Hague, 1971.
El-Khawas, Mohamed A. "Foreign Economic Involvement in Angola and Mozambique." *African Review* 4 (1974): 299–314.
———. "An Involvement in Portuguese Africa: The Legacy of the Nixon Years." *Ufahamu* 6, no. 1 (1975): 117–30.
———. "South Africa and Angola's Civil War." *Africa Today* 24 (April–June 1977): 35–46.
———. "U.S. Foreign Policy towards Angola and Mozambique, 1960–1974." *Current Bibliography of African Affairs* 8 (1975): 186–203.
Eloy, Jean. "La Coopération publique belgo-zaïroise." *Afrique contemporaine* 11 (March–April 1972): 3–13; (May–June 1972): 2–13.
Emerson, Rupert. *From Empire to Nations*. Cambridge, Mass., 1960.
Erny, Pierre. "Aspects de l'évolution de l'enseignment colonial belge." *Revue zaïroise de psychologie et de pédagogie* 3 (1974): 93–106.
———. "Bilan de l'enseignement colonial au Rwanda." *Dialogue* (Kigali), November–December 1978, pp. 22–45.
———. "L'Enseignment au Rwanda." *Revue tiers-monde* 15 (1974): 707–22.
———. "L'Enseignment au Rwanda de 1916 à 1948." *Dialogue* (Kigali), March–April 1976, pp. 24–49.

———. "Une Page d'histoire coloniale. La Mission pédagogique Coulon-Deheyn-Renson et la crise scolaire de 1955 au Congo et au Ruanda-Urundi." *Informateur*. 7 (February 1974): 31–43.
Ezera, Kalu. *Constitutional Developments in Nigeria*. 2d ed. Cambridge, Eng., 1960.
Fabian Colonial Bureau. *Downing Street and the Colonies*. 1942.
Fage, J. D., and Oliver, Roland, gen. eds. *Cambridge History of Africa*. Vol. 3, *c. 1050–1600*, edited by R. Oliver. Vol. 4, *c. 1600 to c. 1790*, edited by R. Gray. Vol. 5, *c. 1790 to c. 1870*, edited by J. E. Flint. Cambridge, Eng., 1975–77.
Farson, Negley. *Last Chance in Africa*. London, 1949.
Faujas, Alain. "La Politique étrangère du Niger." *Revue française d'études politiques africaines* (December 1971), pp. 41–60.
Favoreu, Louis, and Maestre, Jean Claude. "L'Accession des Comores à l'indépendance." *Annuaire des pays de l'océan Indien* 2 (1975): 15–34.
Feit, Edward. *South Africa*. London, 1962.
Felgas, Helio. *Guerra em Angola*. Lisbon, 1968.
———. *Os movimentos terroristas de Angola, Guiné, Moçambique*. Lisbon, 1966.
Feltz, Gaëtan. "Les Causes et conséquences de la guerre civile au Rwanda." Thesis, University of Aix-Marseille, 1971.
———. "Considérations sur l'histoire contemporaine du Rwanda." *Revue française d'études politiques africaines* (September 1971), pp. 76–97.
Ferreira, Antonio. *O movimento migratório de trabalhadores entre Moçambique e a Africa do Sul*. Lisbon, 1963.
Ferreira, Eduardo de Sousa. *Aspectos do colonialsmo portugues*. Lisbon, 1974.
———. *Portuguese Colonialism from South Africa to Europe*. Freiburg, 1972.
———. *Portuguese Colonialism in Africa: The End of an Era*. Paris, 1974.
Fessard de Foucault, Bertrand. "Seize Ans de diplomatie mauritanienne." *Revue française d'études politiques africaines* (March 1973), pp. 82–92.
Fetter, Bruce. "Elisabethville." *African Urban Notes, Bibliographical Supplement* 3 (June 1968): 1–33.
Fieldhouse, D. K. *The Colonial Empires*. New York, 1967.
———. *Economics and Empire, 1830–1914*. Ithaca, 1973.
———. *Unilever Overseas*. London, 1978.
Fields, Rona. *The Portuguese Revolution and the Armed Forces Movement*. New York, 1976.
First, Ruth. *Portugal's Wars in Africa*. London, 1971.
———. "Southern Africa after Spínola," *Ufahamu* 5 (Winter, 1974): 88–108.
Fisher, Nigel. *Iain Macleod*. London, 1973.
Fitzpatrick, J. J. F. "Nigeria's Curse—the Native Administration." *National Review*, (December 1924).
Flobert, Thierry. "Les Comores: Évolution juridique et socio-politique," Thesis, University of Marseilles, 1977.
Flores, Michael. "A Bibliographical Contribution to the Study of Portuguese Africa (1965–1972)." *Current Bibliography of African Affairs*" 7 (1974): 116–37.
Fol, Jean-Jacques. "Le Togo pendant la deuxième guerre mondiale." *Revue d'histoire de la deuxième guerre mondiale* 15 (July 1979): 69–77.
Frankel, Sally Herbert. *Capital Investment in Africa*. London, 1938.

"French Somaliland Attains Independence as Republic of Djibouti." *Objective: Justice* 9 (Summer 1977): 38–48.
Friedland, Elaine A. "The Political Economy of Colonialism in South Africa and Mozambique." *Journal of Southern African Affairs* 2 (1977): 61–76.
Friedland, W. H. *Vuta Kamba.* Stanford, 1969.
Frost, Richard A. *Race against Time.* London, 1978.
Fuglestad, Finn. "Djibo Bakary, the French, and the Referendum of 1958 in Niger." *Journal of African History* 14 (1973): 313–30.
———. "Unis and Bna: The Role of 'Traditionalist' Parties in Niger, 1948–60." *Journal of African History* 16 (1975): 113–36.
Fry, Richard. *Bankers in West Africa.* London, 1976.
Fyfe, Christopher. *A History of Sierra Leone.* London, 1962.
Galletti, R.; Baldwin, K. D. S.; and Dina, I. *Nigerian Cocoa Farmers.* London, 1956.
Galvão, Henrique. "Report on Native Problems in the Portuguese Colonies." *Santa Maria: My Crusade for Portugal,* pp. 57–71. Cleveland, 1961.
Gann, Lewis H. "Neo-Colonialism, Imperialism, and the 'New Class.'" *Survey* 19 (Winter 1973): 165–83.
———. "Portugal, Africa and the Future." *Journal of Modern African Studies* 13 (1975): 1–18.
———, and Duignan, Peter, eds. *Colonialism in Africa, 1870–1960.* 5 vols. Cambridge, Eng., 1969–75.
Ganshof Van der Meersch, Walter J. *Fin de la souveraineté belge au Congo.* Brussels, 1963.
Gardinier, David E. "Education in French Equatorial Africa, 1842–1945." *Proceedings of the French Colonial Historical Society* 3 (1978): 121–37.
———. "Education in the States of Equatorial Africa: A Bibliographical Essay." *Africana Library Journal* 3, no. 3 (1972): 7–20.
———. "France in Gabon since 1960." *Proceedings of the French Colonial Historical Society* 6–7 (1981–82): 65–75.
———. "French Colonial Rule in Africa: A Bibliographical Essay." *France and Britain in Africa,* Prosser Gifford and Wm. Roger Louis, eds. New Haven, 1971.
———. *Historical Dictionary of Gabon.* Metuchen, N.J., 1981.
———. "The Impact of French Education on Africa, 1817–1960." *Proceedings of the French Colonial Historical Society* 5 (1980): 70–82.
———. "Schooling in the States of Equatorial Africa." *Canadian Journal of African Studies* 8 (1974): 517–38.
Gatheru, R. Mugo. *Child of Two Worlds.* London, 1964.
Gaudio, Attilio. *Allal al Fassi ou l'histoire de l'Istiqlal.* Paris, 1972.
Gauzé, René. *The Politics of Congo-Brazzaville.* Stanford, 1973.
Gedebien, Paul-Henri. *L'Intervention des Nations Unies au Congo, (1960–1964).* The Hague, 1967.
Geismar, Peter. "De Gaulle, the Army and Algeria: The Civil, Military Conflict over Decolonization." Ph.D. dissertation, Columbia University, 1967.
Geiss, Imanuel. *Pan Africanism.* New York, 1974.
Gendzier, Irene. "Psychology and Colonialism: Some Observations." *Middle East Journal* 30 (Autumn 1976): 501–16.
Gérard-Libois, Jules, and Verhaegen, Benoit, eds. *Congo 1960: Documents belges et africains.* 3 vols. Brussels, 1961.

———. *Secession du Katanga*. Brussels, 1964. Translated by Rebecca Young as *Katanga Secession*. Madison, Wis., 1967.
Gertzel, Cherry. *Party and Locality in Northern Uganda, 1945–1967*. London, 1974.
———. *The Politics of Independent Kenya*. Nairobi, 1970.
Geshekter, Charles L. "Independent Mozambique and Its Neighbors, Now What?" *Africa Today* 22 (July–September 1975): 21–36.
Ghai, Yash, and Ghai, Dharam. *The Asian Minorities of East and Central Africa*. London, 1971.
Gibbons, E. J. "African Local Government Reform in Kenya, Uganda and Eastern Nigeria." Unpublished report, 1949.
Gibson, Richard. *African Liberation Movements*. New York, 1972.
Gifford, Prosser, and Louis, Wm. Roger, eds. *Britain and Germany in Africa*. New Haven, 1967.
———, eds. *France and Britain in Africa: Imperial Rivalry and Colonial Rule*. New Haven, 1971.
Gilis, Charles-André. *Kasa-Vubu au coeur du drame congolais*. Brussels, 1964.
Girardet, Raoul. *L'Idée coloniale en France, 1871–1962*. Paris, 1972.
Glantz, Michael H. "The War of the Maps. Portugal vs. PAIGC." *Pan African Journal* 6 (1973): 285–96.
Goldsworthy, D. *Colonial Issues in British Politics, 1945–1961*. Oxford, 1971.
Gonçalves, José Julio. *O Islamico na Guiné portuguesa: Ensaio sociomissionólogico*. Lisbon, 1961.
Gonidec, P. F. *Les Systèmes politiques africains*. 2d ed. Paris, 1978.
Good, Kenneth. "Settler Colonialism: Economic Development and Class Formation." *Journal of Modern African Studies* 14 (1976): 597–620.
Good, Robert C. *U.D.I.: The International Politics of the Rhodesian Rebellion*. London, 1973.
Gordon, David C. *Women of Algeria: An Essay on Change*. Cambridge, Mass., 1968.
Gordon, King. *United Nations in the Congo: A Quest for Peace*. New York, 1962.
Goutalier, Regine. "L'OAS en Oranie." Thesis, University of Provence, Aix-Marseille, 1975.
Gran, Guy, ed. *Zaire: The Political Economy of Underdevelopment*. New York, 1979. [Essays on colonial background]
Gregory, Robert G. *India and East Africa*. Oxford, 1971.
Grimal, Henry. *Decolonization*. London, 1978.
Guerra, Henrique Lopes. *Angola: Estrutura econômica e clases sociais*. Luanda, 1973.
Guillaneuf, Raymond. "La Presse en Côte d'Ivoire: La Colonisation: L'Aube de la décolonisation, 1906–1952." Thesis, University of Paris, 1975.
Gupta, P. S. *Imperialism and the British Labour Movement*. New York, 1975.
———. *S. A. H. Haqqi. The Colonial Policy of the Labour Government, 1945–51*. Aligarh, India, 1960.
Gutkind, Peter C. W. *The Emergent African Urban Proletariat*. Montreal, 1974.
Hadria, Élie Cohen. *Du Protectorat français à l'indépendance tunisienne: Souvenirs d'un témoin socialiste*. Nice, 1976.
Hailey, W. M. *An African Survey*. London, 1938.
———. *The African Survey*. Rev. ed. London, 1956.

———. "Colonial Administration by European Powers—British Colonial Policy." *Royal Institute of International Affairs,* Nov.-Dec. 1946, pp. 83–97.
———. *The Future of Colonial Peoples.* Princeton, 1944.
———. *Native Administration in the British African Territories.* 5 parts, 1950–54. London, 1954.
———. *Native Administration and Political Development in British Tropical Africa.* Nendeln, Liechtenstein, 1979.
Haines, Charles Grove, ed. *Africa Today.* Baltimore, 1955.
Hall, H. D. *Mandates, Dependencies and Trusteeship.* Washington, D.C., 1948.
Halvorsen, K. "Colonial Transformations of Agrarian Society in Algeria." *Journal of Peace Research* 15 (1978): 323–44.
Hancock, William K. *Survey of British Commonwealth Africa.* London, 1937–42.
Hanley, Gerald. *The Consul at Sunset.* London, 1951.
Harbi, Mohammed. *Aux origines du FLN.* Paris, 1975.
———. *Le FLN, mirage et réalité. Des origines à la prise du pouvor (1945–1962).* Paris, 1980.
Hargreaves, John D. *The End of Colonial Rule in West Africa.* London, 1979.
———. "History: African and Contemporary." *African Research and Documentation,* vol. 3 (1973).
Harlech, W. G. A. Ormsby-Gore. *Chieftainship in Bantu Africa and Indirect Rule in British African Dependencies.* Basutoland, 1943.
Harlow, Vincent, and Chilver, E. M. *Oxford History of East Africa,* vol. 2 (1965).
Harsch, Ernest, and Thomas, Tony. *Angola: The Hidden History of Washington's War.* New York, 1976.
Harshe, Rajen. "French Neo-Colonialism in Sub-Saharan Africa." *India Quarterly* 36 (1980): 159–78.
Hastings, Adrian. *Wiriyamu: Massacre in Mozambique.* Nairobi, 1974.
Hatch, John. *Two African Statesmen.* Chicago, 1976.
Hayter, Teresa. *French Aid.* London, 1966.
Hazlewood, A. *African Integration and Disintegration.* London, 1967.
Heggoy, Alf Andrew. "Arab Education in Colonial Algeria." *Journal of African Studies* 2 (1975): 149–60.
———. "Education in French Algeria: An Essay on Culture Conflict." *Comparative Education Review* 17 (June 1973): 180–97.
———. "French Algeria and Equality—the Death of an Ideal." *Illinois Quarterly* 36 (February 1974): 51–64.
———. *Insurgency and Counter-Insurgency in Algeria, 1954–1958.* Bloomington, Ind., 1972.
———. "Kepi and Chalkboards: French Soldiers and Education in Revolutionary Algeria." *Military Affairs* 37 (1973): 141–45.
———. "The Two Societies of French Algeria and the Failure of Co-Existence." *Africa Quarterly* 13 (April–June 1973): 23–27.
Heggoy, Alf Andrew, and Zingg, Paul J. "French Education in Revolutionary North Africa." *International Journal of Middle East Studies,* 7 (1976): 571–78.
Heimer, Franz-Wilhelm. "Décolonisation et légitimité politique en Angola." *Revue française d'études politiques africaines.* June 1976, pp. 48–72.
———. "Les Dilemmes de la décolonisation en Angola." *Cultures et développement* 8, no. 1 (1976): 3–42.

———. *Educação e sociedade a áreas rurais de Angola.* 2 vols. Luanda, 1972.
———, ed. *Social Change in Angola.* Munich, 1973.
Heisel, Donald F. "The Indigenous Populations of the Portuguese African Territories." Ph.D. dissertation, University of Wisconsin, 1966.
Henderson, Ian, and Goodhart, P. C. *The Hunt for Kimathi.* London, 1958.
Henige, David P., comp. *Colonial Governors.* Madison, Wis., 1970.
Henriksen, Thomas H. "Marxism and Mozambique." *African Affairs* 77 (1978): 441–62.
———. *Mozambique.* Totowa, N.J. 1978.
———. "People's War in Angola, Mozambique, and Guinea-Bissau." *Journal of Modern African Studies* 14 (1976): 377–400.
Hermassi, Elbaki. "Impérialisme et décadence politique." In Anouar Abdelmalek, ed., *Sociologie de l'impérialisme, VIIe Congrès mondial de sociologie*, pp. 123–40. Paris, 1971.
———, ed., *Leadership and National Development in North Africa: A Comparative Study.* Berkeley, 1972.
Hesseltine, Nigel. *Madagascar.* London, 1971.
Hewitt, Arthur R. *Guide to Resources for Commonwealth Studies in London, Oxford and Cambridge.* London, 1957.
Higgott, Richard. "Structural Dependency and Decolonisation in a West African Land-Locked State: Niger." *Review of African Political Economy,* January–April 1980, pp. 43–59.
Hill, Polly. *The Migrant Cocoa Farmers of Southern Ghana.* Cambridge, Eng., 1963.
Hinden, Rita. *Fabian Colonial Essays.* London, 1945.
———. *Plan for Africa.* London, 1941.
Hinden, Rita, and the Fabian Colonial Bureau. *Colonial and International Conscience.* London, 1945.
Hodges, Tony. "Guinea-Bissau: Five Years of Independence." *Africa Report* 24 (January–February 1979): 4–9.
———. "Mozambique: The Politics of Liberation." In G. M. Carter and P. O'Meara, eds., *Southern Africa in Crisis*, pp. 48–88. Bloomington, Ind., 1977.
Hodgkin, T. L. *African Political Parties.* Harmondsworth, 1961.
———. "A Note on the Language of African Nationalism." In K. Kirkwood, ed. *African Affairs* No. 1 (London, 1961), pp. 22–40.
———. *Nationalism in Colonial Africa.* London. 1956.
Hoisington, William A. "Commerce and Conflict: French Businessmen in Morocco, 1952–55." *Journal of Contemporary History* 9 (April 1974): 49–68.
Hopkins, A. G. "The Burden of Empire Building." *African Affairs,* January 1978.
———. *An Economic History of West Africa.* New York, 1973.
———. "Imperial Business in Africa." *Journal of African History* 17, no. 1 (1976): 29–48; no. 2 (1976): 267–90.
Horne, Alistair. *A Savage War of Peace, Algeria 1954–1962.* London, 1977.
Horowitz, Dan. "Attitudes of British Conservatives towards Decolonization in Africa." *African Affairs* 69, no. 274 (January 1970): 9–26.
Horrell, Muriel. *Action, Reaction and Counter-Action.* Johannesburg, 1963.
Hoskyns, Catherine. *The Congo since Independence.* London, 1965.

Houbert, Jean. "Réunion—I: French Decolonisation in the Mascareignes." *Journal of Commonwealth and Comparative Politics* 18 (July 1980): 145–71.
Houser, George. *No One Can Stop the Rain: Angola and the MPLA.* New York, 1976.
Hovet, Thomas. *Africa in the United Nations.* Evanston, Ill., 1963.
Hugon, Philippe. "Conjoncture et politiques économiques à Madagascar depuis l'indépendance." *Annuaire des pays de l'océan Indien* 1 (1974): 325–44.
Hugot, Pierre. "Les Comores et la France dans l'océan Indien." *Comptes rendus trimestriels des séances de l'Académie des sciences d'outre-mer* 34 (1974): 755–74.
———. "Le Vide politique du Tehad musulman." *Revue française d'etudes politiques africaines,* July–August 1979, pp. 27–40.
Hutchinson, Martha Crenshaw. *Revolutionary Terrorism: The FLN in Algeria, 1954–1962.* Stanford, 1978.
Huxley, Elsbeth. *Four Guineas.* London, 1954.
———. *The Sorcerer's Apprentice.* Westport, Conn., 1975.
———. *White Man's Country.* 2 vols. London, 1935.
———. *With Forks and Hope.* New York, 1964.
Huxley, Elsbeth, and Perham, Margery. *Race and Politics in Kenya.* London, 1944.
Hyden, Goran. *TANU Yajenga Nchi. Political Development in Rural Tanzania.* Lund, 1968.
Hymans, Jacques-Louis. *An Intellectual Biography: Leopold Sedar Senghor.* Edinburgh, 1971.
Ibingira, Grace. *The Forging of an African Nation.* New York, 1973.
INCIDI, Development of a Middle Class in Tropical and Subtropical Countries. 1956.
Ingham, Kenneth. *Foreign Relations of African States.* London, 1974.
———. *A History of East Africa.* New York, 1962.
Institute of Race Relations. *Angola, A Symposium: Views of a Revolt.* London, 1962.
International Monetary Fund. *Survey of African Economies.* Vol. 5: *Botswana, Lesotho, Swaziland, Burundi, Equatorial Guinea, Rwanda.* Washington, D.C. 1973.
Issacman, Allen. *A Luta Continua: Creating a New Society in Mozambique.* Binghamton, N.Y., 1978.
———. "Mozambique." *Issue* 8 (Spring 1978): 1–49.
———. "The Tradition of Resistance in Mozambique." *Africa Today* 22 (July–September 1975): 37–50.
Issacman, Allen, and Davis, Jennifer. "United States Policy toward Mozambique since 1945: 'The Defense of Colonialism and Regional Stability,'" *Africa Today* 25 (January–March 1978): 29–56.
Issacman, Allen, and Wiley, David, eds. "Southern Africa and United States Policy in the 1970's." *Isuse* 5 (February 1975): 3–72.
Jackson, Henry. *The FLN in Algeria: Party Development in a Revolutionary Society (1954–1965).* Westport, Conn., 1977.
Jackson, Kennell A., and Clough, Marshall S. *A Bibliography of a Syllabus of Mau Mau.* Sacramento, 1975.
Jalloh, Abduh A. *Political Integration in French-Speaking Africa.* Berkeley, 1973.

Jeanneney, Marcel. *La Politique de coopération avec les pays en voie de développement.* Paris, 1963.
Jeffries, Charles J. *Transfer of Power.* London, 1960.
Jewsiewicki, Bohumil. "Le Colonat agricole Européen au Congo-Belge, 1910–1960: Questions politiques et économiques." *Journal of African History* 20 (1979): 559–72.
______. "La Contestation sociale et la naissance du prolétariat au Zaïre au cours de la première moitié du XXe siècle." *Canadian Journal of African Studies* 10 (1976): 47–70.
______. "The Great Depression and the Making of the Colonial Economic System in the Belgian Congo." *African Economic History*, Fall 1977, pp. 153–76.
______. "Notes sur l'histoire socio-économique du Congo (1880–1960)." *Etudes d'histoire africaine* 3 (1972): 209–41.
______. "Unequal Development: Capitalism and the Katangan Economy, 1919–1940." In Robin Palmer and Neil Parsons, eds., *The Roots of Rural Poverty in Central and Southern Africa*, pp. 345–64. Berkeley, 1977.
Johnson, R. W. "French Imperialism in Guinea." In Roger Owen and Bob Sutcliffe, eds., *Studies in the Theory of Imperialism*, pp. 230–47. London, 1972.
Jones, Arthur Creech. "British Colonial Policy—Current Scene and Outlook." *Yale Review* 38, no. 2 (1948): 204–21.
______. *The Future of the African Colonies*, Nottingham, 1951.
Jones, William I. *Planning and Economic Policy: Socialist Mali and Her Neighbors.* Washington, D.C., 1976.
Joseph, Richard A. "The Gaullist Legacy: Patterns of French Neo-Colonialism." *Review of African Political Economy* 5 (May–August 1976): 4–14.
______. *Radical Nationalism in Cameroun: Social Origins of the U.P.C.* London, 1977.
______. "Ruben Um Nyobe and the 'Kamerun' Rebellion." *African Affairs* 73 (1974): 428–48.
Journiac, Medécin-Général. "La Coopération franco-africaine dans le domaine de la santé." *Comptes rendus trimestriels des séances de l'Académie des sciences d'outre-mer* 36 (1976): 363–71.
Jouve, Edmond. "Le Tchad de N'Garta Tombalbaye au General Malloum," *Revue française d'études politiques africaines*, February 1978: 21–53.
Julien, Charles-André. *L'Afrique du Nord en marche.* 3d ed. Paris, 1972.
______. *Le Maroc Face aux impérialismes, 1415–1956.* Paris, 1978.
July, Robert W. *The Origins of Modern African Thought.* London, 1968.
Jundanian, Brendan. "Resettlement Programs: Counterinsurgency in Mozambique." *Comparative Politics* 6 (1974): 519–40.
Junior, Alfred D. *Angola perante uma conspiração internacional.* Luanda, 1961.
Kaba, Lansiné. *The Wahhabiyya: Islamic Reform and Politics in French West Africa.* Evanston, Ill., 1974.
Kabongo, Tshijuke. "Les Cultes comme manifestation de la résistance au colonialisme belge (1920–1948)." *Présence africaine* 4 (1977): 46–59.
Kadalie, Clements. *My Life and the ICU.* New York, 1970.
Kadzamira, Z. D. "Local Politics and the Administration of Development in Malawi." Ph.D. dissertation, University of Manchester, 1974.
Kagame, Alexis. *Un Abrégé de l'histoire du Rwanda de 1853 à 1972.* Butre Butare, 1975.

Kaggia, Bildad. *Roots of Freedom, 1921–1963*. Nairobi, 1975.
Kalck, Pierre. *Histoire de la République Centrafricaine*. Paris, 1974.
———. "Le Mouvement pour la restauration de l'indépendance nationale malgache, l'échec de 1947." *Cahiers du Centre de Recherches des Relations Internationales de l'Université de Metz* (1973), pp. 151–89.
Kalibwami, Justin. *Au Coeur de l'histoire contemporaine du Rwanda*. Paris, 1973.
Kalonji, Ditunga Albert. *Mémorandum: Ma Lutte au Kasai pour la verité au service de la justice*. Barcelona, 1964.
Kanet, Roger E. "The Soviet Union, the French Communist Party, and Africa, 1945–1950." *Survey* 22 (Winter 1976): 74–92.
Kanza, Thomas. *Conflict in the Congo: The Rise and Fall of Patrice Lumumba*. Baltimore, 1972. 2d rev. ed. Boston, 1980.
———. *Tôt ou tard*. Brussels, 1960.
Karis, Thomas G., and Carter, Gwendolyn M. *From Protest to Challenge: A Documentary History of African Politics in South Africa, 1882–1964*. Stanford, 1972–77.
Kariuki, J. M. *Mau Mau Detainee*. London, 1963.
Kaunda, Kenneth. *Zambia Shall Be Free*. New York, 1962.
Keita, Sidiki Kabélé. "Les Réalités coloniales en Guinée (1945–1958)." *Banda*, March 1977, pp. 14–23.
Keller, Edmund E. "Urbanisation and the Emergence of the Politics of Independence, Belgian Congo (Zaire)." *Mawazo* 4, no. 2 (1974): 37–52.
Kemal, Said. "Les Comores et le problème mahorais: Hier et aujourd'hui," *Comptes rendus trimestriels des séances de l'Académie des sciences d'outre-mer* 37 (1977): 763–74.
Kilson, Martin. *Political Change in a West African State*. Cambridge, Mass., 1966.
Kimbambo, I. N., and Temu, A. J. *History of Tanzania*. Nairobi, 1969.
Kimble, David. *The Machinery of Self-Government*. London, 1953.
———. *A Political History of Ghana*. Oxford, 1963.
Kimena, Kekwawha K. "La Politique scolaire de l'état colonial vis-à-vis des missions religieuse au Congo Belge." *Cultures au Zaïre et en Afrique* 5 (1974): 163–98.
Kiraranganya, Boniface. *La Verité sur le Burundi*. Sherbrooke, Quebec, 1977. [Eyewitness account of decolonization]
Kirei, Nikolai I. *Algeria and France, 1962–1971*. Moscow, 1973.
Kirk-Greene, A. H. M. *Lugard and the Amalgamation of Nigeria*. London, 1968.
———. *The Principles of Native Administration in Nigeria*. London, 1965.
———. "Public Administration and African Studies." In Christopher Fyfe, ed., *African Studies since 1945*. London, 1976.
Kirkman, W. P. *Unscrambling an Empire*. London, 1966.
Kirkwood, K., ed. *African Affairs No. 1* (St. Antony's Papers No. 10). London, 1961. (See articles by Thomas Hodgkin and Wilfred Whiteley.)
Klein, Jean. "Un épisode de la décolonisation: la guerre d'Algérie (1954–1962)." *Francia* 6 (1978): 64–145.
Klinghoffer, Arthur Jay. *The Angolan War: A Study in Soviet Policy in the Third World*. Boulder, Colo., 1980.
Knowles, Asa, ed. *International Encyclopedia of Higher Education*. 10 vols. San Francisco, 1977.
Koerner, Francis. "Décolonisation et économie de plantations dans les régions

côtières du nord et de l'ouest Malgache. *Revue économique de Madagascar* 5 (1970): 317-31.

———. "Les Evénements de 1947 à Madagascar." *Esprit*, September 1974, pp. 315-26.

Kola, Kabongo-Kongo. *Traités des rapports franco-africains*. Kinshasa, Congo, 1972.

Kolodziej, Edward A. *French International Policy under De Gaulle and Pompidou: The Politics of Grandeur*. Ithaca, 1974.

Kraiem, Mustapha. "C.G.T. et syndicalisme tunisien après la prise de la Tunisie par les alliés: 1943-1944." *Revue tunisienne des sciences sociaux* 12 (1974): 273-308.

———. "Les Evénements du 5 Août 1947 à Sfax." *Revue d'histoire maghrébine*, July 1977, pp. 314-33.

Kuczynski, R. R. *Demographic Survey of the British Colonial Empire*. London, 1948-49.

Kuder, Manfred. *Moçambique: Eine geographische soziale und wirtschaftliche Landeskunde*. Darmstadt, 1975.

Kuper, Leo. *Passive Resistance in South Africa*. New Haven, 1971.

Labouret, Henri. *Colonisation, colonialisme et décolonisation*. Paris, 1952.

Labrousse, André. *La France et l'aide à l'éducation dans 14 états africains et Malgache*. Paris, 1971.

"La Coopération entre la France, l'Afrique noire d'expression française et Madagascar." *Notes et études documentaires*, vol. 3330 (Oct. 25, 1966).

La Documention française. "Le Service de la coopération culturelle scientifique et technique avec les états francophones africains et malgache: Bilan et perspectives." *Notes et études documentaires*, vol. 3787 (May 4, 1971).

Lagrange, E. de. "Le Général de Gaulle et la décolonisation." *Etudes gaulliennes* 1 (1973): 180-95.

Landraud, M. "Justice indigène et politique coloniale: L'Exemple de la Côte d'Ivoire." *Penant* 87 (1978): 205-50.

"La Politique gouvernmentale et l'Eglise dans les territoires portugais d'Afrique." *Pro Mundi Vita* 43 (1972): 18-40.

Larkin, Bruce. *China and Africa, 1949-1970*. Berkeley, 1971.

La Rose, J. "Africa and Portugal." *Race* 16 (July 1974): 1-28.

Laurence, Margaret. *This Side Jordan*. Toronto, 1960.

———. *The Tomorrow-Tamer*. London, 1963.

Lawless, Richard. *A Bibliography of Works on Algeria in English since 1954*. Durham, Eng., 1972.

Lazreg, Marnia. *The Emergence of Classes in Algeria—A Study of Colonialism and Socio-Political Change*. Boulder, Colo., 1974.

Lebrun, Patrice. "La Décolonisation du droit pénal algérien." *Journal of African Law* 21 (Autumn 1977): 153-68.

Leca, Jean, and Vatin, Jean Claude. *L'Algérie politique: Institutions et régime*. Paris, 1975.

Leclercq, Hugues. "L'Enjeu économique de la décolonisation en Angola." *Cultures et développement* 8, no. 1 (1976): 43-88.

Leduc, Michel. *Les Institutions monétaires africaines des pays francophones*. Paris, 1965.

Lee, J. M. *Colonial Development and Good Government: A Study of the Ideas*

Expressed by the British Official Classes in Planning Decolonization, 1939–1964. Oxford, 1967.

Lefever, Ernest W. *Crisis in the Congo: A United Nations Force in Action.* Washington, D.C., 1965.

"Le FLEC et le problème du Cabinda." *Revue française d'études politiques africaines,* October 1977, pp. 84–110.

Legum, Colin. *Congo Disaster.* London, 1961.

Lemarchand, René. *Political Awakening in the Belgian Congo.* Berkeley, 1964.

———. *Rwanda and Burundi.* London, 1970.

Leonard, Willy. "Madagascar et la C.E.E. de 1958 à 1968." *Revue économique de Madagascar,* January–December 1971, pp. 81–135.

Levgold, Robert. *Soviet Policy in West Africa.* Cambridge, Mass., 1970.

Le Vine, Victor T. *The Cameroons, from Mandate to Independence.* Berkeley, 1964.

Leymarie, Philippe. "Début d'indépendance difficile à Djibouti." *Revue française d'études politiques africaines,* October 1978, 60–84.

———. "L'Agence de coopération culturelle et technique ou la francophonie institutionnelle." *Revue française d'études politiques africaines,* February 1976, pp. 13–29.

———. "La Ligue populaire africaine pour l'indépendance." *Revue française d'études politiques africaines,* April 1976, pp. 91–113.

———. "La République de Djibouti entre l'Afrique noire et le monde arabe." *Revue française d'études politiques africaines,* November 1977, pp. 58–72.

Leys, Colin. *European Politics in Southern Rhodesia.* Oxford, 1959.

———. *Underdevelopment in Kenya.* London, 1975.

Liebenow, J. G. *Colonial Rule and Political Development in Tanzania.* Evanston, Ill., 1971.

Ligot, Maurice. *Les Accords de coopération entre la France et les états africains et malgache d'expression française.* Paris, 1964.

———. "La Coopération entre la France et le Rwanda." *Revue juridique et politique* 18 (1964): 107–20.

Linden, Ian. *Church and Revolution in Rwanda.* New York, 1977.

"Livre blanc sur la réunification du Togo." *Revue française d'études politiques africaines,* January 1976, pp. 21–57.

Listowel, Judith. *The Making of Tanganyika.* New York, 1965.

Livingston, William S. *Federalism in the Commonwealth.* London, 1963.

Lloyd, Peter C. *Africa in Social Change.* Baltimore, 1967.

———. *The New Elites of Tropical Africa.* London, 1966.

Lokossou, Clement Koudessa. "La Presse au Dahomey, 1894–1960: Evolution et réaction face à l'administration coloniale." Thesis, University of Paris, 1976.

Lonsdale, J. M. "Some Origins of Nationalism in East Africa." *Journal of African History* 9, no. 1 (1968): 119–46.

Loucou, Jean-Noël. "La Vie politique en Côte d'Ivoire de 1932 à 1952." Thesis, University of Provence, Aix-Marseilles, 1976.

Louis, Wm. Roger. *Imperialism at Bay, 1941–1945.* Oxford, 1977.

———. *Ruanda-Urundi, 1884–1919.* Oxford, 1963.

Low, Donald A., and Lonsdale, J. M. "Towards the New Order, 1945–1963." *Oxford History of East Africa* vol. 3 (1976).

Low, Donald A., and Pratt, R. C. *Buganda and British Overrule.* London, 1960.

———. *Lion Rampant.* London, 1973.
———. *Political Parties in Uganda, 1949–1962.* London, 1962.
Low, Donald A., and Smith, Alison (eds.) *Oxford History of East Africa,* vol. 3 (1976).
Lowenkopf, Marvin. "Political Parties in Uganda and Tanzania." M.Sc., University of London, 1961.
Luc, Jean-Claude. "L'Economie du Niger depuis l'indépendance." *Revue française d'études politiques africaines,* December 1971, pp. 61–84.
Lugard, F. J. D. *The Dual Mandate in British Tropical Africa.* Edinburgh, 1922.
———. *Political Memoranda.* London, 1970.
Lumumba, Patrice. *Le Congo, terre d'avenir—est-il menacé?,* Brussels, 1961. Translated as *Congo, My Country.* London, 1962 (foreword by Colin Legum).
Luthuli, Albert J. *Let My People Go.* New York, 1962.
MacDonald, R. J., ed. *From Nyasaland to Malawi.* Nairobi, 1975.
Machel, Samora. *Establish People's Power to Serve the Masses.* Toronto, 1976.
———. *Mozambique: Revolution or Reaction? Two Speeches.* Richmond, B.C., 1975.
———. "The People's Republic of Mozambique: The Struggle Continues." *Review of African Political Economy* 4 (November 1975): 14–25.
———. *Le Processus de la révolution démocratique populaire au Mozambique.* Paris, 1977. [His speeches, 1970–74].
Mackenzie, W. J. M., and Post, K. W. J., eds. *The Nigerian Federal Election of 1959.* London, 1963.
Mackenzie, W. J. M., and Robinson, K. E. *Five Elections in Africa.* Oxford, 1960.
Mackintosh, John P., ed. *Nigerian Government and Politics.* London, 1966.
MacMillan, W. M. *The Road to Self-Rule.* Freeport, Me. 1959.
Madjarian, Grégoire. *La Question coloniale et la politique du Parti communiste français, 1944–1947.* Paris, 1977.
Maestre, J. C. "L'Expérience révolutionnaire d'Ali Soilih aux Comores (1976–1978)." *Annuaire des pays de l'océan Indien* 4 (1977): 25–42.
Maguire, G. A. *Towards 'Uhuru' in Tanzania.* London, 1969.
Mair, Lucy Philip. *Native Policies in Africa.* New York, 1936.
Majdalany, Fred. *State of Emergency.* London, 1962.
Makedonsky, Jeanne. "L'Épineuse Décolonisation de la Guinée-Bissau." *Revue française d'études politiques africaines,* September 1974, pp. 43–55.
Makonnen, Ras. *Pan Africanism from Within.* Nairobi, 1973. Recorded and edited by Kenneth King.
Malecot, Georges. "Djibouti demain l'indépendance." *Afrique et Asie modernes,* no. 1 (1977): 40–50.
Manouan, A. "L'Evolution du conseil de l'Entente." *Penant* 84 (1975): 19–92, 211–36, 309–75.
Maquet, Jacques. *Eléctions en société féodale.* Brussels, 1959.
———. *The Premise of Inequality in Rwanda.* London, 1961. (Translated from the French text, *Le Système des relations sociales dans le Ruanda ancien,* Tervuren, 1954.)
Marchat, Henri. "La France et l'Espagne au Maroc pendant la période du protectorat (1912–1956)." *Revue de l'occident musulman et de la Méditerranée* 2 (1971): 81–110.

Marcum, John. *The Angolan Revolution.* Vol. 1: *Anatomy of a Revolution, 1950–1962*; vol. 2: *Exile Politics and Guerrilla Warfare, 1962–1976*, Cambridge, Mass., 1969 and 1978.

Markovitz, Marvin D. *Cross and Sword: The Political Role of Christian Missions in the Belgian Congo, 1908–1960.* Stanford, 1973.

Marshall, D. Bruce. *The French Colonial Myth and Constitution-Making in the Fourth Republic.* New Haven, 1973.

Martin, Marie-Louis. *Kimbangu: An African Prophet and His Church.* Grand Rapids, Mich., 1975.

Martin, Phyllis M. "The Cabinda Connection: An Historical Perspective." *African Affairs* 76 (1977): 47–59.

Masson, Paul. *Dix Ans de malheurs* (*Kivu 1957–1967*). Vol. 1: *La Fin des illusions.* Brussels, 1970.

Matthews, Noel. *A Guide to Manuscripts and Documents.* London, 1971.

Mazrui, Ali. "The English Language and Political Consciousness in British Colonial Africa." *Journal of Modern African Studies* (1966).

Mboya, Tom. *Freedom and After.* Boston, 1963.

McCarthy, Joseph M. *Guinea-Bissau and Cape Verde Islands: A Comprehensive Bibliography.* New York, 1977.

McDonald, Gordon C. et al. "Bibliography." *Area Handbook for Burundi*, pp. 179–87. Washington, D.C. 1969.

McNeill, William Hardy. *America, Britain and Russia.* New York, 1970.

McPhee, A. *The Economic Revolution in British West Africa.* London, 1926.

Meebelo, H. S. *Reaction to Colonialism.* Manchester, 1971.

Meek, C. K. *Land Law and Custom in the Colonies.* London, 1946.

Melo, Guilhermo de. *Moçambique norte—Guerra e paz* (*reportagem*). Lourenço Marques, 1969.

"Mémoire des députés du mouvement mahorais sur le référendum du 22 décembre 1974 aux Comores." *Revue française d'études politiques africaines*, February 1975, pp. 81–94.

Mensah, G. "The Process of Monetary Decolonization in Africa." *Utafiti* 4 (1979): 45–64.

Meredith, David. "The British Government and Colonial Economic Policy, 1919–39." *Economic History Review*, vol. 28, no. 3 (August 1975).

Merlier, Michel. *Le Congo de la colonisation belge à l'indépendance.* Paris, 1962.

Merriam, Alan P. *Congo, Background of Conflict.* Evanston, Ill., 1961.

Meyers, B. O. "African Voting in the U.N. General Assembly." *Journal of Modern African Studies* (1968).

Michel, Viviane. "La Politique de coopération belge." *Afrique et Asie modernes* 2 (1975): 27–35.

Middlemas, Keith. "Twentieth Century White Society in Mozambique." *Tarikh* 6, no. 2 (1979): 30–45.

Miège, Jean Louis. *Expansion européenne et décolonisation de 1870 à nos jours.* Paris, 1973.

Minter, William. *Portuguese Africa and the West.* New York, 1972.

Mitchell, Philip. *African Afterthoughts.* London, 1954.

Mokgatle, Naboth. *The Autobiography of an Unknown South African.* London, 1971.

Mondlane, Eduardo. *The Struggle for Mozambique.* Baltimore, 1969.

Moneta, Jacob. *Le Parti communiste français et la question coloniale, 1920–1963* Paris, 1971.
Monsarrat, Nicholas. *Richer than All His Tribe.* New York, 1968.
———. *The Tribe That Lost Its Head.* New York, 1956.
Moolman, J. H. "Portuguese Guinea. The Untenable War." *Africa Institute Bulletin* 12 (1974): 243–60.
Morgan, David J. *The Official History of Colonial Development.* Altantic Highland, N.J., 1980.
Morgan, Edward. "The 1977 Elections in Djibouti: A Tragic-Comic End to French Colonial Rule." *Horn of Africa* 1 (July–September 1978): 47–50.
Morris, H. F., and Read, J. S. *Indirect Rule and the Search for Justice.* Oxford, 1972.
Morris, James. *Farewell the Trumpets: An Imperial Retreat.* New York, 1980.
Morris-Jones, W. H., and Fischer, Georges, eds. *Decolonisation and After: The British and French Experience.* London, 1980.
Morro, Michel, et al. *Indépendance, inflation, développement: l'Economie congolaise de 1960 à 1965.* The Hague, 1968.
Mortimer, Robert Adler. "Foreign Policy and Its Role in Nation-Building in Algeria." Ph.D. dissertation, Columbia University, 1968.
Mphalele, Ezekiel. *Down Second Avenue.* Garden City, N.J., 1959.
M'rabet, Fadela. *La Femme algérienne. Suivi de: Les Algériennes.* Paris, 1969.
Mulford, David C. *The Northern Rhodesia General Election, 1962.* Nairobi, 1964.
———. *Zambia: The Politics of Independence.* London, 1967.
Mulier, Freddy. "La Coopération technique belge dans l'enseignement zaïrois." *Cahiers du CEDAF* 1 (1979): 2–69.
Munro, J. Forbes. *Colonial Rule and the Kamba.* Oxford, 1975.
Munywzangabo, Corneille M. *L'Internationalisation du conflit Hutu-Tutsi en Afrique interlacustrine.* Mémoire, University of Paris, 1976.
Murray, A. V. "Education under Indirect Rule." *Journal of the Royal African Society* (July 1935).
Mustafa, Sophia. *The Tanganyika Way.* London, 1962.
Mutin, Georges. *La Mitidja: Décolonisation et espace géographique.* Paris, 1977.
Mvuluya, Mulambo. "Forces politiques et décolonisation: Le Cas du Parti national du progrès," *Cahiers zaïrois d'études politiques et sociales,* October 1974, pp. 55–76.
Mytelka, Lynn Krieger. "A Genealogy of Francophone West and Equatorial African Regional Organisations." *Journal of Modern African Studies* 12 (1974): 297–320.
Nadir, A. "Le Mouvement réformiste algérien et la guerre de libération nationale." *Revue d'histoire maghrébine,* July 1975, pp. 174–83.
Nahayo, Simon. "Contribution à la bibliographie des ouvrages relatifs au Burundi (Afrique centrale)." *Genève-Afrique* 10, no. 1 (1971): 92–99; no. 2 (1971): 100–11; 11, no. 1 (1972): 94–104.
Nataf, F. *L'Indépendance du Maroc, témoignage d'action (1950–1956).* Paris, 1975.
Naylor, Phillip Chiviges. "Algeria and France: The Post-Colonial Relationship, 1962–1975." *Proceedings of the French Colonial Historical Society* 5 (1980): 58–69.
———. "French-Algerian Relations, 1962–1978." Ph.D. dissertation, Marquette University, 1980.
N'Dongo, Sally. *La Coopération franco-africaine.* Paris, 1972.

Newlyn, Walter T., and Rowan, David C. *Money and Banking in British Colonial Africa*. Oxford, 1954.
Ngango, Georges. *Les Investissements d'origine extérieure en Afrique noire francophone: Leur Statut et incidence sur le développment*. Paris, 1973.
Ngugi Wa Thiong'o, James. *A Grain of Wheat*. London, 1967.
Nichols, Sheridan. "French Liberals and Moroccan Decolonisation: 1944–1955." *Proceedings of the French Colonial Historical Society* 1 (1976): 74–79.
Nkrumah Kwame. *Ghana*. New York, 1957.
______. *Rhodesia File*. London, 1976.
Nkundabenzi, F., ed. *Rwanda Politique*. Brussels, 1961.
Nkusi, Laurent. "Bibliographie de Kinyarwanda." *Informateur* 10 (June 1977): 154–63.
Nogueira, Alberto Franco. *The United Nations and Portugal: A Study in Anti-Colonialism*. London, 1963.
Nolde, André. "Djibouti: Indépendance, oui, mais." *Défense nationale* 32 (February 1976): 69–78.
Nolutshungu, Sam C. *South Africa in Africa: A Study in Ideology and Foreign Policy*. Manchester, 1975.
Nordman, Curtis R. *Prelude to Decolonization in West Africa: The Development of British Colonial Policy, 1938–1947*. Dissertation, Oxford University, 1976.
Nsanze, Térence. *L'Edification de la république du Burundi au carrefour de l'Afrique*. Brussels, 1970.
Nurse, Ronald J. "Critic of Colonialism: JFK and Algerian Independence." *Historian* 39 (February 1977): 307–26.
Nyerere, Julius. *Freedom and Development*. London, 1973.
______. *Freedom and Socialism*. New York, 1968.
______. *Freedom and Unity*. London, 1967.
______. *Ujamaa—Essays on Socialism*. Oxford, 1968.
Nyrop, Richard F. et al. "Bibliography." *Area Handbook for Rwanda*, pp. 191–204. Washington, 1969.
Nzekwu, Onuora. *Blade among the Boys*. London, 1962.
Oberle, Philippe. *Afars et Somalis: Le Dossier de Djibouti*. Paris, 1971.
Obichere, Boniface. "Reconstruction in Guinea-Bissau: From Revolutionaries and Guerrillas to Bureaucrats and Politicians." *Current Bibliography of African Affairs* 8 (1975): 204–19.
O'Brien, Jay. "Portugal and Africa: A Dying Imperialism." *Monthly Review* 26 (May 1974): 19–36.
O'Brien, Rita Cruise. "Colonisation to Cooperation: French Technical Assistance in Senegal." *Journal of Development Studies* 8 (October 1971): 45–58.
______. *White Society in Black Africa: The French of Senegal*. London, 1972.
Odinga, Ajuma O. *Not Yet Uhuru*. 1967.
Offredo, Jean. *Algérie: Avec ou sans la France?* Paris, 1973.
Ogot, Bethwell A. "Revolt of the Elders." *Politics and Nationalism in Colonial Kenya*. Nairobi, 1972.
Ogunsanwo, Alaba. *China's Policy in Africa, 1958–1971*. Cambridge, Eng., 1974.
Ojo, Michael Adelaye. "United Nations and Freedom for Portuguese Colonies." *Africa Quarterly* 16, no. 1 (1976): 5–28.
Okuma, Thomas M. *Angola in Ferment*. Boston, 1962.
Oliveira, Jorge E. da Costa. *Economia de Angola: Evolução e perspectivas, 1962–1969*. Luanda, 1970.

Opello, Walter C. "The Formation of Social Systems: The FRELIMO Case." *Canadian Review of Studies in Nationalism* 2 (1975): 297–316.
———. "Pluralism and Elite Conflict in an Independence Movement: FRELIMO in the 1960's." *Journal of Southern African Studies* 2 (1975): 66–82.
Owusu, Maxwell K. *Uses and Abuses of Political Power.* Chicago, 1970.
Pachai, Bridglal. *Malawi: The History of the Nation.* London, 1973.
Padmore, G., ed. *History of the Pan-African Congress.* London, 1963.
Paillat, Claude. *Vingt Ans qui déchirent la France.* Vol. 2: *La Liquidation, 1954–1962.* Paris, 1972.
Palley, Claire. *The Constitutional History and Law of Southern Rhodesia, 1888–1965.* Oxford, 1966.
Pascal, R. "Le Statut du territoire des Afars et des Issas après six ans d'application." *Revue juridique et politique* 28 (1974): 63–80.
Patel, Hasu. "Race, Class and Citizenship in Uganda, 1900–1972." Ph.D. dissertation, University of California, Los Angeles, 1977.
Paternostre de la Marie, Baudouin. *Le Rwanda.* Brussels, 1972.
Pattee, Richard. *Anti-Colonialismo, marxismo y Portugal.* Mexico City, 1967.
Paul, John. *Mozambique: Memoirs of a Revolution.* Harmondsworth, 1975.
Pearce, Robert. *The Evolution of British Colonial Policy towards Tropical Africa, 1938–1948.* Dissertation, Oxford University, 1978.
Pearson, J. D., ed. *A Guide to the Manuscripts and Documents in the British Isles Relating to Africa.* London, 1971.
Pedler, F. J. *The Lion and the Unicorn in Africa.* London, 1974.
Peemans, Françoise, and Lefèvre, Patrick. "Les Sociétés coloniales Belges: Archives et données bibliographiques (1885–1960)." *Cahiers du CEDAF* 4–5 (1980); 3–95.
Peemans, Jean-Philippe. "Capital Accumulation in the Congo under Colonialism." In Peter Duignan and Lewis Gann, eds. *Colonialism in Black Africa, 1870–1960,* 4: 165–212. Cambridge, Eng., 1970.
———. *Diffusion du progrès économique et convergence des prix: Le Cas congo-belgique, 1900–1960.* Louvain, 1968.
———. "Imperial Hangovers: Belgium—The Economics of Decolonization." *Journal of Contemporary History* 15 (Apr. 1, 1980): 257–86.
———. "The Social and Economic Development of Zaire since Independence: An Historical Outline." *African Affairs* 74 (1975): 148–79.
Pélissier, René. "Angola: Un Equilibre précaire." *Revue française d'études politiques africaines,* February 1975, 18–21.
———. *La Colonie du minotaure: Nationalismes et révoltes en Angola (1926–1961).* Paris, 1978.
———. "Contribution à la bibliographie de l'Angola." *Genève-Afrique* 15, no. 2 (1976): 136–51.
———. "La Guerre de Batepà, São Tomé—février 1953," *Revue française d'études politiques africaines,* January 1972, pp. 74–88.
———. "La Guerre en Angola oriental." *Revue française d'études politiques africaines,* July 1974, pp. 87–109.
———. *Les Guerres grises: Résistance et révoltes en Angola (1845–1941).* 2 vol. Paris, 1977.
———. "Saõ Tomé et Principe: Les Aléas de l'indépendance." *Revue française d'études politiques africaines,* July 1975, pp. 9–12.

———. "São Tomé on le poids des siècles." *Revue française d'études politiques africaines,* January 1968, pp. 34–51.
Pélissier, René, and Wheeler, Douglas, *Angola.* New York, 1971.
Perham, Margery. *African Apprenticeship.* London, 1974.
———. *Colonial Sequence, 1949–1969.* London, 1970.
———. "Introduction to the Fifth Edition." In F. J. D. Lugard, *Dual Mandate in British Tropical Africa* (1965), pp. xxvii-xlix.
———. *Native Administration in Nigeria.* London, 1937.
———. "A Restatement of Indirect Rule." *Africa* 7, no. 3 (July 1934): 321–34.
———. "Some Problems of Indirect Rule in Africa." *Journal of the Royal Society of Arts,* vol. 82, no. 4252 (May 18, 1934).
Perham, Margery, and Curtis, Lionel. *The Protectorates of South Africa.* London, 1935.
Périllier, Louis. *La Conquête de l'indépendance tunisienne.* Paris, 1979. [Diplomacy of the last stages]
Perinbam, B. Marie. "Fanon and the Revolutionary Peasantry—the Algerian Case." *Journal of Modern African Studies* 11 (1973): 427–45.
Pervillé, Guy, "Quinze Ans d'historiographie de la guerre d'Algerie." *Annuaire de l'Afrique du Nord* 15 (1976): 1337–63.
Pétillon, L. A. M. *Temoignage et Réflexions.* Brussels, 1967.
Pim, Alan W. *The Financial and Economic History of the Tropical African Territories.* Oxford, 1940.
Piret, Baudouin. *L'Aide de la Belgique aux pays sous-développés.* Brussels, 1972.
Poncet, Jean. *La Tunisie à la recherche de son avenir: indépendance ou néocolonialisme.* Paris, 1974.
Porch, Douglas. *The Portuguese Armed Forces and the Revolution.* Stanford, 1977.
Post, K. W. J. *The New States of West Africa.* Baltimore, 1964.
———. *The Nigerian Federal Election of 1959.* London, 1963.
Post, K. W. J., and Jenkins, George D. *The Price of Liberty.* Cambridge, Eng., 1973.
Post, K. W. J., and Vickers, M. *Structure and Conflict in Nigeria, 1960–1966.* London, 1973.
Pratt, Robert Cranford. "Administration and Politics in Uganda, 1919–1945." In Vincent Harlow and E. M. Chilver, *Oxford History of East Africa,* 2: 476–541. Oxford, 1965.
———. *The Critical Phase in Tanzania, 1964–67.* Cambridge, Eng., 1976.
Pugh, Patricia M. "The Oxford Colonial Records Project and the Oxford Development Records Project." *Journal of the Society of Archivists* 6, no. 2 (October 1978): 76–86.
Pugh, Ralph B. *The Records of the Colonial and Dominion Offices.* London, 1964.
Quandt, William. *Revolution and Political Leadership: Algeria, 1954–1958.* Cambridge, Mass., 1969.
Ralaimihoatra, Edouard. *Histoire de Madagascar.* Tananarive, 1972.
Ramamonjisoa, Georges. "La Coopération franco-malgache rénovée." *Bulletin de Madagascar* 23 (1973): 447–68, 561–74.
Ranger, T. O. "Connexions between 'Primary Resistance' Movement and Modern Mass Nationalism in East and Central Africa." *Journal of African History* 9, no. 3 (1968): 437–53, and no. 4 (1968): 631–41.
———. "The 'New Historiography' in Dar Es Salaam: An Answer," *African Affairs* 70, no. 278 (January 1971): 329–49.

Rathbone, Richard. "Government of the Gold Coast after World War II." *African Affairs* 67, no. 268 (1968): 209–18.
Rendell, (Sir) William. *History of the Commonwealth Development Corporation, 1948–1972*. London, 1976.
Report of the Nyasaland Commission of Inquiry (the Devlin Commission Cmd. 814, 1959).
Reuss, C. "Réflexions sur l'aide de la Belgique au Burundi." *Etudes congolaises* 12 (April–June 1968): 81–96.
Rey, Pierre Philippe. *Colonialisme, néocolonialisme et transition au capitalisme: Exemple du COMILOG au Congo-Brazzaville*. Paris, 1971.
Ribs, Jacques. *L'Indemnisation des français dépossédés outre-mer*. Paris, 1971.
Rivière, Claude. *Guinea: The Mobilization of a People*. Ithaca, N.Y., 1977.
———. "Les Partis politiques guinéens avant l'indépendance." *Revue française d'études politiques africaines*, November 1974, pp. 61–82.
Robarts, Richard. *French Development Assistance: A Study in Policy and Administration*. Beverly Hills, Calif., 1974.
Robertson, James. *Transition in Africa*. London, 1974.
Robinson, R. E. "Why Direct Rule Has Been Replaced by Local Government in the Nomenclature of British Native Administration." *Journal of African Administration* 2 (July 1950): 12–15.
Robinson, Ronald. "The 'Journal' and the Transfer of Power." *Journal of Administration Overseas*, vol. 13 (January 1974).
Rocha, Nuno. *Guerra em Moçambique*. Lisbon, 1970.
Rodney, Walter. *How Britain Underdeveloped Africa*. Washington, D.C., 1974.
Rogers, Cyril A., and Frantz, Charles. *Racial Themes in Southern Rhodesia*. New Haven, 1962.
Ronen, Dov. *Dahomey between Tradition and Modernity*. Ithaca, N.Y., 1975.
Rosberg, Carl G., and Nottingham, John C. *The Myth of "Mau Mau" Nationalism in Kenya*. Stanford, 1966.
Rotberg, Robert I. "African Nationalism: Concept or Confusion." *Journal of Modern African Studies*, 1966.
———. *The Rise of Nationalism in Central Africa*. Cambridge, Mass., 1965.
Rotberg, Robert I., and Mazrui, Ali, eds. *Protest and Power in Black Africa*. New York, 1970.
Rothchild, Donald S. *Racial Bargaining in Independent Kenya*. London, 1973.
Roux, Edward. *Time Longer than Rope*. London, 1948.
Ruark, Robert C. *Uhuru*. New York, 1962.
Rudebeck, Lars. *Guinea-Bissau: A Study of Political Mobilization*. Uppsala, 1974.
Sady, Emil J. *The United Nations and Dependent Peoples*. Washington, D.C., 1956.
Saint-Veran, Robert. *A Djibouti avec les Afars et les Issas*. Cagnes-sur-Mer, 1977.
Saloway, R. "The New Gold Coast." *International Affairs* 31 (October 1955): 469–76.
Samoff, Joel. *Tanzania: Local Politics and the Structure of Power*. Madison, Wis., 1974.
Samuel, Michel. *Le Prolétariat africain noir en France*. Paris, 1978. [Mainly Soninke from Senegal, Mali, and Mauritania].
Sanger, Clyde, and Nottingham, John. "The Kenya General Election of 1963." *Journal of Modern African Studies*, vol. 2, no. 1 (March 1964).

Santos, Fernando Barciela. *Angola na hora dramática da descolonização*. Lisbon, 1975.

Saul, John S. "Free Mozambique." *Monthly Review* 27 (December 1975): 8–23.

———. "FRELIMO and the Mozambican Revolution." In Giovanni Arrighi and John S. Paul, eds. *Essays on the Political Economy of Africa*, pp. 378–405. New York, 1973.

———. "Portugal and the Mozambican Revolution." *Monthly Review* 26 (September 1974): 45–64.

Saumagne, Charles. *Journal et écrits (Tunisie, 1947–1957)*. Nice, 1979. [Important for 1954–56]

Scalabre, Camille. "Deux Années d'indépendance à Djibouti." *Revue juridique et politique* 33 (1979): 331–36.

Scherk, Nikolaus. *Dekolonisation und Souveräntität*. Stuttgart, 1969.

de Schrevel, Michel. *Les Forces politiques de la décolonisation congolaise jusqu'à la veille de l'indépendance*. Louvain, 1970.

Schwab, Morton. *The Political Relationship between France and Her Former Colonies in the Sub-Saharan Regions since 1958*. Atlanta, 1968.

Scott, Paul. *Raj Quartet (1967–1975)*. London, 1977.

Scotton, Carol M. M. "Some Swahili Political Words." *Journal of Modern African Studies* 3, no. 4 (December 1965).

Seegers, A. "Strategy in National Revolutions. Some Aspects of FRELIMO's Revolutionary Strategy." *Politikon: South African Journal of Political Science* 4 (June 1977): 64–76.

Seligman, Edwin R. A. *Encyclopaedia of the Social Sciences*. New York, 1932. [See Moritz Julius Bonn, s.v. "decolonization"]

Serapiao, Luís Benjamim. "The Influence of the Catholic Church on Portuguese Colonial Policy." *Current Bibliography of African Affairs* 7, no. 2 (1974): 138–55.

Serapiao, Luís B., and El-Khawas, Mohammed A. *Mozambique in the Twentieth Century: From Colonialism to Independence*. Washington, D.C., 1978. [International aspects of liberation]

Serrano, Carlos M. H. "Angola (1961–1976). Bibliografia." *Journal of Southern African Affairs* 2 (1977): 295–322.

Sharwood Smith, Bryan. *Recollections of British Administration in the Cameroons and Northern Nigeria, 1921–1957*. Durham, Eng., 1969.

Shehim, Kassim, and Searing, James. "Djibouti and the Question of Afar Nationalism." *African Affairs* 79 (1980): 195–208.

Shepperson, George, and Price, Thomas. *Independent African*. Edinburgh, 1958.

Sideri, S. *Trade and Power, Informal Colonialism in Portuguese Relations*. Rotterdam, 1970.

Sills, H. D. "The Break Up of the Central African Federation: Notes on the Validity of Assurances." *African Affairs* 73, no. 290 (January 1974): 50–62.

Simon, Gildas. "L'Espace des travailleurs tunisiens en France: Structures et fonctionnement d'un champ migratoire international." Thesis, University of Poitiers, 1978. [Protectorate backgrounds of postindependence immigration]

Simpson, D. H. *Biography Catalogue of the Library of the Royal Commonwealth Society*. London, 1961.

Sinda, Martial. *Le Messianisme congolais*. Paris, 1972.

Sine, Babakar. *Impérialisme et théories sociologiques du développement*. Paris, 1975.

Siriex, Paul-Henri. *Félix Houphouët-Boigny: L'Homme de la paix.* Paris, 1975.
Sithole, N. *African Nationalism.* 2d ed. London, 1968.
Sivan, Emmanuel. *Communisme et nationalisme en Algérie, 1920–1962.* Paris, 1976.
Sklar, Richard. *Nigerian Political Parties.* Princeton, 1963.
Slade, Ruth M. *The Belgian Congo.* 2d ed. London, 1961.
———. *King Leopold's Congo.* London, 1962.
Smith, Alan K. "Antonio Salazar and the Reversal of Portuguese Colonial Policy." *Journal of African History* 15 (1974): 653–68.
Smith, Tony. *The French Stake in Algeria, 1945–1962.* Ithaca, N.Y., 1978.
Smith, William Edgett. *We Must Run While They Walk.* 1st ed. New York, 1972.
Soret, Marcel. *Histoire du Congo, capitale Brazzaville.* Paris, 1978.
Sorrenson, M. P. K. *Origins of European Settlement in Kenya.* Nairobi, 1968.
Sorum, Paul Clay. *Intellectuals and Decolonization in France.* Durham, N.C., 1977.
Soustelle, Jacques. *Lettre ouverte aux victimes de la décolonisation.* Paris, 1973.
Spence, John E. *Lesotho: The Politics of Dependence.* London, 1968.
———. *Republic Under Pressure.* London, 1965.
———. "South Africa and the Modern World." In Monica Wilson and Leonard Thompson, eds., *Oxford History of South Africa,* 2: 477–527. Oxford, 1971.
Spillman, Georges. "L'Anti-Colonialisme en France du XVIIe siècle à nos jours." *Afrique et Asie modernes* 2 (1974): 3–20.
———. "Colonisation, décolonisation, et néo-imperialisme." *Afrique et Asie Modernes* 2 (1976): 45–54.
de Spínola, General António. *Linha de Accão.* Lisbon, 1970.
———. *Portugal e o futuro: Analise da conjuntura nacional.* Lisbon, 1974.
———. *Por uma Guiné melhor.* Lisbon, 1970.
Spitzer, Leo, and Denzer, La Ray. "I. T. A. Wallace-Johnson and the West African Youth League." *African Historical Studies* 6, no. 3 (1973): 413–52.
Staniland, Martin. "The Three-Party System in Dahomey: I, 1946–1956; II, 1956–57." *Journal of African History* 14 (1973): 291–312, 491–504.
Stengers, Jean. "La Belgique et le Congo politique coloniale et décolonisation." *Histoire de la Belgique contemporaine, 1914–1970,* pp. 391–440. Brussels, 1974.
Stephens, Hugh W. *The Political Transformation of Tanganyika, 1920–67.* New York, 1968.
Stevens, Christopher. "The Soviet Union and Angola." *African Affairs* 75 (1976): 137–51.
Stevens, Richard P. *Lesotho, Botswana and Swaziland.* London, 1967.
Stillman, Calvin W., ed. *Africa in the Modern World.* Chicago, 1955.
Stilwell, F. "The Church in Angola and Mozambique." *Clergy Review* 14 (1974): 409–20.
Stockwell, John. *In Search of Enemies: A CIA Story.* New York, 1978.
Strachey, John. *The End of Empire.* London, 1959.
Suret-Canale, Jean. *Afrique noire occidentale et centrale: De la colonisation aux indépendances (1945–1960).* Paris, 1972.
———. "Difficultés du néo-colonialisme français en Afrique tropicale." *Canadian Journal of African Studies* 8 (1974): 211–34.
Swift, Kerry. *Mozambique and the Future.* Cape Town, 1974.
Symonds, Richard. *The British and Their Successors.* Evanston, Ill., 1966.

Tabata, I. B. *The All African Convention.* Nottingham, 1974.
Tawney, John J., "Personal Thoughts on a Rescue Operation," *African Affairs* 67, no. 269 (October 1968): 345–50.
Taylor, J. Claggett. *The Political Development of Tanganyika.* Stanford, 1963.
Teitler, M. et al. *Elites, pouvoir et légitimité au Maghreb.* Paris. 1973.
Teixeira, Bernardo. *The Fabric of Terror.* New York, 1965.
Tessler, Mark A. "The Identity of Religious Minorities in Non-Secular States; Jews in Tunisia and Morocco and Arabs in Israel." *Comparative Studies in Society and History* 20 (1978): 359–73.
Texeira Da Mota, Avelinó. *Guiné portuguêsa.* Lisbon, 1954.
Thiong'o's, Ngugi Wa. *Petals of Blood.* London, 1977.
Thiong'o's, Ngugi Wa, and Githae, Micere. *The Trial of Dedan Kimathi.* London, 1976.
Thompson, Leonard M. *Politics in the Republic of South Africa.* Boston, 1966.
Thompson, Leonard, and Butler, Jeffrey. *Change in Contemporary South Africa.* Berkeley, 1975.
Thompson, Virginia McLean. *West Africa's Council of the Entente.* Ithaca, N.Y., 1972.
Thompson, Virginia, and Richard Adloff. "French Economic Policy in Tropical Africa." In Peter Duignan and Lewis H. Gann, eds., *Colonialism in Africa, 1870–1960,* vol. 4 (1975), pp. 95–126.
Tignor, Robert L. *The Colonial Transformation of Kenya.* Princeton, 1976. [Article in Kikuya agriculture]
Tixier, Gilbert. "Les Conventions fiscales passés par la France avec les pays en voie de développement." *Revue juridique et politique* 29 (1975): 252–62.
Tordoff, William. *Government and Politics in Tanzania.* Nairobi, 1967.
Tordoff, William et al., eds. *Politics in Zambia.* Berkeley, 1974.
Toumi, Mohnsen. "Le Néo-Destour dans le mouvement national tunisien." *Revue française d'études politiques africaines,* February 1974, pp. 26–53.
Travis, Carole. *Periodicals from Africa.* Boston, 1977.
Tricot, Bernard. *Les Sentiers de la paix, Algérie, 1958–1962.* Paris, 1972.
Tripier, Philippe. *Autopsie de la guerre d'Algérie.* Paris, 1972.
Tronchon, Jacques. *L'Insurrection malgache de 1947.* Paris, 1974.
Tshombe, Moise. *Mémoires de Moise Tshombe.* Brussels, 1975.
Turner, Thomas. "La 'Politique indigène du Congo Belge, Le Cas du Sankuru." *Cahiers du CEDAF* 1 (1973).
Twaddle, Michael, ed. *Expulsion of a Minority.* London, 1975.
Udokang, Okon. "Portuguese African Policy—A Critical Re-Appraisal." *African Review* 6 (1976): 289–312.
United Nations publication. *Objective: Justice,* vol. 9, no. 2 (Summer 1977).
Vail, Leroy, and White, Landeg. "The Struggle for Mozambique: Capitalist Rivalries, 1900–1940." *Review,* Fall 1979, pp. 243–76.
Vallier, André. "Les Comores indépendants: Bilan en 1977." *Afrique contemporaine* 16 (July–August 1977): 14–21.
Van Bilsen, Antoine A. J. *L'Indépendance du Congo.* Tournai, 1962.
———. *Vers l'indépendance du Congo et du Ruanda-Urundi.* Kraainem, Belgium 1958.
Van der Meersch, Walter J. Ganshof. *Fin de la souveraineté belge au Congo.* Brussels, 1963.

Vanhove, Julien. *Histoire du Ministère des colonies.* Brussels, 1968.
Van Lierde, Jean, ed. *La Pensée politique de Patrice Lumumba.* Paris, [1963]. Translated as *Lumumba Speaks: The Speeches and Writings of Patrice Lumumba, 1958–1961.* Boston, 1972.
Vansina, Jean. "Les Kuba et l'administration territoriale de 1919 à 1960." *Cultures et développement* 4, no. 2 (1976): 275–326.
van Zwanenberg, R. M. A. *Colonial Capitalism and Labour in Kenya, 1919–1939.* Kampala, Uganda, 1975.
———. *An Economic History of Kenya and Uganda, 1800–1970.* Nairobi, 1975.
Vatikiotis, P. J., ed. *Revolution in the Middle East and Other Case Studies.* London, 1972.
Vatin, Jean-Claude. *L'Algérie politique: Histoire et société.* Paris, 1974.
———. "Eléments pour une bibliographie d'ensemble sur l'Algérie d'aujourd'hui." *Revue algérienne des sciences juridiques économiques et politiques* 5 (1968): 167–208.
Vaudiaux, Jacques. *L'Evolution politique et juridique de la coopération franco-africaine et malgache.* Paris, 1971.
Vazeilles, Benoît. "L'Evolution politique du territoire français des Afars et des Issas depuis 1967." *Revue française d'études politiques africaines,* April 1976, pp. 36–53.
Vellut, Jean-Luc." "Pour une histoire sociale de l'Afrique centrale." *Cultures et développement* 6, no. 1 (1974): 61–86.
Venter, Al J. *Portugal's War in Guinea-Bissau.* Pasadena, 1973.
Verhaegen, Benoît, ed. *A.B.A.K.O, 1950–1960, Documents.* Brussels, 1962.
———. "Les Associations congolaises à Léopoldville et dans le Bas-Congo avant 1960." *Cahiers économiques et sociaux* 8 (September 1970): 389–416.
———, ed. *Congo 1961: Documents belges et africains.* Brussels, 1962.
———. "Contribution à l'histoire politique de Kinshasa: La Consultation communale de 1957." *Cahiers zaïrois de la recherche et du développement,* special number (1971): 11–44.
———. "Dix Ans de nationalisme au Congo. Le Cas de l'ABAKO." *Bulletin de l'Académie royale des sciences d'outre-mer,* vol. 2 (1971).
———. "Les Premiers Manifestes politiques à Léopoldville (1950–1956)." *Cahiers du CEDAF* 10 (1971): 3–42.
———. *Rébellions au Congo.* Brussels, 1966.
Vidal, Claudine. "Colonisation et décolonisation du Rwanda: La Question Tutsi-Hutu." *Revue française d'études politiques africaines,* July 1973, pp. 32–47.
Vignes, Daniel. *L'Association des états africains et malgaches à la C.E.E.* Paris, 1970.
Von Albertini, Rudolf. *Decolonization: The Administration and Future of the Colonies, 1919–1960.* Garden City, N.Y., 1971.
Von Strandmann, Harmut Pogge, and Smith, Alison. "The German Empire in Africa and British Perspectives: A Historiographical Essay." In Prosser Gifford and Wm. Roger Louis, eds., pp. 709–95. *Britain and Germany in Africa,* New Haven, 1967.
Wall, Irwin. "Communism, Decolonization and the Fourth Republic." *French Colonial Studes,* Spring 1977, pp. 82–99.
———. "The French Communists and the Algerian War." *Journal of Contemporary History* 12 (1977): 521–44.

Walshe, Peter. *The Rise of African Nationalism in South Africa.* Berkeley, 1971.
Wasserman, G. B. *Politics of Decolonization: Kenya Europeans and the Land Issue, 1960–1965.* Cambridge, Eng., 1976.
Watson Report on the Commission of Enquiry into Disturbances in the Gold Coast (col. no. 231, 1948).
Watts, R. L. *Administration in Federal Systems.* London, 1970.
Wauters, Authur, ed. *Le Monde communiste et la crise du Congo belge.* Brussels, 1961.
Wauthier, Claude. "France and Africa: 'Long Live Neo-Colonialism." *Issue* 2 (Spring 1972): 23–27.
Webster, John B. *The Constitutions of Burundi, Malagasy and Rwanda.* Syracuse, N.Y., 1964.
———. *The Political Development of Rwanda and Burundi.* Syracuse, N.Y. 1966.
Weexststeen, Raoul. "Colonisation, décolonisation et structures urbaines: Une ville d'Algérie, Blida." Thesis, University of Strasbourg, 1974.
Weinbuch, Helmut Konrad. *Entkolonisierung föderales Prinzip im spiegelder französischen Gemeinschaft.* Berlin, 1968.
Weinstein, Brian. *Eboué.* New York, 1971.
Weinstein, Warren. *Historical Dictionary of Burundi.* Metuchen, N.J., 1976.
———. "The Limits of Military Dependency: the Case of Belgian Military Aid to Burundi, 1961–1973." *Journal of African Studies* 2 (1975): 419–31.
Weinstein, Warren, and Grotpeter, John. *The Patterns of African Decolonization.* Syracuse, N.Y., 1973.
Weiss, Herbert. *Political Protest in the Congo.* Princeton, 1967.
Weissman, Stephen R. *American Foreign Policy in the Congo, 1960–1964.* Ithaca, N.Y., 1974.
Welch, Claude. *Dream of Unity: Pan Africanism and Political Unification in West Africa.* Ithaca, N.Y., 1966.
Wheare, Joan. *The Nigerian Legislative Council.* London, 1950.
Wheeler, Douglas L, and Pélissier, René. *Angola.* New York, 1971.
Whitaker, C. S. *The Politics of Tradition; Continuity and Change in Northern Nigeria, 1946–1966.* Princeton, 1970.
White, Dorothy Shipley. *Black Africa and De Gaulle: From the Empire to Independence.* University Park, Pa., 1979.
———. "De Gaulle and the Decolonization of Black Africa." *Proceedings of the French Colonial Historical Society* 1 (1976): 52–63.
Whiteley, Wilfred. "Political Concepts and Connotations." *African Affairs. No. 1,* edited by K. Kirkland, pp. 7–21. London, 1961.
Wicker, E. R. "Colonial Development and Welfare, 1929–1957: The Evolution of a Policy." *Social and Economic Studies* 7, no. 4 (1958): 170–92.
Wight, M. *British Colonial Constitutions, 1947.* Oxford, 1952.
———. *The Development of the Legislative Council, 1606–1945.* London, 1946.
———. *The Gold Coast Legislative Council.* Westport, Conn., 1947.
Willame, Jean-Claude. *Patrimonialism and Political Change in the Congo.* Stanford, 1972.
Williams-Mayers, A. J. "Mozambique: Regional Aspects of a Historical Legacy of Resistance." *Journal of Southern African Affairs* 2 (1977): 43–60.
Wilmot, Chester. *The Struggle for Europe.* New York, 1952.
Wilson, Henry. S. *The Imperial Experience in Sub-Saharan Africa since 1870.* Minneapolis, 1978.

———. *Origins of West African Nationalism.* London, 1969.
Wilson, Monica [Hunter], and Thompson, Leonard, eds. *The Oxford History of South Africa, 1870-1966.* Vol. 2. New York, 1971.
Windrich, Elaine. *Britain and the Politics of Rhodesian Independence.* London, 1978.
Winks, Robin W. "On Decolonization and Informal Empire." *American Historical Review* 81, no. 3 (1976): 540-56.
Wiseberg, Laurie, and Nelson, Gary F. "Africa's New Island Republics and U.S. Foreign Policy." *Africa Today* 24 (January-March 1977): 7-30.
Wohlgemuth, Patricia Blair. *The Portuguese Territories and the United Nations.* New York, 1973.
Woolf, Leonard. *Empire and Commerce in Africa; A Study in Economic Imperialism.* London, 1920.
Wolff, R. D. *The Economics of Colonialism: Britain and Kenya, 1870-1930.* New Haven, 1974.
Worthington, E. B. *Science in Africa.* London, 1938.
Wraith, R. E. *Local Government in West Africa.* London, 1953. Revised in 1972 as *Local Administration in West Africa.*
Wright, Robin. "Machel's Marxist Mozambique." *Munger Africana Library Notes,* March 1976, pp. 1-53.
Wrigley, Christopher. "Changes in East African Society." In Roland Oliver et al., eds., *History of East Africa,* 3: 508-43. Oxford, 1976.
Yacono, Xavier. *Les Etapes de la décolonisation française.* Paris, 1971.
———. *Histoire de la colonisation française.* Paris, 1969.
Yansané, Aguibou Yan, ed. *Decolonization and Dependency: Problems of Development of African Societies.* Westport, Conn., 1980. [Essays on French West Africa]
———. "Monetary Independence and Transition to Socialism in Guinea." *Journal of African Studies* 6 (1979): 132-43.
———. "Some Problems of Monetary Dependence in West African States of French Colonial Legacy." *Review of Black Political Economy* 7 (Fall 1976): 22-39.
———. "Some Problems of Monetary Dependency in French-Speaking West Africa States." *Journal of African Studies* 5 (1978-79): 444-70.
———. "The State of Economic Integration in Sub-Saharan North-West Africa." *Ufahamu* 8 (1978): 88-131.
Ydevalle, Charles d'. *L'Union minière du Haut-Katanga de l'âge colonial à l'indépendance.* Paris, 1960.
Young, Crawford. "Decolonization in Africa." *Colonialism in Africa* 2 (1970): 450-502.
———. *Politics in the Congo: Decolonization and Independence.* Princeton, 1965.
Young, Roland, and Fosbrooke, Henry. *Smoke in the Hills.* Evanston, Ill., 1960.
Zartman, I. William. "Europe and Africa: Decolonization or Dependency?" *Foreign Affairs* 54 (1976): 325-43.
———. *The Politics of Trade Negotiations between Africa and the European Community: The Weak Confront the Strong.* Princeton, 1971.
Zingg, Paul J. "The Cold War in North Africa: American Foreign Policy and Postwar Muslim Nationalism, 1945-1962." *Historian* 39 (November 1976): 40-61.

CONTRIBUTORS

DENNIS AUSTIN (M.A. Manchester University) is dean of the faculty of Economic and Social Studies and professor of government at the University of Manchester. He is the author of *Politics in Ghana* (Oxford, 1964), *Britain and South Africa* (Oxford, 1966), *Malta and the End of Empire* (London, 1971), *Ghana Observed* (Manchester, 1976), *Commonwealth in Eclipse* (London, 1976), and *Politics in Africa* (Hanover, N.H., 1978). He is now completing a history of the transfer of power within the former British Empire.

HENRI BRUNSCHWIG (Agrégé de l'Université, Docteur ès Lettres, and Licencié en Droit) is director of the School for Advanced Study in the Social Sciences at the University of Paris. He is the author of *L'Expansion allemande outre mer* (Paris, 1957), L'Avènèment de l'Afrique noire (Paris, 1963), *French Colonialism* (London, 1966), and *Le Partage de l'Afrique noire* (Paris, (1971).

DAVID K. FIELDHOUSE (M.A., D.Litt. Oxford University) is Vere Harmsworth Professor of Imperial and Naval History and fellow of Jesus College, Cambridge University. He is the author of *The Colonial Empires* (London, 1966), *The Theory of Capitalist Imperialism* (London, 1967), *Economics and Empire, 1830–1914* (London, 1973), and *Unilever Overseas* (London, 1978).

DAVID E. GARDINIER (Ph.D. Yale University) is a professor of history at Marquette University. He is the author of *Cameroon: United Nations Challenge to French Policy* (London, 1963) and *Historical Dictionary of Gabon* (Metuchen, N.J., 1981). As a senior Fulbright scholar in Paris in 1979, he continued his research on education in the four Equatorial African states. He prepares the Africa section of *Recently Published Articles* for the American Historical Association and is a past president of the French Colonial Historical Society.

PROSSER GIFFORD (Ph.D. Yale University) was formerly dean of the faculty and professor of history at Amherst College. He is now deputy-director of the Woodrow Wilson International Center for Scholars at the Smithsonian Institution. He is coeditor of and contributor to *Britain and Germany in Africa* (New Haven, 1967), and *France and Britain in Africa* (New Haven, 1971).

JOHN D. HARGREAVES (M.A. University of Manchester) is professor of history at the University of Aberdeen. He has taught in Sierra Leone and Nigeria. His books include *Prelude to the Partition of West Africa* (London, 1963) and *West Africa: The Former French States* (Englewood Cliffs, N.J., 1967). The first volume of his *West Africa Partitioned* appeared in 1975, and a volume of essays, *The End of Colonial Rule in West Africa*, in 1979.

GRACE S. IBINGIRA (LL.B. University of Wales) is a former Member of Parliament and minister of justice in Uganda. He has served as Uganda's ambassador to the United Nations. He is the author of *The Forging of an African Nation: A Political and Constitutional History of Uganda, 1894–1962* (New York, 1971), *African Upheavals since Independence* (Boulder, Colo., 1979), and a political novel, *Bitter Harvest* (Nairobi, 1979).

ANTHONY H. M. KIRK-GREENE (M.A. Cambridge University) is a senior research fellow in African Studies at Oxford University. He is the author of *Crisis and Conflict in Nigeria, 1966–70* (Oxford, 1971), *Principles of Native Administration in Nigeria, 1900–47* (Oxford, 1965), and numerous articles on both the African and colonial bureaucracies. He is presently engaged in writing a history of the British Colonial Service.

D. A. LOW (D.Phil. Oxford University) is a historian of both Africa and India. His recent major publications include the editorship of the *History of East Africa*, vol. 3 (with Alison Smith)(Oxford, 1976) and *Congress and the Raj: Facets of the Indian Struggle, 1917–47* (London, 1977). He has also published a volume of his collected essays, *Lion Rampart*. As well as being a professor of history, he is vice-chancellor of the Australian National University.

HOLLIS R. LYNCH (Ph.D. London University) is professor of history at Columbia University and formerly the director of its Institute of African Studies. His books include *Edward Wilmot Blyden: Pan-Negro Patriot, 1832–1912* (Oxford, 1967), *The Black Urban Condition: A Documentary History, 1866–1971* (New York, 1973), *Black Africa* (New York, 1973), and recently *The Selected Letters of Edward Wilmot Blyden* 1973), and *Black American Radicals and the Liberation of Africa* (Ithaca, N.Y., 1978).

WM. ROGER LOUIS (D.Litt., D.Phil. Oxford University) is the author of *Ruanda-Urundi 1884–1919* (Oxford, 1963), *Germany's Lost Colonies* (Oxford, 1967), *E. D. Morel's History of the Congo Reform Movement* (with Jean Stengers)(Oxford, 1968), *British Strategy in the Far East* (Oxford, 1971), and *Imperialism at Bay: The United States and the Decolonization of the British Empire, 1941–1945* (Oxford, 1978). He is professor of history, and curator of Historical Collections at the Humanities Research Center, University of Texas.

KENNETH R. MAXWELL (Ph.D. Princeton University) is a specialist in Iberian and Latin American History. He is professor of history at Columbia University and senior research fellow at the Research Institute on International Change. He is also program director of The Tinker Foundation Inc., New York, and the author of *Conflicts and Conspiracies: Brazil and Portugal, 1750–1807* (Cambridge, 1973), and a forthcoming history of the Portuguese revolution and decolonization.

ELIKIA M'BOKOLO, who studied at the Ecole Normale Supérieure of Paris, is an agrégé of the University and docteur en histoire. He is also director of the African Studies Center at the Ecole des Hautes Etudes en Sciences Sociales at the University of Paris. He has published *Noirs et Blancs en Afrique équatoriale: Les Débuts de l'etablissement français, 1839–1874* (Paris, 1979) and *L'Afrique au XXe siècle* (Paris, 1979, and is preparing a major book on the decolonization of French Equatorial Africa.

YVES PERSON (Docteur ès Lettres, Sorbonne) is professor of African history at the University of Paris. He is the author of *Samori—Une révolution dyula*, 3 vols. (Dakar, 1969–75), and many other publications on West Africa. He is presently at work on a volume about the contradictions between the nation-state and socialism in Africa.

CRANFORD PRATT (B.Phil. Oxford University) is the author of *The Critical Phase in Tanzania, 1945–1967: Nyerere and the Emergence of a Socialist Strategy* (Cambridge, 1976 and Oxford, 1979), and coeditor, with Bismarck Mwansasu, of *Towards Socialism in Tanzania* (Toronto and Dar es Salaam, 1979). He is a professor in the Department of Political Economy at the University of Toronto and was Commonwealth Visiting Professor at the University of London, 1979–80, and first principal of the University College, Dar-es-Salaam, 1961–65.

RONALD ROBINSON (Ph.D. Cambridge University), formerly Smuts Reader in Commonwealth Studies at Cambridge University, is Beit Professor of Commonwealth history at Oxford University and a fellow of Balliol College. He is the coauthor (with the late John A. Gallagher) of *Africa and the Victorians: The Climax of Imperialism in the Dark Continent* (English subtitle *The Official Mind of Imperialism;* London, 1961); and editor of and contributor to *Developing the Third World: The Experience of the Sixties* (Cambridge, 1971).

TONY SMITH (Ph.D. Harvard University) is the editor of *The End of European Empire* (Lexington, Mass., 1975) and author of *The French Stake in Algeria, 1945–1962* (Ithaca, N.Y., 1978) and *The Pattern of Imperialism: The United States, Great Britain, and the Late-Industrializing World since 1815* (Cambridge/New York, 1981). He is presently associate professor of political science at Tufts University.

JEAN STENGERS (Docteur en Philosophie et Lettres, University of Brussels) is professor of contemporary history at the University of Brussels and chairman of the Commission on History of the Belgian Académie Royale des Sciences d'Outre-Mer. In the field of Belgian colonial history, his books include *Combien le Congo a-t-il coûté à la Belgique?* (Brussels, 1957), *Belgique et Congo. L'Elaboration de la charte coloniale* (Brussels, 1963), and *E. D. Morel's History of the Congo Reform Movement* (with Roger Louis)(Oxford, 1968).

JEAN SURET-CANALE (Agrégé de l'Université, Docteur de 3° cycle en Géographie, University of Paris-Sorbonne, and Doctor of Historical Sciences, African Institute, USSR Academy of Sciences, Moscow) teaches at the University of Paris VII. Former Deputy Director of the Center for Marxist Studies and Research (1964–79) in Paris, his principal works are *Afrique noire occidentale et centrale,* of which three volumes have been published (Paris, 1958, 1964, 1972), *La République de Guinée* (Paris, 1970), and *Essais d'histoire africaine* (Paris 1980.

LEONARD THOMPSON (M.A. Oxford University, D.Litt., Rhodes University) is the author of *The Unification of South Africa* (Oxford, 1960), *Politics in the Republic of South Africa* (Boston, 1966), *Survival in Two Worlds: Moshoeshoe of Lesotho* (Oxford, 1975), and, as coauthor, with Philip Curtin et al. of *African History* (Boston, 1978), editor of *African Societies in Southern Africa: Historical Studies* (London, 1969), coeditor with Monica Wilson of *The Oxford History of South Africa* (Oxford and New York, 1969, 1971), with Jeffrey Butler of *Change in Contemporary Africa* (Berkeley, 1975), and with Howard Lamar of *The Frontier in History: North America and South Africa Compared* (New Haven, 1981). A Rhodes scholar, he was formerly professor of history at the University of Cape Town and at the University of California, Los Angeles, and is now professor of history at Yale University.

INDEX

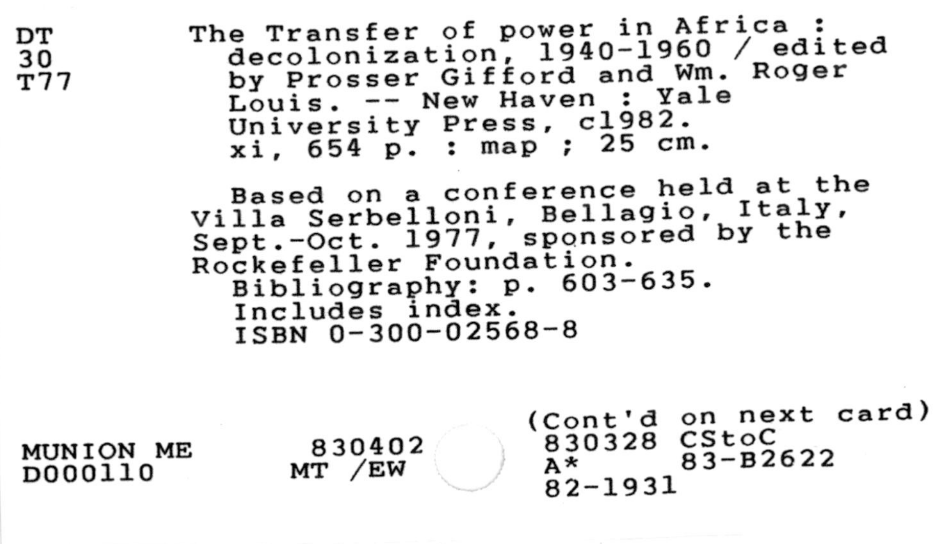

The Transfer of power in Africa : decolonization, 1940-1960 / edited by Prosser Gifford and Wm. Roger Louis. -- New Haven : Yale University Press, c1982.
xi, 654 p. : map ; 25 cm.

Based on a conference held at the Villa Serbelloni, Bellagio, Italy, Sept.-Oct. 1977, sponsored by the Rockefeller Foundation.
Bibliography: p. 603-635.
Includes index.
ISBN 0-300-02568-8

(Cont'd on next card)